THE LIFE OF RICHARD WAGNER

1848-1860

ERNEST NEWMAN

The Life of

RICHARD WAGNER

VOLUME TWO : 1848–1860

NEW YORK · ALFRED · A · KNOPF · MCMXXXVII

FOREWORD

O WING TO a variety of causes, some of which it was beyond my power to control, this volume has taken an unconscionable time to produce. My difficulty came, in part, not only from the extent and the nature of the subject itself but from the constant inflow, during the last few years, of new material relating to this epoch of Wagner's life, necessitating on the one hand the rejection of much in the Wagner story that has hitherto been accepted as authentic, and on the other hand the fusion of the new material with the old at the appropriate points.

While much new material has recently seen the light, there must still be a great deal to come. The contents of the Burrell Collection, now in America, are not yet available to students. A great many letters from and to Wagner are said to have been destroyed by Cosima, but there must still be many in existence that have not yet been made public, notably those that passed between Wagner and King Ludwig. The gaps in our knowledge, however, are being steadily, if slowly, filled up, either by the revelation of letters, or portions of letters, that were omitted from the first " official " editions, or by the publication of quite new material. Dr. Max Fehr, for instance, has recently given us a considerable number of new documents relating to Wagner's Zürich period. It is a matter of the greatest regret to me that I have to send this book to the press before the appearance of the second volume of Dr. Fehr's *Richard Wagners Schweizer Zeit,* in which further new letters are promised us. To delay the issue of the second volume of the present Life any longer on that account, however, is impossible: to wait, indeed, until all the possible or probable future material is available would mean the indefinite postponement of any modern Wagner biography. Any new documents bearing on the years covered by the present volume will have to be dealt with in appendices to the next, which, I have every reason to hope, will follow this one at a much smaller interval of time than has elapsed between it and its predecessor.

Some peculiarities in the lay-out of this second volume will, I trust, commend themselves to the reader in the long run, if not at the first glance. I have made a connected story, for instance, of Wagner's concert and operatic activities in Zürich between 1850 and 1855, even though to do so means a momentary departure from the strictly chronological method. I thought it better to give the reader a bird's-eye view of such a subject as this than to compel him to dig out and join up for himself, over half a dozen chapters, the full story of Wagner's public activities during those years.

If it be thought that the narrative moves rather slowly during the first half of this volume, and the plain biographical sequence is occasionally broken by the insertion of not strictly biographical matter, I venture to justify my procedure in two ways. In the first place, the years from 1848 to about the *Tristan* period are the great formative years in Wagner's life both as man and as artist. The epoch of revolution (1848–9) had the profoundest reactions not only on his life but on his thought. The years between 1848 and about 1856 were one long spiritual convulsion for him, during which his attempts to shape and to understand himself inwardly were sometimes of even more importance than the events of his outward life: after *Tristan* the story settles down upon more purely biographical lines. In the second place, the story of Wagner's life during the years covered by the present volume is a matter not merely of biography pure and simple but of the history, the physiology and the psychology of a major change in European musical life. Wagner was not only making history by his own works: he was also the focal point of a revolution in modern culture-conditions. I have tried, accordingly, to show him not only as he was in himself but in his relation to other leading personalities of the period and to the swiftly moving forces around him.

In the appendices will be found a *précis* of some letters from Wagner to Meyerbeer recently published for the first time, and a further discussion of the problem of Wagner's origin, particularly in connection with the theory that he may have been descended on his mother's side from the royal house of Weimar.

The chances of error in a work of this kind are infinite, and I cannot hope that, for all my care, I have escaped them. I shall be grateful for corrections: at the same time I ought to warn my readers that I have not always thought it necessary to burden my text with footnotes giving my reasons for rejecting a hitherto accepted fact or date. Wagner's dates in *Mein Leben,* for example, are frequently wrong.

I have to correct an error that has been pointed out to me in Volume I. For some reason or other that is now a complete mystery to me — though I suppose I must have had what seemed to me a good reason at the time — I corrected the accepted date of Morlacchi's death from 1841 to 1842. The former is the true date.

My thanks are due to many friends for help of one kind and another, notably to Mr. Robert Lorenz for many fruitful suggestions, and to Mr. William Steinway, of Hamburg, for the vast amount of trouble he has cheerfully given himself in looking out for new Wagner material in the German Press. I am also indebted to Dr. Otto Strobel for his kindness in keeping me in touch with his own many valuable articles dealing with new material in the Wahnfried archives, and to Dr. Hans Wahl, the Curator of the Goethe National Museum, Weimar, for procuring for me the two portraits of Prince Constantin of Weimar that appear in the second Appendix.

E. N.

Tadworth, 6th July, 1936.

CONTENTS

ILLUSTRATIONS

ADDITIONAL SOURCES AND REFERENCES

A

AKL = *Anregungen für Kunst und Wissenschaft . . . herausgegeben von Franz Brendel und Richard Pohl.* 6 vols. Leipzig, 1856–61.

B

BBBW = *Billroth und Brahms im Briefwechsel.* Berlin, 1935.

BBCS = *Briefe von Hector Berlioz an die Fürstin Carolyne Sayn-Wittgenstein: herausgegeben von La Mara.* Leipzig, 1903.

BFF = *Bayreuther Festspielführer:* Cited by year of issue.

BGKL = JAKOB BAECHTOLD: *Gottfried Kellers Leben, Seine Briefe und Tagebücher.* 4th ed. 3 vols. Berlin, 1895–7.

BLTM = M. BEER: *The Life and Teaching of Karl Marx, translated by T. C. Partington and H. J. Stenning.* London, 1921.

BLW = *Briefwechsel zwischen Franz Liszt und Hans von Bülow, herausgegeben von La Mara.* Leipzig, 1898.

BMEN = *Memoirs of Hector Berlioz, annotated by Ernest Newman.* New York, 1932.

BTNJ = C. F. BECKER: *Die Tonkünstler des neunzehnten Jahrhunderts: ein kalendarisches Handbuch zur Kunstgeschichte.* Leipzig, 1849.

BWSW = WALTER BOHE: *Richard Wagner im Spiegel der Wiener Presse.* Würzburg, n.d. [1933].

BWZ = HANS BÉLART: *Richard Wagner in Zürich, 1849–1858.* 2 vols. Leipzig, 1900, 1901.

C

CABT = PETER CORNELIUS: *Ausgewählte Briefe, nebst Tagebuchblättern und Gelegenheitsgedichten, herausgegeben von Carl Maria Cornelius.* 2 vols. Leipzig, 1904–5.

CAMK = PETER CORNELIUS: *Aufsätze über Musik und Kunst, herausgegeben von Edgar Istel.* Leipzig, 1904.

COD = J. CORNET: *Die Oper in Deutschland und das Theater der Neuzeit.* Hamburg, 1849.

D

DMW = HENRY DAVISON: *From Mendelssohn to Wagner, being the Memoirs of J. W. Davison, forty years music critic of " The Times ".* London, 1912.

DS = *Die Sonne* (Monatsschrift für Nordische Weltanschauung). Leipzig. (Cited by date).

DWGE = HUGO DINGER: *Richard Wagners geistige Entwickelung.* Leipzig, 1892.

E

EV = W. ASHTON ELLIS: *1849, A Vindication.* London, 1892.

EWLW = ERICH W. ENGEL: *Richard Wagners Leben und Werke im Bild.* 2nd ed. Leipzig, 1922.

F

FWSZ = MAX FEHR: *Richard Wagners Schweizer Zeit.* Vol. I (1849–55). Aarau and Leipzig, 1934.

G

GW = A. DE GASPERINI: *Richard Wagner.* Paris, 1866.

GWS = FRITZ GYSI: *Richard Wagner und die Schweiz.* Frauenfeld and Leipzig, 1929.

H

HBD = MARCEL HERWEGH: *Au Banquet des Dieux: Liszt, Wagner, et leurs amis.* Paris, 1932.

HFS = *Fürstin Marie zu Hohenlohe und Ferdinand von Saar, ein Briefwechsel: herausgegeben von Anton Bettelheim.* Vienna, 1910.

HM = ROBERT VON HORNSTEIN: *Memoiren, herausgegeben von Ferdinand von Hornstein.* Munich, 1908.

HRTW = P. D. HURN and W. L. ROOT: *The Truth about Wagner.* London, 1930.

HSD = MARCEL HERWEGH: *Au Soir des Dieux: des derniers reflets Wagneriens à la mort de Liszt.* Paris, 1933.

HWN = KURT HILDEBRANDT: *Wagner und Nietzsche, ihr Kampf gegen das neunzehnte Jahrhundert.* Breslau, 1924.

I J

ILL = *L'Illustration,* Paris, 11th February, 1933.

JLVB = *Jahrbuch der literarischen Vereinigung Winterthur.* 1919.

K

KBWM = GEORG KINSKY: *Fünf ungedruckte Briefe Wagners an Meyerbeer.* (In the *Schweizerische Musikzeitung,* Zürich, 15th November, 1934).

KDW = FRIEDRICH KUMMER: *Dresdner Wagner-Annalen, 1814 bis 1914.* Dresden, 1914.

KEK = BERTHOLD KELLERMANN: *Erinnerungen, ein Künstlerleben,* herausgegeben von S. Haussmann und H. Kellermann. Zürich, 1932.

KFW = ERNST KREOWSKI und EDUARD FUCHS: *Richard Wagner in der Karikatur.* Berlin, 1907.

KWBO = JULIUS KAPP: *Richard Wagner und die Berliner Oper: Die Berliner Staatsoper dem Gedächtnis Richard Wagners.* Berlin, 1933.

KWRN = ERNST KOCH: *Richard Wagners Bühnenfestspiel Der Ring des Nibelungen, in seinem Verhältnis zur alten Sage wie zur modernen Nibelungendichtung betrachtet.* Leipzig, n.d.

L

LCD = J. C. LOBE: *Consonanzen und Dissonanzen.* Leipzig, 1869.

LMG = LA MARA: *Aus der Glanzheit der Weimarer Altenburg.* Leipzig, 1906.

LPF = ALBERT LEVY: *La Philosophie de Feuerbach et son influence sur la littérature allemande.* Paris, 1904.

LRRW = AUGUST LESIMPLE: *My Recollections of Richard Wagner.* London, n.d. (A translation of Lesimple's *Erinnerungen,* Leipzig, 1884).

LWF = RUDOLF LÜCK: *Richard Wagner und Ludwig Feuerbach: eine Ergänzung der bisherigen Darstellungen der inneren Entwicklung R. Wagners.* Breslau, 1905.

LZGS = *Gesammelte Schriften von Franz Liszt, herausgegeben von L. Ramann.* 6 vols. Leipzig, 1881–96.

LZLT = FRANZ LISZT: *Lohengrin und Tannhäuser de Richard Wagner.* Leipzig, 1851.

LZMA = *Correspondance de Liszt et de Madame d'Agoult, 1833–1840, 1840–1864,* publiée par Daniel Ollivier. 2 vols. Paris, 1933, 1934.

M

MDM = G. H. MÜLLER: *Die Dresdner Mai-Revolution, 1849.* Dresden, 1924.

MJJ = ANDREAS MOSER: *Joseph Joachim, ein Lebensbild.* 2 vols. Berlin, 1908, 1910.

MMI   = MALWIDA VON MEYSENBUG: *Memoiren einer Idealistin. Der Lebensabend einer Idealistin.* 2 vols. Berlin, n.d.

MRCG   = KARL MARX: *Revolution and Counter-Revolution, or Germany in 1848.* London, 1904.

MRW   = G. H. MÜLLER: *Richard Wagner in der Mai-Revolution 1849.* Dresden, 1919.

MWA   = PAUL MOOS: *Richard Wagner als Aesthetiker.* Berlin, 1906.

MWK   = MAX MOROLD: *Wagners Kampf und Sieg, dargestellt in seinen Beziehungen zu Wien.* 2 vols. Vienna, 1930.

N

NML   = ERNEST NEWMAN: *The Man Liszt.* London, 1934.

NULT   = *Neues Universal-Lexikon der Tonkunst . . . bearbeitet und herausgegeben von Eduard Bernsdorf.* 3 vols. Leipzig, 1856, etc.

NZUB   = FRIEDRICH NIETZSCHE: *Unzeitgemässe Betrachtungen. (Kröners Taschenausgabe).* Leipzig, 1930.

O

OLPF   = DANIEL OLLIVIER: *Lettres d'un Père [Liszt] et de sa Fille [Blandine].* (In *Revue des Deux Mondes,* 15th December, 1935, and 1st January, 1936).

R

RCT   = GUSTAVE ROGER: *Le Carnet d'un Ténor.* Paris, 1880.

RFLS   = PETER RAABE: *Liszts Schaffen.* Stuttgart, 1931.

RJR   = HELENE RAFF: *Joachim Raff, ein Lebensbild.* Regensburg, 1925.

RLKM   = LINA RAMANN: *Franz Liszt als Künstler und Mensch.* 3 vols. Leipzig, 1880, 1887, 1894.

RLW   = SEBASTIEN RÖCKL: *Ludwig II und Richard Wagner.* 2 vols. Munich, 1913, 1920.

RSE   = AUGUST RÖCKEL: *Sachsens Erhebung und das Zuchthaus zu Waldheim.* Frankfort-am-Main, 1865.

RWAR   = *Briefe an August Röckel von Richard Wagner, eingeleitet durch La Mara.* Leipzig, 1894.

RWBA   = *Richard Wagners Briefe, ausgewählt und erläutert von Wilhelm Altmann.* 2 vols. Leipzig [1925].

RWEB   = RICHARD WAGNER: *Echte Briefe an Ferdinand Praeger: Kritik der Praeger'schen Veröffentlichungen, von Houston Stewart Chamberlain.* Bayreuth, n.d. [1894].

RWEW   = *Richard Wagner an Eliza Wille: fünfzehn Briefe. . . .* 2nd ed. Leipzig, 1911.

RWF   = JOACHIM RAFF: *Die Wagnerfrage*. Brunswick, 1854.

RWJR = *Richard Wagners Briefe an Frau Julie Ritter*. Munich, 1920.

RWTS = FRANZ RÜHLMANN: *Richard Wagners theatralische Sendung: Ein Beitrag zur Geschichte und zur Systematik der Opernregie*. Brunswick, 1935.

RWWK = *Richard Wagner an Mathilde Wesendonk: Tagebuchblätter und Briefe, herausgegeben von Julius Kapp*. Leipzig, n.d. [1915].

S

SGW   = OTTO STROBEL: *Genie am Werk: wie Richard Wagner schuf*. (In *Velhagen und Klasings Monatsheft*, Berlin, March, 1934).

SNW   = ADELHEID VON SCHORN: *Das nachklassische Weimar unter der Regierungszeit Karl Friedrichs und Maria Paulownas*. Weimar, 1911.

SRWZ = A. STEINER: *Richard Wagner in Zürich, 1849–1858*. (*Neujahrsblatt der Allgemeinen Musik-Gesellschaft in Zürich*, 1901, 1902, 1903).

SSE   = OTTO STROBEL: *Richard Wagner, Skizzen und Entwürfe zur Ring-Dichtung, mit der Dichtung, Der junge Siegfried*. Munich, 1930.

SVW   = DANIEL SPITZER: *Verliebte Wagnerianer*. 6th ed. Vienna, 1880.

SWJ   = ADOLF STAHR: *Weimar und Jena*. 3rd ed. 2 vols. Oldenburg, n.d.

SWLL = OTTO STROBEL: *Wagners Leben im Lichte der Randbemerkungen seiner Originalhandschriften*. (In *Allgemeine Musikzeitung*, Berlin, 25th March, 1932).

SWM   = EDUARD STEMPLINGER: *Richard Wagner in München, 1864–70: Legende und Wirklichkeit*, Munich, 1933.

SWMF = OTTO STROBEL: *Richard Wagner: "Mitteilung an meine Freunde"*. (In *Zeitschrift für Musik*, July, 1931).

SZM   = ADELHEID VON SCHORN: *Zwei Menschenalter: Erinnerungen und Briefe*. Berlin, 1901.

T

TLFW = JULIEN TIERSOT: *Lettres françaises de Richard Wagner: recueillies et présentées par J.T.* Paris, 1935.

V

VKG   = FRIEDRICH THEODOR VISCHER: *Kritische Gänge*. 2 vols. Tübingen, 1844.

W

WEWL = Wendelin Weissheimer: *Erlebnisse mit Richard Wagner, Franz Liszt, und vielen anderen Zeitgenossen.* Stuttgart, 1898.

WHSC = *Cosima Wagner und Houston Stewart Chamberlain im Briefwechsel, 1888–1908, herausgegeben von Paul Pretzsch.* Leipzig, 1934.

Z

ZGMO = Max Zenger: *Geschichte der Münchener Oper: Nachgelassenes Werk herausgegeben von Theodor Kroyer.* Munich, 1923.

THE LIFE OF RICHARD WAGNER
1848-1860

CHAPTER I

WAGNER AND POLITICS IN 1848

1

THE GALLANT Wagnerian Old Guard, anxious to minimise the extent of their hero's connection with the practical business of revolution, used to insist that during the greater part of 1848 Wagner could have taken little part in politics, revolutionary or other, from simple lack of leisure for anything of the kind.[1] He had finished the scoring of *Lohengrin* at the end of March. From then until about the middle of May he was fully occupied with his *Plan for the Organisation of a German National Theatre for Saxony*. In the summer he took up again the sketch of October, 1846, for a drama on the subject of Friedrich Barbarossa, and made some additions to it; the actual amount of new writing in which this resulted is trifling, but there must have been a great deal of hard thinking at the back of it.[2] During that summer he wrote also an essay entitled *Die Wibelungen: Weltgeschichte aus der Saga* (*The Wibelungen: World-History as revealed in Saga*), that runs to forty large pages in the modern reprint, and another essay, *Der Nibelungen-Mythus, als Entwurf zu einem Drama* (*The Nibelungen-Myth, as Sketch for a Drama*), that occupies eleven.[3] Each of these must have involved a considerable amount of reading as well as of condensation and arrangement of the material. In July, having realised that the Barbarossa subject was actual history, and therefore, according to his rapidly developing aesthetic sense, unsuitable for drama — which, he henceforth held, should concern itself with the " purely human " as revealed in myth, — he turned again

---

[1] See, for instance, ELW, Vol. II, Chapter X. The first part of this chapter is Ellis's own, not Glasenapp's.

[2] The sketch was printed for the first time, from the manuscript in Wahnfried, in RWGS, Vol. XI. It is not to be found in Ellis's English version of Wagner's Prose Works.

[3] Reprinted in RWGS, Vol. II. The *Wibelungen* essay was printed in 1849; Wagner had expanded the original in the interval.

[3]

to the figure of Siegfried that had so long been hovering in the background of his consciousness, and by November he had written the whole poem of *Siegfrieds Tod,* the basis and the main substance of the later *Götterdämmerung.* This is a full-fledged drama running to sixty-two printed pages. To all this was added, by the end of the year, the minutely detailed sketch for the drama *Jesus von Nazareth* (fifty-two pages), which again must have involved a huge amount of reading, reflection and modelling. If we further take into consideration his almost daily duties, of one kind and another, in and about the theatre, it is evident that the great bulk of Wagner's spare time until the autumn of 1848 must have been so taken up with purely intellectual work that he could have had little leisure for political agitation.

2

But it would be absurd to suppose that, in a Germany in which political affairs had been the chief subject of discussion for several years, so eager a mind as Wagner's was alone uninterested in such things, at least in the abstract. Socialism and communism, says Karl Marx, had been fashionable in Germany since France began to coquet with these formulae, " and as far back as 1843 all newspapers teemed with discussions of social questions. . . . A school of socialists very soon formed itself in Germany, distinguished," he comments acidly, " more for the obscurity than for the novelty of its ideas," [4] — a judgment from which few readers of Wagner's prose writings of this period will dissent. Wagner was undoubtedly involved to a minor degree even in 1848 in the political agitations of the period, and one can only marvel at his finding any energy at all to expend upon these in addition to his other labours. Following upon the risings in Paris, Vienna, Berlin and elsewhere in the spring of 1848, a Parliament had met at Frankfort-on-the-Main on the 31st of March to draw up a constitution for a united Germany, while in Saxony the Könneritz cabinet had been dismissed to make way for one of more liberal, even democratic, ideas. In Dresden there was the usual feverish republican theorising, but the King himself had as yet lost nothing of his personal popularity. Wagner's colleague Röckel had adopted enthusiastically all the newest

---

[4] MRCG, p. 23.

theories, including the fantastically idealistic one of a National Guard that should drill with the regular soldiers! During part of the years 1848 and 1849 Röckel issued a democratic sheet of his own, the *Volksblätter*,[5] that ultimately brought him into bad odour both with the theatre management and with the Government. Like Wagner, unable to live on his small salary, he also had got deeper and deeper into debt; he had often thought of emigrating with his family to America and beginning life again there as a farmer. The excitements of 1848 threw him completely off his balance. He developed a surprising facility for plausible argument along social-istic lines, and quickly became one of the heads of the revolutionary movement in Dresden. It has long been a subject for debate whether he or Wagner " influenced " the other more. The truth seems to be that each regarded the other as, on the whole, more speculative than practical. Even Wagner could not quite follow Röckel in all the latter's fanciful reconstructions, on paper, of man and society: while Röckel must have seen clearly that Wagner's nebulous ideal of a new theatre could never be realised in the Germany they both knew.

Röckel had come to Dresden in 1843 with the seeds of revolution already in him. In 1830, as a boy of sixteen, he had been an eye-witness of the July revolution in Paris, and had there made the acquaintance of several of the democratic leaders; later he con-sorted a good deal with Spanish, Portuguese, and Polish political refugees. From 1832 onwards he had lived in England, where he saw, he tells us, how easily popular reforms could be effected when a Government recognised itself to be the servant, not the tyrant, of the people. His warm human sympathies, his intellectual pride as a man of extensive culture, and his generous social and political ideals were alike outraged by his experiences as a Court servant in Dresden — with a King who, for all his personal amiability, would tolerate no criticism of his divine right; a Court given up to a pomp as puerile as it was solemn; a witless, arrogant nobility, despising

---

[5] It had a circulation of more than 2,000. Several other democratic journals were published in Saxony, of which the chief were the *Turmwart* and the *Vaterlandsblätter*, the latter being the recognised organ of the Vaterlandsverein. The *Volksblätter*, however, was the most outspoken and thoroughgoing of them all, and the most eagerly read. See the contemporary testimony of B. Hirschel, quoted in DWGE, pp. 104, 105.

the common people and spending all its time in social follies and in the scramble for Court orders; self-satisfied military officers; and everywhere an immovable bureaucratism.[6] Röckel was one of the many Germans who, like Wagner, had outgrown the old feudal docility towards the petty princelings and nobility of the country, and were exasperated at the pomposity of these absurd homunculi;[7] and the pair of Royal Court musicians must often have sung a canon on this congenial theme. We shall find Wagner, in 1849, thundering out his hatred of courtiers and officials in terms the scorn and venom of which could not have been surpassed by any of the German political pamphleteers of the day, rich as these were in invective.

3

In *Mein Leben* he tries to make out that his motives in joining the democratic movement in Dresden were artistic rather than political. Broadly speaking, this was true of him throughout 1848. He was sincerely moved by the spectacle of the hardships of the common people, and as sorry for them as he was for himself. The central impulse of his being, of course, was to realise himself as artist in the new theatre of his Utopian dreams. But this new German theatre could be born only out of a new German culture; and the new culture would be possible, he thought, only when the " Folk " were " free " — free not only in the political sense, but free to exhibit the abundance of those natural virtues with which he so naïvely credited them, but which, he thought, were held in check by the self-seeking, unintelligent privileged classes. And since the prerequisite social changes could be brought about only by political means, he naturally took, in time, to practical politics, but as yet,

---

[6] See Röckel's own account in RSE, pp. 16 ff.

[7] The general mentality of them may be illustrated by a classical example. In 1845 Prince Heinrich the Seventy-second of Reuss-Lobenstein-Ebersdorf, "most insignificant but longest-named of German principalities," condescendingly ordered the following announcement to appear in the official Gazette of his realm: "His most Serene Highness has most graciously deigned, His All-Highest Self, most graciously to praise before the assembled troops those militiamen, six in number, who hastened to the fire which broke out in Tonna and gave their services there with the most self-sacrificing alacrity, and then with his own All-Highest hand to shake that of the oldest (on proof by birth certificate that he was so), as a mark of his All-Highest highest satisfaction." The incident called forth an amusing satirical poem by Hoffmann von Fallersleben. See LRRG, pp. 168–9.

for the most part, less for mere politics' sake than for art's sake and for Richard Wagner's sake. In the spring and summer of 1848 the Dresden political group with which he was most closely associated, the Vaterlandsverein, was a perfectly legal and reputable association, the subjects it discussed being those that occupied the thoughts of most German democrats of the time. Even its scheme for a national " Folk-arming," fantastic as it may have been, was in no way treasonable in intention. In May, a meeting at which the arming of the people was discussed was held in Wagner's garden at the Marcolini Palace, some army officers being present by invitation — a fact that of itself would seem to guarantee the harmlessness of the proceedings in the official eye.

The representative of Saxony in the Frankfort National Assembly was one Professor Wigard, to whom Wagner wrote a peremptory letter on the 19th May, 1848, laying down what in his opinion were the principles that ought to guide the Frankfort meeting.

> " I am apprehensive of much harm," he said, " if the German Parliament does not in the first instance resolve on the following: (1) that Parliament at once vests the sole constitutive power in itself, as well as the authority to nominate a Provisional Executive from among its members; (2) immediate introduction of Folk-arming after the model known to us; (3) an offensive and defensive alliance with France. . . . Let the fourth step be the Territorial question of the German States. If the Frankfort Assembly intends to create a constitution that will unite Germany, it must first address itself to the inequality of the individual States: it must appoint a commission to formulate proposals for a rational and natural construction on the basic principle that no single State shall have less than four or more than six million inhabitants. That is the definitely decisive point, without the establishment of which all our labours would be merely patchwork ";

and so on, princes, Parliament and public all being told what they ought to do on pain of incurring the disapproval of the second Kapellmeister of the Dresden Opera.[8]

---

[8] RWKK, II, pp. 266–7. The "four millions" in the Kapp-Kastner version of the letter are "three millions" in Glasenapp's. In either case it meant, as Ellis points out, that as Saxony had only two million inhabitants "it would have to be enlarged either at the expense of lately encroaching Prussia, which was many times more populous, or of the smaller princedoms," which were "likely to protest." It is little wonder that the realistic Bakunin contemptuously called Wagner a visionary: but the literary

4

Busy as he was with his purely artistic plans, he still found time, at the end of May, to express his approval of the conduct of the Viennese, who, earlier in that month, had staged a counter-reaction to such purpose that the Emperor had fled the city. On the 1st June there appeared in the *Allgemeine Oesterreichische Zeitung,* over Wagner's signature, a poem entitled *Gruss aus Sachsen an die Wiener (Greeting from Saxony to the Viennese).* This was printed by Glasenapp as an appendix to the second volume of his Wagner biography; and an English translation will be found in the eighth volume of Ellis's version of Wagner's prose and poetical works. As Glasenapp and Ellis gave it, it is in nine eight-line stanzas; but we now know that it originally ran to fourteen. On the basis of the curtailed version given in Glasenapp one's summing up would be that as a poem the thing is no better and no worse than thousands of similar effusions which the time called forth all over Germany and Austria; and though its sentiments would hardly be welcome in Dresden Court circles as coming from a Royal Kapellmeister, still there was nothing in it that would seem aggressively revolutionary, the times being what they were. But the verses omitted by Glasenapp give it another colour altogether; in these, Wagner commends the Viennese " heroes " for having " drawn the sword," and exhorts the Saxons to follow their example — a dangerous piece of advice in those hectic days.[9]

---

records of the time show that, amateur as he visibly was in politics, he was no more of an amateur than thousands of his voluble German contemporaries.

[9] See RWGS, XII, 356–7, 430–1. Glasenapp's handling of the poem is typical of his occasional lack of conscience as a biographer. He twice tells us that he "reproduces it according to the reprint of it in Freiherr von Helfert's collection, *Der Wiener Parnass im Jahre 1848.*" In view of these explicit statements that he gives his readers the poem "according to the reprint," one naturally assumed, after Richard Sternfeld had printed it in full in the twelfth volume of Wagner's works, that only the nine verses given by Glasenapp had been available to him in Helfert. It occurred to me one day, however, to obtain Helfert's book (a large collection, published in 1882, of poems from the Vienna Press of 1848); and then I discovered that the complete poem had been under Glasenapp's eyes all the time! He had deliberately omitted the five final stanzas, presumably because the sentiments expressed by Wagner in them did not square with the official Bayreuth thesis that Wagner had never been animated by revolutionary principles of the more crudely realistic kind. The incident is characteristic of Glasenapp's way of manipulating or suppressing documentary material to suit his own purposes. Even in his later edition of Wagner's poems, published

There were other activities of his that would hardly be likely to commend themselves to his employers; for, after all, he was still a Court servant. In May he and Röckel joined the recently founded [10] Vaterlandsverein (Fatherland Association), which, as has been said, was a quite respectable organisation, holding views inclining to the democratic Right, and not hostile in principle to the monarchy. For the issue of 16th June of the Dresden *Anzeiger* Wagner wrote an article bearing the title, " What relation do republican endeavours bear to the Kingship? " In this he gloated over what he imagined to be the approaching extinction of the aristocracy, or at all events the abolition of their privileges at Court, where they were to be replaced by a " free Folk." Saxony was to have a single chamber, universal adult suffrage, a Folk-army without class distinction, freedom, in some Utopian way the details of which are no clearer to us than they were to Wagner, from servitude to gold — that " sallow metal " — free and flourishing trade (without any more " usury, bill-swindling, interest, and bankers' speculation "), and sundry other benefits. Germany would begin its Providence-appointed task of civilising mankind; its sons — " the noblest of children, like unto gods " — would plant new Germanies across the seas, behaving there much better than the Spaniards, " to whom the New World was only a priestly slaughterhouse," and better than the English, " who had made of it merely a tradesman's till ": the rays of German freedom and German mildness, in fact, would " light and warm the Cossacks and the French, the Bushmen and the Chinese." All this, however, it seems, is not merely quite consistent with the Saxon Kingship but inseparably bound up with it; the King is to be the " first and truest republican of all." Mon-

---

in 1905, he still printed no more than the nine stanzas. He was evidently determined that if *he* could help it the ordinary reader of the Wagner story should never know that in the original there had been five verses more.

[10] I.e., towards the end of March 1848. These Vereine sprang up all over Saxony; in a very little while they had some 100,000 members, drawn from all classes of society, including professors, mayors, government officials, clergymen, and even army officers. They contained a "Right" element and a "Left," the one "progressively democratic," the other "social-revolutionary" and anti-capitalistic. To this latter wing belonged the more thoroughgoing spirits such as Röckel. The Vaterlandsverein had 3,600 members in Dresden alone. There was also a Deutscher Verein, composed of the liberal bourgeoisie who feared revolution as likely to be bad for business. See DWGE, pp. 136 ff., and GRW, II, 225 ff.

The population of Dresden in 1849 was about 94,000.

THE LIFE OF RICHARD WAGNER

archy, the rule of one, has " become a lie "; at the same time, says Wagner, there is no objection to an hereditary Prince so long as he allies himself not with the aristocracy but with the people. The monarchs of the other German States are mostly degenerates, " weak and wicked; their weakness has waxed from generation to generation." But Saxony is fortunate in the possession of a Prince whom his people love, not for dynastic reasons but purely for his own sake. So it is he who is to proclaim the republic, and the first law passed by the Free State must be, " the supreme executive power is vested in the *ROYAL HOUSE OF WETTIN*, and descends therein from generation to generation by right of primogeniture." Thus will be saved not only Saxony, not only Germany, but Europe. Monarchy will be extinguished, but Kinghood will be emancipated; and the King will be " the first of the Folk, the freest of the Free." [11] This article was brought up against Wagner seventeen years later, when, in the course of his meddling with Bavarian politics, he urged King Ludwig to place himself at the head of the " German " movement, get himself chosen by the people as German Emperor, surrender all his prerogatives except that of pardon, and replace the standing army by a Folk-militia on the Swiss model: the Munich *Volksbote* of the 31st December, 1865 seized the opportunity to remind its readers of Wagner's equally fantastic advice to the King of Saxony, in 1848, to relinquish the throne in order to receive it back again at the hands of the people.[12]

---

[11] Hugo Dinger (DWGE, p. 143) said he was unable to find anything corresponding to this idea in the democratic literature of the period: the compromise between monarchy and republicanism advocated in the address was "the product of Wagner's heart of hearts." It is tolerably certain that the very unpractical compromise came from the desire on Wagner's part not to place himself, in spite of his theoretical republicanism, in open opposition to the King for whom he had so high a personal regard. It would appear, though, that other people at the time believed in the possibility of such a compromise. Eduard Avenarius regarded a "monarchical republic" as the ideal. See MKRW, II, pp. 142, 143.

Wagner's article and his Vaterlandsverein speech in themselves would not have been sufficient to account for the gradual alienation of the King's regard from him in the last weeks of 1848. Wagner did not include the Vaterlandsverein speech in his issue of his prose writings, either because he did not think it advisable to revive too many memories of his political past, or for the simple reason that he did not possess a copy of the speech; nor does he even mention it in the sketch of his career that he gives in *A Communication to my Friends*. It was printed for the first time by Wilhelm Tappert in 1883, from the files of the Dresden *Anzeiger*. (See TRW, pp. 33–42). It is given in Vol. XII of RWGS, and in Vol. IV of Ellis's translation of the prose works. [12] See SWM, pp. 47, 48; RLW, I, 207.

The article did not bear Wagner's signature, but was signed " A Member of the Vaterlandsverein." Though the issue of the *Anzeiger* in which it appeared is dated the 14th June, the paper appears not to have been actually published until the 16th. On the 15th Wagner attended a meeting of the Vaterlandsverein, having in his pocket either the manuscript or a proof of his article. It was not in his nature, at that time, to remain in the background in any assembly; so it is not surprising that he seized the first opportunity that presented itself to read the article to the meeting, which numbered 3,000 persons. Delivered in the superb oratorical style of which he was a master, the article was received with wild enthusiasm. What attracted most attention was the boldness of the frontal attack of the Royal Court Kapellmeister on the Court officials; the address and the article itself, which appeared in print the next day, at once became the talk of the town. On the 17th *Rienzi* was to have been given, under Wagner's direction; but the theatre authorities, fearing political demonstrations and counter-demonstrations, forbade the performance. Wagner's article, the authorship of which, of course, by now was no secret in Dresden, brought him eulogies from some quarters, abuse from others; the " little tin king," the " Wagner who thought himself a Faust," [13] was advised to mind his own business, or at all events to be a little more lucid and practical. It is said that the hand behind at any rate one of these contemptuous rejoinders was that of Gutzkow. Wagner countered with a public announcement that he would not deign to reply to the anonymous attacks of " these scoundrels and ruffians." He was made to realise that it is dangerous to joke with worthy people who are not very quick in the uptake: a bright little remark of his about the necessity for a real Folk-Defence-Force, instead of " a standing Army and a recumbent Communal Guard," touched a couple of members of the latter well-meaning body so neatly on the raw that they challenged Wagner to duels. [14]

---

[13] The reference is to the Wagner who figures as Faust's absurd famulus in Goethe's poem.

[14] The quip was quoted in the town for a long while after, as Röckel testifies. (RSE, p. 129.) The Guard seems to have been a somewhat futile body, not only before but during the revolution. The Government was naturally unfriendly to it, for it was ostensibly a democratic body; while the proletariat distrusted it because it numbered in its ranks too many of the "bourgeoisie," whose interest in revolution

5

He had clearly gone rather further than was pleasing to his official superiors. He and his views might in themselves be harmless. The Government organ, the Dresden *Journal*, in its report of the meeting in its issue of the 17th, referred indulgently to the marked contrast between " the coldly intellectual men of the Vaterlandsverein " and " the politics of the romantic poet and composer of *Tannhäuser*," in terms that suggest a slight wonder what Wagner was doing in such company; and it drily hinted that his address " abounded more in problems than in the solution of them." But the more realistically purposeful members of the Verein, among them Röckel, were not theoretical but very practical republicans, who were only playing the monarchical card until they could win over the mass of the people to the more extreme republican way of thinking.

While Wagner was indulging himself in his romantic delusion that the millennium would be amicably reached in Saxony by the King and Court voluntarily surrendering their feudal powers and privileges, Röckel was boldly proclaiming in the *Volksblätter* that the coming fight would be " the extremest, the hardest, the bloodiest that had ever yet been fought." Wagner's open association with firebrands of this kind could do him no good in the eyes of those whose business it was to maintain public order.[15] Even the King, forbearing as he was, seems to have taken some slight offence, and word of his private " censure " came to Wagner's ears: Lüttichau, for his part, could not fail to be annoyed by his Kapellmeister's openly expressed contempt for Courts and animus against courtiers. So Wagner thought it prudent, on the 18th June, to address a letter

---

was purely academic, their main concern, as Karl Marx angrily noted, being for domestic peace and consequent business profits.

[15] Hugo Dinger, in his reprint (1892) of the *Anzeiger* article, placed against it, in parallel columns, extracts from other Saxon papers of the time in which similar opinions are expressed. Ashton Ellis and Houston Stewart Chamberlain, anxious, as always, to minimise the extent of Wagner's co-operation in active politics, were inclined to pooh-pooh these resemblances. In substance, of course, much the same ideas were being expressed by many other German publicists of the period besides Wagner. But from certain finger-prints of style it is tolerably evident that some of the anonymous articles in the *Volksblätter* are from Wagner's hand. See DWGE, pp. 107–35, and Richard Sternfeld's remarks in the appendix to RWGS, XII, 425.

to the Intendant, in which, after a request for a fortnight's leave of absence from Dresden in order to submit himself rigorously to a diet for a gastric trouble that was threatening him, he explained just how the Address came to be delivered, and precisely what he had meant by it. His own position, he says, was that of a moderate; as against the anti-monarchists he wanted to show that, in Saxony, republicanism and Kinghood were not incompatible, and that social and political peace depended upon some such compromise as he had in view. His logic on this question had been quite sound in the abstract. He had pointed out to his Vaterlandsverein hearers that they could have either Kingship of the current type or a republic, but not a combination of the two in the form of the constitutional monarchy desired by some people. For " constitutional monarchy " is really a contradiction in terms; in so far as a King is bound by a constitution, Wagner had argued, he is not king in the sense in which the word was then understood. " Monarchy " meant the rule of one man, and could mean nothing else: " every step forward on the democratic basis is a fresh usurpation of the powers of the monarch, the *sole-ruler:* the principle itself is an utter mockery of monarchy, which is inconceivable except as the positive *rule of one man.*" Wagner's own plan of a republic with the King at the head of it would, he had held, not only save the State and free the citizens but " emancipate " the King. The latter's comment on all this was that it was not practical politics, but only " a poetic picture of Kingship." Wagner's " poetry " would not of itself have created so much disturbance in the royal household as the speech as a whole seems to have done. What really set alarmed ears pricking was the matter in the speech on which he does not dwell in his letter to Lüttichau — his declaration that if the aristocracy did not voluntarily surrender its privileges it would have to be destroyed, that " the contest will be a bloody one," and that the King and his party would both be involved in it. Wagner's intentions were honourable, his sincerity beyond dispute; and had his poetic views on kingship been the beginning and end of the matter, Lüttichau could have found no great reason for complaint, however strongly he may have resented the intrusion of this Court servant into politics.

But even in this letter Wagner tactlessly showed his hatred of those very Court circles to which the Intendant himself belonged; and in his concluding sentences he could not refrain from hinting threateningly at what would happen if his views were not adopted.

"I see, to my great sorrow," he said, "that the time for warfare with the weapons of the spirit is past. I am possessed with a gloomy, fearful foreboding that the war will now soon be waged only by the rougher elements among the masses. Prague is not far from us; [16] in Austria frightful things are preparing, that may take the horrible form of regicide. I have cast a glance at the masses of Dresden: for the moment there is no open sign of criminal activities; but who can answer for the tempest of madness when it bursts on us from outside?"

If his forebodings should prove unfounded, all the better; "but if the step I have taken has given offence, it has failed in its object; if it has only shocked instead of reconciling, then it rested on a delusion for which I sincerely ask pardon of all whom I have annoyed." Clearly he was not quite comfortable as to the effects of what he had said and done; and that Minna was anxious as to the possible results of his launching into politics is shown by his telling Lüttichau that he has given his wife a promise not to mix himself up again with the dangerous questions of the day. Poor Minna no doubt saw herself, if her husband did not mend his crazy ways, once more driven out into the wilderness. But events were too strong for him; it soon proved impossible for him, constituted as he was, to keep his promise to her.

6

Even yet, however, Lüttichau and the King, deeply as they must have been grieved, saw no reason to rank their Kapellmeister definitely among their political enemies, though Lüttichau, by this time, could have been under no illusion as to Wagner's contempt for him as an Opera Intendant. In 1850 — Wagner, of course, being then

---

[16] Alongside the German agitation for freedom and national unity there ran a desire on the part of the Czechs, Slavs and Magyars of the Austrian Empire for independence of their German masters and of each other. There was a revolt in Prague in the early days of June, during which the wife of the Austrian military commandant, Windischgratz, was killed. The insurrection was crushed after a twelve-hours' bombardment of the city.

in exile in Switzerland — a suggestion came from Dresden that he should allow his *Plan for the Organisation of a German National Theatre for the Kingdom of Saxony* [17] to be published. He had no objection to this, he told Uhlig in a long letter on the subject, though, as he said, the *Plan* had no practical meaning now, the conditions under which it might have been realised in 1848 having ceased to exist. In this letter he expresses frankly his poor opinion of the courtiers whom it had been the German tradition to place in command of Court theatres. It appears that the malevolent story had circulated in Dresden, at the time, that Wagner wanted to oust Lüttichau in order to become Intendant himself: as he says, let any one propose, however disinterestedly, any artistic reform whatsoever that implies the limitation of someone or other's ill-exercised powers, and the threatened man immediately assumes that the reformer is anxious to step into his shoes. " The courtier," says Wagner — speaking in general terms of Royal Intendants but meaning, of course, Lüttichau — " may have had an idea of resigning his position in the art institution, but feels compelled, by retaining it, to offer himself as a sacrifice as soon as he reflects that he, as a personage, is expected to give way, not to another person of the same qualifications, but to the fundamental dictum that all persons of his quality are incapable." [18]

From this it is manifest enough what Lüttichau's feeling about the matter was in 1848. Though Wagner's *Plan* had been submitted only to the Ministers of the Interior and of Public Worship, many people must have known of it, for, as Wagner tells us, the actors had petitioned the King to let the Court theatre continue as it was. Lüttichau would certainly feel that his unruly Kapellmeister was making a vigorous frontal attack not only on Court Intendants in general but on himself in particular; and probably few men in his position would have shown such forbearance as he did — a forbearance to be accounted for only on the dual theory that, with all his faults, he was a man of essentially fine character, and that Wagner was held in high esteem as an artist both by him and by the King. They turned decisively against him only when he forsook artistic theorising for practical politics.

---

[17] See Vol. I, pp. 495 ff.
[18] The letter will be found in RWUF, pp. 51–8.

Wagner's letter of apology was kindly received, and he obtained permission for the desired holiday. Apparently Eduard Devrient had been commissioned to bear him a friendly message; for two days later we find Wagner writing in the warmest terms to Lüttichau, addressing him familiarly and informally as "Excellent Man," wishing there were more like him in the world, and enclosing a communication to the King which he asks Lüttichau to pass on to the monarch if it meets with his approval. He had every reason to be grateful to the calm good sense and self-control of his Intendant. Some of the members of the orchestra had petitioned for Wagner's dismissal, their request, however, being countered by one in Wagner's favour from another section of the players, at the head of whom was Uhlig. Lüttichau took the part of his Kapellmeister — yet another proof of the exceptional esteem in which he and the King held Wagner, however much of a trial he might be to them in one way or another.[19]

It was during the next few days that Wagner, as has already been told, implored Liszt to come to his financial rescue by taking over the rights in the scores that he had published through Meser.[20] On

---

[19] By the time he came to write *Mein Leben* Wagner had persuaded himself that he had been mistaken in regarding Lüttichau as his friend during this and the immediately later period that was so critical for him — that Lüttichau, while friendly to his face, had really been trying to have him dismissed, and that these machinations had been foiled by the King himself. But there seems to be no evidence whatever in support of this theory. Considerable pressure must have been put upon Lüttichau, by high persons at Court, to deal firmly with this firebrand of a Kapellmeister; and had Lüttichau really joined the ranks of Wagner's enemies the composer's shrift would have been short. Wagner himself, as we have seen (Vol. I, p. 459), paid tribute later, during his exile, to the Intendant's forbearance towards him in those difficult last years in Dresden. There can be no doubt that, out of admiration for his genius, sympathy for his sufferings, and a keen sense of his box office value, both the King and Lüttichau endured patiently from him an amount of provocation they would not have put up with from any other employé. When Röckel went a step too far he was promptly dismissed from his post. Lüttichau can be excused a little peevishness now and then. Even a theatre Intendant is a human being; and Lüttichau's task of ruling his theatre both firmly and justly must have been a far from easy one. He stood to be shot at from all quarters. The opera and Wagner were not his only troubles: the government of the dramatic side of the theatre brought with it plenty of others. "What frame of mind is Lüttichau in just now?" the Dresden dramatist Gutzkow writes angrily to the actor Emil Devrient on the 28th March, 1848. "I have parted company with him after a very violent scene. He is an insupportable person, who more than anyone else deserves to fall with the representatives of the aristocratic system. I believe that the King, who wants to show his popular sympathies, needs only the slightest push and Lüttichau will have to go." (HED, p. 339).

[20] See Vol. I, p. 506.

the 2nd July he writes two letters — one to the Dresden bookseller Reimann, regretting he cannot pay his bill, and a cordial one to Lüttichau, asking for an extension of the leave that has been granted to him to " three or four weeks," so that he may " go on a little journey in order to strengthen soul and body and refresh them with new impressions." We gather that Lüttichau had been giving him, in private, some fatherly advice, for Wagner adds that after his holiday they will both be able to see more clearly whether there is any future for him in Dresden; meanwhile he will ponder quietly on Lüttichau's " kind counsel," and, " according to his conviction," willingly conform to Lüttichau's " judgment of what is necessary and suitable." At the same time he writes to Reissiger, asking him to be kind enough to fall in with the suggested arrangements for his leave; he is, he says, " a deadly sick man, who simply cannot be counted on at all."

Reissiger consents, in spite of the extra work that will necessarily fall on his own shoulders. Wagner, for his part, will enter into an arrangement that will make things easier for his older colleague " when I return to service — if," he writes to Lüttichau, " this should be possible for me again "; which seems to point to Lütti-chau, for all his forbearance, having given him a hint that he must mend his ways or have his appointment at the theatre terminated. Wagner is friendly and respectful; but he makes it clear that his desire for a temporary absence from Dresden is due not merely to ordinary overwork but to the fact that he has reached a moral crisis in his life. He obtains the desired extra leave; and the " deadly sick man," who is supposed to be in search of change and rest and a diet that will cure him of his physical ills, promptly betakes himself, not to the quiet of the country, not to a watering place, but to Vienna, the centre of a political upheaval to which anything that had so far happened in Dresden was the merest picnic. It is impossible not to believe that he had acted with a certain duplicity towards Lüttichau.

CHAPTER II

THE LITERARY WORK OF 1848

1

BEFORE WE follow him to Vienna, it will be as well to turn an eye for a moment on his non-political activities of the summer and autumn of 1848, and the frame of mind they indicate.

Until now, Wagner's prose writings had been mainly concerned with artistic actualities — reports of musical activities in the various towns to which he had wandered, programme notes for his Dresden concerts, replies to his critics, plans for the improvement of the orchestra and for the organisation of a National Theatre, and so on. To all these matters he brought the mind not only of the idealist but of the expert practician. But in the summer of 1848 a new Wagner comes into view — a boldly speculative philosopher who takes not only music but all literature, history, and life for his province. At the same time that his aspirations as an operatic artist had outgrown the circumstances of his immediate environment, his mind in general, in its enormous overplus of energy, was pursuing apparently the most roundabout paths towards a dimly seen new creative goal. For years he had been steeping himself in Germanic history and legend; and from the centre of the chaos of all he had read and pondered upon there was slowly shaping itself, deep down in his subconsciousness, a drama that should centre in the figure of Siegfried and the fate of the Nibelungen Hoard. But it was only by the most devious ways that he could clarify and concentrate his thinking on these subjects. All kinds of personages and motives from the most diverse fields of history and saga were swirling about within his mind, in a haze through which, as yet, he could not see his way clearly. The long essay on *The Wibelungen*, written in the summer of 1848, was a desperate effort on his part to blaze a trail through the jungle of it all — at once to reduce the mass of fact and legend to manageable artistic form and to find a point of con-

[18]

tact between his new ideas upon art and his solution of certain pressing social and political problems, including that of his own disharmony with the economic world around him.

In the *Wibelungen* essay he examines German political history from the foundations up, in the light of that problem of the Hoard that was perplexing him. But he sees all history through a fantastic mist of his own making. He speculates and generalises in a way that would often be comic did not our respect and sympathy for the great artist, struggling with a burden of thought such as no musician in the whole history of mankind had ever before been plagued with, repress in us every impulse to smile. He crystallises the complicated world of medieval German politics, religion, economics, dynastic struggles, and so on, into a few purely imaginative formulae, that owed their existence only to the fact that a dim instinct in him was driving him towards a great drama of which Siegfried was to be the central personage, and the Hoard, as the symbol of certain unpleasant aspects of politics and economics, the central point of struggle. Rejecting peremptorily the ordinary theory of the historians that the Wibelings — the medieval opponents of the Welfs [1] — took their title from the circumstance that Friedrich Barbarossa was born at the hamlet of Waiblingen, in Swabia, he identifies the Wibelings with the Nibelungen of the sagas. Siegfried, he held, was originally the sun-god, whose destiny it was to be slain, as Day is slain by Night. Just as, at first, Light vanquishes Darkness, so Siegfried vanquishes the Nibelungen dragon, thus winning for his own the Hoard guarded by the dragon. But the dragon's heir plots to win it back; and so the struggle for the possession of the Hoard sets up a vast cycle of revenge. The Hoard is really " the metal bowels of the earth " and all that these imply for humanity — arms, gold and power. In some mysterious way, it appears, the Nibelungen Hoard became identified in the minds of Charlemagne, his successors, and the German people with the idea of universal Kingship. With Barbarossa, the Hoard became essentially one with the Grail; and that last excursion of his into Asia, in which he lost his life, was made, says Wagner, in obedience to a mystical impulse to grasp the Hoard, that had now " ascended " spiritually into the Grail.

[1] The antagonists known later as Guelfs and Ghibelins.

2

It is almost impossible to condense the nebulous haze of Wagner's argument, expressed as it is in a German prose of peculiar obscurity, into lucid statement in any other language. His interpretation of history is often fantastic; the connection between the various elements of the picture he paints is sometimes not apparent to any eye but his own. Fortunately it is no part of my task, as a mere biographer, to re-write Wagner's prose works for English readers; we are here concerned less with his ideas in themselves, and the intrinsic value, or lack of value, of them, than with the temporary state of mind they reveal. One asks oneself in wonder, at first, what all this reading and theorising had to do with Wagner's real business of writing operas. At first sight the answer appears to be, Nothing; no other " librettist " in the world would have gone to all this trouble merely to fashion an " opera book " out of the legends of the Nibelungen Hoard. But Wagner had now arrived at a stage when he could take up no subject without bringing to bear upon it the whole weight of his extraordinarily active brain, of his wide reading, and of his troubled spiritual experience. In some strange way or other the Hoard became symbolical, for him, of the factors in modern society to which he attributed most of his own troubles. On the one hand the Hoard, in the course of time, had " become volatilised into the realm of Poetry and the Idea "; on the other hand there remained of it, on earth, a sediment that took the form of " real property," under the malign influence of which the ordinary man has more and more lost the sense of his primal freedom, while the " nobleman " has become more and more vain and arrogant, " never reflecting that exactly by his deriving his worth from a rigid family possession he was openly disowning and rejecting any actual *human nobleness*." The distinction, in short, in concrete terms, was that between a Lüttichau and a Richard Wagner. In the beginning, Man had conferred rights on Property: in our degenerate civilisation, it is Property that now confers " rights " on Man, and over men. And Richard Wagner, having no property of his own, and being always under the disagreeable necessity of borrowing from those who had, naturally thought there was something fundamentally wrong with a state of society in which so flagrant an injustice was possible.

Ellis sums up the *Wibelungen* essay in these words: for Wagner, " the Hoard was also the Grail, and Friedrich was Siegfried, and Siegfried was Baldur, and Baldur was Christ." Plainly nothing could be done with this huge and confused material for ordinary artistic purposes until it had clarified and sorted itself out in Wagner's subconsciousness. For a considerable time he could not see whither it was all leading him. It was long before he could quite separate the overlapping images of Barbarossa and Siegfried. He concludes the *Wibelungen* essay with the picture of the great Kaiser as the German people had always seen him, guarding the Hoard in the Kyffhäuser, " by his side the sharp sword that had once slain the fierce dragon." That, at least, is the concluding sentence of the essay as we now have it. But when he was reprinting the essay in the Collected Edition of his works in the 1870's he struck out a couple of paragraphs that had formed the real ending in the edition published about the end of 1849: " When comest thou again, Friedrich, thou glorious Siegfried, and slayest the evil gnawing Dragon of humanity? " . . . " Two ravens fly around my mountain — they made themselves fat on the theft of the Kingdom! From the south-east hacks the one, from the north-east the other — chase away the ravens and the Hoard is yours! — But leave me at rest in my gods'-mountain." [2]

Friedrich, Siegfried, the Hoard, the two ravens (of the later *Ring*) and the Dragon are here evidently hovering more or less connectedly but still confusedly before Wagner's fantasy. It cost him much subconscious gestation and much hard conscious thinking before the seething, whirling nebula solidified at last into *Siegfrieds Tod*. Even while he was working upon *Lohengrin* he had had floating before his mind's eye, concurrently with the Siegfried subject, a more or less definite notion of a poetic drama on the subject of Barbarossa; he himself has told us that he saw Friedrich as " a historical re-birth of the old-pagan Siegfried "; and we have his own account in *A Communication to my Friends*,[3] of how the contest between the two themes within him gradually convinced him

---

[2] See RWGS, XII, pp. 227, 425.   [3] RWGS, IV, p. 311.

that in myth and music, not in history and the spoken play, lay the only possibility of the true drama of the future. He actually got so far with the Friedrich subject at that time as to commence the draft of a projected five-act drama upon it.[4]

3

This *Friedrich I* was to have been a spoken play in five acts. The plan begins with the difficulties of the Kaiser with the Lombard cities and with the Church, and ends with the conclusion of peace with the Pope and the Lombards, the news of the fall of Jerusalem, and Friedrich's resolve to go upon a crusade. The additional sheet of 1848 contains a somewhat detailed analysis of the motives of the second act; so that it looks as if, even as late as that time, Wagner was still seriously occupied with the idea of a spoken drama on the subject. And in this supplement of 1848 there are certain passages that link up with his political activities of the period, with those views on property, and the theory of the King as " the first of republicans," which he had set forth in the Vaterlandsverein Address. Nature and its fruits, Friedrich is made to say, belong of right to men. When, however, men wish to constitute themselves into races and countries, they quarrel as to what belongs to each of them; and now is seen the value of " Kaiser-right," in virtue of which the land and everything on it belongs by divine right to the Kaiser; he distributes between his subjects, each according to his need, as a good father divides his property among his children.

> " Therefore I say unto you, everything you have and enjoy, unless you be vested with it by the Kaiser, you hold and enjoy without right, and any robber can take it from you with the same right, for whatever is belongs to him as much as to you; and so the Kaiser, in his wisdom and justice, endows each of you with what it is meet for him to have,

---

4 Wagner did not include this in the Collected Edition of his writings. It remained at Wahnfried, unpublished, until Richard Sternfeld printed it in the first of the two supplementary volumes of the Collected Works (XI, 270–2). The draft of the first act is dated in the manuscript "31st October, 1846." That of the second act, beyond which Wagner did not proceed with the scheme, is undated. It is written on a different kind of paper from the other, and whereas the first draft is in German script, the second is in Latin characters, with small first-letters for the nouns. As it was not until about the end of 1848 that Wagner adopted this procedure, the addition cannot be earlier than that time.

and your feudal lord is your highest and constant protector. Each of you cares for himself alone: the Kaiser's care is for you all! "

No doubt Wagner, in the hectic days of 1848, had more than once paused in the course of his vaporous theorising about the " Folk " to ask himself what, after all, would happen if the existing laws of property and inheritance were suddenly abolished: would not each man try to seize what he could, the strongest and most unscrupulous be victorious, and the last state of the innocent " Folk " be worse than the first? To this awkward question he found, for the moment, a satisfactory answer in his theory of the all-wise and all-good Kinghood — an " authority " indeed, for without authority society would go to pieces, but an authority accepted by all for the benefit of all. All were to be free, but the King was to be the Freest of the Free. The draft of the speech of Friedrich in Act II correlates closely with the following passage in the Vaterlandsverein Address: .

" What individual could be more destined than the Prince to belong, with all his feelings, all his senses, all his endeavours, *entirely* to the affairs of the Folk? Convinced of his glorious calling, what could move him to belittle himself to such an extent as to wish to belong to merely a particular *smaller* section of his people? However warmly each of us must feel for the good of all, none of us could ever be so pure a Republican as the Prince, for *his* cares are undivided; they are for the One and for the Whole, whereas each of us must needs distribute his cares according to the common round of daily life."

It could not have needed very much reflection to convince Wagner that historical subjects and the spoken drama could never draw the best out of him. For that, music as well as poetry and drama were needed: and so we find him, even while he was brooding upon the Barbarossa subject, getting to closer grips with that of Siegfried. In the summer of 1848 he made a lengthy " Sketch for a Drama " as he calls it, to be derived from the Nibelungen myth. Broadly speaking, this scenario covers the whole of the ground of the later *Ring*, from the first theft of the gold from the Rhine by Alberich to the restoration of the Ring to the Rhine-Maidens after the death of Siegfried and the sacrifice of Brynhilde. Shortly afterwards, the essence of the subject, or what seemed to Wagner at that time to be the essence of it, was cast into what has generally been regarded as the first form of *Siegfrieds Tod* — the text of a drama, virtually corresponding to the present *Götterdämmerung*, which Wagner himself did not disdain to issue in the Collected Edition of his works, though by that time the full text of the *Ring* as we now know it had already been published for some time. The complete story of the stages through which the text of the *Ring* drama went has only recently been made available through the researches of Otto Strobel; [5] and the facts, so far as they concern *Siegfrieds Tod*, had better be set forth connectedly at this point, even though, in doing this, we shall be carried for a moment somewhat ahead of the year at which we have now arrived.

4

Few people realise the enormous labour that went into the creation and polishing of the text alone of the *Ring*. From first to last, Wagner's manuscripts relating to the subject — prose outlines, poetic drafts, fair copies, and so on — run to more than 760 pages. He had to do an immense amount of reading, during his Dresden period, in and around the sagas and their attendant modern literature. In 1856 Franz Müller, of Weimar, conceived the idea of writing a book on Wagner's *Ring* poem. He applied to the composer for information as to the sources to which he had gone, and Wagner, in reply, set them forth thus:

(1) *Der Nibelunge Noth und Klage*, edited by Lachmann.
(2) *Zu den Nibelungen, etc.*, by Lachmann.
(3) Grimm's *Mythologie*.
(4) The *Edda*.
(5) The *Volsunga-Saga*, in Hagen's version.
(6) The *Wilkina and Niflunga-Saga*, ditto.
(7) *Das deutsche Heldenbuch*, Hagen's old edition, re-edited, in six volumes, by Simrock.
(8) *Die deutsche Heldensage*, by Wilhelm Grimm.
(9) Mone's writings on the German sagas.
(10) The *Heimskringla*, in Mohnike's translation.

---

[5] See SSE, *passim*.

Nowhere, apparently, does he make any mention of a work which, strictly speaking, is not a " source," yet which almost certainly played its part in the conception of the *Ring*. In the second volume of his *Kritische Gänge* (1844) the aesthetician Friedrich Theodor Vischer published a long essay entitled *Vorschlag zu einer Oper* (*Suggestion for an Opera*), which is interesting in many ways to-day. Vischer was of the opinion that the time was ripe for a new development in German opera. So far, he said, it had been occupied with exploiting the world of subjective feeling; now it was time to turn to the objective. German music had had in Mozart its Goethe, in Haydn its Klopstock, in Beethoven its Jean Paul, in Weber its Tieck; but it had not yet had its Schiller or its Shakespeare. The foundation for a genuine German national opera would have to be the ancient heroic myths of the race. What was now needed was an indigenous national music, answering to the indigenous poetry that modern Germany had created for itself; and this music would have to be heroic. Gluck, indeed, had been, in his way, heroic, but his subjects had been taken from a world not only remote from but alien to the present. The strength of Mozart — " this Italian-feeling Austrian " — had been the representation of " the fiery world of southern passion." He had expressed only private, subjective passion: heroes and the mighty figures of life on the grand scale were outside his range: though he was German at the core, his operatic art was Italian or Spanish. Spontini had a touch of the heroic in him, and for one of his operas, indeed, *Agnes von Hohenstaufen,* he had chosen a German subject: but he aimed too much at external effect, thinning down the true heroic into the merely pompous and military. Beethoven was too romantic and symphonic for the national musical drama that the new Germany needed. Weber had been dramatic enough, but had lived too much in the romantic wonder-world of elves and fiends. Among living composers, Meyerbeer had perhaps strength enough for a heroic subject, but his strength was not pure — it had been corrupted by the French love of effect for effect's sake. The genuine German opera would have to be national in the ways that the myths were national: the heroes of the Nibelungenlied were the true German types, expressive of German mildness, German wrath, German fidelity and good-nature, German love and valour, the tender diffidence, the stubborn toughness, the stern defiance, in a word the deep humanity of the German character. All these natural qualities of the German folk were incarnated in the saga, and there set forth in their primal strength and purity. Out of the saga, then, the national music-drama would have to be made: but " we have no such subject in our music, and no music for such a subject, just as we have no Shakespeare." [6]

The predestined theme, then, Vischer opined, was the Nibelungen saga. But the theme, he argues acutely, is not suitable for the spoken drama. For if, he says,

> " we give these iron men, these giant women, the eloquence required by the drama, the sophistication of passion, the reflectiveness, the capacity to make their volitions clear, to justify them, to cast doubts on them (all which is necessary to the characters of a drama), they at once cease to exist. Their very greatness is so inseparable from their sparingness in the matter of words, their wordless concentration in the depths of their own being, their ruggedness, that they cease to be what they are and yet fail to become anything else that could please and move us."

A form, therefore, would have to be found " in which this material shall be made acceptable to modern feeling, without, however, any sacrifice of its true character." This form would have to be that of opera; for in music the harsh and rugged come to us in an agreeably tempered form. Vischer accordingly suggests the Nibelungenlied as the ideal stuff for " a grand heroic opera ": " it is as if it were made for opera; it wells up out of the most splendid musical motives; it has long awaited its composer, and now calls to him imperiously." [7]

He sees difficulties in the way — the unclearness of the action as a whole, the epic quality of the story, its superabundance of incident. But these difficulties, he is sure, can be surmounted; and he proceeds to draw up an elaborate scenario for a five-act Nibelungen musical drama, to be given on two evenings. There is little similarity between this and Wagner's work: Wagner's genius enabled him at once to condense the action and give it its maximum of significance in a way that was beyond the powers of the pedestrian

---

[6] VKG, II, 399–404.   [7] Ibid., pp. 406–10.

Vischer. In the summer of 1845 Louise Otto, who had read the latter's essay, published three articles on the subject in the *Neue Zeitschrift*, following these up, in October, with the text of the first three scenes of a Nibelungen drama of her own — an appalling specimen of the libretto-German of the period.[8] As Wagner read the *Neue Zeitschrift* it is possible that if he did not already know Vischer's book his attention was drawn to it by Louise Otto's articles. The conclusion that he had read Vischer seems inescapable. It was in 1845, during his work on *Lohengrin*, that he first became interested in the Siegfried subject; but it was not until 1846 that the figure of Siegfried began to force itself upon him as the central theme of his next drama; and it is not an unreasonable assumption that Vischer's arguments, which coincided at so many points with his own ideas, played a determining part in his thinking during these years.[9]

---

[8] Gade appears to have coquetted with the idea of writing music to this text. See TRW, pp. 78–82.

[9] The Nibelungen subject occupied the minds of many poets and composers in the first half of the nineteenth century. A play on the subject by Raupach, *Der Nibelungenhort*, was produced in 1828 and printed in 1834. Wagner may or may not have been acquainted with this. In 1837 A. W. F. von Zuccalmaglio published in the *Neue Zeitschrift* (under the pseudonym of Wedel) an article on *Die deutsche Oper* in which he spoke of the suitability of myths and legends for music, and especially singled out "the hero Siegfried" as one of the characters "that await the artist, the awakener, who can bring him to life again in a rejuvenated form." Schumann seems to have been impressed by this suggestion, for in his note-book he entered "Faust, Eulenspiegel, the Wartburg Contest, Nibelungen, etc.," as likely subjects for an opera of his own. In 1840 Mendelssohn was inspired by his sister Fanny with enthusiasm for a Nibelungen opera, but the idea was soon dropped. Dorn's opera *Die Nibelungen* was produced in 1854. Hebbel worked at his impressive drama from 1855 to about 1860.

Wagner tells us in *Mein Leben* that in Paris, about 1842, his interest in the Tannhäuser legend was stimulated by a "Volksbuch" that had accidentally come into his hands. No such "Volksbuch" is known to German scholars, and the problem connected with it has been given up as insoluble. Recently, however, Dr. Henri Colomb has pointed out the resemblances between Wagner's *Siegfried* and a story by Alexandre Dumas that appeared in the numbers of a popular Paris magazine of the period, the *Musée des Familles*, for September, October, and November, 1841. The story was entitled *Les Aventures merveilleuses du Prince Lyderic*; but the adventures are those of Siegfried. The narrative, according to Colomb, is "a first attempt at a condensation of the legends, aiming at a fusion of the several Siegfrieds presented to us episodically in various epic sources. A number of features which appear neither in the Edda sagas, nor in the Nibelungenlied, nor in the Hürnen Siegfried, are common to Dumas and Wagner."

Colomb thinks it probable that Wagner read Dumas's story while he was in Paris, for the magazine in which it appeared was a "best seller" of that epoch. He surmises also that the so-called Tannhäuser "Volksbuch" was merely another story of the

5

In dealing with the material for *Siegfrieds Tod,* Wagner followed his general practice in these matters. He first of all made a number of detached sketches: then came an elaborate Prose Sketch, that not only outlined the whole drama but developed each episode in some detail, even the future dialogue being prefigured here and there. After that came the actual poem in its first form; and then the fair copy, in which the final wording was decided upon, though Wagner would occasionally alter even this during the composition of the music, sometimes to get a syllabic accent or an order of the words that would fit the melodic and rhythmic scheme of his music better than the original line had done, sometimes to obtain more elbow room for the musician in him, who, being fairly launched upon a " development " that fascinated him for its own purely musical sake, and finding that the words in front of him did not quite space out over the whole of the desired musical area, did not hesitate to add as many words or lines as were necessary.

The first sketch — *The Nibelungen-Myth as Sketch for a Drama* — is dated, at the end of the manuscript, 4th October, 1848. It differs in several respects from the *Ring* as we now know it: Freia is not among the characters; Alberich has obtained the gold without the renunciation of love; the Hoard and the Ring, after they have come into the possession of the Giants, are watched by a dragon appointed by themselves (not, as in the present *Ring*, by one of themselves changed into a dragon); Siegmund already has a wife, but this union, like that of Sieglinde and Hunding, being barren, the twins Siegmund and Sieglinde have to wed to beget the genuine Wälsung wished for by the gods; the sword forged by Siegfried is called Balmung; before killing the dragon, Siegfried avenges his father's death upon Hunding; at the end, Valhalla does not perish in flames, but Brynhilde conducts Siegfried to Wotan, the long-threatened power of the gods being at last restored to them. It will be observed that this sketch is " for a drama." No doubt

same type, of which several appeared in the *Musée des Familles* and the *Magasin Pittoresque* at that time. There may be something in this ingenious conjecture, though it hardly seems likely that by "Volksbuch" Wagner means not a "Folkbook" of the Middle Ages but simply a "popular publication." See HSD, pp. 189 ff.

during the elaboration of it, and when making a fair copy of it, which he did on the 8th October, 1848, Wagner realised that there was a first-rate theme for *musical* treatment in it. Accordingly he immediately set to work on the poem of *Siegfrieds Tod*. This concentrates on the final stage of the long story: after a brief scene for the Three Norns, we have Siegfried parting from Brynhilde in quest of adventures, his arrival at the court of Gunther, and so on as in the *Götterdämmerung*. The long chain of events precedent is merely hinted at, first of all by the Norns, then in a colloquy between Brynhilde and a troop of Valkyries circling round her rock (the forerunner of the scene, in the *Götterdämmerung*, between Brynhilde and Waltraute).

The stages by which *Siegfrieds Tod* developed into the final form in which we now have it were, until recently, to some extent a matter of speculative detective work. The researches of Otto Strobel in the Wahnfried archives have at last established the real facts; the difficulty confronting the earlier investigators had been that although all the manuscripts are still in existence, some of them were not previously accessible.

Wagner himself is responsible for one slight misunderstanding. In *Mein Leben* he tells us that when, immediately after completing the poem of *Siegfrieds Tod*, he read it to Eduard Devrient, the latter shrewdly pointed out to him that he had taken for granted too much knowledge, on the public's part, of the events antecedent to the drama; the bitterness of Brynhilde's hostility to Siegfried in the second act, for instance, could be fully understood only if the audience had seen something of the pair in their former loving relationship. Wagner goes on to say that he had, in fact (as in the first act proper of the present *Götterdämmerung*), opened his poem of *Siegfrieds Tod* with the scene in the Hall of the Gibichungs, the audience being left to surmise the earlier episodes between Siegfried and Brynhilde from the short colloquy, in a later scene, between Brynhilde and a band of Valkyries riding through the air about her rock. Wagner's manuscript of *Siegfrieds Tod*, however, which is dated on the first page " 12th November, 1848," begins, *not* with the scene in the Hall of the Gibichungs, but, as in the present *Götterdämmerung*, with a prelude that opens with the colloquy of the Three Norns and then proceeds to the scene between Siegfried and Brynhilde. The explanation of the discrepancy is clearly that Wagner has made a slip in *Mein Leben:* what he read to Devrient must have been not the *poem* of *Siegfrieds Tod* but the first prose sketch (dated the 20th October, 1848), which *does* plunge at once into the scene between Gunther, Hagen, and Gudrune.

6

Recognising the force of Devrient's criticism, he must have proceeded at once (about the end of October) to make a supplementary Prose Sketch [10] of (*a*) a conversation between the Norns, (*b*) a following scene between Brynhilde and Siegfried, as in the *Götterdämmerung.* Then, on the 12th November, he began the poetic version of *Siegfrieds Tod,* commencing with this new prelude; the final page of the poem is dated 28th November.[11] He at once read the poem (early in December) to a group of his closest friends, Gustav Kietz, Semper, Fischer, Ferdinand Heine and his son Wilhelm, Hans von Bülow, and Karl Ritter. A discussion followed: Fischer shook his serious old head, unable to see how such a poem could be treated in music, whereupon Wagner explained the part that the orchestra would play in the drama, and insisted that the time had come when more importance should be attached to " the word " than had hitherto been the case in opera.[12]

The first Prose Sketch, it will have been noted, was for " a drama "; but *Siegfrieds Tod* is styled in the manuscript " a grand heroic opera in three acts."

Indefatigable as always, Wagner made a fair copy [13] of his poem in December, leaving the text virtually unchanged, but making several alterations in the scenic directions. At a much later date he worked once more over this manuscript; of this redaction Nietzsche, long afterwards, made a fair copy,[14] from which was printed the version published by Wagner himself in the Collected Edition of his works in the 1870's. This printed version, there-

---

[10] This is now published for the first time in SSE, pp. 55–8.
[11] This manuscript is now in the possession of Dr. Siegmund von Hausegger, Munich.
[12] See Kietz's account of the afternoon and evening, in KW, pp. 69–70.
[13] Now in the possession of the Winterthur Town Library.
[14] Now in the possession of the Richard Wagner Gedenkstätte in Bayreuth.

fore, represents not the first but a relatively late form of the text.

In the early part of 1849 he subjected the poem as it then was to a drastic revision, the results of which are summarised thus by Strobel:

" The first act receives the form of the first act of the present *Götterdämmerung*.

" In the second act, Siegfried's speech at the end of scene 4 is slightly expanded, and scene 6 completely cut out, with the exception of the *Weihgesang* of the vassals and women. The trio between Brynhilde, Gunther, and Hagen at the end of scene 5 (with which the act now ends) was expanded, this expansion, together with the *Weihgesang*, being built up into a regular operatic finale.

" The third act is unchanged."

All this necessitated the making of yet another fair copy [15] (the third in a few weeks), presumably in January or February, 1849. The full title now becomes *Siegfrieds Tod, a Heroic Opera in Three Acts*. Even in this copy he made sundry changes in Brynhilde's words at the end of the third act. To complete the record, it may be stated here that at Villeneuve, on the Lake of Geneva, in May, 1850, having decided to publish the text of *Siegfrieds Tod*, Wagner made a fourth fair copy of the poem. (At this period, under the influence of Jacob Grimm, he still preferred the Latin to the German script, and used small letters for all nouns except proper names. The publisher with whom he was negotiating — Wigand, of Leipzig, — told him that if he insisted on the use of Latin characters in the book he could not count on the sale of a single copy; the plan for publication consequently came to nothing.) This fourth fair copy was extensively altered later, in November and December, 1852, when Wagner was casting *Siegfrieds Tod* into the final form it assumes in the *Götterdämmerung*,[16] except, of course, as regards the closing words of Brynhilde, which belong to a still later date. In this last redaction Wagner expands the opening scene of the Norns to its present proportions.[17]

---

[15] Now in the possession of Herr Sulzer, of Zürich.

[16] Ellis's conjectures as to a revision in the summer of 1851 are shown by Strobel to be without foundation in fact.

[17] The prose sketch for this scene was discovered only recently in the Wagner archives. It was published by Otto Strobel, for the first time, in DM, 1933, No. 5 (February).

7

With all these varied tasks in hand, to say nothing of his work at the theatre, Wagner could hardly have found very much time in 1848 for political activity of the cruder kind. Interested as he undoubtedly was in outer events, it would be a mistake on our part to regard these as the prime factor in his life at this period. The changes that were going on within him had their origin in the artistic and spiritual core of him, and they were profound. For the first time in the history of music, a composer was subconsciously driven to compass a whole world not only of literature and aesthetic but of social and ethical speculation before he could attune his mind to creation, and before he could find the appropriate material on which to let his imagination work. The period of formal theorising about music and the drama came rather later, when he was free of Dresden and the routine work of the theatre; but the incandescent mass of ideas of all kinds that could later be reduced to coherence only by formal theorising was already swirling within him. With his eager mind full of speculations so vast in their range as these, we can understand how the commonplace traffic of his daily life and the crude business of the Dresden theatre came to seem utterly unreal to him: when his thought was ranging excitedly over the whole world of history and legend, of musical history, of poetic, dramatic, and musical aesthetic, and trying to cut its way through the inchoate mass to a new theory and practice of musical drama, it must have seemed tragi-comically fantastic to him that he should be expected to take a burning interest in such problems as " whether the Kriete could sing the part or not." [18] His mind was elsewhere, on remote mystical heights whither none of his associates could follow him.

Least of all would the Reissigers, the Lüttichaus, the Gutzkows, the Hillers, or the Schumanns have been able to plod after him in the new world of music towards which his instinct was slowly leading him. It must have been clear to him from the first that such an opera as *Siegfrieds Tod* would be a pure impossibility on any German stage of that epoch. His best friends shook their heads over

---

[18] See Vol. I, p. 480.

the poem when he read it to them: if Schumann had been at a loss to understand how even such a text as *Lohengrin* could ever be set to music, that of *Siegfrieds Tod* must have seemed to the friendliest well-wisher utterly impracticable. It could be envisaged in terms of no musical " form," as musical form was then understood. The curt, pregnant utterances of the characters, often amounting in their quick give-and-take to no more than a single line of three or four words, obviously allowed no scope for vocal expansion of the conventional lyrical kind; the old structure of solo, duet, ensemble, and so on would manifestly have to go by the board. What was to take their place would be quite beyond the comprehension of his Dresden friends, however great their faith in his genius might be. Nor could he himself have had, at that time, much more than the first dim notion of how a text and a subject of this kind were to be clothed with music. He must have had an intuition that the key to the solution of the impending problem lay in a vast expansion of the *symphonic* resources of orchestral music along post-Beethoven lines; but of all that this implied in practice he could as yet have had only the haziest vision. The realisation of *Siegfrieds Tod* in the musical idiom of *Tannhäuser* and *Lohengrin* would have been frankly impossible; yet musically he was not anything like ripe, in 1848, for the drastic change of idiom that would be required. For that he had to wait in patience till what was still only confusedly implicit in the darkest depths of his musical consciousness should have developed into the explicit; and it was in obedience to the surest of artistic instincts that after finishing *Lohengrin* in August, 1847, he wrote no more dramatic music until, at the end of October, 1853, he began the composition of the *Rhinegold*.[19]

---

[19] In June, 1853, he had written a little "sonata" for Frau Wesendonk's Album. The same year saw the composition of the *Züricher Vielliebchen-Walzer*, a humorous trifle of some thirty bars written for Frau Wesendonk's sister Marie.

It is true that in 1850, as the reader will learn later, he began the composition of the opening scene of *Siegfrieds Tod*, but he did not proceed very far with this. It is true also that during the years between 1848 and 1853 he must have drafted a number of the leading motives. But the statement in the text remains correct for all that: a sound instinct told him that he was not yet ripe for the steady evolution of the great drama in terms of music, and for the welding of the details of it into a whole.

CHAPTER III

LEADING UP TO REVOLUTION

1

W E HAVE seen that as soon as he had obtained the desired leave he betook himself, on the 7th July, 1848, to Vienna, where he arrived on the 9th; he found modest quarters in the Goldschmied-gasse, No. 594, near the Stephansplatz. He had gone by way of Breslau, where he spent an evening at the house of Mosewius, examining the old scholar's rich collection of manuscript copies of as yet unpublished church cantatas of Johann Sebastian Bach, and talking politics. One of his objects in visiting Vienna may have been to get *Rienzi* produced; and it is evident now that he had already thought of settling there if circumstances should compel him to leave Dresden.

Wagner, of course, was at this time no more than a name in Vienna, not a note of his music having as yet been heard there. The Austrian capital, in spite of its long association with Haydn, Mozart, Schubert, and Beethoven, was now not much more than a backwater in German music. The local taste had steadily declined since the death of Beethoven (1827) and of Schubert (1828): in the theatre the Viennese cared for little else than Italian opera, and in the concert room for little else than star instrumental performers. Apparently the only musical journal existing in the town when Wagner arrived there was the weekly *Allgemeine Wiener Musik-zeitung* (founded in 1841), the editor of which was Dr. August Schmidt. Its chief contributor was a Dr. Alfred Julius Becher, a man of remarkable parts. Born in Manchester, of German parents, in 1803, he had forsaken law for music, functioned for a time as a professor at the Royal Academy of Music in London, and settled in Vienna in 1842 as a journalist. Wagner describes him in *Mein Leben* as " a passionate and exceedingly cultured man," remarkable for " a certain distractedness and vehemence." Berlioz, who met

Becher in Vienna in 1845, speaks of him as a critic of distinction and a composer of ambitions: " a dreamy concentrated soul, whose harmonic audacity goes beyond anything yet attempted, who endeavours to enlarge the form of the quartet and give it new turns." [1] Becher plunged into politics in 1848, took part in the rising in October of that year, was captured by the imperial forces, and was shot on the 24th November.

Such connection as Wagner had already had with Vienna was not particularly happy. The success of *Rienzi* in 1842 had been duly recorded in the Press there, the notices, of course, coming from correspondents in Dresden. At first the tone was friendly: a certain " Germanus," in the *Allgemeine Theaterzeitung*, recorded the enthusiastic reception given to the new work in Dresden, said that " with this, his first opera, Wagner has placed himself by the side of the best living composers," and prophesied the foremost place for him if he could " fulfil the expectations aroused by this brilliant début." The *Allgemeine Wiener Musikzeitung*, in the leisurely fashion of those days, did not discuss *Rienzi* until the 7th and 9th February, 1843, when an anonymous critic (obviously writing from Dresden) treated the work in the fashion that is only too familiar to-day to students of Wagner criticism: a certain amount of praise was doled out to the young composer, but he was solemnly censured for his unkindness to the human voice, his lack of melody, and the vehemence of his orchestration: " one step further," the critic summed up, " and music ceases to exist." A reply by a Dresden musician, Morgenroth (signing himself " Abendroth "), appeared in the issues of the 25th, 28th, and 30th March, interspersed with editorial comments that suggest anything but friendliness towards Wagner on Schmidt's part. Six months later, on the 14th September, Wagner himself addressed a letter of protest to the paper, complaining of the " animosity " shown to a young German composer at the beginning of his career. To this the editor had no difficulty in making a forensically effective reply in the issue of the 5th October.

The Dresden productions of the *Flying Dutchman* (January, 1843) and *Tannhäuser* (October, 1845) had been briefly recorded

---

[1] BM, II, 201.

in various Vienna newspapers, with the customary lack of insight on the part of the writers into the vital new elements of Wagner's operatic purpose. Between the 28th November and the 29th December, 1846, however, there appeared no less than eleven articles on Wagner in the *Allgemeine Wiener Musikzeitung* from the pen of the twenty-one-years-old Eduard Hanslick, who had heard a performance of *Tannhäuser* in Dresden and studied the work in a piano score which he had borrowed from Schumann. Hanslick hailed Wagner as " the greatest living dramatic talent," and pronounced *Tannhäuser* to be the best opera of the last twelve years (the *Huguenots* had been produced in February, 1836). Wagner thanked Hanslick in the long and thoughtful letter of the 1st January, 1847, to which reference has already been made.[2]

Subsequent references to Wagner in the Vienna press were scanty; but already there was the tendency, always so bitterly and so justly resented by him, to condemn him without knowing anything of his works at first hand: it is probable, indeed, that Hanslick was the only Viennese journalist of that period who had seen a Wagner opera on the stage.

The political unrest in Austria in the spring of 1848 had turned men's minds exclusively in the direction of politics: even the literary and musical papers (among them the *Musikzeitung*) either ceased to exist or temporarily diverted their energies to the problems of the moment. This was the atmosphere into which the optimistic Wagner, with his idealistic dream of a theatre re-born, plunged in July, 1848.[3]

He sought out Professor Josef Fischof, a teacher of the piano at the Conservatoire. Fischof possessed not only the scores of Wagner's operas but some Beethoven manuscripts, including that of the C minor piano sonata, Op. 111, which Wagner examined with interest. In *Mein Leben* he curtly dismisses Fischof with the remark that he was " somewhat dry," whereas his contemporary letters to Minna tell quite another story. He made the acquaintance of Vesque von Püttlingen (a mediocre composer whom he chaffs, in *Mein Leben*, for having modestly been content, for a pseudonym, with

---

[2] See Vol. I, pp. 451–2.

[3] For a mass of information as to the Vienna Press in the first half of the nineteenth century, and its attitude towards Wagner, see BWSW, pp. 1–27.

only the last five letters of Beethoven's name, the fact being, however, that " Hoven " was the name of the family estate near Brussels); the journalist and author Friedrich Uhl (who will come into the Wagner story again in 1865); Dr. Ludwig August Frankl (whom Wagner, in his account of the matter in *Mein Leben*, confuses with the poet Adolf Franckel, who published an " epic-lyrical " poem, *Der Tannhäuser*, in 1854); a Dr. Josef Bacher [4] (a journalist and notorious celebrity hunter whom he describes to Minna as " rich and enthusiastic," but who turned out later, he says, to be " a pettifogger and an agent of Meyerbeer "); the poet Grillparzer; the hypochondriacal comedy writer Eduard von Bauernfeld (who apparently was so little impressed by his new acquaintance that he makes no mention of Wagner in his diary); and Dr. Alfred Julius Becher, who, as we have seen, had now forsaken music for politics.

2

Wagner's letters to Minna place it beyond doubt that his true reason for asking for leave had not been to try a diet, as he told Lüttichau, but to go straight to Vienna, to lay before influential people there a certain " plan " with which Minna was already familiar, and to secure, if possible, an engagement at the Kärntnertor Opera. The local enthusiasts were just then under the spell of that " national " exclusivist feeling that always comes uppermost, for the moment, in times of heightened political self-consciousness: the age-long Italian musical domination in Vienna was to be broken; German operas were to be the staple fare; even the customary " Madame " and " Demoiselle " on the playbills were now to be replaced by " Frau " and " Fräulein." [5] Wagner's " plan " was to combine the five competing Vienna theatres in one co-operative organisation, under the control of a committee constituted partly of the players, partly of the writers for the theatres. Something of the kind, it will be remembered, had been in his mind in connection with his *Organisation of a National Theatre for Saxony;* no doubt the momentary success of the rising in Vienna seemed to him to hold out a promise of democratic control of the theatre, and there-

---

[4] Not Pacher as in *Mein Leben*.   [5] See MWK, I, 69, 70.

fore of freedom from the Court officials he so hated and despised. The plan must have been committed to paper before he left Dresden, for he read it in Vienna to a small meeting convened for that purpose. The document, unfortunately, has not survived. However much his hearers may have agreed with him in theory, — they went so far as to ask him for copies of it, to be sent to the Ministers concerned, and the question of his leaving Dresden to take over the direction of the Kärntnertor was actually discussed [6] — nothing could be done immediately, in view of the unrest and uncertainty of the times; and after his departure from Vienna the scheme was quietly shelved. For the rest, his letters of the period show him to have been greatly excited by the democratic ferment all around him: like so many others, he felt that a golden era was dawning for humanity in general and for artists in particular. And just as in 1847 he had felt that Dresden was small and provincial in comparison with Berlin, so now his pulse quickens at the sight of Vienna, with its half a million inhabitants, its eight thousand students in old-German costume, its traditional blitheness, its pretty, well-dressed women. "I have found Paris again," he writes to Minna, " only more beautiful, gayer, and German. . . . God, how common and greasy a certain town looks to me in comparison! "

In Frankl's paper the *Abendzeitung* [7] there appeared, on the 20th July, an announcement that " Richard Wagner, the interesting composer of *Rienzi*, the *Flying Dutchman*, and *The Contest of Song on the Wartburg*," had been in the town for some days, and had brought with him an " ingenious programme for a reorganisation of the Vienna theatres from the standpoint of the Theatre as a National Institution," which was to be put before the Minister for Education and then before a committee of authors and musicians. This notice was reproduced by the Leipzig *Signale* in its first August number. It could hardly have failed to come under the notice of Lüttichau, who, putting two and two together, would not have much difficulty in guessing what had been in the mind of his some-

---

[6] See RWMW, I, 50.

[7] Thus in MWK, I, 76. According to Walter Bohe, who has made a first-hand study of the Vienna Press of the period, the news was given in much the same words in the 22nd July issue of the *Demokrat* (formerly the *Wanderer*). See BWSW, p. 28.

what evasive Kapellmeister all along. The strained nature of the relations between Wagner and his employers, and the composer's increasing interest in practical politics, seem, indeed, to have been by now a matter of common knowledge in other towns than Dresden. We actually find Lortzing, on the 26th August, writing thus from Vienna to Lüttichau: " The latest news from Dresden being to the effect that important reforms are to be effected in the musical direction, I take the liberty of humbly offering myself for the vacant Kapellmeistership." We can imagine Lüttichau's feelings on thus learning that the differences between himself and Wagner were common talk as far afield as Vienna. On the same day Lortzing writes to his friend Schmidt in Dresden on the same subject: " A few days ago the Munich Lachner [Franz] called on me and told me of a vacancy in the musical direction in your town: Tichatschek himself had told him that important changes were pending. So on the strength of this news I wrote to your Intendant, saying to myself that if nothing can be done for the moment, they may remember when the time comes. Herr Wagner is an ungrateful fellow, and my cousin Röckel, who should thank God he has such a post, ought to get it hot. Fancy pitying such people when things go badly with them! " [8]

More than one incident, at this time and a little later, indicates that Wagner was showing his interest in revolutionary politics rather more openly than was wise for a man in his official position. Uhl took him to meetings at Clubs of " advanced " political complexion, where, however, Wagner soon had his fill of democratic oratory. He himself tells us that on his re-entry into Dresden he was accompanied by a Count Nostitz, whose courage he commends for not concealing his acquaintance with one who, " only a few weeks before, had caused such a terrible commotion in the city." And a little while after his return, just as he was entering the theatre to conduct *Rienzi*, he was publicly greeted by half a dozen dubious-looking political refugees from Vienna, who, hailing him as a " brother democrat," asked him to obtain free tickets for them. He admits that the incident was embarrassing, and that it did him no good in the eyes of the theatre personnel and others. Clearly he was

---

[8] LGB, p. 207.

already being talked about by reason of his revolutionary sympathies, though his real entrance into practical politics did not take place till some months later.

3

The news from Vienna probably led to a hardening of Lüttichau's manner towards Wagner, for on the Kapellmeister's return to Dresden the relations of the pair became decidedly worse, though there was still nothing in the nature of an open breach between them. Wagner learned of the trouble there had been with some of the members of the orchestra: once more he began to despair of his financial situation; and though he settled down again doggedly to his theatre duties, it was with the feeling perpetually at the back of his mind that his affairs in Dresden were coming to a crisis. In September he was compelled to approach Lüttichau once more on the subject of his debts. The opportunity was taken to remind him of the conditions on which assistance had been given him seven months before: [9] it had been understood then that he was not only to regulate his financial affairs but put his heart into his work at the theatre and perform his duties there to the satisfaction of his employers. Lüttichau's latest report to the King suggests that not only had Wagner not fulfilled this obligation but, in the light of recent events, there was no guarantee that he would be able to do so. The Intendant raises the question of the Kapellmeister's dismissal, referring back to Wagner's letter of acceptance of the post in January, 1843, in which he had said that he would not regard the life-engagement as binding on the Court if, on the one hand, he should feel later that he could not serve the theatre as he wished, or if, on the other hand, Lüttichau should come to feel that his confidence in him had been misplaced. [10] It is thus highly probable that even without the revolution of May, 1849, there would have come a crisis as the result of which Wagner would either have resigned from the theatre or have been dismissed from his post.

Though his application to Liszt for 5,000 thalers in June had been unsuccessful, he had still not quite given up hope in this

---

[9] See Vol. I, p. 488.   [10] See PGHD, pp. 550, 551.

quarter; and so, before he had been settled more than a week or two in Dresden again after his return from Vienna, he went off to Weimar to see what he could do in person. Liszt having made it clear to him that so large a loan was beyond his powers, Wagner had to make that temporary arrangement with his creditors the story of which has already been told.[11] For the remainder of the year 1848 his time must have been mostly taken up with his work upon the sagas and the drafting of the plan for *Siegfrieds Tod,* with a slight diversion in September, when the Kapelle celebrated the three-hundredth anniversary of its foundation. At the concert on the 22nd the programme consisted of Weber's *Jubilee* overture, the overture to Reissiger's *Yelva,* and the finale of the first act of the still unperformed *Lohengrin.* Reissiger received a decoration: Wagner was passed over in this respect, while the *Lohengrin* fragment, which must have been mostly unintelligible to the audience in this form, fell rather flat. At the supper that followed, however, Wagner was sufficiently master of himself to make a long impromptu speech in support of the toast of the Kapelle, in which he spoke warmly of the King, congratulated the orchestra on the worthy way it performed its task of upholding the Spirit of German Music as it had been revealed to the world by Beethoven, and hoped for its continuous growth in conformity with the needs of the future.[12] The general tone of the speech suggests that at this time Wagner had become, for the moment, rather more reconciled to the idea of remaining in his post at Dresden.

A little incident that preceded the festivities gives us a hint of the strained relations between the Kapellmeister and some of his players. Some time before, a sounding-board had been installed in the orchestra for acoustical reasons; this was now set aside in order to provide room for a decoration lauding the King. Wagner, on purely artistic grounds, protested against this being done, and was at once accused by his enemies in the Kapelle of wishing to insult the King. He had to make his position clear in a letter of the 15th September to the orchestra. Evidently there was a section of the Kapelle that suspected his loyalty and thought it prudent to disassociate itself from him in the eyes of its superiors.

---

[11] See Vol. I, pp. 506–8.
[12] The toast (*Trinkspruch*) will be found in Vol. II of RWGS.

For all his work on his *Nibelungen,* however, Wagner could still spare an odd hour or two for politics. That there was as yet no serious ill-feeling against him at Court seems to be indicated by the fact that *Tannhäuser* was put down for performance on the 24th September. (An earlier date than this had apparently been impossible, owing, on the one hand, to the illness of Tichatschek, and, on the other, to some guest appearances of the celebrated bass Carl Formes, to whose repertory, of course, that of the theatre would have to be temporarily adjusted.) Wagner hoped in vain that Liszt would be able to attend this performance. Meanwhile Röckel's affairs were proceeding in a way that must have excited still further the already sufficiently febrile Wagner. On the 9th July Röckel had come out publicly as one of the signatories of a manifesto by the Vaterlandsverein; while a few weeks later he began publication of the *Volksblätter.* Some members of the opera company, concerned about their bread and butter, now objected to being associated with him even at rehearsals. Röckel's enthusiasm for the " cause " made him go too rapidly and too far: the climax came with an " Open Letter to the Soldiers " that was calculated, and intended, to undermine their loyalty to the State. The tolerance that, for his genius' sake, could be shown to a Wagner could not be extended to a mere Röckel: Lüttichau went straight to the point, and the Musical Director was dismissed from his post at the end of September.

4

We have Röckel's testimony, many years later, that Wagner had returned from Vienna disappointed and somewhat disillusioned: there was evidently no prospect of the immediate arrival of the only revolution in which he was really interested at that time — a revolution in the theatre. For an anodyne for his chagrin he plunged into the work of shaping his Nibelungen matter; and in proportion as he rid himself of this burden he became more and more interested in politics for politics' sake, and in revolutionary propaganda as a means of working off the excess of his hatred of all who, unlike himself, had place and power and money. On the 15th October there appeared in the *Volksblätter* an article on *Germany and her Princes* which, though anonymous, was attributed in the town to

AUGUST RÖCKEL

him; in this there is a notable cooling down of his former regard for the King of Saxony as a paragon among German rulers. On the 8th January, 1849, he sent to the Augsburg *Allgemeine Zeitung* a review of the recently published third volume of his friend Eduard Devrient's *Geschichte der deutschen Schauspielkunst:* here he lauds the " Folk," in his usual style, as the fountain of all that is worthy in the world, rejoices over the disapproval that is shown by the publics of Vienna and Berlin of the fare put before them by the local theatre directors, and hopes that out of the turmoil of the time there will emerge a condition of affairs under which it will be possible at last for the theatre to play its true part in culture — it should set itself no other object than that of " invigorating and ennobling the manners and taste of the people." Moderate as the article was in tone, it was not accepted by the *Allgemeine Zeitung*.[13]

Devrient had further published a pamphlet on *The National Theatre of the New Germany,* in which he put forward certain suggestions for reform that did not commend themselves to the Saxon authorities. In a letter of the 18th December to Devrient, Wagner bitterly derides his friend's naïve belief that any real help can come from Court circles — by the co-operation, for example, of the present Intendants as ministerial councillors in the projected new Department for the Theatre; but he sprang publicly to his colleague's aid in an article on *Theatre Reform* that appeared in the Dresden *Anzeiger* of the 16th January, 1849.[14] Devrient had protested against the system under which the control of the German theatres was placed in the hands of courtiers ignorant of art, men who had formerly been marshals, equerries, masters of the hounds, and so on. Wagner, in his review, took up this so congenial thesis and developed it in his own way: Who ever heard, he asked, of " an art-struck Major of Hussars " being made the head of an Academy of Painting? Had not musicians and actors, then, a right to feel aggrieved when they were placed under the control of some mere lord-in-waiting? Lüttichau had formerly been Master of the Forests: the shaft, he knew, was aimed straight at him; and the rankling

---

[13] The manuscript has survived, and the review will be found in RWGS, Vol. XII.
[14] It was signed "J. P. F. R.: Actor out of an Engagement." It is reprinted in RWGS, Vol. XII. Wagner humorously assured Gustav Kietz that the initials stood for Jean Paul Friedrich Richter!

barb would hardly be likely to sweeten his temper in his dealings with his obstinate and, judged by the etiquette of those days, impertinent Kapellmeister. The result, Wagner continues, of this system is to endow Germany with a theatre that is merely " a mournful, wretched slip-slop, a makeshift failure, a straining without an object, fatigue without reward."

The *Anzeiger* flourished by the pleasant practice not of paying authors for their contributions, but of making them pay; and for a man as poor as Wagner then was to pay ten thalers for the insertion of the article is at any rate a proof of his unselfish idealism. We have Gustav Kietz's own piquant story of Wagner sending him to the newspaper office with the article and the ten thalers, bidding him to keep the name of the author a secret. Wagner followed up the article with another (*Further on the Subject of Theatre Reform*),[15] presumably once more at his own cost. This article made a sensation in the town: there was much curiosity in the *Anzeiger* office as to the identity of the author, and the youthful Kietz's bland assurance that *he* was responsible for it was received with frank scepticism. In this second article Wagner repeats his assault on the German Intendants, and pleads once more for a rational democratisation of the theatre; in place of the despotism of an individual he desires the willing, intelligent co-operation of artists and public.[16]

5

As the weeks went on, with his personal affairs worsening and public opinion in Germany becoming more and more inflamed, his temper rose, and his language became bolder and angrier. One reason for this was the sudden refusal of the management, towards the end of 1848, to produce *Lohengrin*.

We can perhaps see this matter more objectively now than Wag-

---

[15] Reprinted in RWGS, Vol. XII. (This second article is not in Ellis's English version of the Prose Works). In this article Wagner made use of some of the material of the review that had been rejected by the Augsburg *Allgemeine Zeitung*.

[16] These views, like so many others that are now supposed to have been personal to Wagner, were really current coin at that time. In Prussia, Wilhelm von Humboldt had pleaded for a theatre which, under the guidance of a Ministry of Culture, should be a veritable instrument of national culture. The incentive to Devrient's pamphlet on *The National Theatre of the New Germany* had, as a matter of fact, come directly from the Ministry of Culture in Berlin. See MKRW, II, pp. 141, 142.

ner could, either at that time or later. In spite of all the provocation he had given Lüttichau, there can be no question that as an artist he continued to be held in high regard in Dresden. The *Flying Dutchman*, it is true, still remained out of the repertory, but that was largely because of Johanna Wagner's antipathy to the part of Senta. But *Rienzi* and *Tannhäuser* were given seven times between the 24th September and the 26th December, while *Iphigenia in Aulis*, which, in virtue of all the work he had done upon it, now counted in the Dresden theatre as almost a Wagner opera, was performed twice during that period. *Lohengrin* had been formally accepted soon after its completion, and Lüttichau had gone so far as not only to pay for the copying of the parts but to commission the son of Ferdinand Heine, who had been studying scene-painting in Paris under Desplechin, to prepare new settings for the work. But one day towards the end of 1848 the young Wilhelm Heine came to break the news to Wagner that Lüttichau had counter-manded this order. In later years Lüttichau assured Minna that he had no choice but to do so, the Court being by now decidedly hostile to Wagner.

It may well have been so; but at any rate a partial explanation of the sudden change of front may perhaps be found in the political and economic circumstances of the time. In Saxony, revolution was still in the offing: there was grave doubt whether the theatre could continue to exist much longer on the old basis. We have already seen [17] Breitkopf & Härtel, in the summer of 1848, declining even to consider the publication of *Lohengrin*, in view of the difficulties of the time and the uncertainty of the future for art. As Vesque von Püttlingen said, in a letter of the 24th July, 1848, to his brother, "Unfortunately this is no time to be thinking of the theatre." At the same time, the Dresden rejection of *Lohengrin* was undoubtedly motived, in part, by the desire to teach the recalcitrant young Kapellmeister a lesson.

In the latter part of 1849 one C. F. Becker published in Leipzig a *Calendar Handbook to Art-history*, in which he set forth, under monthly headings, the principal events in music since the beginning of the century — productions of new works, birth- and death-dates

---

[17] See Vol. I, p. 506.

of the leading composers, and so on. An analysis of this shows a decided tendency on the part of the German theatres to refrain from new operatic productions in 1848 and 1849: in the latter year, indeed, up to the time when Becker was writing, only four new operas had been produced in all Germany — Elmenreich's *Gundel oder die beiden Kaiser* in Schwerin in January, the Duke of Sachsen-Coburg-Gotha's *Tony oder die Vergeltung* at his own theatre in Gotha in January, Wallace's *Maritana* (which had been very successful in London since 1845) at Hamburg in February, and Nicolai's *Merry Wives of Windsor* in Berlin in March.[18] As regards the last-named, it is to be noted that order had been restored in Berlin by military means as early as September 1848. By the early part of 1849, when the troubles in Dresden were coming to a head, Berlin had settled down to its normal life again, and the Opera could confidently resume its old activities.

When Wagner wrote a *Communication to my Friends*, in 1851, he painted a picture of his mental condition in the Dresden years that was undoubtedly coloured by later reflection. But although, at that later date, he may have read into *Tannhäuser* and *Lohengrin* something that was not consciously present in his mind at the time he wrote those works, we may believe him when he says that from *Tannhäuser* onwards the sad conviction grew on him of his loneliness in an uncomprehending world. The Dresden public took readily enough to his music, but failed to understand his deeper dramatic intentions — as, indeed, the public, the singers, and most of the conductors and critics have done to the present day. He felt, he says, that in *Tannhäuser* he had signed his own death-warrant: " I could hope for no further life in the modern art-world." *Lohengrin* was in many respects an expression of his increasing sorrowful sense of isolation: like his hero from Monsalvat, he had demanded of men more trust than they were willing to place in him, a purer love than they were ready to give him as artist and thinker. This withdrawal into a world remote from the actual is, indeed, implicit not only in the drama but in the curiously supersensual quality of the music of *Lohengrin*. The rejection of the new opera by the Dresden theatre management must therefore have been

---

[18] See particulars in BTNJ.

the last dash of wormwood in his cup, the last blow to his idealism; and with *Siegfrieds Tod* germinating within him — an opera which, he must have realised from the beginning, was destined to break so completely with every tradition, dramatic and musical, of the stage as it then was that a production of it was conceivable only in a new world of culture — a rupture with the old world around him was sooner or later inevitable.

He could no longer feel much interest in the ordinary repertory of the theatre; and he must have put a sore strain on Lüttichau's forbearance by refusing, about this time, to take any further part in the deliberations of the management. On the 12th February, 1849, Wagner addressed a meeting of the Orchestral Players' Union. (He tells us, by the way, that the " highly treasonable " talk at some of these meetings was always reported to Lüttichau by his " spies," chief among whom was the hornist Levy; and it is worth noting with what little hesitation he brands, in *Mein Leben,* some of these associates of his as " traitors," while invariably trying to make out that *he* was never more than a guileless spectator of the actual revolution — a thesis the fundamental falsity of which will be demonstrated later). At the meeting in question he explained his projected — and rejected — plan for the reform of the orchestra of the Opera; he confessed that he had lost all hope of influencing the Direction, and " must now recommend the players to take the initiative vigorously into their own hands." [19] The remark was greeted " with enthusiastic applause." The " spies " reported the matter to Lüttichau, who sent for Wagner two days later, and apparently spoke more pointedly and angrily to him than he had ever done before, even going so far as to threaten him with dismissal. Wagner was equally exasperated. He would, he said, appeal to the King; whereupon Lüttichau not unreasonably asked how it was possible

---

[19] This is how he puts it in *Mein Leben.* According to the protocol relating to the matter (now in the Dresden archives), he advised the players to continue for the present with their duties in the spoken plays, but promised them the coming of "a better time," in which they "would all be freed of this service." See PGHD, pp. 551, 552.

Prölss's book, which was based on a study of the official documents, was not liked by Glasenapp and his fellows, because it failed to idealise Wagner. In this connection it should be remembered that the book was published in 1878, during Wagner's lifetime. It is hardly likely, then, that Prölss would say, or even hint at, anything that Wagner could prove to be untrue or exaggerated.

for an Intendant to co-operate with a Kapellmeister who behaved as Wagner had done and was doing. Wagner was to learn, before long, that he had exhausted even the patience of the King and forfeited his goodwill. He and Lüttichau parted in anger, and Devrient's attempts to effect a reconciliation between them were in vain. The protocol in the Dresden archives shows that Wagner had insisted that only works of the highest class should be given in the theatre; he particularly objected to the production of Flotow's wretched *Martha*. The points of view of the two men were fundamentally irreconcilable: Wagner cared now for no theatre but the ideal one of the future: Lüttichau saw only the present problem of a practical theatre that must have a popular repertory in order to pay its way. Matters clearly came to a head at this angry interview: Wagner told Lüttichau that he felt himself out of place in the opera house, and would gladly resign his position were it not that he had his wife and his " domestic situation " (a euphemism for his debts) to consider.[20] Prölss admits that Lüttichau went rather too far when he alleged that Wagner, apart from doing his routine job as conductor of the operas allotted to him, had not shown the general zeal for the institution that was due to the King in return for his favour: " it was a failing of this generally upright and well-intentioned man that when he wished to assert his official authority or high rank he fell all too easily into a vehement, wounding tone and became unjust in his judgment." But Wagner had undoubtedly tried his patience and forbearance severely during the past twelve months.

Wagner had now so little heart for his ordinary duties that he even became careless in his conducting, thereby bringing on himself the pointed censure of the Court itself. And with his financial affairs in a more hopeless condition than ever — for if Dresden would not produce *Lohengrin* no other town was likely to do so, and with this new work of his dead on his hands there was unlikely to be a general outburst of enthusiasm in Germany as a whole for his older works, so that the chances of his making a success of his mad publishing venture became more remote than before — it is little wonder that, out of a combination of idealism, sheer desperation,

[20] PGHD, p. 552.

nervous excitement, and ill-temper, he now plunged up to his neck into the political agitation of the time. No world, it must have seemed to him, could conceivably be worse than the world in which he was living; a political revolution might not only better his lot and that of the art for which he lived, but afford a welcome opportunity for revenge upon the Court Junkers whom he had come to regard as the source of all his woes as a man and of his frustration as an artist.

<h2 style="text-align:center">6</h2>

On Palm Sunday, the 1st April, he conducted his last concert in Dresden. The occasion was the annual concert for the benefit of the Kapelle: the central feature of it was the Ninth Symphony. At the conclusion of this, Bakunin, who was in the audience, walked up to him and said in a loud voice that if all the other music ever written were to be destroyed in the coming world-conflagration, this work at any rate ought to be saved, even at the peril of their lives. The episode could have done Wagner no good in the eyes of the authorities. Bakunin, who had notoriously come to Dresden to stir up trouble, was under such close and suspicious observation by the police that as a rule he found it prudent to keep to his lodgings. Wagner's association — now of some months' duration — with this uncompromising firebrand must have been already known to the police; and the handshaking of the pair in public was not likely to endear Wagner to them.

Bakunin seems to have exercised an uncanny fascination over him. The famous anarchist was nothing if not thorough in his views on social wrongs and their remedies. He was one of those who hold that revolutions are not made with rose-water; and with strange prescience he looked to the Russian peasant's hatred of his oppressors to ring up the curtain on a world-drama that should mean the destruction of civilisation. " He cited," says Wagner, " the delight, at once childlike and demoniac, of the Russian people in fire, on which Rostopchin had reckoned in his strategic burning of Moscow." Bakunin's main argument has a sinister ring to-day: " all that was necessary," he told Wagner,

> " to set in motion a world-wide movement was to convince the Russian
> peasant — in whom the natural goodness of oppressed human nature

had maintained itself in its most childlike form — that the burning of their lords' castles, with everything that was in and about them, was completely right in itself and pleasing in the sight of God; from this there must result the destruction of everything which, rightly considered, must appear, even to the most philosophical thinkers of civilised Europe, the real source of all the misery of the modern world. To set this annihilating force in motion seemed to him to be the only worthy activity for any man. . . . This destruction of our whole civilisation was the goal of all his enthusiasm."

The undersized and under-nourished Wagner was impressed by the colossal stature, the boundless physical energy, and the reckless courage of the Russian; and though, even speculatively, he could not go as far as Bakunin in the way of anarchy, he was spellbound by his tirades. Bakunin, for his part, seems to have had little but good-natured contempt for what his present-day disciples would call the " ideology " of Wagner: he even refused to take seriously the musical and dramatic and other schemes of the eager little Kapellmeister. When Wagner outlined his *Jesus von Nazareth* to him, Bakunin gave him the sage advice to show Jesus as a weak character, and to confine the collaboration of the music in the drama to the setting of just one text — the tenor was to sing " Off with his head! " the soprano " Hang him! " and the bass [21] " Fire! Fire! " That Bakunin was not wholly a lunatic in matters of art, however, was shown by his praising the first act of the *Flying Dutchman* when at last Wagner succeeded in inducing him to listen to his singing and playing of it.

Wagner saw a good deal of the anarchist during these early months of 1849: Röckel, and one or two of the more advanced thinkers of the Vaterlandsverein seem to have become his chief companions now. It would be interesting to know the subjects of some of their conversations. Bakunin had been intimate with Marx, Engels, and other leading socialists and communists since the early 'forties, so that it is highly probable that he set the views of these people before Wagner and Röckel. It would be further interesting to know how much reading of Marx and his associates had been done by Wagner on his own account at this time. A German translation

---

[21] By a strange slip of the pen Wagner writes "basso continuo." Or was this, perhaps, an unfortunate excursion of Bakunin's into musical technology which Wagner records for our benefit with a quiet smile?

MICHAEL BAKUNIN

(From Erich W. Engel's "Richard Wagners Leben und Werke im Bilde", by courtesy of Fr. Kiftner and C. F. W. Siegel, Leipzig)

of Proudhon's *What is Property?* had been brought out in Germany in 1844. We shall find Wagner studying this in Paris in 1849, after his flight from Dresden; but this does not preclude the possibility of the book having been read before that by one who was as absorbed in the social problems of property and exploitation as Wagner was in 1848. Marx's *Holy Family* had been published in 1844, and his *Poverty of Philosophy* (in which he deals polemically with Proudhon's *Philosophy of Poverty*) in 1847. In 1848 appeared the historic *Communist Manifesto,* which was mainly the work of Marx. Was Wagner acquainted with any or all of these works, either before or during his association with Bakunin and Röckel? The ideas and the phraseology of them certainly find more than one echo in his own writings. It is a thousand pities that his brother-in-law Brockhaus confiscated his library on his flight from Dresden: [22] the mere titles of some of the books might have told us a good deal we should like to know about Wagner's reading and thinking in those critical days.

What is certain is that in the early part of 1849 he was being drawn nearer and nearer to the centre of the revolutionary movement. He had joined the Communal Guard in June, 1848, but in March of the following year he asked to be allowed to resign, by reason of physical disability (a double hernia). His release was granted on the 1st May, on the medical certificate not of the doctor appointed by the Guard, but of his friend Pusinelli.[23] It is generally admitted now that, in virtue of his long and close association with Röckel and Bakunin, and his attendance at meetings of the revolutionary party, Wagner must have known that a rising had been planned in Dresden for the month of May. His leaving the Communal Guard on the 1st May therefore looks, to unfriendly eyes, like a prudent avoidance of possible physical danger; but, as Müller points out, it is more likely to have been due to the desire to " remove clearly foreseen difficulties from his path." It is highly probable also that Minna, to whom his growing infatuation with politics was a constant anxiety, had insisted on his leaving the Guard.

---

[22] See Vol. I, p. 377.
[23] Evidence from the archives of the Communal Guard, given in MRW, p. 10.

7

In the following chapters will be told the story of the rising in Dresden in May, 1849, and Wagner's connection with it. Though to set forth in full the political conditions of the period would carry us too far afield, a few words of preliminary explanation are necessary.

The high hopes of a new order of things, that had sprung up in Germany in 1848 immediately after the March revolution in Paris and the expulsion of Louis Philippe, had mostly died out by the spring of 1849. For a time it looked as if the risings that had taken place in various parts of Germany in 1848 would be crowned with success, especially those in Austria and Prussia. But the balance of power had swung round again into the hands of the various governments, and by the end of 1848 the triumph of the reaction was complete. The conviction of this led to a general desire for an all-German Constitution; there was an agitation for more popular representation, the abolition of the harsh Press censorship, and a curtailment of the privileges of the nobility. In Saxony, in particular, men had been shocked by the fate of the popular democratic leader and orator Robert Blum, who had at one time been secretary of the Leipzig Theatre: he had taken part in the disturbances in Vienna in October and November, 1848, and had been captured and shot. One result of the anger aroused by the execution of Blum was the election of a Saxon Chamber that was overwhelmingly democratic: among the new deputies was Röckel. Vereine of all shades of political opinion were formed throughout Saxony; several radical journals were started.

As Röckel himself admits sadly,[24] the democratic party had no real unity of view even in the field of theory, and no organisation or discipline at all for purposes of action. It was therefore ill-fitted, even when the revolution broke out, to withstand a government that knew its own mind, was skilled in all the arts of evasion and delay, had its own military force to back it, and in case of need could count on the assistance of Prussian troops. The King was personally popular, and in most respects he was sincerely anxious

---

[24] RSE, pp. 25 ff.

for the welfare of his subjects; but his political judgment was poor, and he clung obstinately, through thick and thin, to the theory of his divine right to govern. In the spring of 1849 the more thorough-going democrats in Dresden, despairing of making any headway by appeal or argument against the chicaneries of the politicians, began to feel that their sole salvation lay in force.

CHAPTER IV

WAGNER AND THE REVOLUTION

I · THE LEGAL CASE AGAINST HIM

1

W AGNER HIMSELF, and his biographers of the Wahnfried
school, would have us believe that his participation in the
Dresden rising of 1849 was trifling in extent and innocent in nature. Later documents bearing on the subject, however, — some of
them the result of recent research in the Dresden State archives —
and a critical study of his own designedly ambiguous account of
the matter in *Mein Leben,* lead us to another conclusion.

Unless the Dresden police were greater imbeciles, and their
secret service less efficient, than we have any reason to assume them
to have been, they must have known that an anonymous article entitled *The Revolution,* in the *Volksblätter* of the 8th April, 1849,
— that is to say, just when matters were beginning to look ugly in
the town — was from the pen of the Royal Kapellmeister. It is a
paean to the red goddess in her most incarnadine aspect:

> " The old world is in ruins from which a new world will arise; for
> the sublime goddess *REVOLUTION* comes rushing and roaring on
> the wings of the storm, her august head rayed round with lightnings,
> a sword in her right hand, a torch in her left, her eyes so sullen, so
> punitive, so cold; and yet what warmth of purest love, what fulness
> of happiness radiate from it towards him who dares to look stead-
> fastly into that sombre eye! Rushing and roaring she comes, the ever-
> rejuvenating mother of mankind; destroying and blessing she sweeps
> across the earth; before her pipes the storm; it shakes so violently
> all man's handiwork that vast clouds of dust darken the air, and where
> her mighty foot treads, all that has been built for ages past in idle
> whim crashes in ruins, and the hem of her robe sweeps the last re-
> mains of it away."

The contemporary reader of the article was invited to turn his
glance on the once powerful but now quaking princes of the earth,

the rascally ministers and diplomats, the scented courtiers, the higgling financiers, the stolid government clerks entangled in their red tape, and all the other knaves and fools who are traditionally supposed to be the obstacle to that embodiment of all the natural virtues, the Folk, enjoying the full fruits of its arduous toil. But Revolution, Wagner continues, is on the way, to bring down the lofty and raise the humble. She sends the Folk her greeting and her blessing:

"I am the ever-rejuvenating, ever-creating Life; where I am not is Death. I am the dream, the balm, the hope of all who suffer. I annihilate what exists, and whither I turn there wells forth fresh life from the dead rock. I come to you to break all the fetters that oppress you, to redeem you from the embrace of Death and to pour young life into your veins. Whatever is must pass away: such is the everlasting law of Nature, such is the condition of Life; and I, the eternal destroyer, fulfil the law and create eternally youthful life. From its roots upwards I will destroy the order of things under which you live, for it has sprung from sin, its flower is misery and its fruit is crime; but the harvest is ripe and I am the reaper! I will destroy every illusion that has power over men. I will destroy the domination of one over many, of the dead over the living, of matter over spirit; I will break down the power of the mighty, of law, of property . . . I will destroy this order of things, that divides what should be one mankind into hostile nations, into powerful and weak, into privileged and outlawed, into rich and poor; for it makes unhappy men of all. I will destroy this order of things that makes millions the slaves of a few, and makes these few the slaves of their own power, their own riches. I will destroy this order of things, that cuts enjoyment off from labour, makes labour a burden and enjoyment a vice, makes one man wretched through want, another through superfluity. I will destroy this order of things, that wastes men's powers in the service of dead matter, which condemns the half of mankind to inactivity or to useless toil, that compels hundreds of thousands to devote their vigorous youth, in the busy idleness of soldiers, officials, speculators and money-makers, to the maintenance of these abject conditions, while the other half must support the whole edifice of shame at the cost of the exhaustion of their powers and the sacrifice of all the joys of life. Down to its very memory I will destroy every trace of this insane order of things, compact of force, lies, care, hypocrisy, want, sorrow, suffering, tears, trickery and crime. . . . So up, ye peoples of the earth! Up, ye mourners, ye oppressed, ye poor! And up, ye others, who strive in vain to cloak the inner desolation of your hearts with the idle show of might and riches! Up, follow my steps in all your multitude and variety, for no distinction can I make among those who follow me! Two peoples only are there henceforth: the one, that follows me, the other, that withstands me. The one I lead to happiness: over the other I tread, crushing it as I go; for I am the REVOLUTION, I am the ever-creating life, I am the one God whom all creation acknowledges, who comprises and animates and fills with happiness all that is." [1]

The passionate indictment was historically hardly more than just, the warmth of heart from which it came was beyond dispute; but this was not the kind of outburst upon which any Government, desperately concerned to save, according to its lights, the working order of things, could be expected to look with an approving eye. In 1911 some anarchist journals in Berlin and Vienna reprinted Wagner's article for propaganda purposes: their proprietors were haled before the courts and the offending issues were confiscated.[2] If that was the view taken of the likely effects of the article some three generations later, we can imagine how it would strike the nervous Saxon authorities in 1849, at a time when all Europe seemed to be heading for chaos. Ashton Ellis calls the " dithyramb " " as pure a piece of poetry as ever clothed itself in prose ", and asks incredulously whether " a man who could express himself in ' music ' so sublime as this was concurrently engaged in ' treasons, stratagems, and spoils '? " But the military authorities and the police — two orders of men notoriously more practical than poetic in their views — would not be likely to have either the time or the inclination to settle back in their chairs and turn an aesthetic connoisseur's eye on Wagner's dithyrambics. The only question they would ask themselves would be, " What is likely to be the effect of this incitement to revolution on certain elements in the community that have been planning violence for some time and now look like getting out of hand? " They would take the view that even if this " poet " were not himself actively engaged in treasons, stratagems and spoils — and as a matter of fact they must already have had reason to suspect that he was — the more inflammable among his readers would assuredly translate the dithyramb into

---

[1] The article will be found in RWGS, Vol. XII.
[2] MKRW, II, 167.

treasonable action. If the Court Kapellmeister was not already under unfriendly observation by the authorities, this article must certainly have made him so. And his conduct during the actual rising, which could have been no secret so far as the police were concerned, was decidedly not calculated to endear him to those who had to maintain order in Dresden.[3]

2

Owing to his having escaped the clutches of the law by his flight to Switzerland in May, 1849, no formal legal indictment, such as was prepared in the case of the Saxon conspirators who were arrested and brought up for trial, was drawn up against Wagner at the time. It was not until some seven years later that his case was gone into systematically by the Dresden authorities, in connection with his appeals for an amnesty; and the charges against him could only be roughly systematised then from the references to him occurring in various documents of 1849 relating to other offenders. It is consequently only fair to him for us to bear in mind that he had no opportunity to correct, at the time, whatever errors there

---

[3] In RWGS, Vol. XII, will be found a poem, *An einen Staatsanwalt* (*To a State Attorney*), that bears the date 22nd March, 1849. In this, Wagner pours out his scorn on "the State, that absolute great egoist," and on the Attorney who has been elected "to wrangle for its highest abstract nothing".

It was natural that both in *Mein Leben* and in *A Communication to my Friends* (1851) Wagner should try to make it appear that his interest in the revolution was merely that of the artist. Broadly speaking, that is true: but it is not the whole truth. His prime concern was with the theatre, which he regarded as not only the expression of a nation's culture but the most powerful of instruments in the shaping of that culture; and if circumstances had supplied him with the means to reform the theatre from the inside he would probably have taken no more than an academic interest in politics. But his own words, guarded as they are, show that in or after 1848 he became convinced that the theatre could not work out its own salvation from the inside. It was so much at the mercy of political and social factors that not until the grip of these upon it was relaxed could it win the freedom to develop along ideal lines; and the moment came when he recognised that the only way to escape from its grip was the way of political revolution.

Alfred Meissner (MGML, pp. 169 ff) tells us of a conversation he had with Wagner in the autumn of 1846, in which the latter laid it down confidently that there would soon be "a fundamental political change," but that this would be easily and quickly effected, as "the binding factors of political and social forms" were "purely external". The revolution was "already complete in men's heads"; the "new Germany" was like "a bronze statue fully cast, that only needed the hammer-stroke on the clay envelope to step forth". It was made clear enough to Wagner, between then and the early months of 1849, that he had been over-optimistic in his idealism.

may have been in the statements of the witnesses of 1849, or even of knowing in detail what they were. Some of the alleged evidence against him would probably not have survived a searching cross-examination.

Glasenapp and Ellis fought heroically to convince the world of his innocence; but we know rather more about the matter now than they did. For a long time the main source of information respecting Wagner and the revolution was Hugo Dinger's book *Richard Wagners geistliche Entwickelung* (1892), which, so far as the period with which we are now dealing is concerned, was based on an examination — the first of its kind — of documents and depositions in the Dresden State records, and on the reminiscences of contemporaries of the events of 1849. It goes without saying that Dinger made himself seriously disliked by the older Wagnerians for having unearthed so much that was unfavourable to their idol's case, and it was easy to make small debating points against him. Glasenapp, in the Foreword to his second volume (1896), tried desperately to discredit Dinger's researches and conclusions: he sneered at his concentration on factual detail, and contrasted unfavourably his realistic method with the more idealistic one of Chamberlain. But a biography must surely aim at being, in the first place, a record of things as they actually happened. A writer may pride himself, as Chamberlain's recently published correspondence shows him to have done, on not only not knowing a great deal about the life of his subject but not wanting to know a great deal, preferring to evolve his picture of the subject out of his own inner consciousness. For those, however, who are more interested in past things as they really were than in some idealist or other's fancy picture of them, there is nothing for it but to put in some hard work at research into the facts. This is what Dinger did.

3

Since Dinger wrote, a good deal of other evidence relating to the years 1848 and 1849 has come to light. In 1901 one Ludwig Schmidt published some new documents from the papers of Franz Adolf Schmidt, the Dresden lawyer who acted on Wagner's behalf when the latter, in 1863, asked for an epitome of the accusations made against him.[4] The lawyer, as we can now see, did not do his work with ideal thoroughness, at any rate from the point of view of the modern Wagner biographer. Ashton Ellis, however, writing in 1902, took the line that the evidence as summarised by Schmidt discredited Dinger.[5] In 1919 there appeared an exhaustive study of the whole matter by Dr. Georg Hermann Müller — *Richard Wagner in der Mai-Revolution 1849* — in which not only are the crowded events of that decisive May fortnight set forth in logical sequence but new facts from the archives are brought to light. (Müller was the Dresden Town Council archivist and Town Librarian.) In 1927 Woldemar Lippert, the Director of the Saxon State archives, went through the whole official material again, and added greatly to our knowledge of the subject in his *Richard Wagners Verbannung und Rückkehr, 1849–62.*

With all these official documents to work upon, plus Wagner's own story in *Mein Leben,* the various political histories and memoirs of the epoch, Röckel's later account of the rising in his book *Sachsens Erhebung,* and a number of contemporary and later letters of Wagner [6] and other people, it becomes possible to make at any rate a tentative reconstruction of the whole affair so far as it concerned Wagner. To do that, mere forensic niceties of the Glasenapp type must be put aside. Owing to the fact that Wagner was neither examined nor cross-examined at the time, and that he had no opportunity, at the trial of Röckel, Bakunin, and the others, of countering witnesses' statements in which his own name occurred, the case against him naturally bristles with points with which a clever lawyer for the defence could have made effective play. But

---

[4] *Wagner-Akten,* in ZIMG, 1901, Heft I.

[5] See the Supplemental Note, pp. 409–18, in ELW, Vol. II.

[6] In his letter, for instance, of the 19th June, 1849, to Liszt (i.e. about a month after his flight from Dresden), he as good as confesses that he had staked his all on the success of the rising: "You know the bitter source of the discontent that sprang from my practice of my beloved art; I nursed these feelings passionately until at last I let them overflow into every field that seemed to me to be connected with the cause of my deep-lying ill-humour. The result was that violent impulse for which the only expression is 'There must be a change! Things cannot continue like this!' I need not give the assurance, for it must be self-evident to any rational being, that, having learned my lesson from my participation in the rising, it is out of the question that I should ever again take part in a political upheaval: what rejoices me, and what I can swear to, is that I have become entirely an artist again."

There could hardly be a clearer admission that his rage and despair over his art had led him to look to a political revolution as the only way to artistic betterment.

a trial before a court and a trial before the bar of public opinion are two very different matters. In the former, everything is rightly stressed that can possibly tell legally in favour of the accused; and he is entitled to acquittal if the case against him is not proved according to the strictest punctilio of legal procedure. But everyone knows that many a defendant wins, on technical grounds such as these, a verdict to which the common sense of the world decides he is not really entitled. That is what might happen to-day if Wagner were put on trial in an English court for some such affair as that of the rising of 1849: his counsel might secure an acquittal, or at least a mitigation of sentence, on technical points connected with the manner of the collection and presentation of the evidence, the uncertainty of some of the witnesses' memory, the difficulty of deciding whether an incident testified to by this or that person occurred on this day or that, or even the precise form in which it occurred, and so on; but the verdict of public opinion would be that in securing a legal acquittal the prisoner was a very fortunate man. The case of Wagner and the revolution of 1849 is a matter nowadays not for legal hair-splitting but for plain common sense. Let us try to summarise the evidence as we now have it.

4

The first clause in the digest of the evidence that was drawn up for the first time in 1856 is to the effect that he " was on intimate terms with the leaders of the rising, Bakunin, Heubner, and Röckel ". Wagner himself admits this in *Mein Leben*. (Röckel, it appears, was not popular in the town. His political proclivities had been no secret long before 1849; and Wagner had apparently quite early come under suspicion through his association with his musical colleague. The remark used to be made, when the two were seen together, " Here comes Mephistopheles [i.e. Röckel] with Faust.")

One Hering, the keeper of the Menagerie Garden in Friedrichstadt (the suburb in which Wagner lived), alleged that in the house of the law-student Naumann, in a secluded part of the garden, there were frequent meetings of sometimes as many as twenty or thirty conspirators, among whom he recognised Kapellmeister Wagner, who was personally known to him. (The Naumann house was No.

24, now No. 58, in the Friedrichstrasse: it was opposite Wagner's apartment in the Marcolini Palace — Friedrichstrasse 20a, now 41 Stadtkrankenhaus, Friedrichstadt. The fact that it could be approached from four sides made it possible for a number of people to enter it without attracting particular observation. Opposite Wagner, in No. 29, was Röckel.) Naumann was the responsible editor of the Dresden *Zeitung*, the daily organ of the more advanced section of the Vaterlandsverein. Hering, under pressure from the Naumann family, withdrew much of what he had said, but it remained established, apparently, that part of the Naumann house had been let to a " Dr. Schwarz ", who had been visited by several people concerned later in the rising, among them Wagner. This " Dr. Schwarz " was none other than the redoubtable Bakunin. Stores of firearms and ammunition were said to have been found in the house. It is significant that in *Mein Leben* Wagner says nothing about these meetings, at which the practical steps to be taken in the coming revolution must certainly have been discussed.

There can be no doubt whatever that Wagner had interested himself, along with Röckel, Semper and others, in the arming of the people: Röckel himself, in the evidence he gave at his trial, testified that Wagner had lent his garden for a discussion of this plan. On one occasion a Lieutenant Schreiber sent Wagner a letter explaining his inability to attend a meeting: Wagner passed the letter on to Röckel, among whose papers it was found. The evidence further showed that at a meeting in Wagner's garden, at which Wagner, Röckel, Semper and others were present, Schreiber " especially dealt with the question of the volunteer artillery ". It may be added that Röckel, in his story of the rising (written after his release from prison in 1862), said that the plan for the arming of the people was one that was particularly dear to Wagner, who urged his colleague to publish the memorial on *The Organisation of Folk-arming in Germany, with special reference to Saxony*, which Röckel had submitted to the National Assembly at Frankfort.

The knowledge of Wagner's interest in practical politics at this time had spread even to Leipzig. Writing from there to Franz Hauser on the 3rd February, 1849, Moritz Hauptmann says that " in the Vaterlandsverein he [Wagner] is strongly in favour of

arming the nation and getting rid of the soldiers " (HLLC, II, 69).
The fact is that Wagner's participation in politics gave rise to so
much gossip everywhere because he was a Court servant, with a life
appointment and with a pension to look forward to: furthermore,
the Court's forbearance with him in the matter of his notorious
debts was generally held to entitle it to more consideration from
him than it received. It was therefore regarded as not quite
" cricket " that he should be at the same time profiting by his connection with the ruling powers and plotting against them. No musician in that epoch was blamed merely for having aspirations towards a better social condition of things: he became an object of
suspicion only when he stepped out of the sphere of art into that
of practical revolutionary politics. Liszt himself, in 1848, took up
again and recast his *Revolution Symphony* of 1830, and could do
so without any sense of disloyalty towards the Weimer Court in
whose service he was; but it would have been a different matter
had he taken an open part in the activities of a revolutionary organisation. One of the Marches of Schumann's op. 76 (written in
1849) was known in the composer's intimate circle as the " Barricades March ". But Schumann, in spite of his democratic opinions,
had the sense to keep out of practical politics; and when Wagner's
Art and Revolution was published, his quiet comment was that he
would have been better pleased had Wagner written a novel.[7] The
more we know of Wagner's political record in the latter part of
1848 and the first months of 1849, the more we wonder at the
Court's continued indulgence towards him.

The fourth article in the summary of evidence runs thus: " The
notorious brassfounder Oehme, one of the persons most deeply
implicated in the rising, and known more particularly for his attempts to burn down the Royal Palace, asserts that Wagner and
Röckel, before Easter, 1849, gave him an order for a considerable
number of hand-grenades: these were said to be wanted for Prague,
and were sent to the office of the Dresden *Zeitung*. It seems, however, that they were not sent to Prague, as Oehme declares that on
the 4th May, 1849, Wagner commissioned him to fill the grenades,
which were still at the office of the *Zeitung*." This evidence was
given in July and August of that year. (The rising had taken place

[7] KRW, p. 106.

in the early days of May.) The official document adds that while Oehme maintained firmly that the grenades had been ordered by both Wagner and Röckel, the latter denied this, asserting that they were commissioned by Wagner alone. This was contradicted by Oehme. The upshot of it all would seem to be that complicity of some kind on Wagner's part in the matter of the grenades is beyond question.

Ellis [8] calls Oehme a "tinsman (or pewterer — *Zinngiesser*)". The term used in the official reports, however, is *Gelbgiesser* (brassfounder). Ellis opines that "from this very fishy evidence" there is "nothing further to be deduced" than that the invariably innocent Wagner "possibly may once have gone to Oehme's shop — to get a kettle repaired, perhaps — in the company of Röckel"! But this really will not do. The actual evidence of Oehme at the trial is summarised thus by Dinger from the Court archives.

"In all I made about 1,400–1,500 grenades, though I cannot be sure of the exact figure. I made them all before the rising in Dresden. Before Easter of this year [1849], acting on instructions, I sent some 24 or 26 to an associate in Leipzig. The remainder of the 140–150 [9] I made about the same time, on the previous instructions of Musical Director Röckel and Kapellmeister Wagner. The others, which were ordered by Wagner and Röckel jointly, were to be sent to Prague to a friend of Röckel's, whose name I do not remember." Röckel admits ordering the hand-grenades, but denies that he directed any to be sent to Prague: "it may be that I was once at Oehme's with Kapellmeister Wagner, but I don't remember it, and I deny the ordering of the grenades". After Röckel's decisive denial, and his insistence that there has been a confusion of persons, he is confronted with Oehme. The latter categorically maintains the correctness of his statements, while Röckel gives evasive replies or flat denials: "It may be that I was once at your place with Wagner, but I know nothing of the order; perhaps Wagner gave it himself; I know nothing whatever about the matter". One

---

[8] ELW, II, p. 411.

[9] It is not clear whether the discrepancy between "1,400–1,500" and "140–150" is in the original document or is due to some error in transcription on Dinger's part. In the "Summary of Evidence" against Wagner, drawn up in 1856, the reference is to "a considerable number of hand-grenades" made by Oehme "to the order of Wagner and Röckel".

batch of grenades was not sent away, but lodged in Dresden; during the rising, Oehme received an order to fill these. Oehme cannot say for certain whether Wagner or a Herr M. brought the order.[10] [M. is probably Minkewitz, Röckel's lawyer.]

Too much weight need not be attached to Röckel's evasions and denials: prisoners on trial for their lives are not expected to admit anything that may incriminate them or others, and there is ground for believing that all through his own trial Röckel was anxious not to damage Wagner more than he could help. But on the face of the evidence no reasonable person can doubt that both Röckel and Wagner were somehow or other concerned with the ordering of a number of grenades. In his letter of the 2nd May to Röckel, that was found on the latter when he was arrested, Wagner says, " Your wife is sending your things [wearing apparel, washing?] to you this evening [to Prague]. What you particularly wanted I have forbidden to be included with them, for reasons which I take upon myself." [11] Who can doubt, in the light of all we know now, that these other " things " that Röckel so particularly wanted in Prague, but that Wagner took it upon himself to retain in Dresden, were the grenades, or a portion of them? [12]

5

The fifth article deals with a matter about which Wagner is discreetly silent in *Mein Leben*. About the beginning of May, Röckel had gone to Prague to stimulate the revolutionary activity there. On the 2nd of that month Wagner wrote him as follows:

> " I hope you have arrived safely in Prague. Just now I am very flustered and distracted owing to a long and violent dispute with Römpler & Katz,[13] who have as yet had no instructions from Minkewitz: nevertheless I think you may rest assured that, after the precautionary measures I have taken, there will be no interruption in the progress of events. . . . Come back as soon as your patient [*sic:* according to Röckel's evidence at his trial, this meant his constituents

---

[10] DWGE, p. 180.

[11] Glasenapp (GRW, II, 302) suppresses this passage from Wagner's letter. His procedure on this occasion is typical of his peculiar conception of biographical honesty.

[12] An alleged "Wagner hand-grenade" that is preserved in the Dresden Museum is, according to Müller, "apocryphal".

[13] The printers of the *Volksblätter*.

in Limbach!] makes it possible for you to do so. Everything is in a state of unrest here; all the Unions, this afternoon also the whole of the Communal Guard, even Prince Albert's regiment, which is stationed here, have declared in the most energetic terms for the German Constitution; the Town Council too. It all points to a decisive conflict, if not with the King, at least with the Prussian troops; people's only fear is that a revolution may break out too soon. . . ." [14]

On the strength of this document, which was found on Röckel when he was arrested, the court could do no less than assume that Wagner was closely connected with the leading Dresden revolutionaries and with Röckel's mission to Prague: it was this letter, indeed, that was the prime cause of the issue of the warrant for Wagner's arrest after the collapse of the rising. The remark about the possibility of the revolution breaking out " too soon " decidedly suggests knowledge on Wagner's part of the plans made by Röckel and the other leaders for a rising shortly. That conjecture finds support in an episode the details of which we owe to Fürstenau, one of the members of the Dresden orchestra. On the 2nd May the *Anzeiger* announced a concert, to be given on the 5th, for the Saxon soldiers wounded in the Schleswig-Holstein war. The programme was to include Berlioz's *Symphonie funèbre et triomphale* (written in 1840). The orchestral parts for this not having arrived by rehearsal time (on the 1st or 2nd May), Fürstenau offered to go to Berlin to obtain them. Wagner replied, " to the astonishment of all present ", that " in all probability the concert would not take place, for the revolution would certainly break out before then, and who could say what would become of the Royal Kapelle in that case? " [15] When Fürstenau returned from Berlin the revolution was in full swing, as Wagner had hinted might be the case. It is of course possible to argue that, the trend of events being what it was, a forecast of that kind might have been made by almost anybody at the time. But the evidence implicating Wagner is largely made up of a number of similar incidents; and while each of them would no doubt be of small importance if it stood alone, the cumulative effect of them is irresistible. Röckel, in his evidence at his trial, said that a *general*

---

[14] This letter was not quite accurately printed by Chamberlain in RWEB, and in the later redaction of that book, RWFP. In one place Wagner speaks of Röckel's "patient" (feminine singular), in another of his "patients in Limbach" (masculine plural).

[15] DWGE, p. 181. Dinger received his information direct from Fürstenau.

German rising had been planned for the 9th; his visit to Prague had for its object the co-operation of the Bohemian revolutionaries with the Saxon.

After the King of Saxony, on the 3rd May, had refused to grant the demands of the democratic party, the Communal Guard was dissolved by a government edict, so that anyone who chose to continue his membership after that date became, *ipso facto*, a rebel.

The two final counts in the dossier of 1856 will be best dealt with later, in the course of our narrative of Wagner's actions during the actual rising, as set forth by himself in *Mein Leben*.[16]

---

[16] Space does not admit of a detailed narrative of the events of the actual rising. The reader will find convenient accounts of it in ERW, Vol. II, and EV. More modern and rather better-informed descriptions will be found in MDM and MRW. The latter is the completest thing of the kind that we have at present. Müller, besides having a thorough first-hand knowledge of the subject, based to some extent on the official archives, had, of course, Wagner's own story in *Mein Leben* to work upon; and his book, MRW, contains a full and careful reconstruction of the events of the period. In the present volume we shall have to restrict ourselves, in the main, to such of the episodes of the rising as bear directly on Wagner.

CHAPTER V

WAGNER AND THE REVOLUTION

II·HIS SHARE IN THE REVOLT

1

WAGNER'S LONG account of the revolution, and of the personalities with whom it brought him in contact, is one of the most vivid pieces of writing in the whole of his autobiography. In broad outline it can clearly be taken as accurate: we may safely assume that it was committed to paper, in essentials, not long after the event, for in 1866 or so, after a lapse of some seventeen or eighteen years, he could hardly have reconstructed all these details so accurately, day by day, by an effort of the memory alone. Let us recall his earlier statement that when writing *Mein Leben* he had before him that journal of his life which he had begun on his tour through Germany, in search of singers for the Magdeburg troupe, in 1835.[1] He expressly tells us that he had added to it ever since at various periods of his life, *" in uninterrupted sequence ".* He could hardly, however, have found leisure to record the daily events of the rising at the actual time; the probability is that he wrote up his record either at Weimar or as soon as possible after settling down in Switzerland. It should be observed that in his account of the affair in *Mein Leben* he allots the wrong days of the week to the dates of the month — he begins by calling the 4th May a Thursday, whereas it was a Friday, and each successive day is named with corresponding inaccuracy. This is just the sort of error a man might make who, when writing up his journal some time later, had calculated the dates backward a trifle too hastily.

On 9th February, 1849, Liszt had invited him to a performance of *Tannhäuser* that was to take place in Weimar on the 16th — the first production of the work outside Dresden. Wagner was deeply moved by this, the first of many services that his new friend was

---

[1] See Vol. I, p. 194.

to render him. For the moment he lost that sense of utter loneliness in the world that had been growing on him for so long, and felt encouraged in his struggle against what he called, in his letter of the 20th to Liszt, "the despotism of malignant ignorance" [of Lüttichau], under the strain of which he had come to doubt whether he could continue any longer in his Dresden post. Tichatschek had sung as guest tenor in the first two Weimar performances; in the third, which was to be given in May, the part of Tannhäuser was to be taken by an ordinary member of the Weimar company. Wagner obtained from Lüttichau the promise of leave to visit Weimar in the second week of May for this third performance. By the second week of May, however, his destiny, thanks to the events in Dresden, had taken a decisive new turn, and it was as a political refugee that he suddenly appeared, to Liszt's astonishment, in Weimar.

Early in February the King of Saxony had dismissed the Liberal Minister Oberländer, substituting for him the Conservative Count von Beust; and on the last day of April the Chambers had been dissolved. On the 29th and the 30th April, Dresden was full of the wildest rumours of successful risings in other parts of Germany, the deposition of Kings, the defection of troops, the mobilisation of Russian and Prussian forces, and so on. The town was working up to the highest pitch of excitement it had yet known; the more militant sections of the democratic front began to tighten up their organisation. The Saxon troops were kept in barracks: there were comparatively few of them in the town, for some regiments were fighting in Schleswig, while others had been drafted off to preserve order in the Vogtland. Röckel's position as a deputy had so far guaranteed him immunity from arrest on the score of his journalistic escapades: [2] now no longer safe, by reason of the dissolution of the Chambers, he had to fly, on the 30th April, to Bohemia — provided with letters from Bakunin to the revolutionary leaders there — and Wagner admits that in his friend's absence he himself saw to the publication of the *Volksblätter*.[3]

---

[2] He had been dismissed from his post as Music Director about the end of September, 1848.

[3] He probably did no more than see to the printing of the issue of the 29th April, the contents, or the main contents, of which had no doubt been prepared by Röckel before his flight. No further numbers were ever published. MRW, p. 8.

Röckel himself admitted that his mission in Prague was to induce the revolutionary leaders there to delay local action until the expected rising in Germany as a whole should materialise. He discovered, however, that Bakunin had overestimated the possible contribution of the Czechs; all Röckel found in Prague was a dozen or so young men with more imagination than practical capacity.[4] He returned to Dresden as soon as news reached him that the revolution had actually broken out there. Wagner's taking charge of the *Volksblätter* must surely have been known to the authorities, for he must have been a marked man already. He would have the readers of *Mein Leben* believe that he had been actuated solely by the humanitarian motive of wishing to provide for Röckel's family; but this is as difficult for us to believe now as it must have been for the Dresden police at the time. He was present, in the early afternoon of Thursday, the 3rd May, at a meeting of the Committee of the Vaterlandsverein, which by this time had become a more openly revolutionary organisation than it had been at first; the meeting passed a resolution to offer armed resistance to the authorities. On his way home from the meeting, when he had reached the Semper fountain in the Postplatz, he heard the clang of bells from the tower of St. Anne's Church.[5] They announced the real beginning of the revolt; the exasperated populace had at last got out of hand. (An attack had been made on the arsenal, and the soldiers had had to fire on the crowd, five of whom were killed. The crowd retaliated with a hail of stones and bullets; an officer was killed, and several soldiers were wounded).

2

At the sound of the bells there came over Wagner that feeling, to which I have already drawn attention, of strange serenity and even exaltation in a moment of crisis: " I experienced ", he says, " a sensation of vast, indeed extravagant, delight. I had a sudden sense of pleasure in playing with something that was in itself serious." He made straight for Tichatschek's house, which was only a few yards away (Marienstrasse 30, at the corner of Annenstrasse,

---

[4] See his own story in RSE, pp. 143, 144.
[5] This would be about three or four o'clock in the afternoon.

now Hauptpost). The tenor was away on tour. Wagner asked the terrified wife for her husband's sporting guns, ostensibly on the ground that, to prevent their falling into the hands of the mob, they ought to be handed over to the Committee of the Vaterlandsverein. Assuming his usual air of sadly misunderstood innocence, he affects astonishment, in *Mein Leben*, that this incident was afterwards brought up against him as evidence of his guilt. Knowing, as we do, his record in the matter of the arming of the people, we cannot but believe that his object was purely and simply to obtain the guns for use by the active revolutionaries of the Vaterlandsverein. One of the grievances, indeed, of the democratic party, as Röckel tells us, was that at the beginning of May the Communal Guard, which previously had been called out for service by the Government on the slightest pretext, was now deprived of ammunition, the excuse being made that there was none available.[6] What other explanation can be put forward of the fact that, suddenly realising that the revolution had really broken out at last, Wagner's self-confessed first thought was to go to the house of a man whom he knew to possess guns and whom he knew to be out of Dresden, and try to cajole or terrify his wife into handing over these useful arms to an organisation that was likely to play a leading part in the struggle? And is it not manifest that, knowing or surmising that this incident had figured in the indictment against him, he mentions it in *Mein Leben* simply in order to have an opportunity to put his own gloss upon it? Had it been a matter of which he thought no one was aware but himself, he would as assuredly have preserved the same silence with regard to it in *Mein Leben* as he has done with regard to certain others.

From this point onwards he was always at the centre of events. In the Altmarkt he found Schröder-Devrient haranguing the crowd from the first-floor window of an apothecary's shop: horrified at the sight of the corpse of a man who had been killed in the disturbance outside the arsenal, she had said rather more than was prudent, and in the enquiry after the rising even she, for all her popularity in Dresden, had some difficulty in exonerating herself.

---

[6] RSE, pp. 92, 98, etc. Röckel's remarks and judgments throughout his book are of course coloured by his political opinions, the revolutionary party being, in his eyes, wholly virtuous and the Government wholly vile; but his first-hand knowledge of the actual events of the rising is valuable to the present-day historian.

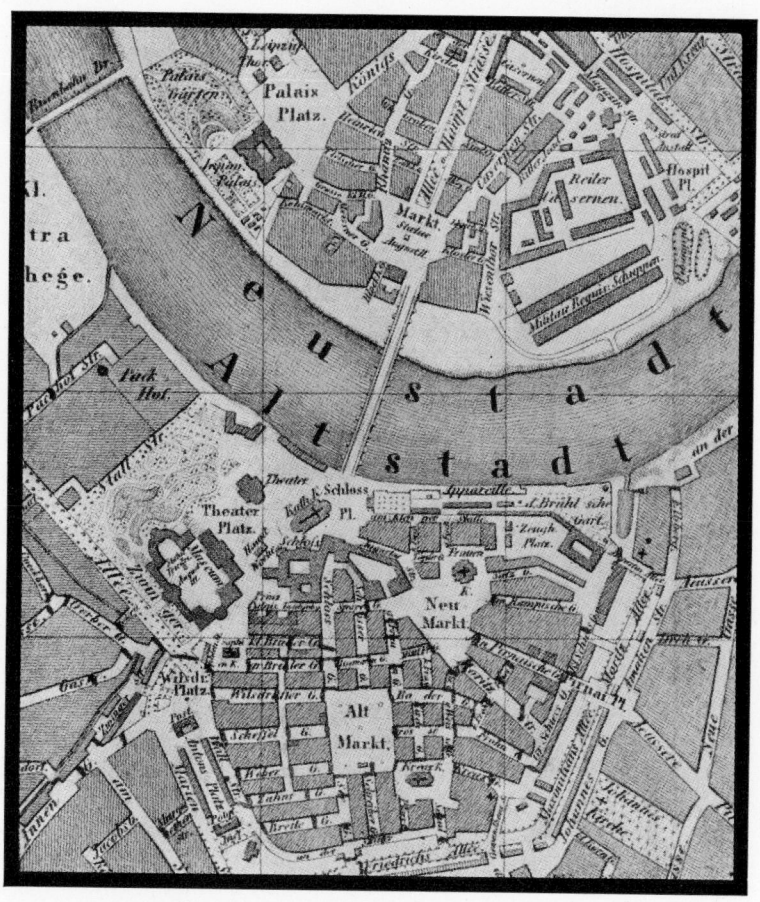

DRESDEN IN 1849 — THE AREA OF THE REVOLT

(*From " Die Dresdner Mairevolution 1849 "*)

When passing through the town in October, 1851 (she was not a member of the Dresden opera company at that time), she was " summoned by the police to answer for her inflammatory speech of the 3rd May, 1849. . . . Further proceedings in connection with this serious charge were graciously quashed by the King; but she had to pay the costs." [7]

Wagner now went by way of the Badergasse, the Neumarkt, and the Rampische Gasse to the neighbourhood of the arsenal, where he met a retreating battalion of the Communal Guard, which had suffered when the troops had fired on the crowd. The cry " To the barricades! " was raised. He drifted back with the mob to the Altmarkt. According to his story in *Mein Leben,* it was only *now* that he began to " take an interest in the drama ", out of pure sympathy, " without feeling any desire to join the combatants "; out of mere curiosity, he says, he went to the Town Hall, where, unobserved, he managed to get into the crowded council chamber itself. All was confusion there; and after making his way through the barricades in the Altmarkt at night he returned, by way of the Wilsdruffer Strasse and the Postplatz, to his home in the Friedrichstadt suburb.

During the night of the 3rd–4th May the King fled, by way of the river, to the fortress of Königstein. (The revolutionists alleged later that there was no need for this step — that the King had been in no danger, but the Court and Government officials wanted him out of the way; they feared that, being as humane as he was, the bloodshed in the town might have caused him to weaken in his resistance to the insurgents' demands).[8] The distracted Town Council had now to make what provision it could for the ordering of affairs in the city. The rumour having spread that Prussian troops were on their way, measures were hastily adopted to deal with this new menace. It was still hoped, in the town, that the King would ally himself with his own people against the foreign forces; the Saxon troops themselves were believed to be mostly with the people at heart. On Friday, the 4th, a Provisional Government had been constituted by the insurgents, who were now beginning to be confident of success: at its head were Tschirner (a barrister from Bautzen),

[7] LWV, pp. 219, 220.
[8] Röckel (RSE, pp. 107 ff.) is very bitter on this subject.

Bürgermeister Adorf Todt, and Heubner (a district prefect in Freiberg, a man of high character). Lenz, the commander of the Communal Guard, having resigned his post, a Lieutenant Heinze, with Zychlinsky as his adjutant, had already been given command of the popular forces, such as they were. Karl Marx, in his retrospect of the years 1848–9, was bitterly contemptuous of the incompetence of the German leaders in general to make a success of a revolution; and those in Dresden seem to have been as amateurish in this field as their fellows elsewhere. The new government was proclaimed from the balcony of the Town Hall in the early afternoon: Wagner is said to have led the cheering with a " Hoch! " [9] There was the usual ringing of bells, the usual issue of a manifesto by the Provisional Government to the citizens; there was further an appeal to the " brotherhood " of the troops. Before this had happened, the Wagner who would have us believe that his interest in the rising was one mainly of detached curiosity had fastened on Römpler, the printer of the *Volksblätter*, and made him produce a large number of placards bearing the words " Are you with us against the foreign troops? " These were pasted on the barricades

---

[9] The contemporary letters of the nineteen-years-old Bülow (from Leipzig to his mother in Dresden) throw one or two side-lights on the rising and on Wagner's share in it: Bülow derived his information from the letters of student friends of his in the capital. On the 7th of May he writes, in great agitation, "If only Wagner has not been shot! I can't think of it without weeping passionate tears: I understand he is in the fourth battalion of the Communal Guard, and he will not neglect his duties, even if death should call." (Bülow evidently did not know that Wagner had ceased to be a member of the Guard on the 1st May).

"About Wagner," he writes later (the letter is not dated, but it must belong to the days just after the rising), "I know more than you do. Rietz told us, in the Conservatoire here, that Wagner has been active as secretary to the Provisional Government." [Whether this be true or not, it indicates that his confidential connection with the leaders was common talk at the time]. "Meser, whom I met yesterday at the booksellers' exchange, could not answer for this, but assured me that Wagner took a prominent part. Ritter's mother wrote him yesterday that Wagner has gone away with his wife; at his house they either do not know where he has gone, or will not say. A student heard him address the crowd from the balcony [of the Town Hall]. So the operas of the arch-traitor are now, as a punishment for him, banned from the repertory for ever, and perhaps he himself is by no means out of danger" (BB, I, 164–7). Wagner says nothing in *Mein Leben* about having harangued the crowd, and he may not have done so.

Ellis tries to discredit this testimony, calling it merely "odds and ends of gossip". The point that Ellis never set himself to meet squarely is why so many of these contemporary "odds and ends of gossip" should centre in Wagner; and presumably Ellis did not know, in 1902, the extent to which *Mein Leben*, which was not published until 1911, either confirms this "gossip" or makes it credible. Once more I may remark that the whole matter is one not for juridical subtleties but for plain common sense.

and at street corners, where it was hoped they would catch the eye of the Saxon soldiers. " Of course ", he says in *Mein Leben,* " no one took any notice of them but intending informers " — another tacit admission that his conduct had already drawn on himself, the King's Kapellmeister, the unfavourable notice of the authorities.[10] On his way to the printer's he had called at the actor Heine's house, where he exhorted his friend to go to the Neustadt quarter and implore the commanding officers not to fire on the people — a naïve suggestion of which Heine sensibly took no notice.[11]

In his treatment of the episode of the placards, Glasenapp rises to a height of naïveté to which even he seldom attained. He tells us, to begin with, that this is the only authenticated instance of Wagner's participation in the struggle — which is flatly untrue. Then he assures us that not only is the episode vastly to Wagner's credit, but if the placards had had the desired effect on the soldiers the revolt would have petered out; there would have been no bloodshed in Dresden, the German constitution would have followed as a matter of course, and throughout happy Teutonia all would have been gas and gaiters! But to attempt to seduce soldiers from their duty, to attempt to persuade them to disobey their officers' orders in face of the enemy (even if the enemy of the moment happens to be a mob of their own nationality), is surely, in the eyes of the law, as much a criminal proceeding on the part of a composer as on that of a coalheaver. One suspects, moreover, that if there had not been irrefragable evidence as to the printing and distribution of the placards Glasenapp would have pooh-poohed this story, as he did so many others, as being " mere tittle-tattle ". The fact being beyond question, the only resource left to Glasenapp was to try to make out that Wagner's action was just another illustration of his all-wisdom and all-virtue, and that the subsequent bloodshed and imprisonments in Saxony were the direct consequence of the purblind authorities having refused to accept Wagner's super-

---

[10] One of the placards is still in existence in a Dresden collection. It is about 19 inches long and 3½ inches deep: the large letters are nearly an inch high, the smaller about half an inch (MRW, p. 19). These placards figure in many of the later accounts of the revolution: they evidently created much excitement at the time.

[11] The story was told by Heine's daughter to Gustav Kietz. See KW, pp. 95, 96. Römpler, who died at Melbourne in 1892, told the story of the placards in an article in a Melbourne Calendar for 1890. This was reprinted in the *Musikalishes Wochenblatt,* No. 27, 1894.

guidance! Karl Marx, who had an incomparable first-hand acquaintance with the German history of that epoch, tells us more than once that throughout the German States one of the most serious difficulties the authorities had to face in 1848 and 1849 was the doubtful loyalty of the troops:

> " The western half of Germany had taken up arms in its [the National Assembly's] behalf: the military everywhere were vacillating; in the lesser States they were undoubtedly favourable to the [revolutionary] movement. . . . In the Palatinate and Baden . . . the soldiers of the regular army themselves joined the insurgents, nay, in Baden they were amongst the foremost of them. . . . Two-thirds of the armies of the smaller States, one-third of the Prussian army, the majority of the Prussian Landwehr (reserve or militia) were ready to join it [the democratic party] if it only acted resolutely and with that courage which is the result of a clear insight into the state of things." [12]

This being the case, any attempt on Wagner's or anyone else's part to undermine the fidelity of the Saxon troops could be regarded only in the most serious light by the authorities.

Kietz, who was in the ranks of the Communal Guard, tells us that on this same afternoon he met Wagner with a number of the placards under his arm. He thrust some of them into the young man's hand, bidding him help him distribute them among the Saxon soldiers stationed on the Brühl Terrace. Kietz was on the point of doing so when a captain snatched them out of his hand, called him a " misguided boy ", and told him to go away. " I saw ", he says, " that my Guard's hat made me an object of suspicion, so I got out of eyesight of the captain as quickly as I could ".[13] Wagner meanwhile had gone on his way, distributing his placards, ignorant or careless of the fact that his conduct at this juncture was not merely rash but treasonable. The loyalty of the Saxon troops to their officers was at that moment anything but certain; the authorities were actually debating the wisdom of taking the extreme step of abandoning the town to the insurgents and withdrawing the troops to another quarter. The arsenal itself was in danger until troops arrived from Leipzig and elsewhere; [14] but the insurgents

---

[12] See MRCG, pp. 119, 127, 135, etc. These articles of Marx's were written in 1851 and 1852.
[13] KW, pp. 96, 97.   [14] MRW, p. 21.

had neither the intelligence nor the organisation to act promptly and effectively when the omens were in their favour. They contented themselves with putting up more barricades.

3

Semper, who had also been bitten by the revolutionary maggot, having complained to Wagner (at the Town Hall) of the poor construction of the barricades in the Wilsdruffergasse and the Brüdergasse, Wagner sent the famous architect, whose technical knowledge would of course be valuable, to the office of the Military Commission for the Defence.[15] Wagner's own account of the further events of this day shows that he was a good deal in the company of Bakunin — who, as usual, was loftily contemptuous of the amateurishness of the revolutionaries, — and the other leading advocates of destruction. He was evidently thoroughly pleased with himself at taking so pronounced a part in these world-shaking events; no doubt the " vanity " that the pitilessly critical Minna so often commented upon in him was drinking its fill of satisfaction. At a late hour he walked back to his suburb thinking out, he tells us, a drama on the subject of Achilles.[16] This is quite credible: it was in moments of excitement such as this, induced by outer events, that his creative genius often functioned at its easiest.

Once more, however, he omits an important detail from his *plaidoyer*. About six o'clock on the following afternoon (Saturday, the 5th), he is said to have approached the Communal Guard on the Zwingerwall (the Guard was protecting the Museum), and, as spokesman for others, to have asked permission to sprinkle the Prince's Palace and the Castle with sulphuric ether, vitriol and spirits, in order to set them on fire. The request was peremptorily refused. The facts are given, though without mention of Wagner's name, in a letter of one Schwender to Köchly of the 14th June,

---

[15] In Zürich, in 1854, Wagner talked to his young friend Hornstein about the revolution days, and made merry at the expense of what he called the great architect's "Corinthian barricades". Hornstein elsewhere refers to Semper as Wagner's "barricade companion". Wagner plainly had a closer acquaintance with the Dresden barricades than would appear from his story in *Mein Leben*. See HM, pp. 143, 144.

[16] It had apparently been occupying his thoughts for some time. His brief sketch for it will be found in RWGS, Vol. XII.

1849. Schwender (who died in Dresden in 1901 as a much-respected merchant) repeatedly and emphatically maintained that it was Wagner who acted as the leader of the men and did the talking: the Kapellmeister was very well known to him, he said.[17]

Wagner had " noticed," he tells us in *Mein Leben,* " the particularly prominent activity " of a former university friend of his, the lawyer Marschall von Bieberstein, who was now an officer in the Communal Guard. He remembered, too, that one Heinze, formerly a Greek colonel, was now made commander of the popular forces: Bakunin, who seems to have had no belief in Heinze, and who never ceased to insist that the dispute with the authorities would never be settled by " moral persuasion ", especially in view of the probability of the coming of Prussian troops, urged his colleagues to enlist the military services of some experienced Polish officers who happened to be in Dresden just then. The suggestion was greeted with horror: with a spinelessness that justified Bakunin's contempt for them, the insurgents preferred to base their hopes on the futile Frankfort Reichsgewalt: " everything was to be done as far as possible in legal form, according to parliamentary ideas ", says Wagner ironically. It will be seen that he is particularly well informed as to what was said and done at the very centre of the revolt, in the inner councils of its leaders. He would hardly have spent so much time there had his interest in the proceedings been purely academic, nor would anyone have been allowed to spend so much time there who was not regarded by the captains of the revolution as virtually one of themselves.

The excitement in the town had by now increased: there were rumours of risings in Baden, the Palatinate, and other places: volunteer student corps from Leipzig arrived, while armed revolutionaries from Chemnitz and from the Erzgebirge, the latter with four cannon, were said to be on their way. But at seven o'clock in the evening the first Prussian troops arrived in Dresden; and these had no hesitation in doing work which some of the Saxon soldiers might possibly have refused. Among these Prussians, by the way, was a certain lieutenant of grenadiers, Botho von Hülsen, who was destined to become, in June, 1851, Intendant of the Ber-

---

[17] MRW, p. 24, on the basis of documents in the Dresden archives.

lin Opera in succession to Küstner, in which capacity it fell to him to produce some of Wagner's works. Did the pair actually meet in these hectic Dresden days? Wagner makes no mention whatever of Hülsen in his account of the rising in *Mein Leben*: but in 1863 we find Hülsen, in a letter to Bülow, declining in the following terms to receive a call from Wagner, who was about to visit Berlin:

> " As regards the visit of Wagner which you suggest, I must confess to you quite openly and honestly that I do not desire it. You will find it both natural and excusable if I do not attempt to disavow my personal feeling, which compels me to say that after our meeting in Dresden in May, 1849 it would be repugnant to me to enter into any kind of personal relations with him." [18]

The inference from this would seem to be that Wagner and Hülsen *did* meet, somehow or other, during the Dresden revolt; but how or when is a mystery. Had they an angry colloquy, perhaps, across some barricade or other? Wagner would presumably not know the Prussian officer to whom he had been speaking — which fact might account for the absence of any reference to him in *Mein Leben* — while even if Wagner's features were not already familiar to Hülsen from the Berlin *Rienzi* performances of October, 1847 (which is quite possible), he would learn from a dozen sources that the man he was talking to was the Royal Kapellmeister Richard Wagner. The intriguing features of the reference to May, 1849, in Hülsen's letter to Bülow are the use of the very definite word " Begegnung " (meeting), and the implication that this " meeting " was a matter of such general knowledge that any enlargement upon it was unnecessary.

In the small hours of the morning of Sunday, the 6th, firing was general in the disturbed area; to the struggle at the barricades there was now added house-to-house fighting. All hope of a peaceful settlement of the matter was now at an end; and the Provisional Government was forced to call in Polish officers to eke out its own inexperience in military affairs. At seven o'clock [19] the " old " opera house was seen to be in flames; apparently it had been set on fire for strategic reasons — to protect the barricades. It was

---

[18] BB, III, 514.

[19] Wagner seems to be wrong in giving the time of the outbreak, in *Mein Leben*, as eleven o'clock.

burnt to the ground, to the no small danger of the surrounding buildings; and as it was the storehouse for theatrical costumes and properties, the loss to the town was serious. It looked like proving no less so to the theatre company; performances now being impossible, the King, on the 11th May, gave the company notice that all appointments other than for life would terminate as from the 31st August following: he added that in view of the circumstances of the time he could not at present decide whether the theatre would afterwards be continued as a royal institution or wholly cease to exist. In the latter case, of course, the dismissals would be final: at the same time the members of the company were asked not to enter into engagements elsewhere without previously informing Lüttichau. A week later, however, the King announced that out of consideration for art, the theatre would continue to be maintained as a charge on his Civil List, though on a somewhat reduced scale, owing to the fall in receipts to be expected after the disturbances in the town and to the expense of replacing the properties and costumes.[20]

4

Wagner's narrative now becomes a little confused in itself, and apparently not quite accurate as regards the order of events. He must have been back in the town, at the centre of things, at a very early hour on the Sunday, for about six in the morning, after leaving the Town Hall, he fell in with one Bromme, a bookseller from Meissen, who told him that an adjutant of the Communal Guard (Zychlinsky) wanted " a safe man " for a special job — to ascend the tower of the Kreuz Church and observe the disposition and

---

[20] See PGHD, pp. 553 ff. The burning down of the old opera house was laid to the charge of Wagner. It appeared probable later that a certain Heinrich Woldemar Wagner, a confectioner's assistant, had something to do with the matter.

The story went about that Semper had assisted Wagner in his alleged incendiary operations. Dinger tells us how this canard arose. On one of the early days of the revolution Wagner and Semper were discussing, in the street in front of Meser's music shop, the staging of Lohengrin. Wagner complained that the stage of the "new" theatre (i.e. the building of which Semper had been the architect) was insufficiently deep for his requirements; whereupon Semper, half-angrily, half-humorously, replied, "Ah well, I'd like to burn the place down myself!" The conversation was overheard by Reissiger and the singer Chiarelli, who repeated it to their friends. After that, of course, it only needed the conflagration at the "old" opera house for the crime to be fixed on Wagner and Semper! See DWGE, p. 193.

movements of the soldiers.[21] Wagner accepted the commission and ascended the tower, which, being about 300 ft. high, made an excellent observation post: it commanded a view not only of the Old Market Place (on the south-east side of which it stands), not only of the adjacent streets and the principal buildings, such as the castle, the Zwinger, and the theatre, but also the surrounding country and of the bridges crossing the Elbe. He saw, about eleven o'clock, that one of the cannon had retired from its former position to the Schlossplatz. Röckel, who was now back in Dresden, called at the tower to see Wagner, but missed him: he had gone to the Town Hall. There he had found Bakunin, who was at last beginning to take his revolutionary colleagues seriously, as a result of a decisive piece of action on Heubner's part at one of the barricades. While the Polish officers carried out the military operations in detail, the central direction seems now to have passed into the hands of Bakunin. Food and reinforcements for the Provisional Government were arriving from the surrounding country; the State military seemed to be weakening; and the hopes of the revolutionaries were correspondingly beginning to revive.

Wagner returned to the tower: Gustav Kietz told Houston Stewart Chamberlain that Wagner had tried to induce him to accompany him, declaring that " the view was splendid and the combination of the bells and the cannon intoxicating ".[22] The Viennese littérateur Ludwig Eckardt said later [23] that at some time or other

---

[21] Wagner's activities there were testified to by several witnesses at the enquiry after the rising: see DWGE, pp. 183, 184. Müller (MRW, p. 27), who re-examined the records for himself, says that Dinger has not reproduced the whole of the depositions bearing on this matter.

[22] CRW, p. 52.

[23] In an article *Über Richard Wagners Entwicklung und Richtung*, in the *Hamburger Literarische und Kritische Blätter*, 1857, cited in MRW, p. 28. "My personal meeting with Wagner took place during these stirring days," said Eckardt. "I can still see him, excited, eagerly asking for news, giving advice, always with the agitation of a man who was a personal participator in the events." See DWGE, p. 226.

This article, be it remembered, was published in 1857. It undoubtedly came under the notice of the police; it is little matters of this kind that help us to understand the implacability of the Dresden authorities towards Wagner during his exile. The association thus indicated with Eckardt was brought up against Wagner by his Munich enemies in 1865: the *Volksbote* reminded its readers of Wagner's former activities in conjunction with "Semper, who constructed barricades in Dresden", and "Eckardt, who, according to the Vienna criminal registers, was one of the intellectual instigators of the assassination of Latour". (See SWM, p. 37.) According to a record of the period, during this period Wagner met him and asked excitedly for news of what was going on in the town. Wagner and a schoolmaster named Berthold protected themselves by means of a straw mattress from the bullets of the Prussian sharpshooters, who were posted in the tower of the Frauenkirche; the pair lightened their task as observers with a discussion of religious and philosophical problems. The Prussians, says Wagner in *Mein Leben*, had made the Kreuzkirche their target, a fact which of itself indicates that it was a recognised observation post of the revolutionaries. He spent the night in the tower, under the great bell; as the rope was close to his hand, we have no difficulty in believing that he got to work on it occasionally.[24] He tells us in *Mein Leben* that Prussian shots " from the distant tower of the Frauenkirche " kept beating against the walls of the Kreuzkirche tower. Mr. William Wallace doubts this, as the weapon then in use by the Prussian troops is said to have carried no more than 400 yards, while the distance between the two towers was 600 yards.[25] There cannot be the least question, however, that, from whatever spot the shots came, the tower was persistently fired upon. There were some seventy rebel sharpshooters in the Kreuzkirche tower, who kept up an incessant fire on the troops below; and the latter, of course, retaliated.

Another occupant of the tower, one Thum, who afterwards became a Professor-Doctor, is not mentioned in *Mein Leben*. Thum left it on record later that during the night Wagner debated eagerly with him, at great length, such questions as the ancient and the Christian conception of the world, the relations of master and apprentice, the Leipzig Gewandhaus concerts in comparison with those of Dresden, Berlioz, Beethoven, " absolute " and " poetic "

he "was arrested in Vienna in 1846 for disseminating seditious literature: afterwards he took part in the Dresden rising and in the Palatinate revolution. . . . From Vienna, where he fought with the insurgents in the October revolution, he escaped in women's clothes."

[24] Frau Hesselbarth, the daughter of Alexander Müller, with whom Wagner found refuge during his first days in Zürich, says that "we learned later that on the outbreak of the revolution Wagner had rung the storm bells". (See SRWZ, I, 16.) She may, of course, have only been repeating hearsay; but in view of the close association of herself and her father with Wagner during the Zürich period it is not improbable that the information came from Wagner himself. He says in *Mein Leben* that he and Berthold "took turns in watching and sleeping, in the immediate neighbourhood of the horribly clanging bell".

[25] WRW, p. 112.

music, etc.[26] It is yet another instance of Wagner's astonishing power of detachment from his immediate surroundings. In his exaltation he is said to have assured another comrade, Ferdinand Götz, in reply to a warning as to the sharpshooters, that " the bullet that could lay him out had not yet been cast."

Wagner omits another detail that we owe to a Herr von Bosse, who saw him and another man (perhaps Berthold) write messages on pieces of paper, attach them to stones, and throw them to the sentinels below; plainly Wagner was in the tower for that very purpose, commissioned by the leaders at the Town Hall to observe and make reports upon the various movements in and round the town, the position of the troops, and the approach of revolutionary reinforcements from the country. Bosse's assurance on this point was confirmed by one of the custodians of the tower, as the official records show. Some of these interesting documents have actually survived: the handwriting on them resembles Wagner's.[27] Berthold's own statement, during the trials that followed the rising, was that " another man ", whose name he did not know, " and Herr Kapellmeister Wagner " were responsible for the messages attached to the stones.[28] Thus while neither Berthold nor Bosse is anxious to implicate himself, each of them expressly names Wagner. Glasenapp reproduces Berthold's statement without comment: Ashton Ellis, while professing to translate Glasenapp, deliberately garbles the passage — " Some say that, like others round him, he [Wagner] pencilled messages on scraps of paper and dropped them overboard ", omitting Glasenapp's " whereupon the sentinels posted below took these reports to the Town Hall " — and then adds a sentence of his own that is designed to suggest the perfect innocence of the mere " spectator " Wagner — " one of these terrible messages was to his wife for a bottle of wine, which he must badly have needed." [29] Wagner's own account of this minor matter is that when night came he sent a *messenger* (the assistant of the tower warder) to Minna for provisions.

---

[26] AMZ, 1893, p. 439. See MRW, p. 29, and CRW, p. 52.
[27] MRW, pp. 30, 31.
[28] DWGE, pp. 183, 184.
[29] ERW, II, p. 349.

That evening there had been severe fighting in and near the Neumarkt; the barricade in the Frauenstrasse had been captured by the troops and the " Hôtel de Saxe " and the hotel " Stadt Rom " occupied, and the soldiers were pressing inward towards the Altmarkt and the Town Hall. A proclamation was issued by the authorities that any citizen taken with arms in his hand would be shot. Matters were now looking critical for the insurgents; there were signs that some of those from the surrounding country were more anxious to return to their homes than to see things through. The Provisional Government was beginning to lose its head: one of the leaders, Tschirner, would occasionally be missing; another, Todt, went off to Frankfort; Heubner alone continued to act with courage and decision. His steadfastness, as we have seen, had already won him the active support of Bakunin, who till then had been contemptuous of so amateurish a " revolution ".

The next day, the 7th (Monday), was one of the most beautiful days of the year. Awakened early by the song of a nightingale in an adjacent garden, Wagner heard the strains of the *Marseillaise* coming from the Tharandterstrasse; columns of well-armed miners from the Erzgebirge were entering the town. They were followed, during the day, by other reinforcements. Hurried steps were taken to defend the insurgent position near the Kreuzkirche; but about nine in the morning the troops attacked and took the Gewandhaus (in the present Gewandhausstrasse); the barricade in the Kreuzgasse, however, between the Gewandhaus and the Kreuzkirche, still remained intact. Wagner, it will be seen, was decidedly in the danger zone; nay, he was in a building and in a company not at all suitable to any one who would fain be taken for just a sober citizen with no more than a spectator's interest in the events. The troops were working their way through the streets between the Gewandhaus and the Altmarkt: they were driven back by shots from the Kreuzkirche, and about midday the tower came under cannon fire.

By now the tower was filled with armed insurgents, whose job it was to defend the approach to the Altmarkt. They were joined by Bakunin, and Wagner once more sent to Minna for provisions, this time ordering *two* bottles of wine. Taking the view that, as an unarmed man,[30] he was only in the way, Wagner now made his way home, by circuitous routes, to appease the anxious Minna, who, having heard that the dangerous Bakunin was with him, had threatened to leave the house unless he returned at once. He found the place full of distracted women, among them being Röckel's wife, who had not seen her husband for days: Wagner's two young nieces, however, the daughters of Luise Brockhaus, found nothing but childish feminine amusement in the shouting and the shooting that were going on in the town. Minna was furious with Richard; to prevent him from going out again she locked the front door and hid the key.[31]

Early in the morning of Tuesday, the 8th, Wagner, having either evaded Minna or succeeded in talking her over, once more made his way to the Town Hall. As he was passing through the barricades near St. Anne's Church — the fact that he was allowed to do so, by the way, seems to indicate that he was known by the insurgents to be one of themselves — one of the Communal Guard, who evidently knew his Ninth Symphony, shouted to him, " Herr Kapellmeister! *Der Freude schöner Götterfunken* has set fire to things! " [32] On his further way he met the first oboist of the theatre, Hiebendahl, who warned him, though in vain, of the danger he was running, as a Court servant, in identifying himself so openly with Röckel and the other thoroughgoing revolutionaries. Wagner merely laughed at him; as Müller puts it, he knew by now that he had burned his bridges. Röckel now appeared on the scene, black with smoke and tar, breathing fire and slaughter; his plans for defending some of the barricades by setting them on fire had been too much for the distracted amateurs in such things who formed the

---

[30] According to Dinger (DWGE, I, p. 179), he had previously lamented to Minna that he "could not shoulder a musket". Even if he had been able to do so, we cannot imagine him ever using it, even on a Prussian soldier. It is practically certain that he took no part at any time in the actual fighting.

[31] DWGE, I, p. 184.

[32] This is the form in which Wagner tells the story in *Mein Leben*. He appears to have given Gustav Kietz another version of it, according to which the incident took place, at some unspecified time, at the main barricade in the Wilsdrufferstrasse, when Wagner was making for his home (DWGE, p. 178). Müller (MRW, p. 35) points out that this barricade is ruled out by the fact that the Postplatz was already exposed to the fire of the troops.

bulk of the Provisional Government. Leaving Röckel to attend to his own duties, Wagner once more made for the Town Hall. It was not until thirteen years later, after Röckel's release from prison in 1862, that the friends met again.

6

While the two were talking, a troop of some hundreds of students from the gymnasium, well armed, had appeared on the scene, coming, apparently, from Zittau. Röckel, says Wagner, undertook to conduct them over the barricades to the mustering-place in front of the Town Hall. According to Röckel's testimony, however, it was Wagner who guided them. This seems to be confirmed by a letter of Wagner's to Röckel's younger brother, Eduard (who had settled in England), of the 15th March, 1851: " Although I had not accepted a special rôle, yet I was present everywhere, actively superintending the bringing in of convoys; and indeed I only returned with one from the Erzgebirge to the Town Hall, Dresden, on the eve of the last day." [33]

At the Town Hall he found that the Provisional Government, despairing now of success in Dresden itself, was counselling a withdrawal of the insurgent forces to the Erzgebirge, where reinforcements could be gathered in, and whence, it was hoped, civil war could be stirred up in Germany as a whole. At this point in his story Wagner unwittingly makes it clear that his participation in the rising had been all along anything but academic:

" I must confess ", he says in *Mein Leben,* " that this idea seemed to me magnificent and full of significance. Whereas hitherto I had been moved only by a spirit of sympathy for a procedure entered upon at first with almost ironical incredulity, then taken up with surprise, now what had previously been incomprehensible unfolded itself before my eyes as of great and hopeful significance. Without feeling within me either the urge, or, more especially, the call to have assigned to me any kind of rôle or function in these happenings, I now, with full consciousness of what I was doing, threw to the winds all consideration for my personal position, and resolved to abandon

---

[33] PW, p. 189. The context, however, makes it doubtful whether this occasion and that dealt with in the text were the same.

myself to the stream of events flowing in the direction towards which my feelings about life had driven me, with a delight that was full of despair."

The wording, it will be observed, is somewhat cloudy, perhaps designedly so. At this stage of his narrative, in fact, he finds himself in a difficulty. He has to account for his conduct in throwing in his lot completely with the revolutionaries in the last stage of their desperate gamble, when it would have been so easy for him, had he been as innocent hitherto as he has tried to make us believe, to go back to his house, let events in the town take their inevitable course, and calmly await, like other sober and prudent citizens, the reorganisation of the national life that would follow the collapse of the rising. The truth was that he had been too deeply involved in the troubles from the beginning to withdraw now that the authorities knew he had been so involved, and that with the failure of the revolution his position would obviously be a serious one. So, to explain his conduct from this point onwards, he tries to make out, clumsily and unsuccessfully, that it was only *now* that he decided to do what other leaders of the rising were doing, but that even now he did not accept " any rôle or function in these happenings ". His acts, and even his words, belie him.

Three of the charges against him in the summary of evidence of 1856 were that " he had been in the Town Hall on the day of the election of the so-called Provisional Government, and had invited Bakunin to accompany him ", that " he had been seen on the tower of the Kreuzkirche ",[34] and that " he had accompanied revolutionary reinforcements from Zittau ".[35] It is manifest that the authorities knew much more about him than he imagined; and we can hardly doubt that he had been under observation for a long while before the actual disturbances broke out. The Town Hall was the recognised headquarters of the people who were most

---

[34] The Leipzig *Neue Zeitschrift für Musik*, in its issue of the 21st June, 1849 (i.e. some five weeks after the suppression of the rising), said that no member of the Dresden theatre company had taken part in the fighting, but "Herr Kapellmeister Wagner has fled, he having been actively engaged in the rising; mindful of his lofty position as Kapellmeister, he was in the Kreuzkirche tower, conducting the storm-bells and the signals, he being in less personal danger in that way than if he had been at the barricades."

[35] LWV, p. 19.

active in directing the revolution: it was there that reports were received and strategy decided upon. The Kreuzkirche tower was a central observation post of the revolutionaries; no one who was not actively and willingly concerned in the revolution had any call whatever to be in either of these two places. We have, in large part, only Wagner's own story of the events of this crowded week so far as they concern him; but this of itself places his complicity in the rising beyond question. On his own showing, wherever the Provisional Government is, there is Richard Wagner; wherever the recognised leaders of the rising — Röckel, Bakunin and Heubner — are, there is Richard Wagner; whenever there is a general movement of the revolutionary headquarters staff to this point of the scene or that, among the other figures is that of Richard Wagner; when things look black for the revolutionary cause, Richard Wagner is one of the first to fly from the town; at the slightest indication that his fears were needless, that reinforcements are arriving, and that the great *coup* may yet succeed, the first to return to Dresden and to get into touch again with the revolutionary leaders is Richard Wagner. Glasenapp is only burking the real issues and misleading his readers when he says that Wagner frequented the company of the leaders during that fateful week only in order " to learn accurately what was going on and to observe the behaviour of the revolutionary party ", that he merely followed events " step by step, always from the loftiest and most wide-reaching point of view, participating in them as an anxious observer, openly demonstrating where his sympathies lay." Wagner has said enough in *Mein Leben* to place it beyond question that, so far from his being a mere curious spectator of events, he was as active a participator in them as most.

7

" For all that ", he continues in *Mein Leben,* " I did not want to leave my wife helpless in Dresden, so I rapidly devised an expedient for drawing her thence into the path I had chosen, without immediately letting her know what was implied by my resolve." He would fain persuade us that all he had in mind was the possibility of an occupation of the Friedrichstadt suburb by the Prussian troops, from the uncomfortable consequences of which he nobly wished to protect Minna. So far he had not shown her much consideration; she had throughout tried to keep him from knocking his hot head against the hard wall of politics, she could be under no illusion as to where all this dabbling in revolution was likely to land herself as well as him, and her unappeasable anger with him in the weeks immediately following the failure of the rising is both comprehensible and pardonable. But in his rage against the society that was not giving him what he felt to be his due as an artist, in his despair of ever rehabilitating his finances so long as things remained as they were, and in the overwhelming self-confidence that led him to believe himself as capable of handling a revolution as anyone else, he had gone on from folly to folly, and now, as even he could not help seeing, the hour of reckoning was at hand. Neither he nor his associates could now doubt that, failing a general rising, the game was lost. And so, not primarily because he was particularly concerned about Minna, but because he saw the possibility of a final flight from Dresden becoming necessary, and in his new life, whatever that might be, Minna would be as domestically necessary to him as she had been in the old, he returned home that morning (Tuesday) and told her to make arrangements to go to his sister Klara in Chemnitz.

Minna having undertaken to follow with the parrot, he himself went on in advance (about eight o'clock in the morning) with the little dog Peps — two small but significant details that prove that he hardly counted just then on seeing Dresden again; [36] he admits, indeed, that as he traversed the ground his walks had made so familiar to him it was with the consciousness that it was for the last time. From Dresden came the continuous thunder of the guns; " accompanied by this terrible music ", he says, " I called out my farewell greeting to the towers of the city that lay behind me, and said

---

[36] The piano teacher Justus Dietz, who had formerly been a Royal Kammermusikus, met him in the Grosse Oberseergasse (now Trompeterstrasse), on his way to his house in Friedrichstadt; Wagner, who was in a great hurry, had been buying a pair of trousers, presumably for his flight. (In another account of the episode, the pair of trousers became a pair of stockings). The story comes through Kohut, who had it from Dietz himself. Dietz says also that he heard two of the rebels, Dr. Herz and Advocate Blöde, call out to Wagner, "The revolt is stamped out here. Let us go to Zittau [more probably Zwickau], and continue the work there." (See EV, p. 58, and MRW, p. 37.) Blöde himself, however, elected to go to the Town Hall, where he was taken prisoner on the morning of the 9th.

to myself with a smile that if, seven years ago, my entry there had been quite unostentatious, at all events my exit was accompanied by a certain pomp and ceremony." But why he should be thus flying from Dresden and arranging for Minna and his household pets to follow him, unless he knew that he had done enough to bring him well within the scope of the law in the event of the failure of the revolution, neither he nor any of his advocates pauses to tell us.

It would seem, however, as if, before leaving Dresden, he plunged once more into the inner part of the town — the neighbourhood of the Annenstrasse — in order to take a last glance at the condition of affairs there. Some time before this, a young Galician violinist named Haimberger had been recommended to him by Bakunin, who wished Wagner to obtain for him a post in the Opera orchestra. If Praeger is to be believed, Haimberger told him in later years that at about eight o'clock one morning (presumably the 8th) he was with Wagner at the barricades when a young girl of eighteen was shot by a Prussian; whereupon Wagner, mounting a cart, cried out, " Men, will you see your wives and daughters fall in the cause of our beloved country, and not avenge their cowardly murder? All who have hearts, all who have the blood and spirit of their forefathers and love their country, follow me, and death to the tyrant." " So saying ", continues Praeger, " he seized a musket, and heading the barricade they came quickly upon the few Prussians who had strayed too far into the town, and who, perceiving that they were outnumbered, gave themselves up as prisoners." [37] Praeger adds that he told the story afterwards to Wagner, " and he agreed entirely as to the truth of Haimberger's recital ". While Praeger is, in general, an unreliable witness, there is no apparent reason, as Müller points out, why he should have invented a story of this peculiarly circumstantial kind. While it may be doubtful whether the episode occurred precisely as he tells it, the probability is that something of the kind did happen.[38] Further according to Praeger,

---

[37] PW, p. 184.

[38] Dinger (DWGE, p. 184) says that some time during this day Wagner was grazed by a bullet, chance insurgent bullets reaching the suburb in which he lived. This seems improbable. If Wagner was touched at all, it is much more likely to have been in the barricade area. He makes no mention himself of this "grazing".

Haimberger fled to Switzerland after the rising, and in January, 1851, Wagner found a place for him among the violins of the Zürich orchestra for the season of that winter. With his usual kindness towards deserving young musicians, he did all he

Haimberger alleged that on an earlier day Wagner, who was at the barricades with him, sent him for an ice for the relief of his parched throat — again an incident which we can hardly believe anyone taking the trouble to invent. Finally Max von Weber, the son of the composer, is said to have told Praeger that he had seen Wagner with a gun on his shoulder, and that Wagner had advised the insurgents to strip the lead from the house-roofs for the casting of bullets. Of this, however, we have no confirmation.

Minna followed her husband to a neighbouring village — perhaps Löbtau; thence they proceeded in a carriage together, by way of Kesselsdorf and Freiberg, to Chemnitz, presumably about ten in the morning. In Freiberg they met armed reinforcements for the insurgents *en route* for Dresden, as well as some weary regular troops, going, as they say, " to do their duty in the town ", but rather reluctantly,[39] — apparently their sympathies were with the people. Wagner was greatly impressed, however, by the numbers and the ardour of the reinforcements for the popular cause. He told them how things, to his personal knowledge, were shaping in Dresden, and the " naked truth ", as he puts it, " sufficed to stimulate them to march on rapidly." In the evening he came, in Oederan, upon the whole of the Chemnitz Communal Guard, proceeding towards Dresden, accompanied by some fourteen hundred volunteers. The men stopped his coach and asked for the latest news from

---

could to assist Haimberger later, recommending him first to Röckel's brother Eduard in London, then to Vieuxtemps in Brussels, and using his influence with Sulzer in the matter of a passport for the young man. See the letters in FWSZ, pp. 361–3.

His innocent association with Haimberger in Zürich did him no good in the eyes of the police, to whom, of course, all political refugees were more or less criminals, carrying on their nefarious activities under the pretext of being concerned with art. In January, 1851, it was reported to Dresden that Wagner, "one of the coryphaei of the Swiss revolutionary party", was much in the company of "the Lemberg fugitive Haimberger", both of them having sinister connections with Austria.

[39] "In all cases", says Karl Marx, speaking of the German risings as a whole, "the real fighting body of the insurgents, that body which first took up arms and gave battle to the troops, consisted of the working classes of the towns. A portion of the poorer country population, labourers and petty farmers, generally joined them after the outbreak of the conflict." In Dresden "the shopkeepers . . ., 'the Communal Guard', not only did not fight but in many instances favoured the proceedings of the troops against the insurgents. These again consisted almost exclusively of working men from the surrounding manufacturing districts. They found an able and cool-headed commander in the Russian refugee Michael Bakunin." See MRCG, pp. 122, 126. Wagner's excursions into the country districts were evidently made in order to get into touch with the real fighting spirits among the revolutionaries.

the town. They did not believe his account of what had recently happened there; their own information, they said, was that the Prussians were already in possession of the place. He was forced to go with the men to the Town Hall, for closer enquiry into his statement: he realised that they were marching to Dresden under compulsion from the volunteers, and were greedy for false news that would give them an excuse for returning home forthwith. Wagner's story not being what they had expected or desired, they arrested him as a fugitive under suspicion; he obtained his release only by promising them that, after depositing his wife in Chemnitz, he would return to Dresden early next morning.

These details we get not from *Mein Leben* but from Wagner's letter of the 17th May to Eduard Devrient. They are partly confirmed and amplified by depositions, now in the Dresden archives, of two officers of the Communal Guard, who said that the Guard were unwilling to go to Dresden, but that they were encouraged to do so by Wagner. " In Oederan ", the depositions run, " the mood of the volunteers became threatening. It was decided that we were not to return on any account, but to push on without delay, in which resolution we were encouraged by the emissaries of the Provincial Government, among them Kapellmeister Wagner." [40]

Back to Dresden, accordingly, Wagner went as quickly as possible.[41] Undeterred by difficulties and dangers, and with new hope in his heart, he found his way by devious routes once more to the Town Hall. (He tells us that any unarmed man who tried to make his way through the barricaded streets was " sharply challenged ": the inference seems irresistible, then, that *he* was allowed to pass to the Town Hall because he was regarded by the insurgents as one of themselves). In his letter of the 17th May he says that at the Town Hall he found only the steadfast Heubner,[42] — the

---

[40] DWGE, p. 185.

[41] The chronological threads are difficult to disentangle at this point. From Wagner's own narrative, in *Mein Leben* and in his letter to Devrient, one would assume that he left Chemnitz the next day. But Müller's reconstruction of the events is probably correct: Wagner no doubt left Chemnitz the same afternoon or early evening on which he had deposited Minna there, and was in Dresden again either late on Tuesday or in the small hours of Wednesday.

[42] In 1887 Heubner, in a letter to Kohut, and again in a verbal communication to Dinger, said that he had seen and spoken to Wagner only once during the rising — on the 9th in Freiberg. Wagner, however, states quite definitely, in *Mein Leben*, that on the occasion with which we are now dealing Heubner was "delighted" to "*see him*

"nervous Todt" and the "cowardly Tschirner" having fled: in *Mein Leben*, however, he tells us that these two had unwillingly returned "after their first panic-stricken flight". The insurgent leaders were all exhausted; Heubner had not closed his eyes for seven days. The troops had been methodically capturing the barricades not by frontal attacks but by working round them through the houses, the inner walls of which they tore down. They were pressing in upon the Altmarkt by way of the Schlossgasse and the Badergasse. The incessant roar of the guns was everywhere breaking down men's nerves. Bakunin alone, inseparable, as usual, from his cigar, preserved his unshakeable *sang froid;* part of his time he spent consoling and heartening the young Haimberger, who quivered with fear at every roar of the cannon. Bakunin's calm proposal that all the available powder should be assembled in the lower rooms of the Town Hall, and the place blown to fragments, had met with no approval. Upon the Town Hall, as the headquarters of the Provisional Government and of the rebel leaders in general, the troops were slowly but surely closing: and the fact that at this supreme moment Wagner should have chosen to plunge once more into the very centre of the revolt is surely another proof that his association with the whole affair was anything but that of a curious spectator, or, as Glasenapp would have us believe, of a mere artist compulsorily interested in political events only because they touched by accident upon the outer edge of his artistic dreams.

8

Röckel was not there: it transpired later that in the night of 7th–8th May he had run into some Saxon troopers in the Plauen suburb and had been taken prisoner. His wife fled the town, having

---

again", "as he regarded my coming as a good omen for the cause he was defending." Again, in his letter to Devrient, written only some nine days after the event, Wagner says that he now had the opportunity to make Heubner's closer acquaintance by interceding for young Fürstenau, who apparently had been accused of firing on the insurgents, had been captured, and was now in danger of his life. He was saved only by Wagner's personal appeal to Heubner. Either the latter's memory was at fault in his old age, or he was anxious not to implicate Wagner too deeply. It is just possible, however, that during the early days of the revolt, though he must have come into contact with Wagner, he did not know who he was. Heubner was not a Dresdener: his home was in Freiberg. It is conceivable, therefore, that he did not know the Kapellmeister by sight.

first asked her friend Julie Haase — as the latter deposed at the enquiry — to hand over to Wagner Bakunin's trunk, which was in Röckel's study. This she forgot to do. Once more, then, we see how intimate was the connection between Wagner on the one side and Röckel and Bakunin on the other.

" It was now decided ", he tells us in *Mein Leben*, " that as everything was ready, the retreat to the Erzgebirge, which had been planned for the preceding day, should be carried out early next morning; young Zychlinsky had already had orders to make the road to Plauen strategically safe." This passage is undesignedly illuminative: it is difficult to resist the conclusion that Wagner's hurried exit from Dresden on the preceding day had been, in part, the result of his knowledge of this plan; it all points in the first place to his having been from first to last in the inner circle of the insurgent council, and in the second place to a commendably prudent resolve on his part not to be the last to stir his shanks when the *sauve qui peut* should begin. He further implicates himself by saying that he now told the other leaders of the sights he had seen on his way to and from Chemnitz, and of his consequent belief that adequate reinforcements from outside were coming to the rescue. " I was begged ", he continues, " at once to go back and convey the opinion of the Provisional Government [i.e. that all would be well if the loyalty of the wavering troops from outside could be undermined] to the people whose acquaintance I had made." Once more he commits himself out of his own mouth: not only is it clear that he was a person whom the leaders knew to be one of themselves, heart and soul, but the phrase about " the people whose acquaintance I had made " makes it fairly obvious that on his way to and from Chemnitz he had been rather more active in the cause than he explicitly states in *Mein Leben*.

He set out with his friend Marschall von Bieberstein, who, as he says, " being an officer of the Provisional Government, was much more qualified than I was to communicate its orders ": the plain inference being that Wagner himself would have carried these orders from the seat of war in Dresden to the insurgents outside the town had his military authority been sufficient to ensure their being obeyed. Marschall, exhausted by lack of sleep, and so hoarse that he could hardly bring a sound out of his throat, took him first of all, by devious ways, to his house in the Plauen suburb, there to requisition a carriage from someone whom he knew and to say good-bye to his family, which he was not likely to see again for some time. It was midnight: after a hurried supper the pair set out for Freiberg, where they must have arrived about four o'clock on the morning of the 9th. Wagner admits that he " set out forthwith to find the leaders of the reserve reinforcements whose acquaintance I had previously made." Marschall, he says (he draws a discreet veil over his own activities), told these leaders to requisition horses and carts wherever they could find them in the villages. The mere thought that, after all, there was still some hope for the rising was enough to make Wagner want to return to the town once more. Marschall, his heart, perhaps, no longer in the business now, went his own way — " to carry his commission further afield ", says Wagner: the latter, in great excitement, took a coach in the direction of Tharandt. He fell asleep, and was awakened, apparently in Plauen, by shouts and a confused parleying with the postilion. The road was filled with an excited crowd of armed revolutionaries flying from Dresden; they were trying to commandeer the coach to facilitate their escape. Wagner asked them what was the matter, and where they were going: the reply was, " Home! It is all over in Dresden. The Provisional Government is behind us in the carriage down there." What had happened was that at three o'clock that morning a retreat to Freiberg — along the Tharandt route, the only one now open — had been proclaimed from the Town Hall and elsewhere, and those who, not being occupied at the barricades, were consequently free to move, had decided on flight. The troops were closing in on the insurgents from all sides: at about four o'clock the Town Hall was evacuated; barricades were abandoned wholesale; white flags appeared everywhere. At eight o'clock the great bell in the tower of the Kreuzkirche gave out a ninefold boom: it was the signal to the last gallant defenders of the barricades to seek safety in flight. At nine o'clock the Saxon troops took possession of the Town Hall. The rising was at an end; little remained for the victors to do but to pursue those of the insurgents who had fled in the direction of Freiberg.

Wagner, by his own account, " shot out of the carriage like an arrow ": he could not have the least illusion now as to the danger he was in. It would seem that for a moment, in his agitation, he tried to get back to Dresden: at Potschappel he entered an old inn, the " Zum Steiger ", where he asked the landlady for some bread and meat, and water for washing: " as quickly as you can ", he said, " for every minute brings me nearer to death." A humorous and characteristic Wagnerian touch in the proceedings is that in the hurry and confusion he got what he wanted without paying for it: he drank some beer, and the hostess's son showed him the road he was to take. His own account is that he hurried " forward " to meet the Provisional Government; but it would seem, from the evidence of Heubner and Bakunin, that they and some 2,000 other fugitives fell in with him between Tharandt and Freiberg. The two leaders of the revolt were in an elegant Dresden carriage, along with the post-office secretary Martin, who lived, by the way, in the same house as Oehme. Martin and Heubner carried muskets. On the box, and following or hanging on to the back of the carriage, were other leaders of the revolution. A fourth inmate of the carriage was one Semmig, who, many years later, gave Dinger his recollections of the meeting. Heubner introduced the pair with a " Herr Kapell-meister Wagner ":

> " Conversation ", said Semmig, " was out of the question; before us, around us, behind us, was nothing but a crowd of armed men in great agitation. But all the din, all the shouting and rattling of arms, was drowned by the flaming talk of Wagner. Never have I seen a man so excited. . . . ' War! ' he kept shouting. This was all he had on his lips and in his mind: he poured out such a flood of words that it is impossible for me now to remember it all. . . . The paroxysm lasted perhaps more than half an hour; and so overwhelmed was I by the storm of words of this man sitting next to me — shall I call him Wotan or Siegfried? — that I could not address a single word to him. The scene remains with me as one of the most thrilling of my memories of those terrible stormy hours." [43]

While the others were engaged in a parley with the distracted coachman, who implored them to spare his carriage, which was not built for so heavy a load, Bakunin made Wagner acquainted with the events of the final hours in Dresden. Heubner, for his part,

---

[43] DWGE, pp. 226, 227. By a printer's error the date is given there as the 19th May. It should, of course, be the 9th.

harangued the new contingents that had come on the scene, exhorting them still to have faith in the cause: they were to retire to Freiberg and there await further orders.

9

At Freiberg, which was reached about two o'clock, Heubner —
who, by the way, had his home there, and now had the mournful
satisfaction of seeing his unhappy wife again — was implored by
some of the citizens not to bring ruin on the town by establishing
the Provisional Government there. Ignoring their appeal, he tried,
after breakfast, to come to a final understanding with Bakunin.
Was the Russian all for a Red Republic, or for a rational new government in place of the old? Bakunin replied frankly that he had
no faith in any kind of government; he had always regarded the
Dresden rising with contempt, and had continued to take part in
it only out of admiration for the courage and devotion of Heubner;
but things having gone so far as they had, they must now throw to
the winds all consideration for themselves and for others, and see
the thing through for honour's sake. Wagner's account of the conversation is admirably detailed and vivid: what he has failed to
notice is that his presence at this meeting is yet another proof that
he ranked with the others as a leader of the revolt; once more we
have to observe that whenever policy is debated and resolutions
are taken at the very heart of events, there Richard Wagner is sure
to be found. He refrains also, in his account of the conversation in
Mein Leben, from adding that, as we learn from Bakunin himself,
he too counselled Heubner to keep up the struggle; he described
the promising state of affairs in Chemnitz, on the strength of which
he advised a march thither, where a call should be made for a Con-
stituent Assembly for all Saxony.[44] In *Mein Leben* he tells us that
the necessary summons for the Assembly was at once sent out by
Heubner: he does not tell us, however, that the decision was taken
as a result of his own representations. Wagner, in fact, had once
more managed to persuade himself that all was not yet lost: Chemnitz and the whole of the Vogtland, he assured his associates, were

---

[44] MRW, p. 49, quoting from the evidence of Bakunin at the trial.

strong for the revolution. Bakunin, at his trial, deposed that " it was Wagner's account of the state of affairs in Chemnitz that determined us to make for there." [45] In a sense, then, the subsequent capture of the other leaders at Chemnitz was the direct result of Wagner's harangues. He was the one man who, in virtue of his recent visit to the town, could presumably speak with assurance of the hopefulness of the conditions there. The others listened to him, and as a consequence went to their doom.

The decision in favour of Chemnitz was strengthened by the entry upon the scene of Stephan Born — a young Leipzig compositor who had played a prominent part in the recent fighting in Dresden — with the announcement that he had brought the gallant band of 2,000 safely and in good order to Freiberg. The defence of the town against the regular troops was, however, he said, a matter for a trained military officer, not for an amateur like himself; if only to gain time, therefore, it would be advisable to fall back on Chemnitz. This part of the story is told correctly enough in *Mein Leben*; but Born, in an account of his life which he published later, adds a detail omitted by Wagner. The latter, he says, ran to meet him with open arms, kissed him, cried out, " Nothing is lost! Youth, youth, youth will redeem everything, save everything! " [46] and embraced him again. The exhausted Heubner left the others to try to get an hour's sleep: Wagner and Bakunin fell asleep on the sofa. Frau Heubner, in her evidence later, supplied a detail of which there is no mention in *Mein Leben*. About four o'clock a man entered the room and asked for " the Government ". Wagner was the first to awake; he pushed Bakunin's huge head off his shoulder, where it had fallen from weariness, threw back his hair from his forehead, and said " A pleasant dream! " — " still full of optimism! " as Müller comments.[47]

According to his own story Wagner, followed after a little while by Bakunin, went to the Town Hall, where he was surprised to find Heubner, who, it seems, had after all been unable to sleep. An excited meeting of townspeople and revolutionaries was in progress,

[45] DWGE, pp. 185, 186.
[46] BORN, *Erinnerungen*, p. 231; quoted in MRW, p. 49.
[47] DWGE, p. 186. It is not certain, however, whether Wagner or Bakunin uttered the words.

and Heubner was trying to evolve some sort of order out of the chaos around him. A retreat to Chemnitz was decided upon; hereupon, Wagner tells us, he informed the others that he would go to Chemnitz in advance of them, and meet them there next day. The reason he gives is that he " longed to be out of this chaos ". Why should this " longing " come upon him precisely now? Did he see that the revolution, though it seemed for the moment to be struggling to its feet again, was really at an end, and, sobered at last, resolve to get out of the danger zone as quickly as possible? It is rather odd that his resolution should be taken just at the hour when the coach from Freiberg to Chemnitz was timed to set out. He actually took his seat in it; but the road was so obstructed by revolutionaries on the march that it would be some time before the coachman could hope to start. Suddenly, says Wagner, the desire came over him to see once more the friends he was leaving behind, and, if possible, to travel with them. The phrase about " the friends I had left behind " may perhaps be significant. He found they had left the Town Hall; he ran to Heubner's house, where he was told that Heubner was asleep. He went back to the coach again, but once more found the road impassable, and the coachman unable or unwilling to start. Once more his pen slips into a phrase that may be undesignedly illuminative. " I walked nervously up and down for some time ", says the English version of *Mein Leben*. The German word, however, — *beklommen* — means rather more than " nervously "; it signifies rather " with my heart oppressed ".[48] Plainly he was becoming desperate; there seemed no chance of the coach ever setting out. Again he went back to the house, to offer himself to Heubner as a travelling companion; the latter and Bakunin, however, had gone, whither he could not discover. " In desperation I went back once more to the coach, which I found now ready to depart." Late at night he reached Chemnitz; he slept a few hours at the first inn he saw, and then, at five in the morning, set out on the fifteen minutes' walk to Wolfram's house, which lay a little distance out of the town. On the way he met a sentinel of the Com-

---

[48] The reader will remember that "beklemmt"—the past participle ("beklommen" is another form of it) of the verb "beklemmen"—is Beethoven's marking for the profoundly moving episode in the great Adagio (the Cavatina) of the posthumous B flat major quartet. It may be translated "with a tightening at the heart".

munal Guard, whom he asked for news of the Provisional Government. " The Provisional Government? " was the reply: " it's all up with that." Not understanding what this meant, Wagner trudged on to Wolfram's, where, of course, he found Minna. His brother-in-law was not at home; he had been sent into the town to do duty as a special constable. It was only when he returned, late in the afternoon, that Wagner learned what had happened. Heubner, Bakunin and Martin had come to Chemnitz in a coach of their own and alighted at another inn than Wagner's. There they collapsed from fatigue; they were betrayed by some former adherents of the cause, and arrested by the police in their sleep. Once more the Fates had intervened to save Wagner for the world: it is no wonder that, as he tells us, there flashed across his mind the memory of those miraculous escapes of his from death in the prospective duels of his boyhood.

The captured men were taken to Dresden by a roundabout route — through Altenburg and Leipzig — and put on trial. They were condemned to death, but this sentence was afterwards commuted to one of life-long imprisonment. Each was released after a term of years. Röckel spent thirteen years — two of them in solitary confinement — in Waldheim. He was released in 1862, and immediately plunged once more into political journalism in Coburg and Frankfort, moved on to Munich in 1866,[49] where Wagner, now the favourite of King Ludwig, was able to befriend him, and then to Vienna. He had a paralytic stroke in 1871, and went to live with his youngest son, Richard, at Pesth, where he died in 1876. Heubner survived Wagner some ten years, dying, at the age of eighty-

---

[49] We find Liszt, in October, 1867, passing him on with a recommendation to his uncle Eduard Liszt: "August Röckel will shortly be calling on you. The name will probably suggest to you, as to many others, an ultra-revolutionary demagogue; instead of which you will find a gentle, cultured, humane, and excellent creature." LZB, II, 106.

This is not quite the whole story, however. Röckel mixed himself up with Wagner's affairs and with the "progressive" political party in Munich in 1865 in a way that did Wagner no service in government quarters. See SWM, pp. 42, 49.

The tough, obstinate nature of the man is shown by his refusal, when at Waldheim, not only to sue for pardon—which would probably have been granted him after a few years—but by his conduct when the King's clemency was at last extended to him. He refused to leave Waldheim: he had been brought there by force, he said, and only by force would they get rid of him. In the end he had to be thrown out of prison! See WEWL, p. 134. Cosima's comment on him, in 1872, was that "Röckel's weakness was that he always thought he alone knew everything." (MECW, I, 616.)

one, in 1893. Bakunin, after a series of romantic adventures, including a daring escape from Siberia, died in 1876, at the age of sixty-two. Todt fled, like Wagner, to Zürich, where he died in March, 1852.

10

Had Wagner been captured with the others, a sentence of death, commuted, as in the other cases, to a long term of imprisonment, would have been practically certain, unless the indulgent King had especially intervened on his Kapellmeister's behalf. There has been much argument as to Wagner's " ingratitude " to the King. His own view was that he had given ample, indeed over-generous, service to the Dresden Opera, and, as we have seen in Volume I, it would have been well for the town had he been better paid and his schemes for reform accepted. But there are two sides to every case. The Dresden authorities could hardly be expected, in 1848 or 1849, to look at the matter from the historical point of view of half a century later. As they saw it, Wagner had been a troublesome servant, who had been persistently quarrelsome towards his superiors and brought considerable discredit on the establishment by reason of his notorious debts, had had exceptional consideration shown to him on account of his exceptional genius, and had finally chosen to bite the hand that fed him.[50] The conviction of his ingratitude rankled in the royal mind for years. King Johann (who succeeded his brother Friedrich August on the 9th August, 1854) laid particular stress on this ingratitude when, in April, 1856, he rejected an appeal of the Grand Duke Carl Alexander of Sachsen-Hesse for clemency towards the exile: in return for the " benefits " his brother Friedrich August had conferred on him, he said, Wagner, in 1848-9, had incited the members of the Kapelle against the Court, and had finally taken an active part in the May rebellion: " had he

---

[50] His contemporaries, of course, could not be expected to appreciate his artistic idealism during these years of suffering: they saw only the externals of the situation. The conviction of his "ingratitude" was universal. His niece Johanna wrote to Lüttichau from Hamburg (where she had been "guesting") on the 20th May, expressing her sorrow at the disasters that had overtaken Dresden and its theatre, and speaking of "the indignation that overmasters us at the insane ingratitude of certain people to whom his Majesty has shown special favour, among whom is one who unhappily is closely connected with me." PGHD, pp. 555, 556.

not fled the country, he would probably have been condemned to death for high treason." [51] Röckel, in his history of the affair, does not mention Wagner: it would have been no kindness to him in 1865, when Wagner was a King's protégé, to lay stress on his friend's former activities as a revolutionary.

It is useless for the Wagner apologists of the old school to insist on the fact, now quite obvious, that Wagner was completely innocent of the gross charges, made against him in 1849, of having burned down the " old " opera house and having wished to set fire to the Royal Palace. As Lippert points out, Wagner — and we may add, some of his modern apologists — seemed to have a rather curious conception of the meaning of the term " guilt " in connection with a revolution; his naïve idea of a " guilty " person, says Lippert, was apparently " one who shoots at the King or a member of the royal household, or sets fire to the royal castle with his own hands, or leads the insurgents in person against the royal residence or the troops." It is true Wagner had done none of these things. Nor, for that matter, had Röckel, Heubner, or several of the other leaders; but their technical innocence in these respects did not save them from drastic punishment, and we can hardly believe that Wagner, had he been put on trial, would have fared any better. It is even possible that his position as a prominent royal employé and his " ingratitude " might have been regarded by some of the judges as an aggravation of his offence. He had every reason to be thankful that his lucky star, assisted, perhaps, by a certain amount of prudent calculation on his own part, had prompted him to make that final entry into Chemnitz in no company but his own, and that an admirably forethoughtful Providence had endowed him with a brother-in-law in that very town.

But even had the May catastrophe not come, it is difficult for us to-day to conceive how Wagner could have continued to live much longer in Dresden, if only by reason of his debts. We probably have not the full tally of these at the moment when the storm broke; but we know for certain that in 1848 he owed in various quarters at least 12,000 thalers exclusive of interest, in addition to 5,000 thalers granted him from the theatre funds. He had had to agree

---

[51] LWV, p. 61.

to a deduction of 650 thalers per annum from his salary (of 1,500 thalers) to pay the interest on this loan and to meet the premiums on the covering policy he had been required to take out on his life; while the gratuity of 300 thalers given him by the King had gone to his private creditors. He could not possibly have managed to carry on existence upon these terms much longer, even allowing for an occasional fee as this or that German theatre took up one or other of the operas of his that were already available.

11

It may be convenient here to summarise broadly the further course of his works in Dresden during the next few years, leaving details to be filled in later in the appropriate places.

As we have seen, the refusal of *Lohengrin* by the Dresden management towards the end of 1848 may be partly accounted for in terms of the political and economic difficulties of the time; and with whatever bitterness Wagner may speak of Lüttichau in *Mein Leben,* it has to be noted that in a letter of 1856 to Tichatschek he absolves the Intendant from blame in the matter. At the same time the General Direction was no doubt not unwilling to find, in the circumstances of the period, a good excuse for doing what it must have long been aching to do — hit back at the aggressive young Kapellmeister for the trouble he had been to them by keeping his works out of the repertory until they felt they had humbled him sufficiently. He did not receive a single performance of any kind in the first four months of 1849, a circumstance that may have contributed to drive him into the camp of the revolutionaries; and of course there could be no question, after a flight that was in itself an admission of guilt, of giving any of his works in the Dresden theatre, though the King, who still seems to have been genuinely attached to him, used to have selections from them performed before him at his seat in Pillnitz. In October, 1852, there was a sufficiently strong demand in the town, especially on the part of the younger element, to bring about a revival of *Tannhäuser* in spite of the protests of the political enemies of the " rebel ". Five performances were given, and then the forces working against Wagner were powerful enough to keep him out of the Dresden theatre until 1858.

King Friedrich August's successor, his brother Johann, was a man of a harder type; he was not so well disposed towards Wagner, whose part in the May rising he personally could not and would not forgive. But *Rienzi*, for all that, appeared on the bills again in August, 1858; eleven performances of it were given during that year, and seven of *Tannhäuser*; and after that there was no question of his exclusion from the Dresden repertory. The figures for the performances in the years immediately following are as follows:

1859: *Rienzi* 7; *Tannhäuser* 6; *Lohengrin* 9.
1860: *Rienzi* 7; *Tannhäuser* 3; *Lohengrin* 5.
1861: *Rienzi* 6; *Tannhäuser* 8; *Lohengrin* 5.
1862: *Rienzi* 4; *Flying Dutchman* 4; *Tannhäuser* 4; *Lohengrin* 2.
1863: *Rienzi* 5; *Tannhäuser* 5; *Lohengrin* 2.
1864: *Rienzi* 5; *Tannhäuser* 4; *Lohengrin* 3.

Wagner was amnestied in 1860. In 1864 his fortune took a new turn under the protection of King Ludwig; his bigger works soon came into general demand, and before long a change in the copyright law made it possible for him to demand a royalty on each performance of each of them, instead of his having to be content, as in the old days, with a single fee from each theatre for the sale of the score of an opera. He, and his heirs after him, rightly took full advantage of his immense popularity and his stronger legal position. The *Meistersinger*, which had been produced at Munich in 1868, was given in Dresden fourteen times in 1869 (on a seven per cent. royalty basis), and remained permanently in the repertory, apart from a temporary disappearance in 1878 and 1879. After 1869, none of the other works of Wagner's maturity were given in the town until 1884, the year after his death. Everyone had wanted to hear *Tristan* and the *Ring*, but Wagner had refused the Dresden theatre permission to produce them except on his own terms. At last, in 1884, the management was obliged to capitulate. As the reader knows, the Dresden theatre possessed the right to perform *Rienzi*, the *Flying Dutchman*, *Tannhäuser* and *Lohengrin* as often as it liked in virtue of its first and final payment for the scores. For some years before his death, Wagner had insisted on his moral, if not legal, right to royalties on all the past performances of these highly popular works. He demanded 21,000 marks in settlement of this claim; and until Dresden came round to his way of thinking they would not get permission to perform his latest operas. The consequence was that Dresden was for a long time barred from performing works that were being enthusiastically received everywhere else. In 1884 — the year after his death — the public resentment became so great that the management was forced, as a condition to being granted permission to give *Tristan* and the *Ring*, to cancel Wagner's still unpaid debt to the theatre, — which now amounted to 15,000 marks plus interest, — and further to agree to pay royalties on all future performances of the four earlier operas; in addition it had to undertake to produce the *Ring* within a certain specified time. At long last, then, Wagner won a complete victory, if only a posthumous one, over the theatre in which he had suffered so much.[52]

---

[52] For details see KDW, *passim.*

CHAPTER VI

BETWEEN ZÜRICH AND PARIS

1

Röckel, as his book shows, had the incredible naïveté to imagine that the tribunal would take the view that his participation in the revolution had not constituted a " crime "; and he was confident of being almost immediately released.[1] Wagner had a clearer perception of realities; however he may have prevaricated later, in *Mein Leben,* as to his state of mind in May, 1849, he knew that what he had done had brought him well within the scope of the law, and his one immediate concern was to get to some safe spot as quickly as possible. Weimar was only some seventy miles away, and at Weimar a prescient Providence had placed Franz Liszt. Wolfram smuggled Wagner away in a conveyance of his own at dead of night, the coachman not knowing that he had another passenger besides his master. They went by way of Altenburg, arriving at Weimar on the morning of the 13th; the penniless Wagner had borrowed some money from his brother-in-law, as is clear from his letter of the 1st December, 1849, to Klara, in which, apparently, he remembers this little service for the first time.[2] In Weimar he made straight for Liszt's hotel, the " Erbprinz ". He seems, at first, to have tried to conceal from his friend the full extent of his share in the events in Dresden; but Liszt must have heard enough to see at once that a return was out of the question.[3] He took Wagner to the house of the Princess Wittgenstein, where they discussed the plan of *Jesus von Nazareth* — a subject which,

---

[1] RSE, pp. 77, 95.

[2] RWKK, II, 375.

[3] An alleged letter of the 14th May from Liszt to his former secretary Belloni, in Paris, urging him to see what he could do to help Wagner to get *Lohengrin* produced in London, seems to be a forgery. (LZB, I, 75.) It was first published by Tappert, in a German translation, in the *Neue Musik-Zeitung* of the 1st October, 1881: Tappert admitted that he had not seen the original.

Wagner saw, commended itself to neither of his hearers. He dared not risk being seen at a public performance of *Tannhäuser*, but he was present (hidden in a box) at a rehearsal, during which he was agreeably astonished at Liszt's imaginative sympathy with his music, though an understanding of his dramatic purpose was less obvious.

Liszt being called away to Carlsruhe, Wagner accompanied him as far as Eisenach, where the fugitive was presented to the Grand Duchess; he discovered later that, having heard that the Dresden Kapellmeister had been implicated in the rising there, she wished to make his acquaintance while it was diplomatically possible for her to do so — that is to say, before he was formally " wanted " in Dresden. Wagner took advantage of his proximity to the Wartburg to pay his first visit to the ancient halls he had immortalised in *Tannhäuser*.

It was perhaps the Grand Duchess's kindly interest in him that not only made him imagine that he could remain as long as he liked at Weimar but actually made him think, for a few days, that when the storm in Dresden had blown over he would be able to return there and even resume his post at the theatre. In the Burrell Collection is a letter of his to Minna (undated), in which he hopes she will be able to be present on the Sunday (the 20th) at the Weimar performance of *Tannhäuser*: " here ", he adds, " I am surely safe." According to another letter in the Collection, dated the 18th, he assures one of his brothers-in-law (whether Wolfram or Avenarius is not certain) that he is as safe in Weimar " as in Abraham's bosom ", and that he intends to settle there should he lose his post in Dresden. On the 17th — i.e. about the date when he was received by the Grand Duchess — he sent his friend Eduard Devrient a long letter that runs to eight closely printed pages of type. In this he goes into the minutest details with regard to his activities during the rebellion; and as we can hardly suppose either that he felt it an imperative necessity to tell Devrient all this, or that Devrient was consumed with the desire to know it, the inference is justifiable that the long letter was really intended for other eyes — that it was a *pièce justificative* addressed at second hand to Lüttichau and the King. In the light now thrown for us, by *Mein Leben* and the depositions and recollections of various participators in the revolt, upon Wagner's activities during that eventful period, his contemporary account of the affair is decidedly interesting.

He begins by saying that his sympathies had long been with the people in their political aspirations, but that he had allied himself not with the red republicans but with the constitutional party. The revolution had not been planned in advance, he says: had that been the case, so many strategic positions would not have been left free for the military to occupy. As for himself, he had followed the events of the opening days with great interest, believing that some means of reconciliation would quickly be found. On the second day he had done all he could to prevent further conflict between the people and the troops: he had told two soldiers whom he had met at the barracks by the arsenal that all they had to do was to assure the people that they would be with them against foreign troops: he had exhorted the people here and there at the barricades not to exasperate the soldiers but merely to ask them the same simple question: this question, again, appeared on posters affixed to the barricades. The one thing that seemed to him important was that populace and soldiers should unite against the Prussians if they came. The formation of a Provisional Government had not disconcerted him, because Heubner and Todt had guaranteed that the agitation would not be diverted from its true aim and that appropriate negotiations would be carried on with the King.

But on the third day his hopes were shattered. The truce had been ended: Prussian troops had arrived, who fought with the Saxon soldiers against the people: this had created " the utmost bitterness ". " Although from that time onwards ", he says, " I was not much in the immediate neighbourhood of the disturbance, I can assure you that it was neither Poles nor Russians, neither the red not the blue republic, that henceforth drove the barricade-defenders to the bitterest and most unrelenting resistance, but simply the quite subjective personal fury of the citizens against the military . . .", especially against a contingent from Leipzig that had been anxious to pay off a long-standing score of hatred against the Dresdeners. He himself had spent the Saturday and Sunday in the tower of the Kreuzkirche, but only as " a calm spectator of the contest ". Early on the Monday he had gone to the Town Hall to discover the then condition of things. He found a great change there: circumstances had made it necessary for the Provisional Government to adopt regular military measures: a Pole [Heinze] with some knowledge of strategy had been asked to elaborate a plan of defence.

2

" Being uncertain now as to my subjective attitude towards the disturbance ", he continues, " I quitted the town at 8 in the morning and took my wife, who had already packed up, to one of my married sisters in Chemnitz." On his return to Dresden the next day, he learned that the only place to which it would be possible to proceed in safety was the Town Hall! To the headquarters of the Provisional Government, therefore, he betook himself. After an hour in the Town Hall, Wagner, finding it impossible to get to his relations, tried to return to Chemnitz, but could not find a coach to take him. Learning, however, that a former university friend of his, now an officer in the militia [Marschall von Bieberstein], was being sent as a courier to Freiberg, with orders to hurry the Chemnitz Communal Guard to Dresden, he accepted a seat in his friend's coach.

On the next day he took advantage of the coach posting back empty from Freiberg to Tharandt to return on his tracks once more and discover how events were now shaping. He met, half-way, some 2,000 men from the barricades: among them was Heubner, who told him that it was proposed to set up the Provisional Government in Freiberg. The inhabitants, however, were not anxious for the honour, while a delegate from the Chemnitz militia arrived with an invitation to make that town the seat of the government. There follows the familiar story of Heubner's arrest in Chemnitz, and a warm eulogy of his character and combination of idealism and energy during the attempted revolution. " But I see ", says Wagner, " that none of us was a real revolutionary, and I least of all: we wanted the revolution in order quickly to construct something good upon it; and it was this consideration that made us misconceive it utterly: the true, the successful revolutionary only wants to destroy, and his sole strength is hate, not love, which was *our* guide."

" I have sent you this precise account ", he tells Devrient, " so that you may know exactly what my participation in the recent events was — full sympathy with the rising at first, exasperation during the two middle days, the utmost excitement and tension, mingled with curiosity, during the last two days. But never was I active, either with weapons or public speech: never had I any official position of any kind in the Provisional Government." [4]

He foresees, however, the depths of commonness to which the reaction would sink under the protection of Prussian bayonets: in Chemnitz, indeed, he had already sensed that he had come under suspicion as a traitor, owing to his previous meeting with the militia of the town, while from his relations in Leipzig he had heard that he had been calumniated and denounced in Dresden. He feels, therefore, that it would be unsafe to return to Dresden now, or while matters there remain as they are at present. But apart from all that, he has to make a decisive resolution as to his future. He tells the story of the wreck of his idealism during the last few years, of his bitter disappointment at the shelving of his *Lohengrin*:

" So I became, in the end, a revolutionary, if not in deed, yet in conviction, and can no longer find joy in creating. The recent catastrophe has brought me to myself to the extent that it made me fully conscious of my unhappy, frustrated condition, and already I hoped nothing, desired nothing, but to get away with my poor sorely tried wife and live my life in quiet seclusion somewhere, without action, yet also without guilt."

He goes on to tell of the encouragement he had met with in Weimar, and of the conviction of his friends there (Liszt and the Grand Duchess) that his artistic future lies outside Germany — his immediate future, perhaps, in London. But what of Dresden? However harshly he may be judged there, it must surely become manifest that no really punishable guilt can be laid to his charge: if *he* is a criminal, half the Saxon population must be so likewise:

" It would be well, therefore, to try to discover indirectly, on the basis of the true statement I have here made to you, whether there is any valid legal ground for proceedings against me. No one but your-

---

[4] This is very dexterously put: but though it is all true, it is not all the truth. He had not carried a musket; he had not harangued the crowd from the Town Hall; he was not on the official list of members of the Provisional Government. But all the same he had been up to his neck in the revolt.

self can be in a position to adopt the right line of action in this respect, and to take what steps may be possible to preserve for me the
right of return to my Fatherland, perhaps even a motivated retention
of my post there. If all went well, the form of the contract might run
somewhat as follows — an immediate half-year's leave of absence to
enable me to go to London and Paris to attend to the production of
my operas at the theatres there, and to see about a commission for a
new work of mine in one of these places. Assuming that the present
storms pass away and that it soon appears that I am much less compromised politically than may be the case at the present moment, why
then should a Dresden art-institute permanently keep me at a distance,
while perhaps already it would not dishonour it if one of its members
were to win fame in the capitals of the world? I at any rate offer
Dresden, with my whole heart, my hand on it to return there later,
and perhaps Dresden would not have cause to regret having accepted
that hand. It is clear what a benefit and comfort this would be to me —
only now, *now* let me remain free, free in every respect! " [5]

3

It will be seen that Wagner at this time would not have been
unwilling to return to his post as Kapellmeister — on his own conditions: no doubt Liszt had been giving him sage advice about politics, while he could be under no illusion as to what Minna would
have to say to him when they met again. With that end in view he
tries to put the best face possible on his recent activities in Dresden,
stressing the idealism of his political outlook, saying no more than
is necessary about his day-to-day share in the revolt, mentioning
only a few incidents his participation in which would be common
knowledge in the town, and in general making it appear that his
interest in the rising had been merely that of a patriotic spectator.
Unfortunately for him he did not realise how much the Government
must already have known about him and how much more would
come out at the trial of the prisoners — he did not even know that
his compromising letter of the 2nd May to Röckel had been found
on the latter when he was arrested. He was soon to discover that
his situation was far more serious than he imagined.

Meanwhile, throughout Saxony, the police were on the track of

---

[5] The letter will be found in RWBA, I, 183–91. It was published for the first time
in the *Deutsche Revue* in 1922.

all who were suspected of complicity in the revolution. Numerous arrests were made, while warrants were issued against several of those who had escaped, including Bieberstein, Zychlinsky, and Semper. Röckel tells us that no less than twelve thousand persons were seized — the number is significant as to the seriousness of the events with which Wagner had been connected — but that the great majority were allowed to go free because of the pure impossibility of the court ever finding time to deal with them. " Naturally ", says Röckel, " the prosecutions were limited to the leaders of the rising and to some of those who had taken part in the actual fighting. . . . Among the men who were charged were about thirty mayors, the majority of the members of the dissolved Landtag, a number of officials, town councillors, lawyers, teachers, military men, and even clergymen." [6] As the warrant for Wagner's arrest was the eighth to be issued, it is clear that the Government regarded him as one of the ringleaders, no doubt primarily because of the Röckel letter. Heubner and Bakunin, as we have seen, had been taken at Chemnitz on the 9th May. The warrants for the arrest of Marschall von Bieberstein and Zychlinsky were issued on the 11th, Semper's on the 17th, Wagner's on the 19th. Of the fifteen persons, beginning with Röckel, either arrested or posted as " wanted " immediately after the rising had been suppressed, six had been the close associates of Wagner during those critical days. It was apparently on the 15th May that a police agent called upon Minna in Dresden, saying that he had orders to arrest her husband and examine his papers, but that he had been empowered to hold the warrant over for three days. (It has been surmised that the King, at this stage, was reluctant to proceed rigorously against Wagner; it is certainly significant that though the warrant was not published until the 19th, it is dated the 16th). Minna was to inform her husband that " if he liked to come back, he could; if not he could stay where he was." The distracted woman at once wrote to Richard,

---

[6] RSE, p. 137. The Hanover *Zeitung für Norddeutschland* said in its issue of the 20th June, 1853, that "of those condemned for the May rising, one hundred and nine are still in Saxon prisons; while the enquiries based on later denunciations seem to be without end, and have only lately resulted in a number of fresh incarcerations in Wurzen and Leipzig." LWV, p. 34. This was four years after the rising.

WARRANT FOR WAGNER'S ARREST — THE STECKBRIEF

(From Erich W. Engel's " Richard Wagners Leben und Werke im Bilde ", by courtesy of Fr. Kiftner and C. F. W. Siegel, Leipzig)

urging him to leave Weimar, and indeed Germany, at once for some safer place. The story goes — seemingly Dinger had it from Natalie in her old age — that Minna was astounded to receive from Richard a letter saying that he was enjoying his walks in the country, and hoped she would come and share them with him. A second and still more urgent letter from Minna was followed by another from Wagner, still making no reference to the Dresden danger but again urging her to come to him. The explanation of it all was that Minna's letters had been sent under cover to Liszt at the " Erbprinz ", and Liszt's servant had placed them with other letters to await his master's return, which took place on the 18th.[7] Legal advice was at once taken; and the Weimar minister, von Watzdorf, advised Wagner to return to Dresden. This, however, he had no intention of doing. On the 19th the warrant (*Steckbrief*) was made public in the Dresden *Anzeiger:*

" The Royal Kapellmeister Richard Wagner, of this place, who is more particularly described below, is wanted for examination on account of his active participation in the recent rising here, but as yet he has not been found. The police are therefore instructed to look out for him, and, if he is found, to arrest him and communicate at once with me.

" Dresden, the 16th May, 1849.

" Von Oppell,

" Deputy Town Police.

" Wagner is 37–38 years old [this, of course, is an error], of middle height, has brown hair, and wears glasses." This was reprinted in the *Anzeiger* on the 14th, 20th, and 28th June. There is probably some truth in the conjecture that the very vague description of Wagner's appearance — concerning which the fugitive himself is said to have gaily remarked, " Well, that applies to a lot of people! " — was deliberately framed with a view to giving him a chance to escape.[8]

---

[7] DWGE, pp. 187, 188. Wagner's account of the matter in *Mein Leben* agrees with this in essentials.

[8] See DWGE, p. 189. At the same time, as Dinger points out, the danger of arrest was very real.

4

The Weimar performance of *Tannhäuser* took place on the 20th. Wagner was unable to be present at it, as by that time the matter of the *Steckbrief* was known everywhere in the town. The Court could no longer countenance his presence in Weimar, as the treaties between the various German states laid on it the obligation to arrest the rebel and surrender him to Saxony. Escape from German soil was now a matter of life or death to him. But in spite of the fact that at this time there was little love lost between him and Minna — a subject which will be dealt with more fully later — he was unwilling to leave Germany without seeing her. Living in the " Erbprinz " at the time was a Professor Siebert, a friend of Liszt. Provided with a letter from him, and with sixty thalers from Liszt (who, having no spare money of his own at the moment, had had to borrow the amount from the Princess Wittgenstein),[9] Wagner went on the morning of the 19th to the village of Magdala, between Weimar and Jena (at that time three hours' journey from Weimar), where he was taken charge of by a local agriculturist, one Wernsdorf. He passed by the name of Professor Werder, from Berlin; he confided, however, the secret of his identity to his protector. A meeting of would-be revolutionaries who had returned in disorder from Dresden was held in the neighbourhood of the farm; Wagner could not keep away from this, but he soon left, with a comprehensive contempt for both the orators and the crowd.

In the early hours of the 22nd Minna arrived. Dinger, again relying, presumably, on Natalie's reminiscences, tells us that she travelled with a false passport: she was recognised at the Dresden station by the police official who was controlling departures from the town, but he good-naturedly allowed her to proceed on a mission the object of which he divined, and with which he sympathised.[10] Wagner, wakened out of his sleep, greeted her without enthusiasm: " What, my wife? " he said, and then, passing his hand over his brow, " My God, this is my birthday! " " The pair ", says Wernsdorf, " greeted each other somewhat coolly. Tea was quickly prepared, and we all sat chatting over this until three in the morn-

---

[9] See LZB, IV, 35.   [10] DWGE, p. 188.

ing, when the married pair retired to their room: Wagner did not reappear until midday." [11] For some reason or other it was decided that Minna and he should have their final parting, for the time being, in Jena. Thither, accordingly, Minna went the next day, to the house of a Professor Wolff, another friend of the ever-helpful Liszt: Wagner, on the 24th, did the six hours' walk by a different route. At Wolff's house he found Liszt and a Professor Widmann: a conference was held, and Liszt's counsel was adopted — that Wagner should make his way as soon as possible to Paris. For safety's sake, however, he was to go by way of Bavaria and Switzerland rather than by the direct route through Baden and Frankfort, which were still disturbed areas, closely watched by the police. After a tearful parting from Minna, and armed with Widmann's passport, he set off on the 25th through Coburg, Rudolstadt and Lichtenfels to Lindau. Here he spent an anxious night, doubtful whether his passport would be found in order, and afraid that his attempts to disguise his Saxon accent and speak passable Swabian (Widmann's passport had been issued in Tübingen) would arouse suspicion in the minds of the Bavarian officials. In the morning, however, the easy-going policeman in charge handed him three passports from which to choose: Wagner seized his own, hastened to the steamer, and was soon on Swiss soil in Rorschach. It was the 28th May. At six o'clock that evening (not, as he states in *Mein Leben,* on the 31st May) he arrived by coach at Zürich, the first sight of which was so enchanting that, as he says, he half-unconsciously resolved to avoid doing anything that might prevent his settling there. If he saw the *Neue Zürcher Zeitung* of the 28th, he must have read that two of his fellow-revolutionaries, Tschirner and Todt, had also escaped. He was still unaware of the full magnitude of the danger that threatened him in Dresden, and would have been astonished had he been told that it would be eleven years before he would set foot in Germany again.

---

[11] Wernsdorf published his reminiscences in a German paper in 1886. A summary is given in GRW, II, 332 ff. In essentials Wernsdorf's account agrees with that of Wagner in *Mein Leben;* it is rather odd, however, that while Wagner mentions everyone with whom he came in contact at this period, he nowhere refers to Wernsdorf by name.

5

Penniless as he was, he had of course had to borrow money again from Liszt, who, indeed, for some time now had to help not only Wagner but Minna, though to nothing like the extent that is generally supposed. We have already had occasion more than once to note approvingly the long foresight of Providence where Richard Wagner was concerned, and especially in connection with the Dresden rising. It had seen to it that his brother-in-law Wolfram and Liszt should be living, the one at Chemnitz, the other at Weimar, just when Wagner was in urgent need of a trusty friend in each of these nearby places. With equal foresight it had removed to Zürich, some fifteen years before the rising, Wagner's Würzburg acquaintance Alexander Müller, a former pupil of Hummel: in Zürich he made a modest living by teaching the piano and conducting a local Choral Society. Wagner, on arriving in the town, made straight for Müller's house, " zum Tannenberg ", Rennweg 55: he was probably unaware at that time that Providence, with a humorous eye to the future, had made Müller the composer of an opera entitled *Die Flucht nach der Schweiz (The Flight into Switzerland)*, which had had a brilliant run of two performances in the Zürich theatre in March, 1841.

Müller being at a picnic in the country that day, Wagner had to spend the night of the 28th–29th in the Hotel " Schwert ", where, by the way, Goethe had more than once stayed. Frau Henriette Hesselbarth, Müller's daughter, has told us how her father, in answer to the ringing of the house bell on the night of the 29th, put his head out of the window (he had only that evening returned from the picnic), and cried, " Who is that, so late as this? " " It is I, Richard Wagner: open quickly! " was the reply. Wagner threw his arms round Müller and said, " Alexander, you must give me shelter. I am safe here. I have fled from Dresden, leaving my wife and property behind me." As Müller was out teaching or rehearsing all day, and Wagner felt lonely, he used to invite the two little girls of the house into the room that their father had placed at his disposal: they went rather unwillingly, for they had to sit quite still, not being allowed even to turn the leaves of a book. Wagner would play to them pieces out of his operas, and ask them " Do you like that? " " Like the stupid children we were ", said Frau Hesselbarth in later years, " we would say ' No! ' Then he would say, ' In that case you must listen to it until you do.' He would often say to us, ' When anyone asks you who your teacher was, say Richard Wagner.' " [12]

The day after his arrival Müller and his pupil Wilhelm Baumgartner (who was already known to Wagner, Baumgartner having called on him in Dresden some years before) introduced the fugitive to two Swiss cantonal secretaries, Jakob Sulzer and Franz Hagenbuch. His name and fame were probably already known to them. Wagner writes to Uhlig that he is astonished to hear that he is " famous " in Zürich, where several copies of his operas exist: two years before his entry into the town, on the 10th June, 1847, Müller and his Choral Society had given the first act of the *Flying Dutchman*. Through the instrumentality of Sulzer and Hagenbuch, Wagner received on the 30th a federal passport for Paris, valid for one year: a note on the document records that it was given " gratis ". We learn from it that he was five feet five-and-a-half inches in height, with brown hair and eyebrows, blue eyes and round chin; his famous nose is tactfully put down as " medium ". He is described as a " compositeur de musique " from Leipzig: apparently it was thought unwise to let it be known that the fugitive came from Dresden, the scene of the recent attempt at revolution. In *Mein Leben* he tells us that these new friends of his showed the greatest sympathy with him and a welcome understanding of his aims; they consequently arranged for him a gathering of a few friends to whom he read the poem of *Siegfrieds Tod*, " the immediate result " of which was the granting of the passport. He is in error here, however, as to the sequence of events: the passport is dated the 30th May, and the reading must have been later.[13]

6

In a few days he was off by coach to Paris, which was now, in the eyes of all his friends, his only hope; for with his black record in the matter of the Dresden rising he could safely reckon on all

[12] SRWZ, I, 16.

[13] For authentic details relating to these first Zürich days see FWSZ, pp. 5 ff.

the German theatres, with the possible exception of that of Weimar, being closed to him for a considerable time. Counting on Liszt's influence, he half-hoped to get a commission to write an opera for Paris, though it must have been fairly evident to him from the start that a scheme of that kind could not be expected to work. Belloni did what he could for him in the way of introductions. One day Wagner went into what had formerly been Schlesinger's shop, but was now the property of a successor, Brandus. There he caught sight of Meyerbeer, obviously trying to avoid him, and as obviously embarrassed when the clerk tactlessly brought them together. After a few minutes' conversation on the subject of Wagner's intentions in Paris, Meyerbeer went away, pleading that he had pressing proof sheets to see to. " You must yet come to a clear opinion about this man ", Wagner writes to Liszt on the 5th June. . . . " Can you have failed to be aware, long ago, that natures like Meyerbeer's are diametrically opposed to yours and mine? Did you not see long ago that the bond between you and M. was one of generosity on your part and of shrewdness on his? . . . Meyerbeer is small through and through, and unfortunately I meet no one now who doubts this." It will be observed that, smarting as he is under Meyerbeer's rather pointed rebuff, there is still no suggestion on Wagner's part that Meyerbeer had played him false in the years since 1839, still no denial of those obligations to him that are plentifully admitted in Wagner's letters of those years.[14] The attitude he takes towards Meyerbeer in *Mein Leben* was plainly the result, in part, of bitter retrospective brooding in the later years, in part of the necessity he felt himself under of justifying his own savage attacks, in the eighteen-fifties, on the man to whom, in one way and another, he had owed so much. As for Meyerbeer's avoidance of him in Paris, that is readily understandable: the Dresden Court Kapellmeister who was wanted by the police, and about whom all kinds of sinister reports were already current in Germany (as to his supposed incendiary activities in particular), would be a person with whom a man in Meyerbeer's official position in Berlin music and in Berlin Court circles would feel it pru-

---

[14] Some letters from Wagner to Meyerbeer, covering the years 1840–46, have recently been published for the first time (November, 1934). A digest of them will be found in Appendix I.

dent not to have his name too closely associated. But Wagner, of course, could never see any matter from any point of view but his own.

That he still took some interest in politics is shown in the first place by his discouragement, which he admits in *Mein Leben*, when he heard of the suppression by the Prussians of the rising in Baden, and in the second place by his avowal, in this same letter to Liszt, of his conviction that there was " no hope for art in the field of anti-revolution." He soon saw the hopelessness of a quick frontal attack on Paris; he lacked the money for an affair of that kind, he had no appetite for the usual opera house intrigue, and it was impossible for him, as he says, to set a Scribe or Dumas libretto to music. He was fretting over Minna, — not that he really wanted her at the moment, but that her implacable silence perplexed and distressed him. He renewed his acquaintance with Ernst Kietz and Anders: Lehrs had died in 1843. Wagner also ran across two of his late associates in the revolt who had been fortunate enough to escape from Dresden — Semper, who was preparing to begin his career as architect over again, and young Wilhelm Heine, who had taken up work once more in the studio of his old master Desplechin, the painter of the scenery for the *Tannhäuser* production of 1845.

The excitement of the stirring May days was dying down in Wagner. His Weimar friends, who had a keener sense of reality than he, managed to make it clear to him not only that it was preposterous for him to think he could ever resume his work in Dresden but that there was no likelihood of his finding employment, as he had hoped, at the Weimar Court. In spite of his detestation of Paris and its musical life, only there could he even remotely hope, at present, to get an opera produced; as it was, he would be dependent for his bread, till that happened, upon Liszt and other friends. He sketched his plans for the immediate future in a letter of the 18th June to Liszt. He could not endure existence in Paris, he said, without a home of his own: he intended to settle in Zürich, whither Minna could bring Natalie and what was left of his household goods: he would have the libretto of a new work done into French by Belloni's friend Gustave Vaez; this being ready by October, he would then go to Paris again, make arrangements to have the work produced, and return to Zürich to write the music; meanwhile he would occupy himself with the composition of *Siegfrieds Tod*. But on one thing he was resolved: never again would he submit to Kapellmeister servitude. So Liszt was to set to work to procure for him a small yearly pension from his own patroness (the Grand Duchess of Sachsen-Weimar), the Grand Duchess of Sachsen-Hesse, the Duke of Coburg, and Princess Augusta (daughter of the Weimar Grand Duchess, the wife of the Prince Wilhelm of Prussia who afterwards became Kaiser Wilhelm I). The proceeds from his Paris opera, he nobly declared, he would apply to the liquidation of his debts in Dresden. The next day he recognises, he tells Liszt, that his conduct in the Dresden rising, innocent as it was, bars his friend from approaching these crowned heads; he can therefore look for help to Liszt alone. Liszt accepts with his usual open-handedness this new responsibility that had so suddenly been thrust upon him. He maps out a plan of campaign for Wagner — (1) a production of *Rienzi* as soon as possible in Paris (its revolutionary subject, he thinks, ought now to be of service to it); (2) a new Paris opera for the winter of 1851; (3) journalistic work, but with a careful avoidance of politics. Meanwhile he sends Wagner 300 francs with which to get back to Zürich; we know also that he came to the assistance of Minna. (Wagner, however, did not take kindly to the *Rienzi* idea; he had long outgrown this work, he tells Liszt, and could not work up enthusiasm enough to remodel it for the Paris Opéra: he would much rather create something new.)

7

As cholera was raging in Paris, Wagner took cheap lodgings in the house of a wine merchant in Reuil, where he was near Belloni. He spent a good deal of his time reading; and it is significant of his frame of mind just then that the books that occupied him most were Proudhon's *Qu'est-ce que la propriété?* and Lamartine's *Histoire des Girondins*. If his story in *Mein Leben* is correct, he at last, " after a long silence ", received a letter from Minna in which she reproached him for having ruined them both by his conduct in Dresden, and refused to live with him again. The date of this letter cannot now be determined. The catalogue of the Burrell Collection shows that he wrote to her from Paris on the 4th and the 8th June:

perhaps these letters remained unanswered. On the 19th June he tells Liszt that he has now received a letter from her; she " feels that she must continue to live under the burden of the dregs of Dresden commonness ", and informs him of " a thousand disagreeable things " which make it appear as if he had been more deeply compromised in the rising than, he says, was actually the case; and as these reports are spreading far and wide he fears that they may have affected the feelings of the Weimar Court towards him. He says nothing, however, of a refusal on Minna's part to live with him again. He tells Liszt that " my wife is suffering and bitter. I hope that time will help her."

On the 26th June (after his return to Zürich), he writes to her again, telling her that " he has already got a plan for an opera to be given in Paris that will be suitable for all languages, and set a new standard for the theatre." [15] On the 9th July he tells Liszt that " my good wife lives in the midst of this [Dresden] slough of bourgeois excellence and great-heartedness; I give up trying to persuade her by means of words to come to me, for I feel that only positive facts could prevail upon her "; and on the 10th he writes to Natalie asking for news of his wife, and complaining of " Minna's treatment of him and her reluctance to join him." [16]

Minna might well hesitate, in view of the uncertainty of his position, and indeed of his future place of residence, to burn her Dresden boats, such as they were. But it is clear enough, from the evidence we now possess, that at this time she had not the slightest insight into him as an artist, not the slightest understanding of, or sympathy with, the deep pain of soul that had driven him to wreck his career, as it seemed to her, by plunging into politics. She saw only the crude outward facts, had no room for any other thought in her mind than that he had once more brought material misery upon *her*. In the end it was only by " positive facts ", as he puts it in his letter to Liszt, that he could assuage her fury. The " positive

---

[15] CBC, No. 180. According to the Catalogue, the letter is dated from Zürich, "Tuesday, 20th June, 1849." This, however, must surely be an error; Wagner, after having written to Liszt from Reuil on the 19th, asking for money to enable him to leave France, could not possibly have received this in time for him to be back in Zürich on the 20th. The Tuesday in that week was the 26th, so it is practically certain that this is the correct date for the letter.

[16] CBC, No. 181.

fact " that ultimately enabled him to do so was a promise on his part to try to get a footing in the operatic world of Paris. This is manifest now from a letter of his to Uhlig that was omitted from the official volume of Wagner-Uhlig correspondence: writing on the 15th April, 1850, he says, " I see now that it was only in consideration of the Paris prospect that she decided last year to return to me, a prospect to which, unhappily, she attached a much more definite meaning than I myself ever conveyed to her regarding it." [17]

8

As we have seen, he was back in Zürich by the 26th. The Strangers' List shows that he stayed with Müller from the 11th July to the 3rd September: after that, partly because he was unwilling to embarrass his kind host any longer, partly because Frau Müller showed Minna no sympathy when the latter (who by this time had rejoined her husband) began raging against him for his " frivolous " conduct in breaking up their Dresden home, he took a couple of rooms in a house known as the " Akazie ", in the Schanzengraben, Ötenbachgasse No. 7. In spite of the fact that he had to do his writing in the common room of the establishment, he managed to make there a final copy of the *Wibelungen* essay. It was in order to have more privacy for his work that he removed, in mid-September, to one of the " back Escher houses ", Steinwiessstrasse No. 3, Zeltweg, in the Hottingen Commune. The Escher houses were the property of one Frau Clementine Stockar-Escher, a scion of an old and rich patrician family, several members of which held high office in the State: she took a fancy to Wagner and took special pains to provide for his comfort. She was a talented amateur painter, and made an excellent portrait of him in 1853.

Minna, as is implied in the foregoing paragraph, was with him now. Her heart had at last melted towards him: about the middle of July she wrote him a moving letter saying she was willing once more to bear his burdens with him. " See ", he writes to Liszt on the 19th July, asking him to send Minna the necessary money for the journey, " I have no home to cling to, but I cling to this poor,

---

[17] Letter published for the first time in DS, Heft 2, 1933, p. 70.

good, faithful woman, to whom I have brought little but sorrow, who takes things very seriously and is without exaltation, but who, for all that, feels herself shackled to me for ever, rapscallion as I am. Give her to me again, and you will give me all you could desire me to have; and see — I will be grateful to you for it — grateful! . . . I will do whatever you bid me, but give me my poor *wife*, make it possible for her to come quickly to me, cheerfully and with some confidence; which, unfortunately, in the language of our sweet nineteenth century, means ' Send her as much money as you can raise! ' " [18]

Minna rejoined him about the end of August or the beginning of September, bringing with her Natalie, the dog Peps, the parrot Papo, and as much as she had been able to rescue of their Dresden goods, including the still unpaid-for Breitkopf piano, which, Wagner says, looked better than it sounded. He hung the portraits of his trusty Fischer and Heine on the walls, placed on his desk the engraving of Peter von Cornelius's " Nibelungen " that had stood there in Dresden, and in spite of the deathly cold of the sunless rooms, he tried to persuade himself that he had a home once more. To his mortification, however, Minna had come without his library, which Hermann Brockhaus had kept as security for Wagner's debt to him.[19] The debt remaining unliquidated, Wagner never saw his beloved books again. From Liszt he received his scores, which had been sent to Weimar some time before by Minna.

Not being yet in the right frame of mind for music, but with the ideas and the events of the last few years, and more especially the last few months, still vibrating within him, he addressed himself to the double object of making up his account with the world of politics and art and of earning a little money. In fourteen days in July he dashed off a treatise on *Art and Revolution*, which, in his innocence, he sent off at once to a Paris political journal, the

---

[18] Liszt, who had little superfluous money of his own, and who by this time must have found Wagner somewhat of a drain on his resources, sent Minna 100 thalers, telling Richard that it was "from an admirer (unknown to you) of *Tannhäuser*" who wished to remain anonymous. This "admirer" was probably the Grand Duke. Acting on a hint from Liszt, Wagner now proposed to dedicate the *Tannhäuser* score to the Duke, who, however, did not think it wise to accept publicly, just then, a dedication from so notorious a political refugee.

[19] See Vol. I, p. 377.

National: but its Teutonic philosophising and generalising being beyond the Gallic understanding his manuscript was politely returned to him. At the same time he sent his essay, through Liszt, to Wigand, the radical Leipzig publisher, who accepted it and paid him five Louisdor for it. The pamphlet had sufficient success to warrant a second edition very soon; and Wigand accepted also Wagner's old essay on *The Wibelungen,* for which he paid him another five Louisdor. By the end of November Wagner had produced also *The Art-Work of the Future;* this he had written in eight weeks. It was published, with a dedication to Feuerbach, by Wigand in 1850. He certainly could not be accused of idleness. He thought also of giving a series of lectures in Zürich in the winter, but this plan came to nothing.

9

The clearer it became that no return to Germany would be possible for him for some time, the more pressing became the problem of money. Frau Julie Ritter (the widowed mother of his friend Karl), who as yet scarcely knew Wagner personally but had succumbed to his genius, generously made him, later in the year, an annual allowance out of her anything but large income. Liszt did all he could, but his own money did not suffice, after his own needs had been met, for much more than maintaining his mother and his three children in Paris; while Princess Wittgenstein, on whose wealth Wagner had no doubt permitted himself to build hopes, was herself slightly embarrassed at this time, her Russian estates having been sequestrated by order of the Czar. Wagner's projected solution of his own problem was simple, and, looked at from a lofty standpoint, perfectly rational. If he could sell the score of *Lohengrin* and get a commission from some theatre for *Siegfrieds Tod* he could maintain himself for a year or so while he worked at another opera; as an alternative, the small circle of people who believed in him might, he thought, combine to help him till he could fend for himself. In his letter of the 14th October, 1849, to Liszt he analyses his own nature quite objectively. He is purely and simply an artist, he says: the less he has to do with the outer world, which he does not understand and which does not understand him, the better. His conception of art being what it is, he cannot seek out the public; it must seek *him* out. But the public he has in mind is a small one, composed of the few people who love him enough, as artist, to make it possible for him to develop his creative faculty in freedom. Is his *Lohengrin* worth nothing? he asks. Is the new work (*Siegfrieds Tod*) to which his instinct is now impelling him worth nothing? " What of the few who love these labours of mine? Ought they not to grant to the poor, sorely suffering creator of them, not a reward, but simply the possibility to go on working? " He would appeal to the public for support, he tells Liszt, but Minna would die of shame if he did that.

But neither his friends nor his wife had his capacity for living in a world of idealistic illusion. It was obvious enough to them that with all the Court theatres of Germany closed to him with the exception of the tiny one of Weimar, his only hope lay either in London or Paris; and for a time Wagner tried to fight down the instinct that told him these places were impossible for so purely Teutonic an artist as himself. He hoped for a moment, though with no very clear notion of how it was to be done, to get *Lohengrin* produced in English at some London theatre. He overcame his repugnance to Paris and to the French language sufficiently to indulge in the quite fantastic dream of producing there either *Achilleus, Jesus von Nazareth,* or a new opera he had sketched on the subject of *Wieland der Schmied.* Liszt, who still did not thoroughly understand him, suggested his bringing out a saleable volume of songs and ballads! Even his dire necessity — he tells Liszt that he lacked firewood and a warm overcoat; he suffered terribly from the cold of his lodgings, and contracted a rheumatism that affected his heart, — could not bring him to consider a proposition so alien to his whole artistic being as that. He rejected also the suggestion — no doubt made by Liszt as a delicate way of giving him some work for which he could be remunerated — that he should write for his Weimar friend the text for an oratorio based on Byron's " Mystery ", *Heaven and Earth.* His need was indeed great at this time. He and his wife have been maintained so far, he tells Liszt, by the kindness of a friend in Zürich; but by the end of the present month (October) his last gulden will have been spent. A letter of his to his Zürich friend Sulzer that has lately been published [20] shows that in this very October he has had to pawn his watch; we gather that it rests with Sulzer whether it shall be forfeited or redeemed. To this piteous appeal Liszt has to reply that he cannot at the moment help Wagner, for his own purse is empty. At last, unable to continue the combined physical and spiritual struggle any longer, Wagner resigned himself to another attack on the Paris he mistrusted and loathed.

10

It is very doubtful whether, in his heart of hearts, he could have believed even for a moment in the possibility of his making an impression on Paris just then. He indeed hoped that some orchestral work of his might be produced at a Conservatoire concert; and Seghers, the conductor of the St. Cecilia Society, had promised Liszt that he would give the *Tannhäuser* overture. But as regards the Opéra Wagner could surely have had no illusions: at the best it would be some years before a still unwritten work of his could be produced there — he was convinced that Meyerbeer would use his influence against him — while he must have been as well aware as we are to-day that *Wieland der Schmied* was no subject for Paris. The sketch for this has survived. If we were to take it at its face value, our judgment would be that it indicated a temporary weakening of his instinct as an artist. It plunges back into a German romanticism that was even at that time antiquated; [21] and it handles the old apparatus with decided naïveté. Its sole interest to us of to-day is biographical and psychological. Nothing that had once found its way into Wagner's mind was ever lost; and several of the incidents, moods, and even phrases of *Wieland* reappear later in *Tristan*, the *Ring*, and *Parsifal*, where they are put to much better use; as was always the case with him, his protecting daemon now held him back from setting seriously to work on the subject until, in the process of time, it should have undergone a thorough spiritual digestion. His temporary interest in the theme no doubt came

[20] See FWSZ, p. 355.
[21] See, on this subject, Vol. I, p. 350.

from the fact that it helped him, for the moment, to bear his terrific burden by a symbolical outer projection of it and himself: Wieland, tricked, maimed, frustrated, mocked, is obviously the artist in general and Richard Wagner in particular, kept by a materialistic society as its singing bird to amuse its hours of ease, but economically held in thrall.

Wieland was both a song of the spirit's yearning for release and an expression of Wagner's own unconquerable will in the face of overwhelming odds. But it is perhaps as well for him as for us that he never wrote the music, or even completed the poem.[22] For the Paris of that, or indeed any other epoch, it was a perfectly hopeless subject; and Liszt showed a curious lack of understanding both of Wagner and of the French when, in his letter of the 14th January, 1850, he told his friend that his mission was " to Germanise the French in *your* sense, or, better, to inspire them with a passion for a more universal, more comprehensive, nobler dramatic artwork." Paris, then and for a long time after, was still the Paris of Meyerbeer, Halévy, Adam, and the others. Liszt had evidently not yet realised that Wagner stood for a purely German art that could have nothing in common with Paris as it then was: being himself far more French than German in his taste, his culture, and his general outlook, Liszt of course saw Paris as the centre of the operatic world, and could not conceive of a resounding success for a German opera composer except via Paris. " I hope ", he wrote to the violinist Ernst on the 30th May, 1849, " that he [Wagner] has by now arrived safe and sound in Paris, where his career as a dramatic composer is bound to expand, and that greatly. He is a man of evident genius, who is bound to win general admiration and take a high place in contemporary art. I regret that you have not had an opportunity of hearing in Weimar his *Tannhäuser*, which in my opinion is the most remarkable opera, the most harmonic, the most complete, the most original and independent as regards both substance and form, that Germany has produced since Weber." [23]

---

[22] He tried later, but in vain, to induce Liszt to set the subject as he had sketched it to music; but Liszt was resolved never to write a German opera. Berlioz also turned it down. Still later Wagner offered it to Weissheimer. An opera based on it, by Kurt Hoesel, was unsuccessfully produced in Berlin on the 11th January, 1913.

[23] See the article *Zu Liszts Gedächtnis*, by Victor Joss, in DM, Vol. I (1901–2), p. 210.

Plenty of people in Dresden, of course, had long been of that opinion: but neither they nor Wagner would have agreed with Liszt, in 1849, that Wagner's way to the German heart lay through Paris.

" At the present moment ", Liszt writes to Carl Reinecke on the 30th May — the same date as his letter to Ernst — " he ought to have reached Paris, where he is sure to find a field more favourable [than Dresden] to the unfolding of his dramatic genius. As I have often said, with luck he will even end by being recognised as a great German composer in Germany if only he can first have his works given in Paris or London, after the fashion of Meyerbeer — to say nothing of Gluck, Weber and Handel." [24]

Liszt's French prepossessions were still too strong, and he had as yet too little insight into the real Wagner, for him to be able to see that the latter's purely Germanic genius had already carried him into a region to which the French public of that day could not possibly follow him.[25]

11

Wagner's frame of mind at this time is revealed in a letter to his sister Klara of the 1st December, 1849. He could hold out, he says, little hope of repaying Wolfram the money the latter had lent him when he fled from Chemnitz. But he had no compunction about relying on his friends for his maintenance, for he is resolved never again to try to compromise between his instinct as an artist and the demands of a society that is sunk in barbarism; and to him it seems self-evident that he has only to state his case to those who love him, understand him, and believe in him, for them to stand by his side in the long fight that is coming:

" You good people are quite blind to the worthlessness of all our public artistic life. That I always stood so much alone in my passionate struggle for true art that I could never successfully combat the pitiable ruling fashion by means of my own works; that even where I had most chance to be heard — in Dresden — I achieved absolutely nothing but fleeting excitements, that were forgotten the next day or gave place to others of a quite opposite kind; that consequently I

24 LZB, I, 76.
25 On the 5th June Liszt wrote to Schumann to much the same effect as in his letters to Ernst and Reinecke.

kept wearing myself out without any real result, and, since I remained true to my own artistic convictions, became more and more estranged from the whole modern egoistic journeyman world of art, saw myself delivered over, hand and foot, without defence, to every kind of commonness, won nothing for all my striving but bitterness and grief; all this you people never noticed, or, if you did, you rated it all at so little that you could not understand why I could not go on tranquilly writing operas [26] which, you thought, I was so capable of doing; you never for a moment considered how I felt when, as was the case with *Lohengrin*, I had by me for two years a work I could not get produced even in Dresden, where my work had been successful and had brought the theatre a reputation; you merely wondered why I did not just write yet another opera and remain indifferent to all that was going on around me. But what you would not do, I had to do — reflect upon the causes and the sum of the circumstances that at present bring to naught every honourable and eager endeavour, in art as in everything else. And to reflect upon all this means to rise in revolt against the whole state of things as they are; and the stronger my artistic enthusiasm is, so much the more imperative and the more uncompromising is my rebellion against everything common, philistine, shameless and pitiful in the present blessed condition of affairs. A more important thing now, it seems to me, than to write operas and still more operas, about which nobody will trouble, is for me to express my views publicly upon the state of art. I address myself to *the thinking artist*: he who is an artist and is capable of thinking will understand me; the fact that our literary mechanics will tear me to pieces does not trouble me, for it is to be expected, seeing that it is against them that I am taking up arms."

His one desire is to settle in Zürich — which pleases him because it is not a large town — and develop in tranquillity the new world that is shaping itself within him: " I am full of hope for the future, and in this hope I find joy and strength to fulfil the best that is in me." But before he could settle down again to creation pure and simple it was necessary for him to balance his account with him-

---

[26] Soon after his flight to Switzerland his brother Albert had written to him giving him the sage advice to be "more practical" in his works, to "take into consideration the small theatres, the wishes of the singers, etc." So little comprehension had anyone of him as he really was! He was so angered by this attitude of his family towards him that when, in 1851, there was some talk of their co-operating with Frau Ritter in his support, he declared that he would rather forfeit his allowance from that lady than accept the help of Albert, Johanna and the others. (This passage in his letter to Uhlig of the 20th October, 1851, was omitted from the official Uhlig correspondence: it was published for the first time in JKJ, pp. 52 ff.)

self and the world by means of some prose works. These show that the idea of revolution was still pulsating within him, though now it had resumed the mainly idealised character it had had before the events of the preceding May. That hectic week had been an attack of something like madness in him; fretted, exasperated, underfed, excited by the commotion and the din around him, half-believing that, after all, the route to the new Jerusalem — a Jerusalem in which art would be run only by artists for art's pure sake, and there would be no more humiliations and no more debts for idealists like himself, — could best be opened by the sword and the gun, he had taken a part in the rising of which he would never have believed himself capable before, and on which he looked back with a sort of dazed incredulity for ever after. His outlet from most disagreeable situations was through an explosion of uncontrollable rage, as poor Minna had good cause to know; and the May week in Dresden was just a piece of insane anger that had lasted for a few days instead of dying out in an hour. The long emotional tension within him had no doubt found its final liberation in the hysterical tirade in which he had indulged in the coach on the way to Chemnitz.[27] He was quite sincere when, in his petition of the 15th May, 1856, to King Johann he said that he had fled to Switzerland in 1849 not merely because he was afraid of the verdict of the court but because, even if he were to resume his Kapellmeistership, he had no hope of realising his artistic ideals in Dresden. In his despair as an artist, he said, he had too easily let himself be persuaded that a political and social upheaval would bring about a condition of affairs in which his ideal of the relation of art to life could be realised. While denying that he had had any real interest in politics for politics' sake, he admits that in his fury at the conditions under which he lived he " lost his head completely ".[28] When the fit was over, the hysterical impulse to destroy with tooth and claw died down, and the earlier impulse to displace and recreate by argument and example came uppermost once more. This is the explanation of his theoretical works of this period: he is as convinced as ever of the need for a European regeneration before

[27] See p. 94.
[28] LWV, pp. 62, 63.

true art can come into its own, and he cherishes the pathetic delusion that men have only to have an ideal put before them for them to forsake everything and follow it.

12

It was a delusion that the greatest of his German predecessors had shared. One of the paradoxes of his being is that in many respects he was at the same time a daring pioneer and a throwback to a much earlier stage of German culture. In music, as he assured Dannreuther in his old age, he regarded himself as a conservative. And in most of his views upon the true function of culture in the world of modern Europe, and especially of German culture, he was simply taking up a thesis at which Schiller and his contemporaries had hammered half a century earlier. As Carlyle pointed out in his *Life of Schiller*, the Germans had always attributed what seemed to the rest of mankind an exaggerated importance to the drama as an instrument for national regeneration:

" The interest excited by the stage ", says Carlyle, writing in 1825, " and the importance of everything connected with it, are greater in Germany than in any other part of Europe, not excepting France, or even Paris. Nor, as in Paris, is the stage in German towns considered merely as a mental recreation, an elegant and pleasant mode of filling up the vacancy of tedious evenings: in Germany it has the advantage of being comparatively new: and its exhibitions are directed to a class of minds attuned to a far higher pitch of feeling. The Germans are accused of a proneness to amplify and systematise, to admire with excess, and to find, in whatever calls forth their applause, an epitome of a thousand excellencies, which no one else can discover in it. Their discussions on the theatre do certainly give colour to this charge. Nothing, at least to an English reader, can appear more disproportionate than the influence they impute to the stage, and the quantity of anxious investigation they devote to its concerns.

" With us, the question about the moral tendency of theatrical amusements is now very generally confined to the meditation of debating clubs, and speculative societies of young men under age; with our neighbours it is a very weighty subject of inquiry from minds of almost the highest order. With us, the stage is considered as a harmless pastime. . . . The Germans, on the contrary, speak of it as some new organ for refining the hearts and minds of men; a sort of lay pulpit, the worthy ally of the sacred one, and perhaps even better fitted to exalt some of our nobler feelings; because its objects are much more varied, and because it speaks to us through many avenues, addressing the eye by its pomp and decorations, the ear by its harmonies, and the heart and imagination by its poetical embellishments and heroic acts and sentiments. Influences still more mysterious are hinted at, if not directly announced. An idea seems to lurk obscurely at the bottom of certain of their abstruse and elaborate speculations, as if the stage were destined to replace some of those sublime illusions which the progress of reason is fast driving from the earth; as if its pageantry, and allegories, and figurative shadowing-forth of things, might supply men's natures with much of that quickening nourishment which we once derived from the superstitions and mythologies of darker ages. Viewing the matter in this light, they proceed in the management of it with all due earnestness."

In his attitude towards the theatre, as in so many other matters, Wagner is the final term in the long, slow development of certain German culture-forces. We ask ourselves in amazement to-day how any artist could persuade himself that the theatre is at once the measure of a nation's civilisation and the most potent shaping factor of that civilisation, and how he could make his life one long agonised struggle to impose such a conception on the world. Nevertheless that was Wagner's view of the theatre's mission and of his own; and for at least a century before him the same vein of idealism had run through the German attitude towards the theatre. Wagner had had a notable forerunner in the actress and entrepreneuse Friederike Karoline Neuber (1692–1776)— known in theatrical history as " die Neuberin " — who ran a travelling company that was famous in its day. It was her view, as it was Wagner's, that the function of the theatre was not merely to entertain men but to make them better — not, of course, through preaching but through the refinement of their taste and their spirit. For this ideal, die Neuberin and many others, actors and dramatists alike, had been willing to labour and to suffer all their lives.[29] German idealism where the theatre was concerned had never quite died out; but between 1795, when Schiller issued his *Letters on the Aesthetic Education*

---

[29] For a convenient summary of the German theatrical history of the Neuberin epoch see Joseph Gregor's *Weltgeschichte des Theaters*, Phaidon-Verlag edition, pp. 482 ff.

of Mankind, and 1850, when Wagner was producing *Art and Revolution* and *The Art-Work of the Future,* there had taken place a considerable change in the attitude of the German public as a whole towards the theatre. For the German of the latter half of the eighteenth century, politically impotent as he was, with drastic restrictions on his freedom of speech in most practical matters, literature in general and the stage in particular had been fields in which he could give expression to ideas for which there was no outlet elsewhere; though it would be unsafe for him to criticise, for example, the tyranny of his own Grand Duke, he could put all he wanted to say on the subject of freedom into the mouth of some historical or fictive character. But towards the middle of the nineteenth century the scene had changed: the tone was no longer given to the German theatre from above but from below — no longer by a few ardent intellectuals but by a bourgeoisie that had made itself comfortable by trade, and saw in the theatre nothing but a medium for providing it with an evening's easy entertainment. It was this spirit against which Wagner had fought almost from his first days in Dresden. To make the theatre financially dependent on the gratification of mob-taste, he realised, meant a constantly changing repertory, with two attendant necessary evils: since masterpieces are always scarce, a great deal of poor stuff would have to be drawn upon to eke out the repertory — to the consequent corruption of the public taste — and, with the theatre open every night, there was inadequate time for the intensive study of the greater works. He fully recognised, of course, that an ideal theatre would be an economic impossibility so long as it depended for its existence on box office receipts: the State, therefore, would have to make the theatre its charge to an extent hitherto undreamed of, and the direction of it would have to be taken out of the hands of Court officials and placed in those of artists. It was a dream impossible of realisation in any such world as ours. Bayreuth itself is not a solution of the whole problem: it is a quasi-solution of only part of it, and an evasion of the rest.

Wagner's prose works of the first Zürich period were a spiritual katharsis. While they did him the double service of working off the excitement still left in him by the events of May, and of sweeping up the mere intellectual débris that was encumbering the ground of his complex being, and so clearing a space for the laying of the foundations of his next big creative work, they seem to have done him no good in many quarters. With the stigma of a violent revolutionary of the Röckel and Bakunin type still on him, it was only natural that many readers of these excited prose manifestos should miss the purely artistic purpose of them and regard them as just so many contributions to the ordinary revolutionary literature of the time. In Dresden they appear actually to have deepened the conviction of his guilt, for in his petition of May, 1856, he sets himself to clear up the misunderstanding:

" The only thing that sustained me ", he writes to the King, " under the painful impressions involved in my breach with my past [in 1849], was an unusual and indeed morbid exaltation, to which I abandoned myself with a certain desperate eagerness during the first years of my exile. To justify myself to myself I was driven to formulate and develop systematically, and to publish, those ideas upon art and life that had conducted me to so violent a catastrophe. As a matter of course, these publications gave renewed and serious offence, since they made it clear to everyone that my conduct, which was necessarily looked upon as thoroughly criminal, was the result of a system worked out from the foundations. But though these literary works could only worsen my position in the eyes of my judges, they were of service to me in that they gradually cooled my excitement and brought me back to health by the expulsion, as it were, of the poisonous matter from my system." [30]

[30] LWV, pp. 64, 65.

CHAPTER VII

JESSIE LAUSSOT

1

HAVING RECEIVED 500 francs from Liszt, Wagner set out for Paris again on the 29th January, 1850. His nerves were beginning to give way under the terrific strain of the past six months: when he was taking his ticket at the Zürich station he felt so ill that he returned to the house and tried to win Minna over to the idea of his abandoning the abhorrent Paris plan. But Minna, anxious that he should rid himself and her of the continual ignominy of borrowing, convinced, as everyone but Wagner himself was at that time, that his only hope of salvation lay in the production of an opera in Paris, and callously incredulous as to the reality of his illness, drove him relentlessly forth, his heart black with bitterness against her and the whole world. In Paris he took a wretched room in the Faubourg Montmartre, from which he was speedily driven by a woman in the room above him practising an aria from Bellini's *Puritani.* He settled the next day but one in an apartment on the fourth floor of 59 Rue de Provence, Cité d'Antan. He at once called on Seghers with regard to the promised performance of the *Tannhäuser* overture, only to learn that the Society had been unable to obtain the orchestral parts. They arrived, through the instrumentality of Liszt, in the early days of March; but as the final concert of the Society was to be given at the end of the month, and no more rehearsals were possible just then, nothing could be done for him that winter.[1] " I had to laugh out loud! " he writes bitterly to Minna. Wagner found Semper once more, as well as Anders and Kietz, the latter being as far as ever from finishing any of his pictures.[2] Anders he found enjoying better health than of old,

---

[1] The performance of the overture did not take place until the 20th November, 1850, on which occasion the programme contained an explanatory note taken from Liszt's brochure on *Tannhäuser.*

[2] See Vol. I, p. 272.

thanks, paradoxically, to a broken leg that had necessitated a rest in a hydropathic establishment.

To add to Wagner's misfortunes, Wigand now informed him that, having been disappointed in the sale of his books, he could send him only half of the promised 20 Louisdor. As against this, a German fugitive, one Adolph Kolatschek, commissioned from him an article for a new journal he had recently started, the *Deutsche Monatsschrift*. Wagner wrote for him the essay *Art and Climate*, in which he developed further one of the lines of thought in *The Art-Work of the Future*. As he quite reasonably pointed out to Minna, he had to " rig himself out " for his Paris campaign, his present clothes not being likely to impress the Parisians. For a hat, an umbrella, a black tie, two pairs of undergarments, a purse, and a paletot he presumably had to pay cash, grievous as that operation must have been to him. But for some clothes made to measure — a coat, a pair of trousers, a black velvet waistcoat and one of ordinary cloth — he went to his tailor of former days, Loizeau. We have seen him [3] paying this gentleman 400 francs on account in January, 1843, since which time, apparently, he had not troubled himself in the least about Loizeau's existence. He still owed him money for the 1839–42 period, so that it must have taken some courage on his part to walk into the shop, renew the acquaintance, and blandly order more clothes. In vain did poor Loizeau protest that times were bad and that he had had losses — had been " considerably set back ", as he plaintively put it. Under the spell of the enchanter he was as helpless as a rabbit in front of a snake. In music, as Wagner was not unwilling to admit, he had learned much from Beethoven, Weber, Berlioz and others; but his technique as a borrower was his own creation. To talk over the sympathetic and generous Liszt, who yielded loans and gifts in every direction as a gusher yields oil, was one thing; but to get further credit from a tailor, and a French tailor at that, to whom he had already owed money for seven or eight years, was an achievement deserving, in its way, to rank with his other works of art. Wagner hoped to liquidate the debt by the sale of his arrangement of *Iphigenia in Aulis* to the Weimar theatre for 500 francs; but as this did not materialise, Liszt, in July, was good-hearted enough

[3] See Vol. I, p. 409.

to place 300 francs at his disposal in Paris to meet the bill of M. Loizeau.

There was really nothing Wagner could do in Paris. Belloni was away, and *Wieland* was still, even in the German, a mere sketch. (He worked over it again in Paris, finishing a second fair copy of it on the 11th March). A shattering blow was dealt him by a hearing of Meyerbeer's *Le Prophète* — the forty-seventh performance of the work. His disgust at this, which found vent in a bitterly ironic letter to Uhlig, drove him raging out of the theatre in the middle of an act. (This is his account of the matter in *Mein Leben:* from his letter to Uhlig, however, it would appear that he stayed to the end. Perhaps he made an unsuccessful attempt to sit through another performance later on). What hope was there for *him*, he asked himself in sorrow, in a city in which a piece of charlatanism of this kind could be so successful? [4]

He was in a woeful state of overstrain, unable to sleep, and suffering from rheumatism: " deliverance from this hell ", he writes to Minna on the 2nd March, " is all I wish for." Some ten days before this he had poured out his woes to his friend Sulzer in Zürich:

---

[4] In this same letter Wagner tells Uhlig that while he would willingly forgive the "bad taste" of Berlioz, he holds aloof from him, regarding him as a "bodyguard of Meyerbeer". This was a curious misunderstanding, for Berlioz himself knew only too well that, as he puts it in his *Mémoires*, "Meyerbeer's influence, and the pressure exercised by his immense fortune, not less than by his *genuine* eclectic talent, on managers, artists, critics, and public alike, are such as to render any serious success at the Opéra impossible. That deleterious influence will probably continue to be felt ten years after his death"; and he quotes, in part, the brilliant epigram of Heinrich Heine, who had said that "Meyerbeer will be immortal during his lifetime, and perhaps for some years afterwards, for he pays in advance." The truth seems to be that a little while before Wagner's arrival in Paris, Berlioz the critic had unjustly come under the suspicion of being "influenced" by Meyerbeer, who had apparently arranged for two extracts from *The Damnation of Faust* to be performed at a Conservatoire concert. Perhaps I may be allowed to quote from a note of my own, dealing with this matter, in my edition of Berlioz's *Mémoires* (New York, 1932): "Berlioz is alleged to have been the dupe of Meyerbeer in the matter. *Le Prophète* was to be produced at the Opéra on April 16th [1849], and for a long time before the great day Meyerbeer had been paying his usual flattering attentions to whoever was likely to be either useful or dangerous. Berlioz, of course, could not be bought in the ordinary way; but Meyerbeer and Girard (who had recently succeeded Habeneck as conductor of the Conservatoire concerts) paid the musical critic of the influential *Débats* the delicate compliment of including two pieces of his in the programme of the concert of the 15th. Their immediate purpose achieved, poor Berlioz had no more to hope for from them." Wagner had no doubt heard the malicious tittle-tattle of the town in connection with this episode.

" I cannot write you much from here: my life is very melancholy. Inaccuracies in the information given me, and the slowness with which things are moving, make it clear to me that I have come to Paris a good four weeks too soon. Imagine then my ill humour and profound depression, which unfortunately are aggravated by persistent bad health. I am heartily sick of Paris, which goes altogether against my grain: the conflict between my own inner inclinations and the urging of some of my friends, and especially of my good wife, no doubt laid the foundations of my present indisposition, by making me spiritually discontented and resentful of compulsion. O you people who will not see that no satisfactory and happy, or in general useful, activity is possible that does not correspond to one's whole and real being! Paris, for me, is nothing but constraint and burden."

It was while he was in this mood that something occurred that was to lead at lightning speed to one of the major crises of his domestic life — the affair with Jessie Laussot.

2

In order to understand this fully we must take a backward glance at his relations with Minna at this time and during the immediately preceding years.

Too much importance has perhaps been attached to a passage in which Kietz tells us how Wagner, during the last period in Dresden, broke into angry denunciation of his wife: " It is frightful! " he said. " While other men have their adversaries only outside their homes, my worst enemy sits at my own table "; to which Minna merely replied, " Oh, you clever men, how foolishly you behave! " [5] Minna, with the fear of another banishment into the wilderness ever present in her mind, had naturally tried to induce him to be a little more conciliatory towards Lüttichau, and above all to keep out of politics. She could not be expected to understand all that was going on in the spiritual depths of him, and to believe, with him, that finally nothing, not even poverty and misery, mattered a straw as against his inner good faith with himself as an artist. But an occasional outburst of the kind related by Kietz is not uncommon in the households of fretted idealists, and there is

[5] KW, p. 86.

no reason to believe that Wagner's bitter words point to any real estrangement from Minna at that epoch; as a matter of fact, after each of these outbursts, as Kietz testifies, Wagner, distressed by the pain he had given his faithful comrade, would redouble his kind attentions to her. His letters of the Dresden years do indeed hint at a cooling-off of the first fire of his physical passion for her; but they also place it beyond doubt that he was still very fond of her in a humdrum domestic way. The general tone of the letters to her of that period is that of a household in which, though romance may have faded, an easy-going good-fellowship has replaced it well enough for all practical purposes.

"See now", he writes to her from Berlin on the 26th September, 1847, "it's really splendid for us to be calling each other ' Old Minna ', ' Old Richard ': what is a youthful passion compared with so old a *love*? Passion is only beautiful when it ends in love of this type — in and for itself it is a suffering; but a love like ours is pure enjoyment. A brief separation always makes this plain — from a long separation may a kind Fate preserve us! Isn't that so, good wife? "

And again, from Vienna on the 11th July, 1848,

"My good dear wife. . . . I have saluted you morning and night; and you have returned it, no doubt? for we two old grown-into-one are always together. You walk by my side all the day here; I point out this and that to you and talk to you."

This tone, in spite of the graver note that has necessarily crept into it now, is maintained in the weeks following his flight from Dresden: home and Minna are blended for him in the one nostalgia; there will be no happiness for him until he and she are together again. But already a change, physical and mental, had taken place in each of them, but unfortunately in reverse directions. When Minna rejoined him in Zürich he was aghast at the visible evidence of how hard she had been hit by the Dresden catastrophe. She seemed suddenly to have grown old: her heart trouble was already well developed; and her affection for him was not proof against the rage that flamed up in her when she thought of the straits to which he had reduced her once more. She was forty, and daily becoming less attractive, sexually, to her younger husband. He, on the other hand, was now taking, in some directions, a new lease of life. He experienced at first a curious elation at having shaken off the fetters of his Dresden servitude. Not for years had he been so blithe; in his own words, he felt like a dog that had got over a beating. His huge debts were no longer a trouble to him; being now penniless and out of the country, his creditors had no alternative but to wait till his ship came home; as for his daily bread, some heaven-sent raven or other, he was convinced, would provide him with that. To Liszt, it is true, he invariably paints his situation at this time in the blackest colours, but this was to some extent a matter of technique; Liszt, for the moment, was practically his only resource. But with some of his other correspondents he maintains a tone that is cheerful to the point of gaiety. It was in the summer that he had fled from Dresden, and that to the south: he had been physically and mentally exhilarated by the sunlight and the pure air of Switzerland and by the beauty and majesty of the Swiss landscape. Notwithstanding his ill-health, which was largely a matter of overwrought nerves, he was full to the brim with an energy of a kind to which he had long been a stranger; and, his temperament being what it was, he was ready to succumb to the charm of a woman, younger and more sympathetic than Minna, should one come his way. And just at that moment Fate threw in his way Jessie Laussot once more.

3

A letter of the 6th February, 1850, from Paris, to Liszt, which is not to be found in the official Wagner-Liszt correspondence, is in the Burrell Collection, where it is described as " unpublished ". A copy of it evidently existed, however, for it was published recently by Ernst Fouqué in a German magazine.[6] Wagner tells Liszt that he is willing to try his fortune with *Wieland* in Paris, but he feels that it is not sufficient for him to be merely a poet and a composer: help of another kind is necessary if success is to be obtained at the Opéra, and for this he hopes he can count on Belloni. He has definitely decided to settle in Zürich, where he will go to compose *Wieland* as soon as an arrangement has been made with the Paris Opéra. He has some good news for Liszt: a young English lady

---

[6] A French translation of it will be found in HBD, pp. 34–7.

whom he hardly knew in Dresden has since married and settled in Bordeaux, and " a third person " has just informed him, " in delicate fashion ", that this Madame Laussot is willing to put aside a " very respectable sum of money " in order to ensure his material existence in a modest way. (The " third person " was Frau Ritter, who, from Dresden, was doing all she could to help Wagner financially. Her own resources being too small at that time for her to take the whole burden on herself, she had enlisted the help of her wealthy Bordeaux friends.)[7] " You know, my dear Liszt ", Wagner says, " that I have few friends: but you also know, better than others do, that each of them is devoted and energetic. In this lady [Madame Laussot] you have a spiritual sister, your equal." He goes on to say that he needs another 500 francs if he is to stay any length of time in Paris, especially as he has had to get clothes from his tailor; and he hopes that Liszt will be able to obtain this sum for him by inducing the Weimar theatre to purchase his arrangement of *Iphigenia in Aulis*. He further hopes that if this can be done it will be the last occasion on which money will be mentioned between them. The hope, as we know, was not realised: in the end it fell to Liszt to discharge the tailor's bill.[8]

Evidently Wagner had as yet not encountered Jessie in Paris: and at this time she was almost a complete stranger to him.

A note in the Catalogue of the Burrell Collection informs us that Wagner " tells Liszt he has just met Madame Laussot." There is nothing to this effect, however, in the letter as published. He tells us in *Mein Leben* that he received a letter from Jessie asking about his health, and then, in reply to *his* reply, an invitation to go to Bordeaux to recuperate. This is borne out by his letter of the 13th February to Minna, in which he says that he has had a letter from " our friend (for she is yours no less) in Bordeaux ", exhorting him to remain true to himself and to his art, and to undertake nothing that will set him in conflict with himself, " as she and her friends

---

[7] The Ritters were originally Germans of Lübeck who had settled in Russia, for business purposes, in the seventeenth century. On the death of her husband, Julie Ritter, who was a native of Hamburg, had left Narwa and made her home in Dresden. Her elder son, Karl, had been powerfully attracted to Wagner in the Dresden days. (See Vol. I, p. 456.) The second son, Alexander, married, in 1854, Wagner's niece Franziska (the daughter of Albert Wagner).

[8] See pp. 134–5.

consider it their highest duty to relieve me of all anxiety as to my outward circumstances. I fancy that I shall soon be able to tell you something more precise on this head." Minna evidently did not like this idea of dependence on others, for in his next letter, dated the 2nd March, he argues with her, quite reasonably, that it is better for him to accept help from idealists who believe in him as an artist than to launch once more, for mere subsistence' sake, into the ignoble traffic of the opera house.

On the 13th March he tells Minna that he has taken " a swift decision " to accept an invitation of the Laussots to Bordeaux; they have even sent him his travelling expenses. Jessie, it seems, had already written to Minna, no doubt telling her of the scheme that was on foot to help her and Richard. To Bordeaux, accordingly, he went by diligence on the 14th March, by ways of Orleans, Tours, and Angoulême. In spite of his assurances to Minna that it was quite useless for him to hope to do anything for his art in Paris, she was deeply displeased with him for having gone to Bordeaux. She could have had no reason as yet to suspect his fidelity, but she resented what she thought was his heartlessness in going off on what seemed to her a mere pleasure jaunt at such a time, instead of returning to Zürich and relieving her, ill as she herself was, of the hard work of finding a suitable new apartment for them.

At Bordeaux he was delighted not only with the town but with his reception by Jessie, her mother (a Scottish widow, Mrs. Taylor), and her husband Eugène, a wine merchant, who spoke German fluently. There was a colony of well-to-do Germans in the place, whose attentions were very flattering to him. Still, he assures Minna a few days later, he could not endure Bordeaux for long: " to lead a happy undisturbed life with you, dear Minna, in that glorious fresh Alpine world, is the highest bliss I can desire." But Minna was not to be appeased with mere words; and the longer he remained in Bordeaux the more suspicious she became as to his object in going there; she knew Jessie to be seventeen or eighteen years younger than herself, rich, musical, cultivated, and attractive. On the 7th April Jessie wrote her a letter that is described in the Catalogue of the Burrell Collection as " charming ": Minna, however, has scrawled across it, probably at some later time, the equally charming comment, " False, devastating creature! "

4

Events had been moving rapidly in Bordeaux. Wagner's normal wretchedness had been increased by the false news published in a French paper that Bakunin and Röckel were about to be executed. He sent them a grave and affectionate letter of farewell, in which, however, singularly enough, he could not refrain from saying that he himself, " protected by the most blessed friendship and love ", was now " looking to the future in freedom and cheerfulness ", and " so, with youth renewed and fresh strength in my wings, I am carrying on, in my own way and according to my own powers, the work for which you heroes are now laying down your lives " — a reflection that perhaps was hardly calculated to bring much solace to men presumably about to die.[9] Ill, depressed, and almost hopeless, the one beam of sunshine in his life was the understanding and sympathy of Jessie. They made music together, for she was an excellent pianist: he read *Siegfrieds Tod* and *Wieland der Schmied* to her; and her romantic young imagination made her see herself as the fettered Wieland's bride. She was secretly as unhappy in her own marriage as Wagner in his. Soon they came to the resolve to fly to Greece or Asia Minor together; and nothing could be more eloquent of Wagner's despair of ever being understood by the world than this mad resolution to fly from it. He brooded sombrely over the knowledge that Minna had only been induced to rejoin him in 1849 on the understanding that he would write an opera for Paris, a project that each successive day since then had made more hateful to him, for he saw in it only a prostitution of his art. Their points of view were fundamentally irreconcilable. The Laussot family and Frau Ritter had offered to support him jointly to the extent of 3,000 francs a year. This he was willing to accept, for it would have enabled him to keep his soul clean as an artist. But the scheme did not commend itself to Minna, who saw in her husband

---

[9] In *Mein Leben* he tells us that he sent this letter to Frau Lüttichau, as the only person likely to be able to transmit it to the prisoners, but, he was informed later, Lüttichau got hold of it and threw it into the fire. It would seem, however, from a letter of Wagner's to Uhlig that has recently come to light, that it was sent to Frau Ritter's daughter Emilie, in Dresden. The letter to Bakunin and Röckel, which was originally published in the *Münchener Neueste Nachrichten* of the 9th February, 1904, will be found in RWKK, II, p. 438. For no reason that I can discover, Altmann (RWML, II, 1039) queries the authenticity of it.

only a German composer and conductor like the rest of the breed, and could never understand why he could not settle down like the others and maintain his wife by conducting and opera-composing on the best commercial lines, instead of plaguing himself and her with fantastic ideals that had no place in this real world — especially when his indulgence in his dreams meant, for her, either a constant succession of duns at the door or living on the charity of women who provoked her feminine jealousy.

His resentment against her came to a head in a letter of the 15th April, to Uhlig, that has recently been published for the first time.[10]

" The disharmony between us ", he writes, " which developed on every side from the time when I began to be what I now am, goes down to the deepest roots of our natures: in not a single trait of my being does my wife now comprehend me. The communication to her, in the most sisterly way,[11] of the fact that my friends would assure our future produced in her only a feeling of humiliation; she does not understand the true meaning of it all. She writes to me of her resolve to separate from ' a man who can no longer support his wife respectably and honorably before the world '. I had hoped, after my reunion with her in Switzerland, to bring her round gradually to my point of view; but so far from this hope being realised, I soon saw that only silence and concealment of my real nature could make it possible for us to live together without quarrelling violently every day. Under this devastating constraint, with no possibility of communing with the one nearest to me, forced all the time to disavow my real thoughts and plans, I fell sick and often thought of death. When I think of returning to Zürich I feel the evil at work in me again; I feel crippled, melancholy, wretched; only love can heal me, I feel, and that I shall not find in my house. I have no longer the strength to engage in fruitless daily wrangles with the one who ought to be closest to me, yet whom I shall never be able to convince."

He had left Bordeaux on 3rd April. He put up in Paris at the Hôtel Valois, where, for ten days or so, he thought things out thoroughly, and in the end resolved to end matters, not only with Minna but with Europe. It was apparently in order that Minna should have some difficulty in finding him that he went, about the

[10] In an article by Otto Strobel — *Unbekannte Lebensdokumente Richard Wagners* — in DS, February, 1933. The proper place of the letter is between Nos. 11 and 12 of the official volume of letters to Uhlig.

[11] This evidently refers to a letter either from the Laussot family or from Frau Ritter concerning the proposed allowance.

middle of the month, to Montmorency, near Paris, where he put up at a small inn kept by one Monsieur Homo, whose name, sombre as his mood was, brought a smile to his lips. It was from there that he addressed his letter of the 15th to Uhlig. Two days later, his mind now being fully made up, he wrote a long and agitated letter to Minna in reply to one from her in which she had carried implacability so far as to tell him to address her in future not as " Du " but as " Sie " — a distinction that means a great deal to the German mind. He reviews their past life together. He pays tribute to her devotion in hours of trial, but insists that she was always actuated not by love but by duty; real love, had she been able to feel such a thing, would have shown itself, he says, in some comprehension of him as an artist, some support of him in his agonising struggle against the Philistinism that surrounded him in his Dresden Kapellmeistership, some faith in his ideals, some perception of how his soul sickened at the thought of plunging once more into the filth of the Paris opera world. " You are true to yourself ", he says bitterly: " in every line of your letter it stands out clear and distinct that you do not love me, for you mock at everything that is dear to me, even at the ' Du ' . . ."

5

The more closely we study him during this period, the more evident does it become that what we have to do with is not simply a " love affair ", in the crude sense of the term, with Jessie Laussot, a mere erotic desire for a new woman to replace the old, but also a revolt of everything that was best in him against domestic conditions that had reached the point when either he must break free of them or come to shipwreck as an artist. It is probable also that his recent experiences of an ampler air and a richer scenery than those he had been accustomed to for so many years played their part in making him long, for the time being, for the East. He had been impressed by the southern French landscape on his first journey to Bordeaux. The sublimity of the Swiss scene had given wings to his cramped and harassed soul: it is fairly safe to say that the *Ring* would have been something less titanic than it is had Wagner not lived in Switzerland during the years when he conceived and realised the main portion of it. And in his parting letter of the 4th May to Minna, in which he tells her that he is on the point of taking boat from Marseilles to Malta, whence he will make his way to Greece and Asia Minor,[12] he says that for a long time, and more especially of late, he has felt the necessity of breaking away from the " mere life of books and ideas ", that " eats him away ", and seeing something of the world.

> " For the present, the modern world is closed behind me, for I detest it and want to have nothing more to do with it, or with what people call its ' art '. Germany can never again become a field to stimulate my activity until conditions there are radically changed: any effort on my part to put myself in tune with them could only make me boundlessly unhappy and disgust me more and more with my life. So my longing had of late been turned again to distant travel, to abstracting myself completely for a time from present-day conditions, and to restoring body and soul by change of sight, of sound, and of abode in other climes. In these last decisive days, therefore, I conceived the plan of a journey to Greece and the East, and am fortunate enough to have the means of executing it placed at my disposal from London, where I have gained a new protector, one of the leading English lawyers, who knows my works, and, in return for a certain obligation — the assignment to him of the original manuscript of everything I may write in the future — will give me his support."

This, of course, is fiction; his English " protector " would have been not the deceased Mr. Taylor but his daughter Jessie. But setting that little fib aside, we must sympathise with the long-fretted man in his desire for escape from the ugliness, restriction and hardness of the life he had so long led, into a world of air and sunlight in which he could find respite for a while from the pressure of thought within his overwrought brain, from the incessant brooding upon plans of artistic and social reform that were unrealisable in the European world as it was. But all this, of course, would be incomprehensible to Minna, whose sole desire was that he should find fresh work to do in the theatre, that very theatre from which the artistic soul of him turned away in loathing.

The situation could no doubt even now have been saved had Minna shown even ordinary affection for him and the smallest

---

[12] On the same day he wrote to Kietz, telling him of his intention to leave Europe.

comprehension of, and belief in, his mission. But into the profounder part of his being she was never able to penetrate, and least
of all now, when her whole mind was concentrated on the effort to
prevent the bottom dropping out of her simple bourgeois world,
and when, in addition, she was blinded by jealousy of the more cultivated women who saw in her husband rather more than she could
see in him. Her letter, to which Wagner's of the 17th is a reply,
was largely answerable for precipitating the catastrophe. When she
had rejoined him in Switzerland in 1849 she had told him frankly
that if he could not or would not support her by work of the ordinary kind she would leave him. He now takes her at her word. In
Mein Leben he says he told her, in this letter of the 17th, that they
must part: he would allow her half of whatever income might be
his in the future. There is nothing to this effect in the letter as we
have it; but there is no reason to doubt his word, for it is fairly
clear that the published version of the letter is incomplete.

We have no letters from Wagner to Jessie, or from her to him,
so that for the immediately following stages of the story we have to
rely mainly on *Mein Leben*. According to this, he now wrote to
Jessie informing her of the step he had taken, and was disturbed
to hear from her that she too was anxious to be free, and would
join him in his flight from the world. He pointed out to her the
difficulties attaching to this course, but she persisted in her purpose.
More than ever perturbed, he says, he sought refuge in Montmorency: here, however, he appears to have got the sequence of events
wrong, for while his letter to Minna is dated the 17th,[13] he had
already written to Uhlig from Montmorency on the 15th. The
probability is that the flight from Europe had been, in essentials,
agreed upon between him and Jessie before he left Bordeaux.
Meanwhile the course of events there had been no secret from
Minna. Somehow or other the news that Richard was deep in a
" love affair " had reached Dresden, from which place, apparently,
Minna had received anonymous letters on the subject.[14] Utterly

---

[13] In the Burrell Collection (No. 204) there is a letter of four pages, "from Paris,
to Minna Wagner at Zürich", dated 16th April, in which he "sets out all his grievances
against Minna and proposes separation. He professes great esteem for her, but will
not live with her."

[14] That the "affair" was pretty widely known is shown by the fact that about two
months later, in the middle of June, Minna received an offer of marriage from some

blind as she was to what was going on in the profound depths of Wagner's artistic nature — the tragedy of his long and vain fight for his art in Dresden, followed by the collapse of his dream of a new world that was to have risen from the ashes of the Revolution, and this in turn by the maddening conviction that Minna and the rest of them, even Liszt himself, misunderstood him and his art so grievously as to think salvation for him lay in his going to Paris and fighting for a place in the Meyerbeer sty, — she was merely true to her rather ordinary feminine type in assuming the attraction of Bordeaux to consist simply in a pretty and well-to-do young woman. The Laussots and the Ritters at least understood him better; they knew that he was not searching for some one to maintain him in order that he might live a lotus-eater's life, but that there were splendid, unique things in him that could come to fruition only if the burden of his material existence were lightened for him, so that he might have leisure and peace of soul for his work.

What is certain is that Minna, alarmed by his letter, now hurried to Paris to have an explanation with him; she brought with her a joint letter from Sulzer and Baumgartner to her husband, whose conduct was evidently perturbing his truest Zürich friends. As he did not wish to see her he returned to the capital (where it would be less easy to trace him than in Montmorency), and told Kietz, at whose house Minna had already called, to assure her that he knew nothing more of Richard than that he had left Paris: then he fled to Clermont-Tonnerre, and from there, by way of Geneva, to the Hotel Byron in Villeneuve, at the other end of the Lake.[15] In the Burrell Collection is a letter to Kietz, dated Geneva, 4th May, in which, if we can rely on the summary of it given in the Catalogue, he tells his friend he is " going for a tour in the East ", " means having suddenly been provided from London. . . . Kietz is to write to him Poste Restante, Marseilles." As the documents relating to this epoch were obtained by Mrs. Burrell from Natalie, the pre-

---

admirer whose name is unknown, the signature having been deleted from the letter, which is now in the Burrell Collection (No. 212). In his letter of the 3rd June to Uhlig, Wagner refers to reports in the Press that he was on his way to the East. How the matter had thus come to be public property we do not know. Perhaps Minna had communicated her troubles to her friends in Dresden.

[15] The old hotel is no longer available for travellers who wish to visit the stations of Wagner's many pilgrimages. It was burnt down in 1933.

sumption is that Kietz sent the letter to Minna. In the second week of May, Wagner was joined at Villeneuve by Karl Ritter. Detaching his mind from the circumstances of the moment, he wrote a short preface, on the 3rd June, to *Siegfrieds Tod*, and sent the manuscript of the poem, through Uhlig, to Wigand, who declined to publish it if the author insisted (as he did) on having it printed in Latin characters and with the " Germanistic " affectation, then current, of using small letters at the commencement of all nouns except proper names.

His peace of mind, such as it was, was broken by a letter from Jessie. She had not been able to resist telling her mother of her plan for flight: her husband had heard of it, and he was now threatening to put a bullet through Wagner. We have, in the main, only Wagner's account of what followed. According to this, he made an appointment with Laussot, wrote to Jessie exhorting her to be calm, went to Bordeaux, and informed Laussot of his arrival. The only result was a summons to the police station (Eugène had communicated with the police), and, his passport not being in order, Wagner was ordered to leave the town within two days; the Laussot family, he was informed, had left Bordeaux. He wrote to Jessie, and took the letter himself to the house; the front door having sprung open at his ring he walked into Jessie's boudoir, where he left the letter in her work-basket. Then he returned to Villeneuve and Karl. His frame of mind at this time may be estimated in a letter he sent to the faithful Frau Ritter on the 11th May, just before setting out on his three days and two nights' journey to Bordeaux: " I am summoning up the last remnants of my strength for the journey to Bordeaux, to see, not Jessie, but Eugène. Look upon me as a dying man, for there lies before me either a speedy death or a new life: my forces are at an end; only a prodigy of love can bring me back to life again." As usual he needs feminine company and feminine comfort: he begs Frau Ritter to come to him, or, if that be impossible, to send him her daughter Emilie.

It is evident from this letter that he still cherished some hopes of a happy ending to the Bordeaux adventure. He returned disillusioned, and fast on the heels of disillusionment came a blow from which it took him a long time to recover. Frau Ritter had answered his piteous appeal by coming with her daughter to Villeneuve, where she spent his birthday (22nd May) with him; and after a while he and Karl left her there while they wandered off for a few days in Valais. He writes to Frau Ritter from Zermatt on the 9th June: he is neither dead nor alive, he says, but suspended painfully between memory and hope, living only in his thoughts, for all contact with the outer world is a martyrdom to him; he is longing for death. (To his niece Franziska he had written on the 4th June: " I am now going far away, and will be for a long time alone: I cannot do otherwise. You will have news of me from Karl: write to me through him when you feel a desire to do so "). That he regards his separation from Minna as final is clear. He thinks, he tells Frau Ritter, of settling in some such place as Thun: there is a possibility, however, of war breaking out in Southern Europe, in which event, he, as a political refugee, would not be safe in Switzerland; if it comes to the worst he will fly to London.

6

Twelve days later came the final catastrophe.

It appears that as a consequence of the pressure put upon Jessie by her family she had undertaken not to see Wagner, or write to him, for a year. His letter of the 9th to Frau Ritter indicates that there has been domestic trouble in Bordeaux, and that he must resign himself, if he can, to not seeing Jessie for a year. " A year! " he cries: " Good God! Are we not all experienced enough already to know what a year is? Are we children, that we are so free with years? Is our life so superabundant that we can wantonly let a year fall out of it? Do you realise, dear Mother [i.e. Frau Ritter], what a year must be to *me*, the no longer living? " Somehow or other Mrs. Taylor and Jessie had come to see his conduct in the worst possible light. Letters had passed between them and Minna, and although the documents that would clear up this part of the story are lacking, it looks as if the ladies in Bordeaux had been won round to Minna's view that what had been planned was neither more nor less than an " elopement " of the ordinary kind. In Thun, on the 15th June, Karl received a curt letter from Jessie saying that she had " broken with the immediate past ", and that any further letters in Wagner's handwriting would be thrown into the fire unread; and in a letter of the 26th (continued on the 27th) — a long letter occupying seventeen pages in print — the wretched man pours out his heart to Frau Ritter, who has the imperishable distinction of being the one woman in the world who at this time understood him and believed unshakeably in him. In *Mein Leben* he affects to make light of the whole affair, and would have us believe that he soon came to the conclusion that, as Karl put it, Jessie was simply " a mad Englishwoman " with whom nothing could be done (all English people, of course, being of questionable sanity in the opinion of the rest of Europe at that time), whereupon he calmly dismissed her from his mind and went back to Minna. His letters to Frau Ritter, however, which were not published until 1920, tell a very different story. His long letter of the 26th–27th June, he tells Frau Ritter, is intended as " the testament of a love of which I shall never be ashamed, and which, even if bodily dead, will perhaps fill me to my dying day with the gladdest memories and an afterglow of happiness."

He complains that, by the machinations of others, Jessie has been persuaded to take the most Philistine view of him, of his intentions, and of his conduct towards Minna. Jessie's passion, her purity of purpose, her faith in him, had led him to take too lofty a view of her strength of character; this, he now finds, was unequal to the last and greatest demand the situation made on her.

" How I rejoiced never to find in her letters a trace of that horrible and unworthy bourgeois hypocrisy! She was wholly nothing but *love:* to the *god of love* we dedicated ourselves, and despised all the idols of this miserable world so deeply that we did not even think them worthy of mention. How then could Jessie suddenly have become so enslaved by one of these idols that she could swiftly and willingly sacrifice her god to it? " . . . " And yet how is the unhappy one to be pitied! My heart breaks with sorrow over the depth of her fall. O Mother, dear, faithful woman, had you seen the jubilation of love that broke forth from every nerve of the rich-souled woman as she not so much confessed as let me see, through herself, through the involuntary, clear and naked revelation of love, that she was mine! . . . No, we will not revile it, the dead one, the murdered one, for it was love! Never, dearest Mother, will I be ashamed of this love: if it has died, if I am convinced that it can never come to life again, yet was its kiss the richest delight of my life. Not honour, nor splendour, nor fame will ever outweigh it for me. Farewell, thou fair one, thou blessed one! Thou wert dear above everything to me, and never will I forget thee! Farewell! "

7

It is easier for the modern reader to jeer at the suffering man, and to censure him for the subterfuges and mendacities to which he resorts when telling the story in *Mein Leben*, than to understand him. Understanding, indeed, of Wagner in this and a score of other matters, is possible only when we cease trying to measure him by the yardstick we are accustomed to apply to ordinary men. This does not mean that, as some of his partisans have contended, genius is entitled to take its own course through the world in callous disregard of the rights of others. That is a superficial reading of him against which he himself would have been the first to protest. In the Laussot affair he was, as always, right in his own eyes, and it would have shocked him to be told that in the eyes of the world he was acting heartlessly towards Minna. On the contrary, his own view of the matter was that he was behaving with the utmost humanity towards her. We have had occasion more than once already, and will have further occasion in the future, to remark on the cool, clear logic in the working of that unusual brain of his; the trouble too often was not that he was wrong in either his arguments or his conclusions, but that logic so clear as his is unrealisable in a world so crude and at the same time so complex as this. Upon this point something will fall to be said when we come to consider his views upon the place of art in modern life, and upon the economic situation of the artist in a modern community. In the present instance he was, as so frequently happened with him, honestly perplexed that those around him could not see the matter through his eyes. It is to be observed that at no time during this Laussot episode does he say a single really unkind word about Minna, or express any dislike of her. His sole reproach against her is that she does not love him according to his conception of love. He is filled with gratitude towards her for all she had done for him, her staunch endurance of so many physical hardships on his account. The root of his complaint against her, which we now know to be fully justified, was that she was intellectually incapable of understanding the new artist that had lately come to life within him. Perfect love, as he saw it, would have cast out doubt; a Minna who really loved him would have linked her fate with his without question — would have believed, even if she could not understand, that he was living and dying for his art as the saint lives for his God and the martyr dies for his faith, and would have borne anything that he himself was willing to bear for the realisation of his lofty ideal.

But Minna was too much the perfect bourgeoise to understand this side of him. One cannot blame her for not seeing, in 1850, whither his daemon was driving him, for not being able to see that he was painfully fighting his way at this time towards a new form of art that even to himself was not quite clear; no one else, not even Uhlig, not even Liszt, had the least perception of what was going on in the depths of him, and what would be the ultimate outcome of it all. To all of them, Minna included, he was just an opera composer among the others, very much better, no doubt, than the others, the Meyerbeers and Aubers and Halévys and Marschners and all the rest of them, but still just another worker in the same conventional field. Had Liszt at this time had the least inkling of the real Wagner he would not have kept pushing the desperate, unhappy man towards Paris as the one goal that mattered. Neither he nor Minna could perceive that the real Wagner, who was now in process of making according to the subtle unconscious laws of genius, could have nothing more to do with the older operatic world as typified by Paris, or, indeed, by any of the larger German towns. Minna thought it would be easy enough for the composer of *Rienzi*, the *Flying Dutchman*, *Tannhäuser* and *Lohengrin* to produce, if he only would, another " opera " of the same kind that would bring in money. She could not comprehend his strange unwillingness to settle down to work — an unwillingness that kept him from writing more than a page or two of music for six years after the completion of *Lohengrin*, and that had its roots in the sound instinct that musically he was not yet ripe for the realisation of so novel a dramatic scheme as that of *Siegfrieds Tod*. She could not understand why he had set his heart on destroying the theatrical world in which, after all, he would have to take his wares to market, why he could not settle down to opera-conducting as a business as other men did.

She could not understand why he wasted so much of his time, as it seemed to her, in writing cumbrous treatises that were incomprehensible to her and to most other people just then. All she could see was that he had forfeited a life-position and a pension in Dresden by what seemed to her his folly, that he had accumulated a monstrous load of debt from which it would take him a lifetime to get free, and that he was facing with inexplicable equanimity the prospect of being supported in what she would call idleness by other people, a prospect that filled her honest bourgeois soul with disgust.

Of the two, he was much the more clear-sighted, and, paradoxical as it may sound, from his point of view the more humane. While there was no chance of Minna's ever coming to understand him as he really was, he understood her through and through. He had had experience enough of her by this time to know that, owing to the intellectual disparity between them, life with her meant, at the worst, constant bickerings that fretted his nerves and put him out of tune with the world, and, at its best, a monastic silence about his innermost self, about his dreams and his visions, a silence that was torture to one who, like himself, could not live without communicating himself lavishly and seeking sympathy. He was unerringly logical, as usual, when he insisted, both to her and to his other correspondents at this time, that it was his very love for Minna that now drove him to leave her. Together, they were a perpetual strain upon each other's nerves and she a drag upon his creative activities; apart, he would be able to remember with love and gratitude and profound pity all she had done for him in her own way. She would not have starved: now, as later, he was scrupulous in his division with her of whatever money he had. The trouble was that he was so constituted that he could not live without feminine society, for he always found women more sympathetic than men. It was not a mere sexual impulse that was at work within him; he turned, upon occasion, with equal eagerness to elderly and unattractive women as to young and pretty ones; the essential things were that they should be women and that they should understand him and be sympathetic to his ideals. But if, as was sometimes the case, they did happen to be young, there followed the consequences that were only to be expected: he " fell in love ", and it was no more clear to others than it was to himself that the love was not much more than a by-product of the situation. The process within him was always the same. During the gestation of a big work the temperature of his whole being was raised: some of the abnormal heat overflowed upon the woman who happened to show him most sympathy at the moment: if she was young and attractive he idealised her, and for the time being identified her with his work: when the work was completed — as in the Mathilde-*Tristan* case — or faded into the background — as in the Jessie-*Wieland* case — the scales gradually fell from his eyes, and he came to see the woman not as an ideal but as an ordinary reality.

8

And so, we may surmise, it was with Jessie Laussot: without question he was passionately in love with her at the moment, but the love was only a by-product of the sense of euphoria he experienced in finding a woman of intelligence and refinement who, he thought at the time, understood him as a man and believed in him as an artist. As always, it was the economic rock upon which his barque had foundered. Life might have been possible even with the uncomprehending Minna had she not been perpetually nagging him to earn a living by ways against which his soul revolted; and when, as happened in the case of Jessie Laussot and that of Mathilde Wesendonk, economic relief came to him through the medium of a woman younger, better bred, more attractive, and more intelligent than poor Minna, it was only to be expected that her feminine jealousy should be aroused, and that she should see nothing in it all but an " affair " of the usual commonplace kind. When each of these " affairs " was over, she had a bourgeois conviction of having triumphed over her " rival ". She shocked and angered Wagner by the crude incomprehension she showed of the underlying meaning of it all when, after what she thought was the termination of the Wesendonk " affair ", she signalised his return to her by flaunting in the Wesendonks' eyes a triumphal arch of flowers outside the little " Asyl ". And now, the Laussot " affair " being at an end, she welcomed back the prodigal at the thought of losing whom she had been genuinely alarmed, for, tragically enough, he was as necessary to her happiness as she was, domestically, to his. Karl Ritter, who had gone to Zürich to see how the land lay, came back to Wagner with the news that she was inclined to be conciliatory; so the friends made their way back to Zürich forthwith, arriving there on the 3rd July. On the 7th Wagner could write philosophically to Kietz that his plan for a flight to the East was at an end, that Minna's love had overcome all her suspicions, and that they were once more living happily together. " I arrived ", he says humorously, " without the horse's tail and turban " — the Turkish symbols of marital authority.[16]

It was not merely that the golden road from Bordeaux to the East had been suddenly closed. The fact was that once more the artist in him had suddenly come uppermost: new ideas were thronging in him and imperiously demanding their reduction to plastic form. Even in the seemingly despairing letter of the 26th–27th June to Frau Ritter he speaks of his desire to get to work again. With *Wieland*, he says, he will not proceed any further: " the faults of this poem are too evident to me to permit of my being in any doubt about them in my present exhausted subjective condition." Just as the angelic aureole faded away from Mathilde Wesendonk's golden head when *Tristan* was finished, so now the vision of Jessie grows weaker within him as he no longer sees himself as *Wieland* and her as the redeeming Swanhilde. " Wieland is dead ", he says: " he will never fly. I think now of writing, first of all, a book on the genius — the common and the lonely (*das gemeinsame und das einsame*). Then, when my strength has returned to me, I will set to work at *Achilleus*." In Minna, he tells Frau Ritter on the 10th July, love has overcome doubt and error; " she has won, after the recent experiences, the strength to believe wholeheartedly in me." She has had only one wish — " that I should return to her, for she had realised, to the very marrow of her being, that she could not live without me. . . . In this strength of love of which she has become conscious during the late decisive catastrophe, in which she has won the victory over all doubt and error, she has become for me a wholly new creature, different from the old. I have realised what I am to her, and so I must set about being this in reality."

[16] CBC, No. 207.

Zürich seems once more to him the ideal place in which to live; he hopes that the Ritters will settle there with him. There can be no question now, of course, of an allowance from the Taylor-Laussot quarter, and he seems to have returned the money, or part of it, that had been sent to him or to Minna from Bordeaux. Frau Ritter's modest purse, however, was still at his service.

It is a fact of the highest significance for our understanding of the true inwardness of the Laussot affair that Frau Ritter's loyalty to him never wavered for a moment during it or after it. She was a calm, wise, high-minded woman of middle age: she was on terms of the closest friendship with Jessie: she knew Minna and felt a profound sympathy with her: and if, in the face of all this, she still saw something to excuse in Wagner's conduct, and did not, like the Laussots, withdraw her financial support from him, it is evident that she, alone among them all, saw that at heart the tragically suffering man had been honest with himself and the others in his own peculiar way, that what looked to common eyes like a common " love affair " was at bottom simply the attempt of the distracted artist to keep his soul free from the corruption that was eating into it from the world outside.

How deeply this brief experience, with its momentary rapture and its enduring disappointment and despair, had bitten into him can be seen from a letter of his of the 7th August, 1852, to Frau Ritter. He had just returned from a month's excursion, in search of health, over the Alps into northern Italy; and perhaps the sight of Geneva, which he had reached on the 3rd, had brought back memories of the final troubled Laussot days. The journey, he tells Frau Ritter, has opened his eyes and rid him of his last illusions with regard to himself. He has, it is true, been entranced by Italy: " but I can no longer blind myself to the fact that for me there is henceforth no happiness in life. It was precisely there that I realised that I am no longer capable of a cheerful enjoyment of life — for youth has left me. Yes, dearest friend, until the event in my life with which you are so familiar I was still young: now I know that hope has deserted me. On that single decisive occasion I desired to seize upon real life, hold it fast to me, and rescue myself in it. But it slipped out of my grasp, and I sank back again into the world of imagination; I now had to seek my life's nourishment once more not in my heart but in my brain, and this frantic harass now wears me out: it will destroy me."

9

The complexion that the Laussot episode has assumed in the course of years is entirely the result of the somewhat untruthful and unpleasant way in which Wagner chose to deal with it in *Mein Leben*, at a time in his life when he was blinded with rage against all those who might have " saved " him but, as he held, had failed him in his hour of need. He tries to make out that Jessie, in 1850, meant nothing in particular to him. His reasons for taking this line were, in the first place, the resentment that had rankled in him for some sixteen years, in the second place a certain unwillingness to let Cosima and King Ludwig know more than was necessary about one or two episodes in his past. When he came to tell the story of his relations with the Wesendonks he once more manipulated the facts to suit his present ends. To do this with the success he hoped for in the eyes of posterity he had to destroy, as he thought, all first-hand evidence of the contemporary truth about these matters — for apparently he never contemplated the possibility of the publication some day of his letters to Otto and Mathilde Wesendonk and others. How he went about this business of destruction has now to be told.

The reader has already learned how, in August, 1835, Wagner began to enter dates and details of his life in a large red pocket-book, " for my future biography ": the book, he tells us, lay before him when he was dictating *Mein Leben*.[17] This passage in the autobiography was dictated in the spring of 1866. We know, from one of his letters to King Ludwig, that he kept up the red book regularly till at least November, 1864; and it now appears that the entries continued for nearly four years after that. There was little in his early life — as far, at any rate, as 1848 — that he was particularly anxious to conceal or re-colour when he was dictating his autobiography; and, as we have had many opportunities of seeing, his account of these years is substantially correct. But as the story developed there came up episode after episode upon which he felt

---

[17] See Vol. I, p. 194, of the present *Life*.

it necessary to put his own gloss for the benefit of future generations, or which, in some cases, he thought it advisable to conceal
altogether. There came a point, therefore, at which the red book
had to be dealt with drastically. By April, 1867, he had progressed
with the dictation of *Mein Leben* as far as the events of 1846 — to
the period at which he had been compelled to ask Lüttichau to obtain for him an advance from the King to help him out of his financial difficulties. At this stage the autobiographer seems to have
realised that he was approaching a period in his life in which frankness unadorned was likely to become more and more difficult. He
naturally wanted to give his own version of his dealings with the
Intendant and the theatre, to conceal the amount of his borrowings
from friends, to minimise his complicity in the Dresden revolt, and
so on. It was not advisable that the young King, who had given him
the incentive to his autobiography and who saw him in so ideal a
light, should read anything that was likely to lower him in his estimation. A little further ahead of him lay the Jessie Laussot and
the Wesendonk affairs, upon neither of which, and more particularly the former, was he inclined to tell the truth, the whole truth
and nothing but the truth. But manifestly the red book, if it ever
came into the hands of posterity, would show his accounts of these
and other matters in *Mein Leben* to be somewhat lacking in completeness, or even, at times in ordinary veracity. And so sentence of
death was passed upon the red book.

It was reprieved only long enough to enable him to extract from
it the details of dates and places that were necessary for the frame-
work of the autobiography. Suspending work upon this latter at
the point in the story he had now reached (Easter, 1846), he spent
some weeks, from February, 1868, onwards, in extracting what he
wanted from the red book after 1846 (perhaps down to 1867) —
and then he destroyed the book. The remainder of his life-story, extending from Easter, 1846, to his rescue by King Ludwig in May,
1864 (at which date *Mein Leben* ends),[18] was dictated, between the

---

[18] Though *Mein Leben* ends with May, 1864, the "Annals," which, by the way,
are in Wagner's own handwriting throughout, extend over another four-and-a-half
years — down to the end of 1868. His original intention was that the story of his life
from 1864 onwards should some day be written by Cosima. *Mein Leben* is in four
parts, comprising respectively the years 1813–42, 1842–50, 1850–61, and 1861–
May 1864. When the dictation of Part III was completed we do not know, as the

28th July, 1868, and some date in 1880 that cannot now be determined precisely, not from the red book but from certain " Annals " that took its place. (These " Annals," now in the Wahnfried archives, contain many details not made use of in *Mein Leben*). Otto Strobel, the Wahnfried archivist, opines that there were two reasons why Wagner substituted the " Annals " for the red book — there were things in his life which he did not wish even Cosima to know, while as regards several matters he preferred to place on record his later view of them, rather than the view he had taken of them at the time of their happening. This latter consideration may well have been operative; but as regards the former it is difficult to believe that Cosima was not an accessory after the fact to the manipulation of the red book for Wagner's own purposes.[19] It is true that he began the " Annals " in February, 1868, at a time when he was living in retirement at Triebschen, while Cosima (who was still Bülow's wife) was in Munich with her husband. In the summer of that year (after the production of the *Meistersinger* in Munich in June) she boldly made a final end of a situation that had become intolerable, and joined Wagner at Triebschen. It is hardly credible that, when Wagner resumed the dictation of his memoirs on the 28th July, Cosima did not ask what had become of the red book that had accompanied all previous dictations, and what was the meaning of these " Annals " that had suddenly taken its place.[20]

---

final page of Cosima's manuscript, which presumably bore the date, has been lost; but Part IV was begun on the 10th January, 1876. The page dealing with the three Vienna concerts of December, 1862, and January, 1863, is dated "20th March, 1880." The remaining pages must have been dictated during the remainder of that year.

Parts I–III only were privately printed in Basel between 1870 and 1875; consequently Part IV is not in the copy of this edition which Mrs. Burrell managed to acquire. This circumstance gave rise, in time, to the fantastic legend that Part IV was Cosima's own work, added by her after Wagner's death. As we have just seen, however, the dictation of Part IV was begun by Wagner in January, 1876; and this Part was privately printed by him (at Bayreuth) in 1881.

[19] In August, 1865, we learn from Cosima's diary, she made extracts from the red book to send to King Ludwig. (See MECW, I, 256). She must have been well acquainted with the book.

[20] Strobel's detailed account of the matter will be found in an article on *Die Originalhandschrift von Wagners grosser Autobiographie, Mein Leben*, in BFF, pp. 30 ff. From a later article by Strobel (in BFF, 1934, pp. 113 ff.) it appears that somehow or other the first two leaves — i.e. four pages — of the red book have survived, and are now in the Wahnfried archives; they summarise his biography from the day of his birth until the 17th September, 1839 (the day after his arrival in Paris).

At a still later date Strobel printed the whole matter of these four pages of the red book in the *Allgemeine Musikzeitung* of the 28th March, 1936, together with a

10

We have seen that in May and June, 1850, he had made a fair copy of the poem of *Siegfrieds Tod* with a view to publication. In Villeneuve, on the 3rd June, he wrote a preface to the work; and he was back again in Zürich on the 3rd July. A document published for the first time in 1933 makes it clear that it was his intention at that time to set the drama to music at once. In *L'Illustration* for the 11th February, 1933, there is given a facsimile of Wagner's setting of the whole of the opening scene of the Norns (fifty lines), and of the first twenty lines of the following scene between Brynhilde and Siegfried — i.e. as far as the latter's words " Brünnhildes zu ge-denken." [21] The music is a continuous " Composition Sketch " [22] running to 150 filled-in bars, spaces being indicated here and there for repetitions. It obviously represents what *Siegfrieds Tod* would have been had Wagner carried out his intention of writing the opera in 1850. We may congratulate ourselves that he did not: in general the music is very much in the style of *Lohengrin,* with scarcely a hint of the *Ring* as we now have it; the orchestral prelude to Bryn-

facsimile of the fourth page. This unique document puts us in possession of a few details as to Wagner's early life not hitherto known. We learn, for instance, that in 1807 as a boy of four, he attended the school of one Hofcantor Schmidt. Three times, in 1829 and 1831, he notes periods when he was "dissipated". There are occasional references to his debts and his general misery during the Magdeburg and later years.

The drastic brevity of the entries — a brevity which enables him to get all the essential facts into a very small space — is seen at its best in the story of the voyage to London:

"15th [July, 1839] arrived in Pillau. 19th early, board the 'Thetis' with Minna. 25th, off Copenhagen and past Helsingör. 27th in Skager Rack storm. 28 Storm. 29 Stormy west wind: had to run into a small Norwegian harbour near Arendal. Evening on shore with Minna. Marvellous rocks out at sea. Place Sand-Wigke. On the 31st we tried to sail again; going out of the harbour the ship strikes an invisible rock: 2 shocks. Back again. Excursion in the boat to Trommsond. 1st August, safe on sea again. Sunday evening, 4th, stormy north wind: favourable. 6th evening, contrary storm. Wednesday, the 7th, bad day. Storm at its worst 2.30 in the afternoon. 8th, mild contrary wind. 9th evening, off English coast off Southwould [sic]. Pilot taken on board. Evening 10th to evening 11th, fierce storm from the west between the sand-banks. Night 11th–12th, tacked to within a mile of Gravesend; 12th by the Gravesend steamship to London. Arrived in London at London Bridge; Tower Hill. Found lodgings in Compton Street." From jottings of this kind his astonishing memory enabled him to reconstruct accurately almost every detail of his life nearly thirty years later. The reader will find it interesting to compare the curt entries about the voyage with the graphic description of it in *Mein Leben.*

[21] The manuscript is in the collection of M. Louis Barthou. It is dated the 12th August, 1850.

[22] The explanation of this term will be given later.

hilde's opening words, for instance, is cast in the rhythmic formula the tyranny of which over him in his earlier works Wagner himself recognised in later years:

Interesting features of the sketch are (1) the choice of the same key (E flat minor) for the Norns scene as later for the prelude to the *Götterdämmerung,* though the later music is completely different, (2) a hint, in the opening words of the first Norn, of the theme that was afterwards to be associated not with the Norns but with the Valkyries, (3) what looks like a foreshadowing, in the music accompanying the transition from the Norns scene to that between Brynhilde and Siegfried, of the downward-striding figure which we now associate with Wotan, and (4) the glimpse of a figure:

out of which the motive of "Love's Rapture" in *Siegfried:*

may have ultimately grown. Here and there one meets with a vocal phrase that suggests, in embryo, something that is familiar to us in the present *Ring.*

Particularly interesting is the evidence the Sketch affords that from the first, in the very shaping of his text, Wagner must have had *musical* forms in his mind. In the printed text of *Siegfrieds Tod* the scene opens thus:

> *The First Norn*
> In Osten wob ich.
> *The Second*
> In Westen wand ich.
> *The Third*
> Nach Norden werf' ich.

(*to the Second*)
Was wandest du im Westen?
The Second (*to the First*)
Was wobest du im Osten?

after which each of them in turn tells us a fragment of the Nibelung story. Then the lines quoted above are repeated, to be followed by further episodes of the story; and the same procedure recurs for the third time. Before each repetition of " In Osten wob ich ", etc., Wagner has left a blank bar with the words " 3 Tacte ": his intention here was evidently to carry on with the orchestra alone for three bars each time, no doubt modulating away from the main key and returning to it, as the Sketch shows, with each " In Osten wob ich ". He does not write out in full (except, of course, on the first occasion) the music to the lines quoted above, but contents himself with indicating the words and the melody of the first line and adding a " u.s.w." (" und so weiter ": " and so on "). The opening section of the first scene was therefore conceived in a kind of rondo form, the same melody recurring three times after various branchings-out from it, with a connective tissue supplied by the orchestral interludes.

CHAPTER VIII

FRIENDS AND PUBLIC WORK
IN ZÜRICH

1

IN APRIL, 1850, during Richard's absence in Paris (at the time of the Laussot episode), Minna had found rooms by the Lake of Zürich in a house known as " Zum Abendstern ", in the commune of Enge, about a quarter of an hour's walk from the town. It stood in what was then the Sternengasse: [1] it was pulled down in 1876 when the railway along the left bank of the Lake was constructed. The situation of the house corresponded practically with that of the present No. 22 in the Sternenstrasse. Wagner had a small garden that ran down to the Lake, across which he had a superb view; he could boat on the Lake, or run down the garden in an old coat and bathe there. Karl Ritter was lodged in an upper room. The house was re-baptised by Sulzer and Wagner's other friends, rather unfortunately, the " Villa Rienzi ": the " Villa " set all sorts of malicious gossip going among Wagner's Saxon creditors and friends as to the unwarrantable luxury in which he was supposed to be living. In a letter to his sister Cäcilie in December, 1852 (after he had left " Zum Abendstern "), he thought it necessary to correct this impression. He now styles his former " Villa ", indeed, a " filthy little place by the Lake ". He was contented enough with it at the time, however; and during the fifteen or sixteen months he spent there he wrote a number of important prose works, including *Judaism in Music, Opera and Drama, A Theatre in Zürich*, and *A Communication to my Friends*, as well as the *Recollections of Spontini*, an *Explanatory Note on Beethoven's Eroica*, and the *Letter to Franz Liszt concerning the Goethe-Foundation*.

---

[1] A contemporary picture of "Zürich seen from the Sternengasse", showing the roof of what was in all probability the "*Zum Abendstern*", may be seen in FWSZ, p. 36.

In time he found the distance from the town inconvenient, especially in bad weather; so about the middle of September, 1851, he removed to the Escherhäuser once more, this time, however, taking apartments on the ground floor of one of the " front " houses — No. 11 in the Zeltweg.[2] In 1852 he indulged himself in the dream of a little house of his own in the country, where he could get more quiet for his work than in Zürich itself, but these plans broke down over the financial problem: so about the middle of April, 1853, he removed to the adjacent No. 13 of the Zeltweg, on the second floor of which he had more room than in No. 11, besides more sun in the winter. In No. 13 [3] he remained until the spring of 1857, when he took up his abode in what he called the " Asyl ", a small house on a plot of land adjoining the Wesendonk property.

Being built somewhat on the pattern of Catharine Morland in *Northanger Abbey*, who " voluntarily rejected the whole city of Bath as unworthy to make part of a landscape ", Minna made it quite clear from the first, both to Richard and to Zürich, that she did not think much of the town, which was hardly important enough, in her estimation, to be the permanent abode of the wife of a one-time Dresden Kapellmeister; " she is already ashamed of our living here ", Wagner complains to Uhlig on the 16th September, " and thinks we ought to lead everyone to believe that we are in Paris." She was loftily critical of most of his new friends, notably of Jacob Sulzer, a brilliant young cantonal secretary who gradually rose to high office in the republic; Minna's patronising verdict on him was that he was only a town clerk who would not be thought anything of in Germany. When it became evident, however, that there was no immediate prospect of Richard being able to return to Germany, she resigned herself to her new surroundings, and the likeable creature soon made many friends among people of her own type. In April, 1852, Wagner could assure Frau Ritter that " my wife is radiantly happy: she has fine clothes and many friends of her own sex: never and nowhere has she spent a more amusing

---

[2] A photograph of the house as it is now will be found in FWSZ, p. 118. The rooms remain very much as they were in Wagner's day: the same Empire stove is still in what was his work-room.

[3] A photograph of No. 13 is given in Fehr's book, p. 220. A memorial tablet has been placed on the house.

winter than this last, as she herself admits." [4] Mathilde Wesendonk, it should be added, had not yet made her stage entry as leading lady.

Wagner's own circle of acquaintances widened rapidly. Zürich at that time housed several men of wide culture; and it was the recognised rallying-place for political revolutionaries from not only Germany but other countries. For some time after his flight Wagner still believed in a coming transformation of society through a general political upheaval; but as these hopes gradually faded, and at the same time the new artist within him began to take more and more definite shape, he lost most of his interest in politics for its own sake and conceived a distaste for the company of the majority of his fellow-revolutionaries. It is probable also that he took to heart the advice of Minna and Liszt and his friends generally, and saw the folly of adding still further to the ill repute that had gathered about his name in Dresden. The German police spies, he knew well, were very active in Zürich.

He was shown considerable attention from the first by many of the leading intellectuals of the place, and became especially intimate with Sulzer, whose character commanded his lifelong respect, with Franz Hagenbuch (another important state official), with Professor Ludwig Ettmüller (a leading German scholar of the day, with whom he could discuss problems connected with the northern sagas, in which Ettmüller was a specialist), and with Alexander Müller's pupil Wilhelm Baumgartner, a young piano teacher and composer of no outstanding ability but of an agreeable disposition, whose only fault, and one that operated to his own disadvantage rather than that of other people, was that he was a little too fond of the bottle.[5] Sulzer, though by no means rich at that time, placed his purse, his cigars, and the products of his vineyards at Wagner's

---

[4] So again in a letter of the 21st March to his niece Franziska: "Everything is all right with Minna; she gets much more amusement here than she did in Dresden, has friends of her own sex and plenty of entertainment." He, on the other hand, suffers incessantly from his nerves, and "probably will not last out much longer", though he longs to be able to finish his Nibelungen drama. See JKJ, p. 57.

[5] He died in 1867, in his forty-seventh year. He was a boon companion of Gottfried Keller, several of whose poems he set to music. Keller corresponded with him while absent from Switzerland, and mentions him occasionally in his diary. See BGKL, I, 264–5, 267, 295–6, etc. Keller's biographer Baechtold describes him as "unpretending, true-hearted, companionable, humorous."

service; Baumgartner also helped him for a while out of his own modest means. With Friedrich Theodor Vischer, the famous author of an *Aesthetik* the final volume of which was published in Zürich in 1857, Wagner does not seem to have become intimate.[6] Like most writers on the subject of aesthetics, Vischer was not very musical; and though Wagner appreciated the intellectual honesty of the man, he no doubt wrote him down as belonging to the " professor " class which was sure to be the last to understand the essence of his own new thinking about the relations of poetry and music in the drama of the future.

The philologist Hermann Köchly, who had formerly lived in Dresden, where he had been impressed by the performance of the Ninth Symphony under Wagner in 1846, and who had taken part in the formation of the Provisional Government three years later, did not take up his abode in Zürich until 1851, when he was appointed to the chair of classical philology in the University. Wagner's efforts to provide for another of his Dresden co-revolutionaries, Semper, did not bear fruit until 1855, when the great architect was made professor at the Zürich Polytechnic.

Another fugitive from Dresden was Adolph Kolatschek, who, operating from Zürich, founded in Stuttgart a monthly journal with the ambitious title of the *Deutsche Monatsschrift für Politik, Wissenschaft, Kunst und Leben*, to which both Wagner and Uhlig contributed: it was in the pages of this paper, as we have seen, that Wagner's essay on *Art and Climate* appeared in February, 1850, as well as selections from *Opera and Drama* at a later date. It was not until the early part of 1851 that he met the poet Georg Herwegh, who, after an ignominious failure as a practical revolutionary, but still basking in the reputation that his outspoken *Gedichte eines Lebendigen* (*Poems of a Live Man*) had brought him some ten years before, had now settled in luxury in Zürich on the income of his rich wife. Herwegh, who himself was exceedingly fond of good living, is said to have encouraged Wagner's inborn tendency to indulge in an expenditure beyond his means.

---

[6] Vischer did not settle in Zürich until 1854. He was another exile from Germany, but on religious, not political grounds. This is the Vischer whose essay, *Vorschlag zu einer Oper*, it has been suggested may have been read by Wagner in the late 1840's, when he first conceived the idea of making an opera out of the Nibelungen saga. (See *supra*, p. 25.)

The poet and novelist Gottfried Keller, a native of Zürich who had lived for some time in Germany, returned to his home-town in 1855, and, introduced by Sulzer, soon became a member of Wagner's circle. In Wagner's house, as in others, he seems to have indulged liberally his passion for alcohol. Wagner was rather alienated by the strain of helplessness in the man that hindered him from realising the best that was in him; but he found a good word to say for his lyrics in an article on Baumgartner's songs (1852),[7] and according to Emilie Heim he was never tired of reading to his Zürich friends whole sections of Keller's *Die Leute von Seldwyla.*

Other Zürich friends were Bernhard Spyri, a lawyer, who edited the *Eidgenössische Zeitung,* which journal was at Wagner's service whenever he needed it; the Wesendonks, who came upon the scene in 1852, and of whom more will be said later; the Willes; and the Heims. It was at Herwegh's house that Wagner met François Wille (a former newspaper editor in Hamburg), and his wife Eliza, the daughter of a wealthy Hamburg shipowner, whose means enabled the pair to live in good style on a small estate at Mariafeld, a short distance further down the Lake. Wagner never got on particularly well with Wille, who argued with him too obstinately about political and other matters for Richard's liking, besides being quite insensitive to music; it is probable also that he did not approve of the composer's habit of borrowing from his well-to-do friends. Frau Wille was much more sympathetic to him, and did him many a kindness in later years: it was to Mariafeld that he fled in March, 1864, when his debts made it necessary for him to leave Vienna in a hurry. Born in 1804, she was some seven years older than her husband, and nine years older than Wagner; and even he, though he respected her character and admired her intellect, had to admit that she was painfully plain. The theory lately put into circulation by a pair of irresponsible intruders into Wagner literature that he was ever in love with her, either in the 'fifties or in 1864, may be dismissed as a ridiculous invention. He was much more attracted to the singer Emilie Heim, the wife of Ignaz Heim, the conductor

[7] Reprinted in RWGS, XII, 283 ff.

of a local choral society, the " Harmonie "; what appealed to him most in her was not so much her voice, which, though good, was untrained, as the wealth of golden hair that reminded him of the Sieglinde of his dreams. The Heims, who settled in Zürich in the autumn of 1852, were his close neighbours in the Escherhäuser, and it is alleged that it was not long before Minna, who was decidedly watchful since the Laussot affair, began to believe, with what justice we cannot now be certain, that she had cause for jealousy.[8] She is said also to have had her suspicions of Johanna Spyri, the wife of the editor of the *Eidgenössische Zeitung*.[9]

Only Wagner's extraordinary personality can account for the rapidity with which he, a friendless, penniless exile, made himself the centre of a circle of intelligent men and women in Zürich, who realised his intellectual power even if they did not always blindly accept his rulings. It had been the same in Paris in 1839: " we young Germans ", says Pecht, " were attracted by the endlessly bubbling richness of his mind. . . ." Poor as they were themselves, he continues, " we could only give him the consolation that he was not absolutely forsaken, that there were people round him who believed in him, and who formed about him a little community of which he was the undisputed centre." [10]

As was to be the case in Venice later, the authorities showed the distinguished fugitive every consideration, in spite of the malevolence with which the Saxon officials pursued him. By a law of 1836, fugitives from other countries for purely political reasons were allowed to settle in Switzerland for good after at least a year's residence. After the events of the summer of 1849 in Germany the authorities naturally felt it their duty to be more than normally alert, but Wagner seems to have escaped their attentions until the autumn of 1850. He had no difficulty in procuring a residence permit from the 17th October of that year to the 27th October, 1851; but this had hardly been granted when, on the 4th November, 1850, the Federal Council, at the instance of the Zürich police, de-

---

[8] Emma Heim survived Wagner nearly thirty years, dying in 1912. She was the last survivor of the Zürich circle of the 1850's. Sulzer lived to attend one of the performances of *Parsifal* in Bayreuth in 1882.

[9] JKWF, pp. 120–33. Kapp gives no documentary evidence in support of his suggestion.

[10] PAMZ.

leted his name from the official list of refugees. As a formality he had to find securities for the sum of 1,600 francs, a matter in which Sulzer and Hagenbuch were delighted to oblige. The Police Director, Bollier, was always friendly and considerate towards Wagner.[11] It was true that the latter's German friends always addressed their letters, until as late as January, 1851, not to him but to " Fräulein Natalie Planer, c/o Frau Hirzel, Sternengasse, Enge," or to Karl Ritter; but this was merely to safeguard them against being seized by the German post offices and opened.

3

Zürich, when Wagner settled there, was a small town of some 33,000 inhabitants, not yet boasting the luxury of street lighting.[12] It possessed a Musical Society of a sort, giving its concerts in the Casino,[13] and employing an orchestra of about two dozen professional musicians, reinforced on occasions by amateurs of the town. One or two of the professional players were very competent, notably the oboist, Fries, whose talent won Wagner's admiration, and an excellent hornist, Bär. Some of the amateurs were unusually capable, especially the rich Konrad Ott-Imhof, who was a sensitive clarinettist; while the cantonal secretary Hagenbuch performed upon the flute. All in all, however, the orchestra must have been a poor one enough, judged by any modern standard.

Attached to the Casino was the theatre,[14] — not run by the town

---

[11] See FWSZ, pp. 13, 14; SRWZ, I, 25.

[12] Apparently it had developed rapidly since the early 1830's, when its population was only some 10,000. The first railway, from Zürich to Baden, had been constructed about 1845. The town still preserved a good deal of its mediaeval aspect. Its government in the 1830's was still aristocratic: as in the German "Residenz" towns, the upper and lower classes, the state officials, the rich traders and the bourgeoisie were sharply marked off from each other in the theatre and the concert room.

[13] The concert hall was a tiny affair, about 66 ft. long by 40 ft. broad and 23 ft. high.

[14] This was the theatre the conductorship of which had been offered to the twenty-year-old Wagner when he was acting as chorus master in Würzburg. (See Vol. I, p. 101). The theatre was at that time in course of construction: it was opened in November, 1834. It appears that "neither in the minutes of the Music Society, which supplied the theatre with its own orchestra and conductor (C. von Blumenthal), nor in those of the company running the theatre, is there any mention of such an offer: probably it was made by the first director of the theatre, the Berliner Deny, and represents the first desire of the institution not to be dependent on a borrowed

[168]

itself but leased to an impresario acting for a company. In 1850 the lessee was one Philipp Waldburg Kramer, who, quick to perceive the esteem in which the Dresden fugitive was held by some of the most influential citizens of the town, offered him the post of opera conductor. Wagner was unwilling to pledge himself at all definitely, for he was resolved never again to sell himself for any length of time into the slavery of the theatre; but he undertook to superintend the first efforts of his young protégé Karl Ritter, who was anxious to take up music as a career. He had been well grounded in the theory of music by Schumann in Dresden, and the gifted but somewhat eccentric youth had now managed to persuade himself that nature had intended him to be a conductor. It was mainly on Wagner's recommendation that in October, 1850, Karl was made musical director of the theatre for the coming winter at the magnificent salary of 100 francs a month. From the first he proved himself incompetent: he was so short-sighted that he had to keep his head down in the score, to the consequent neglect of the stage, and he was lacking in the most elementary of a conductor's qualifications, that of keeping time. The result was that Wagner, who regarded himself as responsible for him to the management, had to conduct, on the 4th October, the opening work of the season, *Der Freischütz*, in which Karl should have made his début.

Wagner's reforming and organising genius had, in fact, quickly got to work at the problem of music in Zürich. He saw at once that the first practical steps should be to amalgamate the orchestra of the Concert Society with that of the theatre, to increase the number of concerts, under better conditions than of old, and to reduce the number of opera performances, with a corresponding improvement in their quality. He gained the ear of some of the leading men of the town for his scheme, and apparently was commissioned, either by them or by Kramer, to enquire of Uhlig, in September, if he knew of any string players who would be willing to come to Zürich for the five or six winter months, at a salary of 15 thalers a month (which

orchestra." (See SRWZ, I, 5). The offer to Wagner no doubt came through one of the many relations of his who were connected with the stage. Steiner says that Wagner's reason for refusing it had been not only his hope of having *Die Feen* produced in Würzburg or Leipzig but also the difficulty he was likely to have in obtaining a passport to Switzerland, he being then of military age.

might be increased to 20 thalers by extra engagements) and their travelling expenses. His projected reform, however, came to nothing, the committee of the Musical Society deciding unanimously that a plan that also involved the theatre was no concern of theirs. But meanwhile Kramer, counting too soon on securing Wagner as conductor and so attracting large audiences, had engaged a few leading singers of a quality above the Zürich average, at more than ordinary expense. This being so, Wagner felt himself under an obligation to do what he personally could for the theatre after Karl Ritter had proved to be untrustworthy. One of the difficulties facing the director was that the competent amateurs of the town would consent to assist in what Wagner called " the horribly weak orchestra in the matter of strings" only if and when Wagner himself conducted. His name did not appear either on the play-bill of the *Freischütz* performance on the 4th October or in the press announcements; the object, of course, was not to discourage the booking for performances under any other conductor. But a secret of this kind was obviously impossible to keep, except by muzzling everyone connected with the rehearsals; and the Zürich public proved that it was in possession of the secret by filling the theatre on the 4th October.

Wagner was luckier in his recommendation of the young Bülow, who, about this time, had definitely decided that his vocation was not the law but music. His parents had separated in the autumn of 1849, owing to incompatibility of temperament: almost the only point on which they were agreed was that the profession of music was not one for a young German of good family with a " von " to his name, and when Hans showed so manifestly his adoration of Wagner, his parents joined forces in a common dislike of the latter. The mother, indeed, who was of a neurotic type, positively hated him, regarding him as a dangerous revolutionary likely to lead her son into wrong paths. At this time the father was living on a small estate at Ötlishausen, near Kradolf on the Lake of Constance. From there Hans addressed a despairing letter to Wagner, who, in his reply, urged him to risk everything rather than abandon an ideal to which his heart was plainly given. The letter was taken to the Bülow villa by Karl Ritter. The two comrades went out for a walk together and did not return; as neither of them had any money, they tramped it back in the rain to Zürich, arriving there two days later, exhausted and considerably soiled, but radiant with happiness. It was arranged that Bülow should share Karl's duties at the theatre with him. Hans at once convinced Wagner that a brilliant career lay before him as a conductor; but, as happened so often in later years, his uncompromising idealism, his irritable disposition and his sharp tongue soon got him into trouble, especially with the singers; while the orchestra, as a matter of course, had not the same confidence in this untried young man of twenty as he rightly had in himself. He, for his part, was not the man to take lying down any disrespect either to himself personally or to his art. Wagner stood faithfully by his side in the storm that soon arose: he threatened the opera personnel with the withdrawal of his sympathy and supervision if they did not behave themselves better with regard to his protégé, and as they had the greatest respect for him, and, for business reasons, did not wish to lose him, they promised to mend their ways. So, for a few weeks, Bülow carried on with fair satisfaction to himself and others. Apparently he and Karl between them received a salary of 50 gulden a month: they ate their midday dinner at Wagner's, where Minna cooked excellently for them and mothered the two boys generally; while Wagner himself was so unfailingly kind to Bülow that Hans describes him in a letter to his mother as " the noblest and kindest of men, the one most deserving of veneration ", who has the greatest claim imaginable on his love and gratitude, and to whom he is willing to commit the fateful decision as to his future.

Wagner, indeed, must already have seen in the youthful Bülow, with his incorruptible conscience where art was concerned, a man after his own pattern. Hans showed his mettle in the first real operas he conducted [15] — Lortzing's *Czar und Zimmermann* and Rossini's *Barbiere*, the scores of which he had practically learned by heart in a few days. With his third opera, *Fra Diavolo,* he had less success; the public was cold towards the work itself, and the singers found it convenient to lay the failure to the charge of the young conductor. The truth seems to have been that already the

---

[15] He had been tested first of all, on the 9th October, in a musical farce, *Einmal-hunderttausend Thaler*. He had to conduct in a suit of Karl Ritter's, having brought no change of clothes with him from Ötlishausen.

public wanted no conductor but Wagner, and him only in works on its own rather low intellectual plane. Matters came to a crisis at the beginning of December, when Bülow conducted his last opera in Zürich, *Masaniello*. The leading soprano (Frau Rosa Rauch-Wernau) and her husband took offence and stood on their dignity, as leading sopranos and their husbands are always inclined to do; and as the director thought, with reason, that the lady counted for more at the box-office than Bülow did, there was nothing for Hans to do but resign. He went to another miserable operatic post at St. Gallen, where, as Wagner says, there was " a wretched theatre, an abominable set of singers, and a ghastly orchestra." Ritter accompanied him, to act mainly as chorus master in this delectable temple of the Muses. Karl, after a final demonstration of his incompetence as a conductor, sensibly gave up all ambition in that quarter. Bülow endured one winter at St. Gallen, and then, having quarrelled with the director, went, at his mother's request, to Weimar, at Easter, 1851, to continue his piano studies under Liszt.

4

Meanwhile Wagner had been doing his best to raise the standard of opera in Zürich. As we have seen, he opened the season on the 4th October, 1850, with *Der Freischütz*. He further conducted *La Dame Blanche* of Boieldieu on the 11th and 18th, *Norma* on the 21st, *Freischütz* again on the 27th, *Don Giovanni* on the 8th and 18th November (again on the 26th March, 1851), the *Magic Flute* on the 29th November, *La Dame Blanche* again on the 6th December, 1850, and the 7th February, 1851, and *Fidelio* on the 4th April, 1851. It was apparently in connection with the third performance of *La Dame Blanche* that Wagner's name appeared for the first time on the theatre bill, though the newspapers had announced in advance his co-operation in other works. He seems to have had quite a good opinion of the powers of the leading lady of the company (Rosa Rauch-Werner), the first tenor (Joseph Baumhauer), and the first bass (Joseph Dupont).

He took particular trouble over *Don Giovanni*, a work that had been greatly disadvantaged, since Mozart's time, by the difficulties of all kinds that are inseparable from a modern performance of it.

Wagner spent three days and nights with Bülow and Ritter correcting the orchestral parts and writing substitute parts for instruments, such as the trombones, that were missing from the local orchestra; he made a working German dialogue version of some of the Italian recitatives, retaining others in their original form; he simplified the scenic arrangements so as to avoid too many changes of the settings; he transposed Donna Anna's aria to the graveyard scene, writing, by way of introduction to it, a short musical recitative for Ottavio and Donna Anna.[16] "I was furious", Bülow wrote to his father, "when I remembered how it used to be said in Dresden that Wagner conducted Mozart's operas badly on purpose, because in his vain self-esteem he could not tolerate this music! He shows towards Mozart a warm, living, unselfish, but rational piety to which none of Mozart's pseudo-worshippers will ever attain." The theatre, according to Bülow, was sold out, but the Zürich public was somewhat irresponsive and ungrateful. Though Wagner, to get Kramer out of a difficulty, consented to conduct *Don Giovanni* again on the 26th March, 1851, and to close the company's season with *Fidelio* on the 4th April,[17] his more or less official connection with Kramer seems to have terminated when Bülow resigned, Wagner feeling that he had no longer any moral responsibility towards the management.

On the evening of the performance of *Norma* — the 21st October, 1850 — the Fates brought to Zürich a young couple who were destined to play a great part in the life of Richard Wagner; they put up at the Hôtel Baur au Lac for what was intended to be a month's stay while they looked round for a suitable property in the

---

[16] The Zürich score with Wagner's revisions in it has unfortunately disappeared. Perhaps it was destroyed when the theatre was burnt down on New Year's Day, 1890; but Max Fehr conjectures that it may have been deliberately consigned to oblivion by the Saxon nobleman Friedrich von Friederici, who had taken part — on the King's side, of course,— in the Dresden rising of 1849, and was an embittered anti-Wagnerian; during his régime at the Zürich theatre (1860–1) he did not permit a single performance of any of the "traitor's" works. He may consequently have thought it a sin to preserve the Mozart-Wagner score. See FWSZ, p. 64. Du Moulin Eckart, according to Fehr, is in error when he implies (MECW, II, 150) that the score is still in the Zürich archives.

[17] Not on the 30th, as in some biographies. The 4th April was the final night of the season. Nor did Wagner, as has been supposed, conduct *Fidelio* on the 31st March. Max Fehr gives sufficient reasons for deciding that this performance was under Abt. See FWSZ, p. 71.

neighbourhood. They were described in the Strangers' List next day as " Wesendonk, Merchant, and Wife, from New York." They settled down definitely in Zürich in the following April. Frau Mathilde in particular soon became interested in the intellectual, and especially the musical, life of the town; and she seems to have been impressed almost at once by the personality of Wagner. She was present at a performance of the *Tannhäuser* overture conducted by him on the 16th March, 1852, an experience which, in common with many other people in the audience, she regarded as the most overwhelming in her life until then. It seems to have been mainly at her urging that Wagner at last consented to produce the *Flying Dutchman* with the local forces on the 25th April; he had at first been unwilling to accede to the request of Gustav Schöneck, the able young conductor of the opera company, that he might have the work for his benefit night; and he groaned at the ever-increasing labour that the rehearsals and the superintendence of the production imposed on him. The new director, Löwe, tried to secure a scenic artist from Munich, but the latter was too busy to undertake the task. Löwe then found what Wagner calls " a vagrant scene-painter and machinist " from Hamburg — one Ludwig Caësmann — who, though working under the composer's directions, seems to have performed his task only moderately well; Wagner, at any rate, could not recommend the scenery to Liszt for the production that was being contemplated in Weimar. The orchestra was augmented for the occasion, but part of the expense of this was borne by Wagner, who had to pay for the ten-days' sojourn in Zürich of musicians from Aarau, Burgdorf, and Donaueschingen, besides compensating the director for the necessary closing of the theatre for a final scenery rehearsal on the night before the first performance! Frau Rauch-Werner was the Senta, Pichon the Dutchman, and Benno Fischer (a nephew of Wagner's old Dresden friend) the Daland; under Wagner's inspired coaching they obtained results that gave him more satisfaction, in some ways, than the Dresden production had done. Four performances, all of them conducted by him, were given, on the 25th, 28th, and 30th April and the 2nd May, all at raised prices and to full houses: Löwe regretted being under engagement to take his company to Geneva on the 4th May, as he saw the possibility of yet another four or five performances in Zürich. It was on this occasion that Wagner toned down the orchestration of the *Flying Dutchman,* which in its original form had been too brazen, and changed the ending of the overture. (It appears from a letter of Wagner's to Uhlig that he had already revised the orchestration in a score he had sent to the Leipzig theatre director in 1846: but although the projected performance did not take place, and consequently no fee was paid to Wagner, the score was never returned to Dresden).

5

He concerned himself no more with the Zürich theatre until 1855; but meanwhile he had been active also in the concert life of the town. On the 15th January, 1850, before he set out on his fruitless journey to Paris, he had conducted a concert of the Allgemeine Musikgesellschaft, the regular conductor of which was Abt. With a scratch orchestra consisting only of some thirty professional players and a few amateurs he gave a performance of Beethoven's Seventh Symphony that astonished the Zürichers, who had never before heard Beethoven's music nuanced so delicately or filled with such fire.[18]

Zürich was naturally anxious to learn what it could of the music of the distinguished composer and interesting political refugee from Dresden; and Abt, at first, showed no hostility to Wagner. On the 20th November, 1849, at a concert for the benefit of Alexander Müller, Abt had included in the programme the duet from the

---

[18] The complete programme is interesting as showing the general standard of musical taste in the average small town of the period, and the type of mind on which Wagner had to force his reforms:

(1) Overture to *William Tell.*
(2) Cavatina from Verdi's *Attila.*
(3) Two songs by Kücken.
(4) Introduction and Variations for guitar, by Vois.
(5) Aria from *Figaro.*
(6) Beethoven No. 7.
(7) Songs by Ciccarelli and Malibran.
(8) Adagio and Polonaise for horn, by Körnlein.
(9) Duet for two sopranos from Donizetti's *Maria Padilla.*

Wagner, of course, conducted only the symphony.

The Donizetti duet was sung by Fräulein Luise Corrodi and Fräulein Josephine Morra. The former of these young ladies survived Wagner by some seventeen years, dying, at the age of eighty, in 1900 or 1901.

second act of the *Flying Dutchman,* and, with the best intentions, a Fantasia (by Müller) for clarinet and piano on themes from *Tannhäuser.* At a concert for his own benefit on the 27th January, 1850, he gave the Sailors' Chorus from the *Flying Dutchman;* and he was interested enough in Wagner to attend the first performance of *Lohengrin,* at Weimar, in August of that year. But the coming of Wagner to the town was bound to be fatal before long to a conductor of the calibre of Abt. Even Zürich felt there was something lacking in him, as is shown by the fact that after the concert of the 20th November, 1849, his reading of a Haydn Symphony was criticised by the *Eidgenössische Zeitung* as having been " too slow, and faulty in ensemble "; while a few days later the committee of the Music Society passed a resolution expressing its dissatisfaction with him, and adjuring him in future to be " somewhat more stringent in his conducting." [19] As Wagner, presumably, was present at this concert, and as the *Eidgenössische Zeitung* was the organ of his friend Spyri, it seems not improbable that this sudden awakening of the critical spirit where Abt was concerned was the result of some remarks by Wagner. Abt was so disturbed at the increase in the attendance whenever Wagner conducted that he threatened to resign his post: but when the committee showed signs of accepting the resignation he thought better of it. He remained in Zürich for more than two years after Wagner began his activities there.

To talk of any " rivalry " between the two men is of course absurd: Abt was never of sufficient stature even to bring him into consideration as a " rival " where a Wagner was concerned. The latter merely went his own way, and after his performance of the Seventh Symphony it was not his fault if orchestra, committee, and public alike began to be acutely conscious of the shortcomings of Abt as a conductor. But the Wagner-Abt case inevitably became one of local musical politics: there has never been a bad conductor yet, in any town, who has not had a circle of admirers who resented the coming of a better conductor, for the simple reasons that he *was* better and was not their man. Abt's cause became that of the various little choral societies with which he was connected: the composer of *When the Swallows homeward fly* was bound to be the darling of

---

[19] FWSZ, pp. 19, 20.

the Philistines. A curiously paradoxical situation soon developed in the local press. These choral societies had been taken under the special protection of the radical journal, the *Neue Zürcher Zeitung*, which might have been counted on, *a priori*, to espouse the cause of the revolutionary refugee from Dresden. On the other hand, the conservative *Eidgenössische Zeitung*, by all the rules of the game, should have looked askance at Wagner. But the editor, Bernhard Spyri, was too much interested, from the first, in Wagner the man and Wagner the artist to care anything about his political record; and so the paper dealt generously and sympathetically with his plans and achievements. The mere fact that the *Eidgenössische* had adopted the newcomer as its own was sufficient to earn him the hostility of the *Neue Zürcher*, for the two papers had always been at daggers drawn with each other. We may conjecture, too, that Wagner's decision to have nothing more to do with practical politics, his studious avoidance of political hotheads, and his openly expressed contempt for their mentality, had not helped to endear him to the radicals of the *Zürcher*. Thus it came about that his work as conductor was ignored by the radical paper virtually from first to last,[20] and, human nature being the charitable thing it is, he was even accused of writing his own commendatory notices in the *Eidgenössische*. Wagner, of course had no desire to occupy either Abt's or anyone else's post: he was concerned simply with getting the best results possible out of the local forces in the great works he was specifically invited to conduct. When Abt left the town, in the third winter after Wagner's arrival, it was not Wagner, but Alexander Müller, who succeeded him as head of the Musical Society,[21] though the latter had formerly invited Wagner to accept the post.

---

[20] Not that it was indifferent to the interests of art when something came along that was really worthy of its high approval. In January, 1853, the local company presented Verdi's *Nabuco*. This was something so much superior to Beethoven and Wagner that the *Neue Zürcher* could not repress its enthusiasm: "Warm thanks to the whole opera company for yesterday's excellent performance of Verdi's opera *Nabucodonosor!* Let us soon have something more in this style! Then, from near and far, all you who want to hear something good, something exquisite in the opera line will come, full of faith, to Zürich!" The lunge, of course, was an indirect one at Wagner.

[21] See FWSZ, pp. 17 ff. Fehr's book (1934) which is based on a good deal of original research in the Swiss journals of the time, is invaluable for our knowledge of Wagner's Zürich period.

6

At the commencement of 1851, after he had severed his connection with the theatre, Wagner took part once more in the concerts of the Society, still refusing, however, to concern himself with anything but the large-scale works — overtures and symphonies, — for which he insisted on improvements in the personnel of the orchestra. Between 1851 and 1855 he officiated at twenty-two of the Music Society's concerts, conducting forty works; the orchestra never seems to have numbered more than about fifty, and was often no more than forty. He had been annoyed by the senseless practice, still prevalent in our concert halls, of following up a great work with some paltry vocal solo: even Zürich seems to have been stirred to protest when Fräulein Morra, at the concert of the 15th January, 1850, had burst into Malibran's *Rataplan* a minute or two after the strains of the Beethoven No. 7 had died away. After the third of the concerts in which he took part, Wagner insisted on the symphony either occupying the whole of the second half of the programme or at all events being the final item; while the doors were closed during the performance of the last movement.

On the 28th January, 1851, he gave the Beethoven C minor Symphony and the *Euryanthe* Overture; on the 25th February the overture to Spontini's *Vestale* and the Eroica, while Bülow made a sensation with a piano performance of Liszt's transcription of the *Tannhäuser* overture. On the 18th March, at the orchestra's benefit concert, Wagner conducted the Beethoven No. 7; [22] on the 20th January, 1852, the Beethoven No. 8 and the whole of the *Egmont* music; on the 17th February the Beethoven No. 5 and the *Coriolan* Overture; on the 16th March, at Herwegh's urgent request, the *Tannhäuser* overture (with an exceptional orchestra of fifty-two) and the Pastoral Symphony. On this occasion the committee had the orchestra reinforced by capable players from various other towns, so that Wagner had under him some twenty violins, six violas, and five 'cellos; to meet the extra expense the charges for

---

[22] The biographers are in error when they say that at this concert he conducted also the *Jubel* overture of Weber: the bill makes it clear that he took charge of the orchestra only in the symphony. The minor pieces in the programme were conducted by Abt.

admission were raised. Frau Wesendonk, who was present at the rehearsals, has left her testimony as to the care Wagner took to explain the overture to the bandsmen, and the electrifying effect of his personality on them; while the music critic of the *Eidgenössische Zeitung* recorded the encouraging fact that after the concert performance " everyone was convinced that Wagner was not only a distinguished conductor but also an eminent composer." The enthusiasm was immense; indeed, the stunned critic added, " nothing but a glance at the orchestra, prostrated by its great exertions, could prevent the overture from being played all through again." Even Wagner was forced to admit, in a letter to Uhlig, that the effect was " terrific "; the women especially were " turned inside out " and had to find relief for their emotion in " sobs and weeping." It is worth noting that he now realised that the proper place for the *Tannhäuser* overture is in the concert room: operatic conductors may be interested to learn that in the theatre Wagner now proposed to play only " the first tempo of the overture " — i.e. the andante statement of the Pilgrims' Chorus: " the remainder — in the fortunate event of its being understood — is, as a prelude to the drama, too much; in the opposite event, too little."

The first three concerts of the following season (1852–3), under Müller, were so poorly attended that on the 8th January the committee had to send a deputation to Wagner to ask him to come to the rescue of the Society. He accordingly conducted the Beethoven No. 7 once more on the 15th February, 1853, and the Eroica on the 8th March: the concert on this latter occasion opened, no doubt to Wagner's amusement, with Alexander Müller's overture *The Refugee.*

By 1853 a general desire had sprung up in the town and neighbourhood to hear more of Wagner himself as a composer. He would not consent to the performance even of the *Flying Dutchman* in the local theatre; but after a guarantee fund had been raised to cover the exceptional expenses,[23] he gave, in May, a kind of Wagner fes-

---

[23] His letter of the 22nd February, 1853, to the committee of the Musical Society is given in FWSZ, pp. 381–2. He tells them that to meet the public wish adequately an orchestra much better than anything to which Zürich has been accustomed will be necessary. Reinforcements must be summoned from outside. (Only fourteen of the local players could be regarded as efficient, and he would need seventy). The concerts are to be given in the theatre, the stage of which is to be reconstructed for the occa-

tival — the first of its genre. A competent orchestra was assembled from near and far, the engagement being for the whole week from Sunday, the 15th May, to Sunday, the 22nd; the players came not only from all parts of Switzerland but from Mainz, Wiesbaden, Stuttgart, Weimar, and Frankfort; apparently some of them gave their services gratis. Half the week was spent in rehearsals: the concerts were given in the theatre on the Wednesday, Friday, and Sunday — the 18th, 20th, and 22nd — the programme being the same on each occasion — from *Rienzi*, the *Friedensmarsch;* from the *Flying Dutchman*, Senta's Ballad (Emilie Heim), the Sailors' Chorus and the overture (described as "The Dutchman's Voyage"!); from *Tannhäuser*, the entry of the guests into the Wartburg, with the chorus, "Freudig begrüssen wir die edle Halle," the orchestral introduction to the third act, with the Pilgrims' Chorus, and the overture (described as "The Venusberg"); from *Lohengrin*, the prelude, the *Männerszene* and Bridal Procession (with an ending especially written for the occasion), and the orchestral prelude to the third act, with the following Bridal Chorus. (Wagner added a few transitional bars after the Chorus, and then repeated the orchestral prelude with a new ending). There was an orchestra of 70, a chorus of 110. He had done what he could to make sure that his listeners should understand his dramatic aims, as well as his music, by reading the poems of the operas to them in the Casino on three evenings.[24] The concerts were such a success that he was asked to duplicate them during the following week, and requests for a repetition of them came in from various towns; but he wisely concluded that their "festival" character would best be preserved

---

sion so as to secure better acoustics. He estimates the total cost of the festival at 6,000 francs: the ordinary prices would need to be revised, so as to bring in, if possible, 2,000 francs a concert. He desires no fee for himself.

On the 16th April the committee writes to him that the appeal for combined subscriptions for the three concerts had so far brought in only 3,600 francs: "and if we estimate the total cost at 7–8,000 francs, it cannot be denied that the outlook is anything but brilliant." Guarantors came forward, at the urging of Otto Wesendonk and Konrad Ott-Imhof, as soon as Wagner gave the committee a positive assurance that the orchestra engaged would be of exceptional quality. A great deal of labour must have fallen upon Wagner's shoulders in connection with the engagement of orchestral players, the arrangements for selling tickets, and so on: and already we see at work the energetic organising genius that was later to call up Bayreuth out of the void.

[24] He had already read the poems on three evenings to an invited audience at the Hôtel Baur au Lac in the preceding March.

by not repeating them. At a final banquet given in his honour on the day after the second concert, following a merry excursion on the Lake in the afternoon, he was deeply affected by the speech of Herr Ott-Imhof, the venerable President of the Musical Society, who impressed on those present the unique significance of these concerts: [25] but probably what gave Wagner most satisfaction of all was having heard, at last, a few pages from the *Lohengrin* that had been completed five years before. Another eight years were to elapse before he could hear and see his work in its entirety (in Vienna).

The expenses of the festival exceeded the receipts by 1,190 francs: this small loss was borne by eight or nine guarantors; among them were Otto Wesendonk, Sulzer, Ott-Imhof and Ott-Usteri. There is no truth in the story, circulated by some writers,[26] that " Wesendonk paid the major portion of the costs, which amounted to 9,000 francs."

7

These festival concerts had repercussions not only in Switzerland but abroad. German visitors to Zürich returned home with glowing accounts of what they had heard; the German press found the concerts good " copy ", both before and after the event. The exile's star was steadily rising. Even the inimical *Neue Zürcher Zeitung* had to admit that " such an assembly of art-masters is a rarity in itself, something that only an artist like Richard Wagner could have brought about "; while the *Eidgenössische* trumped this with " We too [as well as the Residenz towns of Germany] have a king in our midst." The *Zürcher*, however, was plainly perturbed at the enthusiasm evoked by a man to whom it had behaved so churlishly

---

[25] Wagner's speech in reply was thus reported in the Augsburg *Allgemeine Zeitung* of the 24th May: "Wagner, in simple but heartfelt words, told them what was the goal of his endeavours — not fame, not riches, not a brilliant position in the world, but to express his feelings warmly and truly, to bring home to the heart, in word and tone, his visions of what was noble, pure, and godlike, so that his hearers should feel with him and be blessed in love." See FWSZ, pp. 229, 230.

From a recently published letter of Wagner's it appears that he himself bore the cost of the dinner for the orchestra. The singers were to pay for their own food; Wagner asked Ott-Imhof to arrange that the *couvert* should not be more than $1\frac{1}{2}$ francs. See FWSZ, p. 394.

[26] See, for instance, BRWB, p. 18.

in the past: it felt it its duty, after the second concert, to give this
" distinguished man ", this " Orpheus ", the solemn advice to " beware of his friends, who damage him more than they benefit him by
their excessive homage."

The third concert had taken place on his fortieth birthday, the
22nd May; and not only his friends but the public seized the opportunity to demonstrate their love and admiration for him. Before
the concert began, one of Otto Wesendonk's servants went from
box to box distributing flowers. At the end, bouquets were rained
on the stage; a singer stepped forward and recited a poem in Wagner's honour; " the most beautiful of the ladies " presented him
with a laurel wreath, which, however, the Press reporter informs
us, " the modest Master declined to have placed on his head ";
another lady handed him a silver goblet in the name of the feminine
portion of the choir. The poem seems, from internal evidence, to
have been the work of Mathilde Wesendonk. It was preserved
among the papers of Emilie Heim, and has recently been reprinted
by Max Fehr.[27]

On the 13th July the choral and orchestral musicians of the town
assembled in the Zeltweg for a torchlight serenade to Wagner: a
song of Baumgartner's and the Sailors' Chorus from the *Flying
Dutchman* were sung, and a speech was made. Wagner, in his reply,
thanked Zürich for the kindness it had always shown him, and,
according to the newspaper report, " promised he would soon surprise the public with something extraordinary, unprecedented."
That the little town had been able to rise to such an effort as that
of the preceding May seems to have given him, for the moment,
the pleasing illusion that he could summon it to ascend with him
to still greater heights. This illusion did not last long, however. But
a few, at any rate, of the more intelligent inhabitants of Zürich
had realised by this time the potential importance of Wagner to
the musical life of the town; and another effort was now made to
organise this more rationally. As early as January, 1850, he had
tried to induce the leading men of the place to co-operate with him
in a comprehensive scheme for the provision of a better orchestra.
He had renewed his efforts in the autumn of that year, and in the

[27] FWSZ, pp. 231–233.

summer of 1851 he had published his appeal for the rationalisation of the Zürich theatre. All his work on these lines, however, had been in vain: his Zürich friends were willing enough to do what they could to improve the orchestra for this or that special concert under Wagner's baton; but a far-reaching plan for the future seemed to have no attraction for them. Wagner and Ott-Imhof had evidently had a conversation on the subject at the banquet that took place on the 21st May, 1853, for on the 24th June we find Wagner sending Ott-Imhof (from Interlaken, where he had gone for a brief holiday) his promised plan for the reorganisation of the concerts. A draft of this is in the Burrell Collection,[28] and so, for the present, inaccessible to enquirers. But in the archives of the Musical Society there is a minute to the effect that the committee had considered Wagner's scheme for nine concerts under himself between October and May of the following winter: " as, however, no satisfactory way can be found for raising the necessary funds, the undertaking was not proceeded with." [29] From the information we possess on this subject we may probably take it that, as usual, Wagner's plan was too rational to be adopted. As a practical man, he saw that Zürich was too small a town to run an adequate opera and an adequate series of concerts in complete independence of each other. The first thing to be done was to form a permanent orchestra that would in time become an artistic ensemble, instead of a fresh set of players being engaged for each season: the next was to solve simultaneously the artistic and the financial problem by using the same orchestra for both the concerts and the opera. But in the first place there were too many divergent local interests for a scheme of this intelligent kind to be adopted, and in the second, as Wagner tells us in *Mein Leben,* what the people responsible for music in Zürich really wanted him to do was to become the permanent musical director and conductor of the reorganised theatre. To this, of course, he would not consent, partly because he was firmly resolved never to tie himself to any theatre again, partly because he needed all his strength now to realise the colossal *Ring* in music.

---

[28] CBC, No. 337. It consists of three closely written pages, suggesting "the establishment of a permanent orchestra by the [Musical] Society, which is to be placed at the disposal of the theatre."

[29] FWSZ, p. 239.

The plan that Wagner had worked out with such care therefore came to nothing. The loser was not he but Zürich; the centre of music in Switzerland soon became not Zürich but the smaller town of Winterthur. Zürich did not create for itself a permanent orchestra until 1862; until that time it carried on from hand to mouth in the old style, changing its orchestra and its theatre management from season to season. A small group of musicians in Winterthur, among them Kirchner and Friedrich Hegar, supported by the publisher Rieter-Biedermann, steadily fostered the musical life of the town in the 1850's according to their lights, cultivating Mendelssohn, Spohr and Schumann as a counterpoise to the growing vogue elsewhere of Wagner; and the result was that from the time when Hegar began, in 1863, his forty years' service as conductor of the Zürich Musical Society's concerts, the town lost the " modern " direction that Wagner had given it for a while. Several of the people who now took music under their care in Zürich, including Brahms's future friend the surgeon Billroth and the art-historian Lübke, were irreconcilably anti-Wagnerian.[30]

In spite of the rejection of his schemes for the better organisation of music in Zürich, Wagner was still willing to do what he could to help the Musical Society. In the winter of 1853–4 it gave six subscription concerts, at all of which he assisted. The committee fell in with his wish that a good bassoonist should be specially engaged, and apparently by this time the concert organisation and the theatre had been driven by force of circumstances to work together to some extent, to the consequent improvement of the orchestra in general. The concerts, of course, were under the general direction of Müller: Wagner conducted, as a rule, only the second half. His contributions were: 29th November, Beethoven No. 5; 13th December, a Haydn symphony in D minor, the *Egmont* overture, and an *Egmont* entr'acte; 27th December, Beethoven No. 4 and the scene of the Messengers of Peace, with the March, from *Rienzi*; on the 17th January, Beethoven No. 8 and the *Euryanthe* overture; on the 14th February, the Jupiter symphony and the *Fidelio* overture; on the 7th March, Beethoven No. 6 and the overture to *Iphigenia in Aulis*, while at an extra concert for Müller's

---

[30] See BBBW, pp. 14 ff.

benefit, on the 21st February, he conducted the *Freischütz* overture and the fifth piano concerto of Beethoven, Müller being the soloist in the latter.

It was for the concert of the 7th March that Wagner wrote, for the *Iphigenia* overture, the ending that is now in general use for concert performances of the work. Sulzer had expressed the ardent desire to hear some Gluck. A whole Gluck opera, of course, was impossible in the Zürich theatre as it then was, and Wagner could not bring himself, as he says, to give one of the works in concert form, with Iphigenia, for instance, in her best party frock and Orestes in evening dress with white kid gloves. The most he could do to oblige Sulzer was to play the *Iphigenia in Aulis* overture. The score and parts of Mozart's arrangement of this were accordingly obtained from Winterthur. A single rehearsal, however, convinced Wagner that Mozart's concert ending would not do; [31] it was based on a misunderstanding of Gluck's tempo, which in turn came from a misunderstanding of the composer's dramatic purpose in the overture.

Wagner set forth the reasons for this opinion of his in a letter to Brendel that was published in the Leipzig *Neue Zeitschrift* of the 1st July, 1854. Conductors, through lack of insight into Gluck's intentions, had come to regard the *Iphigenia* overture as being cast in the conventional form of a short introduction in slow time followed by a long allegro; and not noticing the change to a quicker tempo *already implied in the notes themselves* of the second section, they trumped this with an "allegro" of their own, the result of it all being that this section, constituting the bulk of the overture, was invariably played *twice* as fast as it should be. Wagner, who had always suspected, on dramatic grounds, that there was something wrong with the way the German Kapellmeisters took the overture, had at last got to the truth of the matter when, in the course of preparing the opera for the Dresden production of 1847, he put aside Spontini's much-manipulated score, which the management had borrowed from Berlin, and obtained a copy of Gluck's original Paris score. This technical point, however, having been satisfactorily

---

[31] As Gluck has written it, the overture merges into the opening scene of the drama.

settled in his own mind in Dresden, did not of itself solve the problem of a close to the overture for concert purposes in Zürich. A conventional close, on the lines of " pure " musical form, would do violence to Gluck's dramatic conception. As he has written it, the overture, says Wagner, consists of (1) a motive of Appeal (the melody sung by Agamemnon as the curtain goes up), (2) a motive of Imperious Power, (3) a motive of Maidenly Grace and Tenderness, (4) a motive of Sorrowing Pity. After ensuring that these motives shall speak as Gluck meant them to speak — above all in the right tempi — Wagner's concern was to round off the overture for concert purposes by means of an added thirty-one bars based on Gluck's material.[32] His arrangement is the one always used to-day for concert performances of the overture.

His concert work for this winter was still not ended when he had conducted the last of the concerts he had officially undertaken. At a performance of *Uncle Tom's Cabin* in Baden, in the Aargau canton, the theatre director Löwe had received an accidental shot in the arm, from the effects of which he died ten days later, on the 16th August, 1853. His widow tried to manage the theatre during the following winter season, but found she lacked the necessary experience; on the following 31st January she was compelled to dismiss the company. The grievous condition of the players and musicians, thus deprived of their scanty living in the middle of the winter, evoked much sympathy in the town. The actors in the spoken plays carried on as best they could for a while on sharing terms. Wagner, who was always sensitive to the sufferings of others, and who knew better than most people how hard was the lot of the average orchestral player in those days, of his own accord offered to take charge of the opera if the shareholders of the theatre would comply with

---

[32] The original Zürich parts of the score containing Wagner's ending were discovered by Max Fehr in 1932. It seems that they contain five bars more than the published arrangement from which performances are now given, the unison motive of Power being introduced again immediately before the end; it is probable that Wagner, on further reflection, cut out these five bars in the interval between the first performance, on the 7th March, and the repeat at the benefit concert for the Zürich oboist, Fries. Wagner's extraordinarily fine shading of Gluck's own music, of which he gives a specimen in his article in the *Neue Zeitschrift*, and which, he says, he taught the Zürich orchestra, does not appear in the Gluck-Wagner score of the overture as published, nor is there any hint of it in the parts discovered by Fehr: the inference is that these nuances were communicated verbally and by example at the rehearsals.

certain conditions the nature of which does not appear from the minute of the committee relating to the matter.

There had gradually grown up a malicious legend in the town that he merely wanted to get the Zürich theatre into his own hands for the realisation of his own ends. This imputation is certainly false: Wagner had no desire whatever to burden himself permanently with theatre duties, while the Zürich opera as it then was, or was likely to become, would have been grossly inadequate to the production of the *Ring*. But misrepresentations of this kind did not deter him in the least from offering his services to the opera musicians and chorus in their distress; and a concert conducted by him was always the surest means of filling the house. He had hoped to arrange for a performance of the Ninth Symphony, but the necessary support for this scheme not being forthcoming he had to abandon it. In its place he offered his services for a benefit concert for the orchestra: this took place on the 21st March, 1854, Wagner conducting the *Iphigenia in Aulis* overture, the *Tannhäuser* overture, and the seventh symphony of Beethoven, Müller taking command in a couple of arias and a violin concerto. Nine days later a second concert, this time for the benefit of the theatre personnel, was given: Wagner conducted the whole of this, the programme consisting of the *Egmont* overture, Beethoven's eighth symphony and fifth piano concerto, the " Entry of the Guests into the Wartburg " and the March from *Tannhäuser*, and songs by Emilie Heim and a member of the theatre company, Franz Orth. The prices were raised for each concert: the first resulted in a profit of 609 francs, the second in a further profit of 695 francs. Wagner, who was in financial difficulties enough of his own at this time, paid for tickets for Minna and Natalie. He seems to have received no public recognition of his services; but the humble Swiss musicians whom he had befriended in their hour of need never forgot his kindness.

For the season of 1854–5 he conducted for the Musical Society the Eroica (9th January), the *Magic Flute* overture, the Beethoven No. 5, and his own *Faust Overture* in its remodelled form [33] (23rd

---

[33] It had been written in 1840, in Paris, as the first movement of a projected symphony. Liszt, who gave the overture in Weimar in 1852, urged him to expand it by the introduction of a tender subject descriptive of Gretchen. Wagner could not do this without a fundamental recasting of the work and the destruction of its organic

January), Beethoven's septet (30th January), the Beethoven No. 7 and the *Freischütz* overture (6th February). On the 20th February, just before his departure for London, he took charge of the entire concert, the programme consisting of the *Iphigenia in Aulis* overture, the *Faust Overture*, the *Lohengrin* prelude and Elsa's bridal procession, and the *Tannhäuser* overture. This was destined to be his last concert in Zürich.

8

In the November of 1854 he had allowed himself to be persuaded by the new theatre director, Walther — " an extremely obtrusive person ", as he calls him in *Mein Leben* — to consent to a production of *Tannhäuser*, on the grounds that as every German theatre had now given the work, it would be unfair to deprive the Zürich public of the pleasure of hearing it. Minna added her pesterings to those of Walther: she had apparently taken under her protection the tenor of the company, who wished to distinguish himself as Tannhäuser. The results of Wagner's rash compliance were precisely what might have been expected: he was dragged deeper and deeper into the business of the coaching of the singers, the supervision of the settings, and the superintendance of the rehearsals, all to his own annoyance but to Walther's profit. The wily director having prevailed upon the theatre committee to make him a grant towards his extra expenses in the matter, one or two new settings were ordered; certain existing settings were refurbished for the present purpose, a stalactite cave, for instance, being metamorphosed into Venus's grotto. The scene-painter's bill of costs is interesting, as throwing a light on the ways and the standards of the average small theatre of the period:

The Venus grotto background with transparency .	Fr.	55
Arch for this	"	12
13 rock pieces @ 3 fr., the Wartburg . . .	"	18

---

musical and psychological being: it was intended to portray Faust alone — "Faust in Solitude", Gretchen having been reserved for the second movement of the symphony. It was not until January, 1855, that he found either the will or the time to re-model the overture. "I have made a completely new score", he tells Liszt, "radically revised the orchestration, altered many things, and given the middle section more extension (the second subject) and significance."

Sky, transparent	"	15
Re-painting the horizon	"	15
The Hörselberg landscape	"	20
An image of the Virgin, 8 fr., 2 tiger skins, 3 fr. .	"	11
A throne with cover and background . . .	"	10 [34]

The Tannhäuser was Stephen Ressler, who, under Wagner's tuition, appears to have surpassed himself: as the *Eidgenössische Zeitung* drily remarked in its notice, " he seems to have become quite a different man since he went to the Hörselberg." For the first three performances the Venus was Katharina Hoffmann, the wife of the Frankfort theatre director Johann Hoffmann: this " guest " having withdrawn when Wagner departed for London, the remaining Venuses were sung by Frau Widmann. The Elisabeth was Maria Jungwirth, a young lady upon whose achievements Wagner looked back with amused irony in later years: having been accustomed to taking soubrette parts, she played Elisabeth in white kid gloves, dangling a fan most of the time. Wagner is in error when he says, in *Mein Leben*, that he conducted the first performance. This and the second were under the direction of the theatre Kapellmeister, Louis Müller: Wagner watched these two performances from a box, in company with Herwegh and his wife and other friends. Six performances in all were given — on the 16th, 19th, and 23rd February and the 2nd, 4th, and 19th March, 1855. Wagner, apparently to please Frau Wesendonk, conducted that of the 23rd February: the later ones he did not see, as he left Zürich on the 25th. In spite of the Elisabeth, with her gloves and her fan, he seems to have been quite pleased with the production as a whole, as is evident from his letter of the 17th February to Frau Ritter, in which he expresses his astonishment at what he has been able to achieve with these mediocre singers — an experience which, he says, gives him hope that some day the *Ring* will prove possible.

According to his own account in *Mein Leben*, he had now " really had enough of these concessions "; and in his speech after the third performance he told the audience very frankly that it was the last time they would induce him to participate in anything of this kind, and that in future they must do something drastic for the local

---

[34] See FWSZ, p. 340.

theatre, of the unsatisfactory condition of which they had just had a demonstration: " at which ", he says, " they were all very astonished." This seems, however, to be another of the many instances in which his memory misled him slightly in later life: according to the report in the *Neue Zürcher Zeitung* the next day, he spoke some words of farewell, promising to return from London: " if the public had received only a faint idea of his work, he was prepared to do everything if Zürich would also play its part. Honour to the Master! "

All six performances were received with the greatest enthusiasm by the public, and, in the main, by the Press. But the comments of one section of the latter show clearly that this revelation, at last, of the real Wagner had warned the supporters of opera routine, in Zürich as in Germany, that danger threatened them and their idols.

CHAPTER IX

LISZT, WAGNER, AND "LOHENGRIN"

1

No one in Europe, about 1850, was conscious of the new Wagner that was silently maturing; but the stage was already being set for a new scene in which the old Wagner was to play the leading part. Liszt had not only given the first performances of *Tannhäuser* outside Dresden: he had been so impressed by the work that in March, 1849, he had written a long article upon it, which appeared in the Paris *Journal des Débats* of the 18th May — the very day on which Wagner, on his flight south from Dresden, had attended a rehearsal of his opera in Weimar. The choice of journal and of town for Liszt's article is not without its significance. That choice can be explained, in part, by the fact that Liszt was at home in no language but French. But there was more in it than that. Liszt, like everyone else at that time, looked upon Paris as the centre of the operatic world, as is shown, incidentally, by his persistent pushing of Wagner towards the French capital in 1850. He had as yet a very imperfect perception of the profoundly German nature of Wagner's art, and did not know that Wagner had already vowed himself to a war on opera as the term was then understood. He knew, of course, nothing whatever at that time of either the music or the text of *Lohengrin;* and neither he nor the pious Princess Wittgenstein had been at all impressed by Wagner's eager outlining of his *Jesus von Nazareth* subject to them during his few days' stay in Weimar in May, 1849. For Liszt in 1848 and 1849, as for everyone else, the composer of *Tannhäuser* was just one operatic craftsman among others, though with a style of his own, a power of his own, and a boldly speculative cast of mind of his own. It therefore seemed as natural to Liszt that Wagner, as an " opera composer ", should look to Paris for a " success " as that Rossini and Meyerbeer should do so. Berlioz, too, evidently regarded Wagner as simply one of the large crowd of German opera composers of the epoch; for though, in his capacity as musical critic of the *Débats*, he kindly introduced his friend Liszt's article with a few lines of his own, he could find nothing more vital to say about Wagner than that he was " a distinguished poet and composer and an expert conductor " who " to-day occupies a brilliant position by the side of Reissiger." Berlioz at that time knew next to nothing of Wagner's work. He had, it is true, heard the *Flying Dutchman* and the last three acts of *Rienzi* in Dresden in 1843, but as he understood scarcely a word of German he was hardly in a position to judge these works very intelligently. With the *Tannhäuser* score he had no acquaintance at all; and it is evident that he was not even aware that *Rienzi* had preceded, not followed, the *Flying Dutchman*. It would have astonished him had he been told that in a few years this raw young German, as he then considered him, would become the leading figure on the European operatic stage.

In a passage in the *Débats* article that was omitted from the subsequent issue of it as a booklet in Leipzig, Liszt drew his readers' attention to the " marvellous instrumentation " of *Tannhäuser*, the " learned and harmonious use of the violins, the flutes, the harps, the trombones, etc., etc.," " the various colours so felicitously applied to the various movements of the drama." He hoped it would not be long before the German theatres took the work into their repertory, and he urged the Paris Conservatoire to give at one of its concerts " the gigantic overture, that contains so much magnificence, so many extraordinary beauties." For the rest, the article, in its original form, consisted simply of an account of the story of the opera, with a final paragraph on the overture — that is to say, pages 117–31 of the *Lohengrin et Tannhäuser* brochure published in 1851, in which year Liszt added to the article another fifty-odd pages of detailed discussion of the overture and of the music of the work in general.

An interesting question arises in connection with this article of Liszt's. How much did he really understand in 1849 — or, indeed, at any time — of the real and total Wagner? Not much, one suspects. We have his own confession, in a letter of the 1st March, 1851, that he had not been able to follow Wagner's reasoning in *Art and Revolution;* and presumably the same is true with regard to *The Art-Work of the Future*. He expresses the hope that he will be more successful with *Opera and Drama*; this, however, was not published until after the brochure *Lohengrin et Tannhäuser de Richard Wagner* had been issued. But long before that time Liszt had produced *Lohengrin* in Weimar, and so had acquired considerable fresh insight into Wagner as a musician; while their correspondence must have given him some small notion of the new ideals towards which Wagner was feeling his way. But on the whole we are driven to the conclusion that neither now nor at any later date was Liszt able to penetrate understandingly, or even sympathetically, into the speculative depths of Wagner's mind. It was his music, in the main, that fascinated Liszt, and that, perhaps, in part, because it fed the stream of his own purpose in instrumental music — to marry a new orchestral form to a poetic subject. It is significant that even in the brochure of 1851 he applies to the *Tannhäuser* overture the title — " symphonic poem " — of the new form he was himself projecting at this time. It is very doubtful whether Wagner could have been quite pleased at Liszt's assuring his readers that a knowledge of the opera was not essential for the understanding of the overture. There is a good deal of self-contradiction in the pages of the expanded article of 1851, indicative of a certain amount of confusion in Liszt's mind. At one point he says that Wagner's opera calls for an audience of a special kind, an audience that will not merely listen to it as music but will grasp the relation of the music to the drama by following a performance with the text-book in their hands — a curious side-light on the customs of the epoch! Wagner, with his ideal of music, poetry and visible action all co-operating to the one end in the theatre, could hardly feel, when he read this, that Liszt had understood him through and through. At another point, however, Liszt says it is not necessary for the listener to the overture to know the relation of the themes to the words and scenes with which they are associated in the opera itself. In proof of this extraordinary thesis he cites his own experience in Weimar, where, he says, the overture, when it was performed before the whole work was as yet known, created the utmost enthusiasm although neither the players nor the public had the least knowledge of the opera, or even of the subject. Here again Wagner probably raised his eyebrows in mild astonishment.

It looks as if it was the overture that had specially attracted Liszt, and that because it seemed to him to prove conclusively the possibility of the symphonic poem. It would be impossible to imagine, he says, any symphonic poem that would conform more fully than the *Tannhäuser* overture to the rules of classical form, or have " a more perfect logic in the exposition, the development, and the *dénouement* of the propositions." It is a poem, he adds, " on the same subject as the opera, but as complete as that: with the same ideas, Wagner has created two different works, each of them being intelligible, perfect, and independent of the other." How a symphonic poem can be fully understood without a knowledge of the characters and the action it describes Liszt does not pause to tell us; and that he should imagine the *Tannhäuser* overture to stand in no need, for its perfect comprehension, of a knowledge of the opera points to a strange confusion in his mind. The truth seems to be that he was predisposed to insist on the self-logic and self-subsistence of the overture as a " symphonic poem " because he found in it a valuable support for the theories to which he himself was just then trying to give practical expression in his own works in the genre.

2

The outward relations of Wagner and Liszt during the earlier years of their acquaintance are clear enough from the records; but the inner psychological threads are less easy to trace. In spite of all Liszt's kindness to Wagner, and in spite of all Wagner's grateful recognition of it, there was something in the nature of each of the two men that never quite commended itself to the other: Wagner in particular was sometimes painfully conscious that certain of his own idiosyncrasies, especially his ebullient humour, found no response in " the starched gentleman ", as Lehmann's Italian servant used to call Liszt in later years. Whether Liszt had or had not been impressed by *Rienzi* when he heard it in Dresden in February, 1844, it was obviously out of his power to do anything practical for Wagner for some time after that, as he did not seriously commence his duties in Weimar until four years later; and at first he would naturally be anxious to develop some technique as a conductor before embarking on anything more ambitious than works of the

Martha type. During all those years there is no evidence that he took any special interest in Wagner, or regarded him as of any outstanding importance until *Tannhäuser* began to be talked about. Apparently he had no knowledge whatever of the *Flying Dutchman* on the stage. In August, 1848, shortly after he had asked Liszt to buy the rights in his Meser scores, Wagner spent a few days with him in Weimar, and seemingly it was only at this time that the two men really drew near to each other: no doubt Wagner's ardent talk about himself, his woes and his ideals — the conversation was certain to have been mainly on that subject! — made Liszt conscious of the unusual quality of his personality and his intellect. Shortly after his return from Weimar, Wagner hoped that Liszt would come to Dresden to see a performance of *Tannhäuser;* but this proving impossible, the Princess went as his deputy, perhaps to be able to report upon the scenic problems of the work before the decision to give it in Weimar was finally taken. It must be remembered, then, that Liszt had not seen *Tannhäuser* on the stage before he produced it himself in February, 1849; and as the tiny Weimar orchestra must have been almost completely out of its depth in such a score, and Liszt was not at that time — if, indeed, he ever was — a first-rate conductor,[1] the probability is that the performances, apart

---

[1] In October, 1853, Ferdinand Hiller criticised sharply Liszt's conducting at the Carlsruhe Festival, at the conclusion of which, says Hiller, "the unanimous opinion was that he is not fit to wield the baton, at any rate in music on a large scale. It is not merely that, in general, he does not mark the beat (in the simplest sense of the term, the way established by the greatest masters), but that by his baroque animation he continually, and sometimes dangerously, causes the orchestra to vacillate. He does nothing but keep changing the baton from one hand to another — sometimes, indeed, laying it down altogether — giving signals in the air with this or that hand, or on occasion with both, having previously told the orchestra 'not to keep too strictly to the beat' (his own words at a rehearsal). Is it any wonder, then, that *not a single work* went with real precision? . . . Is it any wonder that . . . such gross errors are made as in the finale of the Ninth Symphony, where Liszt, apprehensive — and with reason — that a complete breakdown was imminent, had to give the orchestra the signal to stop and commence the movement again from the beginning?" Hiller further accuses him of having failed to give the necessary leads to orchestra, soloist and chorus. "I repeat that not only was the time-beating uncertain, nay, sometimes downright inaccurate, but that often it ceased altogether."

This has always been treated by the Liszt apologists as a typical example of the failure of an academic reactionary to appreciate a genius: they lay stress on the fact that nowadays it is not so much the function of a conductor to indicate every entry as to draw an "interpretation" of the work from the orchestra. Liszt himself took this line in his public reply to Hiller — that the works he had to conduct required a new style of rendering, more care in the matter of accentuation, of rhythm, of the phrasing

from Tichatschek, were of the rough-and-tumble order, although Wagner praises Liszt for his *musical* grasp of the work. Liszt's particular interest in the overture is shown by his arranging it for the piano before the end of 1848.

3

As soon as he reached Zürich after his flight from Dresden, Wagner had asked Minna to send his scores, for safety's sake, to Weimar; Liszt was to retain a copy of the *Flying Dutchman,* take a glance at *Lohengrin,* and then send the latter to Wagner in Paris. Liszt could not have found time just then for an intensive study of the score, but he evidently looked through it. A letter of his to Wagner, written about the end of June, 1849, is unfortunately so damaged that the concluding section, in which he speaks of *Lohengrin,* ends almost as soon as it begins: but it is clear that no thought of producing the opera had as yet occurred to him. He fears, he says, that the " super-ideal tone " which Wagner has " maintained throughout " the work will go against it in performance. " You

---

of certain passages, of the spreading of light and shade over the whole. The letter, he reminded his critics, killeth, while the spirit giveth life; and he ended with a phrase that has become historic — "We are not oarsmen, but steersmen." (See LZGS, V, 227–32). True enough: but if the steersman gives commands that are not understood by the oarsmen, or commands that are contradictory, the boat is liable to founder and the cargo be lost. The probability is that while Liszt was often good at making an orchestra phrase with something of the sensitiveness and elasticity that characterised his piano playing, he was not always technically as assured as he might have been. He had taken up conducting relatively late in life; and it is not in the least incredible that in his desire to impress an idea on the players he should sometimes have been erratic in his mere time-beating. It is not disputed that the orchestra at Carlsruhe *did* break down and that the movement had to be begun afresh. That of itself suggests some error on the conductor's part.

Adelheid von Schorn hints at difficulties of the same kind at a rehearsal, at which she was present, of *St. Elizabeth* under Liszt at Eisenach in 1867. She loyally attempts to excuse him, of course: "He was no time-beater, but *an intellectual leader,* who did not merely conduct with his baton but conveyed his wishes with every feature of his face, nay, every movement of his fingers." "We Weimarers", she says, "understood him; but strange orchestras evidently did not." As the orchestra assembled for the Eisenach festival included such highly skilled players as Ferdinand David (Leipzig), Singer (Stuttgart), Leopold Damrosch (Breslau) and Remenyi, the conclusion seems inevitable that it was Liszt who was at fault.

Much the same thing happened again at a performance of *Christus* in Weimar in 1873. Once more Adelheid von Schorn makes the excuse for Liszt that "orchestra and chorus were not used" to a conductor "sometimes laying aside his baton for minutes at a time." There were consequently "critical hesitations." (See SZM, pp. 123, 233).

will think me a tradesman, no doubt, dear friend ", he writes, " but I cannot help it, and my sincere friendship for you perhaps authorises me to tell you that . . ." There the damaged letter tantalisingly breaks off; but it is manifest that not only had Liszt no intention of producing *Lohengrin* but that he was anything but sanguine about its success with the public. On the 9th July Wagner asked for his scores to be sent to Zürich, hoping that a re-reading of them would enable him to get into the mood for taking up musical composition once more. Liszt sent the scores on the 29th: he was reluctant, he said, to part with *Lohengrin*, his enthusiasm for which increased the more he studied it. He adds, however, " But forgive me my miserable faint-heartedness when I say that I still have some misgivings as to the completely satisfactory effect of the work in performance." Wagner, in his reply of the 7th August, admits that he also often has his doubts on this point, but he is convinced that the opera, " including the final scene ", will " go " on the stage if only the production corresponds to the dramatic conception. It is just a matter, he says, of " daring."

But for some reason or other, or perhaps a combination of reasons, Liszt was not inclined to " dare " *Lohengrin* just then, or indeed for a considerable time yet. Reading between the lines of his letters, we have a faint suspicion that he was finding his new friend something of a burden. He had troubles enough of his own, public and private; and we can understand his feeling now and then that Wagner was making too many demands on his time and his energy, to say nothing of his purse. On the other hand, Wagner's persistency of application to Liszt is comprehensible enough. He was in urgent need of money to maintain him while he wrote a new work for the stage; and there were only two ways, apart from out-and-out charity, by which this money could be raised. One was for some theatre to commission *Siegfrieds Tod* and pay him in advance a fee that would keep him alive for six months. The other was for him to find some one who would buy outright the full score of *Lohengrin* and all future performing rights in the work. He puts forward both proposals in his letters to Liszt, for the simple reason that Liszt was the only man he knew in all Europe who had both the will and the power to help him, by reason of his favoured position at the Court of Weimar and his good relations with another petty Court, that of Coburg — for the Grand Duke Ernst of Sachsen-Coburg-Gotha was not only fond of music but dabbled in opera-composition himself.

In connection with the help given to Wagner by Liszt in Weimar there is a curious point that seems to have been overlooked by the biographers of both men. Liszt had heard *Rienzi* in Dresden in February, 1844; according to Wagner's account in *Mein Leben,* as *Rienzi* was not in the repertory at that time Liszt had asked the management to arrange a special performance for him; he met Wagner between the acts in Tichatschek's dressing room and congratulated him in the warmest terms. In March, 1848, Liszt came unexpectedly to Dresden and spent an evening with the Schumanns; it was on this occasion that the famous quarrel occurred between him and Robert, owing to Liszt's praise of Meyerbeer at the expense of Mendelssohn. Wagner was present and has left us his account of the quarrel.[2] Liszt certainly did not hear *Rienzi* again during this fleeting visit.

Lina Ramann, the authorised biographer of Liszt, began collecting the material for her work in 1876. She had not the slightest firsthand knowledge of the earlier Liszt; her information as to the first part of his career was supplied to her by the Princess Wittgenstein and by Liszt himself in the late eighteen-seventies. In her account of Wagner and Liszt in the first stages of their acquaintance the Princess obviously confused the meeting of 1844 with that of 1848 — an error of memory that is easily understandable after an interval of some thirty years; she thought the meeting at Schumanns had taken place on the occasion of Liszt's hearing of *Rienzi* in 1844, which was not the case. Lina Ramann tells us, accordingly, that at the *Rienzi* performance

> "Liszt was tired after a dinner, and the music could not lift him either out of his fatigue or above the impressions of that disagreeable evening [at the Schumanns]. And so he left the opera house with no particular opinion either for or against Wagner as a composer, but with the impression that *Rienzi* had not wholly escaped the influence of Meyerbeer."[3]

---

[2] See Vol. I, p. 494, and, for another account, LCS, I, 394, 395. Litzmann is in error in attributing the episode to June, 1848: Wagner's date — March — is the correct one.

[3] RLKM, III, 52.

We may be certain that, during the quarrel with Schumann, Wagner did not put up a fight for Meyerbeer; but Lina Ramann, repeating what the Princess had told her, makes out that, owing to Liszt's advocacy of Meyerbeer, Wagner became suspicious of Liszt and ill-disposed towards him:

" from that evening ", she says, " dated Wagner's ill-feeling against Liszt, to which he gave free and angry expression to others. In his letter to Liszt asking for the assistance of the influential artist in the matter of the Weber memorial (1845), and again in those concerning his personal affairs (1846–8), there is indeed no hint of this ill-feeling. But on Wagner's own testimony it existed; and Liszt knew it. It estranged him, though it did not affect his willingness to help Wagner." [4]

This throws a new light on the relations of the pair at this time. The confusion of the two dates in the Princess's mind is of no importance. What *is* of importance is the revelation of Liszt's feelings; and on this point the Princess's testimony can probably be accepted. In her later years she was frankly inimical to Wagner, partly on personal grounds, partly because she was jealous of his enormous vogue and of the relative non-success of Liszt as a composer. It is evident, then, that she wanted to place on record, through Lina Ramann, the true story of the relations between Liszt and Wagner in the years preceding 1849; and her disclosure is yet another illustration of the difficulty of constructing an accurate biography of any man. It is impossible to resist the conclusion that, in the main, her story is true, though it loads the dice, perhaps, against Wagner. The latter may well have been deceived by Liszt's cordiality in 1844. Liszt was always effusive to people's faces; and it is quite possible that, having met Wagner by chance in Tichatschek's dressing-room in one of the intervals — it is significant, by the way, that it was there they should have met; Liszt did not go direct to Wagner — what Schumann called " the French man of the world " in Liszt came to the surface, and he praised the work to the composer's face in his usual rather florid style. It is conceivable, also, that Wagner was anything but pleased at Liszt's championship of Meyerbeer in 1848, and that some remarks of his, derogatory to Liszt, had been repeated to the latter. There is cer-

[4] Ibid., III, 53–4.

tainly no hint of a decided friendship between the pair in their letters of that period. We have evidence enough as to two cardinal traits in Liszt's character — his generous refusal to take purely personal matters into consideration where a question of art and of his ability to help an artist were concerned, and his habit of concealing his personal feelings in his correspondence. It is quite possible, then, that until Wagner descended upon him so unexpectedly in Weimar in May, 1849, he was not particularly well-disposed towards him as a man; and if that be so, it is the most convincing tribute to his generosity that he should have accepted so ungrudgingly this new responsibility that had been suddenly thrust upon him. We may conjecture that the conversations he had had with Wagner during the latter's brief visit to Weimar in July, 1848, and those he now had with him after Wagner's flight from Dresden, had shown him that he had to do with a man who, for all his personal faults, was an incorruptible idealist in matters connected with his art; and the perception of this would be sufficient to win Wagner the whole-hearted sympathy of Liszt.

If Liszt's understanding of Wagner, as distinct from his susceptibility to his music, was not very profound, he was at all events anxious to do what he could to lighten the heavy load of Wagner's material cares. Hence his well-meant schemes for him in Paris and in London, in which latter town, he thought, *Lohengrin* might possibly be produced. Hence his plan for giving the *Tannhäuser* overture at the Hamburg musical festival of April, 1850, with a stipulation that a part of the receipts should be allotted to Wagner. Hence his quaint suggestion that Wagner should bring out an album of songs suitable to the taste and the capacity of the average amateur, and that he should re-arrange other Gluck operas for the modern stage on the lines of his adaptation of *Iphigenia in Aulis*. But the one thing Liszt does *not* seem to have contemplated at this time was the production of *Lohengrin* in Weimar. He was no doubt a little scared at the difficulties it presented, and perhaps none too sanguine of its attracting the public, owing in part to the super-ideal atmosphere in which it moved, in part to the lack of a happy ending. He knew also that the raising of the standard of opera in Weimar depended on his own constant presence in the theatre, for when he was away both the repertory and the performances fell back into the old routine; and as he was not actually the Kapellmeister his authority was limited.

4

So nothing was done in connection with *Lohengrin* until Wagner, on the point of setting out for the East with Jessie Laussot, happened to turn over the pages of the unfortunate work in Paris, felt a passionate desire to see it rescued from oblivion, and, on the 21st April, 1850, wrote Liszt a letter in which he told him of the crisis that had arisen in his private life, and made a direct appeal to him to produce *Lohengrin*. " You are the only man ", he said, " to whom I would address this request. To no one but you would I entrust the ' creation ' of this opera; but to you I deliver it unconditionally, joyfully, calmly. Produce it where you will, even if it is only in Weimar." He suggests that Liszt shall obtain from Lüttichau the corrected copy of the score, for which Dresden is not likely to have any use.

The Wagner-Liszt correspondence was given to the world in an incomplete form, because at the time of its publication there were good reasons for reticence on the subject of the Laussot affair. From internal evidence one surmises that Wagner's letter of the 21st April has not been printed in full, while Liszt's reply is missing altogether.[5] We can only conjecture, therefore, what may have happened; it seems probable that Liszt realised the seriousness of the spiritual crisis through which Wagner was passing, and at once sprang to his help. In view of his previous long dubiety as to the effectiveness of the opera, the suddenness of his resolution to produce it in the following August is rather surprising. It is to be explained, in part, by an increase in his enthusiasm for the work after further acquaintance with the score. A new note of cordiality, almost of affection, is noticeable in Liszt's letters from now onwards; he seems to have acquired a new sense both of Wagner's genius and of his own duty towards him. He is willing, he says, to place himself completely at Wagner's service, though, he adds, " a friend like you is not always easy to serve, for those who are capable of

---

[5] As the next letter in the series is that of Wagner, dated the 2nd July, it is possible that more than one letter is either lost or has been suppressed.

understanding you must before all things serve you in an intelligent and dignified way. . . . You can place complete confidence in me, can listen to what I have to say, and can believe me, as one who is frankly devoted to you without any reservation whatever."

There may have been another reason why Liszt so suddenly decided to produce *Lohengrin*. His mind was at this time full of his plan for a Goethe-Stiftung (Goethe Foundation), the essence of which was to be annual competitions in music, poetry, painting and sculpture, the judges to be drawn from all over Germany, and the successful work of each year to be " crowned " and performed, printed, or exhibited under the auspices of the Stiftung.[6] On the 25th August, 1850, a monument to Herder was to be unveiled in Weimar: delegates from all over Germany would be there in order to discuss on the 28th — Goethe's birthday — the scheme for the *Stiftung*. For this purely Germanic gathering, called together for a purely Germanic ideal, nothing, Liszt may have reasoned, could be more appropriate than the most purely Germanic opera that had yet been written; while it would be doing Wagner the greatest possible service to produce the work before this representative gathering of men of culture, who might be trusted to carry the news of it

---

[6] In addition there was to be a musical festival every four years at the Wartburg. The whole conception did more credit to Liszt's idealism than to his sense of practicalities. He set forth his scheme in detail in a brochure published in the early summer of 1851 — *De la Fondation Goethe à Weimar*. Wagner criticised the scheme in a long letter to Liszt, which was afterwards published, on Liszt's suggestion, in the *Neue Zeitschrift für Musik* of the 5th March, 1852. Wagner pointed out that the four classes of artists whom Liszt had in view — poets, non-operatic composers, painters and sculptors — all work under different conditions and stand in different relations with the world. The man of letters, for instance, can reproduce his work indefinitely by means of the printing press, while the painter or sculptor produces a first specimen of his work that is also the only one; it can belong only to one purchaser. The public to which the plastic or pictorial artist can hope to appeal is necessarily a small one, composed of a few well-to-do individuals of superior taste; whereas the concert room and the Press provide a large miscellaneous public for the musician and the literary worker. What is really wanted, says Wagner, is a new Theatre through which the dramatic poet could mould the mind of the nation; for while the other artists and the men of letters can easily provide themselves with the modest materials necessary for *their* creations — marble, canvas, paint, pen, paper, and so on — the dramatic poet can present his creation to others only through a mass of material too big, too complex, and too expensive for any mere individual. The Goethe-Stiftung cannot be expected to go to the root of the matter in this way, says Wagner; all it will succeed in doing will be to found an "art-lottery" with an annual distribution of prizes. The text of his letter will be found in RWGS, Vol. V.

into every quarter of the land. And so the production of *Lohengrin* was hastily decided upon for the 28th August. As that decision was not conveyed to Wagner until the end of June, it is evident that Liszt was tempting Providence when he undertook to carry out his ambitious project in a mere two months.

CHAPTER X

LISZT AND WEIMAR

1

I T HAS always been held, alike by the biographers of Wagner and those of Liszt, that the latter " made " Wagner by his production of *Lohengrin*. Without at all disparaging Liszt's contribution to the Wagnerian cause, it may be permissible to express a doubt whether the extent of it has not been somewhat exaggerated. We have to ask ourselves whether Liszt in himself, or Weimar in itself, was at that time of sufficient importance in German music for their *cachet* to be of any profound significance to Wagner or anyone else.

Liszt had not settled in Weimar with any end in view even remotely resembling that of creating a new German school on his own account or of furthering the general cause of musical " progress ". It is extremely doubtful whether, before the turn of the half-century, he had the least idea that a musical revolution was in the offing. He had gone to Weimar in the first place for purely personal reasons: he was tired of the life of a wandering piano virtuoso, and he wanted to realise his ambitions as a composer of something more than fantasias, transcriptions and small works for the piano. He was as yet far from sure of himself in the larger field; and he particularly needed a place in which he could not only elaborate his orchestral plans in quietness but try out his works in quasi-seclusion before submitting them to the critical judgment of the greater world. Weimar happened to place at his disposal, for a certain number of weeks each year, the orchestral means for the realisation of this end. There is nothing whatever in his correspondence to suggest that, until *Tannhäuser* took so powerful a hold of him in 1848, it had even dimly occurred to him that little Weimar might be made the centre of a movement of regeneration in the musical life of Germany.

Until Wagner struck a new fire from him his musical outlook had been limited and his ambitions purely personal. His programme as regarded Weimar, he had told Madame d'Agoult in 1844, was to help the young Hereditary Duke Carl Alexander in his plans for reviving the glories of the tiny State as they had been in the days of Goethe: once more it was to have " a Court as charming, as brilliant, as attractive as possible," a University (Jena), a theatre and a literature. His own objects were no more than to make a little public music in Weimar, to practise himself on the Court orchestra, and to take a friendly interest in the *dramatic* side of the theatre. A letter of his to Carl Alexander a couple of years or so later shows him still preoccupied with his old plan — destined never to come to anything — for an Italian opera, *Sardanapale:* it is clear that even at this time Weimar was only a place in which he meant to spend a few months of each year according to his contract, conducting a concert or an opera now and then for the Court, exercising himself in composition and more particularly in scoring, and testing the results with the local orchestra. Hitherto his career as a pianist and a social butterfly had not left him with much time for the study of composition in the deeper sense of the term. Everything connected with the piano was second nature to him; but he was far too good a musician not to know that the limited technique of composition that had served him well enough so far would not avail for larger things.

In reply to the letter of 31st August, 1846, to which reference has just been made, Carl Alexander refers to " the various occupations to which you intend to consecrate your time ", and hopes that Weimar will not be omitted from his plans. Liszt, who was concertising in Hungary just then, sets forth in his reply his plans for the future — he will tour Europe for some time still, with the object of making enough money to allow him to say farewell to the piano and the public, to " break his chrysalid of virtuosity " and let his thoughts fly free, and, once he has settled in Weimar for good, pursue the aim that is now all-important to him, that is to say, " to conquer the theatre for my thought, as I have done for the last six years for my personality as an artist." By this he obviously means writing operas of his own: he has *two* Italian operas on the stocks, he now tells the Duke. It is manifest that even yet he had no thought of Weimar ever becoming an important musical centre, and no conception of any higher operatic ideal than the ordinary one of the period. The mere fact that he was writing an Italian opera would rule the work out so far as a first German production was concerned: the heart of the operatic world, for Liszt, was Paris.

2

So little bent was he at this time on inaugurating a new musical culture in Weimar, or even settling in the town for good, that he was hoping to succeed Donizetti as Kapellmeister in the notoriously reactionary Vienna.[1] He had as yet not the remotest notion of the future, or even the present, significance of Richard Wagner in the world of opera, not the remotest notion that the young Dresden Kapellmeister was already on the way to substituting quite new dramatic values for the old ones. In February, 1847, Carl Alexander had expressed the hope that Liszt would not deny him his counsels in whatever pertained to the improvement of the Weimar theatre — this apropos of the engagement of Zigesar as Intendant to succeed von Spiegel, who had just died. In his reply of the 4th June (from Galatz) Liszt discusses his hopes and fears for the Weimar theatre. He has no illusions with regard to it, he says. They are living in the seven lean years; apart from exceptional people like Jenny Lind, Rachel and Rubini there are few performers of any value, though the price of the remainder has gone up owing to the public's appetite having been whetted for " stars ". Not much can be achieved without considerable expense, and modest Weimar is not in the running in that race. As for the local opera, the most urgent reforms and improvements are (1) the engagement of new leading singers, (2) the organisation of a proper chorus, the present one being beneath contempt. In general, plays and operas must be produced with more care, dramas must not be mutilated by the censor because the author's ideas are too advanced, and dramatic royalties should be legally protected: the Duke's aim should be to attract men of literary standing to the town by a progressive policy.

There is still, it will be observed, no hint whatever of Liszt having realised that he had a vital *musical* mission in Weimar.

---

[1] See LZCA, p. 10; NML, p. 106; LZMA, II, 355.

THE WEIMAR THEATRE, IN THE LISZT PERIOD
(*By courtesy of The Richard Wagner Museum, Eisenach*)

In 1847 he became the lover of the rich Russian Princess von Sayn-Wittgenstein. At first he had looked upon the affair as just one more of those agreeable amorous adventures in which his life had been so rich; and we have evidence that he was a little perturbed when he discovered later that the adoring Princess wished the tie to become a permanent one. Unfortunately her husband declined to take any steps towards divorce. Liszt was consequently faced with the same situation that had proved so embarrassing to him in the case of Madame d'Agoult; there were few European circles in which both he and his " mistress " would have been received. In these circumstances, it now turned out, the contact he had already made with Weimar was fortunate: he was a favorite at the Court, the Grand Duke and Duchess were commendably broadminded, and so long as he and Carolyne occupied separate quarters in the town they provoked the minimum of scandal in the quiet little provincial place.[2] The result of it all was that Liszt gradually became tied to provincial Weimar rather more effectually than he had contemplated when he first took the place into his calculations in 1844, though he still had no thought whatever of settling there permanently. In October, 1847, before as yet the Wittgenstein affair had got him fairly in the net, he had assured Carl Alexander that at the commencement of 1848 he would enter seriously upon his duties, such as they were, at Weimar: he would so arrange his affairs in general, he said, that he could spend the first three months of each year in the town. His reasons for the choice of these months are interesting and characteristic: the fête-days of their Royal Highnesses fall in the early days of February, and " the winter, speaking generally, is the best season for amusements of all kinds, including music." [3] He counts on the support of the Duke in the carrying out of his intentions, which are evidently not in the least revolutionary; nor is there the smallest hint, in the young Duke's side of the correspondence, of anything more having been contemplated between them than a general quickening of the intellectual

---

[2] When, later, the prospect of obtaining a divorce from Prince Wittgenstein receded, Carolyne's Russian estates were sequestrated, and she fell under the ban of the Czar, she could no longer be received at the Weimar Court. After a little while she and Liszt took up residence together in the large house known as the Altenburg. For further details see NML, Chapter VI.

[3] LZCA, p. 19.

life of the little town on very much the old lines. Liszt began his career as an opera conductor in Weimar in February, 1848, in the modest way befitting a learner — with Flotow's *Martha*. Even after the Princess joined him there, in April, 1848, and it gradually became clear to him that Weimar would have to be more or less his headquarters for some time, there is no evidence that he took the place at all seriously as a possible operatic centre.

3

The gradual expansion of his views with regard to Weimar seems to date from his acquaintance with *Tannhäuser*, the overture to which he had given in November, 1848, following upon Wagner's visit in the preceding August. The opera itself was produced in Weimar in February, 1849. This was an event of far more importance to Liszt and to Weimar than to Wagner; the tiny town, with its population of about 12,000, its orchestra of thirty-five, its chorus of twenty-three, a solo personnel that included no famous names, and a conductor who was so far known to Germany only as a pianist,[4] was not in a position to confer distinction on any composer by performing his work.

All this while Liszt had been quietly pursuing the real purpose for which he had gone to Weimar in the first place — that of strengthening the weak spots of which he was conscious in his equipment as a composer. Even after the production of *Tannhäuser* he evidently had no idea of being tied to Weimar, for in his letters of the summer of 1849 to Raff we find him expressing a doubt whether he would be spending the following winter there: as the theatre season extended only from October to June, this makes it evident that he did not regard himself as having anything in the nature of a " mission " in Weimar, or even any consistent, continuous plan for developing opera there. He had, however, a scheme in his mind for founding a conservatoire in the town for the training of piano virtuosi — another indication that he was still very much

---

[4] Liszt was only a kind of honorary Kapellmeister in Weimar; the actual Court Kapellmeister was Chélard. Liszt had virtually no official standing in the theatre; as he himself put it bitterly later, when lamenting his impotence to stir the place up, he "had no vote and no veto."

the Liszt of the old days. Everything points to the fact that but for the powerful impact of Wagner's genius upon him between the autumn of 1848 and the summer of 1850, an impact that gradually suggested to him possibilities he had hitherto not dreamed of in connection with Weimar opera, he would have left the place as soon as he felt able to stand on his own feet as a composer and the Wittgenstein imbroglio had straigthened itself out. He was intelligent enough to realise that at present, apart from his genius where the piano was concerned, he was not much more than a gifted amateur in music. For a long time he was dependent first of all upon Conradi, then upon Raff, for the scoring of his orchestral works, as a whole or in part.[5] But there were other fields in which his life until now had left him too little time or inclination to work seriously at technique — especially that of counterpoint. One of his reasons for engaging Raff as his secretary was that he might profit by the assistance and criticism of the younger but more solidly equipped musician.

4

The pair had first met in 1845, when Raff was twenty-three; and Liszt seems to have drawn at once on his younger colleague's technical knowledge. In the autumn of 1847 there was a temporary estrangement between them by reason of what was apparently too plain a piece of speaking on the part of Raff, who was sometimes embarrassingly frank in his judgments of his friends. His letter to Liszt was seemingly destroyed by the latter; but from Liszt's angry reply to it it is clear that he resented some advice that had been offered him or some criticism that had been passed upon him: " without going any further into the question ", he writes, " of your qualifications to play the part of Mentor, I confess frankly that I am in no way disposed to be your Telemachus." [6]

The quarrel was patched up later; and in November, 1849, Liszt engaged Raff as his secretary and general handyman. Raff's letters

---

[5] It was long before he overcame his distrust of himself in this field. As late as 1853 we find the Princess urging him not to be so dependent on Raff and others for his orchestration. Later he acquired considerable mastery of the art. See, on this subject, NML, p. 140, and RLS, pp. 68 ff.

[6] DM, I, 122; RJR, p. 59.

of the period give us a tolerably clear picture of the situation at that time as regards Liszt's work and plans. Liszt was evidently more inclined than he had formerly been to admit that there were gaps in his musical education to be repaired. Unfortunately the adoring Princess, in this as in so many other matters, was an obstacle to his development. Being the mere sentimental dilettante that she was, she had no notion of the importance of technical accomplishment in music: all she could do was to rhapsodise about the " poetry " of works of art. When Raff, in his conversations with Liszt and the Princess, argued the necessity of technique on the composer's part, she called him " heartless ". He seems to have told Liszt quite frankly of his faults: " I maintain, on the contrary [as against the Princess] ", he writes to a friend towards the end of 1849, " that it is time Liszt stopped treating the piano as if it were an orchestra and the orchestra as if it were a piano, time he ceased to banish utterly from his work one of the most useful elements in music — counterpoint — and time he ceased making a mere stone-heap out of the edifice of form that has been bequeathed to us by the past — spinning out a song, for instance, to 19 pages, while in other works he hasn't the least idea where to find material enough. But some day we will talk more of this *viva voce*. However, I must do Liszt the justice to say that he took my part against the Princess." Liszt, in truth, was less inclined in 1849 than he had been in 1847 to mount his high horse when it was hinted to him that he still had a good deal to learn about composition, that his unsurpassable virtuosity as a pianist would not see him safely through the problems of orchestral and choral music. " This last week ", says Raff in his letter of December, 1849, " I have cleaned up Liszt's first *Concerto symphonique* for him. . . . Now comes the scoring and copying of an overture entitled *Ce qu'on entend sur la montagne*. . . .[7] I must confess that I find Liszt extraordinarily changed. He takes my criticisms in good part, and shows that he is anxious to learn. . . . The object he has in view is to prepare himself for two or three years, in seclusion, for the career of a composer, and then make his début in Paris." [8]

---

[7] I.e. the symphonic poem based on Victor Hugo. Later in his letter Raff again says that the scoring of this work is partly his.

[8] DM, I, pp. 387 ff.; RJR, pp. 70 ff. In a letter of the 14th January, 1850, to

Contemporary Weimar itself saw the whole matter much more clearly than the servile Liszt biographers have done. That he had settled there, for the most part, to learn his job as a composer and conductor was evident to everyone; and even in Weimar, one gathers, he was not taken very seriously except by the Court. Bernhardi, who was in the town in 1851 and 1852, mixing in all circles, received the impression from Liszt's own bodyguard that he was regarded as " so poor a general-bassist that he is no good at composition. He gets, as musical princesses do, a good idea for a cantilena, but he cannot give it shape and body, and more particularly the necessary harmonic breadth. Raff helps him out in this, just like the music master of a musical princess." [9] Liszt, not to put too fine a point upon it, was, as a composer, as yet next to nobody in the larger musical world of Germany: it was not until 1854 that he ventured into the open with his piano sonata, while the first six of the symphonic poems were not published until 1856. The situation in 1850 was precisely as described by Raff in a letter to his friend Frau Heinrich in the February of that year. Raff tells her the story of Liszt's first meeting with the Princess Wittgenstein, and describes the awkward state of affairs that has now made it impossible for him either to leave her, to marry her, or to enter the larger social world with her. He was no longer a wholly voluntary settler in Weimar; in some ways he was for the time being a captive in the place: and, as Raff puts it, " in these circumstances you will readily understand that what Liszt is bent on is a quiet career as a composer." [10] If Liszt had had at this period any idea whatever of making Weimar the spear-point of a new movement, we may be sure that Raff, who was in daily contact with him, would have heard of it.

As late as April, 1850, we find Liszt writing to Joseph d'Ortigue, apropos of his Mass for male voices and orchestra (afterwards known as the Sexard Mass), that he would like to continue in this

---

Breitkopf & Härtel, Liszt says that in Weimar he lives "in retirement, sheltered from the noise and activity of the world."

[9] NML, p. 187, citing Bernhardi's diary.

[10] DM, I, 396. Raff's daughter Helene, in her biography of her father (RJR), unfortunately curtailed many of the letters from which she was quoting. For the full text we have to go to her earlier articles, *Franz Liszt und Joachim Raff im Spiegel ihrer Briefe*, in DM, Vol. I.

path, which is " that of my youth and the most intimate affinities of my heart ", but that " present and pressing necessities " urge him towards " the dramatic element as it is to-day." He has been working at his opera *Sardanapale* (to an Italian text) ; this will be finished at the end of the year. He also has in hand a series of symphonic poems which will take about three years to complete, and some works for the piano. For the rest, he is compelled to " lose much time in unavoidable duties of all kinds." By this he means, apparently, his public musical work in Weimar — another proof that at this period his mind ran almost exclusively on his own inner development as an artist.

Even when, later in 1850, he is writing his brochure in support of the appeal for the Goethe Foundation, he had no thought, so far as music was concerned, beyond the vague one of " encouraging " it, along with literature and the other arts, by the offering of yearly prizes. He dreamed, as his letter of the 24th April to Dingelstedt shows, of making the Foundation " the concentric and virtual foyer of Germanic intellect and talent ", and so bringing about " the regeneration, or, if you prefer it, the *new-generation* of Weimar." Until *Lohengrin* and Wagner's passionate idealism burned their way into him, he was quite content to take Weimar music and Weimar life as they came, to conduct trash like *Tony*,[11] and to go on giving the Hereditary Grand Duchess Sophie lessons in music, in which, he politely assures the Hereditary Grand Duke, " the master has more to learn than the pupil " : he is teaching the royal lady the recitatives and roulades of the *Prophète*, which will " be executed in the most accomplished style possible, thanks to the brilliant vocalisation of a royal *prima donna assoluta*." [12]

---

[11] His notorious respect for titles even made him a propagandist for this work. "In a few days", he writes to Carl Alexander on the 23rd May, 1849, "we shall repeat the opera [*Tony*] of the Duke of Coburg, in connection with which I have sent to a dozen of the French papers, including the Frankfort one, the little article which I now enclose. If your Royal Highness were to deem it advisable to send this to the composer of *Tony*, and at the same time to recall me to the memory of his favour, I should be greatly obliged."

That he had been, as usual, a trifle fulsome in his praise of the royal dilettante seems to be indicated by Carl Alexander's reply: "I do not know whether I can send the composer of *Tony* your eulogy of his work, for I do not know where he is. . . ."

Liszt actually made and published a transcription of the "Halloh!" hunting chorus and Styrienne from this royal masterpiece.

[12] LZCA, p. 24.

Raff makes no mention of Wagner in his letters of this period: the plain inference is that nothing in Liszt's conversation had led him to believe, even as late as February, 1850, that the production of *Tannhäuser* in February of the preceding year had inspired him with any idea of making Weimar the centre of a Wagner movement. That production, indeed, had attracted the attention of the German musical world to Weimar, for this was the first time *Tannhäuser* had been given outside Dresden; and possibly Liszt may now have had an intuition that a new spirit was beginning to stir the dry bones of opera, and that Weimar might play a leading part in the forward movement. *Tannhäuser* had indisputably made a profound impression on him between February, 1849, and the meeting with Wagner in Weimar in the following May. In his article in the *Débats* he had praised the " lofty poetic sentiment " of the opera, the moving nature of its drama, " full of the finest nuances of the heart and of passion ", the " original and daring plan " of the work, the " absolutely new " quality of the music. In the concluding portion of the article, which was not reprinted in the later book — where, of course, it was unnecessary, the whole opera being now subjected to a detailed analysis, musical as well as dramatic, — he made it clear to his French readers that he regarded *Tannhäuser* as a work altogether out of the common, " one of the greatest masterpieces that any artist has ever produced." [13]

But the intuition could have been at the best only a dim one; and dim it remained until after the production of *Lohengrin* in August, 1850. Even after the bold deed of *Tannhäuser*, Liszt seems to have felt his way forward very cautiously as conductor and producer, contenting himself with the Duke of Saxe-Coburg-Gotha's *Tony* in April, 1849, Rossini's *Le Comte Ory* and Hoven's *Abenteuer Karls II* in April, 1850, Saloman's *Das Corps der Rache* in June, and Donizetti's *La Favorita* in September. It is true that in 1849 he had given the second part of Schumann's *Faust*; but in that year celebrations of the hundredth anniversary of Goethe's

---

[13] It is perhaps indicative of Liszt's imperfect acquaintance with the German language at this time that all through the book, as well as on the title-page, he writes "Tannhaüser" for "Tannhäuser."

birth were general throughout Germany, and in those celebrations Weimar, of all places, would have to play its part.[14] It was only after the production of *Lohengrin* that Liszt launched out more boldly into a specifically " modern " repertory for Weimar, giving Raff's *King Alfred* in March, 1851,[15] Berlioz's *Harold in Italy* in April, Schumann's *Braut von Messina* overture in November, Bülow's *Julius Caesar* overture in December, Berlioz's *Benvenuto Cellini* in March, 1852, Wagner's *Faust Overture* in May, Schumann's *Manfred* music in June, and a whole Berlioz week in November. *Lohengrin* is manifestly the turning-point both in Liszt's development and that of Weimar. Liszt's original purpose, of merely using Weimar as a quiet little backwater in which he could experiment with his own essays in orchestral music before submitting himself to the judgment of Paris, has now given way to the more ambitious plan of making Weimar the starting-point of a crusade. Wagner's influence and example had changed the whole current of Liszt's life and the whole orientation of his thought.

It is after his experiences with *Lohengrin* and the long bombardment of Wagner's letters, and not until then, that a complete change of heart is wrought in him. We can still feel, as we read his letters of this period, something of the fire that *Lohengrin* must have kindled in him. It is evident that this was the profoundest artistic experience of his life until then. He had entered upon the undertaking, in the first place, mainly in order to help the needy Wagner. Though the performance had been fixed for the 28th August, he did not obtain the score from Dresden until about the end of May, and rehearsals do not seem to have commenced until July. But as soon as serious work is begun upon the opera, Liszt is all fire and flame for it. " Nothing within living memory has been seen like our efforts for the performance of *Lohengrin* ", he writes to Dingelstedt on the 14th July: " little by little ", he tells Feodor von Milde on the 2nd August, " our whole company will become enthusiastic over this masterpiece, will be penetrated by its substance, live in its life, all which is the *sine qua non* for a performance such as I have in view." Two months after the production of *Lohengrin* he

---

[14] Portions of Schumann's *Faust* were given on this occasion not only in Weimar but in Dresden and Leipzig.

[15] Raff, however, conducted his own work.

writes Dingelstedt a letter in which we see him for the first time mapping out an ambitious plan for the Weimar theatre. " Either ", he says, " our theatre must make the *amende honorable* (or rather the *amende honteuse*) for having dreamed of giving the tragic and lyric masterpieces, including *Tannhäuser* and *Lohengrin*, and surrender itself body and soul to the infernal deities of stagnation, decrepitude, and the stupidest banality, anxiously making its selection among masterpieces of the order of *Weltumsegler, Ochsenhändler, Letztes Fensterl, Haimonskinder, Czar und Zimmermann,* and works that during the last fifteen years have been run to death and at last abandoned by respectable German theatres, or else we must go on developing and acquiring all the lustre possible in the direction we have given the theatre during the last eighteen months [i.e. since the production of *Tannhäuser* in February, 1849]. In the former case, I retire absolutely: Zigesar will also assuredly resign. In the second case (which looks highly probable), the subsidy to the theatre must be increased by 8,000 to 10,000 thalers a year, which would enable us to do what is necessary in the way of new engagements, reforms and improvements, and above all to ensure your valuable co-operation in our dramatic institution as Dramaturg." These questions, he hopes, will be settled one way or another in three or four months' time.[16]

In January, 1851, we find him telling Gustav Schmidt, the Kapellmeister at Frankfort, who wants to give *Lohengrin* there, that Wagner's operas are not for the ordinary theatre, demanding as they do " a decisive understanding of his lofty spiritual and artistic being." He criticises sharply, quite in the Wagnerian way, Schmidt's predecessor Guhr, whom he calls a typical representative of an epoch of routine Kapellmeistership which, he hopes, is now dead and done with. Wherever we look in Liszt's correspondence, indeed, we discover that after the experiences of July and August, 1850, he is a new man and a new artist, thanks to Wagner in general and to *Lohengrin* in particular.

---

[16] LZB, VIII, 72–4.

We must rid ourselves of the notion, then, that Liszt, even when he took the sudden resolution to produce *Lohengrin* in Weimar, was a person of any particular importance in the larger European musical world. He conferred no distinction whatever on Wagner by that production; neither he nor his absurd little theatre was in a position to confer distinction on anyone, least of all on a composer who, during the last six or seven years, had attracted considerable attention by three such works as *Rienzi*, the *Flying Dutchman*, and *Tannhäuser*. All that Liszt did for Wagner in 1850 was to put an end to the legend that had become current in Germany that his works were impossible for any but the larger theatres. As a matter of fact, the works *were* difficult for that epoch: they called for singers of the calibre of a Tichatschek or a Schröder-Devrient, for expensive productions, for better orchestral playing than most German theatres could rise to at that time. The Wagner performances in Weimar, even with an augmented orchestra, must have been lamentably inadequate judged by the standards of to-day. *Lohengrin*, strictly speaking, was impossible there.

The important thing was that Liszt had attempted, and apparently achieved, the impossible, and so had given encouragement to many other theatres that had hitherto shrunk from producing a Wagner opera. All Germany knew that *Rienzi* and *Tannhäuser* had been resounding successes in Dresden, and, artistic considerations apart, each theatre must have seen that these works would mean good business if they were possible at all. After Weimar, there really seemed no reason why any theatre, even the smallest, should be scared of attempting them. It is significant that the first theatre to produce *Tannhäuser* after Weimar was that of Schwerin, a town hardly bigger than Weimar, and ranking even lower in the estimation of musicians. Breslau, Prague and Wiesbaden quickly followed suit, and in a little while *Tannhäuser* was being given practically all over Germany. Wagner's works had not become any less difficult between 1849 and 1851; it was simply that the legend of their being impossibly difficult for any but the richest opera houses had been blown sky-high. And once the ball had been set rolling by Weimar, every theatre was anxious to take its part in the profitable game. Even the big Court theatres were ultimately compelled by the pressure of events to join in it, or at all events to make a pretence of doing so in response to the popular demand, in spite of their animus against the composer as a political revolutionary, in spite of the lack of cordiality towards him on the part of the resident conductors. Even Dresden, as early as 1851, thought of giving *Lohengrin*, and was only deterred from doing so by Wagner's blunt declaration that he had no confidence in the ability of the local Kapellmeisters. It was through his bold deed in connection with *Lohengrin* that a new kind of fame suddenly came to Liszt, and through *Lohengrin* that he became fired with the laudable ambition of placing Weimar on the musical map. By doing what he had done he undoubtedly benefited Wagner; but he benefited himself and Weimar still more, for henceforth his name and Weimar's were gloriously associated with the rising star of German music. Cornelius was as clear-sighted as usual when he said, in after years, that it was Liszt who had " boldly and adroitly " climbed to fame on the shoulders of Wagner.

CHAPTER XI

THE RISING TIDE

1

THE TRUTH is that, owing to a variety of causes, Wagner, at the turn of the half-century, had suddenly become the most eagerly discussed musician in Germany. The fact that he had had to fly from Dresden for political reasons in May, 1849, had focussed the attention of the musical world on him; and whatever harm his revolutionary actions and opinions may have done him in Court circles, they must certainly have commended him to thousands of ardent souls who thought as he did. By a swift succession of blows he had compelled the public to take account of his comprehensive discontent with the old world of music and his bold aspirations for a new and better world. *Art and Revolution* had been published in the autumn of 1849, *The Art-Work of the Future* in December of that year, *A Communication to my Friends* at the end of 1851, *Opera and Drama* in November, 1851, *A Theatre for Zürich* in the *Neue Zeitschrift für Musik* in the summer of 1851, *On Musical Criticism* in the same paper in February, 1852 (in pamphlet form a little later), *Judaism in Music* in the *Neue Zeitschrift* in September, 1850. No matter how small the sale of the books may have been (though it has to be noted that the first editions of some of them were fairly quickly sold out), and no matter how small the circulation of the *Neue Zeitschrift*, the cumulative effect of all these bombardments must have been immense. A large proportion of the German Press of the time is said to have been in the hands of the Jews, who naturally were not well disposed towards Wagner after the publication of *Judaism in Music;* [1] and

---

[1] The article, which was signed "K. Freigedank", raised a storm in Germany. The editor of the *Neue Zeitschrift*, Brendel, was professor of musical history at the Leipzig Conservatoire. A memorial asking for his removal from that post was signed by every one of the other professors: included among them were Joachim, Rietz, David, Hauptmann and Moscheles. Wagner's authorship of the article could have been no secret from the first.

certainly the papers, both musical and general, that had the largest circulation were then and for a long time after hostile to him. But it was something even to be abused by them, for at least it meant publicity. He was beginning to be discussed even in France: in the summer of 1852 Fétis, who, like Hanslick, could generally be trusted to land with both feet on the wrong side of the fence where significant new music was concerned, wrote a series of articles on him in the *Gazette Musicale*. They were full of the stupidest misunderstanding of Wagner's remarks, in *A Communication to my Friends*, concerning his " failures," Fétis being unable to see that the Dresden successes ranked as failures in the composer's eyes because they touched only the musical side of his art, not the dramatic: but at any rate these articles helped a little to bring Wagner into the limelight. He was now too big a figure in the operatic world to be ignored: the Meyerbeer party in the Press saw the danger that was threatening their idol, and henceforth lost no opportunity of attacking the pretender to the tottering throne.

Meanwhile Wagner's own admirers were beginning to be active in such journals as were open to them; and their writing was of a calibre that made thoughtful people take notice of them. It was beginning to be clear to everyone by now that the issue was between Wagner and Meyerbeer, one or other of whom would sooner or later have to go to the wall. Uhlig's writings were symptomatic of the state of the atmosphere. In a series of closely reasoned articles in the *Neue Zeitschrift* during 1850 and 1851 he tore the wretched *Prophète* to pieces.[2] The strong body of German opinion that regarded Meyerbeer as a charlatan devoid of artistic conscience, who had imposed himself upon the opera houses of Europe by the most dubious means, was at last beginning to find public expression. Uhlig was a first-rate musician who knew his subject inside out, and who never wrote upon music without having something vital to say. He thoroughly understood Wagner, and his exposition of the composer's musical and dramatic intentions was all the more convincing because his attitude was not that of an idolater. He did not hesitate, for instance, to hint that the popular *Rienzi* was a work that Wagner had long since outgrown: even the *Flying Dutchman*

[2] The articles have recently been reprinted in UMS; they are well worth reading even to-day.

he regarded as an opera that was only a stage in his progress to the real Wagner, the Wagner of *Tannhäuser* and *Lohengrin*. After the performance of the *Tannhäuser* overture in Paris in November, 1850, Uhlig set himself, in the *Neue Zeitschrift*, to account for the fact that this work, which had " electrified " Dresden and Weimar, had been greeted with laughter in Paris and in Leipzig. He showed the importance of an understanding of the opera for the comprehension of the overture; and in these articles, as in a later series on *The Final Scene of Tannhäuser*,[3] *Three Days in Weimar* (dealing with the production of *Lohengrin* there),[4] and *Richard Wagner's Operas*,[5] he gave the public temperate and reasoned expositions of Wagner's theory and practice.

2

Musical criticism, in fact, was beginning, about this period, to take a new orientation; for the first time thoughtful people were becoming conscious of music as a seminal factor in the general cultural life of an epoch. Musical criticism hitherto had for the most part dealt simply with the aesthetic values, or what the critic imagined to be the aesthetic values, of this or that work of this or that composer; he " liked " or " disliked " this or that symphony or quartet of Mozart or Beethoven, and thought his reactions of sufficient importance to the rest of mankind to justify his placing them on record. There was as yet no conception of an individual composer as the symbol of a new epoch, the standard-bearer of a new faith, no general sense that a stage in the evolution of the art had been reached at which a new development must either slay contemporary conventions or be slain by them. But about the middle of the century a new phenomenon comes into view: a number of the younger and finer spirits were conscious that the battle had been joined between the ordinary operas of the day and the operas of Wagner, between a convention that was visibly outworn and a conception that was rich in promise for the future. The political commotions of the time had quickened men's sensibilities and thrilled

---

[3] *Neue Zeitschrift*, January–June, 1852.
[4] Ibid., 1850.
[5] *Deutsche Monatsschrift*, 1850. These and other articles of Uhlig are now available in UMS.

them with a vision of a brave new world that might be realisable in art, however remote it might still seem in the political or the social sphere. Wagner's black record in the matter of the Dresden rising was in this respect a service to him; the German world could not be indifferent to the unprecedented fact that a Court Kapellmeister had declared war not only on his own institution but on the institution of Court opera in general, and had produced at least three works that challenged the existing genre to a duel *à outrance*.

The controversy that was to rage over Wagner during the next few years attained therefore a range and a significance far beyond the merely musical. While on the one hand the musical critics saw clearly enough that their own standards, such as they were, were about to be sharply challenged, on the other hand a number of people who were not specially interested in music had a vague feeling that if Wagner and what he stood for were not crushed, the world would be, for them, a less comfortable place than it had hitherto been. And so practically the whole weight of the German and, later, the French and the English Press was thrown into the business of deriding and denigrating Wagner. He had made this easier for them by his prose works. The core of truth in these that was so vital for the future was invisible to them. Far easier than to attempt to understand them in their true essence was it to fasten upon the obvious fallacies with which they were strewn. That these fallacies had no seminal connection with the real work of the man, with the significance of it and of him for the musical drama of the future, was something they would not have dwelt upon even if they had been aware of it. And as the prose works were often difficult to understand, partly because of the obscurity of Wagner's style, partly because of the complexity of some of the problems with which he had to deal, it followed as a matter of course that his arguments were re-stated by his opponents in a form in which he could not have recognized them, and that the misunderstanding spread in ever-widening circles as one writer after another, instead of going direct to the works themselves, merely copied the errors of his fellows.

But on Wagner's side were a number of people who were not to be daunted by the mere fact that they were grossly outnumbered in the Press. For them, Wagner represented a new force that was vital to the whole future of opera. The opposition to him did not dismay them; it merely infuriated them. They were out for blood; and anyone who entered the lists against them could count on losing a considerable quantity of it. Foremost among the younger warriors was Bülow, at all times a useful man to have by one's side in a fight, and at this period of his life more than usually careless of possible consequences to himself. Some years later, in an article in the *Neue Zeitschrift für Musik* of the 25th September, 1863, that was motived primarily by the death of his friend Eduard Fischel, who had been run over by an omnibus in Paris, he told the story of the early struggle of the pair on behalf of Wagner, and of the difficulties they had had to encounter. When Wagner's first polemical writings appeared in 1849 and 1850, Bülow looked in vain for any notice of them in the ordinary journals of the day. Furious at this neglect, he wrote article after article of his own on *Art and Revolution* and *The Art-Work of the Future*, for which he tried in vain to find a home in any even of the liberal papers. At last he turned his despairing gaze on a radical paper, the Berlin *Demokratische Zeitung*, which had already dealt with Wagner's books in a way which, if superficial, was at any rate not disrespectful. Connected with the paper were two of his student acquaintances, Adolf Mützelburg (who afterwards achieved a reputation as a novelist) and Eduard Fischel: a League of Youth was formed, Bülow was appointed musical critic of the *Demokratische* — without a salary and without free tickets for concerts or theatres — and he proceeded to wage a furious war against the accredited musical critics of Berlin. The leading representative of these was the one-time famous Rellstab, against whom Bülow launched, in February, 1850, a biting satire, as he calls it, which unfortunately cannot now be traced.[6]

In a very little while Bülow managed, by his attacks on routine and his advocacy of Wagner and Liszt, to make himself a thoroughly unacceptable person in Berlin musical circles. The critics naturally repaid him in kind when, a few years later, he began to

---

[6] It appears that the whole of the issues for February, 1850, are missing from the only copy that survives of the *Abend-Post*. (The *Demokratische Zeitung* had taken the new title of *Abend-Post* in January of that year). According to Bülow in later years, his attack on Rellstab, who was the musical-and-every-other-kind-of-critic of the *Vossische Zeitung*, was entitled *Aunty Voss's Fossilised Critics*.

give concerts of his own in Berlin. By that time all Germany had become either Wagnerian or anti-Wagnerian; even homes that had once been models of domestic harmony were broken up by an unfortunate difference of opinion on this burning subject between father and son, or between husband and wife. Bülow, in a few years, came to be regarded in Berlin professional musical circles as a leper from whom it was safest to be separated as widely as possible: a man of less idealism and less courage would have broken under the strain of the malevolence poured out upon him in the Press of the town. All this while Fischel, who was an amateur musician of wide culture, had been incurring a hostility almost as savage for standing by Bülow's side in his fights; matters came to such a pass that editors who had formerly prized his contributions highly would not print his articles in support of Bülow unless he paid for the privilege.

3

The recognised organ of what was shortly to be known as the New German School was Schumann's old journal, the *Neue Zeitschrift für Musik*, now under the editorship of Franz Brendel. A hint of the importance already attached to the names of Wagner and Liszt is given in the leading article with which the year 1852 began: " This paper will henceforth have for its task the emphatic advocacy, from every point of view, of the transformation upon which the art of music is now entering." For all Brendel's courage, however, he jibbed at the vehemence of some of Bülow's writing. Neither in his youth nor in his old age was Bülow ever capable either of compromise where art was concerned, or of the slightest honeying of his speech where fools who could not or knaves who would not be convinced had to be castigated. From June, 1851, he lived for some time in Weimar, studying the piano under Liszt. Having been dissatisfied with a performance of *Tannhäuser* in Weimar, he made so pointed an attack on the theatre administration in the official journal, the *Weimarische Zeitung*, that henceforth he was barred from its columns; whereupon he transferred his opinions to a rival paper, the *Deutschland*. Most of his critical work, however, was done in the *Neue Zeitschrift*. The Leipzig *Grenzboten* having published in 1851 an article on Wagner, Bülow addressed himself, in a series of articles in the *Neue Zeitschrift*, to the agreeable dual task of setting the world right on the subject of Wagner and putting arrogant academic Leipzig in its place.

Even at this distant date it is easy to imagine the sensation he made in musical circles. Self-satisfied Leipzig had never been spoken to so frankly before. It prided itself on being the intellectual centre of Saxony, if not, indeed, of Germany. It regarded Dresden, the capital of the state, as being sunk in relative barbarism; and it had been an unforgivable crime on Dresden's part to have produced, in *Rienzi,* an opera that rivalled any work of Meyerbeer or Mendelssohn in popularity. Not being fortunate enough itself to have proprietary rights in the young composer and conductor who had given the Dresden Opera a standing it had never had before, even under Weber, Leipzig took the line of disparaging and misrepresenting him, alleging, for instance, that he was a despiser of Mozart and Beethoven and other classics, and of pooh-poohing his musical attainments: as the critic of the *Grenzboten* put it, " Wagner is a dilettante in the opera, as Berlioz is in the symphony." Wagner had given Leipzig serious cause for offence by that section of his plan for the reform of the Dresden Opera in which he proposed to transfer the Leipzig Conservatoire, the pride and darling of the town, to the Saxon capital. Leipzig, in fact, the cardinal virtue of which, according to Bülow and others, was " its exclusive, intolerant local patriotism ", was nettled at the success of this young upstart of a Wagner; and so Leipzig was his declared enemy even before his works were known there. Matters had not been helped by the incompetent performance of the *Tannhäuser* overture under Mendelssohn in 1846, a performance which Bülow characterised as an " execution " in more senses than one.[7] After the death of Mendelssohn, Leipzig had the uncomfortable feeling that its glory was likely to depart from it. It had hoped that Schumann's *Genoveva* and the *Corsar* of the local Kapellmeister, Rietz, would be a counterpoise to Wagner's successes in Dresden; but both these works had been failures, Schumann's in spite of the great beauty of much of the music.

And all at once Leipzig had discovered that so far from Wagner

---

[7] See Vol. I, p. 401.

being socially, politically and musically finished by his rebellion and flight into Switzerland, his star was steadily rising. His prose writings had made a commotion: Liszt had set all Germany talking with his production of *Lohengrin:* however shocked Court circles and the bourgeoisie might be by Wagner's political opinions, the democratic party was all for him: Leipzig visitors who had seen *Tannhäuser* and *Lohengrin* in Weimar had come back with glowing reports of them: whether Leipzig liked it or not, Wagner had now to be reckoned with as the man of the hour. Bülow subjected the *Grenzboten* article to a searching examination. He said, and proved, that the critic did not know what he was talking about: that he had misunderstood Wagner's theories: that he was merely making the usual fatuous mistake in comparing Meyerbeer's " reforms ", his " modernity ", with those of Wagner: that Wagner was now as surely the man of the future as Meyerbeer was the man of the past, let the ignorant public, for the moment, run after the *Prophète* as it liked. Bülow's knowledge of his subject was unquestionable: his language was fiery: his epithets were blunt. He may not have convinced those who perhaps had no great desire to be convinced; but at any rate he made it clear that the battle between the old art and the new had begun, and that there would be no truce on the part of the Wagnerians till the victory was won. He and the few youthful enthusiasts who were working with him must have given not only Leipzig but all Germany something to think about. Towns like Leipzig and Berlin might continue to place local amour-propre before the interests of music in general, but at least they were rudely shaken out of their old complacency: they were no longer autocrats in the operatic world, but worried garrisons on the defensive. Neither suppression nor mangling of the Wagner operas, nor the combined tactics of printing articles attacking Wagner and suppressing testimony in his favour, could long avail. The well-known man of letters Adolf Stahr, who had seen *Lohengrin* at Weimar in 1851, had been so impressed by it that he wrote enthusiastically about the work in the Berlin *Nationalzeitung:* but later the *Nationalzeitung* refused him permission to reprint his articles in his book *Weimar und Jena,* and closed its columns to a contributor to whom it had owed much of its popularity.[8] Incidents of this kind

[8] BAS, II, 24.

merely served to emphasise the growing importance of Wagner in the artistic and intellectual life of the new Germany.

4

The clearest picture of the situation as it was shaping itself during the years after 1850 is obtained by leaping a little ahead of the date at which we have now arrived in Wagner's life, and taking a rapid glance at a book sent to the press in the first days of 1854, and therefore written in 1853 — Raff's *Die Wagnerfrage*. That there should be a " Wagner Question " to discuss as early as 1853 is itself an indication of the sensation he had made by now in German musical circles. Raff was a man of extraordinary ability, a little inclined to the pedantic — for he possessed so much learning of all kinds that he could not refrain from seizing upon the smallest pretext to display it — but undeniably a thinker.

Raff opens his book with the remark that is the justification for the writing of it: the imaginary correspondent to whom the supposed letters are addressed has asked him, it appears, to help him to take his bearings in " the present musical agitation ", an agitation of which Wagner is the recognised centre. Raff first of all sets himself to remove certain misconceptions that have become general. People have read Wagner's *Opera and Drama*, etc., have next listened to *Tannhäuser* and *Lohengrin*, and have then made the pardonable mistake of supposing that these works embody his theories; the truth being, of course, that they were written before his inner development had as yet driven him to theorise about the *future* problem of the music drama. Full light on the theories could only come much later, when Wagner had shown, in his Nibelungen drama, how they were to be realised in practice. In spite of this confusion, or perhaps because of it, Wagner was already being eagerly discussed all over Germany as an innovator without precedent. Raff sets himself to deal in detail not with the problematic future but with the present Wagner. He subjects the poems and the music of the operas already known to the public to a close examination, pointing out what he takes to be excellences and originalities in both of them, but always maintaining an attitude of scrupulous objectivity towards Wagner, in spite of his own close association with the " Weimar School ". No modern writer on musical criticism should fail to take studious account of Raff's book, for it illustrates, as few books do, the eternal difficulties attending the criticism of works contemporary with the critic. Raff is perturbed about all kinds of things in the early Wagner works — in the poetic diction and in the dramatic handling as well as in the music — that no one would dream of discussing seriously to-day: all that he says is well observed and well reasoned, but the verdict of the modern world upon it all is simply that it does not matter; and the thoughtful critic of to-day cannot read these closely argued pages without wondering how many of the defects *he* triumphantly points out in a contemporary work will be regarded by the generation after next as being of any real importance to the work considered as a whole. Raff, progressive as he was in so many ways, was still so much the child of his age and of his musical upbringing that he could not forgive Wagner for not having been more contrapuntal now and then; in the very act of impressing it on the reader that Wagner's operas must not be judged from the standpoint of " absolute " music — a common mistake in those days — he himself blames the composer for not having foisted " absolute " counterpoint upon dramatic situations which, as we now see, not only stand in no need of it but would be all the worse for it. He chooses, to enforce his point, the chorus that greets the arrival of Lohengrin in the first act: he is kind enough to show Wagner how much better this would have been had the composer had the advantage of Raff's tuition in choral polyphony.[9]

On the other hand, Raff disapproves of many of the musical passages that are to-day the most popular. He censures the *Tannhäuser* overture because it is too " homophonic "; once more he cannot reconcile himself to Wagner's scrapping of contrapuntal ingenuity where contrapuntal ingenuity would have been out of place. He is particularly severe on the *Lohengrin* prelude: he sets out the sequence of the modulations in the best analytical-chemist style, and graciously approves of them; but, he adds, while he " understands " what Wagner has done at one point, " I know that it could have been done better and more beautifully." [10] But though

---

[9] RWF, pp. 123–5.   [10] Ibid., pp. 183–5.

the modern critic, as he reads the book, shivers at the thought of how some of his own judgments upon new music will impress posterity, Raff undoubtedly did Wagner a great service by his searching examination of the " Wagner Question ". No composer until then had received such close attention from contemporary criticism; and Raff's readers, whatever their personal prepossessions might have been, must all have felt that Wagner was a new phenomenon in art, a force, whether for good or evil, with which the whole operatic world of the present and the future would have to reckon. And towards the end of his book Raff makes it quite clear that, for all the faults he had to find with Wagner's works, the composer of them was already something unique in the history of art, and likely in the future to re-make the whole fabric of music drama. If Wagner himself, he suggests, should not realise in his later works all that is implicit in the seminal ideas he has thrust upon the attention of the world, it will assuredly be realised in the course of time. " Then at last musical history will know to the full what to make of Wagner. The war-cries of the dissentient parties will be silenced: a new generation will take the new art-work to its bosom and foster it, and allot to its creator a place of honour by the side of Aeschylus, Shakespeare and Beethoven." [11] He honours Wagner not only for the candour with which he expresses his convictions but for " the resignation with which he has sacrificed his material life " to them.[12] Little as Raff's book was liked in the Wagner circle, there can be no question that it did a great deal to focus the attention of the German musical world upon the new developments in opera.

[11] RWF, pp. 251–2. [12] Ibid., p. 253.

CHAPTER XII

UHLIG'S VISIT: EXPANSION OF THE NIBELUNGEN PLAN

1

W E MAY now take up again the main thread of Wagner's life in Switzerland after his return to Zürich and Minna, the Laussot episode being over, in July, 1850. We have found him housed in the " Zum Abendstern " (the so-called " Villa Rienzi ") in Enge. Minna, after a first attempt to assert herself by demanding belligerently if he had returned to her " simply out of pity ", promised never to refer to the Laussot affair again, and settled down to the task at which she really excelled — that of making a comfortable home for the pair of them out of his slender resources. The little dog and the parrot were delighted to make their own contributions to Wagner's happiness; Peps would lie down behind the chair in which he was working, and Papo, whose manners were always engagingly impudent, would sometimes enliven the household by whistling a tune from *Rienzi*, or, if he happened to be in a more classical mood at the moment, a melody from a Beethoven symphony.[1] He would welcome Wagner's friends by name — " Good evening, Müller! " or " Here you are, Boom! " (Baumgartner). One of his most charming leading motives had been taught him by his mistress: when Wagner began to scold her, he would cry, "Bad man! Poor Minna!" (Papo's talents as a biographer seem to have been inherited by Messrs Hurn and Root). The slug in an otherwise fairly palatable salad was Natalie, whose quarrels with her " sister " Minna became more and more frequent; Wagner often had to leave the world of his dreams to pacify the nagging pair. For a time, at a rather later period than that at which we have

---

[1] Poor Papo died in February, 1851, and Wagner was inconsolable: the bird, he told Uhlig, was "something indispensable" between, as well as for, Minna and himself.

now arrived, Natalie obtained work in one of the hotels in the neighbourhood.

In 1850 Wagner did his best to induce not only the Ritter family but Uhlig to settle in Zürich, suggesting that they should all live together in the same house. This plan, of course, came to nothing, Frau Ritter and her family having their own circle of interests in Dresden, and Uhlig being unable to give up his post, ill-paid as it was, in the Dresden orchestra. Karl Ritter, however, shared the " Villa Rienzi " with Wagner for a time, occupying a small attic and taking his meals with Richard and Minna. But his peculiar nature made him at all times difficult to live with; and after Wagner, who felt a certain responsibility to Frau Ritter for him, had remonstrated with him for ruining his digestion by eating too many sweets, and so impairing his appetite that he began to slight the family meals, Karl took a room of his own in the town. Wagner seems to have been genuinely fond of the gifted but cross-grained young man, and to have borne more than one trial in connection with him with exemplary patience. The trouble apparently was that Karl's ambitions exceeded his powers. He was not without gifts, either literary or musical: but he lacked the ability to pursue any end with sufficient thoroughness to win even his own approval. He played a not inconsiderable part in Wagner's life for a few years, and then disappeared from it almost as suddenly as he had entered it.

On the 12th August Wagner made a sketch for the music of the opening scene of *Siegfrieds Tod*, and by the 24th he had completed his article on *Judaism in Music,* to which he had been impelled in part by his growing disgust with Meyerbeer and all he stood for, in part by the news that seems to have reached him of the unfriendly spirit towards him that his former friend, Ferdinand Hiller, was now displaying in Cologne, where he had recently settled as head of the newly founded local Conservatoire and conductor of the choral and orchestral concerts. We have seen that in Paris Wagner's gorge had risen at *Le Prophète.* On his return to Zürich he read the articles in the *Neue Zeitschrift für Musik* in which Uhlig handled Meyerbeer in general and *Le Prophète* in particular with relentless thoroughness. In one of these articles occurred the expression " Hebraic art-taste "; and this may well have provided the starting-point for Wagner's savage article.

Two days after finishing *Judaism in Music*, having received a welcome gift of a hundred thalers from the Grand Duke of Weimar (sent anonymously through Liszt), he took Minna off on an excursion to the Rigi; the arduous climb brought to light the first sure proof of the heart disease from which the poor woman was now to suffer constantly. The 28th found them in Lucerne. It was the day of the first performance of *Lohengrin* in Weimar. Wagner listened to it, in imagination, in the hotel " Zum Schwanen ": Minna, apparently, was so little interested in his emotions that when telling the story of that evening years later in *Mein Leben* he was moved to add, " every similar attempt on my part to pass an hour or two of sentiment with my wife resulted only in distress, discomfort, and a sense that we were out of tune with each other." [2] He was appalled to hear, a few days later, that the performance had lasted from six o'clock till nearly eleven, whereas by his own timing of the work it should have been over by about a quarter to ten, the first act playing " not much over an hour ", the second an hour and a quarter, the third " just over an hour." His first thought was that Liszt must have dragged the tempi. Having learned that this was not the case, he could only assume that in the passages in which the conductor had least power to dictate the tempi — in the so-called recitatives — the singers had slowed down the time in their customary fashion: and he treated Liszt to a long dissertation on the

---

[2] It was apparently only in intellectual matters that the disharmony between the pair showed itself at this time. "I presume", Wagner writes to Uhlig shortly after his return from the Rigi expedition, "that you have been informed, through Frau Ritter, of the change in my affairs; let me, then, be silent about the immediate past [the Laussot episode], and only briefly tell you this much, that I have a new wife. Though, speaking generally, she is the same as of old, yet now I know that, whatever may happen, she will stand by my side till death. I, for my part, certainly had no thought of trying her in any way: as circumstances have turned out, however, she has passed through an ordeal by fire such as all must endure who nowadays consciously wish to stand by the side of those who recognise the future and steer straight towards it. My friends here have proved their quality splendidly. I have aged a good deal: I now know for certain that I have entered on the second half of my life and have left many a hope behind me."

Once more, in all probability, *Mein Leben* represents the embittered retrospect of the later years. But the sentence "though, speaking generally, she is the same as of old" points clearly to Wagner's disappointment with Minna's failure to understand the idealist in him, highly as he appreciated her ordinary human qualities.

sins of German singers in this regard, which he attributed to two causes, in the first place their natural dullness of apprehension, in the second place their loss of all sense of the true relations of words and music in opera, owing to their being compelled to sing so many of their parts in bad translations from the French and Italian.

The whole letter is interesting as showing the difficulties he had to contend with in the performance of his works, and especially the virtual impossibility of making the singers realise the drama as well as the music. He had, he says, carefully inserted in the Dresden voice parts the fullest instructions as to the way the actors were to conduct themselves on the stage, but could never get Tichatschek and the others to observe them. He gave Liszt the sensible advice, that might be followed with advantage in our opera houses to-day, to take the singers through a few rehearsals in which they would merely *speak* their parts — advice, however, that would be lost now, as it was in Wagner's own day, on people who cannot see that anything matters in any opera but the music. He insisted to Liszt, again, as he always did in cases of this kind, that if the audience found the work rather long it was because his *dramatic* intentions in it had not been made clear to them. He was rather annoyed by a well-intentioned but undiscerning article on the performance by Dingelstedt,[3] from whom, as a man of the theatre, not a musician, he expected some understanding of the opera as the realisation of a dramatic idea. Dingelstedt, however, had merely rambled on amateurishly about the score — the orchestration, and so on; and Wagner felt that if this was the best that a man of culture, himself a dramatist, could make of the new problem that was put before him, there was not much to expect of the ordinary Philistine. Reading between the lines of his letters of this period, we gather that while exceedingly grateful to Liszt for all the trouble he had taken over *Lohengrin*, he suspected that it had been easier for his friend also to feel the beauty of the music than to grasp the drama, to re-live it in rehearsal, and to make the actors re-live it in performance.

It is difficult to-day to form an accurate idea of what these

---

[3] Franz Dingelstedt, more famous now as producer than dramatist, was Intendant of the Munich Court theatre from 1850 to 1857; in the latter year he became General Director of the Weimar Theatre, in which capacity he soon came into collision with Liszt.

Weimar performances of *Lohengrin* were like; but one suspects that they were grossly inadequate, except in the orchestral nuancing of the music, to which Liszt must have given close attention. With some difficulty he had managed to have the tiny orchestra augmented for the occasion, a bass clarinet, for example, which the Kapelle did not possess, being specially bought; and the management had spent nearly 2,000 thalers on the production — an expenditure, as Liszt told Wagner, till then unheard-of in Weimar. Even with a grand total of 16–18 violins the score could hardly have sounded as Wagner intended it to do, and as we are accustomed to hearing it to-day: the balance between the strings and brass must have been completely destroyed at times. But there were not even the 16–18 violins that Liszt had promised Wagner in his letter of the middle of July. Uhlig, who was present at the first performance, and who knew the opera by heart — it was he, indeed, who made the piano arrangement of it — tells us in his article in the *Neue Zeitschrift* that there were only six first violins, and asks what so small a body of strings could do against " a wind orchestra that is sometimes written not merely in two but in three parts in each section." The Lohengrin, one J. N. Beck, was obviously unequal to his task: the best that Uhlig can say for him is that he hears that Beck has done quite well in certain other operas.[4] All in all, the presumption is that these first performances of *Lohengrin* were hardly on the level of those of a small English touring company to-day.[5]

---

[4] As Beck was only twenty-three in 1850 he could not have had much experience of opera.

[5] See Vol. I, pp. 135, 136, for Liszt's frank admission, some years later, of the gross inadequacy in many respects, orchestral and scenic, of the Weimar performances of *Lohengrin* and the *Flying Dutchman*.

The first performance of *Lohengrin*, on the 28th August, took place as an "extra", after the conclusion of the theatre season. Only one more performance was possible just then: this took place on the 14th September. The third was given on the 9th October of that year, the fourth on the 12th April, 1851, and the fifth on the 11th May. The long intervals between the performances are accounted for, in the main, by the fact that Liszt spent only a small part of these years in Weimar, and when he was not there the theatre relapsed into its normal provincial sluggishness. *Lohengrin* was too exacting a work for the standard forces and the standard mentality of the place.

2

Wagner and Minna returned to Zürich on the 29th August. The story of his co-operation in the musical life of the town in the winter of 1850–1 has already been told. During this time the political spies were busy watching him and reporting to their superiors about him. It was difficult for these gentry, with their purely professional outlook, to believe that the Dresden ex-Kapellmeister was not still carrying on his nefarious political activities under the cloak of music. The Police Commissioner in Prague, one Weimann, sent off an anxious enquiry concerning Wagner to Councillor Eberhardt in Dresden — the editor of the *General Police Intelligencer*. Eberhardt at once got into communication with Captain Nötzli, the Chief of Cantonal Police in Zürich, who, after reporting that " Richard Wagner, the fugitive from Dresden ", was conducting concerts and operas in the town, though without any fixed appointment, went on to say that " the Jewish swindler Samuel Lehmann, known as Braunschweig ", had been handed over to the High Court at Hall on 1st February, and that " the notorious impostor and forger Mitalis Georg, alias Fürst, from Smyrna ", who had been expelled from Switzerland for life, was to be brought up before the authorities at Basel.[6]

Wagner, however, was blissfully unconscious of all this inter-State curiosity concerning him and of the distinguished criminal company in which his name was appearing in the police reports. Zürich as a whole was interested in him only as a brilliant composer and conductor who had settled in the town, very much to the town's advantage. His numerous admirers wishing to have a portrait of him, the local publishing firm of Orell Füssli & Co. engaged a local lithographer, Kaspar Scheuchzer, to touch up Kietz's drawing of 1842 in conformity with the changes that had taken place in Wagner in the interim. The difference between the two portraits, however, are infinitesimal, apart from a look of greater concentration in the eyes in the later one. Having been pressed, no doubt, by the enterprising publisher for a " message " to accompany the new lithograph, Wagner wrote underneath it, " The be-

[6] LWV, pp. 27 ff.

getter of the Art-Work of the Future is none other than the artist of the Present, who looks out upon the life of the Future and longs to be taken up into it. He who nourishes this longing within himself out of his own powers lives already a better life. But only the artist can do this." It is to be hoped that the good Zürichers understood the sentiment: perhaps its very obscurity impressed them.

The good air of Switzerland, the freedom from restraint in his life, and above all the production of *Lohengrin* in Weimar were now doing their beneficent work within him. It is true that the Weimar affair had made him realise once more that the public with the right intelligence for the new Wagner did not yet exist and would have to be made; and so he plunged, in October, 1850, into the writing of the voluminous *Opera and Drama*, the 330 large pages of which he dashed off, in spite of his other occupations, in the four months between October, 1850, and February, 1851.[7] Spontini having died on the 14th January, 1851, Wagner wrote for the *Eidgenössische Zeitung* of the 25th of that month the *Recollections of Spontini*, in which he praised the dead master, at the expense of the frivolous Rossini and the charlatan Meyerbeer, as the last dramatic composer to be impelled by enthusiasm for a lofty purpose: " Spontini is dead, and with him a great, highly estimable and noble art-period has manifestly gone to its grave." On the 8th May he wrote his long letter to Liszt apropos of the latter's brochure *De la Fondation Goethe à Weimar*. It was Liszt's desire that this letter should be published; but this did not happen until the 5th March, 1852, when it appeared in the *Neue Zeitschrift für Musik*. Meanwhile, in April, 1851, Wagner had been busy with his pamphlet on *A Theatre in Zürich*, which appeared in the summer of that year in pamphlet form in Zürich, portions of it also being reproduced in the *Neue Zeitschrift* of the 27th June and the 4th and 11th July. *A Communication to my Friends* occupied him during August of this year: it was published by Breitkopf & Härtel at the end of the following December. He was assuredly not idle all this time, whatever Minna might think of him. Only his unconquerable idealism could have sustained him in the face of her indiffer-

---

[7] It was published in three volumes by Weber, of Leipzig, in November, 1851, in an edition of 500 copies, for which Wagner received 20 Louisdor. The second edition was brought out in 1868–9.

ence, nay, hostility, to everything that was most vital to the artist in him. He tells Liszt, on the 9th March, 1851, that if he is to undertake a new musical work he must have his mere maintenance ensured by somebody or other for at least the remainder of the year,

> " as otherwise, on account of my wife, I shall not be able to find the necessary serenity and concentration. With all her excellent qualities, she unfortunately has no understanding whatever of my innermost being; the poor woman cannot find, in what I am and what I am doing, anything to help her to bear what has to be borne for the sake of that higher something; she perceives only the clouds about our lot, and cannot find consolation for that in any of my activities. My real self is alien to her. At the same time I pity her deeply for this very reason."

His passionate interest in his own inner intellectual world made it at all times a necessity to him to " communicate " himself liberally to his friends. To the ordinary unsympathetic observer of him this looked like mere egoism: Minna bluntly called it vanity.[8] His character, however, has to be accepted as a whole: without his burning conviction that the message he had to deliver to the world was of prime importance to it he would never have won through in the face of so many difficulties: he was fighting, he felt, not merely for himself but for the culture that alone could save civilisation. We have seen him, in 1848, reading the text of *Siegfrieds Tod* to his Dresden friends. In 1849 he had read a chapter of *The Art-Work of the Future* to a gathering in a small room in the Steinwiesstrasse. And now he had no sooner finished *Opera and Drama* than he must needs read the whole of that formidable work to his friends, and probably also to some strangers, on twelve evenings in February and March, 1851. The readings were given first of all in the Abendstern; the final ones took place perhaps in the Guild

---

[8] So it appeared to other unfriendly observers also. Frau Emma Herwegh, who was always Minna's friend rather than Richard's, described him as "this pocket edition of a man, this folio of vanity, heartlessness and egoism." (See JKWF, p. 120.)

Frau Herwegh's full-length portrait of Minna as *she* saw her will be found in HBD, pp. 133–4. She admits that she had little culture, little tact, that her conversation was "not precisely sparkling with wit", and that it was difficult for her to keep pace with a man of Wagner's quality, to follow him from height to height. She credits Minna, however, with a good heart, a charm of her own, and all the domestic virtues: "the world will never know all that this good and faithful proletarian soul did for her husband."

House in the Waag, his own rooms being unable to hold the gradually growing numbers of his auditors. Encouraged, no doubt, by the interest thus shown in his ideas, he proceeded to read *Siegfrieds Tod*, about the middle of March, to an audience so large that he had to take for the purpose either a room in the Hochschule or the smaller Casino hall. These readings were talked about in the German Press: and the *Neue Zeitschrift*, on the 30th May, informed its readers that Wagner was already engaged on the composition of the music of *Siegfrieds Tod*. This announcement was a trifle premature: there could be no question of setting *Siegfrieds Tod* to music now or for a long time to come, for already Wagner had conceived the idea of a preliminary drama to it. The resolution to write a *Young Siegfried* seems to have been taken shortly before the 10th May: the first extended Prose Sketch [9] for it was made, as is shown by Wagner's dates at the beginning and at the end, between the 24th May and the 1st June: two days later he began to work at the poem, completing it on the 24th. He had entered upon a path that meant the complete recasting of the great work that had been germinating in him since 1848, and the end of all his plans for an opera of his to follow *Lohengrin* fairly swiftly in Weimar and possibly other German theatres.

3

With the poem of *Young Siegfried* off his hands he could at last gratify an old desire of his — a visit from his faithful Uhlig, who had served him with unshakeable loyalty since his flight from Dresden. Uhlig was now to take his summer holiday in Switzerland. The friends were to meet at Rorschach, whither Wagner betook himself in the early days of July, tramping on foot through Rapperswil, Utznach, the 2,500 ft. high Ricken Pass, Lichtensteig, and

---

[9] It runs to 27 printed pages. It has recently been discovered that it was preceded by a very short sketch made rapidly on the third of four pages obtained by folding a sheet of large paper in two. A facsimile of this is given in SSE, p. 66. A few lines of notes, by way of further elucidation of one or two points, seem, by the character of the handwriting, to have been added at some later date. Later still, Wagner added to the upper part of the sheet two short paragraphs that fix further details. This historic sheet of paper was afterwards used by Wagner as a kind of wrapper for the poem of *Young Siegfried*, with the original manuscript of which it has fortunately been preserved for us.

St. Gallen, where he arrived on the 5th. There, of course, he hunted out Karl Ritter, and, equally of course, read him the poem of *Young Siegfried*. At Rorschach he was appalled to observe the ravages that Uhlig's consumption had wrought in him since last they had met. At the sight of him Wagner wanted to give up the idea of going back to Zürich by way of the Säntis (over 8,000 ft.), but Uhlig would not be dissuaded. The ascent, which was a more difficult one in those days than it is now, must have told severely on both of them, and especially on Uhlig. Wagner, for his part, was probably taxing his physical strength unduly, as he was to do on more than one occasion later in his excursions; his frequent bad health during this and the following years was almost certainly the result, in part, of his resorting to violent physical exercise after a prolonged period of intellectual strain, instead of resting. But rest was at all times impossible for a nature so energetic as his: and he enjoyed these climbs not only for the splendour of the views they brought him, but because of the curious feeling of exhilaration that always came over him in dangerous situations. Few men, and of artists fewer still, have had heads as steady as Wagner's. The perfect correlation between brain and body, the completeness of nervous control that shows itself in his copperplate handwriting and in the neatness of the fair copies of his scores, which, for the most part, are as legible as if they were engraved, manifested itself again in an exultant freedom from anything like giddiness at great heights: he would have made an excellent steeplejack or tight-rope walker. (His exploits in the matter of his debts, indeed, may be regarded as a kind of financial tight-rope walking. Only in an occasional moment of overwhelming strain did he lose his balance over these things; in the main, he showed a coolness and ingenuity and fertility of device that would have made him a Napoleon of finance had the Fates cast him for a business career).

But his companions, especially Karl Ritter, were not made of the same steely stuff. Karl's nerves finally gave out; and after one terrifying scene near the top of the Säntis, in which it became clear that the descent of the mountain on the precipitous side would cost Karl his life, and perhaps Wagner's and Uhlig's as well, the pair had to leave him behind in the care of a guide, who later shepherded him back to Zürich by an easier route. Uhlig and Wagner completed their itinerary according to plan, the former regaling his old Kapellmeister with spicy stories of events in the Dresden theatre since he had left it, and of Reissiger's complacent lapse back into the old ruts now that he was free of the embarrassing pressure of the idealism of his one-time colleague.

The two valetudinarians, of course, talked a great deal about their various symptoms. Uhlig had a pathetic belief in the virtues of a water-cure; according to a certain Dr. Rausse, who had made some stir in Germany by three portentous medical treatises on the subject, every real medicine can do what it does within us only because it is a poison, and therefore people who find themselves weak after a prolonged course of medicine-taking can restore their health only by driving out the poison through the skin by means of water. Wagner, after reading one of Rausse's books which Uhlig had brought with him, fell an easy victim to the man's arguments. Like most men whose health is constantly subnormal, he was given to thinking too much about his symptoms, and too ready to listen to any new theory that professes to cure the malady while all the time it does little more than expatiate on the symptoms. Never to the end of his days, apparently, did Wagner realise that a physician is never such a menace to his patients as when he is suffering from a rush of theory to the head. He tried, during his Swiss years, all sorts of cures, beginning with this of Rausse's. The results were always the same — the momentary sense of well-being that results from almost any change of diet and habit, followed inevitably by a worse state of health than before, the fundamental causes of his malaise having been left untouched.

4

Wagner and Uhlig were back in Zürich about the 8th or 10th July. The mere suggestion of a second Alpine trip was enough to send the scared Ritter back to St. Gallen; so the two old cronies set out without him about the end of July, going through Brunnen, on the eastern shore of the Lake of Lucerne, by way of Beckenried (on the southern shore) and the Surenen Pass (7,560 ft.), Attinghausen, the Reuss valley and Amsteg to Flüelen, and from there back by boat to Brunnen. The prime object of the two Schiller enthusiasts had evidently been to traverse the William Tell country from end to end. Uhlig returned to Dresden about the middle of August, apparently in as good health as he could ever be said to enjoy. The friends were destined never to meet again: the devoted Uhlig, who was one of the few men whom Wagner ever really loved, died six months later.

Between the first and the second of these excursions Wagner was visited in Zürich by the twenty-one-years-old Robert Radecke, who was later to become a Kapellmeister in Berlin and Director of the Stern Conservatoire there. He came armed with a letter from his Leipzig violin teacher Ferdinand David — a circumstance that seems to suggest that the effects of *Judaism in Music* in Leipzig professional circles had somewhat worn off by this time. Radecke had two audiences (on the 19th and 21st July) with Wagner, who received him as kindly as he always did young people who had come to worship at the shrine. Radecke's contemporary notes on the meetings are interesting to-day:

> "How sad it is", he records, "that so eminent an artist as Wagner, who is the most important German opera composer of the day, should have marred his fortunes by his revolutionary bias in politics, and consequently has to live now in Switzerland, far away from the musical world. He is very industrious in his solitude, however, and active both as composer and as writer on music."

When Radecke left Zürich he took with him, as a gift from Wagner, a piece of music paper that contains the earliest known record of the theme of the Ride of the Valkyries.[10] It runs thus:

<small>[10] Radecke's reminiscences, together with a facsimile of the musical quotation, will be found in an article by his son Ernst Radecke, *Schweizerreise eines jungen Musikers im Jahre 1851*, in JLVB, pp. 136 ff.</small>

These were the words — the first two of the following four lines —

> Nach Süden wir ziehen, Siege zu zeugen,
> kämpfenden Heeren zu kiesen das Loos,
> für Helden zu fechten, Helden zu fällen,
> nach Walhall zu führen erschlagene Sieger.

sung by the Valkyries in their colloquy with Brynhilde in the third scene of Act I of *Siegfrieds Tod.* (They do not appear, of course, in the *Götterdämmerung,* this scene having been entirely recast by Wagner when, after having prefaced *Young Siegfried* and *Siegfrieds Tod* with the *Valkyrie* and the *Rhinegold,* he gave the *Götterdämmerung* its present form).

The Radecke fragment is dated 23rd July, 1851: at that time Wagner's plan embraced only *Young Siegfried* and *Siegfrieds Tod.* On the 12th November, 1852, he contributed another sketch of the motive to an " Autographic Album " that was published in Bremen in 1855: this sketch runs to *four* lines,[11] but the final line appears as " wehrliche Sieger zu senden nach Walhall ". This affords an illustration of the way in which Wagner, all through the *Ring,* would modify his first poetic text when necessary, in order to make it conform with his *musical* idea. He had evidently felt that the last line, in its original form, led to musical monotony; the unaccented " nach " and " er- " would have necessitated an up-take before the strong beat of the next bar on " Walhall " and " -schlagene ". This would have meant five up-take phrases in eight bars. By altering the line to " wehrliche Sieger zu senden nach Walhall " he was not

für Hel–den zu fech–ten   Hel–den zu fäll–en.

wehr–lich–e Sieg–er   zu send–en nach Wal–hall.

---

[11] It has frequently been reproduced — see, for instance, GRW, Vol. II (Part I), p. 441, and TRW, p. 77.

only able to make this last phrase begin on the strong beat of the bar but to clinch the whole line with the vital word " Walhall ".[12] (It is unnecessary to quote the music of the first two lines, as it is the same as that in the preceding quotation). As the conversion of the text of *Siegfrieds Tod* into that of the *Götterdämmerung* took place between the early part of November and the Christmas of 1852, there could be no question at that time of his composing these four lines at all. The motive probably dates from long before the Radecke sketch of July, 1851. It is a pity we cannot have the whole of the sketches Wagner made for the *Siegfrieds Tod* music between 1848 and 1851. It is curious, by the way, that for the " Autographic Album " he should select, as illustrative of his new work, a passage which he now knew would never appear in it! [13]

Soon after Uhlig's departure Wagner finished *A Communication to my Friends* — on the 16th August. He had offered the book to Breitkopf & Härtel on the 4th June, saying that lately there had been so much critical discussion of his works, particularly of *Lohengrin*, that he now felt it necessary to elucidate for his " friends " — by which he means, of course, all who have become interested in his art — the seeming inconsistency between those operas of his by which the public knew him and his maturer views on the nature of the musical drama as set forth in *Opera and Drama*. He thought it desirable in Breitkopf & Härtel's own interests, he hinted to them, that they should be the publishers of this treatise of his, for it was

---

[12] A systematic exposition of the changes of this kind in the *Ring* text during the act of composition of the music would throw a most interesting light on Wagner the musician. It would call, however, for a whole volume.

[13] It may be observed that underneath the Radecke sketch Wagner has written: "Nehmen Sie diesen altfränkischen Vers aus den Zeiten der Grenzboten zum Andenken Ihres Aufenthaltes in Zürich." Gustav Freytag, in his *Erinnerungen*, tells us that Wagner had told him and others, in the autumn of 1848, of his plan for an opera on the Nibelungen subject, mentioning in particular the scene of the Valkyries riding through the air. In 1849 Freytag and Julian Schmidt bought the Leipzig journal *Die Grenzboten*, which distinguished itself during the remainder of Wagner's lifetime by its attacks on him. "From the frontiers [*Grenzen*] on which they have set themselves up", Wagner wrote ironically to Uhlig, "they send out their runners [*Boten*] right and left, and so make use of all occasions. . . ." The *Grenzboten* jibe about "Old-Frankish stuff" seems to have originated with one Riccius, to whom, apparently, Liszt (or someone else in Weimar) had been indiscreet enough to show the manuscript of *Siegfrieds Tod*, and who, in turn, had been indecent enough to make public use of this private confidence in a *Grenzboten* article. (See Bülow's assault on him in an article reprinted in BAS, pp. 18 ff.) Wagner's inscription on the Radecke sketch is an ironic reference to this *Grenzboten* catchword about "altfränkisches Zeug".

largely concerned with *Lohengrin,* the score of which the Leipzig firm had at last taken over on its own account. It is significant of the attention Wagner had attracted by this time, and a refutation of the absurd thesis that recognition only came to him after his death, that Breitkopfs should now decide not only to engrave the *full* score of *Lohengrin,*[14] but to publish the *Communication* and the three accompanying opera poems. As is often the pleasant way of publishers where authors and composers are concerned, they impressed it on Wagner that they were obeying the promptings of their noble hearts rather than the prudent dictates of their business heads: they pointed out to him that the book he was now offering them was of a kind that could appeal only to a small circle of readers, and that this sort of publication involved special dealings with the booksellers — a point, they hinted, which he had perhaps not taken into consideration. They delicately refrained from pointing out to him something he already knew quite well, that as the poems of the *Flying Dutchman, Tannhäuser* and *Lohengrin* were to be printed along with the *Communication,* and as the text of *Lohengrin* now belonged to them, it might have been difficult for him to negotiate with any other publisher.

Wagner was still so overwhelmed by their decision to engrave *Lohengrin* — an act of *noblesse,* he said, which almost made him feel ashamed, — and so anxious for the *Communication* to appear, that he was willing, he told them, to forgo any honorarium, though perhaps they would deign to remember him if the book should happen to sell well; they might even allow him a trifling commission on so many copies of the proposed edition of five hundred as the booksellers might take. Though a few thalers would be very welcome, the really vital thing to him is that the book shall appear. At the same time, he says, they are not to think of undertaking the publication if it is going to be a burden to them: in that case he will offer the book elsewhere. Having read the first page or two of the manuscript, the firm had no hesitation in proceeding with the printing of it, in spite of the fact that Wagner had already informed them that another work of his — the huge *Opera and Drama* —

---

[14] Wagner could hardly believe his eyes when he read their letter of the 25th June. It was almost "fabulous", he wrote to Liszt — engraving the full score of an opera that had been given only in Weimar!

was in process of publication by J. J. Weber. The conclusion is forced on us that Wagner was already too important a figure in German music for the firm to wish to lose touch with him: they accordingly offered him a hundred gulden for the *Communication* — " a very small honorarium, of course ", they tell him, " but you have yourself seen the matter through our eyes, and so we ask you not to despise it." [15]

5

That they had accepted the book not out of that almost reprehensible tenderness of heart that has always been a danger to publishers but with the knowledge that anything with Wagner's name attached to it would be a fair business proposition, is shown by their letter of the 23rd October to him. They had sent the manuscript to the printers without having read beyond the opening page or so. Now, when the proofs are coming through, they find, to their " dismay ", that in his Foreword he has indulged in certain reflections on Christianity and on his own connection with Saxon politics that are likely to result in confiscation of the book; and as *he* is secure from pursuit by the German authorities, owing to his residence in Switzerland, the consequences will be visited on them — plain business men who, as they put it, " keep utterly aloof, as a business firm, from politics of any kind, especially of the party order." As Wagner had not felt the slightest interest in politics for its own sake when he was writing the *Communication*, but was concerned solely with tracing his inner development as artist, and as he could think of no passage in the work likely to agitate the authorities, political journalism being what it then was, he could only assume that Breitkopfs were anxious to be rid of the book. He accordingly asked his brother-in-law Avenarius, who was now a publisher on his own account in Leipzig, to call on Breitkopfs and inform them that *he* would take over the publication of the *Communication*. Thanks to Avenarius's diplomacy the affair was amicably arranged. When the passages that had been objected to were specified by Breitkopfs, it turned out that they were of so little significance to Wagner that he did not in the least mind altering

---

[15] See the correspondence on both sides in RWBV, I, 21 ff.

them to placate these " apprehensive bourgeois with perhaps a dash of piety." [16] The only result of all the bother was a delay of a few weeks in publication; and as Wagner, during that time, had conceived (at Albisbrunn) the idea of two further dramas to precede *Young Siegfried* and *Siegfrieds Tod*, he had to alter the final pages of the *Communication* accordingly: his bold scheme, the no doubt astonished public now learned, was for a " special festival at some future time ", at which his Nibelungen drama [17] would be produced " in the course of three days and a fore-evening."

A day or two after he had removed to his new house in the Zeltweg, Wagner went off, on the 16th September, to Albisbrunn for his ardently desired cure. Uhlig, when he had lauded the virtues of water during that tramp through the mountains, had only been preaching to the converted, or at any rate the half-converted; for as early as December, 1850, Wagner had written him that he was taking baths in the morning and drinking cold water in bed; a month later he had got as far as wearing what seems to have been known at that time as a " Neptune-girdle " — presumably a cold wet belt of some kind; and on the 2nd February, 1851, we find him telling his brother-in-law Hermann Brockhaus, who was troubled about his wife's health, that the doctors do not understand the lady's

---

[16] The manuscript of the *Communication* is now in the possession of Herr Hausegger, Munich. The concluding paragraphs, which were omitted from the published book, have been printed for the first time by Otto Strobel in SWMF, pp. 564–5. In the last paragraph Wagner says that though he does not know whether his new "artistic undertaking" (the Siegfried drama) will attain its end under present European conditions, the doubt leaves him unperturbed. But if, he says, the foundations of his present activity as an artist should be destroyed, then "Welcome! I do not oppose where I myself, as artist, am contributing to the creative annihilation of the modern world. So if you ask what you are to understand, by that, what I am, I reply: I am neither a republican, nor a democrat, nor a socialist, nor a communist, but — an artistic being; and as such, everywhere that my gaze, my desire and my will extend, an out-and-out revolutionary, a destroyer of the old by the creation of the new!"

This was evidently one of the passages that frightened the publishers, who had evidently missed the significance of the "as such" — i.e. "as an artist." Uhlig, however, in an article in the *Neue Zeitschrift* of the 26th July, 1852, said in Wagner's own words what Wagner himself had not been allowed to say: "In fact only one description fits Wagner — that of revolutionary, that is to say, an out-and-out destroyer of the old and builder of the new; nothing more and nothing less." The proofs of the *Communication* had passed through Uhlig's hands.

[17] "I will write no more operas", he says. "As I do not wish to invent an arbitrary title for my works, I call them dramas, a term which will at least indicate clearly the standpoint from which the thing I offer should be accepted."

malady. According to Wagner, " in her case the blood is working on the nerves " — a truly luminous diagnosis: what she needs is " a rational diet, good air, and *water* ", all of which, of course, she will be able to obtain in Switzerland. (It was perhaps owing to Brockhaus's neglect to take Wagner's advice in medical matters that Ottilie survived until 1883). At the end of August, before he has gone to Albisbrunn, Wagner tells Uhlig that for the last week he has been on a strict water diet, which suits him extraordinarily well. As yet he has not read much of Rausse, he says, but he has grasped the principle of the thing — " no wine, no beer, no coffee, only water and cold milk. No soup, but everything cool or tepid. Early in bed, three or four glasses of cold water, then a wash. At midday, a bathe in the lake, or a hip-bath. . . . During the day I continually drink much water; after a meal I go out for half an hour, and so on." He is sure he is feeling better already, even though his head has become not merely light but rather giddy; this, however, is probably only the first effect of the treatment. He is confident that very soon he will have more health than he knows what to do with.

6

For Wagner, if a thing was worth doing at all it was worth doing thoroughly; and so he remained in Albisbrunn (in the hills south-west of Zürich), heroically undergoing his murderous cure, until the 23rd November. The institution was in charge of a doctor from Winterthur, one Christoph Zacharias Brunner. At first Wagner occupied a room on the ground floor; later he removed to a quieter one on the first floor, known to this day as the " Wagner room "; there still stands in it a small piano of the 1850 period, made by Huni & Hubert, on which Wagner may or may not have beaten out a theme for the *Ring* now and then. A co-inmate of the establishment was the Saxon Lieutenant Hermann Müller — in former days the lover of Wilhelmine Schröder-Devrient, and now, like Wagner, one of the exiles of 1849. By the end of September Karl Ritter had come from Stuttgart to join the other victims of medical science. He had latterly been trying to restore his health by drinking large quantities of water: but Wagner, with all the zeal of a convert, had persuaded him that this was highly dangerous unless one submitted to all the rest of the water-discipline. But Karl's enthusiasm for the ordeal by water was more theoretical than practical. He objected to cold milk, as being indigestible and unnatural: was not mother's milk always warm? He took more pleasure in cards and billiards than in cold baths and cold packs, which he dodged whenever he could; as for diet, he soon found a pastrycook's shop from which he could draw, unknown to Dr. Brunner, the supplies upon which he felt his life really depended.

The Albisbrunn regimen was certainly calculated to appal any-one but a fanatic, and to slay anyone who had not the constitution of a horse: Wagner details it in a letter to Uhlig:

> " 1. At half-past five in the morning, wrapping up in a wet sheet until seven; then a cold tub and a walk. Eight o'clock, breakfast — dry bread and milk, or water.
>
> 2. Another short walk; then a cold compress.
>
> 3. About twelve, a rub-down with damp towels; a short walk; another compress. Then dinner in my room, to avoid unpleasant consequences. An hour's idleness; a stiff walk of two hours, alone.
>
> 4. About five, another damp rub-down and a short walk.
>
> 5. About six, a hip-bath, lasting a quarter of an hour, followed by a walk to get my circulation up. Another compress. Supper about seven — dry bread and water. Then a whist party until nine, after which another compress, and about ten o'clock to bed."

His constitution was sound enough to stand even this murderous treatment, which included giving up his beloved snuff-taking; and for a while he felt rather better. Some time before this, a Zürich medical crank had put him on a sulphur regimen; and no doubt the Albisbrunn treatment did him a certain amount of good by cancelling out the previous error: for four weeks, he tells Uhlig, he has sweated sulphur, and then his wet cloth has become a light red, the result, he was assured in the establishment, of the expul-sion of mercury. Probably what did him most good of all was the escape from Minna — though she paid him a four days' visit at the end of October — and the considerate action of a rich uncle of Karl Ritter, who died suddenly, leaving a fortune to each member of the family; for now Frau Ritter was able to guarantee Wagner a regular income of eight hundred thalers.[18] Under the stimulating influence of this splendid exhibition of tact and timing on the part of a rich uncle, he was able, in spite of the rigours of his cure, to write Liszt, on the 20th November, a letter that runs to ten printed pages, in which he describes at length the changes in his mental outlook since 1848, his plans for the *Ring*, and his dream of a special festival production of the work. The letter must have been something of a shock for Liszt, for it meant, in fact if not in word, a great change in the relations between Wagner and Weimar: and as the charge has been made against Wagner that he was now showing " ingratitude " to Liszt, the chain of circumstances leading up to this point must be set out in full.

---

[18] It was from Albisbrunn that he wrote Uhlig the letter referred to on page 127, in which he angrily refused even to consider receiving assistance from his niece Johanna, who was now one of the "stars" of the Berlin Opera. It appears from a letter from Wagner to his other niece, Franziska, that Uhlig, on his way back to Dresden from Zürich, had met Johanna in Frankfort. She had apparently been moved by what Uhlig told her of Wagner's plight, and would have visited him and tried to do something for him had her parents not prevented her. See JKJ, p. 55.

CHAPTER XIII

WEAKENING OF THE LINK
WITH WEIMAR

1

O NE EFFECT of Paris on Wagner in 1850 had been to deepen his consciousness that he was in blood and bone a German artist, and could never be anything else with profit either to himself or to the world. In a letter to Uhlig he compares himself, after he had taken the definite resolution " under no condition whatever to write a work for Paris ", to the horse in the desert that cures itself by biting open a vein; " I rejoice in the feeling ", he says, " of this unhealthy, stagnant blood passing out of me. . . . Should I not live to see the fulfilment of the prophecy of the star-wise cobbler [in *Lumpacivagabundus*], grant me a death in that Alpine valley, but do not compel me to die like a rat in the great sweet-smelling flue. From the Alps I will write you a German *Wieland*, all complete, which the Folk will some day understand." But Paris had also disheartened him for the moment: how could one so fundamentally different from the rest of the operatic world as he now knew himself to be ever hope to find minds to understand him? So, he adds, " *Siegfried* and *Achilles*, for which the interpreters are not yet born, I will bequeath, printed — black upon white — to a more fortunate posterity."

The phrase " for which the interpreters are not yet born " is significant: with this depressing conviction within him, we ask ourselves, what hopes could he really have built on the one tiny town — Weimar — on which his artistic destiny seemed in 1850 and 1851 to depend henceforth? Liszt's production of *Lohengrin* there had indeed proved of benefit to him in that it sent the ball rolling towards the other German theatres, and that it gave him the heartening sense that at least one man in high places believed in him and would serve him through thick and thin. But it is clear enough that from the beginning he had not much faith in the capacity of Weimar to realise his new ideal, though for a time he fought down his disturbing doubts. Nor did he, in his heart of hearts, attach much real importance to a production of *Lohengrin* at Weimar or anywhere else. He already felt that he had himself outgrown this work, and that he had a much more important message to deliver to the world in *Siegfrieds Tod*. He was so different psychologically from any other musician who has ever lived that it is not always easy to see him as he saw himself; but it is manifest enough that the central impulse of his being was not to achieve honour and pile up riches by his work but to turn civilisation and culture into the only channel which, he felt, could save them. Modern art, he had told Liszt on the 20th July, 1850, is dying, and the thought fills him with joy. It is not art itself that is on its deathbed, but art as that lost generation understood it. The " monumental ", as he calls it — by which he means the more or less mummified art that was alive in its own day but is no longer representative of contemporary man, and, by its sacred prestige, has a stranglehold upon contemporary man's free expression of himself —

" all this cleaving to the past, must go; we must cast from us the egoistic anxiety for our own immortality: we will let the past be the past and the future be the future, and live only in *to-day*, in the full present, and create for this. . . . Having won this conviction, it cannot concern me any more to write works which I must condemn to death in advance in the present, in order to endow them with a flattering visionary immortality: what cannot become true for to-day will remain untrue for the future. So the illusion of creating over and above the present for the future no longer has any hold on me; but if I am to create anything for the present, this present must show itself to me in a less disgusting form than it does now. I renounce fame, and particularly the lunatic spectre of posthumous fame, because I love humanity far too much to want, for vanity's sake, to condemn it in thought to the poverty on which alone the posthumous fame of the dead is nourished. What impels me to artistic creation now is not ambition but the longing to communicate myself to my friends, the desire to give them pleasure: whenever this desire, this longing, is appeased I am happy and completely satisfied. If now you produce my *Lohengrin* in tiny Weimar with delight and love, joy and success . . . I shall feel so blessed thereby, my purpose so fully achieved, that I shall have no further concern with this work, and can then strive to present you [i.e. his friends] with something new of the same kind. Now give your verdict! Can you chide me for these convictions, seeing that they rob me of all egoism, all the petty passion of ambition? Surely not! "

It is not surprising that a man who took this view of his art should be for ever complaining of his loneliness: he would have been an intellectual solitary in any epoch. It is noteworthy that never, in his letters, does Liszt really discuss matters of this kind with Wagner. For all his admiration for his friend's *musical* genius and for the courage of his idealism, he never quite understood his nature in its totality. Nor, perhaps, did any one individual in Wagner's lifetime ever succeed in fully doing so, with the exception of Cosima: the key to the peculiar mental constitution of the man is possible only to us who, at half-a-century's remove from him, and in the possession of countless documents that throw a light on him, can at last see him to the centre and in the round.

2

Let us try to visualise the situation as Wagner must have seen it about 1850. On Weimar itself he could never have built much hope: the town counted for nothing whatever in German musical life, and was hardly likely ever to do so. Weimar, for him, meant simply Liszt, as he tells his friend: and from the first he must have felt that Liszt's power to help him would apply only to the operas he had finished and put behind him, not to the very different works he was planning for the future, — though he did not give definite expression to this feeling until, having attained to full consciousness of all that the *Ring* drama implied, he could no longer cherish the smallest illusion about Weimar. What, in all probability, played a large part in his desire to have *Lohengrin* produced there was the hope that he himself might hear it; for he felt it necessary to see this last work of his on the stage before settling down to compose the music to a new one. Liszt no sooner tells him of his resolve to give *Lohengrin* than Wagner throws out the suggestion that it shall be arranged for him to go to Weimar incognito for the first performance: the Grand Duchess, he hopes, will consent to " snap her fingers at the German police " and provide him with a safe conduct under another name. Liszt, of course, had to tell him frankly that anything of the kind was impossible. Wagner's hope of hearing his work being thus frustrated, the production had little more significance for him, at the moment, than the small fee it brought him.

Though he did not learn the worst about the Weimar production till later, he must have suspected from the first that the event had not answered to his desires; and if Weimar could not be trusted to perform *Lohengrin* adequately, what could it hope to do with something so unprecedented as *Siegfrieds Tod?* A month or so before *Lohengrin* was given, Liszt had told him that if this proved a popular success he would propose to the Grand Duke that he should commission *Siegfrieds Tod* for Weimar, and send Wagner an advance honorarium to support him for the six months presumed to be necessary for the writing of the music. Encouraged by these signs of friendliness on everyone's part towards him, Wagner tells Liszt, on the 20th July, 1850, that if *Lohengrin* turns out satisfactorily from the local point of view he will compose *Siegfrieds Tod*, but only for Liszt and for Weimar. He actually seems to have contemplated beginning work at it there and then: " the music to my *Siegfried* ", he writes to Liszt on the 16th August, " already runs through every limb of me." But a certain disillusionment must have crept over him soon after the production of the 28th August. He knew well that neither the actors, the singers, the producers, nor the public as yet existed for the adequate realisation of his ideals; a revolution would be necessary in the theatre before this could happen. Weimar had been pressing him to allow *Lohengrin* to be cut — a sure sign that neither the players nor the producer nor the audience had grasped the *drama* of the work, which was all in all to him.

" If I do not win this victory [over the indolence and stupidity of all concerned]," he had told Liszt on the 8th September, 1850, " if I must capitulate in the present instance, in which I have so many powerful allies, yourself, for example, by my side, then I fight no more battles. If my *Lohengrin* can only be kept going by the sacrifice of the artistic unity that was my plan in writing it . . . then I give up opera entirely: Weimar has for me no more interest than any other theatre, and I have written my last opera."

Liszt, in his soothing reply, agrees with Wagner that a reformation is necessary in the theatre generally, but thinks that, unintelligent as the singers are, the real root of the trouble is first of all the critics, who are hopelessly sunk in routine, and secondly the public, which has become Philistine through force of habit and lack of guidance. Wagner's rejoinder to this is the one that he was to make many times in the following years — that the public is by nature sound enough in its instincts, but is misled by the critics and by the art-intelligentsia in general, people who know nothing in reality, but to whose dogmatic judgments the public has become accustomed to pay a quite preposterous respect. He asks for nothing from his hearers but " healthy senses and a human heart ", the dictates of which they will follow without concerning themselves with the nonsense talked by their self-appointed guides in matters of art. Time proved that he was right: the majority of the public took him to its heart in defiance of the enmity of the greater portion of the European Press.

3

That he was now becoming decidedly dissatisfied with Weimar is shown by his letter of the 20th September, 1850, to Uhlig. Liszt, he says, had held out to him hopes for a fee of 30 Louisdor for *Lohengrin*, but the theatre has actually paid him only 130 thalers. Liszt had talked of the commissioning of *Siegfrieds Tod* for Weimar, and of a subsidy to keep him alive while he was writing the music; but not a word more had reached him on this subject. If now he is asked whether he will give *Siegfrieds Tod* to Weimar, his answer, " as matters now stand ", must be " an unqualified No! " " I really *abandoned Lohengrin* when I permitted its production in Weimar. . . . I need not give you my further reasons when I declare that I want *Siegfried* brought into the world in a different fashion from what would be possible to the good people there." Then comes the famous passage in which he foreshadows the " festival " idea that was to come to fruition a quarter of a century later in Bayreuth. If he had his way, he says, he would erect, in some beautiful meadow near Zürich, a wooden theatre built to plans of his own, furnished merely with what was necessary to produce

Siegfrieds Tod. For chorus he could rely on the amateurs of Zürich. The best singers to be found anywhere, and an orchestra correspondingly good, would be " invited " to Zürich for six weeks. The production would take place in the summer of the selected year; and in the preceding January all friends of the musical drama would be invited, through the newspapers, to visit Zürich. Admission would be free to these travellers: he would also invite the local young people, the students, the choral unions, and so on. He would give three performances of *Siegfrieds Tod* in one week; after the third, the theatre would be pulled down, the score burnt, and he would say to " those who had been pleased with the thing ", " Now do likewise! " If they ask for something new from him, his reply will be, " You get the money together! " For the fulfilment of this plan he would need 10,000 thalers.

There is a touch of whimsical exaggeration in all this, but, for those who understand the peculiar nature of the man, no more than a touch. He would probably, when it came to the point, have refrained from committing his score to the flames. Even as to that, however, we cannot be too sure. He held that when a work has been written the creator of it should put it definitely from him and pass on to the acquisition of a new life-experience, to be incarnated in its turn in a new work of art. We have to remember his thesis that " egoistic " art would have to pass away, to be replaced by an art that should be the work of the community: " the free artistic Fellowship ", he had said in *The Art-Work of the Future*, " is therefore the foundation and the condition of the art-work itself." In this fellowship he had included the performer as virtually coequal with the dramatist — not, of course, the performer as he then was, and unfortunately still is, but the performer as he might be, taking up the work into himself and creating it afresh on the stage from the centre of the spirit that had given birth to it on paper. When writing *The Art-Work of the Future* he had already in mind something corresponding very closely to the ideal of a festival production, followed by the setting aside of the accomplished endeavour and the passing on to a new one, that he sketches in his letter to Uhlig. The free giving of service on the part of the performing artist is also hinted at in *The Art-Work of the Future*, in the passage in which Wagner speaks of " that artistic fellowship which comes together for no other aim than the satisfaction of a common artistic impulse "; in the passage, again, that runs, " when once the [creative] artist has raised his project to a *common* one by the energy of his own enthusiasm, the artistic undertaking in its turn becomes thenceforth a *common one.*" In *A Communication to my Friends*, which was not written till rather later than the period of the letter to Uhlig, he sets forth his conviction that each truly vital dramatic work of the present demands, as the very condition of its being, a presentation that shall aim at calling out in the spectators the life-conditions that had animated the dramatist in the creation of the work. He held that men can never truly express or represent anything but the art of their own epoch — a theory for which there is a good deal to be said.

" The poet's purpose ", he says, " would only be fully realised not merely when he saw it correspondingly expressed upon the stage, but also when this happened at a definite time, under definite conditions, and before an audience with a definite affinity to himself." " A poetic aim which I have conceived with a view to certain definite relations and surroundings ", he continues, " achieves its wholly correspondent effect when I impart it in the same relations and the same surroundings, . . . but not when all these life-giving conditions shall have disappeared and the relations have changed." He selects, in support of this thesis, a character like Mozart's Don Juan. This was the natural product of an eighteenth century mentality; it was fully understood by everyone in its own epoch because in the first place it enshrined the mind of its own civilisation, in the second place because not only the author, the composer and the public but the performers also had the type in their blood and bones. It is no longer the same thing, he goes on to say, when the drama of Don Juan is performed, as in our days, before a totally different public — boursiers, state officials, and so on — and the character is played by an actor who spends so much of his leisure on beer and skittles that he is never tempted to be unfaithful to his wife. " Will not *this* Don Juan be understood in a way quite different from that intended by the poet, and is not this quite other understanding — at best reached only through the medium of criticism

— in truth simply *no* understanding at all of the real Don Juan? " [1]

In proportion, then, Wagner continues in *A Communication to my Friends*, as the work of the modern dramatist springs out of the heart of modern life itself, instead of being the product, as so much art is, of a mere facility in playing the conventional aesthetic game, it can be adequately realised only by performers and adequately grasped by spectators only while these are part and parcel of the same inner forces that brought it into being. Only misunderstanding of the artist and of the art can result if the work is treated " as a ' monumental ' one, which may indifferently be given at any convenient time or before any audience one pleases." Hence the necessity for the artist to look for support and understanding to " fellow-feeling and fellow-creating friends ", who can understand his situation and share in his endeavour.[2] And Wagner proceeds to tell his readers how from the beginning he had never indulged himself in the dream that *Siegfrieds Tod* would be possible in the theatre as it then was. He had written the poem because he had to do so, as some kind of consolation for the disgust he had long felt with modern life and modern art; and when it had been borne in upon him that he was doomed to be a solitary in the modern world of art he had turned to the subject of *Jesus von Nazareth* — a study of one who also had realised his loneliness in a world given up to materialism, and had made his " self-offering the imperfect utter-

---

[1] As so often happened with Wagner, he had unconsciously lighted here on a principle the basic truth of which was to be perceived only much later. In proportion as modern musical criticism calls in history to its aid it becomes evident that no later generation can hear old music precisely as its composer conceived it and as his contemporaries heard it. It is possible, of course, for the men of a later day to hear more in it than its contemporaries did; but whether they hear more or less, it is certain they do not hear quite the same thing. We can get out of a work of art only what we bring to it; and to the extent that we are the product of a society and a culture that did not exist until to-day we must have lost the key to much that was vital in old art for the men of its own epoch. To take an extreme case, it is impossible for us to look at a statue of one of the Greek gods as an ancient Greek looked at it. For us, it is a matter for purely aesthetic contemplation, and that in the light of many a further development in the art of sculpture. Not only did the Greek see it without this purely aesthetic perspective, but for him its meaning as a work of plastic art was intensified by its religious associations. In the same way, an ancient Greek brought to life to-day and taken to see a modern Passion Play would see it with his eyes alone, without the *mental* predisposition towards being moved by it that the modern man — even the Freethinker — possesses as the result of two thousand years of Christian legend and Christian art.

[2] See RWGS, IV, 242 ff.

ance of that human instinct that drives the individual into revolt against the loveless totality of things." [3]

4

It was Liszt's great service towards him, he goes on to say, that after the production of *Lohengrin* he had run to meet its creator with the cry, " See! Thus far have we brought it: now create for us a new work, so that we may bring it further yet! " All this, be it remembered, was written in the summer of 1851, that is to say, nearly a year after he had told Uhlig that he was not satisfied with the way *Lohengrin* had been given in Weimar, that he would like to see *Siegfrieds Tod* brought into the world in a different fashion from what was possible to the good people there, and that he now had the heart to finish his new work only because he had conceived the " chimerical plan ", as he calls it, of producing it under " festival " conditions in a temporary theatre specially created for the purpose. It is clear that at this time he was more or less disillusioned as to Weimar. The " good people " there were taking, with the best intentions, the wrong line with regard to him. Regarding him as just an opera composer who wanted to make his profitable way in the world like the others, they kept assuring him, after the third performance, that *Lohengrin* was already on the way to becoming as popular as *Tannhäuser*, and that only " small concessions " on his part and " zealous propaganda " on theirs were now necessary in order to have the whole German opera public running after him. " I presume ", he says in the letter in which he communicates this news to Uhlig (on the 22nd October, 1850), " that I must appear to them stark mad when, in return for these announcements of theirs, I stubbornly assure them that they are in error about something that is impossible."

Yet at this very time, encouraged, no doubt, by the news that Liszt was preparing an article on *Lohengrin* for a Paris journal, he was once more thinking of embarking upon the music of *Siegfrieds Tod*. The winter, he tells Liszt on the 8th October, 1850, is his deadly enemy; his health is bad, and he cannot begin composing

---

[3] RWGS, IV, 332.

till the spring; the score, however, will be ready in the following summer. He closes the discussion of his own work with a curt " For the present I can't think of anything further "; and asks Liszt to send him some of *his* scores. Six weeks later he informs Liszt that he is clearing his mind of the last vestiges of theory by writing *Opera and Drama*, to be followed by *A Communication to my Friends*, and that after that he will be finished with speculation and will give himself up again to unconscious creation.[4] He is encouraged by all that Liszt has done for him and by his understanding of him; heartened also by a few articles in the German Press that reveal sympathy with his aims.[5]

On the 24th December, 1850, and the 18th February, 1851, he assures Liszt once more that he is only waiting for the spring to begin the composition of *Siegfrieds Tod*. But on the 9th March he evidently feels that the time has come to clear up the situation once for all. He reminds Liszt of the plan the latter had broached in the preceding summer for a sustentation grant to enable him to set to work at the music of *Siegfrieds Tod*, with a view to a production in Weimar: either, he says, he must see this plan being realised or he must cease to think about it. He had at one time intended to print the poem, as a kind of despairing recognition that the opera would be theatrically impossible; but from this step he had been held back by the hopes that Liszt had implanted in him. Meanwhile his pecuniary situation has become desperate. He has not yet found a publisher for *Opera and Drama*. He has had to support himself for the last six months — since the spending of the small Weimar

---

[4] He also thinks, he says, of republishing the best of the articles he had written during the Paris period of 1839–42. The main motive for this, however, was no doubt merely the hope of raising a little money.

[5] For the first time in his life he was meeting with a certain amount of sympathy and understanding in the Press; and the contrast with the atmosphere of journalistic enmity that had surrounded him in Dresden called out all his optimism. The Weimar Court Councillor Franz Müller had written an appreciative article on *Lohengrin* for the Frankfort *Konversationsblatt*. Adolf Stahr had done the already mentioned article for the Berlin *Nationalzeitung;* J. C. Lobe one for the Leipzig *Signale;* Gérard de Nerval one for the Paris *Presse* that was warm in tone if not specially conspicuous for understanding; and Uhlig, musically the most intelligent of them all, had rendered valuable service in the *Neue Zeitschrift*. (Lobe afterwards turned against Wagner on account of *Judaism in Music*. His anonymous article of 1854 on Wagner, in the *Gartenlaube*, was afterwards reprinted in his book *Consonanzen und Dissonanzen*. See LCD, pp. 1 ff.)

fee for *Lohengrin* — on what Frau Ritter has been able to allow him, plus a trifling fee for conducting two Beethoven symphonies in Zürich. He knows that Frau Ritter's circumstances do not permit her to do more for him than she has already done. Consequently, if things remain as they are, he must give up the idea of composing *Siegfrieds Tod,* and, repugnant as this is to him, try to make some kind of a living by journalism. On the other hand, if he is to embark upon a new musical work he must see his immediate future secured — to at least the end of the present year, — otherwise he can neither find the necessary frame of mind for creation nor be safe from the reproaches of his wife. He must therefore speak frankly to Liszt. He knows the difficulties that have beset his friend in the further prosecution of his plan — the Grand Duchess had been ill, and so could not be present at *Lohengrin* until the third performance; then Liszt had been absent from Weimar for a long time; and so on. But " I must know *now* just where I stand." And so, will Liszt tell him once for all whether he is to go on hoping or give up hope. If the latter, he has no hesitation in asking Liszt to send him some money, no matter how little, so that he may win a moment's breathing space in which to adjust himself to the new circumstances that have arisen through the collapse of the Weimar scheme.

5

Liszt does not reply to this urgent appeal until the 9th April. It was not until the 4th that he had returned to Weimar; and reading between the lines we gather that the intervening time had been spent in trying to bring the feeble courage of the Court to the sticking-point.[6] *Lohengrin,* he says, should have been given on the 8th, but Beck is hoarse; anyhow two more performances of the opera will be given during the present season. He sends Wagner the German manuscript of the *Lohengrin* essay, asking him to post it at once, after looking through it, to the publisher Weber in Leipzig, as it will probably appear in the next number of the Leipzig *Illustrirte*

---

[6] On the 15th April he had written to the Princess Wittgenstein, "I am going to open negotiations [with the Court] as to *Siegfried.* Perhaps I shall succeed!" He refers to the matter again in his letter of the 30th. Apparently it was settled in the first days of May.

Zeitung; the French version will be issued by Brockhaus. " Have you received the 100 thalers? " he asks — which looks as if he had responded promptly to Wagner's appeal for funds. Then he sets himself to reply to Wagner's last letter, which, he says, has made him sad. He has not yet " definitely given up the hope " of bringing to a successful end " the somewhat difficult diplomatic affair " of *Siegfrieds Tod.* Perhaps he will be able to do so by the middle of May. Wagner is to make his financial position clear in writing, and to set forth the plan of the work and " the just artistic hopes " connected with it. All this is not for Liszt himself . . . " you know *me* and know that you can trust me absolutely."

Wagner, in the interval between the receipt of this letter and his reply to it (on the 18th), has received the issue of the *Illustrirte Zeitung* containing Liszt's article; and this has been enough to lift him out of his depression. Hope has sprung up in him again. " At the beginning of May I will start on my *Siegfried,* no matter what happens. Away with all guarantees for my existence: I won't starve to death! " Avenarius is going to publish *Opera and Drama* and pay him 100 thalers; [7] " it is next to nothing, but I don't think I can get any more." Liszt will no doubt put aside a groschen or two for him now and then, while Frau Ritter will do what she can: " next winter I shall earn a few Louisdor by conducting symphonies; and so, all in all, the devil won't get me, if only my wife will keep quiet." He will not trouble the Grand Duchess any further; if of her own accord she sees fit to make him an offer, that will be a different matter.

Liszt's next letter is dated 17th May. Before then, however, the Weimar Court had managed to make up its vacillating mind about *Siegfrieds Tod.* On the 3rd, Zigesar had written to Wagner direct,[8] offering him 500 thalers for the new work, 100 to be paid on the 1st July, 100 on the 1st November, 100 on the 1st March, 1852, and, " if the score is delivered by the 1st July, 1852," the remaining 200 on that date. Wagner confirms this in his letter of the 10th

---

[7] In the end, however, it was published by J. J. Weber: Wagner received 20 Louisdor down, and the promise of another 20 when the edition (500 copies) should be sold out. He therefore did rather better for himself by the new arrangement.

[8] The letter has apparently not survived. Our information about it is derived from Liszt's letter of the same day to the Princess.

May to Uhlig. But, he continues, the affair has now taken on a new complexion in his mind; evidently he can persuade himself no longer that *Siegfrieds Tod* is possible in Weimar. As far back as July, 1850, he had told Liszt that he could not compose the music for it " in the air ": for his heroes he needed, he said, actors such as the German stage had not yet seen; and where were these to be found? He was still sanguine enough to believe at that time, however, that Liszt could perform the miracle of calling these actors out of the earth. By May, 1851, when he is writing to Uhlig, this illusion has left him: " Were I to undertake *Siegfrieds Tod* with a serious view to a performance in Weimar next year, I should have to recognise that the thing is utterly impossible. Where could I get actors and public? " Now he has been obsessed all through the winter by a new dramatic subject, that of the old folk-tale of the youth who sets out " to learn fear ", but is " too stupid to learn it." One day it dawned on him that this youth was no other than his own Siegfried, who wins the hoard and awakens Brynhilde. This will be a better subject for Weimar — for the public as a whole, indeed — because the myth is here presented in the clearest and most plastic form, " just as a fairy tale is presented to a child." Two advantages will result: in the first place the public will be helped by this fresh, gladsome tale to understand better the problems put before it in the more serious *Siegfrieds Tod,* and in the second place the training the actors will receive in the lighter work will be of service to them when they have to approach the more exacting one. The two operas are to be connected yet independent: at the first production they will be played in succession, but afterwards they can be given individually as the theatres may desire.

6

Deep down in his subconscious mind the vast subject upon which he had been brooding since 1848 was now evolving organically according to its own imperious inner law. It was not long before he was to discover that even yet the process of gestation was not complete. The conviction of the necessity of a *Young Siegfried* must have come to him quite suddenly: after having told Avenarius on the 3rd May, 1851, that he was about to begin the music of

Siegfrieds Tod, he now, on the 10th, communicates to Uhlig his intention, in spite of the Weimar commission, of putting this work aside and writing a preliminary drama. He writes to the same effect two days later to Bülow, who is on the point of leaving St. Gallen for Weimar. When telling him of the commission he has received from Weimar for *Siegfrieds Tod,* however, he adds that although he is about to set to work at the music of this — which is in direct contradiction to what he had told Uhlig — his plan is now to be extended so as to include a preliminary opera that shall be at once " more produceable " and more within the comprehension of the public.

Was he, one wonders, anxious not to tell Bülow, who of course would tell Liszt, that there was no likelihood of his being able to carry out for some time yet the particular scheme for which Weimar had given him a contract? We can understand his reluctance, his financial position being what it was just then, to say anything that might lead to the cancellation or suspension of the contract and the consequent withholding of the sorely needed 500 thalers. We learn from Liszt's letter of the 13th May to the Princess that " Zigesar has just spent an hour with me and communicated to me Wagner's reply: he accepts, with admirably expressed gratitude, the proposition as regards *Siegfried,* but he will first write a *Young Siegfried* — which will be given in February, 1853, at the latest — in order to prepare the public for *Siegfrieds Tod."* Wagner, of course, *may* have cherished the hope that the none-too-brilliant Weimar singers might prove equal to the easier *Young Siegfried,* and so receive the necessary education for *Siegfrieds Tod.* But in the light of what he had said to Uhlig it is a little difficult to believe this entirely. In all probability he thought he might as well secure the subsidy for the period during which he would be writing *Young Siegfried,* and trust to the gods that when the time came to produce that work, in substitution for *Siegfrieds Tod,* all would be well in Weimar. That Liszt himself was a little doubtful how the news of the change of plan would be received by the Court is clear from his letter of the 17th May. He is wholeheartedly with Wagner in his new scheme — " really you are a quite incredible fellow ", he says, " to whom one has to take off one's hat three times "; but, he adds, it will be as well to preserve absolute silence (he underlines these words) about the matter until the score of *Young Siegfried* is sent in, which will presumably be on the 1st July, 1852. It shall be a secret between himself and Zigesar, who apparently can be trusted.

That a letter is missing from the correspondence seems to be indicated by Wagner's next letter (22nd May), in which he appears to enlarge upon a hint of his intentions that had presumably already been given to Liszt. He has a vision of a new theatre that will bring salvation to German dramatic art, and he hopes a commencement may be made in Weimar: he exhorts Liszt to set at once about the creation of a new breed of singers who will also be good actors, and to get a better régisseur than Genast, who, capable and willing as he is, belongs to the old school, from the routine of which he cannot escape: Wagner would prefer to see at Weimar a man like his former Dresden colleague Eduard Devrient. He urges upon Liszt a drastic reform of the repertory — above all he must make an end of that system of constant fluctuation between all the European styles and genres that makes it impossible for the singers to develop an authentic German style: " To-day Gluck, to-morrow Donizetti, to-day Weber, to-morrow Rossini or Auber, to-day something serious, to-morrow something frivolous — what can come out of all this? Simply that they can perform adequately neither Gluck nor Donizetti, neither the serious nor the frivolous." The evil is aggravated by the German translations to which foreign operas are sung, translations that are not only wretched in themselves — thus confirming the singers in the delusion that only the notes, not the words, matter in opera, — but are so untrue to the original that often neither the actors nor the public are brought into direct relation with the drama, such as it is. If the singers want to solve their purely lyrical problems, they must first grasp the dramatic essence of their parts. He recommends, as the basis of the repertory, the works of the older French school, in which a dramatic idea is set forth naturally and realised clearly.

" If an opera personnel cannot first of all give an effective representation of Cherubini's *Water Carrier*, Méhul's *Joseph*, and things of that kind, how will it ever be able to overcome the enormous difficulties of one of my operas? The end to keep in view is — new works of a kind that are adapted to the capacities of our theatre personnel and specifically planned for our theatre."

The advice was sound enough in itself; it left out of account only two things — the indifference of most opera singers to any consideration but that of winning popularity and making money in the easiest way possible, and the indifference of the main body of the public, which regards the theatre only as a means of entertainment after its day's work, to questions of art and culture pure and simple.

Wagner finishes the poem of *Young Siegfried* on the 24th June, but he is rather reluctant to send it to Liszt: he would prefer his friend to come to Zürich, if possible, so that he may *read* it to him; apparently he distrusts Liszt's ability to see, by a mere silent reading of the poem on his own account, how so novel a scheme will work out in music and on the stage: Wagner knows his own powers as an actor, and feels that he can make the characters and situations live if he reads the poem to his friend in his own way. But Liszt finds it impossible to get to Zürich just then, and indeed he shows no great anxiety to receive a copy of the poem. Wagner, for his part, was perhaps beginning to feel that his optimism had carried him too far with regard to Weimar. Uhlig was with him between about the 8th July and the middle of August, and it is a fair surmise that from him Wagner received, for the first time, full and authentic information about the Weimar *Lohengrin* production. He would realise now how imperfect the performances had been in almost every respect, and how impossible it would be for Liszt ever to carry out, under Weimar conditions, the fundamental reform of the theatre that Wagner had in mind. Brooding, no doubt, over these and kindred matters during the autumn of 1851, he probably welcomed with joy the more or less sudden perception, at Albisbrunn, that two *further* dramas would be necessary to complete his great work. The first hint of this occurs in a letter to Uhlig that is undated, but must belong to some time in October: he has in his head, he says, " some big plans besides *Siegfried* — three dramas, with a three-act *Vorspiel*. If all the German theatres tumble down I will erect a new one on the banks of the Rhine, call people together, and produce the whole in the course of a week." Uhlig may not have gathered from this that the new " big plans " were an expansion of the *Siegfried* plan: but he receives more definite information in Wagner's letter of the 3rd November: " I am planning three dramas (the second and third of which are the two *Sieg-friends*) and a big *Vorspiel*. When all is finished I contemplate producing it in my own way." [9] This of itself suggests pretty clearly that in inner fact, if not in words, he had already parted company from Weimar. Nine days later he asks Uhlig to smuggle out of the Dresden Royal Library for him Hagen's translation of the *Volsungasaga*, which he needs in order to refresh his memory with regard to one or two details; but he has already progressed so far with the treatment of the material that he can give Uhlig an outline of the two new dramas.

7

And now he is fully conscious that Weimar no longer comes into the reckoning. In his undated October letter to Uhlig there was already a hint of this. Uhlig was seeing the *Communication* through the press. Wagner asks him to instruct Breitkopfs to send a complete set of final proofs to Liszt: as soon as he hears that this has been done, he says, he will send Liszt the poem of *Young Siegfried* — but not before. He will tell Liszt that he adheres to his intention of finishing the double work, but that he will not allow it to be produced in Weimar unless he can be present himself: and this, he foresees, will mean the abrogation of the contract. As there was the minimum of prospect of his being amnestied in the near future, and as the plan for *four* Nibelungen dramas was already taking shape in his mind, it is evident that, in whatever diplomatic language he might veil his thoughts in his letters to his friend, all was over between him and Weimar.

" One other thing ", he tells Uhlig, on the 12th November, " determined me to enlarge my plan — the feeling I had of the impossibility of producing *Young Siegfried* also in anything like a suitable way in Weimar, or anywhere else. I cannot and will not endure any longer the martyrdom of things done by halves. With this new conception of mine I withdraw *entirely* from all connection with our theatre and public of to-day: I break decisively and for ever with the

---

[9] Not, as in the English version of Uhlig's letters, "I think of carrying it out in my own manner." The verb that Wagner uses, *aufführen* (not *ausführen*), indicates clearly that what he means is not the "carrying out" of the poetic and musical plan but the *production* of the work in a theatre.

formal present. Do you now ask me what I propose to do with my plan? First of all to realise it, so far as it lies within my poetic and musical powers to do so. This will take me at least three full years. And so I place my existence wholly in the Ritters' hands: God grant *that they may remain unfalteringly true to me!* I can imagine a performance only under quite other conditions than those possible in Weimar or anywhere else. I will erect a theatre on the banks of the Rhine and issue invitations to a great dramatic festival. After a year's preparation I shall produce the whole work in the course of three or four days. Extravagant as this plan may be, it is nevertheless the only one to which I now devote my life and my labours. If I live to carry it out, I shall have lived gloriously: if not, I die for something fine."

Before Liszt received any intimation of this change in Wagner's attitude towards Weimar, others of his friends must have been aware of it. Uhlig had evidently shown Wagner's Albisbrunn letter to Frau Ritter, and she had drawn the logical conclusion from it; for on the 20th November we find Wagner writing to Uhlig,

"Tell Frau Ritter that when she gave me the advice, through you, not to 'break' unnecessarily with Weimar, the matter was quite unclear to her; that I am not inimical to Weimar, through presumption, caprice, or obstinacy, but that I now have something in hand which — by its very nature and by the way it has taken root in me — makes it impossible for me to consider Weimar any more."

He sees quite clearly at this time that the new path upon which he is entering involves a complete break with the existing operatic world, and almost certainly a long wandering in the wilderness. For that reason, he tells Uhlig, the Ritter pension has come in the nick of time. But, he assures him, even without that he would not have submitted to any compromise: "Even without this bit of luck — you know me well enough to believe this! — I would not have budged an inch from my path, and the latest crisis in my artistic plans would not have differed by a hair's-breadth from what it is now." Of that we cannot have the least doubt to-day. "Only", he continues, "I should have had to carry on under such troubles, anxieties and struggles that I would have set to work in a dark and bitter mood, instead of, as now, in the highest spirits."

One wonders how, on his return to Zürich, Minna received the news of what must have seemed to the poor woman the final evidence of her husband's unfitness for practical life, if not of his complete insanity. His immediate difficulty, however, was not Minna but Liszt. From his next letter to Uhlig (11th November) we realise what an embarrassment the contract with Weimar had latterly become to him. The manuscript of *A Communication to my Friends* had been sent to Breitkopfs in August, that is to say, at a time when his scheme embraced only *two* dramas, to be produced, according to the plan, in Weimar. As we have seen, the final pages of the *Communication*, in which he had announced this intention — coupled with a warm eulogy of Liszt for all he had done for him — had therefore to be modified now: perhaps it was as well, after all, that the publishers' scruples had [10] led to a delay in the issue of the book, though Wagner had raged against it at the time. He had now, of course, to alter the final page or two so as to bring them into accordance with the new facts — the expansion of the original scheme from two operas to four, to be produced at a special festival " at some future time." For this startling news to reach Liszt for the first time through the pages of *A Communication to my Friends* would obviously never do: " Now ", he writes to Uhlig, " I shall almost be compelled to let Liszt have earlier warning that our opera compact is at an end, for he will see, from the *Communication*, that it really was my honourable intention to work for Weimar."

On the 20th November, accordingly, he sends Liszt a long letter of self-explanation. He pays generous tribute to all that Liszt had done for him in the theatre and with his pen. He tells him how he had intended to announce, in the *Communication*, the commission of *Young Siegfried* and *Siegfrieds Tod* by the Weimar theatre, and how it has come about that this announcement will no longer hold good in its original form. He goes over in detail the story of his experiences with *Siegfrieds Tod* since 1848; his fluctuations between the desire to compose the music to that poem and the conviction that a fitting production was nowhere possible; his attempts to come to terms with himself and to educate the public by his theoretical writings; the sudden perception — of which Liszt knows already — that *Siegfrieds Tod* ought to be preceded by a lighter,

---

[10] See p. 244.

and, as it were, explanatory work; his reluctance to send Liszt the poem of *Young Siegfried;* his intention, in the summer of 1851, of setting to work at the musical composition of the latter; his having been compelled, by reasons of health, to postpone this for a while; his stay at Albisbrunn; his constant vacillation between the wish to send Liszt the poem and his fear that the written word alone would not enable his friend to see the drama as *he* saw it; then the startling realisation that the myth could be adequately presented only in *four* dramas; the impossibility of presenting the vast work, in the first place, otherwise than as a whole; the necessity, therefore, of a festival production, which cannot in any circumstances take place earlier than three years from the present time; and the fortunate change in Frau Ritter's finances that guarantees his existence during that period, and perhaps for his lifetime. He thinks it necessary to soothe Liszt with the vague promise that if Weimar is " still there " when his big work is finished and properly produced, and if Liszt is still at Weimar and has been more fortunate in his effort to reform the local theatre than appears to be the case now, " we will see what can be done about it." In any case, fantastic as his vast scheme may perhaps seem to Liszt, he has been driven to it, he assures him, by imperative inner necessity.

With his mind rid of the burdensome thought that Weimar would be saddled with *Young Siegfried,* he says, he can at last send Liszt the poem, for Liszt can now read it without being plagued at every turn by anxieties as to its production under the agreement.

"Let us cherish no illusions about this matter! What you, and only you, have so far done for me in Weimar is wonderful. Still more was it to my benefit. Without you I would have completely disappeared by now; instead of which you have turned the public attention of the friends of art to me by means of all the powers at your disposal, with such energy and such success that it is solely due to you that now I am able at all to think of the carrying out of such plans as those I have outlined for you. I am perfectly clear as to all this, and I frankly denote you as the creator of my present position, which, perhaps, is not without promise for the future."

But now, he asks, what hopes can Liszt still have as regards Weimar? Sadly he has to recognise that his friend's efforts for the town are unavailing. If Liszt goes away for a while, the theatre falls back into the old wretched routine; when he returns, he has no sooner uprooted one noisome weed than another springs up. He bids him not to place too much trust in the Court: was it not the much-praised Karl August of a former day who allowed Goethe to be lost to the theatre because the poet objected to the introduction of a performing poodle into a play? And what ground has Liszt for thinking that *he*, in circumstances less favourable to art than existed in former days, can achieve results the means for which are almost totally lacking? Wagner does not regret the impending failure for his own sake but for his friend's. He then comes to the matter of the sustentation fee that had been sent him by Zigesar. Although this had not been granted him by way of a binding obligation on his part towards Zigesar and Liszt, but rather to set him free of material cares while engaged on a new work, it assumes a different complexion now that Zigesar is likely to be succeeded by a new Intendant, who will rightly, in the theatre's interest, regard the friendly advance as a business contract. He had unfortunately drawn 200 thalers of the 500 to be granted him under the Weimar agreement. Karl Ritter, however, came to the rescue, and Wagner was able to enclose the 200 thalers in his letter to Liszt, with an accompanying letter for Zigesar.

For all the politeness of Liszt's reply to this letter, it is tolerably clear that he was relieved, rather than otherwise, to learn definitely that there was no likelihood now of his being called upon to produce even one of the Siegfried dramas in Weimar. On the 1st December he writes to Wagner complimenting him on his daring conception, assuring him of his sympathy, and renewing the expression of belief in his friend's genius. During the three years necessary for the writing of the work, he says, Wagner's material circumstances will no doubt change very much for the better; he may even be able to return to Germany by that time. In three years, also, he himself may have " other means " at his disposal at Weimar than he has at present — a tacit admission that he recognises that the colossal new plan rules little Weimar out. Wagner is to go on with his great work regardless of consequences: Liszt reminds him, in a fine sentence that has become historic, of the direction given by the Chapter of Seville to the architect of the new cathedral — " Build for us such a temple that future generations will say that the Chapter was crazy to undertake anything so extraordinary."

The suggestion that Liszt was relieved, rather than otherwise, when he realised that there was now no likelihood of Weimar being called upon to undertake the impossible task of producing either *Young Siegfried* or *Siegfrieds Tod*, may seem, at first sight, to be negatived by his next letter, dated the 15th January, 1852. In this he urges Wagner to begin work on the complete *Ring* as soon as he can: " perhaps ", he says, " you can manage to finish the whole thing in less than three years "; he is curious, he tells him, " to know how you will work it out musically, what proportion you will give to the sections, and so on." As for the production, he continues, that can surely be managed somewhere if Wagner's directions and stipulations are carried out to the letter, for Wagner is too experienced and practical to ask for the impossible. If, contrary to Liszt's hope, Wagner is not amnestied by then, he is to commit the care of the whole thing to Liszt, merely giving himself the trouble to specify in detail his requirements, which Liszt will follow to the letter. " The necessary people and things will be obtained." Liszt hopes, however, that it will be his good fortune to watch the first performance from his seat in the Dresden or the Berlin theatre, and to entertain Wagner to supper on each of the four evenings.

All of which, of course, meant nothing whatever: Liszt was merely being gracefully polite in his usual way. He knew that as yet not even the poems of the *Valkyrie* and the *Rhinegold* were written; and he could hardly have entertained the idea seriously that an artist of Wagner's type, accustomed to brooding long over his works, would be able to solve in three years the many problems involved in the musical working-out of four huge dramas that would fling overboard every convention of opera as the term had previously been understood. On the other hand, if the *Ring* were actually to be ready within three years, there was not the faintest hope of conditions having so far improved in Weimar during that period as to make a production even thinkable there. The conclusion is irresistible that Liszt, like Wagner, tacitly assumed that Weimar's responsibility in the matter of the Nibelungen drama was at an end, and was content to leave the whole future of the thing on the knees of the gods. Wagner's reply to Liszt's letter had been to the effect that his friend was taking too bright a view of the future: for his part, he does not count on a production of the *Ring* anywhere during his lifetime, and least of all in Dresden or Berlin, for the musical atmosphere of large towns is becoming more and more abhorrent to him. For his possible audience he can imagine only an assembly of friends in some beautiful quiet corner of the earth, " far from the thick smoke and the pestilential odour of industrialism of our city-civilisation." As an afterthought, no doubt to soothe Liszt, he adds, " Such a quiet corner I could behold in Weimar at most, but in no larger town." But all this talk about Weimar now meant nothing, either on Wagner's side or on Liszt's.

Liszt had not replied specifically to Wagner's condolences, in his letter of the 11th November, on the state of affairs in Weimar: he had contented himself with the vague remark that Wagner's anxiety on this score will either be justified or allayed during the next few years. The truth is that Liszt's real troubles in Weimar were now beginning to come to a head. A few weeks after his reply to Wagner he was driven to present the Grand Duchess with something like an ultimatum. It was not merely that the Weimar opera forces, solo, choral, instrumental and scenic, were inadequate for such ideals as his. Liszt had evidently been impressed by Wagner's arguments, in his prose works, as to the impossibility of making the German theatre at once a temple of the Muses and an organisation supplying the bourgeois with nightly entertainment on business lines, with a view to the balancing of the material profit-and-loss account.

"The theatre ", he tells the Grand Duchess in his long letter of the 14th January, 1852, " must necessarily belong to one of two categories: an industrial enterprise taking as its aim the supplying of the public with its daily fare and the attraction of customers, representing, in the main, merely the day-to-day sympathies, good and bad, of this public, its aberrations of taste and its habitual ignorance; or a royal and national institution that represents the protection of the fine arts by those in authority. In the former case it is evident that the expenses must be adapted to the receipts. In the latter case, it seems to me equally evident that the receipts should not influence the choice and the rendering of the works. The *juste milieu* that is admirable enough in domestic matters appears to me to be of little importance here, for if it is a question of economy the Courts can achieve a much more radical solution of that problem by stipulating with a theatre Director that proper performances shall be given on the occasions when the Court is officially present, their good taste, therefore, not being interested in the average level of accomplishment."

An amphibious establishment, he concludes, that has the virtues neither of the one type of theatre nor of the other can live only from hand to mouth, costing a great deal yet at the same time giving little satisfaction. Precisely, in fact, what Wagner had been saying.

Not, Liszt continues, that he thinks it the duty of Court theatres to spend immense sums without getting any return. All he has in mind is a larger expenditure in order to further moral and material interests that are larger still: in any business, big profits can come only from the employment of a big capital. The Weimar theatre, during the last couple of years, has drawn outside attention to itself by its performances of certain new works, some of which have been on the grand scale; but the step forward thus taken makes it clear how much is still lacking. The question now arises whether the institution is to remain a Court theatre or become an ordinary commercial enterprise. If the latter, then " the degree to which it will satisfy the exigencies of the day being a mere question of business, it will depend on the impresario to decide whether it is to his interest to raise it to the standard that will only gradually repay him for his expenditure." As Weimar, however, " does not possess a public capable of estimating the real value of the works put before it, its theatre can gain fame only by appealing to the interests of the neighbouring towns." This other and more intelligent public, having brought about an excellence of performance that would not have been insisted upon by the uncultured Weimarians themselves, will not be without influence on the latter, " who, if they are not very apt at distinguishing for themselves the difference between the good and the bad, will none the less be delighted to pass an evening watching a work that comes to them with a certificate of superiority." If the institution is to remain a Court theatre in deed as well as in name it must abandon what we, in these days, would call the box-office point of view: " if the administration ", says Liszt, " cannot make up its mind to spend enough on important works, without paying any regard to what the natives may have to say about it or to the chance of their patronising these performances frequently, the Weimar stage will never rise above a level that is below the mediocre." He then outlines some of the reforms in the musical department that are immediately necessary — a second Kapellmeister (for the concerts and the opera are too much for one to handle efficiently), a better orchestra, a larger chorus, more adequate scenery.[11] He recognises that the theatre has its dramatic as well as its musical side, that the former, in the nature of the case, is less expensive than the latter, and that there is a party in Weimar that shakes its head over the growing importance of the opera in the theatre at the expense of the drama, which had been the glory of the town in the days of the Grand Duke Karl August and Goethe. He lets it be seen, however, that his own sympathies are mainly musical: the German drama, he says, is no longer what it was in the old days, as regards either poets or actors, while the modern public intelligence is everywhere veering round in the direction of the opera. But whatever view the Grand Duchess may take of these matters, his own position must be made clear. He has done all that he or any other man could do with the means placed at his disposal.[12]

The reply of the Grand Duchess to this manifesto — for such it was — has not been published: perhaps it was given verbally. No doubt some small reforms were promised, for Liszt continued with his progressive work, and even extended the range of it where possible. But the next five or six years were to convince him, to his chagrin, that neither Weimar in general nor Carl Alexander in particular could be relied upon to realise his ideal. The town was too small and too provincial: Carl Alexander was too parsimonious.

---

[11] See Vol. I, pp. 134–6, for further details, and for Liszt's criticism of the deficiencies of the *Lohengrin* performances.
[12] LZCA, pp. 33–9.

CHAPTER XIV

DISTRACTIONS AND DIET: THE "CELLINI" EPISODE

1

IN SPITE of his fevers, his giddiness, his general physical and mental malaise, in spite even of the fact that his shingles were as bad in the last weeks of his stay at Albisbrunn as they had been before he undertook the sulphur cure, in spite of the fact that he was very weak and " terribly emaciated ", Wagner still tried to persuade himself, then and for some time afterwards, that his water cure had made a new man of him. His constitutional reluctance to admit that he could be in error on any subject made him, on his return to Zürich, do all he could to convince his friends (perhaps as the best way of convincing himself) of the superlative merits of water as a means to health. On the 24th November he and Minna gave a party to celebrate the anniversary of their wedding. He was very much annoyed at the hearty way in which Sulzer and the others indulged their carnal appetite for wine and beer that evening; and for weeks afterwards he argued with his friends about the evil effects of strong liquors, with such vehemence on both sides that they often came near quarrelling. He had, as he says in *Mein Leben,* adopted a sort of new religion; and there is no fanatic like a religious fanatic, unless it be a health fanatic. He could not deny that wine in moderation produced an exhilaration that is well worth having for its own pleasant sake, helps its devotees to bear the burden of existence, and unlocks the chambers of the imagination: but he argued, as against Sulzer and Herwegh, that for this spiritual " intoxication " regenerate man should look not to the juice of the grape but to love.

" But the more closely my friends studied my condition ", he says in *Mein Leben,* " the more occasion they had to be anxious about my strange and obstinate extravagances. I was exceedingly pale and

[274]

thin; I hardly slept at all, and showed an alarming excitement in everything I did. But although sleep eventually forsook me almost entirely, I stuck to it that I had never been so well and cheerful in my life: I went on with my cold baths on the coldest winter mornings — to the torment of my wife, who had to light me out with a lantern for the walk that had to follow."

The situation had been, for a time, even worse than he paints it in *Mein Leben*; it was only Sulzer's good sense and good temper that prevented more than one breach between the two over this doctrine of salvation by water. We begin to understand better Wagner's undeviating singleness of purpose in great matters when we see how obstinate he was in small ones. He could never see the world through any eyes but his own. For him the cosmos was always a matter of Wagner *contra* non-Wagner; and whenever *he* adopted a new faith it was the duty of humanity to change with him. In his last years, largely as the result of his horror of vivisection, he preached the virtues of vegetarianism. He laid it down that " the degeneration of the human race has been brought about by its departure from its natural food ", that of the vegetable world. He was not dismayed by the easily foreseen objection that while a vegetable diet might have been well enough for the remote ancestors of European man, living under simpler conditions and in a warmer climate than ours, life in modern Europe could be adequately sustained only on flesh foods. He had his reply ready, and it certainly lacked nothing in thoroughness. " If there is any basis ", he writes, " for the assumption that animal food is indispensable in northern climates, what is to prevent our making a rationally directed transmigration to those other countries of the globe which, in virtue of their luxuriant productivity — the South American peninsula, for example — are capable of maintaining the present population of every country in the world? " [1]

Wagner became more self-centred, less able to brook contradiction, as he grew older, and especially after about 1866, when this inborn tendency was intensified by his relative seclusion from the rough world in the hothouse atmosphere of Triebschen. But there are abundant hints of this trait in him in the earlier years, and it

---

[1] *Religion and Art* (1880), in RWGS, X, 242 About 1870 he had converted Nietzsche *from* vegetarianism!

comes out in a letter to Sulzer after one of those arguments about the water cure during which Sulzer had remained unconvinced, his sober view being that " it was useless to quarrel about matters which neither of them understood." Thereupon Wagner further argued the matter of water in general and his own medical knowledge in particular in a letter of three quarto pages, in which he expressed the fear that the difference of opinion between them on this vital point might transform their intimate friendship into a mere external acquaintance! Fehr prints in full for the first time this letter of the 15th December, 1851, to Sulzer: it shows how desperately bent Wagner was on converting his friend; it was a matter of life and death for him that whatever *he* believed everyone else should believe. He sends Sulzer the Rausse books on the water cure and exhorts him to study them in practical connection with his own health problems. The way in which Sulzer has rejected his arguments, he says, gives him no hope of appealing to his friend's " theoretical reason ". " The reason for this is rooted in the ' alpha ' of our respective views as to life, or rather the ways of living that have formed these views, which must necessarily lead in the last resort to an ' omega ' as divergent in the two cases as the ' alpha.' " He resents Sulzer's remark that he, Richard Wagner, is inclined to dogmatise about things concerning which he has no professional knowledge, and that before laying down the law about hydropathy he ought to study medicine and chemistry. His temper rises as he goes on: it is like telling him, he says, that he ought to justify his philosophical opinions about God by theology, and therefore make theology his professional study, nay, further, that he ought not to talk as he does about art, or indeed produce any creative works, until he has studied Hegel's *Aesthetic*. He admits his " passionate nature " in argument, but hopes that their disputes will not make an end of their friendship: he hopes also that Sulzer will not read Rausse's books predetermined to differ from them and from him (Wagner).

" I confess I already fear that it has come to this — that in this sense I have become, in all that I am and all that I say, an object for your opposition. In proportion as this becomes clear to me, the more sorrowfully do I become absolutely sure about it: and as I am a man to whom it would be impossible to exchange the completest and most sympathetic relations with one who, in a decisive period of my life, was for me what you have been and still are — one whom I esteem in the warmest sense of which that word is capable, — for a calculated superficial intercourse, this certainty *must lead to the final and sincerest consequence of my leaving my Zürich refuge* — a deeply felt necessity which I felt compelled to communicate yesterday to our mutual friends [i.e. Baumgartner and Spyri]."

2

For us to-day the affair has its comic side; but it is illuminative, in its small way, of certain root-elements in Wagner's nature — his persistency in pursuit of a desired object, his pure inability to understand how anyone of any intelligence could think differently from him on any subject, and the intellectual tyranny he tried to exercise over others. But for these elements in him he would never have won through, as he did, in the most terrific conflict that any artist has ever had to wage with the world. Nietzsche, in his *Richard Wagner in Bayreuth,* analysed him acutely. That essay, written in 1876, was the outcome of an impulse to help Wagner in the difficult first days of the Bayreuth undertaking. By that time Nietzsche had known him for seven years: he had had innumerable confidential conversations with him at Triebschen and elsewhere: and he had read the proofs of the privately printed *Mein Leben,* or at all events a good portion of that work. As the result of it all a very clear image of Wagner as a man, independently of his achievement as an artist, had been stamped on Nietzsche's brain; and that image is reproduced for us in *Richard Wagner in Bayreuth.* There is no gainsaying the truth of Nietzsche's penetrating analysis, which shows him divided between admiration and awe and doubt of this masterful spirit, the like of which was not to be found anywhere in contemporary Europe.

Nietzsche had projected a book on Wagner as early as 1874, and his detached notes for this have been published. His general relations with Wagner and his attitude towards him as an artist will of course come up for discussion later in the present Life; at the moment we are concerned only with his view of the personality of the man. Among the chapter headings for the work he had planned we find

"Reasons for the failure [i.e. of the Bayreuth plan]. Above all, the element of singularity. Lack of sympathy for Wagner. Difficult. Complicated ": " Wagner's dual nature ": " Passion. Ecstasy. Dangers ": " Arrogance ": " Late manhood; slow development ": " Friends (arouse fresh doubts) ": " Enemies (awaken no respect, no interest in the hostile thing) ": " The strangeness explained; perhaps overcome? " " One of Wagner's qualities — ungovernableness, lack of moderation, pursues everything to the extreme limit of his strength, of his feeling." " The other quality is a great histrionic gift that has been transplanted into another channel than the nearest one: for that he lacks figure, voice, and the necessary training." " Wagner is by nature a law-giver: he disregards many circumstances and is not in the least embarrassed by minor things; he handles everything in the mass, and is not to be judged by isolated details — music, drama, poetry, the State, art, etc." [2]

What is lacking in clearness in these hurried jottings is remedied in the carefully written *Richard Wagner in Bayreuth.* Nietzsche pierces to the core of the development of Wagner's personality. The reader of the foregoing pages of the present study will have seen the importance of the five-year period from about 1847–52 in the evolution both of the man and of the artist. In those five years the relatively naïve Wagner of the earlier years, working his troubled way through various fields with only a dim consciousness of whither he was tending and what would be the end of it all, gradually hardens into a domineering spirit that has taken full stock of itself, realises its fundamental difference from the rest of mankind, becomes perfectly clear as to its pre-appointed goal, and makes for that goal without a moment's self-doubt, a moment's compromise, a moment's consideration for others. Whoever is not for him is against him; and whoever is against him, if he cannot be convinced and enlisted, must be swept aside. Nietzsche, with not only his personal knowledge of Wagner to draw upon but with the picture before him that Wagner paints of his youth and early manhood in *Mein Leben,* was able to perceive as no one else could at that time the *dramatic* nature of his evolution, as it were a play the fifth act of which would be the necessary result of the contending forces exhibited in the first.

---

[2] FNWN, pp. 181 ff.

> "The dramatic element in Wagner's development", he says, "is unmistakeable, from the moment when his dominant passion attained to self-consciousness and gathered up his whole being into itself; from that time on there is an end of all groping, straying, and pullulation of offshoots, and in all his most tortuous divagations, in the often fantastic trajectory of his plans, a single inner law is seen to rule, a will that explains all these phenomena, however strange the explanation may sometimes appear."

Nietzsche goes on to trace Wagner's inner development in a way that would have been impossible for him had he not read *Mein Leben*. He shows the vacillations of the man's complex and restless spirit in his childhood and youth, that hint at the danger that he might have become a mere cultivated dilettante, sampling everything but mastering nothing. He was the reverse of the precocious type; he was one of those who, like Goethe, simplify their nature as they grow older, resembling in some respects an old man when they are children and discovering their youthfulness rather late in life.

> "When once he had attained to intellectual and moral manhood the drama of his life begins. And how the aspect changes now! His nature seems to have been simplified in terrible fashion, to have been rent asunder into two instincts or spheres. In the depths there rushes headlong a passionate will which makes for the light through every kind of path, cavern and gorge, questing for power."

It was well both for Wagner and for the world that this mighty will was guided by "a force completely pure and free"; had it been allied with a narrow intelligence, such a will, with its uncontrollable impulse towards the tyrannical, must have become a fatality. The obstacles placed by unkind fate in the way of a man's realising his aspirations, Nietzsche goes on to say, often make him bitter and intolerant: he charges the world with his failure. "It thus often happens that fine natures, on the road to the ideal, turn savage." Wagner was saved from this fate by a presiding spirit that was "loving, full of goodness and sweetness, overflowing with mild counsel, that hates violence and self-ruin and the sight of one in bondage. This spirit spoke to Wagner. It descended upon him, enveloped him in its consoling wings, and showed him his path."

The characters created by an artist, continues Nietzsche, are not the man himself; but a succession in his works of character-types to which, it is clear, he is intimately attached tells us something about the artist himself. Nietzsche shows that a strain of moral nobility runs through all Wagner's principal characters. The same, to some extent, is true of other dramatists, Schiller, for example: "but in Wagner the standard is higher, the ground traversed is greater." These characters are all guided by a star whose name is "Fidelity — self-less Fidelity". The experience of all of them is "the basic experience of Wagner himself, which he reveres like a religious mystery . . . the wonderful experience and perception that the one side of his nature has remained true to the other, keeping the faith out of free, self-less love, keeping the creative, blamless, shining side of him square with the dark, the ungovernable and the tyrannical side." [3]

The analysis is searching; and it particularly holds good for the period of Wagner's life with which we have been occupied in the preceding chapters. His character is at its most attractive during these years, when almost the whole force of his nature was being directed into ideal channels. His passion for domination, his inability to see that anything else in the whole world could matter except the realisation of his own aims, were noble enough so long as they were confined to the world of the ideal. But the time was to come when the same tyrannical qualities were to operate in the sphere of the real; and then the picture becomes a less pleasing one. In Munich, in 1864 and 1865, he used his power over the young King so unscrupulously for material as well as ideal ends that it is no wonder outraged public opinion drove him from the town. His belief that he was entitled to be relieved of the commoner financial cares of existence in order to devote himself to his great work — a belief for which posterity finds every justification — gradually expanded and hardened into a belief that it was the world's duty to provide him not merely with necessities but with luxuries on a scale corresponding to his insatiable demands: he became, for a while, completely insensible to ordinary considerations of prudence and decency in these matters. Knowing as he did that his thinking upon matters of art scaled heights and plumbed

[3] NZUB, pp. 307 ff.

depths that were inaccessible to the great majority of his contemporaries, the contemptuously diminishing perspective down which he looked at these people in the field of art gradually extended its tapering lines into the field of life. He became less and less able to bear opposition as he grew older; and in such minor episodes as those of his quarrels with his Zürich friends over the medicinal qualities of water we see the beginning of that belief in himself in every department of life and thought that was to carry him in the end to victory, but along a road that was to be strewn with the wreckage of friendships, and with a hatred such as no other artist in the world's history has had to endure.

3

Two things sustained him during this difficult winter of 1851–2 — the feeling of security that Frau Ritter's pension gave him against ever having again to depend for his existence upon commercial courses that were horrible to him, and the arrival of the printed copies of *Opera and Drama:* as he read his huge work through once more there came to him not only a sensation of intellectual and artistic power but the joyous feeling that at last, and for good, he had squared his accounts with the existing operatic world, conflict with which had been the source of so many of his miseries as man and artist. His perennial optimism had persuaded him once more that sooner or later a new humanity would be born, with a new and better attitude towards the theatre as the central fount of culture, and that the new birth was likely now to come sooner rather than later. Far behind him as the May of 1849 now lay, and cured as he was of all desire to meddle with practical politics, there still lingered in him a feeling that, if only for Richard Wagner's sake, a major crisis in the history of Europe was due — for his sake, for without such a crisis his practical path as a creative artist seemed to be barred. He was still no nearer finding his way out of the intellectual muddle in which the events of 1849 had left him than when he was writing *Art and Revolution.* At one moment he was convinced that the change in men's lives necessary to inaugurate real art could come only after a political revolution: at the next moment he was equally convinced that the impulse to such a revolution could come only out of a change in men's hearts that would in turn demand a change in their lives. As Paul Moos has put it, this was Münchhausen lifting himself out of the bog by his own head.[4] That he was still coquetting with the notion of a revolution that would introduce the new world in which, and in which alone, the *Ring* would be possible, is shown by a passage in his letter of the 12th November, 1851 which, for some strange reason or other, was suppressed in the official edition of the letters to Uhlig. The full text runs thus:

> " I can imagine a performance *only after the revolution,* for the revolution alone can provide me with my artists and my audience. The next revolution must of necessity make an end of the whole of this theatre business of ours: it must and will all come crashing down: that is inevitable. Then I will throw up a theatre on the Rhine and send out invitations to a great dramatic festival. After a year of preparation I then produce my whole work in the course of four days; and with it I make clear to the men and women of revolution the meaning of this revolution in the noblest sense of the word. That public will understand me: the present cannot." [5]

This consolatory illusion, the product of his despair, remained with him for some little time after his return from Albisbrunn. Recent events in Paris had given him the hope that the democratic spirit that had been beaten down by military force at the turn of the half-century was now reviving and would carry all before it, and that the other European states would be compelled to follow the lead of France. The year 1852, he became convinced, would mark the beginning of a new epoch in the world's history. When the 2nd December, 1851, came, and with it the news of Louis Napoleon's *coup d'état,* he could hardly believe what he heard; the universe, he thought, was surely rushing to its doom. When the incredible news was confirmed, he says, he " gave the whole thing up " as a riddle that was not worth the trouble of solving, and made no further attempt to understand this enigmatic real world.

---

[4] MWA, p. 116. Moos's book (MWA) is indispensable to students who wish to get the gist of the contents of Wagner's theoretical writings without going to the trouble of reading the twelve volumes of the *Gesämmelte Schriften.* Moos epitomises each of the articles or treatises, from those of Wagner's youthful days to those of the final Bayreuth period, and adds many sound comments of his own.

[5] The missing passage was restored in an article by J. van Santen-Kolff — *Aus der Geschichte des Bayreuther Gedankens* — in BBW, 1892, p. 99.

With his political delusions went, for a time, all his artistic optimism: once more he was driven to the conclusion that there is no hope of the regeneration of humanity in the sense in which he understood the term:

> " I have now completely given up ", he writes to Uhlig on the 18th December, "every attempt to fight against the reigning stupidity, dull-wittedness, and wretchedness: I shall let the rotten rot, and employ my still robust powers in production and enjoyment, not in agonising and utterly useless attempts to galvanise the corpse of European civilisation. I have in mind only to live, to enjoy — i.e. to create as an artist and bring my works to performance, not, however, for the critical muck-brains of the mob."

Less than a month later, on the 12th January, 1852, he has to admit to Uhlig that his water cure, while apparently beneficial in some ways, has been followed out too thoroughly, and has resulted in a fresh exasperation of his nerves. The failure of the committee of the Zürich Concert Society to fall in with his plans for reform had meant that he was denied the opportunity, so long and so ardently desired, of hearing the prelude to *Lohengrin*. He compares himself mournfully with Beethoven:

> "*He* could not hear his music because he was deaf. . . . *I* cannot hear mine because I am more than deaf, because I no longer live in my epoch, because I wander about among you like a ghost, because the whole wide world is full of . . . hounds! . . . Ah, if I were not to rise from my bed to-morrow, if I were nevermore to wake to this loathsome life, yes — then I should be happier even than the Ritters when they listen to *Tannhäuser*."

He has, in fact, after his brief spell of hope for himself and for the world, " gone back to his old mood ":

> " The devil has hold of me again. No cure in the world can protect me from the vexations of outward impressions: their evil influence must ever trouble the inner spring and bring it to a painful standstill. Here I am stranded again with all my wishes, my whims and strivings. With intolerable clearness I see and feel that everything must remain unsatisfied and aimless. Alas! alas! it matters not at what door I knock! I have to see each of my plans just as it is, in all its desolate, grey impossibility! I can soothe myself with no more illusions. I lack the only thing that could keep me in a happy state of illusion — *sympathy*, true, manifest sympathy! "

Like all men of his type, what he really needed to keep him in health and spirits was not doctors and " cures " but the opportunity to proceed, in peace and comfort and hope, with the work of his heart's desire: he was always ill at ease when he was evolving, in his head, some great aesthetic plan or other, and always well, or as well as an overworked man could expect to be, when he had done with this torturous brooding and could lose himself in the joy of actual creation on paper. Just now he was going through a more than usually difficult period of gestation: the poem of the *Ring* in its final form was struggling towards birth in him. He had made the first prose sketches for the *Rhinegold* and the *Valkyrie* during his stay in Albisbrunn, the former between the 3rd and the 11th November, 1851, the latter between the 11th and the 20th. He wanted now to proceed with the versification; but his work in connection with the Zürich concerts and opera of the winter of 1851–2, his ill-health and general depression during this period, and above all the cold of winter, made this impossible for him just then. In May, 1852, he went off with Minna to the Pension Rinderknecht, about half-way up the Zürich Berg, for a double purpose — to try a new cure and to get to work at his poems. His belief in Rausse and cold water had been gradually waning all through the winter: on the 4th April he had progressed so far towards common sense that he could write to Frau Ritter, " No more water-cure institutions for me! " He had discovered, he says, that for a man with nerves like his something less drastic than his former regimen is required: he must look after his diet and not cut himself off, as they had tried to make him do before, from intellectual work. He has made the useful discovery that " nature's " methods are not for human beings, for " we are no longer nature-creatures "; we need to balance the demands of our mental with the facts of our bodily life. He has now come under the spell of another universal healer, to whose theory he had been introduced by Hermann Müller — a Dr. Karl Lindemann, of Paris, who, it seems, knows Rausse and his hydropathic methods quite well, and, while generously admitting his colleague's ability, sees just where he has gone astray, and himself has the secret of the " new developments " necessary to perfect Rausse's theory and practice — all, it will be seen, in the best tradition of medical wisdom, which consists in confidently affirming

B this year after having as confidently affirmed A last year, with the certainty of an equally confident scrapping of both A and B and the optimistic prescription of C the year after next. Lindemann had effected some improvement in Kietz's health, and Kietz, of course, with the enthusiasm to be expected in the circumstances, had asked the great man to prescribe for his friend Wagner. The latter, in turn, was anxious that Karl Ritter should benefit by the new light that had arisen on the banks of the Seine to shine upon men. Frau Ritter was exhorted to send Karl at once to Paris, with instructions to obey Lindemann to the letter: " I feel that if he goes on as he is doing for another year, your son is — lost! *Follow my counsel!* " [6]

He had no doubt been flattered to learn from Kietz that Lindemann already knew something of him from his writings. He sent off to Paris a description of his condition, and in due course received instructions as to the regimen he was to follow at the Rinderknecht: Lindemann appears to have been one of those sagacious practitioners who find out what their patients themselves have discovered, by past experience, is most likely to do them good, and then prescribe it for them. Having learned that Wagner had once been enamoured of the cold-water cure but loathed its asinine visage now, he sapiently assured him that a glass of good wine now and then and a tepid bath in the evenings would do him no harm; nor would it hurt him to do a little intellectual work. Voltaire gravely agreed with the soothsayers of his time that incantations could destroy a flock of sheep — provided sufficient arsenic were added. Wagner discovered that a medical regimen could effect a certain improvement in his health, provided that he took care of his diet and his skin, spent several hours a day in exercise in the purest air imaginable, kept his mind reasonably free of worry, and let his brain work in moderation at what interested him most. In spite of the depressing effect of the almost incessant rain he was able to finish the poem of the *Valkyrie* on the 1st July, 1852; and about the 7th July he returned to Zürich.

---

[6] Wagner's worst fears for his young friend were realised: Karl lingered on for only another thirty-nine years, dying in 1891.

A pleasing piece of evidence as to the growing vogue of his works in Germany was a call, about this time, from the Berlin Opera manager Mantius, to discuss with him a production of *Tannhäuser* there as soon as a satisfactory tenor could be found. Mantius missed Wagner, however, who had gone on a long walk in the woods, and had to content himself with talking the matter over with Minna.

The weather having at last improved, Wagner set out on the 10th July for a long tramp over the Alps to Italy in search of the perfect health that still eluded him. He had been foolish enough to promise, a little while before, to act as adjudicator at a musical festival in Basel; but having recognised, when the time came, that his was not exactly the temperament to sit patiently through performance after performance of choral music of the Abt kind, he sensibly cried off. He had hoped that Herwegh, who at this time was more sympathetic to him than any other male acquaintance in Zürich, would accompany him on his excursion; but the poet, who had troubles enough of his own just then owing to the mess he had made of his marital relations, disappointed him at the last moment. The funds for the first part of the journey were provided by Liszt, who opportunely sent Wagner a fee of 100 thalers for the proposed production of the *Flying Dutchman* in Weimar; as Wagner humorously put it in a letter to Uhlig, his expenses being 20 francs a day, each day cost him one number of the opera. He started off on the 10th July by way of Lucerne, Alpnach, Brienz, Interlaken, Lauterbrunnen, Wengernalp, the Kleine Scheidegg, Grindelwald, over the Faulhorn (8,800 ft.), down the Grosse Scheidegg to Meiringen, through the Hasli valley to the hospice on the Grimsel, and over the Aare glacier to the Siedelhorn (9,600 ft.). In a week, what with the excessive physical exertion and the fretting sense of being alone and misunderstood in the world, he was dangerously tired. He pushed on, however, through Obergestelen in Valais, through the Eginen valley, and over the Gries glacier (8,200 ft.) to Formazza and Domodossola, where he arrived on the 19th. He had been accompanied part of the time by a rather sinister guide — recommended to him by the landlord of the hospice on the Grimsel — with whom he could not get on at all. Later in the year he learned that these two worthies had conspired to burn down the inn for the purposes of profit: the landlord drowned himself when the crime was discovered, and the servant was sent to gaol. Wagner seems to have had good reason to congratulate himself on having come safely through his adventures with the guide.

On the 20th he went to the Borromean Islands: from Pallanza he wrote to inform Otto Wesendonk that he was sitting on the shore of Lake Maggiore smoking " the first of your godlike cigars." Then by boat and coach he went by way of Locarno and Bellinzona to Lugano, reaching the appointed end of his journey on the 21st.

The first contact with the warmer air of Italy enervated him physically, but his eyes were enchanted with the sudden transition from snow to the luxuriant plant life of the south. His main and sometimes comic difficulty appears to have been with the language. He wanted a drink of milk, he told Uhlig; but as his knowledge of Italian, such as it was, had been derived from Italian operas, and as the word milk did not occur in any Italian libretto known to him, he found himself in a quandary. In Lugano he put up in a dirty room in the Albergo del Lago (now the Town Hall): the building was the headquarters of the government of the Ticino Canton in the winter, and was used as a hotel only in the summer. At Lugano he felt so tired and lonely and depressed that, seemingly on the principle of any port in a storm, he telegraphed to Minna to join him. She came immediately (accompanied, apparently, by Peps), and was followed the next day by Herwegh and Dr. François Wille. Wagner visited the Borromean Islands once more with the other three: then Herwegh and Wille went back to Zürich by the shortest route, while Wagner, who was anxious to see all he could of Switzerland while he was yet in the mood for it, returned with Minna across the Simplon and through Martigny — where, the hotels being full, they used the influence of their postillion with a maid-servant to obtain a night's shelter in a private house the owner of which was away — Chamonix, the Mer de Glace, La Flégère — where Minna fell and sprained her ankle — Geneva, Lausanne and Berne to their home in the Zeltweg, where he arrived on the 5th August. The trip had taken nearly a month; the expenses of the latter part of it had been met by Sulzer advancing Wagner 25 Louisdor on account of the fee he expected from Frankfort and Leipzig for performances of his operas.[7]

We have seen him pouring out his woes to Frau Ritter after his return to Zürich, lamenting his lost youth and thinking sadly of Jessie Laussot.[8] He talks in the same strain to Uhlig on the 9th August:

> " I have spent nearly four weeks on a journey to which I had long looked forward as to the realisation of a beautiful dream. I received many an impression that was delightful enough in itself; but I was always in search of the right one, and — rest I could not find! It is all over, and my youth is gone: there is no longer any *life* ahead of me; all my working and doing can henceforth be no more than a gradual dying. The journey has brought me wisdom with regard to many things."

His main malady, had he but known it, was merely that he was big with the *Ring*. The huge scheme had to gestate at its own pace within him, and until it was brought to birth there could be no peace of mind or health of body for him. His spiritual restlessness, his physical desire for more and yet more exercise and change of scene, were merely an incessant agonised flight from himself in search of himself. The *Rhinegold* poem was still unwritten,[9] and

---

[7] See his cheerful letters of the 22nd and 26th July to Sulzer in FWSZ, I, 375, 378.

From Lugano, three days later, he addressed a letter to one Gottlieb Rabe, of Lenzburg, that throws an interesting light on his attitude towards the theatre. Rabe had evidently asked him to support his application for a post as Kapellmeister. "I sincerely sympathise with you", says Wagner, "in your dissatisfaction with your present position in Lenzburg; but at the same time I cannot comprehend how you think you will be any better off as music director in a theatre. To anyone who functions in that capacity in one of our smaller theatres I can only give the advice — unless, of course, he is just a poor dull beast broken in by routine — to get some post outside the theatre, in which, even if he is bored to death, he will at any rate be spared open shame and infamy. At least you ought not to expect *me* to encourage anyone to exchange any position whatever for one in a theatre. For only a pig can be comfortable there, or even make shift: it means the quick ruin of a decent artist. Think too of the material precariousness of such a post, in which you are not sure of your life from one six months to another, and whence you may be driven out by any female singer you happen to have offended." (FWSZ, p. 377.) Excellent advice, no doubt, for people who had something of Wagner's belief in their star, but not for poor devils who would be glad of anything to keep a roof over their heads and buy them bread and butter!

[8] See *supra*, pp. 155-6.

[9] That of the *Valkyrie* had been finished on the 1st July (1852). The *Rhinegold* poem was completed on the following 3rd November.

those of *Young Siegfried* and *Siegfrieds Tod* had to be revised and recast: and a good deal of preliminary mental sketching and shaping of the musical material would have to be done before he could think of making a systematic start upon the music of the first section of his vast tetralogy. The longer a big artistic or literary scheme keeps seething in a man's head the more discouragingly difficult it comes to seem to him at times: brooding upon it does not so much bring simplification and clarification of his problems as an increase of them through the constant enrichment of the first main stream of the idea by the inflow of many other waters. The secret cause of Wagner's ill-health during these years was probably not so much physical as mental — the sense of difficulty and frustration that grew upon him as his plan for the *Ring* expanded and the day when he could hope to begin the music for it receded further and further into the distance. It was in obedience to the instinct that always made seclusion, or relative seclusion, a necessity to him during a period of musical parturition that he began to dream once more, after his return from Italy, of a little house and garden of his own in the country. He sketches his scheme in a letter to Uhlig of the 9th August, and, as usual, he is practicality itself — on paper. He can count, he says, on substantial receipts from his operas in the immediate future. But it is no use his calculating on putting these receipts aside as they come in, in order to accumulate in time the sum necessary to buy a small estate: for one thing, the immediate necessities of life will probably make him fritter away a good portion of them; for another, this plan will mean that he cannot obtain his house and garden for some years yet, and he needs them now if his work is to be done. Having already discussed the matter with his Zürich friends, he has decided to advertise for a suitable small estate to cost not more than 10,000 francs. All he needs is 2,000 francs for the deposit: out of the fees from his operas he will be able gradually to pay off the interest on the loan and the capital owing. As he and Minna would die childless, the property would some day revert to whoever would advance him the money he needs. It was all perfectly logical, in the way that his proposals to his publishers were logical: but, like the publishers, his friends were unable to look so far ahead as he, and declined to share his optimism. His dream of a quiet house and garden of his own was not to be realised for some years yet; and it had hardly been realised before the sudden harsh awakening from his dream shattered his life for the time being.

5

To a casual observer, or even to his friends, his life in Switzerland during these years must have seemed of a kind that left him with little cause for grousing. The basic necessities of his existence were provided for by Frau Ritter's pension. He made small sums from time to time by conducting or by literary work. His well-to-do friends in Zürich showed him great indulgence as a borrower. His operas were swiftly making their way through the German theatres. He had become the centre of a vigorous movement of regeneration in music, an eager subject of discussion in the German musical papers. He was tied to no disagreeable daily duties as most men are; he had complete bodily and mental freedom, could work when he liked, take exercise when he liked, go away when he liked. He had a small circle of friends in Zürich whose devotion to him could always be relied upon, and whose intellectual interests covered something of the same range as his own. To any other composer the situation would have seemed an ideal one. To Wagner it seemed not far from the last circle in hell, partly because of his feeling that even the most sympathetic of his friends did not understand him as he was in the depths of his being, partly because he was tortured by the stupendous difficulties of his *Ring* scheme, partly because he was not loved in the only sense in which he ever understood the word — in the sense that those who loved him should share his conviction that nothing in the world mattered but the realisation of his mission, and place not only their purses but their minds and their lives at his service. He would have liked some of his Zürich friends better if, instead of arguing so much with him, they had seen everything from his point of view. He got on best with Herwegh because the poet, apparently, in addition to having some natural affinity with Wagner's ideals in art — though he was not specifically musical — felt the imprint of the stronger character upon his own too deeply to assert himself more than Wagner felt was quite becoming in any friend of his. As a rule Wagner preferred the company of women, because the women who did not frankly dislike him — in which case he was happily indifferent to them — were hypnotised by his genius and his eloquence, and moreover had a subtle intuition, that was beyond the capacity of most of his male friends, of the profound and largely undeserved unhappiness of the man.

He saw a good deal at this time of François and Eliza Wille, whose small estate at Mariafeld, close to Zürich, he often visited in 1852. Frau Wille had met him in Dresden for a moment in 1843, before her marriage, at a party at the house of Major Serre: the acquaintance had developed no further then, but she never forgot the impression made on her by Wagner's animated manner, his unusually large head with its pantechnicon forehead, his piercing eyes, his resolute mouth, and the massive chin that seemed, as she says, to be carved out of stone. She and her husband had left Hamburg to settle at Mariafeld in 1851; but it was apparently not until they had been there for some little time that they met Wagner again, through the instrumentality of Herwegh, who took him out to Mariafeld for the first time on a Sunday in May, 1852. The visit was repeated many times during the following summer and autumn, both Wagner and Minna sometimes spending two or three days there at a time. On one occasion Herwegh brought with him the works of Schopenhauer, at that time unknown both to his host and to Wagner. Wille became so fanatical an admirer of the philosopher that henceforth he made a journey to Frankfort every year to see him. Wagner was equally impressed: Frau Wille, in her recollections, speaks of the astounding swiftness of apprehension that enabled him to assimilate this new philosophy at a first reading. He was probably fascinated by it, in the first place, by reason of its chiming with the ideas of world-denial and renunciation — in a purely artistic sense, of course — that had been unconsciously germinating in him during the last few years.

6

The conversations at Mariafeld must have been very interesting. Frau Wille had to the end of her days the deepest regard for Wagner; but she sturdily records that at Mariafeld he was never " deified." It was not in her husband's nature, indeed, to deify anyone, least of all a man whose ideas on most subjects would seem to his harder mind somewhat lacking in realism. At Göttingen University Wille had been, as Marcel Herwegh puts it, Bismarck's companion in studies, duels, and debauches. Having been expelled from Göttingen, the pair betook themselves to Jena, where they lived the same wild life as before. On his return to his native Hamburg, Wille had devoted himself mainly to politics and political journalism; his bellicose disposition involved him in several duels, and his head and face in later years showed scars of more than one kind. Heine has limned him for us in a stanza in one of his poems, in which he describes Wille's face as an album in which his university enemies had written their signatures with their swords. Even in his comfortable Swiss retirement Wille showed the pugnacious qualities of his youth; his unimaginative mind had virtually nothing in common with that of Wagner, and their wrangles about politics often became dangerously heated. He was an early believer in the doctrine of " Deutschland über Alles." Marcel Herwegh (the son of the poet) quotes a passage from an unpublished letter of a certain Colonel Rustow to Frau Emma Herwegh (1871), in which he gives Wille's own story of an episode in Venice that aptly illustrates his arrogance. Being lost, he had asked, in German, an Italian boy to show him his way. " Non capisco " (" I do not understand "), said the boy. " What! " said Wille, " You don't understand the language of your masters? " [10]

Herwegh was no longer the poet of the *Gedichte eines Lebendigen,* the iron lark, as Heine had called him. His spirit had gradually softened and sagged under the strain of ignominious failure in practical politics, a sybaritic manner of life in Switzerland, and the social odium incurred by his liaison with Alexander Herzen's wife. For the most part he preferred to recline languidly on a couch in Frau Wille's drawing room and talk beautifully in his soft voice about Schopenhauer, Pushkin, Gogol, Shelley, and Calderon. But

---

[10] HBD, p. 136. Marcel Herwegh evidently has no very high opinion of Frau Wille and her husband, between whom and his parents there appears to have been no love lost. More light may some day be thrown on the characters of all of them by the publication of the letters of the poet and his wife.

occasionally something of the old angry revolutionary fire would rekindle in him, and he would support Wagner in the latter's furious tirades against nineteenth-century civilisation, which Wille would counter with cool, disillusioned common sense. On one occasion Wagner and Herwegh were railing against all things German: according to them, everything in life and art, in thought and feeling, was rotten to the core and fit only for destruction. Warming to their subject, they maintained that it was the duty of the Folk to burn down castles and palaces, so that their tyrants would have nowhere to lay their criminal heads. Wille's dry comment upon this was, " Yes, that's what they did in Brunswick, and the taxpayers were bled to pay for the rebuilding of the castle." On another occasion a heated argument over the *Antigone,* that began with the subject of translations but soon slipped over, as usual, into politics, was only saved from degenerating into a quarrel by a tactful suggestion on Frau Wille's part that Herwegh should read the company some of his poems.

The pleasantest hours for the hostess were when Wagner would read his opera poems, or play and expound some music of his own or a Beethoven symphony, or when gay excursions would be made over the mountains or the lake. Wille would tell such rich stories of his student days that his delighted hearers would urge him to write a " Decameron of the North." Once, however, Wagner shocked Frau Wille so much by maintaining that the love of the Magdalen for the Prophet of Nazareth could and should be represented on the stage that she fled from the room as the virtuous ladies of the Wartburg fled from the Hall of Song when Tannhäuser launched out into his praise of sensual love. With Frau Wille, however, Wagner could always make peace again; but all in all he never really took to Wille, whom he treats none too kindly in *Mein Leben.* " He was an extraordinarily good story-teller ", he says, adding, however, with a manifest sniff, " which acquired for him the reputation of being entertaining." Elsewhere he calls him " cynical." The day was to come, in 1864, when Wille was to refuse asylum to the hunted composer whom all his friends had come to regard, by that time, as a danger to their pockets and their private peace; and the memory of that wounding refusal was still too vivid in Wagner's mind when he was writing his memoirs for him to be able to look back upon the earlier days at Mariafeld with any great pleasure.

7

It was during this summer of 1852 that the tide in his external fortune definitely turned. Wherever we look we see signs of rapidly expanding interest in both his ideas and his works. The sixth performance of *Lohengrin* was the last to be given in Weimar for some time, owing to the lack of the necessary singers; but Liszt gave *Tannhäuser* again, in May, on the occasion of the visit to the town of the Empress of Russia. Liszt was now setting seriously to work at his lately realised mission of making Weimar the centre of the new spirit in music. As to the nature of that spirit he, in common with many other people, was at that time still a trifle vague. On the one side, clearly enough, there was the ancient world of opera and of instrumental music, and the equally ancient world of the routine Kapellmeisters: on the other side a new sap was visibly rising, but at the moment it was not to be expected that anyone could foresee what the full-grown tree was likely to become. Schumann was regarded rather suspiciously in some quarters as a pioneer, Berlioz was looked upon as co-operating with Wagner in laying the foundations of the future: it was not until some years later that Berlioz was to be recognised as the plougher of his own lonely furrow, while the ideal of art for which Schumann stood was gradually to diverge from that of the " New German School " to such an extent as to bring about a total breach between the two camps. For the moment men were conscious only that an eager new something was in the air; and so we find Liszt, in March, 1852, producing Berlioz's *Benvenuto Cellini* (which had been a failure in Paris in 1838), with the laudable intention of striking yet another blow for " progress."

Wagner saw more clearly than Liszt in this matter. It is easy enough to see only a personal motive in his expression of surprise at this revival and his broad hint to Liszt that nothing could come of it. It is practically certain that he knew neither the score nor even the libretto of *Cellini* at first hand, but had derived his opinion of what was fundamentally wrong with the work from Bülow's two well-informed articles on it in the *Neue Zeitschrift* in April, 1852. But even had he known the opera himself he would have been unable to agree that the revival of it in Weimar could have any influence on the progress of opera as he conceived it — which, of course, was all that mattered to Wagner. French music, however brilliant, however much at war with Parisian tradition, could contribute nothing to the inner force of a development that, so far as Germany was concerned, would have to be wholly German in spirit and in aim. Liszt's attempt to force Berlioz upon the Weimar public could at best be nothing more than a generous reaching-out of the hand to a man of genius whose ill-luck in his own country was notorious. The completely different artistic natures of the two men made it impossible for Berlioz and Wagner ever really to understand each other: but at heart Wagner was not ill-disposed towards Berlioz. It was simply that he divined that it was the imperfect dramatic construction of a work like *Benvenuto Cellini*, rather than a failure of purely musical genius, that made it merely a brilliant flash in the pan, without significance for the future of opera. We may smile at his offer to Berlioz, through Liszt, of his *Wieland* poem, but his intentions were honourable enough. He was right in both his contentions — that Berlioz would never get much further in opera without the co-operation of the right kind of poet, and that in any case the rational thing for him to do now in 1852, at the age of nearly fifty, was not to patch up a failure of some fourteen years earlier but to set to work at a new subject into which he could pour the experience he had acquired since then. Wagner was justified in telling Liszt that he could not agree with him as to the " consequences " to be expected of this Weimar revival of *Cellini*. What Liszt had in mind when he spoke of these " consequences " is tantalisingly obscure. Ellis conjectured that Liszt, who was always delighted to play the diplomatist, may have thought that to give the Frenchman's work in Weimar, which was now regarded everywhere as the Wagnerian headquarters, might facilitate the production of Wagner's works in Paris.[11] That, however, is doubtful. But

[11] When Liszt produced Heinrich Dorn's *Nibelungen* in Weimar on the 22nd January, 1854, he can have had no motive whatever for doing so other than the "diplomatic" ones of currying favour with the Berlin Opera, of which Dorn was

that there was something more in Liszt's resolve to give *Cellini* than simple admiration for the work itself is evident from his own words, obscure as the meaning of them is in a way that is familiar to close students of his correspondence. He once told a friend that if he had not been a musician he would have been " the first diplomatist in Europe." He certainly loved to wallow in diplomatic verbiage, being apparently of the opinion that language was given to diplomatists to conceal their thoughts.

This is how he answers Wagner in his letter of the 7th April, 1852: " Let me just add this, that the reasons that decided me to give this opera have proved completely right, and advantageous to the further success of my activity here. ' Why *Cellini* in Weimar? ' is a question to which I am not bound to provide anyone with an answer, but which will resolve itself practically in a way that may be satisfactory to *us*. Perhaps you have not as yet grasped the matter so practically as you will later. In any case I believe you will agree with me, unless you are bent on shooting into the air." This is decidedly one of the many occasions when we could wish he had plumed himself a little less on his diplomatic subtlety, and tried, in spite of his awkwardness in the handling of the German language, to express himself in such a way as to leave posterity in no doubt as to his meaning. His invitation to Berlioz to revise the score of

---

Kapellmeister, and of wanting to secure Dorn's goodwill for Bülow, who was to play in Berlin in December, 1853. (See Liszt's letter to Dorn of the 21st November, in LZB, VIII, 109.) Unless we are to suppose that Liszt's taste in music was hopelessly bad, we can only attribute to diplomatic insincerity his praise of an aria from the first act in his letter of the 21st January, 1854, to Dorn: "Liebert [who played Gunther] sings with charm and sensibility his aria in the first act, 'Komm' an den Rhein,'— a very grateful piece, which is bound to make a decided effect." Tappert reprints the melody, which runs thus:

Komm' an den Rhein, und folg' mir oh–ne Be–ben,

dort lacht das Le – ben, das Glück al – lein.

With Wagner's heroic figures in his mind, Liszt could actually bring himself to praise banality of this kind in a Nibelungen drama!

Cellini had been issued in July, 1851 — less than a year, that is to say, after his production of *Lohengrin*, and therefore before he had yet realised all that Wagner was likely to mean for the future of Weimar. Some time was still to elapse before it became clear to him and to others that, in the first place, there was no general international movement of musical " progress " in which the French, under the leadership of Berlioz, could play their part by the side of the Germans, and that, in the second place, a breach was imminent between the Leipzig school and the Wagner party, the former deciding that its rôle was not to launch into the future but to conserve what it took to be the essence of the classical past. In 1851 Liszt, in all probability, thought he was really helping the Wagnerian cause by throwing the mantle of his benevolence over all " modern " music and so making " Weimar " a synonym for " modernity." Possibly, also, he believed that this ambitious plan would fire the imagination of the Hereditary Grand Duke, who had every desire to make his little capital a cultural centre without any very clear idea of how to go about it.

A little more light has been thrown on the subject, since Ellis wrote, by the publication of Wagner's letters to Bülow, who was at that time living in Weimar.

" One thing I regard as being of importance," Wagner writes him,[12] " namely your attitude towards Liszt in the matter of Berlioz. You say in your letter, ' and I am compelled to exhibit the greatest sympathy for [Berlioz and his opera], have to praise the opera and so on, *because one must now support Liszt in everything he does.*' " This, by the way, of itself suggests a slight lack of enthusiasm for *Cellini* on Bülow's part. His articles on the Weimar production in the *Neue Zeitschrift* of the 2nd and 30th April, indeed, manifestly " hedge " a good deal, in the style customary with journalists who, for one reason or another, find it diplomatic not to say precisely what they think or all they think. Bülow begins by praising Berlioz as a composer of *instrumental* music. He tells how Liszt's first performance of *Cellini*, which was to have taken place on the 16th February, had to be postponed to the 20th March by rea-

---

[12] The letter is undated, but apparently belongs to January, 1852.

son not only of the indisposition of the chief singer but of " a fairly open ill-will towards the work (that had been Liszt's choice), on the part of other people whose co-operation was unfortunately indispensable." Evidently there was already a party in Weimar that was inimical to everything Liszt did.[13] The bulk of Bülow's first article is taken up with a defence of Berlioz against the charge that his music " ruins the singers' voices ", abuse of the Weimar public, justification of Liszt's action in reviving a work that had been a failure in Paris, and an attack on the powerful Paris trio, Meyerbeer, Auber, and Halévy, who are not particularly well-disposed towards any composer who appears to threaten their supremacy. Of the work itself he simply says that " *Cellini* is not a dramatic art-work in the higher sense of the term, but perhaps only the dramatic study of a musical genius." In his second article he gave his reasons for holding that the opera as a whole is not " an art-work in the higher sense." He praises Berlioz's *musical* gifts, but argues that " the prime condition of a musical drama is the right relation between poet and composer. . . . The absence of this prime condition — which, indeed, had not as yet come into consideration at the time when this work was written and produced in Paris, everyone being sunk in the deepest depths of the *opera fallacy* — virtually bars us from pronouncing *Cellini* to be an art-work in the higher sense." There follows a detailed consideration of the characters, the milieu, the motives and the action of the opera. Then comes the summing-up — " but if I say that *Cellini* is not an art-work in the higher sense I mean that as an art-work it is too defective and in its totality it is too abortive to satisfy *the public of the future*, too noble and intelligent to be sympathetic to *the public of the present*." Bülow goes on to find the root-error of *Cellini* in the faulty conception of the *drama* — an indication of the impression that had been made on him by Wagner's theory and practice.[14]

Even without the evidence afforded by the quotation given above from Bülow's letter to Wagner, it would be tolerably clear that, for

---

[13] I have elsewhere given reasons for thinking that much of the opposition to Liszt in Weimar was less a matter of convictions about art than a personal dislike for Liszt and the Princess. See NML, Chapter VI.

[14] BAS, pp. 61–79. See also a later article of Bülow's on Berlioz and *Cellini*, in BAS, pp. 90–101.

all his admiration of Berlioz as a composer, the young man could not see an epoch-making or future-forming *dramatic* work in *Cellini,* and that he was torn between his desire to speak the whole truth and nothing but the truth about it and his sense of loyalty towards Liszt. Wagner, in his reply — written, be it remembered, some weeks before Bülow's articles appeared — shows that he is fully aware of this contest in his young friend's soul between honesty and expediency. His answer to Bülow's plea that one ought to support Liszt in everything is,

"No, that you must not do! I know only one vice — insincerity, cowardice; and only one virtue — veracity and courage. Beware, my dear Hans, of coming to ruin through politics. [This is manifestly a glancing blow at Liszt]. . . . You think it is for a good ultimate purpose — to prepare the path for *me.* This is fundamentally false, and only weakness can deceive itself in this fashion. A good end can never be achieved through bad means; if it could, the Jesuit *end* would equally have to be recognised as good. The means that Liszt is now employing must of necessity lead to a quite other end than the one he has in view: by productions of Berlioz and Meyerbeer he can merely confuse public opinion still further with regard to myself and still further confuse taste in general. By so doing he can only destroy utterly all that he has so far done for me. Whoever desires to further my tendency [in art] can do so only by specifically showing how it differs fundamentally from that other tendency, and indeed by showing that this other is the wrong one, and in no wise to be encouraged. Liszt could be of service to me by productions of Berlioz and so on only if he said to people, ' See, this is what Wagner does *not* want, for such and such reasons that ought to be evident to you.' Such a procedure, however, would be in the highest degree unpractical, cruel to others, and, at the very least, a mistake. Better therefore that this art that is the opposite of mine should be left untouched in any form. But *this* Liszt will not do, for he is too unclear within himself as to the vast difference between Berlioz and such people as myself. I cannot take it amiss that he is fond of Berlioz, for I myself am truly not indifferent towards him; so if he [Liszt] cannot see what the point really is, but is simply bent on pushing Berlioz, in God's name let him go on doing so. But if he imagines that he is cutting a path for *me* by doing this, you should do all that is in your power to convince him how utterly wrong he is, and to make it clear to him that by doing so he can achieve nothing but the direct opposite. If you can't knock this into him, then at any rate do *nothing* by way of support of him in this connection. On the contrary, try at any rate, without going against Liszt, to make the thing clear to the public. In that way you will be doing what it behoves you to do, and what will keep your conscience clean. And do not imagine that by acting in this way Liszt is furnishing me with the material for the performance of my future works. What is of service to me is not money but the spirit in which the material is shaped.[15] On this point I have already written to Liszt in full, in connection with the Goethe Foundation. Has that letter had no effect upon him? Have you people read *Opera and Drama?* If so, how can Liszt still believe that he can be of help to me *via* Berlioz? " [16]

The conclusion seems to be the one to which other considerations have already led us — that not long after the production of *Lohengrin* it dawned upon Liszt that he and Weimar had a " mission " in music, but that for some time yet he was anything but clear as to the precise nature of that mission. Wagner's attitude towards the whole matter was perfectly logical. If Liszt was merely bent on giving miscellaneous concert and opera performances after the fashion of any other Kapellmeister, then, no matter how superior the Weimar repertory might in time become to that of the ordinary theatre, all this was no concern of Wagner's. If, on the other hand, Liszt, in spite of all his correspondence with his friend, in spite of his presumed reading of his friend's prose works, was still ignorant of the special nature of Wagner's projected reform of the opera, still under the delusion that Wagner was simply one of an international body of composers who were all of them, each in his own way, contributing to the " progress " of music, then there was nothing more to be done with him, nothing more to be hoped for from Weimar. In the light of this *Cellini* episode, Wagner's letters of the

---

[15] The clue to this is given us by a letter from Wagner to Liszt of the preceding May (1851) in which he urged Liszt to make the Weimar theatre unique in that the performers would have a genuine German style and culture of their own, not the bad mixture of all varieties of styles, domestic and foreign, and the total lack of culture, that were the bane of the German theatre in general. It is clear from this letter that Wagner already at that time disapproved of Liszt's reinforcing the Weimar repertory with foreign works. What could this policy bring him, he asked, beyond an increase of fame? "Very good; but will that make you happy — You? No! Only in quite another sense can you be happy. Do something for *your* Weimar!"

It becomes clear now what was his real objection, in the following year, to the production of *Cellini:* this could contribute nothing to moulding the Weimar singers to the shape he needed them to be for *his* purely German works of the future.

[16] RWHB, pp. 19 ff.

latter part of 1851 to Liszt acquire a new significance; the tacit ruling-out of Weimar so far as the *Ring* was concerned was probably not unconnected with the dawning perception on Wagner's part that there was something in him that Liszt had never understood and would never understand, that Liszt merely admired him as a composer without being either able or particularly anxious to comprehend him as dramatist and thinker.

But Liszt continued to work loyally for Wagner according to his lights. He planned to give the *Flying Dutchman* in the season 1852–3. He revived *Tannhäuser,* and aimed at producing it more in accordance with the composer's intentions than had previously been the case. He conducted the *Faust Overture* at a concert of the Montag Singing Society on the 11th May. A production of *Tannhäuser* for the benefit of the Czar of Russia in mid-May being impossible owing to the disability of some of the singers, Liszt gave what seems to have been the first of those " Wagner evenings " that have been staple concert room fare for more than eighty years; the programme consisted of the first act of *Tannhäuser* as far as the Pilgrims' Chorus and the third act of *Lohengrin* to the end of the duet, with Berlioz's *Carnaval romain* Overture and the second act of *Cellini* (minus the baritone aria) to finish up with. The tiny town of Ballenstedt was to be the scene of a two-days' festival under Liszt's direction on the 22nd and 23rd June. This became something of a Wagner festival, the programmes including the *Tannhäuser* overture, the *Liebesmahl der Apostel* and the duet from the second act of the *Flying Dutchman,* Liszt's own *Die Macht der Musik,* Beethoven's Choral Fantasia and Ninth Symphony, Raff's *King Alfred* overture, Mendelssohn's *Walpurgis-Nacht,* and part of Berlioz's *Harold in Italy.* The *Tannhäuser* overture was repeated by request at the end of the second concert, and glowing accounts of the affair were sent to various papers by the Wagnerian bodyguard of the period — Brendel, Bülow, Raff, and Robert Franz. Liszt had by now, in fact, gone completely Wagnerian. In August, 1852, the full score of *Lohengrin* was published by Breitkopf & Härtel, with a dedication to Liszt. There is a marked change in both the number and the tone of Liszt's letters to Wagner from about this time onward: Liszt is henceforth considerably more demonstrative than he had hitherto been. Wagner's genius had made a complete conquest of him: and with the *cachet* given to his own activities by the now universal association of his name with that of Wagner he is inspired with a new ambition both for Weimar and for himself.

CHAPTER XV

THE "HAILSTORM"

1

I T WAS during 1852 that there arose that extraordinary demand for Wagner's scores that showed how swiftly the tide had begun to flow in his direction. It has already been pointed out that the vital core of the service rendered him by the Weimar production of *Lohengrin* in August, 1850, had been the destruction of the legend that his works were too difficult for the average German theatre. Another determining element in the situation was the fact that a Grand Ducal Court had thrown its protecting mantle round the banned " revolutionary ": it gave Wagner the entry, as it were, into respectable operatic society in spite of his black record in 1849. Taking into consideration the fact that operas cannot be produced or repertories changed at a moment's notice, it is manifest that the repercussions of the Weimar *Lohengrin* had been fairly swift and decidedly powerful. As early as the spring of 1851 Frankfort was enquiring after *Tannhäuser*, though the delays incidental to opera houses made a production impossible there until February, 1853. Little Schwerin was the first to take up the ball that Liszt had started rolling: *Tannhäuser* was given there on the 26th January, 1852, and proved such a success that it received three other performances in less than a month. The " hailstorm ", as the astonished Wagner called it, had begun. The quaint legend of a much later day that he had no success during his lifetime will not stand examination in the light of the record of 1852 and the years immediately following. Difficulties of this or that local order sometimes made a projected performance of one or other of the Wagner operas impracticable at the moment, even after negotiations had been entered into with the composer on the subject; but in 1852 and 1853 we find the following towns either planning or carrying out a Wagner production — Leipzig, Frankfort, Wiesbaden, Würzburg, Breslau, Düsseldorf, Rudolstadt, Hamburg, Riga. The work in most general demand was *Tannhäuser*.

The Wagner operas created the greatest enthusiasm everywhere. Special trains were run to Schwerin, Wiesbaden, and other places from the neighbouring towns. Schwerin alone gave fourteen performances of *Tannhäuser* during 1852. In one or two cases Wagner obtained royalties; but from the majority of theatres he received, in accordance with the practice of the epoch, a first fee that was also the last: it varied from about £7/10/0 in English money for a small theatre like the Würzburg one to about £17 for one the size of Breslau. Tichatschek, however, could command, even in a tiny town like Weimar, the equivalent of £40 for a single guest appearance in a Wagner opera — something like three times the sum paid to the composer by the average theatre for the right to perform one of his operas in perpetuity! Had composers in general been treated with ordinary justice in those days, and been given a royalty on each performance of their works, Wagner would have done so well out of his first four operas that he would not only not have been under the necessity of looking to friends for his support but could even have indulged himself in his heart's desire of a house with a little garden, in which he could work at his music without the distraction of pianos in the adjoining rooms and of noises in the street. There is something peculiarly revolting about a social system that legally made it almost impossible for a composer like Wagner to be anything but a mendicant and then sneered at him for borrowing.

2

Wagner's luck, as he himself said, was mainly in the smaller towns, in which the Kapellmeisters were not men who had grown hoary in routine, had become mentally flaccid with the years, and were themselves composers with operas of their own for which a home had to be found, but young men with no personal axes to grind, and with their young veins full of generous new fire. With the larger and richer opera houses his path was not so easy. Franz Lachner had given the *Tannhäuser* overture in Munich in November, 1852, but in all probability it was helped neither by Lachner's conducting nor by the somewhat foolish programme note which the authorities preferred to Wagner's own. The overture had a mixed reception from both public and Press, the most sensible word on the subject being spoken by the critic of the *Bayerische Landbote:* " One ought to read the Foreword to a book twice, once before reading the book and once afterwards. And an overture can be thoroughly understood only after hearing the opera, especially when the composer's trend is new and his aim original, as is the case with Richard Wagner, who has stirred up a huge controversy about opera music that has not yet been fought out either theoretically or practically. Let us not forget that Beethoven himself had to blaze his trail before he was accepted at his full value, and that the beautiful, if it happens also to be new, needs to become familiar." [1]

Wagner jumped to the conclusion that Lachner had given the overture only with the sinister purpose of prejudicing the Munich public against him and so barring the way to a production of the opera. In this, however, it appears that he was wrong, for after the *Tannhäuser* overture had made a sensation in Wiesbaden a fortnight or so later the Munich Intendant, Dingelstedt, sent his theatre inspector, Wilhelm Schmitt, to Zürich to treat with Wagner on the subject of a production in Munich. [2] But as soon as the news of the negotiations became public property there arose an outcry that was curiously prophetic of the storm that was to break over Wagner's head in Munich some twelve years later. Apparently there was a strong party in the town opposed to Dingelstedt himself as an " importation " from the north; and his interest in Wagner was too good a stick to beat him with for his enemies to let the chance go by. " The Court Theatre Intendant ", one journalist said, " intends to give a work by the revolutionary, the red republican Richard Wagner "; while another opined that " the proper place for the Orpheus who, during the May revolt in Dresden, raised barricades with his lyre is not the Munich Opera House but the prison at Waldheim " — i.e. in the company of Röckel. The political rancour against the Zürich refugee was largely due to the close relationship existing between the Wittelsbachs and the Saxon Court. The Saxon President of the Bavarian Council, von der Pfordten,

---

[1] RLW, I, 2.
[2] Wagner makes no mention of this visit in *Mein Leben.*

who was destined to play a large part in Wagner's stormy life in Munich in 1864 and the following years, seems to have advised King Maximilian that it would be impolitic to produce the opera of the " revolutionary " just then, and so the project was allowed to lapse, not to be taken up again till nearly three years later.

3

Wagner's birthplace, Leipzig, which had not yet heard a single opera by its distinguished son, though the *Tannhäuser* overture had been murdered there by Mendelssohn in 1846,[3] began to coquet with the idea of giving *Lohengrin* in 1851: the influential Dr. Härtel had evidently told his friends of the effect of the Weimar production, at which he had been present. Nothing was done in the matter then, however, and it was not until the beginning of 1852 that Wagner came into the Leipzigers' thoughts again, on this occasion, however, in connection with what was at that time regarded as the " easier " *Tannhäuser*. Wagner asked for an honorarium of 28 Louisdor, but made it clear that the fee was a less important matter in his eyes than an adequate production of his work, for which he innocently thought he could rely on the Kapellmeister, Julius Rietz. He learned, to his astonishment, that Leipzig thought him " too exacting " in his artistic demands; but after an interval of some months they approached him once more, no doubt in obedience to pressure from some of the more advanced musical elements in the town. The theatre director, Wirsing, actually called on him in Zürich in July, and got as far as asking for Hähnel's original Dresden sketches for the scenery and costumes, which he wanted to follow for his own production. As these were simultaneously in demand from several other theatres, however, Wagner made the practical suggestion that Hähnel should prepare a number of copies of the sketches, to be supplied by him direct to any theatre that might need them. Wirsing now declined to pay the modest fee of 27 thalers asked for these sketches — 9 thalers for each of the three chief settings — on the ground that it had not been stipulated in the fee originally demanded by Wagner. After further wrangling

---

[3] See Vol. I, pp. 400-1.

Wirsing waived the point, but although he had had the score for some time he still did not pay Wagner the honorarium of which he was sorely in need at the time. In September Wagner was told that the score had been returned to Uhlig, who was acting for him in the matter, and that the work could not be given on account of its " insuperable difficulties ": Rietz and the others, it seems, had read the *Guide to the Performing of Tannhäuser* which the composer, in the innocence of his heart, had sent round to the various theatres presumed to be interested in the opera, and they had taken fright at what was expected of them and of the singers. It looks as if there was never more than the minimum of intention, or even desire, on the part of Rietz and his associates to give the work, and that they jumped at any excuse to turn it down. Presuming on what they thought to be the legal disadvantages of Wagner's position as an exile, they did not even part with the score until he turned a Leipzig lawyer on to them; and they appear to have done their best to prejudice Breitkopf & Härtel against him by scare-talk about the vocal difficulties of his operas and the too exacting nature of his demands in the matter of mounting and of production generally. The publishers, who were just then negotiating with Wagner over the *Faust Overture* and his revised version of the *Iphigenia in Aulis* score, wrote tearfully to him about the difficulties he was in the habit of making for himself, for them, and for the theatres; and it ended in his withdrawing his offers of the two scores.

Apparently, however, the demand for *Tannhäuser* in certain Leipzig quarters was too powerful to be resisted for long. The opera was at last produced, under Rietz, on the 31st January, 1853. The first performance was enthusiastically received, but at the second the house was nearly empty, the public resenting the raised prices by which Wirsing hoped to recoup himself for his extra expenditure on the enlarged orchestra and on the settings. As twenty performances of *Tannhäuser* were given during that year, however, there could be no doubt of its Leipzig success.

4

With Berlin, meanwhile, Wagner's experiences had been still more exasperating. Although Mantius had missed Wagner in

Zürich in June, 1852,[4] negotiations for *Tannhäuser* had subsequently been opened by letter. Wagner, with his bitter memories of the Berlin productions of the *Flying Dutchman* in 1844 and *Rienzi* in 1847, and with the consciousness that no excess of goodwill towards him need be anticipated either from the powerful Meyerbeer — who could hardly be expected to love him after *Judaism in Music* — or the local Kapellmeisters, Dorn and Taubert, could cherish no hope of any great artistic results there: but Berlin was too important in various ways to be cold-shouldered. An outstanding success there would make itself felt all over Europe; moreover, Berlin could not only afford a handsome first fee but was one of the very few German theatres that paid a composer continuing royalties. The difficulties he foresaw aroused both his fighting spirit and his sense of strategy. It was not enough that the Berlin Opera should merely save its face with the public by producing *Tannhäuser* and then shelve it: it would have to be jockeyed into such a position that it would be to its own interest to keep the work in the repertory. So Wagner demanded what both he and Liszt agreed was the " exceptional ", though by no means unreasonable, fee of 1,000 thalers, a sum which the theatre, of course, could recoup only by frequent performance. As on so many other occasions when Wagner was dealing with finance, his proposal, had it been accepted, would ultimately have proved a gold mine for the other party. Ellis pointed out that during the last years of Wagner's life *Tannhäuser* attained its 200th performance in Berlin, so that the honorarium of 1,000 thalers would have represented up to that time an average royalty of no more than about fifteen shillings a performance. But that is not the whole story: by February, 1892, the work had been given [5] in Berlin 300 times, by August, 1898,

---

4 See *supra*, p. 286.
5 For the figures relating to the performances of all the Wagner operas in Berlin see KWBO, pp. 61, 62. It may be driving a further nail in the coffin of the nonsensical legend that it was not until long after Wagner's death that he had any real success if I give the figures for the performances of his other chief operas in Berlin alone:

Rienzi	50	performances by August, 1884.
Flying Dutchman	100	performances by January, 1891.
Lohengrin . . .	300	performances by October, 1892.
Tristan	50	performances between March, 1876, and May, 1896.
Meistersinger . .	100	performances between April, 1870, and December, 1894.
Rhinegold . . .	50	performances between April, 1888, and September, 1898.

400 times, by August, 1907, 500 times, by August, 1916, 600 times, by September, 1930, 700 times. Hülsen would have done well to accept Wagner's terms in 1852.

5

Tannhäuser seems to have been more or less definitely projected for the 15th October, 1852,[6] the birthday of the King of Prussia; and even after that plan had to be abandoned Hülsen agreed that when the opera *was* produced it would be given six times in the first month and at least ten times between the autumn of 1852 and the spring of 1853. By this time arrangements had been made with Wagner for a royalty of 10 per cent. on each evening's takings in lieu of the lump sum of 1,000 thalers he had asked for at first; he was willing to renounce payment altogether if only his artistic demands were conscientiously met. But it was one of his conditions that Liszt should be in charge to ensure that everything was done in accordance with his intentions. Liszt was willing enough to go to Berlin, but rightly stipulated that he should receive a direct invitation to that effect from Hülsen. It indicates a certain innocence on Wagner's part that he should not have seen that this condition was a direct affront to Dorn and Taubert: his low opinion of them may have been fully justified, but they could hardly be expected to share it, and there is nothing surprising in the fact that Hülsen, probably for peace' sake, stood by them; the intrusion of Liszt, armed with powers above those of the regular Kapellmeisters, would have turned the opera house upside down. To Wagner, of

---

Valkyrie. . . .   100 performances between April, 1884, and April, 1896.
Siegfried. . . .   50 performances between December, 1885, and October, 1898.
Götterdämmerung   50 performances between September, 1888, and September, 1900.

Parsifal, of course, could not be produced in Berlin until January, 1914, after the expiry of the copyright. It had 50 performances between then and the end of 1915. From the date of the first performance of the *Flying Dutchman* (7th January, 1844) to the 13th February, 1933, (the fiftieth anniversary of Wagner's death), the Berlin Opera gave in all 3,733 Wagner performances. Hülsen and Meyerbeer would probably turn in their graves if they could see the figures.

[6] Early in October *Lohengrin* had been given for the seventh time in Weimar, in honour of the Prince of Prussia (who was to become later the first German Emperor) and his wife Augusta (the daughter of the Grand Duke of Sachsen-Weimar). Even their interest in Wagner was apparently insufficient to break down the professional opposition to him in the Berlin Opera.

course, the whole thing looked simplicity itself: he saw only the artistic side of the affair. Hülsen, on the other hand, regarded Wagner's stipulation as " insulting " to the Berlin personnel. The negotiations seem to have been carried on at first through the medium of brother Albert (who was at that time stationed in Berlin), Hülsen objecting to having anything to do with Wagner direct.[7] But on the 17th October Wagner had written personally to Hülsen, setting forth his reasons for requiring the presence of Liszt in Berlin. Hülsen now definitely refused the demand. " This Hülsen ", Wagner writes to Liszt, " is personally a quite well-disposed creature, but without a trace of understanding of the things he is supposed to administer; he treats with me over *Tannhäuser* as he would with Flotow over *Martha*. It is too disgusting! "

Still unable to see the matter as Hülsen saw it, he wrote on the 30th November to his niece Johanna (who was now one of the leading " stars " of the Berlin Opera, and who had herself handed his previous letter to Hülsen), in terms that suggest a still lingering belief in his mind that the production would take place, though without Liszt: " Your father and Hülsen will not, I hope, expect any answer from me to their last letters; what could I say to them, seeing that they have no comprehension at all of the real point involved in inviting Liszt? All I can do now is to let the affair go on in its own way, only hoping that it may happen [in Berlin] as in Breslau, where *Tannhäuser* has been given twelve times in six weeks to full houses; for in that case I shall at least get some money from Berlin. Please send me a few lines at once to let me know how the *Tannhäuser* matter now stands there. According to the latest arrangement the rehearsals should already have begun; it would interest me to know how things are going." [8]

A letter of eight days later to Johanna shows him to be decidedly anxious, for material reasons, that the production shall not fall through. Johanna (who of course would sing Elisabeth) can, he thinks, help the not very intelligent tenor to rise for a few hours above his normal self: while if only the conductor will study the Guide he will be able temporarily to make good actors out of quite

---

[7] See *supra*, p. 77.
[8] Letter published for the first time in JKJ, p. 63.

mediocre singers, as had been the case in Breslau and Wiesbaden. But whatever goodwill Johanna may have personally had towards her uncle was probably impotent against the illwill of her father, who had no intention of letting his daughter's fame and pocket suffer through anything so absurdly idealistic as art for art's sake. As early as January she had to tell her uncle that in any case *Tannhäuser* was impossible at the moment, as Auber's thirteen-years-old *Lac des fées* and the wretched *Martha* were to be given first. Thereupon Wagner demanded the return of his score. It was not sent back until February, and then without a single accompanying word from Hülsen or anyone else. There had been little real goodwill towards him on the part of anyone in the theatre; and the negotiations had probably been mostly a blague from start to finish. The time was to come when Hülsen would be glad to eat out of Wagner's hand, but that day was as yet some years distant. When it did come, Wagner had ample revenge for all his sufferings of this winter of 1852–3.

6

Even Dresden succumbed to the general excitement over Wagner at this time; there was plainly a public interest in him there that was too strong for either his political or his musical enemies to ignore. There had been some talk of giving *Lohengrin* in 1851, but Wagner would not hear of it. He would have vetoed a production of *Tannhäuser* if he could, for he had little confidence in the worthy Reissiger, and still less in his own successor, Krebs, who, according to Bülow, was anything but skilled in the reading of even the simplest scores. But Dresden was legally able to do what it liked as regarded *Tannhäuser*. In view of the attitude of the police and the high officials generally towards the escaped revolutionary, only personal goodwill on the King's part could have made a revival of the opera possible. It was given, for the first time after nearly four years, on the 26th October, 1852, before a crowded house; probably many people went to the theatre that evening in the joyous hope of a disturbance, but nothing of that kind took place. The second performance does not seem to have been so well attended; but at the fifth, on the 28th November — at which, by the way, Liszt was present — the house was full. After that, *Tannhäuser* disappeared once more from the Dresden repertory for something like another five years: evidently the forces opposed to Wagner, in the opera house and outside it, were too powerful. There was once more some vague talk about producing *Lohengrin;* Fischer and Heine had certainly gone to Weimar in November to see the opera, but whether officially or not we cannot be quite sure. Presumably Dresden could have insisted on its legal rights in that matter also had it wanted to. Wagner, however, wrote to Lüttichau appealing to his sense of decency, and making it clear to him that he had no confidence in either Reissiger or Krebs; and Lüttichau was no doubt glad of so good an excuse at once to please Wagner's Court enemies and save himself an infinite amount of trouble and annoyance. The *Lohengrin* project was dropped: Dresden did not hear the work for another seven years.

CHAPTER XVI

GROWING ESTRANGEMENT FROM THE WORLD

1

HAVING THUS run a connected line, for convenience' sake, through the history of Wagner's successes and difficulties in the German theatres in 1852 and 1853, we may now take up the thread of his life at the point at which we left it in the summer of the former year.

All this "success" had, for him, a touch of unreality about it. He could be under no illusion as to the character of the great majority of the performances his works were receiving in this or that small town. His exile weighed heavily on his spirit: he had no great desire to hear again any of his earlier works except *Lohengrin*, but it was a torture to him to think how grievously *Tannhäuser* must have been misrepresented all over Germany in his absence. He could have no doubt by this time that even Liszt, for all his good intentions, had produced both *Tannhäuser* and *Lohengrin* in a way of which he himself would not have approved.

Liszt, it cannot be too often reiterated, had virtually no understanding of anything in Wagner but the musician: not only was he unreceptive where Wagner's theories of art and philosophy were concerned but he had the minimum of insight into his dramatic ideals. Wagner had sensed this defect in him on that day in May, 1849, when he attended a rehearsal of *Tannhäuser* in Weimar:

"Liszt's conducting," he says in *Mein Leben*, "though it was more concerned with the musical than with the dramatic side, filled me for the first time with the flattering warmth of a feeling of being understood by another man who entered deeply into my emotions. At the same time, in spite of my dreamy condition, I formed very definite opinions as to the capacity of the singers and the producer."

The remark as to his " dreamy condition " is significant: he was plainly in a highly nervous state after his experiences of the last few days, deeply moved at finding himself, on this of all occasions, in the midst of people who were interested in him as an artist, affected by Liszt's enthusiasm, and impressed by the way in which he brought to bear upon the score all the fineness of nuancing that in the days gone by had made his piano-playing so incomparable. It was the first time Wagner had seen at work in a conductor a temperament and a sensitivity in any degree corresponding to his own: after what he used to call the wood-and-leather of German Kapellmeisters of the type of Reissiger, the elegant superficiality of Mendelssohn, or the merely technical competence of people like Habeneck, Liszt's ardour must have made a tremendous effect on him. Yet even at that time he guessed that Liszt's interest in *Tannhäuser* was mainly musical, not dramatic; and as the months went on he must have become more and more conscious that this was so. He did not personally blame Liszt for the cuts made in *Tannhäuser*, being charitably inclined to place the responsibility for these on the singers; but the cuts were lengthened as time went on, the performances conducted by Götze when Liszt was not there were an outrage on the work, and Liszt never showed any inclination to restore the cuts until Wagner began to appeal to him on the subject in the winter of 1851–2.

2

Liszt, as always where Wagner was concerned, was willing enough to help, but he did so out of respect for Wagner's musical genius and out of goodwill towards him as a man rather than from any sense of what the *drama* of his operas meant for him. For in his heart of hearts Liszt was by now out of sympathy with the opera form. His own words of a slightly later period leave us in no doubt as to this. In his review of A. B. Marx's book *Die Musik des neunzehnten Jahrhunderts und ihre Pflege* (1855), he agrees with the author (who was also the composer of the oratorio *Moses*)[1] that the stage fetters the fantasy of the composer.

---

[1] Liszt had given this work in Weimar in May, 1853.

"Marx is absolutely right", he says, "in regarding the stage as too confined a field for the lofty passions he would like to display upon it: it lacks the indescribable magic of perspective, of mirage, of half-shade that the vision of marvellous pictures permits to the fancy. The inadequate reality of the stage can only hinder these as soon as it tries to replace the resplendent visions of the imagination by the visible scene, which in comparison can only look like a parody of them. To anyone whose fancy can invent for his fictions a landscape frame of inimitable beauty and grandeur it must seem as childish to confine them within the narrow compass of the boards as it would be to try to represent a sea-storm in a park pool. Costumes and sets, decorations and machines, actors and mounting are too clumsy instruments for the realisation of certain sublime scenes. There cannot be any question that in many cases art does not suffer in the least when it renounces the attempt to represent *everything*, realise *everything*, make *everything* clear to the senses; for the mind can conjecture more than can be shown to it, and the listener who supplies his own particular frame for the dramatic action is in no danger of having his attention distracted or his emotions disturbed by this or that illusion-destroying reality. Many a thing gains rather than loses when it is suggested rather than described, or described rather than realised. In many cases, indeed, the imagination so far outsoars the possibility of representation that the latter attempts in vain to compete with it." [2]

All this, of course, is special pleading for Liszt's own — or was it the Princess's? — ideal of the symphonic poem; his first six works in that genre were to be published in the following year. There is a good deal to be said, in certain circumstances, for the aesthetic principle he puts forward in the passage quoted above. With that, however, we are not concerned here. What does concern us is the fact that had Liszt [3] deliberately set out to deny in public all that Wagner stood for he could have hit upon no more drastic

---

[2] LZGS, V, 212–3.

[3] Or, again, was it the Princess? It is impossible now to decide how much in Liszt's literary works of the Weimar period was written by him and how much by Carolyne; but there is reason to believe that in many, if not in most cases, he gave her a sketch which she expanded and embroidered in her own florid way. He sometimes rebelled against her matter or her style, but in the end was always weak enough to surrender. (See fresh evidence on this point, from unpublished letters at Weimar, in RFLS, pp. 175–6). It is rather significant that not a single original manuscript of any of these writings has been allowed to survive. Both Liszt and the Princess, of course, wrote in French; translations for the German papers were made by Cornelius, Raff, or some other member of the Altenburg circle.

expression of his views than this; for it was the very core of Wagner's aesthetic that the highest results in art were to be obtained only by the close co-operation of eye and ear in the musical drama; and Wagner, when he read Liszt's article in the *Neue Zeitschrift*, as he must have done, must have realised at last, if he had never done so before, that what he regarded as the very essence of himself as an artist was a sealed book to Liszt, and always would be. Even after we have given due consideration to the fact that the article on Marx dates from 1855, a period when the Princess had to some extent managed to estrange Liszt intellectually from Wagner, the implications remain the same: a conductor who held these views, even in embryo, upon the inferiority of the theatre to the concert room was constitutionally ill fitted to present a Wagner work to the world according to the intentions of the creator of it.

What we find all through the early 1850's in the correspondence of the pair is an amiable willingness on Liszt's part to listen to all that Wagner has to say on the need for bringing out the *drama* in his operas, and to do what he can to meet his friend's wishes in such matters, without any indication whatever that he himself thought the points on which Wagner insisted so urgently were of supreme importance. In more than one letter of 1852 Wagner gives at great length his reasons for wanting the proposed revival of *Tannhäuser* in Weimar to correspond more closely to his intentions than the earlier performances had done: Liszt assures him that everything will be done " *selon le bon plaisir de l'auteur* ", but still betrays no clear sense of what it all means to Wagner; he agrees with everything Wagner says with the air of one who wants to humour a crotchety friend but cannot attach as much importance to his crotchets as he does himself. It was perhaps fortunate for their friendship that Wagner could not see the Weimar performances; had he done so, he would probably have been tempted to include them in his general denunciation of the German performances of his works, and been more than ever fortified in his resolve not to give the theatres permission to produce *Lohengrin* until they had shown some comprehension of *Tannhäuser* as he had conceived it.

To rid himself, as well as he could, of the torturing suspicion that everything was going wrong with the opera without his being able to be present anywhere to set a standard, he wrote, in August, 1852, a brochure *On the Performing of Tannhäuser*, two hundred copies of which he had printed at his own expense and sent to the theatres that were producing the opera or contemplating producing it.[4] Practically the only result was to add to his troubles and to disillusionise him still further with regard to the German theatre of the day. Here and there a devotee like Schindelmeisser (at Wiesbaden), after reading the Guide, did indeed embark enthusiastically upon a new production of *Tannhäuser* in the light of the fresh insight he had thus acquired into the work. But in general the Guide was either ignored or it produced results exactly opposite to those Wagner had reckoned upon. Six copies had been sent to the Munich Court Theatre: there Wagner found them some twelve years later in mint state, not even the edges having been cut. Leipzig, as we have seen, was so appalled by the revelation of what the composer demanded in the way of intelligence and application from singers, conductors, and producers that it temporarily gave up the idea of producing the work.[5] The average tenor's old dread of a part that had been looked upon as possible only to a Tichatschek was increased when he learned, from the Guide, that even Germany's leading tenor had not come up to the composer's ideal. Both Tichatschek and the Dresden Venus, Schröder-Devrient, must have been deeply hurt by Wagner's plain hints, in the Guide, of their inadequacy to realise his dramatic intentions in the work. There was no real unkindness and certainly no ingratitude in these hints. For Wagner it was not a matter of persons but of principle: his thesis was that the finest singing in the world would not of itself make an ideal Tannhäuser or Venus or Elisabeth, but that once the

---

[4] Portions of the brochure were printed in the *Neue Zeitschrift* of the 3rd and 24th December, 1852, and the 1st, 7th, and 14th January, 1853.

[5] Many theatre directors were no doubt perturbed when they read that Wagner insisted on their increasing the number of their strings for his operas. His demands in this respect would be thought modest to-day. When he urges that no orchestra can do justice to a score like that of *Tannhäuser* with *less than four violas* we get a startling light on the small-town opera orchestras of the period.

essence of the character and of the situations had been grasped the dreaded vocal difficulties would automatically disappear. Time was to prove him to be right: but for the present he had done little more with his well-intentioned Guide than to bring one more charge of " ingratitude " upon himself. The sort of friend who makes it a point of honour to bring to an artist's notice everything that has been said in disparagement of him hastened to " condole " with Tichatschek by word of mouth or by letter. The tenor would hardly have been human had he not felt some annoyance, but this soon passed away. The good-natured fellow was sincerely attached to Wagner personally, and as sincerely enthusiastic over the brilliant — and profitable — parts with which the composer had provided him: and it was not long before his good sense and his good feeling combined to tell him that there were excellent reasons for his old friend's dissatisfaction with him.

4

What with the prolonged birth-pangs attendant on the working out of the *Ring* poem, his fatiguing exertions in connection with the *Flying Dutchman* performances in Zürich, the immense amount of correspondence involved in the negotiations with the theatres during the *Tannhäuser* " hailstorm ", and his increasing financial worries — for he generally spent his theatre fees in anticipation, and the anticipations were not invariably realised — he was in a pitiable state of health all through the summer of 1852. His " success " in Germany was welcome to him for domestic budgetary reasons, but it all seemed a little unreal to him, for he no longer existed in anything but body in the operatic world around him. He knew that the majority of the performances his works were receiving were little more than travesties of his ideal. He knew that in the nature of the case the *Tannhäuser* " hailstorm " could not last much longer, for the list of possible theatres was already nearing exhaustion. The *Ring* would not only take many years to complete but would be wholly impracticable when it was ready, so far as the German theatre as it then was, and was likely to continue to be, was concerned. Yet his will remained unshaken and his belief in his star undiminished: he went on working at the *Ring*, he tells us in

Mein Leben, in utter disregard of existing theatre conditions, confident that what he calls " the ideal theatre I had in my mind " would come of necessity sooner or later.

It was probably his desperate need of money that made him coquet for a while with the idea of producing *Tannhäuser* in Paris. In the autumn of 1852 he received a visit from Belloni, from whom he learned that " owing to the stupidity of Meyerbeer " — who, alarmed at the growing vogue of Wagner, had set his hirelings of the Paris Press to disparage him, — he had " suddenly become famous, or at any rate very interesting " there. Belloni, who took only the impresario's view of the matter and no doubt had an eye to his own ultimate profit, suggested that it would be to Wagner's interest to write an opera expressly for Paris. This, of course, was out of the question: Wagner was resolved never to write an opera to any foreign text whatever. But he would have had no objection to *Tannhäuser* being given in a good French translation provided he were guaranteed a satisfactory performance. At this time Johanna was contemplating leaving Berlin for Paris. The leading French tenor of the period was Roger, good accounts of whom reached Wagner. The omens seemed good, therefore, for a Paris performance:

> " Roger ", he wrote on the 28th September to his niece Franziska (Johanna's sister), " would suit me better than any other tenor in the world — much better than the . . . Tichatschek. What attracts me in the first place is the possibility of a really good performance: in addition, the prospect of a terrific yet momentous and uncommonly successful fight with Meyerbeer stimulates my — call it malice if you like."

All this would be possible, he thought, if Johanna would " enter the lists for me energetically and completely emancipate herself from her dependence on Meyerbeer." It appears from a subsequent letter that Albert had sent his brother particulars of the proposed Paris contract, according to which Johanna was to sing only in Meyerbeer's operas; whereupon Wagner had expressed to Albert his sorrow that Johanna, " who means so much to *me*, should have to sell herself to the greedy Jew: she could surely have found a nobler task for her youthful powers than to sacrifice herself to that rotting carcase." [6] That Johanna, of all people, should squander her talent on the composer whom he had now come to hate more than anyone else in the world was an unspeakable grief to Wagner: he had always had a high opinion of his niece's gifts, and she must often have been present in his mind when thinking out the *Ring*; but the repertory in which she was making her reputation was hardly calculated to mould her mind as he could have wished. He regarded himself as having been " betrayed " by Johanna.

" Could she not win for herself the highest fame ", he asks Franziska in his letter of the 13th October, " by devoting herself to a *noble* task? It would have meant very much to me if *Lohengrin* could be given in Berlin next winter. Everything points that way, but Johanna, for whom I wrote the part of Elsa . . . brings Meyerbeer's *L'Africaine* into the world [7] — all for the sake of her ' career.' If I could only rescue her for true art and show her to the world as an exception among the miserable prime donne of our epoch! "

To Johanna herself, who had sent him her portrait, the wretched man poured out his bitterness and his longing for love:

" I have never cherished resentment against you, but, at the most, a bitter astonishment, distressing doubts. . . . My one need is love! Fame, honour — nothing of that kind can refresh me: only one thing can delight me and reconcile me to life — a sign that I am loved, even if it comes only from a child! "

---

[6] She had been particularly successful during the last three years as Valentine in the *Huguenots* and Fides in the *Prophète*. She had attracted the attention of Meyerbeer during her engagement at Hamburg (where she had gone after leaving Dresden in May, 1849); he obtained a guest engagement for her as Fides in Berlin in May, 1850. Her success in this and other parts led to her being engaged for a year from May, 1851, at a salary of 4,000 thalers, with a bonus of 600 thalers, plus 100 thalers for removal expenses, and with three months' leave. Singers, it is evident, even in those days made more money than composers! Hülsen, who had succeeded Küstner as Intendant in June, 1851, gave her, as from the 1st September, 1852, a ten-years' contract (with a pension to follow) at 1,000 thalers a month, with six months' leave of absence each year. She was not only the best "draw" in Berlin but in eager demand in London, Paris, and America. She was thus exceptionally well placed to further Wagner's interests had her grasping father allowed her to do so. She made, for the time being, box office successes of the now forgotten operas of the two Berlin Kapellmeisters, Dorn and Taubert. See JKJ, pp. 144 ff.

[7] *L'Africaine*, however, was not produced until 1865.

5

The dream of a Paris production of *Tannhäuser* did not last long. It would seem from his letter of the 3rd October, 1852, to Liszt that it had been the latter who had put the idea of it into Belloni's head; but as soon as Wagner began to discuss it with him, Liszt, who was evidently wiser now than he had been two years before, threw cold water on the plan. He had discovered by this time that Wagner was a *German* composer: the present conditions in Paris, he said, were unfavourable for a work like *Tannhäuser;* indeed, the only suitable Wagner opera for the French was *Rienzi.* His sensible advice to his friend was to get on with the composition of the *Ring* and not trouble about anything else; " the rest will come of itself at the proper time." This was true enough, but it did not go far towards solving the most immediately pressing of Wagner's problems — that of making enough money to enable him to live in comfort and pay off his debts. It is significant that from this time onwards Paris came gradually to occupy a larger and larger part in Wagner's plans. A success would not only mean royalties but could be calculated on to impress Germany, and so, perhaps, help to bring about the amnesty for which in the depths of his heart he longed so ardently, for only by means of that could he hope to hear his *Lohengrin.*

He was wearying of Zürich by this time: he had realised that artistically it would never rise to the height of his ideal, and the restricted intellectual life of the place was beginning to pall on him. As his interest in Zürich public music narrowed he probably suffered from a sense of frustration of that lust for power that was always so strong in him. It was one of the paradoxes of his nature that as a creative artist he longed for seclusion from the world, while as a man he could find an outlet for his colossal energy only on the largest public stage. He loathed the big towns, yet it was in these — Dresden, Paris, Vienna, Munich — that he rose to his greatest heights as fighter: even Bayreuth, which was in theory a withdrawal from the world, was in reality the creation of a kingdom in which he could at last gratify his passion for despotic power. In the mid-'fifties, as he watched his growing vogue in Germany and at the same time saw himself condemned to relative impotence in tiny Zürich, the inability to be at the centre of this new operatic world of his own creating must have been a torture to him. In addition, he had come by this time under the spell of Mathilde Wesendonk: although he does not mention her by name in his letters of the period, certain veiled allusions to feminine sympathy, and his own dating of the beginning of the attachment in later years, leave no doubt as to the matter.

Finally, there was the incessant fret of his vast new artistic plans. He tried to persuade himself that with the completion of his great chain of prose works he had finished for ever with theorising about his art. But the theory had now to be converted into practice. The terrific problem of the musical working out of the *Ring* must sometimes have appalled him; and the longer the delay in committing his ideas to paper the more disorganising must the mental pressure have been. " I shall go mad here! " he cries to Liszt on the 9th November. If only he could get permission at least to go to Weimar and hear one of his operas!

> " In that case I might hope for a cure. I might find something to stimulate me as an artist: I might even hear a word of love here and there. But here? Here, before long I must go to perdition; everything, everything will come *too late* — too late! . . . What can I do? Must I beg for grace from the King of Saxony, or more likely from his —— ministers? Make humble and repentant confession? Can anyone expect *that* of me? Among the princes who admire my ' works ' is there not a single one who has sufficient sense of shame to understand that it is unworthy, mean, common, pitiable, to leave me in my present situation, not one who will take the trouble to persuade the thoughtless Saxon royal couple to enable me to return to Germany without exacting self-humiliation of me? "

And he pours out once more his love and gratitude to Liszt: " You, my only and dearest one, you, my prince, my world, my all in all, have pity on me! "

6

To Uhlig, a few days later, he writes in the same hectic strain:

> " There must be a change in my situation; something must happen to tear me away from this mere world of thought-life. This occupa-

tion with art *par distance* is death to me. No joy is lasting — not even the Breslau news — for I cannot appease myself with 'news.' What the change shall be I cannot conceive, for at no price would I apply for an amnesty! But this I know: a trip to Weimar or Berlin to hear my operas and do something real for them — that would have a highly beneficial effect on me."

To Robert Franz, on the 28th October, goes out a similar cry: the most painful thing for him, he says, is that although *Lohengrin* now belongs so much to his past he has still been unable to produce it in his own way — and then forget it.

" If I now still have the desire to produce this opera, it is only in order to make up for an omission, as it were; and this undertaking could bear almost only on the matter of a proper production of it purely and simply as an art-work in itself, for this *Lohengrin* has now only a certain historical connection with what I want to do as man, poet and musician; in any case, a production would show the public only a part of me, not the whole of me as I now am." [8]

So agonising was the desire to hear at least some of the *Lohengrin* music that he conceived the idea of going to Paris with Minna for a few weeks and engaging an orchestra there for the sole delectation of himself and a few friends. For this bold plan, however, the necessary funds were lacking.

The poem of the tetralogy was no sooner complete [9] than, as usual with him, he felt an overwhelming desire to read it to his friends. For this purpose a small company that included, in addition to Wille and his wife, the latter's sister, Frau von Bissing, and Herwegh, met at Mariafeld towards the end of December, 1852. According to his own account in *Mein Leben* he read the *Rhinegold* and *Valkyrie* on the first evening, finishing at midnight, *Siegfried* the next morning after breakfast, and the *Götterdämmerung* the same evening. According to Frau Wille, however, three evenings were devoted to the readings. Wagner was in a painfully excited condition, that was unfortunately exacerbated by Frau Wille's having to leave the company in the middle of one of the readings in

---

[8] Letter printed for the first time in FWSZ, pp. 379–80.

[9] The finishing touches had been given to it, and the earlier *Siegfrieds Tod* and *Young Siegfried* re-cast, in the last days of November and the early part of December, 1852.

order to attend her sick child, who was in a fever. Wagner could never brook interruption or even inattention when he was reading or expounding. The next morning he sarcastically remarked to his hostess that evidently the child's illness was not a fatal one, pointed out to her that for her to leave the room in this way was equivalent to an unfavourable criticism of the author, and called her " Fricka." She took it all in good part. Wagner, after a sleepless night, was disinclined for general conversation; he was silent throughout the walk back to Zürich, and Herwegh was tactful enough to respect his silence.

CHAPTER XVII

DIFFICULTIES IN THE ROUNDING OF THE "RING"

1

THE RECENT publication of the poem of *Young Siegfried* and of all Wagner's prose sketches for the *Ring* enables us to trace accurately, for the first time, all the changes the great drama underwent before it reached its present form. To enumerate all the points of difference between the *Ring* as it now is and the *Ring* as it originally was at this point or that would be beyond the specific scope of this Life; but it is desirable that the reader should become acquainted with some of the more drastic alterations, especially those that reveal a gradual change in Wagner's attitude towards his subject.

Ellis, who made a most praiseworthy effort to reconstruct the stages of that change, an effort, however, which, in the absence of the necessary documents, was bound to be unsuccessful here and there, was puzzled at Wagner's description of the coming *Rhinegold*, in his letter of the 14th October, 1851, to Uhlig, as being in three acts. Ellis conjectured that in its first form the work must have been planned without what we now regard as the second scene, i.e. " the earliest appearance of Wotan and the Giants ". Writing again to Uhlig on the 12th November, Wagner foreshadows an important new psychological motive — Alberich's *renunciation of love* in order to win the gold — and then summarises the further course of the action thus: " The capture of Alberich; the division of the gold between the two Giant brothers; the swift fulfilment of Alberich's curse on these two, one of whom immediately slays the other." From the omission from this summary of all mention of Freia, Ellis concluded that the idea of the scene in which Freia is claimed by the Giants did not occur to Wagner until 1852, perhaps as the result of a hint from Ettmüller. We see now, however, that the Freia scene formed part of Wagner's first short Prose Sketch, which, though undated, appears to have been made some time between the 3rd and 11th November, 1851. From this Sketch we see also what Wagner had in his mind in his curious division of the work into three acts. The first act begins with the scene of the Rhine Maidens, in which, incongruously as it seems to us now, Wotan takes part: he learns from the maidens, for the first time, the peculiar property of the gold. Then follows the rape of the gold by Alberich. The second act includes the scene between Wotan and Fricka, the demand of the Giants for Freia as payment for the building of the castle — they finally ask for as much gold as corresponds to the goddess's bulk, — and Wotan's decision to seize the Nibelung's Hoard. The third act deals with Alberich's domination of Mime and the other Nibelungs by means of the Ring and the Tarnhelm, the entry of Wotan and Loge, the device of the latter by which Alberich is bound, Alberich's cursing of the Ring, the satisfaction of the Giants' demands, Wotan's desire to keep the Ring for himself, his being " warned " (by some one as yet unnamed) to surrender it, the murder of one of the Giants by the other, and Wotan's realisation of the import of the curse. No provision is here made for a change of scene from Nibelheim to the upper air, as in the present *Rhinegold:* at this stage Wagner apparently visualised the whole action of the " third act " as taking place in the one setting.

A later supplementary note shows him still a considerable distance from seeing the action as it now is. He depicts the Giants as having coveted the gold *before the drama opens:* they do not as yet know, however, that Alberich has seized it, and Wotan himself is ignorant of the power attaching to it. He and Loge go to the Rhine Maidens, from whom they learn of Alberich's theft: the Maidens implore Wotan to help them. The remainder of the action of the drama is very much that of the *Rhinegold,* and we now learn that it is the Wala (Erda) who warns Wotan against keeping the Ring. In the Extended Prose Sketch, made between the 23rd and the 31st March, 1852, the action and the motives run on the same lines as in the present work; but curiously enough only two settings are formally indicated — (1) the present opening scene,

(2) the present second (duplicated, of course, in the fourth) scene; the change to Nibelheim and back again (the third scene) is effected by means of a mist that first of all descends and then disperses, without any specific intimation of a break. The transition from the opening scene (that of the Rhine Maidens) to the second (Wotan and Fricka on the heights) is also specifically denoted as taking place " imperceptibly "; Wagner no longer saw the drama as divided into three or any other number of acts, but as flowing on indivisibly from start to finish.

2

Sundry other variations from the first conception of the drama are worth noting.

In both the First Prose Sketch and the Extended Sketch of the *Valkyrie* Wotan appears in the first act, claims hospitality from Hunding, and, as " guest-gift ", strikes his sword into the ash tree, saying, as he leaves the hut, that it shall belong to him who can withdraw it. Hunding tries in vain to do so, but Siegmund succeeds. Wagner's stage sense must later have shown him that Siegmund's withdrawal of the sword ought to constitute the climactic point of the whole act: accordingly when he came to write the poem he held this thrilling stroke in reserve until the moment before the curtain falls. This, of course, meant re-casting a good deal of the earlier matter; as Wotan now does not appear in person, the episode of the placing of the sword in the tree has to be told, in narrative form, by Sieglinde.

At the end of the second act of the present *Valkyrie*, Wotan, after the death of Siegmund, says to Hunding:

> Get hence, slave!
> Kneel before Fricka!
> tell her that Wotan's spear
> avenged what wrought her shame. —
> Go! Go!

There follows the stage direction, " Before the contemptuous wave of his hand, Hunding sinks lifeless to the ground." In neither the First nor the Extended Prose Sketch, however, does Hunding die:

he is merely dismissed by Wotan with the words, " Get hence and tell Fricka, upon whom thou callest [for moral support], that thou hast been avenged by my spear! " This is one of the instances in which Wagner has carried something over from the Sketches into the poem without having made proper allowance for the fact that in the interval his imagination had introduced a new element into the scene. Wotan's words make complete sense in the Sketch, but make something less than perfect sense in the present poem: there is surely no need for Hunding to die to take the message to the living Fricka! Apparently what happened was that Wagner saw that Hunding's exit from the scene in the flesh would be an anti-climax, but that a crowning effect of horror could be made by his falling dead. No valid reason appears why Wotan should visit death upon him. It will be remembered, however, that in the Sketch of 1848 — *The Nibelungen Myth as Sketch for a Drama* — Siegfried, before killing Fafner and Mime, avenges his father's death by slaying Hunding. It may be that when Wagner came to write the *Valkyrie* poem he had an uncomfortable sense that the continued existence of Hunding would be a sort of loose end that would require tying up somehow or other at some later stage, and that the best way to deal with it was to have him finally disposed of by Wotan. But in that case he should surely have sought for other words than those he had originally put into Wotan's mouth under quite other circumstances, when the intention of the god had been merely to send the *living* man to Fricka with the news that her command to him to sacrifice Siegmund on the altar of morality had been obeyed.

Ellis was puzzled, as many other students of the *Ring* have been, by Mime's despairing words to the Wanderer (in the first act of *Siegfried*) after he has been posed with the question of who will forge the sword:

> The splinters! The sword!
> Alas! I know not!
> What shall I do?
> Where shall I turn?
> Accursed steel!
> Would I ne'er had stolen it!

As the reader will remember, it is only a few minutes since Mime had told Siegfried that the splinters of his father's sword had been *given to him by Sieglinde before she died:*

> This had I of thy mother:
> for trouble, food and shelter,
> this was the paltry pay!
> Look then, 'tis a shattered sword!
> She said thy father had borne it
> in the last of his fights, when he fell.

Ellis therefore opined that the line " Verfluchter Stahl, dass ich dich *gestohlen* " could hardly have been written after the scene between Sieglinde and Brynhilde in the *Valkyrie,* act III. It was so, however: the explanation is that when, after writing the *Valkyrie,* Wagner came to re-cast *Young Siegfried,* he forgot that *there* he had treated the incident differently. His first idea had evidently been to make Mime *steal* the fragments of the sword; and in the scene with the Wanderer in *Young Siegfried,* Mime uses precisely the words quoted above from *Siegfried.* With this conception still in his mind when he wrote the Prose Sketch for the *Valkyrie,* Wagner omitted all mention of the fragments in the scene between Brynhilde and Sieglinde at the commencement of the third act: the Valkyrie bids Sieglinde live for the sake of the child she bears within her, hurriedly sends her into the woods for safety, and then turns to face the wrath of Wotan. In the *poem* of the *Valkyrie,* however, he makes an addition at this point: Brynhilde, before she dismisses Sieglinde, " produces ", according to the stage directions, " the pieces of Siegmund's sword from under her armour and hands them to Sieglinde ", saying:

> Preserve thou for him
> these mighty splinters;
> from his father's death-field
> by good hap I saved them:
> he who this sword
> re-wrought shall swing,
> his name from me let him take,
> " Siegfried " — victorious o'er all!

That this had been an afterthought is clearly shown by the manuscript of the Prose Sketch of the *Valkyrie*, for in the margin of that, at the point where Brynhilde sends Sieglinde away, we find a jotting added at some later date: " Preserve for him these swordsplinters: a hallowed sword, Balmung, were they before it was shattered in Siegmund's hand! " This alteration was then incorporated in the poem of the *Valkyrie;* yet, oddly enough, when Wagner re-cast *Young Siegfried* to make the present *Siegfried* of it, he retained the lines about the " stealing " of the fragments, in complete forgetfulness of his own change of plan! [1]

3

The most curious and the most vital instance, however, of the confusion that came from a change of plan in the course of the re-shaping of the drama is afforded by Wagner's successive treatments of the motive of fearing.

In the first act of *Siegfried*, the hero, after having wormed out of Mime the story of his own parentage, runs from the ugly and hateful dwarf into the woods, with the words:

> Gladness floods me
> for my freedom,
> Nothing now binds me here.
> My father art thou not,
> and afar I know my home;
> thy hearth is not my house,
> nor thy cave my rightful roof.
> As the glad fish
> in the flood swims,
> as the finch free
> on the wind soars:
> I fly from here,
> fleetly I flow

---

[1] It was no doubt the feeling that Wagner had blundered that made Frederick Jameson alter the sense of the vital line in his English version of *Siegfried:* he makes Mime say, instead of "Accursed steel! Would I ne'er had stol'n it!" — "Accursed steel! Would I ne'er had seen it!"

> like the wind o'er the woods
> wending my way,
> thee, Mime, no more to behold!

whereupon the Wanderer enters. In *Young Siegfried*, however, Mime recalls the boy and enlarges upon the theme of fearing. He tells him how his mother had urged the dwarf to keep him always with him in the wood, far away from the world, for the world is full of guile, and only he who has learned what fearing is is fit to go into the world. The clever man, says Mime, learns it easily, the stupid man more hardly. For the wise man, he continues, is always on the look-out for danger that threatens his life; " fear it is that teaches us craft: this is fear's fruit " — a sound enough piece of psychologising. In the wood, he continues, the boy is safe in his native element; but in the world he must either be always on his guard or be destroyed, and without fear one is not on one's guard against guile. In the world, Siegfried will perish as his father had done: let him therefore pay heed to his mother's warning and remain with the good Mime. The impetuous boy, however, will not be advised: he is bent on learning what fear is: into the world he will go, he says, for that very purpose, and Mime must forge him the sword upon which he can rely for his protection.

It is only now, after this extended dialogue, that he takes leave of Mime; and before the Wanderer enters, Mime further indulges in a long monologue in which he makes it clear to us why he had fostered Siegfried. His sole aim all these years has been to win for himself the Hoard and the Ring through the prowess of the boy; and now he finds that he has overreached himself. For his own purpose he had brought Siegfried up to be a boy of high courage; and now this courage impels Siegfried to leave him and test himself in the world, away from the wood, away from Mime and his obsessing, racking problem. He had tried to make the boy love him alone and be wholly dependent on him; and now the boy hates him alone. " What I had planned has turned to my evil: I am caught in every one of my own snares: I thought to hold him through fear, and now through fear he holds me! How to keep him now in my cave and make him serve my ends? " He thinks it over — " to the music ", says a note in the text, " of the Fafner motive." He sees the solution. Since the boy is bent on learning fear, it is through fear that Mime will use him. He will take him to Fafner's lair to learn it: in this way he will make the boy win the Hoard for him. But alas, there still remains the difficult problem of forging the sword, " the only one that will avail: weld it can I not! "

As he sinks down in despair in front of the anvil the Wanderer enters. They play their game of questions and answers, as in the present *Siegfried*. Mime, of course, cannot find the answer to the third question — Who will forge Nothung out of the fragments of Siegmund's sword? In *Young Siegfried* the Wanderer supplies the answer: " Only Siegfried himself can forge his sword." He leaves Mime a prey to terror. Siegfried returns and asks if the sword is ready: the cunning dwarf replies that he has not yet had time to make it, as he has been pondering weighty matters for the boy's sake. The sword will be of no use to him until he has first learned fear; and how that is to come about, he says, had fortunately just struck him when Siegfried returned. He knows a place in the wood, " not far from the world," called Neidhöhle, where dwells a fearsome dragon: if Siegfried could find him, from him he would learn fear. The boy asks to be taken there: but Mime tells him he will never learn fear with such a sword as *he* can make for him. Thereupon Siegfried, keen both to leave Mime to enter into the world and to learn what this fearing is, declares that he himself will forge the needed weapon out of the fragments of his father's sword. The central psychological point of the scene, be it noted, is that Mime has had his difficult problem solved for him by the Wanderer. That problem all along has been the dual one of finding someone strong enough to deal with Fafner, and of finding a weapon sharp enough and powerful enough for the deed. The first part of the dwarf's problem he himself had solved by his bringing up of Siegfried. The second part had been the cause of Mime's perpetual anguish. Now, at a stroke, the solution is given him by the Wanderer. Siegfried as a sword-smith had previously never entered into Mime's calculations, because the wayward boy had refused to learn the smith's art. But now Mime learns from the Wanderer that it is Siegfried himself who, in spite of his lack of skill, is destined to forge the sword. He accordingly sets the boy, by means of suggestion, to work at the forging.

As Siegfried does so, Mime congratulates himself on his wits: the Wanderer had thought him stupid, but now he will prove how wise and cunning he is. Formerly he had not wished the boy to be clever enough to learn fear: now he sees that Siegfried's dullness will serve him, Mime, even better than cleverness could have done. It is through Siegfried's fearing, not through his courage as the dwarf had previously thought, that Mime will achieve his ends: " He himself smithies the needful sword: he will slay Fafner for me." Thus Mime will win the Hoard and the Ring: the boy, who knows nothing of them, can be put to sleep, after the combat, with a treacherous potion, and slain; and Mime will be lord of the world.

All this hangs together with perfect consistency in *Young Siegfried*. In *Siegfried*, however, it becomes less clear. For one thing, Wagner evidently realised later that the scene as it originally was in *Young Siegfried* was too long. He accordingly cut out the whole of the lengthy dialogue between Mime and Siegfried after the point at which the former recalls the boy in order to give him sage counsel about the advantage of living in the wood rather than in the world, where safety would be impossible without fear. We thus lose the vital explanation of *why* Mime had brought Siegfried up in ignorance of fear — so that he might be the more capable of killing Fafner. Wagner now, in the final version of the poem, makes Siegfried run into the wood at his first instead of his second attempt; whereupon there follows at once the scene with the Wanderer. This runs on the same lines as it had done in *Young Siegfried* until we come to the final question of who will forge Nothung; but now, instead of the Wanderer saying " Only Siegfried himself can forge the sword ", he says:

> He who to fear
> was ne'er a slave
> forges Nothung anew.
> Thy wise old head
> ward from to-day:
> I leave it forfeit to him
> who to fear has never learned!

At first sight the two answers seem the same, especially to us who know so well the future course of the drama. But in their bearing upon the psychological working-out of the situation they are not at all the same; and in the effort to persuade himself that they are, Wagner falls into some confusion. The new episode lacks the logic of the old one. There it had been made fully clear to us that the whole object of Mime's manner of bringing up Siegfried had been to keep him at once from knowledge of fear and from the attraction of the world, in order that he might slay Fafner. When the Wanderer, in *Young Siegfried*, tells Mime that it is Siegfried who will forge the sword, the dwarf's whole problem, as we have seen, is solved for him almost instantly. The Wanderer's words to him in *Young Siegfried* — " Keep thy wise head: so useless a thing concerns me not. Yet from to-day guard it well: have a care when thy tongue wags: babble no foolishness " — set up only a vague terror in him, for there is here no such definite threat to Mime's life as we find in the correspondence passage quoted above from the later poem. Siegfried, on his re-entry, indeed finds him crouching fearfully behind the anvil (he has been scared by the lights and noises that come from the forest as the Wanderer departs), but Mime's plan for the future has already shaped itself in his mind — to persuade Siegfried that any sword will be useless to him until he has learned to fear, and to promise to take him where fear can be learned, at Fafner's lair, and to set the boy to work at the sword. He himself sits at one side and gloats over his coming victory.

In *Siegfried*, however, much greater stress is laid on Mime's terror after the departure of the Wanderer, a terror due to the fact that here it is not Siegfried himself who has been specifically named as the maker of the sword, but " he who has never felt fear ": for Mime knows that this rules *him* out, while at the same time he does not yet associate it with Siegfried, who has always been too impatient to learn the smith's craft. He has further been told by the Wanderer that his own head is to fall to this unknown maker of the sword:

> Thy wise old head
> ward from to-day:
> I leave it forfeit to him
> who to fear has never learned!

Wagner now reverts to the words used by Mime, in *Young Sieg-fried*, in his self-colloguing after the flight of the boy into the wood; but he gives them a new application, and one that does not explain itself sufficiently.

4

Mime's terror, in *Young Siegfried*, after the exit of the Wan-derer, had been purely physical. In *Siegfried*, however, it becomes mental, and far more intense. For now, instead of finding his eternal problem solved for him, the bottom has dropped out of the world he had so carefully and cunningly built up for his own ends. The only clue he now has to the forging of the sword is that it will be done by someone who has never felt fear. For the moment Mime cannot see who is to make the sword — and yet to the maker of it his own head, according to the Wanderer, is to fall. His mind is, for a while, in utter confusion, whereas in *Young Siegfried* he had seen at a flash the way out of his difficulties and what his next move must be. In *Siegfried* Wagner has to turn the whole psychology of the scene round in another direction; and he does so rather clumsily.

In response to the dwarf's mutterings he now makes Siegfried interject, somewhat irrelevantly,

> Ha! wouldst thou flout me?
> Me wouldst thou fly?

which seems to have no other *raison d'être* than to give Mime the cue for the following, which, however, adds obscurity to apparent irrelevance:

> Him would I fly
> who knoweth fear!
> But that truly I ne'er taught the stripling;
> I fool-like forgot
> the one thing good.
> Love for the dwarf
> was his lesson;
> but alas, no luck had I!
> How now put this fear in his heart?

[335]

Wagner now goes back, in part, to the discarded dialogue between the pair in *Young Siegfried*, but without seeing that what was fully self-explanatory there is not equally so here. He suddenly introduces the subject of fearing:

> What fear is learned I for thee,
> that I, thou dunce, might teach thee.

This remark of Mime's seems to slip in from nowhere in particular, whereas in *Young Siegfried* the long conversation on the subject of fearing had been adequately motived — Mime had wanted to prevent Siegfried from upsetting all his plans by leaving him, and thought the best way to do this was to fill him with fear of the world.

Siegfried obligingly picks up the clue thus palpably dangled before his eyes. He asks " What then is this fearing? " to which Mime's reply is:

> Thou knowest not fear,
> and yet from the wood
> wouldst forth in the world?
> What use were the stoutest of swords,
> if thou no fear hast felt?

Mime proceeds to tell him of his mother's request that the boy should not be allowed to go into the world until he had learned fear as a ward against craft. We know, of course, that it has been Siegfried's desire to leave Mime in search of freedom; but from the text of *Siegfried* alone we cannot gather the full subtlety of the dwarf's argument about fear as a device to keep the youth by him till he has served his ends. That full subtlety is apparent only from the long dialogue in *Young Siegfried*. When the fear motive is now introduced (in the later poem), it is with quite another purpose on Mime's part — that of discovering whether Siegfried is capable of fearing, whether, therefore, *he* is the hero hinted at in the Wanderer's parting words. Wagner carries over from *Young Siegfried*, in a modified form, some of the lines given to Mime in the scene of the dialogue in its first form, but without making their original meaning and significance perfectly clear to us:

> Thou knowest not fear,
> and yet from the wood
> wouldst forth in the world?

he makes Mime ask; and later Siegfried asks if Neidhöhle is " far from the world " — verbal reminiscences of the dialogue in *Young Siegfried* without a full elucidation of the importance they had there.

5

Wagner has done marvellously, on the whole, in condensing the former two scenes into one; but he has certainly left some loose threads hanging. It looks as if from first to last he had been in a little difficulty with the fearing motive. He has told us, via Uhlig, how there had run in his mind for years, as a theme for an opera, the story of the boy who was too stupid to learn fear,[2] and how one day it suddenly dawned on him that this boy was none other than the Siegfried who won the Hoard and awoke Brynhilde. From the moment, however, when he decided to run the two stories in harness he began to pile up trouble for himself. A minute comparison of the Extended Prose Sketch for *Young Siegfried* with the poem of that work, and of this again with the poem of *Siegfried,* shows his difficulties and his vacillations very clearly. In the poem of *Young Siegfried* it is Mime who deliberately introduces the subject of fearing: all that Siegfried does is to declare that his impulse towards freedom is driving him into the world, whereupon Mime, afraid of losing him, paints for him the danger to which he will be open from the craft of the world unless he first knows what fear is. In the Sketch, however, the subject had been first broached by the boy himself, thus:

Siegfried.   Now thou must make me my sword [out of the fragments of his father's sword].
Mime.   Ah, how many times have I tried to forge it; yet never will it yield to my art!

---

[2] In the Dresden days he had told Kietz that if he were to compose another opera it would not be on a historical subject but on one drawn from a fairy-tale, such as that of the youth who set out to learn what fear is. See KW, p. 86.

Siegfried.   Listen now to me: unless thou achievst the sword for me, no art of thine will protect thee.

Mime.   And were I to achieve it, what then wouldst thou do?

Siegfried.   That have I told thee long ago: into the world will I fare and learn fearing, since with thee I shall never learn it.

Mime.   What is in thy mind, stupid child?

Siegfried.   Much hast thou taught me, but the most of it have I had to wring from thee: the best of all have I to-day learned from thee, that thou art not my father: now am I glad and clear. One thing only I could never learn — what fearing is. . . . Forge then the sword for me, that I may fare forth to battle.

Thereupon, according to the Prose Sketch, he runs into the wood. Mime does not restrain him, as he does in the poem, but falls to brooding over his troubles. He thinks it all out along the lines of that monologue of his in the poem to which the reader's attention has already been drawn: having failed to make Siegfried love him — being, indeed, the one object in their little world that the boy hates, — it is clear to him now that Siegfried will never slay the dragon simply for *his* sake. " Now, indeed," says the Sketch, " he is on the point of leaving him: so it is time for Mime to lead him against Fafner: his foolish curiosity to learn fear shall serve him [Mime] to incite the boy against the dragon. But first of all the sword! He despairs of making it, and yet made it must be if Fafner is to be slain! " He accordingly sets to work again at his old task; and while he is engaged on it the Wanderer enters.

Evidently at some slightly later time Wagner considered that this could be improved upon; and the result of his reflections was to transfer the first broaching of the subject of fearing from Siegfried to Mime, as is done in the poem of *Young Siegfried*. This is clear from a note in the margin of the manuscript of the Sketch at the point where the dialogue set forth above begins. The note runs thus: " Siegfried now feels himself quite free of Mime. He will leave him in order to go into the world: for this reason he once more demands the sword. Mime tries to instil into him fear of the world, so as to keep him in the wood. He paints for him one terror after another in the world beyond the wood. . . . Argument over fearing. Mime must explain it. He describes fear. Siegfried cannot learn it, and now will go forth just to learn it. (Mime resolves quickly to teach it to him *himself*. Fafner? *Later*)." It was along these new lines that Wagner wrote the corresponding section of the poem: he now makes Mime recall Siegfried, preach him his sermon on the world, craft, and fearing, and then, when at last the boy has gone, hatch the plot to ensnare him through his very desire to learn fear: he will take him, once the sword has been made, to Fafner's lair.

6

The consistency that runs through all this is maintained, in *Young Siegfried*, when Siegfried returns after the exit of the Wanderer. Having learned from the latter that it is Siegfried who will forge the sword, Mime sees clearly and delightedly what now remains for him to do. The youth, on his return, asks once more how he can learn fearing. " Let me think," says Mime to himself in the Prose Sketch: " thou clever Wanderer, see how dull are the wits of this creature! He himself puts into my cunning hands the means by which to make him serve my end." Then he turns to Siegfried and promises to take him out on the morrow to a place known as Neidhöhle, where dwells a monster who will teach him fear. " Siegfried is delighted ", says the Sketch: " thus will he go into the world a wise man. ' When I have learned fear I shall know enough; and then will I part for ever from thee. Now show me the sword! ' *Mime:* ' Not yet is it ready, but this will I tell thee: fearing canst thou learn only with the sword that thou thyself hast forged.' " Whereupon the boy at once sets to work at the task; while Mime rubs his hands with glee at the thought of how, Fafner being slain, he in turn will slay Siegfried. " He gives vent to his malicious joy over Siegfried's childish zeal, that shall profit only *him* [Mime]. He derides the Gods and the heroes, and praises dwarf's-wit: they shall all bow down to him once he has won the Ring, towards the winning of which Siegfried is now so eagerly co-operating for *his* sake."

But this logical consistency is not so evident in the corresponding scene in *Siegfried*. Here Mime sees that the boy, in spite of his having neglected to learn the craft, is really going to achieve the forging of the sword. But the very perception of this makes him uneasy, for reasons inherent in the Wanderer's final words. Let us look again at the two forms given to these. In *Young Siegfried* Wagner makes the Wanderer say:

> Only Siegfried himself
> forges his sword.
> Thy wise head
> hold for thyself:
> What is useless to me I need not!
> But ward it well
> from to-day:
> Have a care when thy tongue shall wag,
> Babble no foolish things!

While in *Siegfried* what the Wanderer says is this:

> He who to fear
> was ne'er a slave
> Forges Nothung anew.
> Thy wise old head
> ward from to-day:
> I leave it forfeit to him
> who to fear has never learned!

Mime attaches no significance to the final lines of the former of these two speeches: the meaning of them, indeed, only becomes evident to him and to us much later, as we shall shortly see. All that concerns the dwarf is the knowledge that Siegfried will make the sword: armed with that knowledge he goes forward confidently with his plan to incite the boy to begin the forging, to have him slay Fafner, and then himself to slay Siegfried after having given him a numbing drink. But the second form — the *Siegfried* form — of the Wanderer's parting speech perturbs Mime during the forging:

> He will win the sword
> full well I see:
> fearless forge it anew.

> How wise the Wanderer was!
> Where now to hide
> my hapless head!
> To the valiant boy will it fall,
> learns he from Fafner not fear!
> But woe is me still!
> If Siegfried learn fear,
> how then shall the dragon be slain?
> Can he win the dwarf the Ring?
> Oh fate accursed!
> I'm fettered fast:
> where shall I counsel find
> how to master this fearless boy?

It is after this that he discloses the plan that occurs to him for disposing of Siegfried after the killing of Fafner. He dances about with delight:

> Hei, wisest Wanderer!
> Deemst thou me dull?
> Doth it please thee now,
> my playful wit?
> Have I won
> the way to peace?

That is to say, we arrive at precisely the point we had formerly reached in *Young Siegfried,* but in that work without all these unnecessary divagations, delays and complications. And not only have the threads become complicated but they have become a trifle confused. For if it should happen that Siegfried, in virtue of the fact that he does not know fear, turns out to be the destined forger of the sword, then, by logical sequence from the Wanderer's final words, Mime's head is to fall to the boy. Why then should the dwarf so gleefully set him to work?

7

With all respect to the great mind that conceived, in the *Ring,* one of the most stupendous dramas that humanity has ever produced, one is driven to the conclusion that Wagner would have done better to have left the working out of this and the preceding scenes as it was in *Young Siegfried*. Why, we may ask, did he decide to change the Wanderer's direct statement that it is Siegfried who shall forge the sword into the vague statement that the forging shall be done by him who knows not fear, and, inversely, to change the vague warning to Mime not to babble nonsense into the definite warning that his head shall be forfeit to the boy? Partly, no doubt, because the psychological matter as he had first of all elaborated it in *Young Siegfried* needed considerable compression for practical stage purposes. But partly also, one surmises, because he felt that the Wanderer's naming of Siegfried as the maker of the sword was too direct a procedure. Be that as it may, the fact remains that he never quite succeeded in overcoming the difficulties in which he had landed himself through the change. When he came, in *Siegfried*, to the later scene in which, after the hero has slain Fafner, Mime reveals his intention of murdering the youth (who, as we know, perceives the real meaning underneath the dwarf's cajoling words, in virtue of his having tasted the dragon's blood), Wagner forgets that it is precisely the final words (now discarded) of the Wanderer in *Young Siegfried* that explain this scene, while at the same time it is this scene that at last explains those ironic words. The Wanderer had there warned Mime, in vague terms, not to let his tongue wag too freely, not to babble foolishness. Wagner evidently put these words into the Wanderer's mouth with his mind looking forward to the later scene, as is shown by his repetition, in the latter, of the phraseology of the former. This is clearer in the German than it can be made in translation: the Wanderer's words in *Young Siegfried* are:

> Hab' Acht, wenn die Zunge dir schwankt,
> schwatze kein albernes Zeug!

which links up not merely psychologically but verbally with Siegfried's later words when, disgusted with the treacherous knave, he kills Mime:

> Schmeck' du mein Schwert,
> alberner Schwätzer!

This was the hidden meaning of the Wanderer's warning to the dwarf in *Young Siegfried*. But Wagner carries over what are essentially the same words into the poem of *Siegfried*, without noticing, apparently, that by cutting out the Wanderer's words in the earlier scene and substituting a quite different warning for them he has severed a vital dramatic thread. It is true that he finally changes the " alberner " to " ekliger "; but this does not alter the fact that Siegfried's words as he kills Mime are the sinister fulfilment of the Wanderer's veiled threat — a threat that was embodied in the earlier poem but not in the later one! [3]

There are one or two other evidences that in his successive recastings of his vast material during the course of so many years Wagner did not always remember to smooth out discrepancies between his first ideas and his last. In his first draft of 1848, *The Nibelungen Myth as Sketch for a Drama*, he had followed the old sagas in his lay-out of the preliminaries. The reader will recall that in the present *Rhinegold* neither the Gods nor the Giants know anything whatever of the gold until Loge returns from his wanderings to tell of Alberich's rape of it, and to broach to Wotan the scheme of robbing the gnome of it in order to pay the Giants and so redeem Freia. In the sketch of 1848, however, the race of the Giants has known from old time of the gold, the Ring, and the Tarnhelm. They have themselves been ambitious for world-lordship, but have felt that their rather dull wits are no match for Alberich's guile and the superlative power conferred on him by the Tarnhelm and the Ring. Wotan takes advantage of this strife between the rival powers to further his own end of ruling the world in peace and order. He has the Giants build him a castle for this purpose. When it is completed, it is the Giants themselves who ask for, and receive, the Nibelungen-Hoard in payment. Too stupid afterwards to make use of the might conferred by the Hoard and the Ring, but anxious to secure themselves against their passing into other hands, particularly those of Alberich, they appoint as their custodian a monstrous dragon who sleeps on them through the ages.

---

[3] The Wanderer's parting words (in *Young Siegfried*) — quoted above, p. 340 — actually appear in the first printed edition of the *Ring* poem (1853); so it is evident that, even after remodelling the whole drama, Wagner, as late as 1853, regarded this as the final form of the scene. It is not clear when he rejected this handling of the situation in favour of the one now familiar to us in *Siegfried*.

As late as the period when he was writing *Young Siegfried*, Wagner evidently still clung to this conception. Thus in response to Mime's question, " What is the race that dwells on the earth's surface? " the Wanderer says (in the Prose Sketch for *Young Siegfried*): " On the earth's surface go heavily the Giants. . . . They made war with the Nibelungs, coveting Alberich's Ring. They called the Gods to their aid. For the Gods they built a burg on the heights, and asked, as wage, for the Ring. The Gods took the Ring from the Nibelung. The Giants placed a guard upon it. But strife broke out between them over it: into whosesoever hands it came, he was slain by another through envy. Thus the whole race of Giants perished except one, the strongest of all — Fafner now guards the Ring." In Wagner's original conception, then, the Giants knew from the first of the existence and the virtue of the Ring, coveted it, and, with the help of the Gods, took it from Alberich to consolidate their own power. All this was altered later: the Giants were reduced to two; Valhalla is already built when the drama opens; the price promised for it by Wotan, who as yet knows nothing of the Ring, has been Freia; and it is to get out of that embarrassing bargain that he listens to Loge's news of the rape of the gold by Alberich and falls in with the suggestion that he in turn shall rob the Nibelung to pay the Giants. Wagner, in the final form of the drama, re-shaped all references to the Ring to fit in with this changed conception — except two. In the quarrel between the two evil brothers in *Siegfried* he makes Mime say to Alberich:

> Where now is thy Ring?
> Thou coward, the Giants did rob thee;

which had indeed been the case in the first scheme for the drama but is inconsistent with the later scheme. And while Wagner, in *Siegfried*, modifies the passage from *Young Siegfried* quoted above to the extent that now we have only Fasolt and Fafner, instead of, as before, the whole race of the Giants, he still, oddly enough, makes it appear that *the pair themselves* took the Hoard and the Ring from Alberich — as the race of the Giants had done in the Sagas — because Ring and Hoard were a threat to their own power: says the Wanderer to Mime:

> Fasolt and Fafner,
> the Giants' rulers,
> envied the Nibelung's power:
> and the mighty Hoard
> they won for themselves,
> and ravished with it the Ring;

a direct contradiction of the *Rhinegold*, where the Giants know nothing of the gold until Loge tells them of it, and it is Wotan who robs Alberich for *his* ends. Nothing whatever is said in the *Rhinegold* about the Giants wanting Hoard and Ring because they envy Alberich's power: what Fafner says to Fasolt when first he hears Loge's story of the rape of the Gold, is:

> Trust me, more than Freia
> boots the glittering gold:
> for youth eternal it gives
> unto him who masters its might;

and in the later scene Fasolt makes it clear that he desires the treasure only as some kind of compensation for the loss of the lovely Freia. Even the Tarnhelm and the Ring are demanded only because Freia's form is not yet completely covered; and when the Giants quarrel over the division of the booty, Fasolt's sole reason for insisting on retaining the Ring is because to him it is the equivalent of " Freia's glance ". From first to last there is not a word about the Giants " envying the Nibelung's power ".[4]

---

[4] It is true that Loge has just told the Gods and the Giants that should a ring be fashioned from the gold stolen by Alberich it will confer "measureless might" on the owner, and the Giants, mindful of their old enmity with Alberich, begrudge him possession of the gold. Not a word is said, however, to suggest that they desire the gold for world-ruling purposes of their own, which is the suggestion in the Wanderer's words to Mime quoted above — they "envied the Nibelung's power". Wagner fluctuates between two fundamentally irreconcilable dramatic "motives" — (a) that of the *Sketch for a Nibelungen Drama*, in which the Giants have for a long time been perturbed over the power conferred on Alberich by the Hoard and the Ring, and consequently demand the latter from Wotan as the price for the building of Valhalla; and (b) that of the *Rhinegold*, in which neither the Giants nor the Gods know anything whatever of the rape of the gold by Alberich, and his fashioning of a Ring from it, until Loge returns from his wanderings with the story; by that time Valhalla has been built, the wage promised to the Giants by Wotan having been not the Hoard but Freia.

A particularly interesting feature of the text of *Young Siegfried* is the detailed description Wagner gives of Mime, in a passage in the stage directions (for the opening scene) that was not carried over into the *Siegfried* poem. It runs thus: " Mime, the Nibelung, alone. He is small and bent, somewhat deformed and hobbling. His head is abnormally large, his face is a dark ashen colour and wrinkled, his eyes small and piercing, with red rims, his grey beard long and scrubby, his head bald and covered with a red cap. He wears a dark grey smock with a broad belt about his loins: feet bare, with thick coarse soles underneath. There must be *nothing approaching caricature in all this:* [5] his aspect, when he is quiet, must be simply eerie: it is only in moments of extreme excitement that he becomes *exteriorily* [6] ludicrous, but never too uncouth. His voice is husky and harsh; but this again ought of itself never to provoke the listener to laughter." There is nothing in all this to suggest feeble, pitiful old age: and when we recall that the description occurs in the *Young Siegfried* of 1851 — i.e. at what was at that time Mime's first entrance into the drama — it is evident that this is how Wagner visualised the character from the beginning. Obviously he would not have approved of the frequent modern practice of representing Mime as a rather amiable old dodderer who secures the sympathy of the audience by his feebleness and his quaintness. Mime is a powerful thing of evil, one who would do all that Alberich has done were he fortunate enough to possess the Ring: he is dangerous in spite of his appearance and build: and the actor who does not make us conscious of all this, but so handles the character that the audience feels that Mime is pitiable rather than dangerous and loathsome, and Siegfried, consequently, a monster of boyish ingratitude, completely misrepresents the part. The nearer a Mime gets to a caricature of pathetic senility the further he gets from what Wagner intended. Nor, one imagines, would Wagner have recognised very much of the Alberich of his imagination in the crudely grotesque figure that is usually put before us under that name. Wagner's description of Alberich (in

---

[5] Italics mine.   [6] Italics mine.

Young Siegfried) is this: "He resembles Mime in every respect [the pair, of course, are brothers], only his appearance and his expression invariably make a more serious and indeed nobler effect." Here again, evidently, there must be nothing approaching caricature: Alberich must inspire a certain respect in spite of his ugliness. As Ashton Ellis rightly says, "Alberich in his own domain is the counterpart of Wotan."

9

One final point in connection with the psychological changes the *Ring* underwent between its first conception and its final form calls for a moment's examination.

In its first, as in its last form, the drama ends with Brynhilde drawing the Ring from Siegfried's finger and placing it on her own hand before she enters the flaming pyre, the surging of the Rhine into the hall, and the restoration of the Ring to the Rhine Maidens. The ethical implications of the scene, however, are completely different in the two instances. In *Siegfrieds Tod*, Brynhilde not only announces to the Nibelungs that their thraldom is ended but declares the eternal over-lordship of Wotan; and she carries Siegfried with her to Valhalla:

> One only shall rule:
> All-Father! Glorious one!
> Have joy of the freest of heroes!
> Siegfried I bear to thee:
> Give him greeting sweet,
> the warrant of might without end!

To which the Vassals and Women add a comment of their own:

> Wotan! Wotan! Ruler of Gods!
> Wotan, bless thou the flames!
> Burn hero and bride,
> burn too the faithful horse;
> that wound-healed and pure
> All-Father's free consorts
> may gladly greet Walhall,
> joined in a bliss without end!

But in the *Götterdämmerung* Valhalla and the Gods pass away in flames; and in their downfall the Gods are redeemed, by the deed and the death of Siegfried, from the curse that had been laid upon Wotan by his theft of the Ring to establish his own power. " Fly home, ye ravens ", says Brynhilde now:

> Fly home, ye ravens!
> Tell this tale to Wotan
> that here on the Rhine ye have heard!
> To Brynhilde's rock
> first wend your way!
> There flameth Loge:
> bid him hasten to Walhall!
> For the Gods' great ending
> dawneth at last.
> So — cast I the brand
> on Walhall's glittering towers.

Siegfried, in fact, has fulfilled the inmost wish of Wotan's heart, of the God who has willed his own passing; by his dying the hero has brought peace to the Gods:

> Hear my woeful wail,
> thou God of all!,

says Brynhilde:

> The deed of deeds he [7] wrought,
> worked the wish of thine heart:
> then on the hero
> laid'st thou the load
> of the curse that of old consumed thee;
> my woe must he work
> all unwitting,
> that wise a woman might grow!
>
> .   .   .   .   .   .
>
> Rest thou, rest thou, o God!

---

[7] I.e. Siegfried.

The vital motive of the drama, that is to say, had changed completely in the course of the years: the central character is now no longer Siegfried but Wotan; the final solution of the problem raised by Alberich's rape of the gold is no longer that the Gods are made for ever free of the menace of their enemies — through the restoration at last of the Ring, the symbol and the instrument of might, to the Rhine Maidens — but the Gods and Wotan himself go down to destruction. Wagner had begun the expansion and re-casting of his drama with the sole intention, at first, of creating, in his young Siegfried, a joyous youthful being of healthy natural instincts: as he put it in a letter to Röckel, written after the completion of the whole tetralogy, Wotan

> " resembles *us* to a hair. He represents the sum of the intelligence of the Present, whereas Siegfried is the man of the Future whom we so greatly desire and long to create. . . . I have sought to portray in Siegfried my ideal of the perfect human being, whose highest consciousness manifests itself in the fact that all consciousness can find expression only in the most actual living and doing of the present." [8]

That, to be sure, had been Wagner's first conception of the character. He speaks, in his letter to Uhlig, of the stimulating influence exercised on him by the " warmth " of this new subject: he thinks it will appeal much more than the serious *Siegfrieds Tod* to the popular conscience, for it is " less heroic, merrier, human and youthful."

It is clear that in his first conception of the youthful Siegfried he had as yet had no intuition of the way in which the boy was later to become merely a pawn in the tremendous game of Wotan's moral problem, a problem which had not dawned upon Wagner himself at that time; one finds it hard to understand, indeed, why the ideal Man of the Future should crash to ruin as Siegfried does in the *Götterdämmerung*, and the Gods with him. The fact is that in the interval between the conception of *Young Siegfried* and the expansion of the drama into its present form by the addition of the *Valkyrie* and the *Rhinegold*, Wagner's whole poetic attitude towards life had subtly changed: Wotan had gradually come more and more into the forefront of his thought, and his social optimism

---

[8] RWAR, pp. 38, 39.

had changed into resignation. In accordance with this change, not only were the two as yet unwritten dramas of the *Ring*, the *Rhinegold* and the *Valkyrie*, given a central meaning that had not been in his mind when he wrote *Siegfrieds Tod*, but the original ending of that work had to be completely altered for the purpose of the *Götterdämmerung*, the very title of which is in itself significant. Other changes in the text became necessary: in *Siegfrieds Tod*, for instance, the Valkyries merely condole in a sisterly way with Brynhilde on having been condemned to her rock as punishment for having disobeyed Wotan in the combat between Siegmund and Hunding, whereas in the corresponding scene in the *Götterdämmerung* Waltraute implores her sister Valkyrie to give back the Ring to the Rhine Maidens and so redeem the Gods from the doom that is hanging over them.

10

Attempts have been made to show that the changes in the central conception of the *Ring*, from a " yea-saying " to the world to a " denial " of the world, were the direct result of Wagner's gradually changing attitude towards the politics of his time. Kurt Hildebrandt, for instance, holds that the solution of the moral problem as it is first put before us in *Siegfrieds Tod* correlates with Wagner's Vaterlandsverein speech — here " Wotan corresponds to the conception of Germanic kinghood, Siegfried being the vassal who supports his lord by voluntarily taking the latter's guilt on himself "; that the *Young Siegfried* of 1851 is the outcome of Wagner's belief at that time in the speedy coming of a victorious revolution, Siegfried being " the new man who springs from the communistic paradise "; that this Siegfried was modelled on memories of Bakunin, who was " fearless, full of childlike confidence, utterly regardless of consequences to himself, tender in spite of all his passion for destruction "; that at this stage Siegfried, in his relation to Wotan, " expresses Wagner's veering round [in the interval between 1848 and 1851] to anarchism and social optimism ", Siegfried now being " no longer Wotan's rescuer but his foe and inheritor ", who, when the Wanderer questions him, " behaves insolently to his godlike progenitor " and defeats the jealous

God when the latter would bar his way to Brynhilde's rock; that Napoleon's *coup d'état* in December, 1851, drove the disappointed and disillusioned Wagner not only to immediate political resignation but to a pessimistic denial of the world, the result, for the *Ring*, being that now " Siegfried, the man of the [hoped-for] golden age of 1852 fades into the romantic distance ", while " Wotan, the luster after power, becomes, as the representative of resignation, theoretically more interesting but weaker as a figure "; that Wagner, perceiving the fundamental opposition between his first dramatic conception of a restoration of the power of the Gods and his second conception of the downfall of the Gods, sought for a new significance to be attached to the Ring itself, and found it in the idea of the cursing of love by Alberich; and so on.

The thesis is ingenious, and it is ingeniously argued and documented from *Mein Leben*. As we have seen, Wagner did not always succeed in squaring his later ideas in connection with the *Ring* drama with his original conception. Hildebrandt rightly points out that he seems to have been in some confusion of mind as to how to handle Erda's warning to Wotan in the *Rhinegold*. In the 1848 Sketch for a drama on the subject of the Nibelungen myth he had made the Three Norns warn Wotan " of the downfall of the Gods themselves " when the God is reluctant to part with the Ring; and this was elaborated in the first form of the *Rhinegold* into Erda's " A day of gloom is dawning for the Gods: in shame shall thy noble race end if thou givst not up the Ring." " This ", says Hildebrandt, " can hardly be understood to mean anything else than that the Gods will be saved by giving up the Ring — as in the Sketch of 1848. The later decision for a downfall of the Gods, however, takes all sense not only out of Erda's appearance but out of practically the whole of the succeeding action of the drama." Wagner now makes Erda say merely, " All that is, ends: a day of gloom dawns for the Gods: I counsel thee, give up the Ring! " which, Hildebrandt contends, has no meaning at all.

Wagner was certainly not perfectly clear in his own mind as to the handling of the Erda episode. We can admit this, however, without accepting Hildebrandt's explanation of the reason for the fundamental change in the moral issue of the *Ring* between 1848 and 1852 — that Wagner now " conceives the whole myth of the

downfall of the Gods in terms of nineteenth century dejection ",
that " when Wagner saw his Young Siegfried as inheritor of the
abdicating God he saw him, on his own confession, as the ideal of
the optimistic human being who derives from the Greek joy of life,
while Wotan was the representative of State law, of the power-
politics that Wagner so hated "; but that " when Wagner, as the
result of his political resignation, sank into a mood of world-denial,
an extraordinary thing happened — he incarnated himself in his
enemy Wotan. He forgot object and destiny: resignation became
sweet to him for its own sake. . . . Wagner, who had meant to
show us, in Siegfried, the shining rescuer and renewer, now turns
upon us, out of the senile mask of the epoch, out of the death-weary
visage of Wotan, his own death-desiring eyes. His longing towards
the God has changed into the longing for eternal quiet: the sense
of the four dramas is now summed up in Brynhilde's ' Rest thou,
o God! ' " [9]

Hildebrandt's thesis is, in fact, the familiar one of the Nietzsche
partisans, that Nietzsche represented the ascending scale and Wagner the descending scale of political and social morality, Wagner
being the expression of nineteenth-century decay, Nietzsche of the
new birth which, at some date still unspecified, is to produce for us
the superman. Without passing any opinion here upon the Nietzsche-
Wagner problem, or upon the relative merits of a philosophy of
optimism and a philosophy of pessimism, it may be pointed out
that the facts and the dates do not bear out the assumption that
Wagner's final conception of Wotan was determined by the disappointment of his political hopes at the end of 1851. However he
may vacillate in his verbal handling of one or two episodes, this
much is certain, now that the text of *Young Siegfried* and that of
the various Prose Sketches are at last available — that the motive
of the downfall of the Gods had defined itself clearly in Wagner's
mind long before Napoleon's *coup d'état*.[10] Evidently the more he
brooded over the vast canvas of the myth the more he was obsessed by the moral problem of Wotan.

The falsity of the thesis that the " pessimistic " dénouement of

[9] See HWN, pp. 96–117.
[10] See in particular SSE, pp. 66, 67, 88, 89, 174, 204, 211.

the *Götterdämmerung* was motived by Wagner's political disillusionment in December, 1851, can perhaps best be demonstrated by setting forth the full facts of the case, as they are now at last known, in the reverse order of their emergence.

That the solution of the central ethical problem of the Nibelungen drama had always been a perplexity and a trouble to Wagner is made clear to us by a letter of his to Röckel of the 23rd August, 1856. Discussing the difference between our conscious intellectual conceptions (*Begriffe*) and our subconscious intuitions (*Anschauungen*), he tells Röckel of his own " strangest experiences " in connection with the *Ring*. It was only after reading Schopenhauer, he says, that his *reason* made clear to him what had all along been *intuitive* in him as an artist; that is to say, while his instincts had made him realise the tragedy of the *Flying Dutchman, Tannhäuser,* and *Lohengrin* as one of renunciation, of negation of the will, his reason had misled him to an opposite interpretation of the world. The conscious reasoner in him, dealing with the outer world and its immediate impact on him as a man, the bad world as he saw it and the better world he hoped might some day come, made him construct for himself and it an optimistic philosophy; his reason, therefore, was pulling him in those days in the reverse direction to the urge of his feeling as an artist.

Under the influence of this " Hellenic optimism " he had created, in the hero of *Siegfrieds Tod,* " an existence free from pain "; the wrongdoing of the Gods had led to " a whole world of evil ", which could be set right only by " raising in its stead a righteous world ". Gradually it dawned on him that his artistic intuition, as distinct from his political and social self, had from the first been bent on realising something quite different from this, something much more philosophically profound — the conception of the final nothingness of the world. For a long time, however, he could not shake himself free of the concept of social and political regeneration that had been dominant in him when he began *Siegfrieds Tod;* and, still under the influence of this concept, he virtually forced on his drama the " tendencious final sentences " (quoted on pages 365–6), in which Brynhilde impresses on the bystanders the evil inherent in the possession of " goods and gold ", and declares that " love alone can bless " — " without, unfortunately, making it quite clear what this 'love' is which, in the development of the myth, we have seen playing the part of a destroyer." His prose is not very lucid at this point; but apparently what he means is that even while his intellect was thus making his pen talk optimism he intuitively felt that the only logical end to his drama was the downfall of the Gods.

He goes on to admit that the words he had put into Brynhilde's mouth were " always a torture " to him, though he could never quite comprehend why until Schopenhauer made it all clear to him. When at last, under Schopenhauer's guidance, his intuitions got the upper hand of his reflective reason, he found, he says, " the keystone really correspondent to my poem, which consists in the frank recognition of the veritable, profound meaning of things, free from anything tendencious " — i.e. anything in the nature of preaching a doctrine.

11

For a long while he had pondered over a new ending to his drama. In the notebook that contains the sketch of May, 1856, for *Die Sieger* there is a jotting running thus:

" Ending for *Siegfried*.

" Brynhilde, after she has set fire to the funeral pile, turns round to the others: she wishes no re-birth for the fallen ones; but she predicts to Hagen a long coming-to-birth again, ending in redemption, which she goes to meet, since she knows that she will not be born again. To the other living ones she gives the choice between her fate and Hagen's: ' if you love life, then turn your eyes from me to him!' She goes to the horse, and for a long time remains in silent colloquy with him. The chorus expresses its increasing sympathy with her, until at last it directs its gaze definitely on her as she mounts the horse, as it were in triumph, and rides into the flames." [11] This rather confused statement — the lack of clearness in all his utterances on this subject is of itself eloquent of the difficulty the situation was causing him — is elucidated by a letter of the 22nd June of that year to Franz Müller, in which Wagner de-

---

[11] Published for the first time in Otto Strobel's article *Zur Entstehungsgeschichte der Götterdämmerung*, in DM, February, 1933, p. 340.

clares his intention of not publishing the *Ring* poem [12] until the whole of the music has been written — once more an indication of an uncomfortable feeling on his part that the proper ending to the work was still evading him. " Not unimportant changes [from the text of the privately printed edition of 1853] in the concluding parts are impending ", he goes on to say. The title of the fourth drama is to be *Die Götterdämmerung:* he means to re-write entirely Brynhilde's closing words, for " it has become clear to me that the poem has travelled far beyond its original schematic tendency, as still retained in the present ending; this is consequently a cramping and spoiling of the achieved result. Naturally the result remains essentially the same: only the explanation put into the mouth of the now all-knowing Brynhilde becomes something different, wider-reaching, more decisive; the men and women, for the first time in the entire work, will now feel and express a broader sympathetic interest ".[13]

This new solution of his problem was the " keystone " to which he refers in his letter of the 23rd August to Röckel. The prose sketch quoted above was ultimately cast into the following verse-form:

Führ' ich nun nicht mehr
   nach Walhalls Feste,
wisst ihr, wohin ich fahre?
Aus Wunschheim zieh' ich fort,
Wahnheim flieh' ich auf immer;
   des ew'gen Werdens
   offne Tore
schliess' ich hinter mir zu:
   nach dem wunsch- und wahnlos
   heiligsten Wahlland,
der Welt-Wanderung Ziel,
von Wiedergeburt erlöst,
zieht nun die Wissende hin.

If I go no more to Walhall's fastness, know ye whither I fare?
From Wunschheim (home of desire) I depart, flee for ever from Wahnheim (home of illusion);
the open gates of eternal becoming I close behind me; redeemed from re-birth, goes the illumined one [*die Wissende,* the *knower*] to the holiest chosen land, where is no wishing, no illusion.

---

[12] I.e. a public issue: the edition of 1853 was a private one.
[13] Ibid., p. 340. The letter is there published for the first time.

Alles Ew'gen	Know ye how I won to the
sel'ges Ende,	blessed end of all things
wisst ihr, wie ich's gewann?	eternal? Deepest distress of
Trauender Liebe	grieving love opened my
tiefstes Leiden	eyes: I saw the world end.
schloss die Augen mir auf:	
enden sah ich die Welt.	

These words, jotted down on the final page of his own copy of the 1853 imprint,[14] were in the end not set to music, though Wagner printed them as a footnote to the scene in the public imprint of the final *Ring* poem in 1872.

12

Here, as will be seen, he is expressing, somewhat mystically, his artistic conviction that the right ending for the drama was the destruction of the world. But it is quite an error to attribute this radical change from the first conception of *Siegfrieds Tod* either to the influence of Schopenhauer — who did no more than make him intellectually conscious of what had been dumbly stirring all the while in his subconscious [15] — or to the disillusionment following on Napoleon's *coup d'état* of December, 1851. For it is manifest that long before that date he had been groping his way towards a closing scene of " downfall ". Practically from the first he must have had the feeling that the original ending of *Siegfrieds Tod* did not answer to his inner artistic vision. In that ending, the reader may once more be reminded, Brynhilde had cried out to Wotan that she was bringing to him Siegfried, whom the God, now firmly established as sole ruler of the world, was to greet and make free

---

[14] Strobel gives a facsimile of it in the article mentioned, p. 337.

[15] It cannot be too often insisted upon that it was Wagner's artistic intuitions that determined his relations towards men and things, and not *vice versa:* as his inner world changed, his eyes saw outer things in new forms and a new light. The most curious instance of this is given us in an entry of 1878 in Cosima's diary. So long, she notes, as Wagner was engaged on the *Ring* and inhabiting the "sombre yet joyous" world of the heroes of the saga, he could sympathise with Bismarck and his policy; but when, possessed in all his being by *Parsifal*, he was creating a hero whose "guiding force" was pity, he "saw Bismarck with quite other eyes than formerly." "It was not that he had withdrawn from the profane world, but he now saw its problems", and consequently Bismarck, "from another point of view." MECW, I, 829, 830.

of Walhall, the " fortress of eternal power ". Before May, 1849, however, Wagner crossed this passage through in his manuscript, substituting for it the following:

Selige Sühnung ersah ich den hehren heilig ewigen einigen Göttern! Freuet euch des freiesten Helden! Göttlichem Brudergruss führt seine Braut ihn zu.	Blessed atonement I perceived for the august, holy, eternal Gods! Rejoice in the freest of heroes! His bride brings him to the brother-greeting of the Gods.

At some time or other before the spring of 1851 he changed the passage once more, making it now read thus:

Machtlos scheidet
  die die Schuld nun meidet.
Eurer Schuld entspross der froheste
  Held
dessen freie That sie getilgt:
erspart ist euch der bange Kampf
um eure endende Macht:
Erbleichet in Wonne vor des
  Menschen That,
vor dem Helden, den ihr gezeugt!
Aus eurer bangen Furcht
verkünd' ich euch selige Todes-
  erlösung!
	Powerless depart, ye whose
	guilt is forgone.
	From your guilt sprang the
	joyfullest hero, whose free
	deed has redeemed it:
	spared are ye the anxious
	conflict for your ending
	might: pass away in bliss be-
	fore the human hero whom
	ye begat! I proclaim to you
	blessed death-redemption
	from your anxious fear!

This indicates a radical change from Wagner's former conception of the ending of the drama. No longer is there any talk of a " blessed atonement " for the Gods and a continuance of their power: already they are doomed to downfall by reason of their guilt in the theft of the Ring, given a " blessed redemption in death " by the free deed of the hero, Siegfried, who had been born to Wotan. In conformity with this new conception, Wagner, when he drafted *Young Siegfried* a few months later, now made Wotan conscious of his guilt and of the necessity of the downfall of the

Gods. Yet oddly enough, when he came to make the changes in *Siegfrieds Tod* necessitated by the incorporation of *Young Siegfried*, the *Valkyrie*, and the *Rhinegold* in the tetralogy, he could still find no better words to put into Brynhilde's mouth in the closing scene than the oft-quoted " tendencious " moralising about love being more desirable than " goods and gold ", " godlike splendour ", and so on. Clearly the final scene was a never-ending perplexity to him, his developing artistic intuition of the veritable inner ethical purport of his drama being constantly hampered by the conclusion he had been unlucky to hit upon in his " Hellenic optimistic " mood of 1848. It was not until 1872 that his problem solved itself, apparently with the help of Cosima. It was she, at any rate, who persuaded him to leave out the long passage quoted above that commences " Führ' ich nun nicht mehr nach Walhalls Feste ": she thought the references to " Wunschheim " and " Wahnheim " " a little artificial ".[16]

13

The *Ring* has called forth books almost without number, and it still provokes discussion. Whether the course of Wagner's thinking in it can ever be made entirely clear is open to doubt: the more one studies the drama the more conscious does one become that the process by which it was built up over so many years inevitably led to a certain confusion in Wagner's mind with regard to one or two elements in it. Perhaps the root of all his troubles was the impulse that came over him, presumably some time in 1851, to combine the Siegfried myth with that of the downfall of the Gods. The two have no connection in the ancient mythology. It stands to reason that as soon as Wagner decided on the radical turning-round that is implied in the very title of the *Götterdämmerung* — from a final scene in which Siegfried and Brynhilde re-establish the power of the Gods by the death of the former and the restoration of the Ring to the Rhine Maidens by the latter, to a final scene in which the restoration of the Gold to the Rhine brings with it the destruction of the Gods — a complete psychological re-casting of all the earlier material became necessary. The re-casting, however, was never

---

[16] See MECW, I, 597.

complete enough, the consequence being that at more than one point Wagner has either not made the psychology clear to the reader or has been unable to bring two antithetical conceptions into harmony with each other. When, for instance, in the *Rhinegold*, Erda warns Wotan that *unless* he gives up the Ring the Gods will go down to destruction, surely the implication is that *if* he gives it up the Gods will be saved. Yet although Wotan surrenders the Ring the Gods are still doomed! Whatever ingenuity of analysis we may bring to bear upon the elucidation of this problem, we finally cannot fight down our suspicion that Wagner has failed to bring the two motives — that of the redemption of the Gods and that of the downfall of the Gods — into completely satisfying harmony. The common-sense mind of Röckel, to whom Wagner sent a copy of the private imprint of the *Ring* poem in 1853, fastened at once upon the central weakness of the drama: " Why," he asked him, " seeing that the gold is returned to the Rhine, is it necessary for the Gods to perish? " Wagner's reply to this is significantly evasive. He makes no attempt to justify the situation by reasoning; all he can say is:

> " I feel that, at a good performance, the most simple-minded spectator will be in no doubt as to that point. It has to be admitted that the downfall of the Gods does not arise of necessity out of counterpoints. These can indeed be interpreted, turned and twisted in all kinds of ways — any juristic politician could play the lawyer for that purpose.
>
> No, the necessity of this downfall springs from our innermost feelings, as it does from the innermost feelings of Wotan. It was thus important to justify this necessity *by feeling:* and this happens of itself when the feeling follows the total action, with all its simple, natural motives, in complete sympathy from beginning to end. When finally Wotan gives expression to this necessity he only says what we ourselves already feel must needs be. When Loge, at the end of the *Rhinegold*, calls out after the Gods, as they make their way towards Valhalla, ' They hasten towards their end who deem their power to be so enduring,' in that moment he only gives expression to our own thought; for any one who has followed this prelude [i.e. the *Rhinegold*] sympathetically, not cudgelling his brains over it but letting the events themselves work on his feelings, must agree with Loge entirely."

It is manifest enough from this confused statement that the reason why Wagner does not give a plain answer to Röckel's plain question is that he cannot do so. The upshot of it all seems to be that to his own feeling the matter was perfectly clear, but that he despaired of making it equally clear to others by means of words. Some passages in an earlier part of the same letter help us to see what his difficulty was, and how he could persuade himself that if the spectator would only *feel* with him about the drama, instead of coldly reasoning about it, that difficulty would disappear. Wagner's thesis is that the world is governed by an immutable law of change and renewal. To this law we must all yield. " This is the lesson we have to learn from the history of mankind: *to will what is necessary*, and ourselves bring it about." The appointed instrument of this supreme, self-destroying will is Siegfried, the fearless, always-loving human being.

> " The mischief-working power, the poison that is fatal to love, is embodied in the Gold that has been stolen from Nature and misused — the Nibelung's Ring: the curse laid upon this can never be annulled until it is restored to Nature, sunk in the depths of the Rhine. It is only at the end that Wotan realises this, at the culminating point of his tragic career: what Loge had repeatedly told him in the beginning, with touching insistence, the God lusting for power had ignored. Later he merely realises, in Fafner's deed, the power of the curse: it is only when Siegfried also has to be destroyed through the Ring that he sees that only by the restoration of what had been stolen can the evil be annulled, and he links his own desired destruction with this annulling of the ancient wrong." Wotan " now rises to the tragic height of *willing* his own downfall."

In one sense, and that the higher sense, Wagner was right when he pleaded that the spectator, instead of coldly reasoning about the matter, should let himself be carried away by his feeling. We can see how the profounder implications of the moral problems gradually came to take possession of Wagner's imagination as he brooded over the action and the motives of his drama, and how, feeling the compelling power of these implications within him, he turned a tolerant eye on certain flaws of which he was secretly conscious in the external structure of the work, flaws that were the inescapable result in the first place of his trying to accommodate two myths that originally had no connection with each other, in the second place of the difficulty of imposing a new central ethical conception upon material that had been planned some years earlier with quite a different end in view. The marvel is not that the coldly critical eye can now detect these flaws but that any human brain should have achieved so much in the way of welding this vast material into an organic whole. It is possible that what was in his mind all along, through the troubled years of pondering upon his problem, was the feeling that the music would make clear what he despaired of expressing clearly in words. It is to be observed that in the *Götterdämmerung* Brynhilde announces the downfall of the Gods in four lines —

Denn der Götter Ende	For the Gods' ending
dämmert nun auf:	dawneth at last:
So — werf' ich den Brand	So — cast I the brand
in Walhalls prangende Burg,	on Walhall's glittering towers,

and devotes the remainder of her oration to a passionate call to Grane to bear her to a fiery death with Siegfried. But even this is not the real ending: that comes, bringing with it to the spectator an emotional conviction beyond the reach of mere words, in the concluding bars given to the orchestra, where the great motive of " Redemption through Love " soars aloft in the violins as the flames envelop Valhalla and the waters of the Rhine achieve their work of lustration of a world at last redeemed.

14

A curious light has recently been thrown on one famous episode in the *Ring* by the publication for the first time of a letter of Wagner's of 1874. About that period (the book unfortunately bears no date on the title page) a certain Dr. Ernst Koch, a Professor in Grimma, published a study of the sources of the *Ring* — *Richard Wagners Bühnenfestspiel Der Ring des Nibelungen, in seinem Verhältniss zur alten Sage wie zur modernen Nibelungendichtung betrachtet.* Towards the end of the book Koch threw out what seemed, on the face of it, an odd suggestion with regard to the episode in which Mime, imagining himself to be cajoling Siegfried, declares his intention of murdering him — thanks to the taste he has had of the dragon's blood, the boy pierces through the dwarf's deceptive words to the real thought that is in his mind. This scene, said Koch, " has no basis in the northern mythology: but in the well-known farce *Dr. Fausts Hauskäppchen*, by Fr. Hopp, there is a merry character who, by putting on his head a magic cap that ostensibly belonged to Dr. Faust, can compel people to answer his questions fully and truthfully." No doubt, Koch continued, it was the memory, perhaps unconscious, of this device that prompted Wagner to handle the scene of the tasting of the dragon's blood as he has done: " the Nordic Sigurd understands the speech of the birds, Wagner's Siegfried understands the speech of human beings no matter what pains they may take not to be understood." [17]

Koch's suggestion is now proved to be well founded; for it came from Wagner himself! Koch, for the purpose of his book, had evidently asked him for information regarding the powers attributed in *Siegfried* to the dragon's blood. In his reply of the 10th August, 1874, Wagner says it was necessary for him to expand the effect of the " dragon's-blood magic ", which in the Edda extends only to an understanding of the speech of birds, to an understanding by Siegfried of Mime's treachery. He was able to achieve this, he says, in the particular way he did, by reason of the fact that Mime *sings* — the cajoling melody expresses his desire to dupe the boy, while he has no control over his words, which consequently lay bare his true intentions, " all of which is highly comic in its effects." " I cannot remember ", he continues, " any direct source for this: but no doubt Dr. Faust's magic skull-cap unconsciously contributed to it." [18]

---

[17] KWRN, pp. 91, 92. Hopp's farce was first printed in 1843: it had a considerable success in north Germany. It is said to be in the vein of Raimund (1790–1836), the famous Viennese writer of farces in which magic played a large part. Wagner was a great admirer of Raimund.

[18] The letter will be found in the *Berliner Tageblatt* of the 12th July, 1935.

CHAPTER XVIII

MARKING TIME IN ZÜRICH

1

T HE YEAR 1853 opened sadly for Wagner, for his faithful Uhlig died of consumption on the 3rd January, a few weeks before completing his thirty-first year.[1] He was one of the very few men to whom Wagner was ever sincerely attached. Wagner lost in him not only a devoted and understanding friend but an invaluable business man, for Uhlig had taken on himself the burden of many a negotiation with the German theatres, the sending out of scores, and so on, which the exile would have found it almost impossible to attend to himself from Zürich.

The completion of the *Ring* poem brought with it, of course, the imperative desire to " communicate it to his friends ". In the summer of 1852, before the whole poem was as yet complete, he had discussed with Breitkopf & Härtel the question of a lithograph reproduction of some twenty-five to thirty copies for this purpose. Breitkopf & Härtel thought an ordinary printed edition would be better, the balance of copies to be held in reserve for the time when the scores would be ready for sale. (The firm's willingness to take the highly problematic four-barrelled work, by the way, is another evidence of the " success " of Wagner at that time). He pointed out to them, however, the probability of alterations having to be made in the text during the composition of the music, and the inadvisability, therefore, of printing a large edition now. The negotiations for lithographing were accordingly dropped.[2] In the early weeks of 1853 Wagner had the poem printed in Zürich at his own ex-

---

[1] It was said that he was an illegitimate son of the King of Saxony. Three years after his death Wagner tried to induce Breitkopf & Härtel to bring out a collection of his essays for the benefit of his widow, but the firm refused to do so without payment.

[2] See the correspondence in RWBV, I, 48–54.

pense,[3] in an edition of fifty copies. On the 11th February he sent ten copies to Liszt. Three of these, handsomely bound, were for Liszt himself, the Grand Duchess of Weimar, and the Princess of Prussia. Of the remainder, Liszt was to hold two in reserve, give one to Zigesar, two to Bülow (one of which the latter was to send to Röckel), one to the Weimar Councillor Franz Müller, who had already shown his interest in Wagner's works, and one to Alwine Frommann: a further three copies were soon dispatched to Weimar at Liszt's request.[4] Other copies were of course distributed among Wagner's friends in Zürich and Dresden.

The printed copies were hardly in Wagner's hands before he felt an irresistible urge to read the poem to a larger audience than the one that had listened to it at Mariafeld a few weeks before. This he did in the Hôtel Baur on the evenings of the 16th, 17th, 18th, and 19th February. Invitations were issued only to his personal friends; but as these were authorised to bring with them anyone who was likely to be interested, the audience was probably large and miscellaneous. Wagner himself was more pleased with these readings than with those at the Willes': perhaps the larger audience, by reason of its very size, had a more impersonal quality and so helped the actor to lose himself in his part. Herwegh, however, was for some reason or other so out of tune with the company on the first evening that he did not attend the other readings. Wagner received the congratulations and glib assurances of perfect understanding that are usual on occasions of this kind, and for the moment he seems to have been quite satisfied with the results of his undertaking.[5]

But he was soon to realise, to his chagrin and dismay, that in thus printing and distributing his poem he had made one of the greatest mistakes of his life. As was only to be expected, no one at

---

[3] Schopenhauer, to whom Wagner sent a copy later, was particularly struck by the "superb, thick paper". The edition must have cost Wagner a great deal of money.

[4] It is noteworthy that in this first edition of the poem Wotan's name is spelt throughout "Wodan"; the third section bears the title of *Der Junge Siegfried*, the fourth that of *Siegfrieds Tod*.

[5] He is in error when he says, in *Mein Leben*, that he was so encouraged by these signs of understanding that he began to think something might be made out of the local theatre, and accordingly wrote his brochure *A Theatre in Zürich*. That work had been published in May, 1851.

that time could understand how a " libretto " of this kind could be realised in music: in *Lohengrin,* it must be remembered, the music had still flowed along in extended lyrical forms analogous to those of opera as it had hitherto been understood, and it was beyond the capacity of anyone in 1853 to see how musical shape and continuity and inner organic life could be given to the short lines and quick interchange of dialogue in the new poem. His puzzled friends took refuge in diplomatic silence. It was not until the 26th that Liszt acknowledged receipt of the volumes. He assured Wagner that the Princess Wittgenstein had read the poem at once and was " enthusiastic " over it; but for himself he could do no more than call Wagner a " wonder-man " and the work itself " the most incredible you have yet produced ", and say that after the three performances he was projecting of the *Flying Dutchman, Tannhäuser* and *Lohengrin* in Weimar he meant to shut himself up for a few days in order to read the four poems: " Forgive me therefore if to-day I say no more than that I share heartily the joy you must be feeling in the printed copies." Apparently he did not communicate to Wagner his impressions even after having read the poem. On the 30th March, six weeks after the first copies had been dispatched in such high hopes from Zürich, Wagner wrote to him bitterly:

" Why do I still go on living? . . . I print my new poem: I send it to all the friends whom I might presume to be interested in it: I indulge myself in the hope that now I have *compelled* people to show me a sign of themselves: — Franz Müller in Weimar and Karl Ritter have written me about it, but not a single one of all the others has thought it worth his while so much as to acknowledge receipt."

Liszt's only reply to this is:

" Do not take it amiss that I have not yet written you at length about the Nibelungen-Ring. My task is not the criticising and analysing of so extraordinary a work, for which I intend later to do all that I can to win for it its proper place. I have always begged you not to desist from the work, and I am delighted with your poetic accomplishment. Almost every day the Princess greets me with the words:

Nicht Gut, nicht Gold,	Not goods, nor gold,
noch göttliche Pracht;	nor greatness of gods;
nicht Haus, nicht Hof,	not house, nor land,

noch herrlicher Prunk;
nicht trüber Verträge
trügender Bund,
nicht heuchelnder Sitte
hartes Gesetz:
selig in Lust und Leid
lasst — die Liebe nur sein.

nor lordly life;
not burdensome bargains'
treacherous bands,
not wont with the lying
weight of its law;
happy, in luck or need,
holds you nothing but love.

(Alfred Forman's translation.)

There is something gently ironic for us of to-day in the Princess's having picked out for special approbation, and Liszt for sole quotation, a passage from Brynhilde's final oration that Wagner was to reject when he came to write the music to the *Götterdämmerung*, his changed conception of the inner meaning of his drama having necessitated by then a drastic re-writing of the closing scene. It must have been clear enough to him that neither the Princess nor Liszt had been able to see his great dramatic scheme as a whole as he saw it, but had merely been taken by the moral ring of these particular lines, into which they read their own domestic sentimentality; and if it was not further clear to him at the time it is crystal-clear to us to-day that Liszt was in the embarrassing situation of being unable either to be enthusiastic about the poem or to break his friend's heart by frankly saying so. It may have been a sense of the intellectual loneliness to which Wagner now seemed more than ever condemned, quite as much as the cumulative effect of his own troubles, that made Liszt, in this letter of the 8th April, venture, in a way that was quite unusual with him where Wagner was concerned, to recommend to him the consolations of religion.

" Your greatness is the cause of your misery ", he writes; " the two are inseparable, and are bound to be a torment and an agony to you until you let them both be lost in *faith*. . . . I cannot preach, cannot explain; but I will pray to God that he may enlighten your heart through His faith and His love. You may pour bitter derision on this feeling of mine if you like, but I shall continue to see and find in it the only salvation. Through Christ, through resigned suffering in God shall salvation and redemption come to us! "

Wagner, to whom neither Christianity in particular nor religion in general made any appeal in this period of his life, does not " deride ", in his reply, his friend's opinions, but says frankly that consolations of that kind are inefficacious in his case. He too has faith, he says, but a faith of his own, a faith in the future of humanity when love shall have gained the victory over lovelessness.

"Let me ask you this — who, in the depths of his heart, shares my faith more than you do, you who believe in me, you who know love and prove it as perhaps no one else has ever done? You *realise* your faith in every moment of your life. I, for my part, *know* in the depths of me *what* your faith is: could I then scoff at the form out of which such a marvel flows forth? I really would have to be less an artist than I am, not to understand you with delight."

The one thing, however, that more than anything else would have gladdened and heartened him at this time — the assurance that Liszt understood his *Ring* poem and shared his faith in the musical drama that was to come out of it — he never received. Liszt's later letters, though he more than once mentions the poem in connection with other people, never touch on this point.

2

The one man who showed some comprehension of the work, some notion of what it meant for the future, was Louis Köhler, a young musician in Königsberg, who, already a Wagner enthusiast, had come to Weimar in May to hear *Lohengrin*. At Liszt's request, Wagner sent him a copy of the poem. Köhler already had in the press a book on *The Melody of Speech*, which he sent to Wagner in July. He gave Liszt his impressions of the *Ring* poem in a letter of the 3rd July: at first, he said, it had seemed strange to him, but it gradually drew him deeper and deeper into its depths, till now he sees it as one of the noblest creations of the last few centuries. He could realise it mentally, he was bold enough to think, as it would be on the stage, and could see arising from its pithy verses a kind of speech-melody corresponding to the one that had hovered before his eyes as " the ultimate ideal of dramatic tone-speech " when he was writing his book. If, he continues, he could see only ten of the notes that Wagner has given a character to sing in the *Ring* he would be sure of his ground; and he asks Liszt to send him a word or two as to " Wagner's intentions " in the work. But this, of course, neither Liszt nor anyone else could do.

Wagner, in his letter of the 26th July to Liszt, in which he encloses one to be sent on to Köhler, is a little unkind to his eager young disciple:

> " the foolish fellow wanted me to say something about his book; but the moment I even dip my head into theory the nerves of my brain give me such agony that I become thoroughly ill: I can't and won't theorise any more, and he is no friend of mine who would entice me again into this cursed field. *Pereant* all Brendels and Köhlers, so long as they can think of nothing better than this eternal confused speculation about — art! "

This, however, was merely the fretful expression of his bad health and discouragement at that time: he had put exhausting theory behind him, he was longing to begin work upon the *Ring* music and exasperated at the delay in doing so, and it was an irritation to him even to be reminded that merely speculative problems in art occupied the minds of other men. It was about this time that he refused point-blank to have anything to do with a new review projected by Brendel, though the object of it was to make propaganda for the ideal of art now associated with his own name. For one thing, he felt that it was time now, not only for himself but for others, to create, not to talk. For another, he never had much respect for what he called the " literary aesthetes ", and was already becoming rather painfully aware that many even of his own admirers neither understood his prose works nor had any idea of how his new conception of drama would realise itself in a new form of music. " If it is your opinion ", he writes to Liszt, who had been urging him to contribute to the review, " that the journal cannot come into being without me, then I say, ' Good, let it drop; for it has no object and no value.' "

To Köhler, however, he had written more calmly on the 24th, in a way that shows that the book of the " foolish fellow " had really interested him. He sets forth once more his thesis that since modern verse has developed into what it now is independently of music, while modern melody has become what it now is along " absolute " musical lines that have nothing in common with speech, it is useless to try to " set " already existing poetry to music. It was this conviction — in itself, of course, the product not of abstract theorising but of his personal creative instinct — that had led him to discard the long lines, the rhymes, the traditional " poetic " apparatus of the *Lohengrin* text for the drastic concision, and at the same time freedom of line, of the *Ring* poem. It took the world some time to perceive that it was the *musician* in Wagner that made him take the novel view he did of poetry: it was the musician in him choosing words and shaping lines and groups of lines and whole scenes to suit a musical melody and a musical design that were none the less determinant within him because as yet they were mainly subconscious. It was with all this at the back of his mind that, while praising Köhler for the clarity of his ideas on melody-in-speech and speech-in-melody so far as single phrases were concerned, he suggested that the young man should now carry his investigation into the further field of the broader relations of verse-form and musical form. But no one, of course, could do this with any profit until Wagner himself had shown how the theoretical problem was to be triumphantly solved in the *Ring*.

His penetrating, uncompromising mind reached out into the future in his protest, in this same letter to Köhler, against the perfectly useless things with which " musical criticism " and musical journals have always been largely concerned. He had thrown cold water on Brendel's plans for his new paper.

" I have repeatedly impressed on him that his *Zeitschrift* should keep much more to what is learnable — to *technic*.[6] The *content* of an art-work is a matter for the individual, and therefore not a subject for criticism: here it is a question of a feeling of liking or disliking, which again is the affair of each individual. Technic, on the other hand, is the collective property of the artists of all epochs; one inherits it from the other, each adding to it and forming it as well as he can and must. One can talk about *that*, though naturally among artists alone: the layman should never hear anything about it." [7]

That is the common sense of the matter, the day for general recognition of which, indeed, is not yet, though it will some day come.

---

[6] This is perhaps a better rendering of *Technik* than the current English word "technique", which is associated in most people's minds with the conception of craftsmanship, dexterity, and things of that kind. Wagner does not mean this: he means by "technic" something much more fundamental — the problems of the relation between the inner being of an artistic idea and its realisation in a particular medium and form.

[7] His letter to Köhler will be found in RWFZ, pp. 133 ff.

One's emotional reactions to a work of art are one's own affair, determined by one's own constitution: the reactions of other people who are differently constituted being of no importance whatever to us, there is little reason why we should take the trouble to read about them; and conversely, our own reactions being of no importance whatever to them, there is little justification for our writing about them. The only rational basis for profitable public talk about art is that element in it that is deep below and high above merely personal reaction: and this element, which is concerned with the peculiar nature of the individual artist's mind, the problems he sets himself to solve, the means he employs to solve them, his place in the historical perspective, and so on, is beyond the comprehension of the average layman. When the day comes — it may still be far distant but it will assuredly arrive — when " musical criticism " has perished under the weight of its own absurdity, perhaps it will be remembered to Wagner's credit that he saw the absurdity of it a century or so before.

3

With one reader of his new poem Wagner was particularly unfortunate. Adolf Stahr had been so enthusiastic over *Lohengrin* that Liszt, with the best intentions, sent him a copy of the *Ring* poem. His criticism was prompt and devastating, so devastating, indeed, that Liszt tactfully refrained from passing the letter on to Wagner: in his letter of the 8th April he merely tells him that " Stahr has written me a long letter in which he calls your poem point-blank a total blunder, etc." Stahr's letter will be best considered in detail in a later chapter in which we shall deal with the development of pro-Wagnerism and anti-Wagnerism during the first years of the second half of the century. Here it is sufficient to point out, as against the angry tirades of Ashton Ellis, that Stahr's reactions to the work were perfectly natural, the circumstances being what they were. He had only the poem to go upon, the poem as yet unilluminated and justified, in all its seeming strangenesses, by the music. It is true that he might have given more weight to the brief Foreword to the volume, in which Wagner expressly said that " in the nature of the thing " his project " can be fully realised only when the poem here communicated has been worked out in music and shown forth on the stage ": he is perfectly clear in his own mind, Wagner continues, that both these things can be done, though for the full achievement of the latter the necessary forces do not as yet exist in the theatre, except *in posse;* and he asks those into whose hands the poem may come to safeguard it from anyone who is likely to make the mistake of judging it from the literary standpoint alone and of discussing it in the Press from that wrong standpoint. But Stahr or anyone else might reasonably enough ask what sense there was, in that case, in putting the poem, without its music, into people's hands and then expecting them to judge it by any standard *but* the purely literary one. The historian should be grateful to Stahr, who, one gathers, only blurted out what several other recipients of the volume thought but were too diplomatic to say: his letter, an English translation of which will be found in an appendix to Ellis's fourth volume, is invaluable to us to-day in our attempt to reconstruct that epoch as it appeared in the eyes of those who were living in it. Wagner took the matter calmly and philosophically: his verdict was simply that Stahr was talking precisely as a mere literary man might be expected to talk about something he did not understand and had not the natural qualifications for understanding. " Let it pass ", he wrote prophetically to Liszt: " it will one day right itself. Once I have put everything else on one side, to plunge over head and ears into the fountain again, the thing shall *sound* in such fashion that people shall hear what they cannot see."

As time went on, however, he realised more and more clearly that in his eagerness to communicate himself to his friends he had made a sad blunder in submitting the poem alone of the *Ring* to their judgment. It was one thing for *him* to read it aloud in his incomparable fashion, giving such sharpness of definition to the words and the rhythms that his listeners already had a prevision, however faint, of how they would sound in music, suggesting varieties of character by his own extraordinary histrionic powers, making the vicissitudes of the drama clear by changes in the quality of his voice and nuances in the tempo of delivery, and so on; but it was quite another matter when well-meaning disciples without any of his qualifications, and without the least knowledge of the musical contents and build and atmosphere of the work, read it to others as they would any of the purely " literary " poems that were the object of his scorn. He says nothing when Liszt informs him that the Weimar Hofrath Sauppe has read the poem in four evenings at the Altenburg, or when he hears that Moritz — the husband of Röckel's sister, who was attached to the Wiesbaden opera, where she had sung some of the Wagner parts and made enthusiastic propaganda for his works — is about to read it in Wiesbaden. But when he hears from a Leipzig admirer, the singer Lydia Steche, that a certain B. [Brendel?] intends to follow suit, his temper rises. " B. must not read it! " he writes to Liszt. " My God, how I regret ever having printed the poem! It shall not be bandied about like this: it is still *mine*! "

It gave him no pleasure, but only exasperated him, to read, or to be told of, the " critical " literature that well-meaning friends and admirers like Brendel were devoting to him and to what they took to be his purpose in music; for by this time he had realised that from *Opera and Drama* alone they would never be able to see what would happen when his new theory was converted into practice as it would be in the *Ring*. At no time of his life had he much more respect for the generality of his literary advocates than he had for his enemies: their intentions were good, but he could not persuade himself that they understood him as he really was. In these early 1850's in particular he had the maddening conviction that nobody understood him: his older works were given, as a rule, in a form that was not far from parody, his theoretical writings were almost equally misrepresented by his partisans and by his opponents, and it would be years yet before the completed *Ring* could demonstrate practically what had been at the back of his mind throughout all this theorising.

4

We have seen that he was powerless against the forces of reaction in the larger theatres and against the personal ill-will of the Kapellmeisters there; but there was evidently a growing body of public opinion in his favour, or at all events of curiosity regarding him, and the younger and more energetic among his admirers were not at all inclined to leave the field in the possession of his enemies. The Berlin Court Opera having rejected *Tannhäuser*, it seems to have occurred to some ingenious persons to take the position by a side attack. In May the Leipzig director Wirsing considered the plan of taking his opera personnel to Berlin to give the work in the Königstadt theatre. Wagner had not been consulted in the matter, but his only objection to the scheme when he heard of it was that the performances would have been under the baton of the incompetent and inimical Rietz. It was perhaps to overcome this difficulty that Wirsing asked Liszt to conduct. Liszt, however, declined the invitation, and the plan fell through. It may have been conceived in the first place as a counterpoise to one put forward about the same time by Schöneck, who had been, in a sense, the cause of the production of the *Flying Dutchman* in Zürich in April, 1852.[8] For some reason or other Schöneck disappeared so completely from future history that modern biographical dictionaries do not even mention his name. But Wagner evidently thought highly of him in some respects. Schöneck's work at Zürich had evidently won his approval; and even in the mid-'seventies, when he was writing *Mein Leben*, he remembered him as " a young Kapellmeister [9] who had decidedly won me over to him by his indubitable gifts as a conductor." Apparently Schöneck, at the conclusion of the Zürich season, had been looking for another more or less permanent post, but without immediate success; meanwhile, having realised, no doubt, the advantage of having his name associated with that of the rising star in the operatic world, he had conducted some five performances of *Tannhäuser* in nine days at Posen, and others in Freiburg-im-Breisgau. He had now linked his fortunes with those of a travelling impresario of the name of Wallner; and the bright idea occurred to this pair of producing the popular work in Kroll's theatre in Berlin.

The scheme had both Wagner's approval and Liszt's, though Wagner had certain doubts about Schöneck, who seems to have been advertising himself as Wagner's " pupil ". To more than one correspondent Wagner paid tribute to the young man's enthusiasm,

---

[8] See *supra*, p. 174.
[9] Schöneck was only twenty-three years old in 1852.

energy, and technical qualifications as a conductor, but in other respects he did not rank him highly. " As a musician ", he wrote to Schindelmeisser on the 29th May, " he is ordinary and insignificant; as a man he is without any particular culture. His specific talent as conductor, however, is quite extraordinary — nervous, fine in his perceptions, and of incredible activity." The truth of the matter probably was that Schöneck had studied Wagner's conducting at close quarters and had been quick to see what constituted the special virtues of it and the technical means by which very much the same effects could be produced; but, as Wagner tells Liszt, as regarded the conception of a Wagner opera as a whole he would be dubious about entrusting Schöneck with complete powers, and would accordingly like Karl Ritter to supervise the production of *Tannhäuser* in general. But as it happened, neither Schöneck nor Karl was put to the test in Berlin. Alarmed at the prospect of having its thunder stolen, the Court Theatre stepped in with a prohibition of " grand " opera in any other building in the town. Wagner humorously suggested that Schöneck should get round the edict by announcing *Tannhäuser* not as an opera but as a Singspiel. It is to be hoped that he found some consolation in his little joke, for the failure of the plan meant the loss of the opportunity to make a couple of thousand badly needed francs.

However dire his need of money, however, there were things he could not bring himself to do. In the spring of this year the Grand Duke of Coburg, the composer of the immortal *Tony*, approached him, through Liszt, with a suggestion that he should score a new three-act opera that had just had the honour of welling from the Grand Ducal pen. The fee was to be anything between 500 and 1,000 thalers; moreover, the Duke was so well disposed towards Wagner that he had an idea of summoning him to Gotha as his Kapellmeister. Of the two proposals, it was probably the latter that struck most terror into Wagner. He had nothing of Liszt's sycophancy and oily complaisance in these matters, and the prospect of putting on court uniform again in order to conduct the wretched operas of the royal amateur was the last in the world that was likely to appeal to him. His gorge no doubt rose also at the thought that a German royalty, instead of making him a small allowance purely and simply in order that he might get on with his own works, could think of no better way of helping him than inviting him to put that work aside and waste his time and strength on *his*. Though the offer of the Grand Duke reminded him, as he bitterly tells Liszt, of the Paris days when he had to arrange *La Favorita* for two cornets for Schlesinger, he mastered his annoyance sufficiently to send the royal dilettante an admirably polite and diplomatic letter of refusal. Had it not been that Liszt's feelings and his position as an intermediary in the affair had to be considered, Wagner would no doubt have preferred to reply somewhat on the lines of his covering letter to his friend in Weimar:

> "Here is the 'diplomatic' letter! If I could convey to you my profoundedly painful and bitter mood at the moment you would admire me for this 'diplomatic' epistle. If I associated more with people in general I would perhaps judge their actions more superficially; but being what I am I cannot do anything else but estimate all that happens to me according to its inner and basic significance, and so the opera-writing Duke of Coburg comes very badly off with me with his request that I shall score his rubbish. I can see myself, in imagination, as his Kapellmeister, having broken with God and the world simply in order to sit in a Coburg castle co-operating with Frau Charlotte Birch-Pfeiffer [the Duke's librettist], manufacturer of the ducal operas! Really, these people have all become Jews! "

Accompanying this letter for Liszt's private eye, however, was one for the Duke that could leave no sting behind it: Wagner thanks him for his good intentions with regard to him, but points out that in his present state of health even the scoring of his own music is a strain on him, and that for a long time to come he will need all his energy for his *Ring* music. In *Mein Leben* he says that the percipient Duke had told Liszt that he had been particularly struck with Wagner's way of using the trombones, and would be glad to know what his " rules " were in these matters; whereupon Wagner asked his friend to assure his Royal Highness that before he gave the trombones anything to do he had an idea for them in his head. The conversation with Liszt on this subject probably took place during the latter's visit to Zürich in July, 1853. We may take it for granted that Wagner's instructions how to write well for the trombones were *not* passed on to the Grand Duke: it was not Liszt's habit to be so frank as this with royal personages. The Duke seems to have taken

Wagner's refusal in good part, and to have done what he could, at this time and later, to induce the Saxon Court to allow the exile to enter Germany again.

5

Wagner's mood throughout the spring and summer of 1853 was the usual one of alternate optimism and deepest pessimism. The success of his " festival " in May and the many signs that were given him of the esteem in which Zürich held him seem to have revived, for a while, his dream of some day producing the *Ring* there in a theatre specially constructed for the purpose. In his little speech of thanks to his serenaders, as we have seen, he hinted at something " unprecedented " being in store for them. The expression can refer only to his plans for the *Ring*.

> " My musical festival was splendid," he wrote to his Dresden friend Heine in June, " and gave me great hopes of accomplishing unheard-of things here in the future. I will certainly produce my operas here some day, the *Nibelungen* as well, but of course only under quite exceptional circumstances. For that I shall require (*ut semper*) Wilhelm [Heine's son, the scene-painter]. In three or four years from now Wilhelm must come to Switzerland: write him that to Japan! "

About the same time he writes to Röckel in a similar strain. His recent experiences with the Zürichers, he says, have been so encouraging that he has no doubt that when the time comes

> " the means will be placed at my disposal for the production of my dramatic compositions according to my own ideas. This implies, of course, my devoting myself for some years exclusively to training a body of performers such as I need: once I have done that to my satisfaction I shall produce in the course of a whole year all my works, particularly my *Nibelungen* dramas, in a specially constructed theatre, lightly built but suitable to its purpose — and thus attain, if not my ideal, at least as much as is humanly possible to a single being. First, however, I must gather up all my strength and health — which is often very ailing — to write the music to my *Nibelungen*. This, I imagine, will take me three or four years."

Ellis is perhaps in error when he takes this to mean " ' three to four years ' for completion of the *Ring* music, and *after* that ' a series of years ' for the training of a special company "; the " first "

[376]

in Wagner's penultimate sentence does not necessarily mean first in point of time. It is rather more likely that what was in his mind was a gradual training of the local singers and players — somewhat on the lines set forth in *A Theatre in Zürich* [10] — so that when the *Ring* was at last in being he would already have at his hand a personnel more or less competent to take part in it. Zürich, however, appears to have been exhausted by the special effort it had made in connection with the *Flying Dutchman* and the festival performances: in the following year Wagner found it impossible to carry the concert committee with him in his ambitious scheme for giving the town its first performance of the Ninth Symphony. It is just possible that the leading inhabitants, who had already spent more upon Wagner than they had upon any other musician — to say nothing of their private loans to him — were anything but charmed at the prospect of being asked some day for very much larger sums for the building of a theatre which, in the terms of the case, would be almost useless for any purpose but that of one highly problematical four-barrelled opera: and no doubt they made it clear to him as soon as possible — in such ways, among others, as the refusal of his suggestion for the Ninth Symphony — that his ambitions were outrunning the capacity of their pockets.

Very soon after the festival he was made to realise rather unpleasantly that he was living not in a world of agreeable dreams but in one of disagreeable actuality. Reports had appeared in the German press that the exile of Zürich was thinking of repeating these successful concerts of his in Germany; and for some time

---

[10] His main thesis in that interesting brochure had been that it was useless for the small German (or German-speaking) theatres to attempt to ape the ways of the "grand" Opera of Paris. The essential thing was to make a repertory and form a style that should express the natural relation between the performers and the public of the town. Both parties would be better off if they understood the *dramatic* core of an opera. The local theatre should be, not an industrial speculation, but the focus of the spiritual life of the community. Local talent should be trained step by step, beginning with relatively simple works and passing gradually to more exacting works written specially for the local theatre.

He could never, of course, have imagined that the honest burghers of Zürich, no matter how hard they might work at improving their voices and their acting, would be equal to the leading parts in the *Ring*. His general idea was simply to create an efficient and intelligent troupe of local actors and singers for the smaller parts and the chorus: for the principal characters he would have to import the best singers from Germany.

Liszt and his Grand Ducal patrons had been employing every possible diplomatic means to induce the Saxon Court to pardon Wagner. Early in June the King and Queen of Saxony had paid a visit to Weimar. The subject of an amnesty was certainly discussed then; and the Hereditary Grand Duke promised Liszt that he would raise it again on his forthcoming visit to Dresden. The King himself might perhaps have been willing enough to pardon Wagner: but he was in the hands of his Minister Count von Beust and of a party that was determined to push home relentlessly the advantages conferred on it by the political reaction in Germany. The politicians either could not or would not see that Wagner had no further connection with, or even interest in, politics. The spies prejudiced them against him by their reports of his extravagant way of living in Zürich; and it did him no good, in official eyes, to be so constantly in the company of Herwegh, whose *Gedichte eines Lebendigen* were not yet forgotten in German government circles.

The friends and relations of more than one imprisoned revolutionary had hoped that clemency would be granted him on the occasion of the marriage, in July, 1853, of the King of Saxony's nephew, Prince Albert, with the Moravian Princess Carola Wasa; and although Wagner himself took no direct steps to this end, it is probable that his friends in Dresden did so on his behalf. The official reply to all this agitation, public and private, appeared in the *Polizei-Anzeiger* of the 11th June:

" Wagner, Richard, formerly Kapellmeister in Dresden, one of the most prominent members of the revolutionary party, for whose arrest on account of his participation in the Dresden rising in May, 1849, a warrant was issued, is said to intend to leave Zürich, where he lives at present, and return to Germany. To facilitate his arrest we append a portrait of Wagner, who, if he is caught, must be arrested and handed over to the Royal Court of Justice in Dresden." [11]

---

[11] LWVR, pp. 32 ff. The contemporary correspondence (printed by Lippert) between the Saxon and the Hanoverian police makes it clear that the reissue of the *Steckbrief* was expressly designed to put an end to the appeals of Wagner's friends; furthermore, the police authorities seem to have aimed, by public action, at making the King repent of the goodwill he had shown towards Wagner by his sanctioning the *Tannhäuser* revival of October, 1852. The police took the characteristically stupid view that the Dresden movement in favour of Wagner's works was only a blind on

The stab was exquisite in its calculated cruelty and perfect in its timing. There had been occasions in the past four years when Wagner had blithely assured his friends that he would not return to Germany if its frontiers were thrown open to him. But latterly the desire to return had become a torture to him. It was not merely that it fretted him to hear of his works being given in Germany without his being able to supervise any of the performances. More serious than this was the burning longing to hear his *Lohengrin:* he was fairly indifferent by now to *Rienzi,* the *Flying Dutchman,* and *Tannhäuser,* but he yearned to hear *Lohengrin* not only for its own sake but because, for some curious psychological reason or other, he had persuaded himself that he could not settle down to the composition of the *Ring* until he had heard this old music of his at least once. Had the slightest official encouragement been given him in Weimar he would no doubt at any time in 1852 or 1853 have risked arrest by going there for a performance of *Lohengrin,* trusting to the temporary protection of the Grand Duke; but Liszt made it clear to him, sympathetically but firmly, that anything of the kind was out of the question. In the spring and summer of 1853, the *Ring* poem having been completed and the music to it seething within his brain, his sense of frustration and despair at not being able to hear *Lohengrin* became overwhelming. And this was the moment chosen by the Saxon authorities to proclaim to all the world that in their eyes the leader of the new movement in German music was merely an ordinary political offender escaped from justice, and to dash, seemingly for all time, his hopes of seeing any future work of his on the boards of a German theatre! It is more than possible, it is extremely probable, that Liszt and the royalties through whom he was working had put in the forefront of their pleas for clemency for Wagner the fact that he had in hand an opera on a colossal scale, production of which would be possible only in Germany, and that under the composer's own supervision. By so doing they unwittingly showed his Dresden enemies the way

---

the part of the Saxon democrats, their real intention being to bring about the recall of one of their most active political supporters!

Even Frau Ritter and her family became the subjects of the malignant attention of the Saxon police, because of their financial support of Wagner.

to stab him to the heart: it must have seemed to them that now they had ruined him utterly. By the irony of fate, their blow was in the long run to recoil upon themselves. From this time onwards Paris began to occupy Wagner's thoughts more and more — Paris, where the Saxon royal writ did not run. It was eight years yet before *Tannhäuser* was given in Paris; but it was *Tannhäuser* in Paris, and the general indignation created by its brutal treatment there, that at last did more than anything else to break down the political op-position to Wagner in Dresden.

CHAPTER XIX

LISZT AND WAGNER MEET AGAIN: THE "RING" MUSIC BEGUN

1

To HIS Zürich friends, of course, it seemed that he had little real cause for crying out against Fate as he was always doing. As we have seen from Frau Wille's reminiscences, his lot appeared to be enviable in comparison with that of the ordinary refugee: he was admired as a musician, Frau Ritter's pension of itself kept him certainly above the destitution mark, he had well-to-do friends whose purses were always open to him, he had access to the best intellectual society of the town, and his reputation and influence in Germany were increasing month by month. But if few of his friends knew of his vast capacity for suffering, his equally vast capacity for self-pity must have aroused their wonder sometimes, as it still does ours to-day. Only a man as completely self-centred as Wagner was could have written such a letter as his to Röckel of the 12th September, 1852. A letter he has just received from Röckel has given him a high opinion of his friend's fortitude in adversity. But Wagner's talk is mainly about himself. His health is not good, he says:

> "My nervous system is in a bad way and is gradually getting worse — the necessary result of my abandoning myself to that passionate and hectic sensitivity in virtue of which I am the artistic being that I am."

His personal affairs are going pleasantly enough, he continues, and he supposes that he ought to congratulate himself on being secure from anxiety as to his immediate necessities.

> "But I am *very lonely*: I lack congenial company, and I feel more than ever that the exceptional nature of my position has become a veritable curse so far as the enjoyment of life is concerned. A prisoner

[i.e. Röckel] would not be able to understand why I am mostly so depressed and longing for death. . . . Farewell, and go on bearing yourself as well as you do."

There is something almost comic in this insistence, to a man condemned to penal servitude for life, on his own " loneliness "! Yet pitifully, tragically lonely Wagner was in soul.

There is the same cry of anguish in his letters of the following year to Liszt. He has completely lost touch with his Zürich surroundings, he says.

" My life here is only a dream-life; if I awake, it is only to pain. Either nothing allures me and occupies me, or what does so is in the distance. . . . Truly, my friend, it took me till I was thirty-five to realise that I have *never really lived*. It was my art that revealed to me the secret that my life here, bare of joy and love as it has been, has been wretched. What will you say when I tell you that I have never yet enjoyed the real happiness of love? Now I drag out my existence between deprivation and renunciation in face of the confinement of my nearest surroundings, in which I am understood less and less every day. I cannot and will not show my grief openly here . . . but I must at least win the power to get away now and then from this desert, so as to spread the wings of my life-power unhindered. . . . Listen and grant my request! Let me know soon and beyond the possibility of doubt whether I can return to Germany or not."

His need was a dual one — that of hearing his *Lohengrin* (hence his longing to return to Germany, if only for a few days), and that of some one to whom he could " communicate himself " as creative artist. He was interested in the world in general only so far as it could or would contribute to his own realisation of himself. We have seen him admitting, in *Mein Leben,* that as a boy " he cared only for someone to accompany me in my excursions to whom I could pour out my inmost feelings to my heart's content, without caring what the effect was on him." [1] As a grown man he had still very little other use than this for other people; the one thing that mattered in the universe was the soul of Richard Wagner.[2] A rather

---

[1] See Vol. I, p. 81.

[2] It was this incessant concentration on his own problems, and his need of other people only in so far as they were able or willing to help him to solve them, that made so many people turn from him as a master-egoist. Marcel Herwegh (HBD, p. 137) cites a letter to Georg Herwegh from his intimate friend Rustow, who angrily refuses to take part in an excursion if Wagner is to be in it. He calls him "a heartless egoist

curious passage in his *Lebens-Bericht* (written in 1879) suggests that Weimar had come to mean, for a time, so much to him in the 1850's because he thought he saw there the nucleus of the new society he had dreamed of in *Art and Revolution* — a society that would share his conviction that the theatre (the ideal theatre of the future, of course) was the real goal of all mankind's striving, the real fulfilment of mankind's destiny, and that the ideal theatre would be the Wagnerian theatre. Before the new drama could materialise, he had argued, a new humanity must be born. Apparently he had persuaded himself, for a while, that Weimar, under Liszt, was in process of producing this new humanity, and that from Weimar the sun of the new dispensation would gradually shed its beams on all Germany.

" This bold deed ", he says in 1879 [i.e. the production of *Lohengrin*] " was the starting-point of a society that first of all grouped itself round the honoured person of the Master [Liszt]. Here, instructed and inspired by him, there arose adherents to my contemned and forgotten art. My writings might not be read in Germany, my works not performed: but here there had appeared for my sake a real *life* of art, here had been shown the germ of a *future*, here something had been shaped that hinted at the hopeful beginning of what I had dreamed of in my conception of an artistic *Folk*." [3]

As the other people in Zürich had their own lives to live and their own particular circle of interests, however, it is a fair surmise that after a time some of them began to resent Wagner's perpetual assumption that the world seemed to have been created only to make *him* wretched by denying him everything he wanted. There never existed a man less capable of consuming his own smoke. His letters of this period are one long complaint, to Liszt especially — to Liszt, who himself had inner and outer troubles that were enough for one man's bearing, but who had the capacity, which Wagner lacked, to suffer in silence, finding an escape from his sorrows in

who carries on like a hysterical woman, who bleeds all his friends and deceives them, and, when he fails in this, speaks of them ironically and contemptuously."

[3] RWLB, pp. 49, 50.

Nietzsche expressed much the same idea in his *Richard Wagner in Bayreuth:* "If a number of people suffered under the same distress as he [Wagner], these, he said to himself, would constitute the Folk. And when the same distress led to the same impulses and desires, the same satisfaction would necessarily be sought, the same happiness found in this satisfaction." (NZUB, p. 352.)

stimulants, in narcotics, and in prayer. As Wagner's hopes for Zürich faded and at the same time he saw himself apparently condemned to the place for the rest of his days, and in proportion as the music of the *Ring* grew to life within him and he needed someone, at once intelligent and sympathetic, with whom he could talk about his plans for his gigantic work, the desire to see Liszt became a torture to him. His letters show that he would have liked his friend to settle in Zürich, just as in later years he did everything in his power to persuade Cornelius, Nietzsche and others to link their lives inseparably with his. Failing that, he implored Liszt to come to him in Zürich, if only for a few days.

2

It was not until July, 1853, that the two friends met again, for the first time for more than four years, during which so much had happened that was vital to the whole later life of each of them. It was on the 1st July that Liszt arrived in Zürich, and to the fortunate circumstance that he went without the Princess we owe the firsthand record of his impressions during his stay. " Wagner was waiting for me at the post-house ", he writes to Carolyne. " We nearly choked each other with embraces. Sometimes he has a sort of eaglet's cry in his voice. He wept and laughed and stormed with joy for at least a quarter of an hour at seeing me again." Liszt found Wagner " very well housed ", sporting a " modest luxury ": his eye fell on the piano scores of *Rienzi, Tannhäuser* and *Lohengrin,* " superbly bound in red ". Wagner looked well, though rather thinner than when Liszt had seen him last; " his features, especially his nose and mouth, have acquired a remarkable fineness and accentuation." Liszt was writing at eight in the morning of the 3rd. He had arrived in Zürich only at seven on the evening of the 1st, but in the short interval Wagner had evidently talked without intermission. He had assured Liszt that he had no dealings with other refugees or with politics.

> " His relations with musicians are those of a great general with only a dozen tallow-chandlers to discipline. His logic where artists are concerned is pitiless in its sharpness. As for myself, he loves me heart and soul, and never ceases saying, ' See what you've made of

me! ' when the conversation turns on his fame and popularity. Twenty times during the day he fell on my neck — then rolled on the ground caressing his dog Peps and talking nonsense to it turn by turn — reviling the Jews, with him a generic term of a very wide meaning. In a word, a grand and grandissimo nature, something like a Vesuvius letting off fireworks, emitting sheaves of flame and bouquets of roses and lilacs. ' Art is but Elegy ', he said to me among other things; and as he developed this theme of the artist's infinite sufferings, renewed every hour, it led me to reply, ' Yes, and the crucified God is Truth.' "

Liszt found Minna " no longer pretty, and slightly stout; but her manner is pleasant, and she looks after her house, even to the cooking."

In spite of Liszt's scruples as to the expense to which his friend was obviously putting himself on his account, Wagner insisted on keeping open house for him from morning till night, there being, at any rate during the first day or two, about a dozen guests for the mid-day meal and as many for supper: the waiting at table was done by Liszt's servant, Hermann, who reported to his master that Wagner's wine-cellar was well stocked. " He has a decided taste for luxury, and his habits are elegant ", says Liszt, who noted also that while Wagner's allowance from Frau Ritter was 1,000 écus a year (3,000 francs), his way of living seemed to call for at least twice, if not three times, that sum. Liszt was told in confidence by one of their common friends that

" during the first years of his sojourn here, when he was offending everyone by his ways, Wagner only gradually gained ground in the esteem and consideration of the natives; but after the rehearsals and performances of his concerts [evidently the festival of the preceding May] he had become so amiable that they could no longer resist him. This very week he will become an honorary member of several musical societies — which can only be a prelude to his being made a freeman of the city of Zürich, which will carry him straight on to the dignity of Kapellmeister-in-chief, General-Musikdirektor of the Confédération Helvétique. . . . He suspects that one of the spies whose business it is to make reports to Dresden is personally hostile to him, bearing him a grudge because Wagner at one time treated him *de haut en bas*. That, by the way, is his custom in general, even with people who show him a zeal that amounts to obsequiosity. His manner is decidedly dominating. . . ."

Wagner gave Liszt his frank opinion not only of his enemies but of the friends and well-wishers, including Raff and Brendel, who " understood " him only in a way he regarded as not much better than blank misunderstanding, and who misled the public by attributing to him a " system " that had never been in his thoughts: the real Wagner, he said, was beyond the understanding of the public as a whole. He told Liszt of his plan for a theatre for the *Ring* in Zürich: he was confident of his ability to raise the necessary 100,000 francs for the construction of a temporary theatre that was to be open from the spring to the autumn of the chosen year. Liszt promised to help him in every possible way to raise the money: and when Wille, having heard of the grandiose scheme, ejaculated " But this will cost more than a million! " Liszt replied, " Il l'aura! Le million se trouvera! " He and Liszt sang the duet of Elsa and Lohengrin in a way that left Liszt with no regrets for not having gone to hear a projected performance of the opera in Wiesbaden: " *ma foi, c'était superbe!* as our poor friend Chopin used to say." On the 4th and 5th Wagner read the *Rhinegold* and the *Valkyrie* poems to the company, " with incredible energy and intelligence of accent." On the 6th, Herwegh joined the two friends in an excursion to Brunnen, on the Lake of Lucerne: the next morning they were rowed out to Tell's Chapel and Grütli, where Wagner and Liszt drank *Brüderschaft* with Herwegh at the springs. They were back in Zürich again on the evening of the 8th. Presumably, though Liszt does not mention it, Wagner read the poem of *Siegfried* to them some time during the trip.

They were eight glorious days both for Liszt — who was no doubt relieved to escape for a while from the sometimes burdensome adoration of the Princess and to be able to relax in congenial male company — and for Wagner, who now, as he wrote to Otto Wesendonk on the 13th, really got to *know* Liszt for the first time as a man, besides making his first genuine acquaintance with him as a composer: Liszt played for him, he says, from the manuscripts, his *Faust Symphony*,[4] various piano works, and some of the sym-

---

[4] Wagner, however, seems to be in error here. Liszt did not begin work on the *Faust Symphony* until August, 1854, finishing it in October of that year. Wagner is perhaps confusing Liszt's visit of July, 1853, with that of October, 1856.

phonic poems, of which *Ce qu'on entend sur la montagne, Tasso, Prometheus, Héroïde funèbre, Mazeppa* and *Festklänge* were at this period completed. Liszt left Zürich on the 10th, leaving Wagner in the depths of depression, out of which he was lifted for a moment by the presentation of a Diploma of Honour by the local Choral Society, to the accompaniment of a torchlight procession, a serenade and some complimentary speech-making. A platform for the orchestra had been put up outside his house: his first thought on seeing it, he humorously wrote to Liszt, was that they were erecting a scaffold for him. He was so cheered by these evidences of good-will towards him that in reply to the complimentary address he launched out into a hopeful forecast of the realisation of his artistic ideals in Zürich. His remarks were greeted with great enthusiasm — his audience having taken them to mean that he was inexpressibly keen about the development of the local choral societies!

3

After this, exhaustion and depression laid their chill hands on him once more. He was longing to begin work upon the music of the *Ring*, but, as had happened so often in the past, could not find the propitious mood for it. Once more he persuaded himself that what he needed was a change of air and scene. About the 14th, accordingly, he started off with Herwegh on a trip to St. Moritz, in the Engadine, and the Rosegg glacier. The excursion was not a great success: Herwegh's languid habit of life unfitted him for the hard going to which Wagner subjected him, the inns were uncomfortable, and the friends wrangled about literary questions in general and the character of Goethe's Charlotte in particular. Still putting a pathetic faith in " cures ", although he recognised, in one of his saner moments, that " I am no ' cure ' subject ", Wagner conscientiously took the St. Moritz baths and drank the St. Moritz waters, but their powerful impregnation of iron upset his bowels and his nerves. Herwegh seems not to have taken his companion's ill-health too seriously. Wagner, he wrote to his wife (who was now in Zürich again, the pair having lately been reconciled), " busies himself solely with himself ": all the same, Herwegh humoured him, feeling that it was best to " let him have the pleasure of curing himself thoroughly ill for once " as a possible way of getting rid of his hypochondria. The poor man needed all the composure of which his fretted nerves were capable, for Minna, apparently, was pestering him with letters that showed even more than her normal bourgeois stupidity — accusing him of finding fault with her style even before she had written to him (she having taken his request to her to write *punctually* (*pünktlich*) to mean that he was urging her to be more *punctilious in her language*) — and hinting that he had his own reprehensible male reasons for going away with Herwegh, of whose passion for pursuing women she did not approve. Wagner bore patiently with the poor creature, whose natural defects of intelligence were now visibly complicated by gnawing anxieties about her health: she had even begun to imagine that she was consumptive.

Wagner was back again in Zürich by the 10th August, not a particle the better for his mountain-climbing and his " cure ". A fortnight later he was off once more in search of health — this time to Italy. He went by way of Geneva, Mont Cenis and Turin — where he greatly enjoyed a performance of Rossini's *Barbiere* and had the odd experience of meeting Liszt's old rival Thalberg — to Genoa. There everything delighted him, the clement air, the blue sea, the antique palaces, the splendid physique of the men working in the harbour. The night was " divine ": he drank his coffee and smoked his cigar in a quasi-mystic ecstasy, " under flowering oleander trees as tall as a house ". He planned to stay a fortnight in this earthly paradise. But two days later he was ill and homesick, and, though he perhaps did not know it, suffering from the frustration of his desire to work. Some profoundly-seated instinct in him kept calling out not for outer sensuous delight but for a quiet retiring inward upon himself: he was like an animal prowling about uneasily in quest of some corner in which to be delivered of its young. Sick with dysentery — the result of over-indulging in ices — with his nerves harassed beyond endurance by the noises of the harbour, he took boat on the 3rd to Spezia, crawled to a hotel, could not sleep at night for noise without and fever within, took a long walk next day, and in the afternoon flung himself down on a hard couch, intending to sleep. And then, at last, the miracle happened for which his subconscious mind had been crying out for so many weary months.

He had probably never realised precisely why he could not set to work at the *Ring* music. It was much less a matter of his health, as he thought, or of enriching his mind with new impressions to be derived from travel, than of finding an opening gambit for the great work. He had before him a task such as had faced no other composer in the whole history of music, the task not merely of " setting the text to music " but of giving organic musical unity to the enormous dramatic mass. His themes had not only to be expressive in and by themselves: they had to relate to each other in all kinds of subtle musical and psychological ways. More than that, they had to be capable of infinite transformation according to the part they would be called upon to play in the drama at any given moment: beyond that again, they had to be susceptible to contrapuntal treatment. At every point in the score he would have to look both before and after, seeing the whole in each part, and each part as contributing to the whole. He must have done an immense amount of thinking and sketching for the music of the *Ring* during all the years since 1848.[5] He must have seen and heard it all, with his inner eye and ear, very much as it would be at the finish: hence the quiet confidence of his assurances to Liszt that he had within him the clue to the maze that the poem by itself seemed to be to mere readers of it as " literature ", that " once I have put everything else on one side, to plunge head and ears again into the fountain [of music], the thing shall *sound* in such fashion that people shall hear what they cannot see." His difficulty was to *begin* — to find the tiny point of matter which, introduced into the inchoate fluid of his thinking, would effect in a flash the needed crystallisation.

And that tiny point of consolidating matter came to him, unbidden, unanticipated, during his disturbed half-sleep on that hard couch in the hotel at Spezia. Falling into that cataleptic state that

---

[5] See p. 240 for the first record (1851) of the theme of the Ride of the Valkyries. The Fafner motive was one of the earliest to be settled upon. Wagner told Tappert that the fugato on Siegfried's horn motive (in what is now known as "Siegfried's Rhine Journey" in the *Götterdämmerung*) was one of the first pieces to be drafted. See TRW, p. 77.

is the prime condition for all artistic creation of the highest kind, he suddenly felt, he says, as though he were sinking in a mighty flood of water:

> " The rush and roar soon took musical shape within my brain as the chord of E flat major, surging incessantly in broken chords: these declared themselves as melodic figurations of increasing motion, yet the pure triad of E flat major never changed, but seemed by its steady persistence to impart infinite significance to the element in which I was sinking. I awoke from my half-sleep in terror, feeling as though the waves were now rushing high above my head. I at once recognised that the orchestral prelude to the *Rhinegold,* which for a long time I must have carried about within me, yet had never been able to fix definitely, had at last come to being in me: and I quickly understood the very essence of my own nature: the stream of life was not to flow to me from without, but from within."

The experience always remained vivid in his memory. He described it once more, some eighteen years later, in his open *Letter to an Italian Friend* [Boito] *on the Production of 'Lohengrin' in Bologna:*

> " Be it a daemon or a genius that often rules us in hours of crisis — enough: stretched sleepless in a hotel in Spezia there came to me the prompting for the music for my *Rhinegold;* at once I returned to my melancholy home,[6] to carry out that immense work the fate of which now, above all else, binds me to Germany." [7]

4

He at once decided to return to Zürich, and set out by coach the same evening. At Genoa he wavered for a moment: the pull of Italy's loveliness was strong upon him: he thought once more of returning in leisurely fashion by way of Nice and the Riviera. But he had no sooner begun to coquet with this temptation than his daemon intervened. He fell ill again: then, he says,

> " I realised that what had lately refreshed me and brought me healing and vigour was not the renewal of my delight in Italy but the resolve

---

[6] For some reason or other that is not clear to me, Ashton Ellis translates this "I returned to the land of shadow."

[7] RWGS, IX, 290.

to take up my work again. . . . Now I understood myself: giving up the idea of Nice, I went straight home by the nearest way through Alessandria and Novara."

From Genoa (not, as he says in *Mein Leben*, from Spezia) he sent Minna a telegram announcing his return and asking her to have his study all in order for his work. It is significant as to the lack of intellectual communication between them that in his letter of the same day (the 6th September) he attributes his sudden resolve to return only to concern for his health: he says nothing of the real reason — the illumination that had come to him in his dream. *That* was something that Minna would have found it impossible to understand.

In Zürich, however, where he arrived about the 10th, the opportunity to set to work at the *Ring* was still tantalisingly denied him. Minna, not expecting him to return so soon, was taking the waters at Baden-am-Stein, some twelve miles from the town. He visited her there daily, filled with a new anxiety over her worsening health. He sank once more into the deepest pit of depression: " here I am in Zürich again ", he wrote to Liszt on the 12th, " unwell, out of tune, ready for death. . . . I came back to peg out — or — to compose — one or the other: there is nothing else left to me to do." Restless, and exasperated with himself for not being able to conquer his restlessness, unable to find the peace of mind and body necessary for his work, he decided it would be better to postpone it until after the meeting with Liszt that had already been tentatively arranged for the early days of October. At the invitation of the Grand Duke of Baden, Liszt was to conduct some of his own and Wagner's works.[8] in Carlsruhe, where, by the way, Eduard Devrient was now the theatre regisseur: after that, he and Wagner were to

---

[8] The programmes of the two concerts on the 3rd and 5th October consisted, in the main, of the *Tannhäuser* overture, a selection from *Lohengrin*, the Beethoven No. 9, Schumann's *Manfred* overture, Liszt's cantata *An die Künstler* (in its first form, with Raff's scoring), Meyerbeer's *Struensee* overture, and a selection from Berlioz's *Romeo and Juliet*. Joachim played the Bach Chaconne and his own violin concerto: Bülow played Liszt's Fantasia on Beethoven's *Ruins of Athens*.

The orchestral and choral forces had been assembled from Carlsruhe, Darmstadt and Mannheim. The rehearsals must have been inadequate for such works, especially the new or unfamiliar ones: apparently few of the players had any previous acquaintance even with the Beethoven symphony. It was in this work that the orchestra went wrong, with the result that Liszt's enemies said he "could not conduct." See *supra*, pp. 195-6.

meet in Basel, Wagner preferring that town to Paris, where, he said, he was " afraid " of Berlioz — " I shall be lost with my bad French."

Wagner arrived in Basel on the 6th October. In the evening he was sitting in the dining room of the hotel " Zu den drei Königen " when he heard from the vestibule a male chorus singing the trumpet fanfare that accompanies the King's address in *Lohengrin*. It was Liszt and his young bodyguard — Bülow, Joachim, Cornelius, Richard Pohl (who wrote for the Wagner-Liszt cause under the pseudonym of " Hoplit "), Liszt's piano pupil Dionys Pruckner, and the Hungarian violinist Reményi. They were a joyous band of young enthusiasts, the eldest of them, Cornelius, being no more than twenty-nine. But already, perhaps, the seeds of doubt were germinating in the mind of one of them — Joachim. He had gone to Weimar, as first violin of the theatre orchestra, in 1849, at the age of eighteen: but at the time of this first meeting of his with Wagner at Basel he had already (at the turn of 1852–3) taken up his residence in Hanover as Konzertmeister in the local theatre. Wagner found him a little shy, on account, it was explained to him, of the *Judaism in Music* article: all the same, Joachim was so infected with the enthusiasm of the moment that he offered his services for the first production of the *Ring*. But it is probable that Joachim, who had spent the impressionable years of his adolescence in the Leipzig of Mendelssohn, Schumann, David and Hauptmann, was already turning away in secret from what was now beginning to be known as the New German School. He never became a bigoted anti-Wagnerian: [9] his later revolt was against the music of Liszt and, to some extent, against Liszt the man, whose theatricality and other weaknesses of character had been made manifest to him during the years of their close association in Weimar.[10] But at present there was no sign of the rift that was later to declare itself between Joachim and Liszt; and the young violinist seems to have played his part in the uproarious merriment of the rest of the company.

---

[9] It is true that in later life he preferred the music of *Euryanthe* to *Lohengrin*. But he conducted Wagner works at the Berlin Hochschule concerts; and, in general, neither he nor Brahms was so anti-Wagnerian at heart as the too-zealous partisans on both sides imagined. See MJJ, II, 55, 56, 167, 168.

[10] See NML, pp. 12, 204, 214, 244–5.

They all, Liszt included; sobered down when, on the following day, the Princess Wittgenstein arrived with her cousin, Eugène von Sayn-Wittgenstein, and her fifteen-years-old daughter Marie, to whom Wagner at once took a great liking. Her curious combination of childhood and dawning womanhood was very attractive to him: he dubbed her " The Child ", a name by which she was known in the Liszt-Wagner circle for some years.[11] Wagner, of course, read the *Siegfried* poem to his friends, there not being time for a reading of the whole tetralogy. (He also seems to have played for them a few of the *Ring* motives). But as The Child wished to hear the remainder of the poem she persuaded her mother to accompany Liszt and Wagner to Paris, instead of returning to Weimar as she had originally intended to do.

The disciples having gone their several ways — at Baden the exuberance of some of them got them into a little trouble with the police, for they had entered the town roaring out the same fanfare from *Lohengrin* — Liszt, Wagner, the Princess, Eugène and Marie went on the 9th to Paris, where the *Ring* readings were concluded: they put up at the Hôtel des Princes, Wagner being Liszt's " guest " while there. Liszt was in the seventh heaven of happiness, leaving the others very much alone while he renewed his acquaintance with the scenes and the personalities associated with his early triumphs as a pianist. Wagner was less happy: he was unwell and out of tune again, and a performance of *Robert the Devil* to which he was dragged only deepened his depression. He found consolation, however, in attending a concert of the Maurin-Chevillard Quartet, at which, he says, the inner melody of Beethoven's C sharp minor

---

[11] In 1859 she married Prince Konstantin Hohenlohe, and went to live in Vienna. Her intellect and her charm were praised year after year in prose and poetry, by almost everyone who was distinguished in letters, in politics, or in high society in the second half of the nineteenth century; and when one makes the necessary deductions on account of her birth and position one is still left with an impression of a personality of uncommon distinction. An attractive picture of her will be found in HFS. She appears to have had all the best qualities of her mother and none of her defects.

It has to be recorded, however, that according to Cosima's diary for 1871, after Wagner "had received information from Vienna of an extremely ugly piece of behaviour" on the part of the Princess Marie, he "regretted every cordial and enthusiastic word he had spoken to so deceitful a creature." (MECW, I, 571). No doubt Marie, by this time, had been affected by her mother's long-standing hatred of Wagner. Marie refused to go to the first Bayreuth festival in 1876, on the pretext that she "feared the hubbub there". (See HFS, pp. 21, 48).

quartet was revealed to him for the first time, much as the Ninth Symphony had been made clear to him, years before, by the Conservatoire Orchestra's performance under Habeneck. Liszt took him to see his children, who were under the care of their governess: Wagner would no doubt have been surprised had he been told that the younger of the two girls, the shy little sixteen-years-old Cosima, would one day become his wife and the inheritor of his kingdom. He met also Jules Janin, at that time the leading Parisian journalist, Berlioz, who was on the point of setting out on a German tour, and Liszt's friend — rather more than friend, it was said — the beautiful Marie Kalergis, whom Wagner had met some years before in Dresden.[12] Eugène Wittgenstein, who was a sculptor of some ability, made, with Kietz's assistance, a medallion portrait of Wagner which Liszt thought " the best existing likeness " of him, while Wagner could say of it only that " it isn't bad, though a bit sick." [13]

By way of a treat for Minna, he had her join him in Paris on the 20th: for their expenses he borrowed 600 francs on the 12th October from Sulzer which he promised to repay " for certain " early in November: four days later he asked Sulzer to send him, by Minna, as much more as he could, against monies he (Wagner) expected to come in during November and December: he wanted, he said, to give Minna a really good time in the town in which she had suffered so much in years gone by. She arrived on the 20th. Liszt and his ladies had had to leave Paris a day or two before: but by way of compensation Wagner ran into the Wesendonks, Otto having just returned from a business visit to America. For the rest there were always Kietz and Anders to hobnob with, while Wagner allowed himself to be persuaded into consulting that Dr. Lindemann who had prescribed for him at a distance a couple of years before. Lindemann, who seems to have been strong on theory, whatever he may have been in practice, gravely set out on a search for the " metallic poison " that would be best for a nervous system like Wagner's, and advised him to take laudanum whenever he was suffering more acutely than usual, and, for more ordinary purposes, valerian. It may have been in consequence of following these pre-

---

[12] See Vol. I, p. 456.

[13] It has been frequently reproduced in modern books on Wagner, and will be found in EWLW, p. 217. To us of to-day it seems a veracious piece of portraiture.

scriptions that Wagner left Paris on the 27th feeling, as he says, " utterly exhausted, restless, and in the highest degree fretful and excited." He left, he adds, without in the least comprehending why he had spent so much money there. In Basel, on the way back, he met the violinist Ernst, to whom he loyally sang Liszt's praises. Home again in Zürich, where he arrived on the 29th, he at last settled down, early in November, to the composition of the *Ring*.

5

He began the music of the *Rhinegold* on the 1st November, 1853, and finished it on the 14th January following: he took up the scoring at once, completing this on the 28th May. The composition of the first act of the *Valkyrie* occupied him from the 28th January to the 1st September, 1854, the second act from the 4th September to the 18th November, the third from the 20th November to the 27th December. The dates themselves are sufficient indication of the ease with which the music must have flowed from him after his long brooding upon it: and the diagnosis suggested in the foregoing pages — that his ill-health for so many years was largely the result of his being unable to get to real grips with the *Ring* — is confirmed by his own remark in *Mein Leben:* " I remember how greatly my health improved while I was engaged in this work, so that the circumstances of my outer life during that time have left very little impression on me."

He tells us in *Mein Leben* that the peculiar nature of the *Rhinegold* prelude compelled him to resort to a new way of putting his music on paper. His method in the earliest operas had been to begin with a " short " score of three staves, the upper one containing the vocal part, the two lower ones a compressed statement of the orchestral part: from this he made the full orchestral score. For the *Flying Dutchman, Tannhäuser* and *Lohengrin* he had adopted another system: for the three-staves sketch he substituted one on two staves, the vocal part being continuously interwoven with the orchestral: then followed a full-score sketch, and after that the carefully written full score proper. But he found it impossible to sketch out the *Rhinegold* prelude clearly in this way: he had to resort at the outset to a quasi-orchestral lay-out of the chords. This method he adopted

[395]

for the remainder of the work, the music being sketched on sometimes two, sometimes three staves: points in the future orchestration were jotted down here and there, and stage directions were inserted. From this sketch he then made the full score, first of all in a pen or pencil draft, then in a fair copy, in ink, in the copperplate for which he was famous.[14]

This method, he says in *Mein Leben*, " landed me in some serious difficulties later, as the slightest interruption in my work often made me forget what my hasty sketch meant, and I had to recall it to my memory by a painful process." He found the task of making the fair copy of the final score so irksome — it exhausted him physically and put him out of tune for creative work — that in March, 1854, he begged Liszt to find for him a copyist who could " make a neat full score from my wild pencil sketches. Without someone of this kind I am lost: with him I can finish the whole work in two years." But he soon had to abandon this idea, as the elucidation of the sketches would have been impossible for anyone but himself. Frau Wesendonk solved his problem for him by giving him an " everlasting " gold pen, working with which was such a delight that he gladly turned his best penmanship upon the fair copy of his *Rhinegold* score.

Those who believe that Wagner " composed at the piano ", — a legend which seems to derive from some remarks of the foolish Ferdinand Praeger — would be hard put to it to explain how he managed to complete the *Rhinegold* in so short a time. For it did not really take him the ten weeks implied by the dates 1st November, 1853, to 14th January, 1854. The actual period, after allowance has been made for interruptions due to illness and other causes (a feverish cold, for instance, prevented him from doing any work for ten days), was no more than about seven weeks. It was his habit to compose only in the morning; in the afternoon he would take a walk; the evening he would spend with friends, generally the Wesendonks (at that time living at the Hôtel Baur au Lac), to whom he would sometimes play what he had written earlier in the day. As the vocal score of the *Rhinegold* runs, in an ordinary edi-

---

[14] The fullest and most authoritative account as yet available of Wagner's way of working, from sketch to full score, will be found, with a number of facsimiles of the manuscripts, in Otto Strobel's article in SGW, pp. 27–39.

tion such as that of Breitkopf & Härtel, to some 270 pages, he must therefore have composed at an average rate of about five pages each morning, and this in an idiom for which there was no precedent in opera, with new problems of construction of all kinds confronting him. How a feat of this sort could be performed by anyone " composing at the piano " it may be left to the believer in that grotesque legend to explain. Wagner used the piano now and then, as all composers do, to try out audibly what he had put on paper. But the piano sometimes served a further purpose in his case: the *sound* of the music somehow helped him to recall, from the background of his memory, passages, and the connecting matter between passages, that he had shaped for himself in weeks or months or years gone by as he brooded over the characters and episodes of his work; it helped him, in fact, to get into the cataleptic state that is necessary for artistic creation of the finest kind.[15]

We do not lack testimony as to the " raptus " — to employ a term that will be familiar to readers of Beethoven's life — that descended upon Wagner also, submerged and transformed him, when he was in the thick of composition.[16] Weissheimer has told us how, in Biebrich in 1862, he chanced to interrupt him during the composition of the *Meistersinger*.

> " I knocked at his door, and as he did not answer I assumed that he had gone to the hotel to dine. I was just on the point of seeking him out there when I heard a commotion inside. I knocked again. At last he appeared at the door: his features were completely changed, almost wild. ' I am in the thick of it ', he said, and ran back shyly into his bedroom, where he remained until he had calmed down."

On another occasion Weissheimer, after knocking and receiving no answer, was going away when Wagner came out on the balcony

> " and called out to me ecstatically, ' Don't disturb me now: I am in heat! ' His excitement had evidently not quite died down when, an hour later, he came into the hotel, for he gulped his food almost

---

[15] We have his own plain testimony to this effect. He told Cosima in 1874 that "When I sit down to the piano it is only to *recall* things: no new idea occurs to me there." MECW, I, 704–5.

[16] "I am spinning my cocoon like a silkworm," he wrote to Liszt on the 17th December, 1853, when he was in the thick of his work on the *Rhinegold;* "but I also spin out of myself. For five years I have written no music."

without chewing it, although he had to be particularly careful not to eat in a hurry." [17]

In one of his letters to Frau Wesendonk he described the blissful dream-state into which he was wont to fall during the hours of creation, a state in which the outer world was lost to him and he to it. It was to induce this state that he needed a certain " luxury " in his immediate surroundings and the absence of any object in the room likely to wrench him out of his dream-world into rude reality. It was for this reason that he chose for his study soft carpets and curtains that reflected a mellow light, and that he liked the room to be filled with perfume. He could not endure any object in the room the sharp lines of which were apt to cut across his dream: even books had to be removed. Every artist or thinker has his own way of creating the dream-condition and securing the concentration necessary for his work. This was Wagner's way: for other men it may be opium, or wine, or tobacco. It is only the Philistine who will sneer at Wagner for the adoption of his own means to the desired end.

---

[17] WEWL, pp. 99, 100.

CHAPTER XX

WAGNER'S FINANCES IN ZÜRICH

1

HIS ACTIVITIES in connection with Zürich music in the November of 1853 have already been set forth.[1] These of themselves must have interfered somewhat with his work on the *Rhinegold:* but before that was ended he had to pass through so bitter an experience that we can only wonder at the self-detachment that enabled the artist to maintain his hold on the threads of his work. The experience was not only mortifying in itself: it brought with it financial consequences of the gravest kind, that were to affect the course of his outer life for a long time to come.

The full story of his desperate attempt, in November, 1853, to raise money by selling the performing rights of *Lohengrin* outright to Breitkopf & Härtel will be told shortly. Liszt, who had put the business details personally before Dr. Härtel during a visit to Leipzig at the beginning of December, had the unpleasant duty of telling his friend on the 13th that the firm had refused the offer. They had been influenced by their friends in conservative Leipzig musical circles, and especially by the future biographer of Mozart, Otto Jahn — a man, as we can now see, of decidedly Philistine constitution.[2] The cleavage between the Wagner party and the party

---

[1] See Chapter VIII.

[2] To the *Grenzboten*, in the early days of 1853, Jahn had contributed an article on *Tannhäuser*, apropos of the "interest that the work is now creating in Leipzig", an interest that had resulted in its being given "three times in a short period of time to moderately full houses". The article, which is of a quite monumental stupidity, even for a "classicist" of that epoch, will be found in Jahn's *Gesammelte Aufsätze über Musik* (2nd ed., 1867). Further light on Jahn's narrow mind, and on his complete incompetence to deal with any but the simplest problems of musical aesthetic, is afforded by his essays, in the same volume, on *Berlioz's Faust* (1853), *Berlioz in Leipzig* (1853), and *Lohengrin* (1854).

The measure of the mediocre intelligence he brought to bear upon music may be taken by a single quotation from the passage in which he dismisses Berlioz's brilliant *Carnaval romain* overture: "What gives the Roman Carnival its irresistible charm is the immediate freshness, the inexhaustible strength of the unspoilt human nature

that now regarded itself as the divinely appointed defender of the "classical spirit" was becoming very marked in Leipzig; and, as Liszt points out to his friend, Wagner's Press champions, Pohl, Ritter, Bülow and the others, were not *personae gratae* with the cautious Härtel. The Wagnerian element in the town had been strong enough, however, to force a production of *Lohengrin* on the theatre management; and Liszt had hopes that this would be so successful as to bring about an improvement in Wagner's position in Leipzig. The omens were certainly favourable. On the 17th January, 1853, the programme at the Gewandhaus concert had included the *Lohengrin* prelude and the third scene of the first act of the opera: and as the concert was for the benefit of the orchestral players, and it is the rule on these occasions to make the programme up of works that are certain to draw an audience, it is clear that Wagner's name counted for something even in Leipzig. (This was apparently the first time anything of his had been given at a Leipzig concert for some years). So well was the music received that it was repeated at the ordinary subscription concert on the 20th. On the 31st *Tannhäuser* was produced, with such success that the opera director, Wirsing, was emboldened to attempt *Lohengrin*.

Wagner had stipulated, as in the case of Berlin some time before, that Liszt should either conduct the opera or, if this were out of the question, should have plenipotentiary powers of supervision, and even, if he saw fit, of absolute veto. These conditions were of course unacceptable to Julius Rietz, the local Kapellmeister; and he and Wirsing seem to have played a double game with Wagner and Liszt, pushing on, after a fashion, with the preparation of the work without committing themselves too definitely to either of them. After several postponements the production was fixed (at double prices) for the 7th January, 1854. Liszt, who had already been

---

that finds free outlet in exuberant mirth and merriment, without any loss of nobility, dignity or grace. What is insufferable in the Roman Carnival is the foreigners, who think they must *parforce* be boisterous and witty and indulge in droll fancies, and disturb the general joy with their tasteless excesses, so that the Romans shake their heads over these foreigners, who are perpetual barbarians, and who would be quite beyond putting up with if it were not for their money. All this came vividly once more to my mind as I listened to Berlioz's overture."

This was the type of mind that gave its "tone" to musical criticism in those days, the type, entrenched in the authority of the Press or the academic chair, against which Wagner and Berlioz had incessantly to contend.

twice tricked into journeying to Leipzig to survey the situation in Wagner's interests and to superintend the final rehearsals, was in the end able only to be present at the first performance.

His letter to Wagner the next day is one of the worst examples we have of his " diplomacy ". With his extensive experience of *Lohengrin* he must have known that the performance had been a most inadequate one: he tells Wagner, indeed, that while the first act had gone " fairly satisfactorily ", in the second and third there were " many faults and slips on the part both of the chorus and the principals "; that the second act was so " dragged " that " a lassitude in the audience was painfully perceptible "; that the tempi of the choruses in the second act were " decidedly too fast ", while there had been several actual breakdowns in this scene. Yet he not only found it in his conscience to tell his friend that the " magnificent success of the work could not be questioned: we can rejoice at that, and the rest will come gradually of itself ", but actually to ask him, if he had occasion to write to Leipzig in the next few days, to " do me the favour to adopt a friendly attitude and to recognise the good will and the success, which cannot be doubted."

A report of the production in the *Deutsche Allgemeine Zeitung* of the 10th, friendly as it was in general tone, left, however, no room for doubt in Wagner's mind that the work had in reality failed: while Pohl, in an exhaustive article in the *Neue Zeitschrift* of the 13th, bluntly told his readers that the performance had been unsatisfactory from first to last, and that it was well for the composer that he had been spared the pain of seeing with his own eyes such a degradation of his work; though, Pohl added, even a performance of this kind could not kill it. It was presumably Pohl who, as we learn from a letter of the 26th from Wagner to Röckel, informed the composer that the performance had been unspeakably bad, not a word being audible the whole evening, except from the Herald. The immediate consequences of this disgraceful affair were bad enough. But the remoter consequences were still worse; for, as Pohl said in later years, Rietz's reputation in Germany as a " sound " conductor resulted in his *Lohengrin* travesty, with its defects of style and its liberal cuts (made in later performances under him, if not in the first) being taken as a standard in other theatres.

2

Wagner was in despair when he realised the full extent of the catastrophe. " It has come to this," he wrote to Röckel, " that I regret ever having let my works go out of my hands." " I have written to Wagner ", Bülow told Liszt on the 27th January, " to tranquillise him on the subject of the fiasco of his *Lohengrin* in Leipzig. Ritter has joined me in this good work: Wagner was bursting with plans of the most irrational kind — he meant, for instance, to demand his amnesty of the King, to deliver himself up to the Government,[3] and so on: all this as the result of Hoplit's [Pohl's] article." For the first time in Wagner's correspondence we get a hint of a revolt in him against the weaker elements in Liszt's character. He felt that his friend could have put up a sterner fight with the Leipzig people had he really wished to do so. Liszt, he told Ferdinand Heine, had been too " complaisant " in the matter of the plans for him to attend the rehearsals: " it seems that notice was not given to him of these, and he has had the somewhat too diplomatic weakness to leave the affair to take its own course, good or bad." To Bülow, on the 16th January, Wagner wrote in stronger terms. He gives Liszt credit for kindly intentions in glossing over the fiasco as he had done. But, he continues bitterly,

" it is assuredly a joy to know oneself maltreated and mocked with the noblest thing one has: this time, unfortunately, much depended on this joy being spared me! Liszt has behaved in the matter in a way that is rather incomprehensible to me. He seems not to have understood rightly the conditions under which I granted *Lohengrin* to Leipzig: he was to have gone there as my *alter ego*, with the right even of veto. The fatal thing in him is that only in the rarest cases can he bring himself really to fall out with anyone, when that happens to be necessary. He understood my conditions perfectly well — perhaps because he saw that they would not agree to them in Leipzig: but why then did we not put an end at once to the whole affair? Did he look upon the Leipzig production as a necessity, even if it should

---

[3] To Frau Ritter, on the 20th January, Wagner had written: "the day before yesterday I very nearly wrote to the King of Saxony asking for an amnesty. Naturally this did not last long. Then I had it in my mind to go straight off to Germany, and if no other course were possible, to let myself be taken." To such despair had he been reduced by the thought of his impotence, as an exile, to control the German productions of his *Lohengrin*.

turn out badly? Comic politics! Now I have it: it is clear to me that he did not make the slightest use of my stipulation, for he advised me to write to Rietz(!) with regard to putting him right as respects certain tempi(!) which he had so completely mistaken that often they were turned upside down. Consequently either Liszt was not at any of the rehearsals or — he was so weak as not to make a *single* protest. This is sad! " [4]

It is curious that in *Mein Leben* Wagner makes no mention whatever of this Leipzig " outrage ", as he calls it in his letters of the period. He merely records, apropos of the weeks when he was working at the *Rhinegold*, that there had been little change in his home life, where everything was running quite smoothly, but that

" at this time I once more experienced some embarrassment in my economic affairs, because in the preceding year I had counted much too surely, as regards both my household furnishing and my manner of living, on the continuance and increase of my receipts from the theatres for my works. Unfortunately, however, the largest and best-paying theatres still held back: during this year it became painfully clear to me that I could not arrive anywhere with Berlin and Vienna. In consequence, during a great part of the year I was plagued with cares of all kinds."

His financial affairs had, in fact, reached a crisis, the origins and consequences of which must now be described in full. But for these money troubles he would almost certainly not have interrupted his work upon the *Ring* in order to conduct concerts in London in the spring of 1855.

3

Although, of course, he was never more than what most people would regard as a poor man in his Zürich period, taking it as a whole, Wagner was never destitute. He made a trifle occasionally by a book or an article, or by conducting; [5] and for two or three

---

[4] RWHB, pp. 40, 41.

[5] The fees paid to him for his concert work in Zürich do not seem to have erred on the side of generosity even when the standards of the time are taken into consideration. After he had conducted the Beethoven No. 7 on the 15th January, 1850, the committee met to consider what his reward should be. It was at first thought that a mere written expression of thanks would be enough; but after a debate it was agreed to give him, in addition, four ten-gulden pieces (about 83 francs). In February, 1851, he received fifteen napoleons (300 francs) for his services at the two concerts: Bülow, for playing Liszt's piano transcription of the *Tannhäuser* overture, was paid 25 francs!

years after 1851, when one German theatre after another was taking up his operas, he derived quite a fair income from this source. The average payment per theatre, however, was no more than about 16 Louisdor. We have seen that in the autumn of 1851 Frau Julie Ritter, who had been making him a small allowance ever since the summer of 1850, was delighted to be able to guarantee him an income of 800 thalers (3,000 francs) a year, which was about half his salary as Kapellmeister in Dresden. Liszt was able to help occasionally in the early Zürich days, not so much out of his own funds, which were relatively small, as through the medium of the Grand Duke of Weimar, by way of " gifts from an anonymous admirer " or an advance payment for works to be performed.

An income of 3,000 francs a year does not seem much to-day on which to support existence; but the salaries of musicians and intellectuals generally were low in those days and living was cheap, and one gathers that Wagner could at least have kept starvation from the door on Frau Ritter's allowance. The life of the ordinary musician was a hard one in Germany in the first half of the nineteenth century and for some time after: if ever men " scorned delights and lived laborious days " it was they. Moritz Hauptmann, in 1827 (in Cassel), received about half a thaler for an hour's teaching. Peter Cornelius was paid at the same rate in Berlin in 1849. His incomings averaged 25–30 thalers a month: he lived, he tells a correspondent, from hand to mouth, rarely having 5 or 10 thalers put by: the second half of each month was always a time of strain and anxiety. And these small sums could be earned only by running from one end of Berlin to another to pupils' houses! Often the poor musical proletarian, as Cornelius calls him, was glad to " make music " in some well-to-do bourgeois' house for a little soup or bread.[6] To many struggling musicians of that epoch, Wagner's pension from Frau Ritter would have seemed a reasonable competency.[7]

In May, 1852, Wagner received 300 francs for three concerts. For the two concerts in which he took part in the winter of 1852–3 he was rewarded with a coffee service of the value of 273 francs. In April, 1854, he received 500 francs for six concerts.

[6] See his letter of the 25th December, 1849, to Hestermann, in CABT, I, 104 ff.

[7] When Nietzsche had to resign his Basel professorship of classical philology in 1879 he received a pension of only 3,000 francs. Fortunately for him, he had a modest private income.

Wagner was always convinced that popularity and prosperity were waiting for him round the corner; and he could have made rather more money than he did if only he could have brought himself to put his artistic idealism in his pocket. But he would generally rather forgo a fee than grant permission for a work of his to be given under conditions which he had reason to believe would be inadequate; and more than once he saved his artistic conscience at a considerable pecuniary sacrifice. In April, 1851, Frau Ritter, who had five children to maintain, had had to warn him regretfully that there was a possibility of her not being able to help him for more than another year. He was grateful to her, he wrote, for even that respite; he looked forward to the future without dismay, for he had daily evidence, he said, that his popularity was increasing: he had found a publisher for *Lohengrin*, and he hoped that not only his operas but his prose writings would bring him in something. When, seven or eight months later, she tells him that she can now guarantee him 800 thalers a year, he is filled with a new confidence as to the future: now, he says, he can proceed with the bold artistic plans that are taking place within him. It is true that even while he is thanking her for her generosity in the matter of the new allowance he is compelled to ask her for a trifle of 300 thalers immediately — an " oblation ", as he puts it, rendered necessary by the failure of his hopes with regard to a Weimar contract.

Later, on the 4th April, 1852, he tells her that it is she who makes it possible for him to do what he is now doing,

> " for you alone make it possible for me to work in independence. Thanks to you, I do not need to work for money, and only so can I work at all: it is wholly owing to you, for example, that I can give the *Flying Dutchman* here, for thanks to you I can disdain an honorarium, and thus take up the one position that makes such an undertaking possible — the position of complete independence, of concern only with the deed itself."

In the following December, speaking of the recent reawakening of his eternal longing for a little house and garden of his own, in which he will be able to find the necessary quiet for his work, he tells her that Otto Wesendonk has offered to advance him money enough to buy a piece of land, but he dares not accept it. It is true, he says, that he could repay it out of his future receipts from the theatres; but he fears being placed, in that case, in the " terrible situation " of having to consent to performances on any consideration, instead of refusing his permission, as at present, unless he can look forward to " a success in *my* sense of the word." It is possible, he thinks, that as a result of his idealism the theatres will soon cease to be interested in him.

> " In these circumstances ", he continues, " I realise more than ever the value of the allowance made to me by your family, for it is this alone that ensures me freedom and a certain amount of serenity in my dealings. Rest assured once more that I look upon your care for me as the greatest benefit that has ever befallen me."

4

It seems clear from all this that at any rate the basic necessities of existence were secured for him by Frau Ritter's subsidy. But Richard Wagner could never be satisfied with the mere basic necessities for long. When the German theatres began to take up *Tannhäuser* his inveterate optimism made him assume that the process would go on indefinitely, and that as soon as the four operas of his first period had gone the whole round he would be ready with the *Ring*. He accordingly launched out into an expenditure on his house in the Zeltweg 13 that of necessity left him with heavy debts on his hands when the demands from the theatres slowed down. And as landlords and tradespeople became more pressing in their requests for a sight of the colour of his money he had no recourse but to appeal to his friends for assistance. He was astonishingly successful: well might Bülow call him a " genius of finance ", who in each fresh need found fresh sources to tap. Steiner protests, with justice, against Chamberlain's cursory handling of the Zürich period and his slighting references to the help given Wagner by his friends there.

> " That all these friendships had something unsatisfactory about them ", says Chamberlain, " is explained by the very natural circumstance that these worthy helpers in need did not fully realise *whom* they were helping, their good deeds being motived, so to speak, only by a sense of duty. They did not help him unconditionally, as

Liszt did: perhaps a great impulse was lacking in their generosities, in which there was a suspicion of playing the Maecenas; and so these relationships were dissolved one after another by the Master himself. . . ." [8]

The mean shaft — the full meanness of it will be manifest later — was aimed primarily at the memory of Otto Wesendonk; but Chamberlain's injustice, which is to say Wahnfried's injustice, towards the other Zürich friends is no less gross. They all helped Wagner according to their means; and it is hardly credible that they placed their purses and their services at his disposal as they did unless they had some inkling of his unique powers and considerable sympathy with his idealism. If, on the other hand, they had neither, if they helped this mendicant stranger in their midst from no motives but those of common humanity, misunderstanding the artist but being filled with pity for the man, their generosity deserves all the more recognition to-day. The full extent of his obligations to his Zürich friends has only recently become even approximately known.

He himself confesses that Liszt, on his visit to Zürich in July, 1853, raised his eyebrows slightly at the sight of what he called *la petite élégance* of Wagner's house-furnishings; [9] and Otto Wesendonk, in a letter of the 26th June of that year to Sulzer, con-

---

[8] CRW, pp. 61–2. Chamberlain's mind was constructed for the weaving of fancies rather than for the reconstruction of the actual. He confessedly despised biographical details, yet could not see that this constitutional bias on his part unfitted him for the writing of biography. He admitted, for instance, that he had not the slightest interest in "the Albert Wagners, the Laubes, the Dorns, the Stahrs, the Pechts, the Meyerbeers, the Schlesingers, the Lüttichaus," etc., and felt that nobody mattered very much in Wagner's life until Liszt came on the scene. (See his letter of the 27th March, 1895, to Cosima, in WHSC, p. 402). All the others, he said, would be ignored by the biographer of 2895. Which is all very well; but Chamberlain saw that even a professed biography of Wagner on Chamberlainistic lines must concern itself to some degree with facts; and when he was compelled to touch upon these he was far too prone to draw upon his imagination, or be content with mere half-knowledge. Mathilde Wesendonk, who knew well for how many services, financial and others, Wagner had been indebted to his Zürich friends, wrote Chamberlain a dignified letter of protest at his handling of the Zürich period. Chamberlain's self-exculpatory reply was the merest bluff. See the letters in WHSC, pp. 431–435.

[9] In the Zeltweg he appears to have gratified his usual passion for heavy and rich-coloured curtains and hangings, and to have permitted himself a few indulgences in the matter of *objets d'art* and knick-knacks. Gottfried Keller was struck by "a silver hair-brush in a crystal bowl." It would all have looked harmless enough to any visitor who did not know that it had been done on tradesmen's credit or on borrowed money; but manifestly it was a little more than Liszt had expected from a man in Wagner's economic position.

fesses that he used to feel more comfortable in the old house (No. 11) than he does in the new one (No. 13). It must have been evident to everyone that Wagner was living beyond his means; and probably his richer friends were uneasy at the thought that part, at any rate, of this expenditure had been incurred in order to entertain them becomingly. But another reason than this, another reason than even the desire for a little luxury for its own pleasant sake, may be suggested for Wagner's growing extravagance at this time. Not only did his abnormally sensitive physical organisation make it difficult for him to compose during the winter — we know that his skin was morbidly susceptible to cold — but he could not get the mental machine going without a certain amount of comfort and elegance in his home. If he was to compose, he needed plenty of light and warmth, good carpets and curtains, and so on; [10] when he fled from his Vienna creditors, in March, 1864, to Frau Wille's house at Mariafeld, he broke out exasperatedly one day against the world that denied him the luxuries that were a necessity to him if he was to do his work. He was organised, he said, differently from the ordinary run of musicians — from a Mozart or a Schubert, who could compose unconcernedly in the direst penury and the most squalid surroundings.

> " I have excitable nerves; I must have beauty, brilliance, light. The world ought to give me what I need. I cannot live in a wretched organist's post like your Meister Bach. Is it an unheard-of demand if I hold that the little luxury I like is my due? I, who am procuring enjoyment to the world and to thousands? " [11]

We have seen that it was in the summer of 1853 that, the *Ring* poem having at last achieved its own complete digestion within him, he began to experience an irresistible desire to start composing again after an interval of five years. It may well be, then, that in large part it was this desire to get into the right frame of mind for composition that led him to indulge himself in a certain amount of household luxury. Certain it is that not only were his friends, who, for all their admiration of him, hardly understood his peculiar

---

[10] It may not be too far-fetched a conjecture that the heavy curtains and portières of which he was so fond gave him an agreeable sense of temporary seclusion from the world that treated him so roughly.

[11] RWEW, pp. 74, 75.

mentality, inclined to shake their heads over his extravagance, but his enemies, who did not understand him at all and had no desire to do so, were maliciously making the most of it. One Jakob Reithard, taking a characteristically mean and Philistine view of Wagner's disinterested attempts to improve the orchestral music of the town — which necessarily implied an expenditure that the notables of the place would be called upon to meet — hinted maliciously, in a letter of the 16th November, 1853, to Xaver Schnyder von Wartensee, that Wagner was also making demands on the purses of his fellow-citizens for other than public purposes:

> " So much is certain, that in the higher circles of society they are already talking doubtfully about the frightful debts of the Flying Dutchman, and the unbecoming luxury with which he surrounds himself. They are beginning to express a portentous sympathy with his wife, who suffers keenly under his tyrannical extravagance in domestic matters — so keenly that, placid as she is by nature, she is sometimes driven to call him half-crazy, and to find the sacrifice of a burnt-out brain for a famous name a trifle excessive." [12]

Making all allowances for personal enmity on the part of people like Reithard, it is evident enough that Wagner's " luxury " was at this time a subject of general comment in Zürich. In July, 1853, the Vienna police, whose spies were of course very active in a town harbouring so many political refugees as Zürich did, made a report on him to Privy Councillor Körner, one of the officials attached to the Saxon Ministry of the Interior, whose duty it was to attend to offences against public order.

> " Strange reports ", they said, " are again circulating about Richard Wagner. In Zürich he not only lives in ostentatious luxury but also purchases the most valuable articles, such as gold watches, at enormous prices. His apartments are adorned with the finest furniture, carpets, silk curtains and chandeliers; all this creates the utmost astonishment and curiosity among the simple natives of the republic, who cannot help wondering where this man, who was so poor when he came to Zürich, gets his money from. He himself gives it out that he has received a good deal from the performances of his operas in Germany, but on strict investigation this has been found to be untrue: the few theatres that venture to perform his operas pay him

---

[12] See FWSZ, I, 396.

nothing; nor can his literary works bring him in anything, as he generally prints only some fifty or a hundred copies at his own expense." [13]

The police spy conjectures that he must be secretly supported by " one of the princely houses of Germany ", and indulges in an obvious falsehood when he adds that Wagner is " trying to bring about a revolution by means of his art, and to this end is co-operating with all the literary and artistic leaders of propaganda."

The police agent, who had certainly never been in Wagner's apartments, is obviously repeating and exaggerating the tittle-tattle of the town. But though the amount of smoke may have been grossly excessive for the size of the fire, a fire of some sort there manifestly was. Wagner was once more living very much beyond his means. It is accordingly not surprising to find him, a few months later, going through one of his periodical financial crises.

5

The storm had been working up for a long time. It was on the strength of his receipts from the German theatres and his hopes for the future that he had indulged himself in 1852 and 1853 in an expenditure beyond his means. In June, 1853, however, the implacable Saxon authorities had re-issued the *Steckbrief* of 1849; the result was that some of the more prudent among the German theatre directors began to be less desirous of having their names linked with that of the " traitor " who was to be arrested and sent to Dresden if he were found on German soil. His excursions to Italy and Paris in the summer and autumn of 1853 must have involved him in a certain amount of debt: we have seen him, for instance, borrowing at least 600 francs from Sulzer in October of that year.

His difficulties evidently came to a head on his return to Zürich in November, for on the 16th of that month we find him laying the whole case before Liszt. He is so happy in his work on the *Ring,* he says, that he hates to be compelled to abandon it for a single day. If, however, this frame of mind is to last, he *must* put his money affairs in order: this he can do by selling *en bloc* his future receipts from the theatres for *Lohengrin.* He has no doubt that, in time, this

---

[13] LWV, p. 45.

opera will sweep the theatres as *Tannhäuser* has done. But unfortunately his sanguine temperament always leads him to anticipate receipts. The result is that heavy accounts will have to be met at Christmas, without his being able to reckon positively on a single thaler coming in just when he wants it. He can endure this financial sickness no longer: a radical cure is necessary, and Liszt must help him to it by inducing Breitkopf & Härtel to buy from him the performing rights of *Lohengrin*. These rights have already been sold to Weimar, Dresden, Wiesbaden, and Leipzig, and he must further except the Court theatres in Berlin, Vienna and Munich from the agreement: these he will negotiate with himself. But there will remain to Breitkopfs all the theatres " that have already had a success with *Tannhäuser* " or will soon be performing that work. In view of the hard-dying legend that Wagner had no success until after his death, the list of the theatres, besides Dresden, that had already bought the opera from him is interesting. They were these: Schwerin, Breslau, Frankfort, Düsseldorf, Riga, Rostock, Prague, Freiburg, Cassel, Königsberg, Danzig, Stettin, Bremen, Cologne, Magdeburg, Hamburg, Reval, Darmstadt, Carlsruhe, Ballenstedt, Würzburg, and Grätz. The theatres to which he confidently counts on selling *Tannhäuser* shortly are Brunswick, Hanover, Mannheim, Coburg, Stuttgart, Dessau, Pesth, Brünn, Linz, Aachen, Mainz, Augsburg, Nuremberg, Posen, and Lemberg.

The fees he has received from the twenty-two theatres in the first list range from 10 Louisdor in the case of the smallest, such as Magdeburg and Würzburg, to 25 in the case of such as Frankfort and Cassel, and 50 in the case of Hamburg.[14] These, he says, are at least the fees they would have to pay for *Lohengrin*. For the fifteen theatres in the second list, the fees for either *Tannhäuser* or *Lohengrin* would run from a minimum of 10 Louisdor to a maximum of 40.

Before the modern world censures Wagner for his borrowings, it ought, then, to remember that had German composers in those days received anything like justice at the hands of the theatres, a continuing royalty being paid them as is the case to-day, Wagner

---

[14] With Hamburg he had compounded future royalties for a lump sum, as he was in great need of money at the time.

would have been able to live comfortably for a considerable time on *Tannhäuser* alone.

From the twenty-two theatres he has received 362 Louisdor, he continues in his letter to Liszt. From the other fifteen he can reasonably expect another 270 Louisdor, making a total of 632 as the performing value of *Tannhäuser* in the German-speaking theatres. He holds himself to be justified in regarding *Lohengrin* as of the same potential value, for wherever it has been given it has been considered superior to *Tannhäuser*. He suggests (1) that Breitkopf shall bring out " morçeaux détachés " from *Lohengrin*, as is done with all popular operas; in view of the peculiar continuity of the music of *Lohengrin*, he himself will make these selections and write the necessary introductions and endings to them; (2) that instead of sharing the proceeds of the libretti with him, — which, in the case of *Tannhäuser*, have had an extraordinary sale, no fewer than 6,000 having been taken by Breslau alone in a single winter — the firm shall buy his rights in the books for a lump sum; (3) that they shall buy outright the performing rights of *Lohengrin*, not only for the German but for all foreign theatres with the exception of London and Paris. The grand total he asks for is 15,000 francs (the actual or anticipated fees from the thirty-seven German theatres in Wagner's list alone amount to about 13,000 francs, or 632 Louisdor). This amount he wants by the 20th December, so that he may pay off his debts and have something to live on while he is writing the *Ring*. He thinks his demand quite reasonable in a business sense: and the future was to justify him. The deal with Breitkopf fell through, however: the most they did was to pay him, early in January, 1854, 300 thalers for the arrangements he had made of nine " lyrical pieces for solo voice " from *Lohengrin*.[15] They declined, however, to publish some transcriptions from the opera made by Bülow for piano solo, perhaps, as Liszt suggested in his letter of the 13th December to Wagner, because Bülow was not in good odour in Leipzig academic musical circles, owing to his fiery articles in the *Neue Zeitschrift*.

---

[15] For the fullest information as to his dealings with Breitkopf & Härtel during this period see the correspondence in RWBV, Vol. I.

Wagner thought the firm had been quite "flush with their money", he told Liszt: "but", he added, "what use are hundreds to me, when I need thousands?"

It was in the spring of 1852 that what Wagner called " the hail-storm " — the demand for *Tannhäuser* by the German theatres — had set in. In about eighteen months, then, he had received, and spent, some 360 Louisdor (7,500 francs = £300) in addition to the various sums he had made by conducting and so on, and in addition to Frau Ritter's subsidy of 3,000 francs a year. Taking into consideration the average level of income among intellectuals and the average standard of living in those days, he ought, then, not only to have been quite comfortably circumstanced for the time being, but to have saved a little money. Instead of that, he had piled up a mountain of debt, as is evident from some recently published letters of himself and his Swiss friends.

The immediate and disastrous effect of the *Lohengrin* fiasco in Leipzig was that not only did Breitkopf & Härtel take fright, but the Berlin publishing firm Bote & Bock, whom Wagner had sounded through his agent Michaelson, and who had been nibbling quite promisingly at his offer of the performing rights of his works, also withdrew into their shell after the Leipzig catastrophe: they were naturally cautious about purchasing the rights in a work that for the moment looked like becoming a drug in the German market. Wagner suddenly found himself in a financial position of the utmost embarrassment, and even danger. In January, 1854, he was being hard pressed by the firms who had supplied his house-furnishings, and he had to send out desperate appeals for the quick payment of theatre fees to Gustave Schmidt in Frankfort and Louis Schindelmeisser in Wiesbaden.[16]

On the 17th January he made a passionate appeal to Liszt to help him to find someone who would buy his theatrical prospects outright for an immediate sum. Liszt, he said, understood him as an artist, whereas the " Philistines " — by which he meant his Zürich friends — could not do so. Liszt, one cannot help thinking,

---

[16] "Shamefaced as I feel towards you," he writes to Schindelmeisser on the 13th January, 1854, " — for you really shame me by the so-quick decision to give *Lohengrin* in Darmstadt — I must all the same beg you to arrange for the payment of the honorarium for this, for, as usual, I urgently need money: I can't and won't live my last years like a dog! I hope you [i.e. the theatre] can give me 25 Louisdor, as you did for *Tannhäuser*. . . . (Between ourselves — if you can somehow bamboozle your treasurer into sending me the money *at once*, you would be doing me a favour"). RWFZ, p. 143.

might have made an effort to interest one of his own innumerable rich friends in the distracted artist: but all he does [17] is to hold out hopes of Berlin taking up *Lohengrin*, express once more his belief in Wagner's future, and ask him (1) whether he has any pressing debts, and if so, what amount he needs for the immediate liquidation of them; (2) if he can manage to last out the remainder of the year with his present income. Wagner's reply, on the 4th March, is that he has had to give tradesmen and others bills which will fall due in the middle of April, " and God knows how I am to meet them! " He may possibly scrape through to the autumn, when receipts will begin to come in again from the theatres. Can Liszt help him to get a loan of 5,000 francs somewhere? He has exhausted the capacity of his Zürich friends: Sulzer has even been placed in considerable difficulty by Wagner's inability to repay what he had borrowed from him.

Once more all that Liszt can do is to hold out hopes for *Lohengrin* in Berlin: he has heard also that the Königsberg company projected taking *Tannhäuser* there in the summer. But as he simultaneously advised Wagner to adhere to his old resolution not to allow Berlin to give any of his works except under Liszt's supervision, he cannot, in his heart of hearts, have really hoped for much in this quarter.

Wagner tells him, in reply, that following on the production of *Tannhäuser* in Augsburg, Dingelstedt is desirous of giving that work in Munich. Can Liszt use his good offices with Dingelstedt to secure not only royalties for him but an immediate advance in respect of them, or, failing that, to compound with him for a lump sum of 100 Louisdor? But the Munich plan, like so many others, came to nothing: and Wagner, now thoroughly desperate, had to appeal for rescue to those " Philistines " in Zürich to whom he had been ungratefully unjust in his letter to Liszt, and injustice towards whom became an article of the true faith in Wagner circles in later years.

---

[17] It must be borne in mind, however, that Liszt himself was passing through a very difficult period just then: it looked for the moment as if the Princess would be deprived of all her Russian property.

6

In July and August, 1854, he had two bills for 1,500 francs each to meet, and no funds with which to meet them. A desperate attempt to induce Breitkopf & Härtel to make him an advance failed; Wagner could not have gone to the musical festival in Sitten in July had not Liszt sent him 500 francs. The good Sulzer, discouraging as his financial relations with him had been, came once more to the rescue. He wrote to Otto Wesendonk, who at that time was in Schwalbach (Nassau), asking him to join him in helping Wagner. Wesendonk, in his reply of the 26th June, makes it clear enough, as we have seen, that he, like everyone else, had had his doubts about the wisdom of Wagner's expenditure on his new rooms. He had granted him a loan, however, in May, 1853, and another at the end of the year, "which he promised to repay at Easter." Wesendonk had been grieved at Wagner's manifest unhappiness, and was sincerely anxious to help him to regulate his financial affairs; he had, however, shown him clearly that he did not approve of his way of living. At Easter, 1854, Wagner had had to confess that he had been disappointed in his hope of soon being in funds; whereupon Otto, speaking as " a practical business man ", gave him the sage advice that it was as well not to take problematical future receipts into one's balance sheet as certainties, but to make up one's budget in accordance with realities. Otto cancelled the debt, and said that he and Wagner's other friends would now be rejoiced to see him win the peace of mind that was necessary for the continuance of his work. As he had heard that Wagner owed money also to one Kölliker, he begged him to tell him precisely how he stood so that he might advise him as to the future.

Wagner appears to have avoided this rather embarrassing inquisition, and the next thing Otto hears, as he tells Sulzer, is that " Wagner has a whole heap of debts, far, far beyond the sums you mention "; included in them was one to his tailor for about 1,000 francs. The much-enduring Otto was rather scandalised, but he was still willing to do what he could for Wagner, in conjunction with Sulzer; the first thing, of course, was to discover the real extent of his debts. " This much, however, is clear," he writes: " no money must be handed over to Wagner himself. . . . The best thing would be for him to be granted a regular allowance of moderate amount, which will compel him to think about augmenting his income." [18] Otto had already thought of arranging for all moneys to pass through Minna's hands; but he feared that this humiliation of Wagner on his own hearth might not conduce to domestic harmony. This, he concludes, is the situation as it now is: " my pure good nature has reached its limits; and if I may permit myself a word of blame it is that he has too little regard for his friends, or he would not get himself into a situation towards them that is so painful for them all."

Matters appear to have moved slowly, for in the following September we find Wagner asking Sulzer to communicate to Wesendonk " the financial result of our last arrangement "; apparently he did not quite like the idea of tackling the business-like Otto direct. He had already borrowed 1,000 thalers from Karl Ritter, but this was insufficient for his needs; so on the 14th September he had to lay the whole position bare to Sulzer. He admitted that the beginning of his troubles was the expenditure upon his house-furnishing in 1853, which he excuses on the grounds that he needed a certain surrounding luxury to help him in his creative work. He would be willing now to sell all he has to satisfy his creditors, but that would necessitate his leaving Zürich; and he fears this would be a deathblow to Minna. He needs 10,000 francs, exclusive of a debt to Sulzer — 7,000 for local requirements, 3,000 to fulfil his promise to repay Karl by the end of October. If this sum can be raised for him, he will repay it out of his receipts from the theatres, which should amount before long to at least 21,000 francs, not reckoning what Berlin may some day yield: but he himself will need, out of these receipts, 2,000 francs a year for three years for household expenses. Then he suddenly remembers that he has to meet, next day, a bill for 500 francs! To do so he had reckoned on a fee from Breslau for *Lohengrin.* As this has not yet arrived, will Sulzer advance the amount to him? He will go to ruin, he concludes, unless his friends come to his assistance.

As a result of Sulzer's intervention, Wesendonk sent the latter,

---

[18] This ought to be all the easier, he says, as Wagner already has a yearly allowance of 300 thalers [from Frau Ritter]. In fact it was 800 thalers.

on the 29th September, 7,000 francs to be applied to " the liquidation of our friend's debts ", against the hypothecation of the fees for future performances of his operas, out of which Wagner is to receive 500 francs quarterly for the defrayal of his household expenses.

Two days later, however, a bomb drops on the astonished Sulzer. Wagner now tells him that on looking into his accounts he had discovered that he had made " an unfortunate mistake " in estimating his debts at 10,000 francs: he had overlooked sundry small accounts, amounting in all to another 342 francs. The 500 francs he hopes to receive shortly from the Breslau theatre he asks to be allowed to retain in his own hands as the first quarter of the proposed allowance, for he has 350 francs to pay at once to his landlord. He recognises that in future he must live within his allowance; but the extra 342 francs are a present necessity. Sulzer passes the interesting news on to Wesendonk. The latter is obviously astonished and hurt; but he authorises Sulzer to pay the 342 francs on his account, on Wagner's word of honour that the whole tale has now been told. Sulzer is to tell Wagner that in no circumstances will Otto listen to further appeals, and that he relies on the arrangement as to theatre royalties and the quarterly allowance being scrupulously observed.

> " I believe ", he says, " that Wagner fully intends now to keep strictly within his income and to incur no more debts. But I believe also that it will do no harm to let him understand that I will not be responsible for any future debts of his, and that I hope we shall all be spared the pain of hearing any more about such things and having to discuss them. In future I will not concern myself with them, and if Wagner, after the present settlement of his affairs, again brings distress on himself and his friends, he will have only himself to thank if they leave him to himself."

But even this was not the end. Otto paid not only the 342 francs but, the next day, the 350 francs that Wagner owed for rent. In sending the money to Sulzer he insists once more that Wagner shall carry out strictly the arrangements made on his behalf, and reiterates that in no circumstances will he open his purse again. " You and I have had vexations enough over it all, and we must at last become hard. If Wagner has any understanding at all of our sentiments towards him, he will keep a watch on himself in future for his own sake and for ours." [19]

The friends obviously could not have been expected to do more than they did. The wonder is that they were willing to do so much, for Sulzer's means at this time were only moderate, while Wesendonk, from whom Wagner had begun to borrow in May, 1853, had made the latter's acquaintance a bare year and a quarter before that date. In the light of all these and other facts, Wagner's treatment of Otto Wesendonk in *Mein Leben* leaves a very unpleasant taste in the mouth.

7

As for his debts in Dresden, he had virtually washed his hands of these. His view of the matter, to which it would be not only uncharitable but unjust not to pay due regard, was that his creditors there were secured by the arrangement made with his publisher Meser; but the bovine Meser was sadly incompetent either to find new markets for the scores or to go half-way to meet the fair demand that had sprung up for them. For a time there was an estrangement between Wagner and the good Pusinelli over this affair; [20] it was apparently not until 1853 that friendly relations were once more established between them.

Wagner's argument, from that date onward, was that if the creditors would only light a fire under the sluggish Meser the business could be made to pay, and all the creditors would in time be satisfied: it looks as if Meser, unable to cope with the situation in all its bearings, and resenting having to find more capital for the new printings that were occasionally called for, took the simple course

---

[19] The correspondence was published for the first time in 1934, in FWSZ, pp. 296 ff., 403 ff. The letters that follow those dealt with above seem to suggest that Wagner was involved in new difficulties immediately: as usual, he was too optimistic about the immediate future, and kept taking prospects into his balance sheet as cash assets.

Apparently Wesendonk had declined to liquidate the debt to Karl Ritter. In consequence, the payments for the 1st November, 1854, 1st May and 1st November, 1855, in respect of the pension from Frau Ritter were withheld. This, of course, meant fresh embarrassment for Wagner.

[20] See the extraordinary passage in Wagner's letter to Uhlig of the 15th September, 1851, in RWAP, pp. 37–9. This passage was omitted from the official edition of the Uhlig letters.

of retaining the proceeds of sale for himself, as the first creditor, and letting the others rage as they liked. Wagner was probably right in his contention that now there was a fair demand for the scores, all that was necessary was for the practical side of the business to be taken out of Meser's hands. He accordingly asked Pusinelli to call the other creditors together and get them to elect a representative to act vigorously in their own interests. The three principal creditors seem to have been Pusinelli himself, the actor Kriete, and the Dresden Opera oboist Hiebendahl. To Kriete he was indebted to the tune of 2,000 thalers, representing the savings of the actor's wife, the former Henriette Wüst. The sufferings of this unfortunate pair were a grief to the tender heart of Wagner; so he airily suggested to Pusinelli, in the spring of 1853, that *he* should stand aside for their benefit:

> " I feel especially distressed about them ", he writes: " hence I appeal to your generosity with the request that you not only take general charge of the matter yourself [i.e. the appointment of a receiver], but also first of all resign yourself as much as possible to renouncing in Kriete's favour your own share in the receipts anticipated, as long as it will be possible for you to do so without injuring your own interests too much. By doing this you would take an unusual burden from my heart."

The request seems, on the face of it, not to be lacking in assurance; but we must constantly bear in mind that Wagner had no doubt whatever that the creditors would all be fully reimbursed if the business was properly managed, and that in his view all he was asking the affluent Pusinelli to do was to stand aside for a little while for the benefit of one who was less well off than himself.

On the 30th September, 1853, the affair was concluded in the way suggested by Wagner: to Pusinelli, Kriete and Hiebendahl he assigned all his " literary rights " in the three operas published by Meser — that is to say, in the printed words and music, the right to sell the scores for performance being still vested in himself. But in 1855 Hiebendahl, believing that as a result of Wagner's engagement as conductor of the London Philharmonic concerts he was better off than he really was, began to make trouble. He was a creditor for only 400 thalers; but Wagner was unable to meet the bill drawn on him for that amount, because, as he explained to Pusinelli, by that time he had assigned to Otto Wesendonk all his prospective earnings of every kind in return for the guarantee of a small allowance that was barely sufficient to keep him alive and enable him to proceed with his work. By the following year the oboist's claim had been reduced to 300 thalers, for which amount he threatened to sue Wagner; and once more the harried man had to ask Pusinelli to " relieve him of this coarse fellow." Seemingly Pusinelli was unable to do so, for the next we hear of the matter is that Hiebendahl has entrusted the collection of his debt to one Müller, in Berne, who began to put pressure upon Wagner. The latter again appealed to Pusinelli to come to his help, or, if that should be impossible, to apply to Karl Ritter, who was at that time in Dresden on a visit to his mother. In the end, Karl advanced about 400 thalers to pay off Hiebendahl. " This amount was to be repaid to Ritter within a year out of the profits anticipated from the Dresden publishing business, with the additional proviso that, should the money fail to be forthcoming from this source, it would be deducted by Ritter from the annual allowance of 800 thalers paid by his mother, Frau Julie Ritter, to Wagner." [21]

8

As to what Wagner's other creditors in Dresden were doing about his debts to them we have little information, though one Henniger, a tailor, seems to have been disagreeably active about this time. With the debts originally contracted by reason of the publishing venture only Pusinelli and Kriete were now concerned, Meser, in the early part of 1856, having shuffled off this mortal coil and gone, one hopes, to a better land where there were no musicians of the future to plague him. But Kriete now seems to have made up his mind to adopt the technique so successfully exploited by Hiebendahl; in October of this year he told his attorney to proceed against

[21] RWAP, p. 56. Mr Lenrow's volume should be consulted for closer details about Meser and the other Dresden creditors. Many of the letters to Pusinelli are published for the first time in RWAP; passages that were omitted from the official reprint of the letters are restored; and the correct names are given of the persons who, in the official version, were indicated only by an initial or an X. The guesses of earlier commentators as to the identity of these people were sometimes wrong.

Wagner for repayment of his 2,000 thalers plus interest for twelve years. Wagner, of course, could do nothing but implore Pusinelli to take this fresh and final burden on his own shoulders. He himself was even more than usually embarrassed just then, for he had had to submit to the deduction from his pension of the 400 thalers advanced by the Ritters, the sales of the scores not having sufficed to liquidate this obligation. Once more, in justice to Wagner, we must remember that, as he saw the matter, his Dresden creditors were amply covered if they only could and would wait till his ship came home: for all the pessimism as to the future of European culture expressed in his letters to friends, he had no doubt that sooner or later his works would be in general demand, and as he had no heirs, and was not likely to have any, the profits from the sales of his scores would automatically accrue to the benefit of his creditors until his debts were paid in full. In this, as in so many other matters, history has proved the accuracy of his reasoning; and it might have been well for Pusinelli had he seen the logic of it. " You are a man of means now ", Wagner wrote to him on the 9th October, 1856; " you could perhaps look after everything, and if you secured the owner's rights to my works you could then be sure of leaving your children something through this after your death." [22] As he never tired of pointing out, his exile made it impossible for him to infuse the necessary energy into the business himself; this could only be done by someone on the spot, and would be done best of all by someone whose own financial interests were at stake. He begged Pusinelli to " think in large terms "; he offered to give him in addition the rights in the *Tristan* he was now meditating. But Pusinelli, unfortunately for himself, could not think in sufficiently large terms. He and Kriete, in 1856, appointed one Hermann Müller, a music dealer, to be manager of the business; but three years later, being by now utterly weary of the whole affair, they sold out their rights to Müller for a paltry 3,000 thalers. Apparently even Kriete's relatively small claim was never fully met, while Pusinelli's total loss in capital and interest is estimated at 10,000 thalers.

Meanwhile, in 1857, a new claimant for the mythical Wagner

---

[22] RWAP, p. 59.

millions had appeared on the scene — the former double-bassist of the Dresden orchestra, Tietz, who demanded, through his solicitor, 800 rh., with interest in default since the Easter of that year; and it would seem that other Dresden creditors became aggressive just then. Pusinelli had to deal with all these people, with the lawyers, and with Wagner, for by this time the distracted composer, in spite of his genius for finance, was becoming almost unable to disentangle the multitudinous threads he had gradually woven about himself. The worst blow of all had been his having to submit to the deduction from his pension of the 400 thalers advanced by Frau Ritter. This touched him to the quick: he characteristically regarded himself as having been " deprived " of this sum.

CHAPTER XXI

THE YEAR 1854

1

THE SPRING and summer of 1854 had brought Wagner into indirect contact with Berlin once more. In the autumn of 1853 Liszt, who just about this time was more active than ever in trying to further Wagner's interests — though unfortunately not always in the wisest way imaginable — took up eagerly Bülow's idea of repeating in Berlin the Zürich programmes of the preceding May festival, Liszt to conduct the concerts in co-operation with the Wieprecht Male Voice Choir, of which he had been the honorary conductor since 1843.[1] The scheme came to nothing, however, Wieprecht apparently taking fright at the ill-will towards Wagner that existed, or which he imagined to exist, on the part of the King of Prussia, the Opera Intendant Hülsen, and the Kapellmeisters Taubert and Dorn. But Liszt seems to have conceived about this time a bold plan of campaign against the Berlin fortress. It can only have been for " diplomatic " reasons of the most questionable kind that he decided, during this autumn, to give in Weimar the first performance of Dorn's new opera, *Die Nibelungen*. It is impossible to believe that he had any faith or any interest whatever in Dorn as a composer: even as late as December he had not seen the score of even the first act of the work he had promised to produce. His only object could have been to bribe Dorn for the furtherance of Wagner's interests, Bülow's, and his own in Berlin. The opera was given under Liszt in Weimar on the 22nd January, 1854; Dorn conducted the second performance. Evidently the subject of Wagner's concerts in Berlin was discussed between them while he was there, for in April we find Dorn — who has no use for Liszt now that his opera has been floated in Weimar and is on the point of being given in Berlin — making all kinds of excuses and suggest-

---

[1] For Wieprecht see Vol. I, 404, *note*.

ing that the concerts had better be postponed to the following October.

Meanwhile Hülsen, prompted, as we now know, by Dorn — wheels within wheels! — had once more taken up the idea of producing *Tannhäuser* in Berlin. He broached the subject at a meeting with Liszt in Coburg in the early days of April, 1854, and six weeks later asked him for a definite statement of the " conditions " under which he would be allowed to do so. The three-cornered negotiations that ensued between Hülsen, Liszt and Wagner show Hülsen willing, even eager, to carry out the plan — which promised good receipts for the theatre — and Wagner disposed to be conciliatory in the matter of terms. All would have gone well but for Liszt, who, armed with Wagner's old commission to him of plenipotentiary powers, tried to put a pressure on Hülsen which the latter resented. By " conditions ", he explained, he had simply meant financial conditions: but Liszt's " conditions " were that *he* should settle with Hülsen the casting of the parts and superintend the major rehearsals. Hülsen could not agree to this: he naturally regarded it as a slight on himself and on the important institution of which he was the head. The rules of the Berlin Opera forbade the taking of the baton out of the hands of the regular Kapellmeisters to place it in the hands of anyone but the composer of the work to be produced, and even this only by the special permission of the King: whatever suggestions Liszt might have to make about the performances would be gratefully accepted if offered privately, but he could not be given any official control. This was reasonable enough. But Liszt was unreasonable, unyielding, and tactless.

Hülsen laid the correspondence before Albert Wagner, who was at that time with his daughter in Königsberg, where Johanna was making a series of guest appearances. Albert was wholly in favour of the Berlin production, if only because it would have meant good business for the theatre and a personal success for Johanna as Elisabeth. But, like Hülsen, he soon grew tired of what he called Liszt's " stuff and nonsense " (*Quakeleien*), and, in view of the manifest importance of the Berlin affair to both Wagner and Liszt, suggested calling the latter's bluff. He wanted to have as little as possible to do with his brother personally, he told Hülsen, for he had no great opinion of his character, though he valued his talents as highly as anyone. Ellis, as usual, falls foul of Albert for his hard frankness where his brother was concerned. But Ellis did not know what we have recently learned — that at the first hint of a possible production of *Tannhäuser* in Berlin, Wagner, who was desperately in need of money at this time, had approached Johanna with a request for a loan of 1,000 thalers against the expected royalties. This, of course, was too much for the prudent Albert, who had both a keen sense of the value of money and a close knowledge of his brother Richard. He could forgive him, he wrote him in reply, the unkind things he had said in the past about Johanna and her family.

" I can let that pass, used as I am to seeing that you consider people only when and in so far as they can be of service to you: when that is over they no longer exist for you. You have no conception of thankfulness for what is past — all that was simply their duty! It has always been so, with Brockhaus, with the King, with Lüttichau, with Pusinelli, with Tichatschek, with everyone who has been good to you in one way or another. Much as I esteem and love your talent, it is anything but so as regards your character. . . . In Johanna's name and my own I give you this answer: As soon as your opera is put into rehearsal at Berlin, and I receive from you a fully valid assignment, confirmed by the management, of your royalties, I am willing, if you then wish it and need it, to advance you a round sum against them after the second performance. But for me to do at once what you ask, regardless of Johanna's future, would be merely shooting into the blue. Without my going into details, it is enough to say that if Johanna were to satisfy the demands of the various families she herself would soon have to live on very short commons, to say nothing about providing for her future. She supports her parents, has established Marie in our place in Hamburg, and is now going to do the same for Franziska: brother Julius, who is nothing, can do nothing, and is nothing, costs her a great deal — not to mention other matters. She is doing quite enough; as for you, I know that you have enough to live on in a becoming way, if you could regulate your affairs according to circumstances."

Hülsen, he continues, is a trifle dubious about *Tannhäuser*, which he has recently seen in some small town or other where it was badly done. Hülsen does not deny that the work has been a success everywhere, but thinks this is due to the efforts of " a party ". At the same time he clearly sees that Berlin will have to give the work some time or other; but he will have nothing to do with Richard, "because you impose too many nonsensical conditions".

" Convinced as I am ", Albert concludes, " that *Tannhäuser* will one day be given in Berlin, I do not think it will be next winter, for other forces are secretly at work besides the modest hopes, on the part of the Intendant, of its being a success. But unless I deceive myself greatly, *Tannhäuser*, done well, and — which is important — rehearsed with enthusiasm by the conductor, will make a great effect in Berlin, for we can now cast it fairly well. . . . If that happens, we shall really be delighted, and then we can treat of the other matters." [2]

2

So it went on, the sole obstacle to the production being the obstinacy of Liszt. The diplomacy on which he plumed himself failed: he discovered that it was one thing to get what he wanted out of willing givers and personal admirers by means of flattery, and quite another thing to deal *de haut en bas* with people who took a severely realistic view of him and of the business between them. No opera house in Germany would have accepted Liszt's conditions, which would have reflected not only on the Kapellmeisters but on the institution itself. Had Liszt's only object been to further Wagner's interests he would have accepted Hülsen's offer to avail himself of any suggestions he might have to make *in private*. But Liszt evidently had something else and something more than Wagner in his mind all along: and that something was himself. He was tactless and unaccommodating throughout: he certainly did not improve matters by trying to get the Grand Duke of Weimar to influence the King of Prussia behind Hülsen's back, and letting it be known that he was doing so. As Ellis points out, that move, if successful, could have had only one of two results — either Hülsen would have resigned then and there, or he would have bowed to superior force, retained his position, produced the opera as a matter of form, and then withdrawn it from the repertory as soon as Liszt had left the town. The upshot of it all was that in July Hülsen, his patience exhausted, closed the negotiations down for good: he told Liszt frankly that he would never consent to rehearse the opera

[2] JKJ, p. 69.

under *his* tutelage, and wound up by saying, with regret, that as two attempts to come to an agreement about *Tannhäuser* in Berlin had failed, no third attempt would be made so long as he was in command there. An unpleasant feature of the matter is the way in which Liszt kept from Wagner the evidences of relative goodwill that had been manifest enough on the part of Hülsen and Albert, and of the features in his own letters to them that had stiffened their backs. Wagner, for his part, sorely as he needed the royalties the Berlin production would have brought him, stuck loyally to his friend, still leaving the affair entirely in Liszt's hands even when it must have been tolerably clear to him that with a different handling of the matter a way out could have been found that would have been agreeable to all parties.[3]

Towards the end of July, 1854, he went to Sitten (Sion), in Valais, in fulfilment of a promise he had given some time before, in a weak moment, to conduct a performance of Beethoven's Seventh Symphony at a festival there. (He had originally thought of giving the *Tannhäuser* overture also, but had later declined to do so with merely part of one rehearsal of an orchestra largely made up of amateurs). On the way he stopped at Collonges, near Montreux, to spend a week with Karl Ritter and his recently acquired wife: it gave him ample opportunities, he says, for doubting whether the happiness of the young couple would last very long. Karl's tastes, one gathers, reading between the lines here and elsewhere, were for his own rather than the opposite sex. He was engaged just then on a comedy called *Alkibiades,* which had been occupying him since the Albisbrunn days of 1851. At that time he had shown Wagner an elegant dagger, into the blade of which the syllables *Alki* had been burnt; a similar dagger, bearing the syllables *Biades,* was in the possession of a young actor in Stuttgart with whom, presumably, his soul was in more or less mystic communion. Now, in Montreux, he seemed to have found his Alkibiadesian complement in a certain Baron Robert von Hornstein, who joined them at Martigny on their way to Sitten. This Hornstein, on whom the

---

[3] Ellis, in chapter VII of his fourth volume, gives the three-cornered correspondence in fair detail, so far as it was available at the time he was writing. The Hülsen-Liszt-Wagner letters were published, practically in full, by Wilhelm Altmann in DM, March–May, 1903.

angry Wagner, in *Mein Leben,* unloads such epithets as "quaint creature" and "booby", was a young man of property who dabbled in literature and the arts and even fancied himself as a composer. His memoirs nowhere convey the impression that he was one of the world's most massive intellects; and it is readily understandable that Wagner, whose nerves were more than normally on the stretch just now, found him rather trying at times. The true cause, however, of the malice that Wagner everywhere shows towards him in *Mein Leben* will be made manifest at a later stage of our story.

Arriving at Sitten on the 8th July in the middle of the preparations for the festival, in no very good temper — for he was already regretting his rash promise to go there, he resented having to interrupt his work on the *Valkyrie,* and he was in the thick of his latest financial worries [4] — Wagner found that the orchestra was utterly inadequate and the small church in which the symphony was to be given acoustically unsuitable for the purpose. On the evening of the 10th July he fled the town incontinently by the first post-chaise available, not even telling his two young companions that he was going, but leaving an explanatory note for Adolf Methfessel, the Berne conductor who had organised the festival.[5] Perhaps Ritter and Hornstein had unconsciously contributed to drive him forth. On his return to the inn for dinner after his visit to the church, feeling, as he says, miserable and depressed over what he had just heard, he was annoyed to find that the two young irresponsibles took only a humorous view of the situation. This of itself was bad enough: but in his touchy mood he assumed that they had been joking at his expense before he came in; and this was *lèse-majesté.* After spending a few days at Geneva and Lausanne

---

[4] The recent publication of some *Valkyrie* facsimiles shows him able to joke over his miseries in the midst of his work. He had had to lay down his pen to go to the music festival at the point in the first act where Sieglinde says to Siegmund, "Guest, who thou art I fain would learn." Underneath the stave Wagner has scrawled, "Answer when I get back from Sitten 13–4 July." Otto Strobel reads this as "3–4" July, taking the view that this denotes the date when Wagner *broke off* to go to Sitten. But the 1 before the 3 is quite unmistakeable. The chief concert of the festival was on the evening of the 12th, so Wagner was presumably reckoning on returning on the 13th or 14th. When he takes up the threads of his composition again he writes "3 August!!" The double exclamation mark is obviously intended to signify his disgust and alarm at so much lost time. See SGW, pp. 35, 36.

[5] Glasenapp confuses him with Ernst Methfessel, of Winterthur.

he called at Collonges again to see Frau Ritter. There he found the two culprits again, duly penitent and subdued; and as a mark of his restored favour he allowed Hornstein to accompany him, mostly on foot, by way of Vevey to Lausanne. From there Wagner went on through Berne and Lucerne to Seelisberg, on the Lake of Lucerne, where Minna, whose heart disease was now in a fairly advanced stage, was taking a cure. Although, seemingly, she had no great desire for his company, and the social habits of the Kurhaus — the " Sonnenberg " — that gave her bourgeois soul so much pleasure were a torture to him, his sense of duty to her made him last out a week in the place. With Seelisberg itself he was so enchanted that he already planned to go there again next summer for the composition of his *Siegfried*. Towards the end of July they were both back in Zürich, where he plunged once more into the music of his *Valkyrie*.

It was during this month of August that he received a visit from a young disciple from Cologne, August Lesimple, who came with a letter of introduction from Liszt. The young man was struck by the worn appearance of Minna, who by now had lost virtually all the good looks for which she had once been famous. He told Wagner of the fight against him by his enemies in Cologne, of whom Hiller and the critic Bischoff were the leaders. Wagner refused to believe that *Tannhäuser* had been a success there in the meaning *he* attached to the word, attributing its undoubted success to the fact that the tenor had won favour. He spoke of his plans for producing the *Ring* in some quiet place in South Germany before a select invited audience: " a single hearing would suffice for him, because he only desired to embody the conception of a national art-work which floated before his mind and was ever present to his spirit." He spoke warmly of Liszt, but for whom " he would most likely have been entirely forgotten." Now, as on later occasions when they met, Lesimple was impressed by Wagner's eyes. " Whoever has looked once into his eyes will never again forget the deep and mysterious expression which shone there. There was something marvellous about his eyes." [6]

---

[6] See LRRW, pp. 11–28.

Creative work and philosophical brooding were now his only refuge from the fast-increasing miseries of his life. He had grown out of touch with Zürich society, which, he was beginning to realise, would never place at his disposal the relatively large sums necessary to achieve his ideal of a worthy concert and operatic life in the town, to say nothing of the more expansive and expensive ideal of a special theatre for the *Ring*. The intellectual and spiritual cleavage between Minna and himself was widening and deepening daily. The one woman who could have brought him balm — Mathilde Wesendonk — was unattainable. The demand for his early works on the part of the theatres was necessarily a diminishing quantity now. He was more deeply in debt than ever, with little prospect of any increase in his income for a long time to come. He was barred, apparently for ever, from his native land, which meant that not only could he not gratify the immediate desire of his heart to hear his *Lohengrin*, but that the few German theatres that might ultimately take up the *Ring* would have to solve its new and difficult problems without his personal guidance. It is little wonder that under the pressure of all these miseries his health declined; more than once he thought of suicide. It was his artist's imagination alone that kept him going. By the 26th September he had completed the fair copy of the *Rhinegold* full score, sending it, in sections at a time, to Bülow (in Dresden), who was to have another copy made for practical use, while he himself was to make the piano score. It was not until the 27th December that Wagner finished the composition sketch of the *Valkyrie*. By that time several decisive changes had taken place in both his inner and his outer life.

The two most important ones were spiritually correlative. In the autumn he had been introduced by Herwegh to Arthur Schopenhauer's system of philosophy. *The World as Will and Idea* had been published originally as long ago as 1819, a second and enlarged edition following in 1844: but its author had been studiously ignored by the academic world whose ideas the book had flouted, and even the name of the now sixty-two-years-old Schopenhauer was unknown to all but a few readers.[7] " A book, like a person ",

---

[7] He was first brought to the notice of the literary world in general by an article

said Walter Pater, " has its fortunes with one; is lucky or unlucky in the precise moment of its falling our way, and often by some happy accident counts with us for something more than its independent value." It was certainly fortunate for Schopenhauer and for Wagner that the former swept into the musician's ken at the very moment when his inner development made him peculiarly disposed to welcome this philosophy of pessimism. We talk too loosely of " influences " in an artist or thinker's inner life, naïvely conceiving him as a blank page on which this or that external " influence " writes itself. We forget that it is only because the page, and indeed the whole book, are what they already are that they lend themselves to the writing: as Pascal says of all similar phenomena of apparently sudden spiritual revelation and re-birth, " You would not have sought me unless you had already found me." Wagner did not take his philosophy from Schopenhauer: what happened was that *The World as Will and Idea* [8] introduced into his mind the point of solid matter that was necessary to bring about the crystallisation of a philosophy that was already latent in him: Schopenhauer merely reinforced his emotions and intuitions with reasons and arguments. That, and that alone, was Schopenhauer's " influence " upon him; but it was the most powerful thing of the kind that his mind had ever known or was ever afterwards to know.

He talked about Schopenhauer to everyone he met, including even the " booby " Hornstein: he forced him on the attention of

by John Oxenford in the *Westminster Review* of April, 1853. This was reproduced in a Berlin journal.

[8] It should be added that he read the *Parerga und Paralipomena* also.

By this time he had drifted far apart from Feuerbach, to whom he had dedicated *The Art-Work of the Future*, and whom he had tried to attract to Zürich in December, 1851. For some strange reason or other, Wahnfried and some of its partisans have always tried to minimise Wagner's obligations, as a philosopher, to Feuerbach: even the dedication to Feuerbach is suppressed in the modern editions of Wagner's prose works. Wagner's references to Feuerbach are a little confusing in their chronology, but there can be no question that he was reading him at least as early as 1848–9. The similarity between Wagner's opinions about 1850 and those of Feuerbach was long ago pointed out by Albert Levy (LPF, Chapter IX). The question has further been discussed in close detail by Rudolf Lück in LWF.

It has always seemed to me that the style of such works as *The Art-Work of the Future*, a style abounding in clockwork antitheses, was derived from Feuerbach, who, as the English reader of George Eliot's translation of *The Essence of Christianity* will be able to see for himself, was constitutionally prone to the antithetical; and when we come upon the same stylistic finger-prints in some of the anonymous articles in Röckel's *Volksblätter* we shall perhaps not go far wrong in attributing these articles to Wagner.

his correspondents. At Christmas, 1854, he sent the Frankfort philosopher one of his few remaining copies of the *Ring* poem, without an accompanying letter, but with the inscription " With reverence and gratitude." Schopenhauer never realised how much of the vogue that was now beginning for him he owed to Wagner. The old man, whom years of misunderstanding, neglect and disappointment had made excessively self-centred, did not even know that it was Wagner (not Sulzer, with whom the official correspondence was carried on) who was responsible for a movement, which, however, came to nothing, to found a chair of Schopenhauerian philosophy at the Zürich University. We do not know whether the Sage of Frankfort, who played the flute and whose musical gods were Mozart and Rossini, had heard any of Wagner's operas, while it is clear that he knew nothing of his theories concerning the Art-Work of the Future at first hand, but had derived his knowledge of them, such as it was, solely from the travesties the journalists made of them. We cannot even be certain what was the total impression made on him by the poem of the *Ring*. It is true that his marginal comments on it are mostly unfavourable; but it is equally true, as Ellis points out, that these pencillings of points of disagreement do not of necessity imply a lack of admiration for what is left unmarked. Like so many of his contemporaries, he jibbed at Wagner's novel handling of the German language for his own purposes: [9] he thought Siegmund and Sieglinde no better morally than they ought to be, and regarded Siegfried as a monster of ingratitude towards Mime. Some of his comments have become classics: opposite the scene in which Fricka forces her will on Wotan he has a sarcastic

---

[9] Wagner not only habitually used words in senses of his own and made compound words that did not commend themselves to the ordinary German mind, but indulged freely in personal oddities in the matter of construction and grammar. It was the number of these latter in *Mein Leben* that, we may recall, made Mrs Burrell declare that it was "not the German of a German", the implication being, of course, that "this unmentionable book", as she called the autobiography, was the work of the detested Cosima. Professor H. G. Fiedler at one time held that certain "solecisms" in it, "though trifling enough in themselves, are not such as a German would have written" — for instance, the peculiar construction "in meinem Bezug" instead of "in Bezug auf mich." (See NFF, p. 281, etc.). But Wagner was addicted to this peculiar "Bezug" construction almost from the beginning. We find it again and again in his letters — for instance, to Röckel in 1855, ". . . und nicht mehr nach Sophismen zur Beschönigung der Schlechtigkeit der Menschen in diesem Bezuge suchen zu müssen." A good many of Schopenhauer's marginal notes are by way of protest against Wag-

" Wotan under the slipper! " while to the stage direction at the end of the first act of the *Valkyrie,* where the brother-and-sister lovers run into the forest — " The curtain falls quickly " — he appends " And high time, too! " But even his dogmatic declaration to Hornstein that " the fellow is a poet, no musician ", makes it tolerably clear that as a whole the poem *had* impressed him.[10]

4

It is in a letter of Wagner's to Liszt of the end of December, 1854, that we have the first unmistakeable hint of a change in the artistic depths of him that links up with his recent Schopenhauer experiences. He hopes to complete the whole *Ring* in 1856, he tells Liszt, and to produce it in 1858, " the tenth year of my Hegira." But, he continues, he has now in his head a *Tristan and Isolde.* " Since I have never enjoyed in life the real happiness of love, I will erect to this most beautiful of all dreams a memorial in which, from beginning to end, this love shall for once drink its fill." The new work, which he has already sketched out mentally, will be " the simplest yet most full-blooded musical conception: and with the ' black flag ' that waves at the end I will cover myself — to die." The " black flag " refers to an episode that does not appear in *Tristan* as we now have it: it had been his intention at first to bring Parsifal to the couch of the dying Tristan, but this idea was abandoned later.[11] To say, as some writers have done, that *Tristan* owes part at any rate of its origin to Wagner's reading of

---

ner's cavalier treatment of the German tongue: as the shocked philosopher puts it in one place, "Die Sprache muss das Leibeigen des Herrn seyn!" ("The gentleman seems to think the language is his serf!"). "He has no ears, the deaf music-maker!" he laments elsewhere.

[10] A complete statement of Schopenhauer's marginal pencillings will be found in ELW, IV, 440–446. Ellis copied them in 1896 from the book itself, which at that time was in the possession of Alfred Bovet.

[11] I have always been struck by the curiously Parsifalesque quality of the music to King Marke's final words in the third act of the opera, just before Isolde begins the Liebestod, more especially in the lines,

> Dem holden Mann dich zu vermählen
> mit vollen Segeln flog ich dir nach.

Can it be that the music here is a *Nachklang* of some phrase that had already shaped itself in his mind when he first conceived the idea of the opera? "Tristan," he tells us in *Mein Leben,* "wounded but unable to die, identified himself in my mind with Amfortas in the romance of the Grail."

Schopenhauer is to exhibit a woeful misunderstanding of the artistic psychology in general and of Wagner's in particular. *The World as Will and Idea,* with its central thesis of the denial of the Will to Live, may indeed have brought about that final crystallisation of his emotions to which I have already referred: but the emotions themselves, and the philosophy of existence that was interwrought with them, already existed in him as the product of his own bitter experiences and his mournful brooding upon them. The conviction that life is only a bad dream and all our striving merely illusion had been growing upon him for a long time. It found expression in an undated letter of about October, 1854, to Liszt, in which he laments ever having allowed himself to surrender his operas to the traffic of the theatres.

> " The last song of the ' world ' has died on my ear. . . . O let us not mangle ourselves as we do: let us regard the world with eyes only of scorn. It is fit for nothing else: let us hope for nothing from it, for no illusion for our hearts. It is bad, *bad, bad to the core:* only the heart of a *friend,* the tears of a woman, can redeem it for us from its curse. So let us show it no respect, least of all in anything that resembles Honour, Fame, or by whatever name men call its buffooneries. It belongs to Alberich, no one else! Away with it! Enough — you know my mood now. It is no mere ebullition: it is solid and firm, adamantine. It alone gives me strength to bear any longer the burden of life: but in it I must henceforth be unrelenting. I hate all *semblance* with a deadly hatred: I will have no hope, for that is self-deception. But I will work. . . ."

Here already is the mystical withdrawal from hateful reality that is the essence of the *Tristan* conception, and that later was to find such touching expression in his letters to Frau Wesendonk from Venice.

In a later communication to Liszt — about the middle of December — he expressly denies, indeed, that Schopenhauer's book has done anything more than add another note to spiritual concords and dissonances that were already sounding within him. The idea of the denial of the Will to Live, he says, is " frightfully serious, but alone redeeming "; and in truth almost his whole work, from the *Flying Dutchman* to *Parsifal,* deals in one way or another with the problem of man's redemption. The central Schopenhauerian idea, he tells Liszt, is of course not new to him, for, as he rightly says,

> "no one can think it in whom it does not exist already. But this philosopher is the first to make it all clear to me. When I look back upon the fearful convulsions through which my heart, in the storms it has passed through, has clung reluctantly to the hope of life, when, indeed, these storms have risen, as they have sometimes done, to the power of a hurricane, I find a last anodyne that alone brings me sleep in wakeful nights — the profound longing of my heart for death, complete unconsciousness, total nihility, a final end to dreaming, the last and only salvation."

So again in a letter of the 5th December to Röckel:

> "My experience of life had brought me to the point where only Schopenhauer's philosophy could wholly suit me and determine me. In unreservedly accepting his very, very earnest truths I was able to follow my own inner bent to the decisive end; and although he has given me a direction somewhat other than my earlier one, yet this direction is simply one that corresponds with my profoundly sorrowful feeling as to the nature of the world."

We may even go further, and say that *Tristan* itself was something inherent in the German soul of that epoch that *had* to find expression some time or other, somehow or other, needing for its final perfect realisation only the coincidence of the right artist and the right moment, under which latter rubric we may include the reading of *The World as Will and Idea*. As Arthur Prüfer has pointed out, Wagner is connected by a hundred links with his predecessors in German romanticism; even where there is no direct evidence that he had ever read this or that author there is often a curious similarity between his ideas and theirs, for these ideas were a part of the vast romantic heritage. Others before him had toyed with the conception of night and death as the redeemers of man from the glare and turmoil of daylight and life — notably Novalis in his *Hymns to Night* (1800), in which we find some remarkable parallels to the mystical metaphysics of the second act of *Tristan*.[12]

---

[12] See Prüfer's article on *Novalis Hymnen an die Nacht in ihren Beziehungen zu Wagners Tristan und Isolde*, in RWJF, 1906, pp. 290 ff. Compare also several passages in the duet, which have for their theme the longing for escape from day and reality

There could be nothing essentially new, in Schopenhauer's theory of the negation of the Will to Live, to the Wagner who, nearly a year before he met with *The World as Will and Idea,* had spoken to Röckel of Wotan " rising to the tragic height of willing his own destruction."

His first reactions to the book, he tells us in *Mein Leben,* had not been altogether favourable: while grateful for the lucidity — rare in German speculation — with which Schopenhauer had treated the fundamental problems of philosophy, he was perturbed by the clash between this uncompromising pessimism and the " Greek cheerfulness " that had been his own ideal in his writings of 1849–51. It was only gradually that he perceived that the clash was merely between the new doctrine and the conscious reasoner in him, whereas between his world of subconscious thought and feeling and the thesis of " the nullity of the visible world " there was a profound affinity. Once the perception of this affinity had come to him he discovered that for a long time he had been, so to speak, a Schopenhauerian without knowing it; and at last, he says, he understood his own Wotan. It was undoubtedly the reading of Schopenhauer's book in the autumn of 1854 that precipitated into solid matter the nebula of pessimistic emotion that had been forming itself within him for some time past. It was not until August, 1857, that he drafted the actual poem of *Tristan* — for the time being he needed the whole of his creative energy for the music of the *Ring;* but we may be sure that in the interval the fascinating new subject was rarely out of his thoughts.

5

From his accumulating financial difficulties he was rescued temporarily by his friends, and for a brief period he cherished hopes again for a brighter material future. About the end of August,

---

into a night of forgetfulness and mystic union, with the following passage in Schlegel's *Lucinde:* "O eternal longing! But at the last the fruitless yearning and the empty garishness of the day fade away into a night of love of endless tranquillity."

For further passages in Wagner's dramas to which parallels, more or less close, exist in other works of German literature see Arthur Seidl's article *Analogien — Parallelen — Harmonien,* in RWJF, 1912, pp. 79 ff.

Minna — leaving her husband to the congenial company of Peps and the new parrot Jacquot — had gone back to Germany, ostensibly for the benefit of her health and to visit her relations and old friends, but actually to make a last desperate effort to have him amnestied and to bring about an understanding with Hülsen over *Tannhäuser.*

Writing to her about the third week in October, Wagner confesses a resurgence of his longing to return to Germany. So long as he was only theorising and poetising he had found Zürich tolerable, but now that he has plunged into the sea of his own music again he feels the need of surroundings more congenial to the creative artist in him. He is not sure that Minna herself wants to leave Zürich, where she has made so many friends of her own type; and therefore he will not attempt to influence her to do so, for she has borne much on his account. But if the return to Germany would not mean too great a sacrifice for her, he is willing that an effort shall be made to induce the Grand Duke to obtain permission from the King of Saxony for him to live in Weimar, it being understood that he will not leave Weimar territory without permission and that he will undertake never to engage in politics again. Only — no declaration regarding the past that would be humiliating to him and open to misunderstanding by others must be exacted of him!

But Minna had already, apparently, acted on her own initiative. Sensing, no doubt, during the stay she had made in Weimar, that Liszt and the Grand Duke did not think it would be opportune for them to approach the Saxon Court just then — for in the preceding August Wagner's old patron Friedrich Augustus had been succeeded by his brother Johann, a man of a sterner, more unyielding disposition — she went off to Dresden without informing her husband of her intention. There, supported by a letter from the Grand Duke, she personally presented a petition to the King, humbly asking for clemency for " a banished man . . . an erring artist who is quite beaten down because his activities are hampered by the impossibility of hearing his new works." The King's reply was given to the Minister of Justice, Zschinsky, about a month later, to be handed to the petitioner on her personal application. As the document was still unclaimed by the 13th December it was forwarded to Minna at Zürich, where she had by now returned. It was couched in the coldest official terms:

> " The petition for pardon addressed to the King by Minna Wagner on behalf of her husband Richard Wagner, a fugitive for high treason, has been handed by his Majesty to the Minister of Justice. As, however, hesitation is felt as to advising his Majesty to decide upon the matter of a pardon until the fugitive has returned and submitted himself to examination, the petitioner is hereby informed that her appeal above-mentioned is rejected." [13]

Lippert opines that Wagner never knew of this direct attempt of Minna to secure his pardon. That, however, seems improbable, in the light of a letter of the 4th November from Minna to Hülsen, apropos of *Tannhäuser*, in which she expressly mentions her having presented a petition to the King of Saxony, " supported by a letter from the Grand Duke of Weimar to the King himself "; apparently she had come away from the interview with the feeling that the omens were favourable, though she had been given to understand that " no political acts, such as an amnesty, could take place before a quarter of a year " [after the King's accession to the throne]. This letter to Hülsen, dealing as it does with the possibility of permission being obtained for Wagner to go to Berlin to supervise the rehearsals of *Tannhäuser*, could hardly have been written without the cognisance of her husband.

He seems not to have known himself, during these years, whether he really desired to be amnestied or not. His feelings on the matter were in a perpetual flux: he loathed the German theatres from the bottom of his heart, and was convinced that the performances of his works given there were, in the main, little more than travesties. On the other hand, he had an agonised longing to hear *Lohengrin* at any rate once; while, looking some distance ahead, it was clear to him that he must either be allowed to return to Germany for the production of the *Ring*, or, unless he could accomplish his bold dream of a theatre of his own, in non-German territory, for that purpose, resign himself to the virtual non-existence of the great work — for he would probably never have entrusted so novel a conception to conductors and singers and producers who had shown

---

[13] LVW, p. 49.

themselves unequal to the far simpler problems of *Tannhäuser* and *Lohengrin*.

He was in the same constant dubiety of purpose with regard to Berlin and *Tannhäuser*. In his heart of hearts he had not the slightest faith in the ability of Dorn, Taubert and their like to do the work justice. But as a strategic point in his struggle not only with art but with the grim realities of life, Berlin was of the utmost importance to him. He knew, as everyone else did, that *Tannhäuser* would prove the same box-office success in Berlin as it had done elsewhere: and this meant continuing royalties which he estimated, in a letter to Minna, at an assured 1,000 thalers a year. Further, the lead of Berlin was tolerably certain to be followed by the two other great Court Operas — of Vienna and Munich. The money that all this would have meant to him would have been welcome to him not only for his own sake but for Minna's. In spite of the lack of spiritual harmony between them, he never, at this or any other time before or after, failed to pay generous tribute to his wife's domestic devotion to him, and to repay her for it as best he could. He was sincerely anxious for her to be happy in her own way; and even in his hours of direst financial difficulty he never stinted her a groschen in anything that might be necessary for her happiness or her health. He would have borne anything himself to keep his artistic idealism unsullied, even, as he told Liszt, to the extent of selling all he had and going back into the world as naked as he had entered it. But that, he added, would kill his wife, whose damaged health now called for every possible consideration. There are hints in his letters that she looked coldly on the scheme of the *Ring*, which must have seemed, to her as to many others, utterly impracticable: as she saw the matter, he was merely wasting his time on abstractions instead of taking practical advantage of his popularity and producing operas that would be within the scope of all the theatres. As he could not yield to her on this major matter, the arguments were strong in favour of his turning his earlier works to the utmost possible profit. And so we find him once more consenting despairingly to what he regarded as the prostitution of his art:

"For her sake [Minna's]", he cries to Liszt, "I have determined to endure it: *Tannhäuser* and *Lohengrin* must go to the Jews. . . .

Berlin's abstention from my operas causes a stoppage in all the rest of the business, and, by God, the diffusion of my works means nothing to me but *business*. That is the only real thing about it; all the rest is a sham pure and simple."

As it happened, the omens were in favour of an accommodation being arrived at with Berlin. Minna, aided by Alwine Frommann, who, the reader will remember, was in close touch with Berlin Court circles, secured an interview with Hülsen at which, it would appear, all difficulties were removed except the cardinal one — that of the co-operation of Liszt in the production. Liszt had only to withdraw from the matter, with one of those noble diplomatic gestures that came so naturally to him, and everything would have run smoothly. But Liszt, for some reason or other, would not withdraw: the probability is that the pride that was so strong an element in his nature had been roused, and at all costs he was determined not to suffer what he would have regarded as an affront in the eyes of the musical world. The problem was, then, how to remove this one obstacle from the path of the opera. Sorely tried and perplexed as he was, Wagner was too loyal to do anything that could be read as a slight on Liszt.[14] His alleged ingratitude to Liszt, be it repeated once more, is a myth: in one circumstance after another he bore patiently, in a manner that is almost inexplicable to us to-day, with disabilities created for him by Liszt's curious character and his abject subservience to the Princess, because of his profound gratitude for all that Liszt had been to him and done for him in earlier years.

---

[14] "From every possible side", he wrote to Bülow, "I am urged to desist from the 'senseless' condition that *Tannhäuser* shall be given in Berlin only with the co-operation of Liszt: everywhere the cry goes up that they do not think much of him as a conductor; they assure me also that, as matters are, people see in Liszt's demand (for they all believe that it comes solely from him) nothing but boundless vanity. ... How much Philistinism there is behind all this I know quite well; but I also know that in this matter I am acting less for myself than for Liszt, for whom I would right gladly secure a triumph through me. It only surprises me that Liszt remains so completely impotent in this matter: I really thought he was more of a diplomatist and had more influence than seems to be the case. But he knows the fix I am in: and that he has found no way out by which I can get over the loss of the Berlin royalties, rather lowers my faith in his shrewdness and solicitude." RWHB, pp. 56, 57.

Minna and Hülsen between them had seen a way out of the difficulty, and Wagner, in spite of all it meant to him, had agreed to it for Liszt's sake. Liszt's contention was that a responsibility had been entrusted to him by Wagner which he could not relinquish without Wagner's express consent. That consent, in the terms of the case, was impossible; Wagner would not hurt his old friend by anything of that kind. But Liszt's objections would automatically fall to the ground if *Wagner himself* could superintend the production of *Tannhäuser* in Berlin. It was to bring this about that Minna made, unknown to her husband at the time, her journey to Dresden and her personal appeal to the King of Saxony for his pardon. Wagner himself, when he heard of it on Minna's return to Zürich — before the official rejection of the petition had arrived, — made it clear to Hülsen that if he were permitted to go to Berlin he would not ask to be allowed to conduct the work but simply to act as mentor during the rehearsals. As he said in a letter to Alwine Frommann, he would have welcomed the permission to go to Berlin merely because it would have " made retreat easy for Liszt "; the old condition that Liszt should have a deciding hand in the production " would drop of itself, without affront to him." He has no desire either to conduct in Berlin or to take an active part in the production of this early work of his, to which, he says, he has now grown somewhat indifferent. He is willing for it to be given without either Liszt or himself being concerned in it; if he does consent, after all, to go to Berlin, it will be solely out of consideration for Liszt, whom he wishes to " remain unmortified ". " So if *Tannhäuser* is not given in Berlin this winter it will not be due to me but to Liszt, whom I cannot leave in the lurch, for he worked for my music when no one else had done anything for it."

It is true that Liszt, in a letter to Bülow of the 30th September, says that " Wagner is perfectly free to get *Tannhäuser* produced there [Berlin] whenever he thinks fit; and it is certainly not I who will ever make him the shadow of a reproach about it "; and again, some six weeks later to Brendel,

" On the subject of the Berlin *Tannhäuser* I can say nothing at the moment than that I have *all along* left it perfectly free to Wagner to leave me out of the game and to handle the affair directly, according to his own way of thinking, *without me*. But so long as he puts trust in me as a friend the duty is imposed on me to serve him as a judicious friend; and that I can do only by lending no ear to negotiations carried on in that way and letting people tattle as they please."

But these are mere high-sounding words: the plain fact is that all along in this Berlin affair, urged on, it would appear, by the ambitious Princess, he had behaved, now actively, now passively, in a way that put himself in the forefront to the detriment of Wagner; and finally Wagner had to sketch out with Hülsen a tentative plan for saving his friend's face by handing over *Tannhäuser* to Berlin without the supervision of either of them. It was not merely that, as Ellis says, Liszt " had worked himself up to a sense of being indispensable." There was obviously more in it than that. It had not been his habit hitherto to persist obstinately in any course of conduct that would be contrary to Wagner's interests. If he did so in this case — and his touchy letters to Bülow and Brendel suggest that his conscience told him he was doing so — it must have been because a special force must have come into action. That force, in all probability, was resentment against Hülsen. Liszt had been used to seeing his " diplomacy " succeed. In this case it had failed all along the line; and neither he nor the Princess could forgive the wound to his pride.[15]

There, for the present, we must leave the Berlin matter, to take it up again some months later, when the tragi-comedy had at last played itself out to the end.

7

To the end of the year 1854 belongs one of the most curious — indeed almost inexplicable — episodes in the Wagner-Liszt story.

In the autumn of that year Wagner sent his friend, for his private perusal, the manuscript of the full score of the *Rhinegold*. So far

---

[15] " Regarding the Berlin production of *Tannhäuser*," Wagner writes to Minna in October, 1854, "you have done perfectly right: indeed, no one but *you* could have taken the matter in hand — not I. No doubt Liszt feels sore about it: if he draws back, he will be [in his own opinion] shamed: therefore the decision to do so must come entirely from himself." Liszt, for once, was not great enough to take a decision of that kind.

as can be gathered from their published correspondence, Liszt made no comment to Wagner on the music, any more than he had done, in 1853, on the text of the *Ring* poem. About the middle of December Wagner asked Liszt, if he had finished with the manuscript, to send it to Fischer in Dresden to be copied. In his reply of the 1st January, Liszt tells him that he has " permitted himself a little indiscretion " — the writing of an article on the work for the *Neue Zeitschrift*. " I hope you will not be angry with me for this. My intentions have been good, and it will do no harm to draw a little more public attention to the matter." The article appeared in the *Neue Zeitschrift* in January.[16]

It was decidedly an " indiscretion " on Liszt's part thus to discuss publicly a work, still in manuscript and not likely to be published for some time yet, that had been sent to him solely for his private study. But what is still more amazing about the affair is the tone adopted towards the work in the article. When the verbiage in this has been separated from the small amount of real substance, what remains is, to all intents and purposes, an expression of dubiety about the *Rhinegold*. Posing an imaginary question on the part of the reader — " What emotions do the characters inspire in us? " — Liszt answers it by saying that as yet no one *can* answer it properly, " even though the poem and the score lie before us ", because no one as yet, in the absence of a knowledge of the three other operas, can see the colossal building as a whole! If that were the case, we feel bound to ask, why did Liszt write his article at all? One could understand his saying that, knowing only the *Rhinegold*, he could profitably talk only about that, and then proceeding to analyse and expound the poem and the music for the benefit of his readers. But to set out with the profession of writing an article on the *Rhinegold* and then say he could not do so adequately because he had not the *Valkyrie, Siegfried,* and the *Götterdämmerung* before him was a strange procedure. But worse was to follow. After more irrelevant verbiage, — chatter about Michelangelo and so on — Liszt remarks that " opera, as we have hitherto known it, will appear transformed in Wagner's plan. Will it lose or gain thereby in beauty and effectiveness? That is the question! . . . So we will not

---

[16] It is reprinted in LZGS, III, Part 2.

express in advance any opinion as to the effect which this miracle of daring, this mightily planned architectural group will some day produce."

Ellis is right in calling this a " back-hander ". Whether the article, or at any rate the motive force behind it, emanated from Liszt or from the Princess is a matter of no great moment: the point is that Liszt had chosen to go out of his way to create at least a doubt in the public mind with regard to a work that had been sent to him only for his private reading, and about which there was no call for him to have written a single public word. We are driven to the conclusion that in the first place he had not studied the score very closely, in spite of its having been in his possession so long, and that in the second place he had been quite unable to get a connected and lucid view of it. Light is thrown on the affair by an entry in the diary of Cornelius, whose painful job it was at this time to try to turn the French rhodomontades of Liszt and the Princess into intelligible German for the German papers. Cornelius records in his diary one more of those maddening discussions at the Altenburg — this time in connection with this very article — over the best German word for this or that French word in the original. Tired of it all, he politely suggested to the Princess, in effect, that it might have been better if Liszt, instead of talking high-sounding nonsense all round the *Rhinegold* subject but never getting to grips with it, had dealt more specifically with the music itself; whereupon the Princess replied, " Ah, but Liszt can't do that, because he can't praise it! " [17] Why then, we may reasonably ask, did he write his article at all, seeing that there was no external call upon him to do so? Had he been goaded into doing so by the Princess, who by this time was not averse to doing Wagner a bad turn?

Wagner must have been greatly astonished by the article, though his loyalty to Liszt made him take so indulgent a view of it that to-day we are astonished at his moderation. He even went so far as to say that he saw in the article what it would puzzle any modern reader to discover in it — evidence of Liszt's " increasing sympathy " with him. At the same time he could not refrain from remarking that he had been " startled " by the article, and that he

---

[17] CABT, I, 187–8.

doubted the wisdom of giving the public the impression that the plan of the *Ring* was so colossal as to be chimerical. As so often happened with him, he cut to the heart of the matter in a single phrase: it is not that the work is on too big a scale, he says, but that the current notions of the scope of the theatre are on too small a scale: " my work is of proper human proportions, which appear to be gigantic only when we try to confine them within those other unworthy proportions."

CHAPTER XXII

THE LONDON INFERNO

1

IN 1854 he had made a last attempt to induce the patrons of music in Zürich to put the art on a solid and permanent footing at relatively small cost. He had by now sketched out for them three schemes in all; the last of them he put before the Committee of the Music Society in February. The essence of it, of course, was a plan for giving the players continuous employment in both the concert and the opera performances. The Society was to give thirty-six of them a ten months' engagement, the cost of which would have been 26,800 francs. The opera impresario was to hire this orchestra from the Society for 10,000 francs for the season: and to make both ends meet only a guarantee fund of 8,700 francs would have been required. Had the Zürich opera been a municipal institution the scheme might perhaps have gone through. But it had always been a private speculation on the part of some impresario or other: and the new director, Ernst Walther, took the view that the concerts were no particular concern of his. He made impossible conditions: his business being flourishing just then, he offered the theatre musicians higher fees than the Music Society could afford, and forbade them to take part in any of the Society's concerts. By August all hope of Wagner's comprehensive scheme being put into operation was at an end, and he now retired from the hopeless struggle. He permitted himself a little fling at the authorities in the article on Gluck's overture to *Iphigenia in Aulis* which he contributed to the *Neue Zeitschrift für Musik* of the 1st July of that year: in this he speaks of his occasionally having tried to perform " one of Beethoven's symphonies, or something similar ", with the small orchestra, " reformed each year, as chance betides ", of the Zürich Music Society.

His sympathies were decidedly with the theatre management in this affair, not only because of his resentment, on artistic grounds, at the shortsightedness of the Music Society's Committee but because he was moved by the economic plight of many of the orchestral players. The Society managed to scrape together an orchestra of sorts for the following winter season, but their first three concerts, given in December, were so sparsely attended — tickets sold, apart from the subscriptions, being only 27 for the first concert, 21 for the second, and 12 for the third — that finally Wagner had to be invoked to the rescue. To an appeal of theirs in November he had replied in dignified and moving terms, recalling to their memory the personal sacrifices he had made for the musical life of the town, expressing his sympathy with the players — never too well paid — who had suffered in the quarrel with the theatre, and declaring that he would not conduct again unless adequate rehearsals were guaranteed him and the necessary players drafted in from the theatre orchestra. Walther now proved more accommodating; and Wagner accordingly conducted at the fourth, fifth, sixth and seventh of the concerts, as well as the benefit to Alexander Müller.[1] His popularity with the public was shown by the number of tickets sold for the four regular concerts — 118, 181, 142, and 202 respectively.[2] He also, as we have seen, gave his support to the production of *Tannhäuser* in the theatre in February and March, 1855. It was no doubt the desire to secure Wagner's co-operation in this that made Walther willing to meet the Music Society Committee half-way.

Wagner further showed his sympathy with the orchestral players by inducing the string leaders to form a quartet, which he rehearsed, with infinite patience, in Beethoven's great C sharp minor quartet: he also wrote for the programme of the concert the analytical notes on the work that are now to be had in his collected writings.[3] He had the satisfaction of knowing that he had not only helped to make better artists of the men but had put them in the way of adding a little to their meagre incomes.

Anything in the nature of conducting for mere conducting's sake — the normal routine, for business ends, of the concert room — was abhorrent to him. Yet so dire was his need of money during these months that he seriously thought, for a while, of giving con-

---

[1] For particulars as to the programmes see Chapter VIII, p. 187.
[2] See FWSZ, pp. 316 ff.
[3] See RWGS, XII, 348 ff.

certs in Brussels and perhaps other towns. It was while he was in this desperate mood that he received that invitation to London which, although he did not suspect it at the time, was indirectly to have grave consequences for his future life.

2

He had hardly begun work at the scoring of the *Valkyrie* before he received a letter (in the first days of 1855) from the London Philharmonic Society, asking whether he would be willing to conduct their concerts for the coming season. Before definitely committing himself he enquired whether (1) there would be a second conductor for the " fiddle-faddle ", as he described it in a letter to Liszt, i.e. the minor works in the programme — vocal and instrumental solos, for example; (2) whether he could count on what he would regard as sufficient rehearsals. A fortnight or so later he received a visit from Mr. Anderson, the treasurer of the Society, with whom he agreed to conduct eight concerts during the coming season. A " New " Philharmonic Society had been formed some time before this, the competition of which the " Old " Society had to meet by the engagement of a conductor likely to be a box-office draw. Ferdinand Praeger, in his notorious book *Wagner as I knew him*, tried to make out that it was he who was answerable for the invitation to Wagner. The claim has been proved to be false. The prime moving spirit had been Prosper Sainton, the leader of the orchestra — a Frenchman from Toulouse — who had heard enough about Wagner to feel curious about him and to believe that there must be something exceptional in him. Sainton had for crony and housemate a German named Lüders, who, apparently, was one of the few people who had read Wagner's theoretical writings for himself, had understood their drift, and had been impressed by them. The distracted Philharmonic Committee, upset by the unexpected resignation of Sir Michael Costa, and hardly knowing where to look to find a conductor likely to counterbalance Berlioz, who was to be in charge of the " New " concerts in the latter part of that season, took Sainton's view of the Wagner question — that although no one on the committee knew anything at first hand of his capacities, " a man who had been so much abused must have something in him ".

[448]

But on the evidence of a letter of Wagner's of the 21st March, 1855, to Otto Wesendonk it seems clear that Sainton had gone even further than this: " When Sainton, having proposed me to the directors, had to explain how he knew me, he told a fib — that he had himself seen me conduct — since, as he said, the true ground for his conviction regarding me [his talks with Lüders] would have been incomprehensible to these people." [4]

To Zürich, accordingly, came Mr. Anderson in January, 1855, in an impressive fur coat that was not his own but Sainton's. Partly for finance' sake and Minna's sake, partly because a wild hope had suddenly sprung up in him that if he could make an impression on the London concert world he would be able to arrange a season of theatre performances of his works there next year, partly, no doubt, because, in view of the scoring of the *Valkyrie*, he was longing to hear a good orchestra again, Wagner allowed himself to be persuaded to undertake the eight concerts of the coming season for a fee of £200. He left Zürich on the 26th February, spent a few days in Paris with Kietz, Anders and Lindemann, and arrived in London on the evening of the 4th March (not the 2nd, as he says in *Mein Leben*).

His first harbour of refuge was Praeger. This curious creature, the running to earth of whose errors, mendacities, and embroideries upon the truth has been the occasion of infinite trouble to Wagner researchers, was a German born in Leipzig in 1815 who, after a brief career at The Hague and in other continental towns, had settled in London as a teacher and composer in 1834. From about 1845, seemingly, he had been the London correspondent of the *Neue Zeitschrift für Musik*. In later life, anxious to draw all possible glory from what had really been from first to last a rather slight acquaintance with Wagner, he tried to make out that the Philharmonic engagement was *his* work: according to him, it was he who recommended Wagner to Sainton, whereupon he [Praeger] was invited to " state his views " at a meeting of the directors. The truth of the matter is that Wagner, anxious to obtain some light on

---

[4] The directors had first of all tried to obtain Lindpaintner, the Stuttgart Kapellmeister. As might have been expected, there was an outcry in some quarters because the job had not been given to an Englishman, or to some foreigner resident in England. Sterndale Bennett received the appointment in 1856, and retained it until 1866.

musical conditions in London, and not having yet received a reply from the Society, got into communication with J. A. Röckel (the father of the Waldheim prisoner), who was now living in Basel, but who had at one time lived in England, having run, indeed, a season of opera in London in 1832–4. His son, Eduard Röckel, who by this time had removed to Bath, had made the acquaintance of Praeger in London somewhere about the middle of the century. (This was the Eduard Röckel to whom Wagner had recommended the young violinist Haimberger in 1851).[5] Röckel *père* replied, among other things, that

> " the best thing would be for you to write at once to Praeger and get him to enquire of Hogarth [the secretary of the Philharmonic] why you have had no answer. . . . Praeger's address is
>
> Ferd. Praeger Esq.,
> 31 Milton Street, Dorset Square,
> London.
>
> As Praeger occupies a whole house to himself, I am sure it would give him great pleasure if you and your wife were to alight there. Eduard and his wife always do this when they visit London. This would obviate the necessity of any hurry in your choice of a lodging."

It is clear from this that Wagner already knew at least Praeger's name; and indeed he says, in *Mein Leben*, that Praeger, in his youth, " had been a friend of the Röckel brothers, who had given me a very favourable account of him." " Presumably you know ", he now wrote to him (addressing him as " Honoured Sir " and enclosing J. A. Röckel's letter) on the 8th January, " that I am already acquainted with you — through the Röckels — also that I am aware that I am beholden to you "; following this up with a request to Praeger to see Hogarth and discuss with him the two points as to which he was still a little uncertain — the matter of a second conductor and that of the rehearsals. He apologises to his . correspondent for " dropping on him like this ", and says he will welcome the opportunity to become more intimate with him. The inference from it all is that Praeger's name had come up in the correspondence with Eduard Röckel over Haimberger in 1851, but that nothing whatever in the nature of a direct acquaintance had developed between Wagner and Praeger between that date and

---

[5] See p. 88.

1855: the tone, as well as the substance, of Wagner's letter of the 8th January is that of one addressing virtually a complete stranger, whose address, even, he does not know. It is evident at the outset that the claim subsequently made by Praeger of having been the prime cause of Wagner being invited to London has not the smallest foundation in fact.[6] Nor is there any truth in his contention that he had already been the valiant advocate of Wagner in public. On the contrary, as late as the summer of 1854 he had been decidedly scornful in print about " the New German School " and " The Music of the Future ". But once it had been settled that Wagner was to come to London, Praeger saw his opportunity to turn to good account the extremely slight acquaintance he had with the great man. He was undoubtedly of some service to Wagner at first in helping him to find his way about London and in acting as inter-preter — for Wagner knew no English; but before the end of the season it became clear enough, as we shall see later, that to be associated with Mr. Ferdinand Praeger was more of a liability than an asset for any man.

3

Wagner had embarked upon the London venture with a heavy heart: it meant not only the interruption of his work upon the *Valkyrie* score and separation from Mathilde Wesendonk, who by this time had become almost his sole human link with his immediate surroundings, but a resumption of something like the old Dresden servitude — the making of music for other people's ends, and ends,

---

[6] We need not waste any space, at this time of day, in demonstrating the frequent unreliability of Praeger's book. That has been done once for all by Ashton Ellis and Houston Stewart Chamberlain. It may just be said, for the benefit of the reader with no first-hand knowledge of the subject, that Praeger not only garbled Wagner's letters but garbled them in one way in the English edition of his book and in another way in the German: Chamberlain, in 1893, obtained access to the originals, which were then in the possession of the Earl of Dysart, and made exact copies of them. These he published in the following year, with a devastating exposure of Praeger's sins of omission and commission. (*Richard Wagner: echte Briefe an Ferdinand Praeger. Kritik der Praeger'schen Veröffentlichungen.* This, in its second edition, became the RWFP referred to in the list of Sources and References given in the first volume of the present work). The exposure was so complete that the German publishers with-drew Praeger's book from circulation.

Chamberlain's contemporary account of his quest of the original letters in London will be found in the recently published correspondence between him and Cosima Wagner. See WHSC, pp. 353 ff.

at that, which, looked at from his idealistic point of view, had more connection with business than with art. " Going to London and conducting Philharmonic concerts is not my *métier* ", he told Liszt ruefully on the 19th January, just after Anderson's visit. " Believe me ", he wrote to Wesendonk on the 5th April, between his second and third concert, " I ought not to have gone to London! " A month later he cries out to Minna, " My bitterness is frightful: only by means of the most ferocious irony, which fortunately no one here understands, can I go through with it to the end." By the 16th May there was a further crescendo of discontent: " I live here like a damned soul in hell ", he told Liszt. " How wretched I am in these surroundings, that are utterly repugnant to me, is indescribable; and I recognise that it was simply a sin and a crime on my part to accept this London invitation, which in the happiest circumstances could only mean taking me ever further and further from my true path." In after years he was able to look back upon it all with a certain indulgent irony; but at the time he suffered martyrdom.

Praeger being his only acquaintance, however remote, in London, it was naturally to Praeger's house, 31 Milton Street (now Balcombe Street), Dorset Square, that he went on his arrival; but the next day he found lodgings at 22 Portland Terrace, Regent's Park, where he remained until the end of his stay in London. Ellis's researches established the fact that Portland Terrace was not, as Glasenapp had said, at the south-east corner of Regent's Park — which would have been within easy distance of the concert room and the West End generally — but near the North Gate of the Park.[7] There he did his best to make himself comfortable. Through the good offices of Liszt he obtained the loan of an excellent grand piano from Erard; and a carpenter was found to rig up for him a tall desk of the type he was accustomed to use, standing up, when he was scoring. London in February must have seemed to him a depressing place after Zürich; but he found some consolation in taking Praeger's big dog, Gipsy, for an occasional run in the Park, contemplating the sheep there, feeding the ducks, and visiting the Zoological

---

[7] For closer details see ELW, V, 130 ff. Ellis conjectures that the landlady of the house was one Mrs Henry, "a respectable widow", charging Wagner something like "two to four guineas a week . . . according as it did or did not include his board."

Gardens, Westminster Abbey, St. Paul's, and no doubt the other usual London " sights ". At the Guildhall he enjoyed hugely the Gog and Magog figures, which reminded him, according to Praeger, of his Fasolt and Fafner; and at Greenwich he experienced the rare felicity of a whitebait dinner.

Mein Leben makes it evident that while his real intimates were Sainton and Lüders he spent rather more time with Praeger than Ellis was willing to believe. He had no great opinion of his new friend's intelligence: " I am a good deal with Praeger, that good ridiculous fellow ",[8] he writes to August Röckel. In *Mein Leben* he describes him as " an unusually good-natured fellow, though of an excitability out of proportion to his culture." He was certainly very appreciative of the many little things that Praeger and his wife were able and willing to do for him.

He was equally unhappy in the concert room — the old Hanover Square Rooms — and out of it. He was appalled, as all foreigners were in that epoch, by the cost of living in London: he soon realised that his £200 for four months would not leave much margin for saving. Dinner at a restaurant being impossible under six shillings, he soon made arrangements for eating at his lodgings. But coal cost him nearly a shilling a day, and even then he could not keep himself warm: he made what no doubt struck him as an original discovery — that the English fireplace warms you only if you are sitting close to it. Owing to the great distances to be covered he had to spend a good deal of money on cabs. The formality of English social life fretted him: a top hat for calls on such people as the Philharmonic directors was one of his first and probably most regretted expenses. Praeger is perhaps within the bounds of veracity when he describes the difficulty the Regent Street hatter had in finding a top hat that would fit that enormous head. So convinced was Wagner that Englishmen always dressed formally for any occasion out of the common that a day or two after his arrival in London he called at Sainton's house in full evening dress at nine o'clock in the morning. That must have been a sight for the small

---

[8] " Närrisch " may mean all sorts of things — foolish, crazy, strange, queer, ridiculous, merry, droll, etc. All in all, "ridiculous" seems to be the best translation here.

boys of the neighbourhood. He refused to pay any etiquette visits whatever except to the Philharmonic directors, and to Costa, to whom he was taken by Praeger.[9]

Nor was he any happier in his contact with the musical life of the town. Musical London bore in 1855 the same faintly comic aspect it had always had, still has, and probably will have to the end of recorded time. There was the usual mixture of professionalism and dilettantism in the public music-making; there was the usual fatuous confidence that any orchestral concert programme whatever could be adequately carried out with one rehearsal, or at the most two, English orchestral players being so super-competent that they did not need as many rehearsals as their weaker brethren on the Continent; there was the usual crowd of professional and amateur-professional practitioners, several of whom were such manifest mediocrities that to us of to-day it is a mystery how they escaped a knighthood. There was *The Times*, already bearing with conscious dignity the heavy burden of the responsibility that had been laid upon it by Providence of giving the cosmos its A. There were the very British oratorio concerts of the Sacred Music Society at Exeter Hall, at which, as Wagner assured Otto Wesendonk, people sat for four hours at a stretch listening to one fugue after another, with the sure conviction of having done a good deed for which they would reap their reward in heaven, where they would get nothing but the loveliest Italian opera arias.[10] This bent of the English public towards oratorio, he thought, had been perceived by the astute Mendelssohn, who, by ministering to it, had become the Briton's god in music, and had certainly increased the public's

---

[9] Ellis doubted whether Praeger was telling the truth when he said that it was he who took Wagner to Sainton's — opining that Praeger, with his knowledge of London, would have vetoed the evening dress. Ellis declined to believe, again, that Praeger accompanied Wagner on the visit to Costa. Wagner, however, in *Mein Leben*, says that it was Praeger who took him both to Costa and Sainton. Now that we have *Mein Leben* — which of course was inaccessible to Ellis — we find that in small things Praeger was telling the truth rather oftener than, on the face of it, had formerly seemed probable.

[10] He still remembered these appalling experiences when he was writing *Mein Leben*. English musical culture, he says, is bound up with English Protestantism: this accounted for oratorio being more popular in England than opera, for to the delights of music was added the satisfaction of having attended a sort of church service. "Everyone holds a Handel piano score in his hand — in the same way that he holds a prayer-book in church."

appetite for that kind of thing by supplying it. Into the complex question which was cause and which effect Wagner presumably did not feel himself competent to enter. Oscar Wilde, it will be remembered, could never solve to his own satisfaction the problem of whether it was the fogs that were the cause of there being so many dull people in London, or the dull people who caused the fogs. And no scientist has as yet been able to settle for us the question whether it is that the British have been so fond of oratorios because Handel and Mendelssohn wrote them, or that Handel and Mendelssohn wrote oratorios because the British are constitutionally so fond of them.

4

Another strange feature of the British musical psychology which sorely puzzled Wagner has persisted to the present day. He noted with astonishment that while London audiences were commendably enthusiastic in their applause after a good work or a good performance, they applauded with just as much enthusiasm after a bad work or a bad performance. Thirty seconds after the strains of the Eroica had died away at his first concert the audience was listening with the same zest as previously to a wearisome duet from a Marschner opera. He went to a concert of the New Philharmonic Society where he heard, he says, " overtures, symphonies, concertos, choruses, arias, etc." all " conducted *klitsch-klatsch* by Dr. Wylde." The audience applauded everything with its customary heartiness, and the next day Wagner discovered from the newspaper reports that this had been " the finest concert of the whole season." And the robust appetite that enabled people to gorge themselves for four hours on end in Exeter Hall on oratorio fugues without any apparent ill consequences made it possible for them to sit, without turning a hair, through Philharmonic concerts the mere length of which reduced poor Wagner to complete exhaustion. The programmes, which comprised, as a rule, two symphonies, an overture or two, and a number of vocal or instrumental solos, reminded him, he says, of the cry of the London bus conductors — " Full inside ".

The orchestra he found quite good in many respects, though it lacked nuance and favoured a level mezzo forte in everything; a pianissimo such as he desired in certain passages was something unknown to them. Their tepidity in this and other respects may have been due in part to the bad traditions that had continued from the days of Mendelssohn to those of Costa. But it was perhaps due even more to the belief of Victorian England that any display of unusual sensitiveness was bad form, even in art — especially in art, one might almost say. Malwida von Meysenbug, who has given us an incomparable picture of English social life at that period, has an amusing story of one of her London pupils who very much wanted to learn singing, but was deterred by the reflection that singing, in anything like the full sense of the term, was not quite ladylike, and certainly not quite English.

> " She had been given to understand that the first rule was that she must not exhibit any feeling when she was singing: this would be improper for a young girl, particularly as most songs were love songs. ' The Germans ', she said to me, ' do not shrink from showing feeling, nay, even passion when they sing; but that is most improper.' When I replied that it was precisely on this account that most of what we heard from English dilettanti in English drawing-rooms was not really song at all, she laughed and said, ' Strictly speaking I think you are right, and if I were a German I would sing with the utmost feeling: but as it is, I mustn't ".[11]

With a national mentality of this kind it is little wonder that a number of people in Wagner's audiences detected a touch of moral impropriety in his loving nuancing of a beautiful phrase, or saw a direct attack on Victorian morals in the passions unchained in the *Tannhäuser* overture.

Among his few consolations during these months of misery were talks with Sainton and Lüders, whose kindness to him was unfailing: the good Sainton made a special point of keeping their visitor's cigar case filled with good cigars. Wagner's ignorance of English must have made intercourse with the ordinary Londoner virtually impossible. Through the instrumentality of Otto Wesendonk he met a rich merchant of German extraction, one Beneke, whose wife was a relation of Mendelssohn. Beneke took him at least twice in his carriage to his fine house in Camberwell, where, every Saturday evening, relations and friends gathered together to the number of something like twenty-five; there was much singing and piano-

---

[11] MMI, I, 331.

playing, the music, as Wagner says, being naturally all Mendelssohn. He was appreciative enough of Beneke's good nature, but the atmosphere of the house could not have been congenial to him. He could talk German with Karl Klindworth, a handsome young pianist who had been a pupil of Liszt in Weimar, and had now been settled in London for a year or so, where he had already incurred some hostility because of his advocacy of Liszt and Wagner. A congenial subject for conversation between him and Wagner was the lack of idealism in English musical life, public and private. Klindworth was all fire and flame for the *Valkyrie*, of which he began forthwith to make a piano score. Wagner conceived a great liking for the fine young fellow, and only regretted that he had not a tenor voice, in which case his appearance and stature would have made him an ideal Siegfried. Unfortunately the two did not meet as often as Wagner could have wished, owing to the persistent bad health of Klindworth.

With the professional musicians of the town, and with most of the well-meaning dilettanti who clustered round the Philharmonic, he was naturally out of tune from the beginning. He took a liking to the gentlemanly John Lodge Ellerton (brother-in-law of Lord Brougham), whom he describes as " a poet, a music-lover, and, alas! a composer ": a composer indeed, for the encyclopaedias inform us that he had to his credit an oratorio, some eleven operas, and forty-four string quartets, as well as, no doubt, a number of minor works. He commended himself to Wagner by his pleasant manners, by the fact that he was already an ardent Wagnerian, having heard Wagner's operas in Germany, by his reaction against the English Mendelssohn worship, and by a splendid dinner he gave Wagner and his friends at the University Club, from which the generous host had to be taken home by two men, one holding each arm — " quite as a matter of course ", says Wagner, who regarded the incident, perhaps with some reason, as typical of the England of that epoch.

He could not get on with George Alexander Macfarren, whom he regarded as " a turgid, melancholy Scotsman " [12] who was too

---

[12] Wagner would no doubt have been interested in the "melancholy Scotsman's" analysis of himself, at the age of twenty-three, in a letter to his friend and pupil Davison: "I am a miserable being, and it is not enough that I am, like all humanity,

proud to discuss the manner of interpretation of his own works with Wagner, so that the latter was relieved when the symphony of Macfarren which the Society had intended to give was set aside in favour of his *Chevy Chase* overture: this appealed to Wagner " on account of its wild, passionate character ". He was more attracted to the old-fashioned and amiable Cipriani Potter, then a man of about sixty-three, who charmed him by what Wagner thought almost an excess of modesty. He liked also old George Hogarth, the secretary of the Society; [13] but it was an embarrassing moment for everyone concerned when Wagner, on calling at Hogarth's to say goodbye, found Meyerbeer there: he had come to London to conduct his latest opera, *L'Etoile du Nord*. The two composers stared at each other in awkward silence. Hogarth, says Wagner,

> " who had felt sure that we were acquainted, was greatly astonished; and when I was leaving he asked me if I did not know Herr Meyerbeer. I replied that he had better ask Meyerbeer about me. When I met Hogarth again that evening he assured me that Meyerbeer had spoken of me in terms of the warmest appreciation. Thereupon I suggested his reading certain numbers of the Paris *Gazette Musicale* in which Fétis, some time before, had given a less favourable account of Meyerbeer's views about me. Hogarth shook his head, and could not understand 'how two such great composers could meet in so strange a manner'."

Meyerbeer's diary for that date contains only this brief reference to the affair: " 24th June. Visit to . . . Hogarth: there I met also Richard Wagner. We greeted each other coldly without speaking." [14]

5

Anderson, who, it seems, had quarrelled, under Costa's influence, with Sainton, was merely a figure of fun to Wagner, who tells us that " he had succeeded, through the influence of her Majesty's coachman, in elevating himself to the post of conductor of the Queen's Band." (Was " her Majesty's coachman ", one wonders,

---

born to endure misfortune, but I am a perpetual blister — the constant cause of vexation to my friends." (DMW, p. 27). The shadow of the total blindness that was one day to engulf him was perhaps creeping over him even in his youth.

[13] In *Mein Leben* Wagner calls him Mr. Howard.
[14] See RWML, II, 1046-7.

Wagner's misinterpretation of " Master of the Horse "?). His ignorance of music made him the butt of the musicians when he had to conduct at the annual Court concert. Wagner assures us further that Mrs Anderson — whom, on account of her corpulence, he had christened " Charlemagne " — had also appropriated to herself, among other things, the office of a Court trumpeter.

Another old friend whom he saw occasionally was Semper, who had been settled in London for some time, employing his genius in designs for interior decoration and furniture. Soon after his return to Zürich Wagner had the satisfaction of securing a post for Semper as a teacher at the Federal Polytechnic.

The only other persons with whom he came into anything like close contact were Berlioz, the story of whose meetings with him will be told later — and his old friend Hermann Franck,[15] who, being at Brighton at this time, came up to London to see him. Franck told him of the extraordinary stories concerning him that were going the rounds in Germany — how he intended to make for himself in London " a position from which he could wage a war of extermination against the whole race of German musicians ", and so on. Wagner set his mind at rest on this and other points, and the two old friends turned to the more congenial subject of Schopenhauer. It was the last time they were to meet. A few months later Franck's shattered body was found in a Brighton street — the result of a fall from a window — while on the bed lay the strangled body of his sixteen-years-old son, with whose determination to join the English navy he had not been in sympathy. It was the morning of the day on which the boy should have joined his ship.

The Italian Opera at Covent Garden Wagner visited only once or twice: presumably a " rather grotesque " performance of *Fidelio* by " dirty Germans and voiceless Italians " was too much for him. More to his liking was the light fare provided at the Olympic Theatre — where he saw Robson in the *Yellow Dwarf* and in *Garrick Fever* — and some Shakespeare performances at the Haymarket and at a small out-of-the-way theatre in Marylebone which was trying just then to attract the public with Shakespeare — the sempiternal British experience! He also saw the British intellect in

---

[15] See Index to Vol. I.

its full glory in a wonderful pantomime, which began with the Goose that laid the Golden Eggs, passed on, by an easy transition, into the Three Wishes, thence into Little Red Riding Hood — " with the wolf metamorphosed into a cannibal who sang a very comical couplet " — and came to a palpitating end with Cinderella. From all this the creator of the *Ring* and student of Schopenhauer obtained, he says, " a very good idea of the kind of imaginative fare that pleases the [English] people."

One acquaintance made at this time was destined to endure to the end, though chance willed that it should be some years yet before the first meeting was followed by a second one. One of the noblest women of the nineteenth century, Malwida von Meysenbug, had been driven by her idealism out of Germany in the troubled days of 1848. In 1855 she was living in England, earning her living by teaching, and devoting herself largely to the care of the children of Alexander Herzen, the Russian patriot, whose wife had fallen a victim, some years before, to the wiles of Herwegh. It was at the house of Professor Friedrich Althaus, the brother of the great friend of her earlier days in Germany, Theodor Althaus, that Malwida one evening met Wagner. She had long been acquainted with his revolutionary writings, in which, she tells us in her Memoirs, she recognized the gospel of that German future of which she herself had dreamed. She had written to the author in 1852, expressing her understanding of, and sympathy with, his ideals; but the correspondence had gone no further just then. It had long been a great regret to her that owing to her exile from Germany she had never heard any of the music of the man whose aspirations seemed to her to have so much in common with her own. It was consequently with a thrill that she heard that he was to be in charge of the Philharmonic concerts during the spring season of 1855. She lived in Richmond, at that time so inaccessible from London that it was impossible for her to get home again after a concert; she accordingly made arrangements to stay in town for the night after his second concert. The impression she received from this, she tells us, was the profoundest she had ever experienced since she had heard Schröder-Devrient in the singer's great days. She was especially moved by Wagner's performance of the *Freischütz* overture: she had known the opera almost by heart from her childhood's days, yet now, it seemed to her, she was really hearing this music for the first time: Wagner had for the moment lifted the British orchestra out of their normal rut and made it realise the mystery and horror and poetry of Weber's romantic world.

Soon afterwards she received an invitation from Anna Althaus to meet Wagner at her house. At first she was chilled by his reserve, which, however, she soon traced to its cause — the gnawing sense of complete alienation from English life and the English temperament. The Mendelssohn clique had pursued him, in the Press and in private, with unrelenting hatred: they had even said that no one deserved the title of conductor who presumed to conduct Beethoven's symphonies by heart! Suddenly the name of Schopenhauer was introduced into the conversation. Malwida had often seen the philosopher in Frankfort in her youth — an old man taking his daily solitary walk with no company but that of his dog, and, at the table d'hôte in the hotel, openly derided as a madman. At Althaus's request, Wagner entered upon an exposition of the Schopenhauerian philosophy, with its central thesis, so attractive to him at that time, of the denial of the Will to Live; and Malwida found, as so many others in that epoch did, the meaning of the universe laid bare to her in a flash. But even on this occasion there was no special *rapprochement* between her and Wagner. She wrote to him later, asking him to visit her in Richmond, where Herzen was anxious to meet him. Wagner declined the invitation, ostensibly on the ground that all his time was taken up just then with preparations for his return to Germany.[16] It is probable, however, that he felt that his close friendship with Herwegh might prove an embarrassment both to himself and to Herzen.

6

The programmes of Wagner's concerts were essentially as follows, the minor pieces being omitted as being of no interest to-day:

I. 12th March.
　　Haydn's Symphony No. 7.
　　Spohr's " Dramatic " concerto (Ernst).

---

[16] See MMI, I, 445–50.

Mendelssohn's *Hebrides* overture.
The Eroica Symphony.
The *Magic Flute* overture.

II. 26th March.
    Freischütz overture.
    Mendelssohn's violin concerto (Blagrove).
    Lohengrin: the Prelude; the Procession to the Minster; the
        Wedding March and Bridal Chorus.
    Beethoven No. 9.

III. 16th April.
    Mendelssohn's Italian Symphony.
    Beethoven's B flat piano concerto.
    Euryanthe overture.
    Beethoven No. 5.
    Cherubini's *Water-Carrier* overture.

IV. 30th April.
    Lucas's 3rd Symphony in B flat (manuscript).
    Spohr's Nonet.
    Weber's *Ruler of the Spirits* overture.
    Beethoven No. 7.
    Onslow's overture *L'Alcalde de la Vega.*

V. 14th May.
    Mozart's E flat symphony.
    Chopin's E minor concerto (Charles Halle).
    Tannhäuser overture.
    Beethoven No. 6.
    Weber's *Preciosa* overture.

VI. 28th May.
    Cipriani Potter's G minor symphony.
    Beethoven's violin concerto (Sainton).
    Beethoven's Leonora overture No. 3.
    Mendelssohn's Scotch Symphony.
    Spohr's overture to *Der Berggeist.*

VII. 11th June.

> Macfarren's *Chevy Chase* overture.
> Mozart's Jupiter Symphony.
> *Tannhäuser* overture.
> Beethoven No. 8. ·
> Cherubini's *Anacreon* overture.

VIII. 25th June.

> Spohr's 3rd symphony.
> Hummel's A flat piano concerto (Pauer).
> Mendelssohn's *Midsummer Night's Dream* overture.
> Beethoven No. 4.
> Weber's *Oberon* overture.

It will be seen that these programmes contain nothing by Liszt. The reproach has often been made against Wagner, by unthinking people, that although Liszt had done so much for him, he never performed a single work of Liszt's. They forget that Wagner's concerts, apart from those in London, were in the main not those of a touring professional conductor, conducting miscellaneous programmes for conducting's sake, but were designed to introduce his own music to the public in a more representative way than he had found, by experience, the ordinary Kapellmeister capable of doing, and so to pave the way for a performance of one or other of his operas. As a matter of fact, he had offered to include a work by Liszt in his London programmes, but Liszt himself suggested leaving the matter over to the following season. Neither the *Faust* nor the *Dante* Symphony was as yet ready, while the first batch of symphonic poems was only being engraved at the time when Wagner went to London.

The full story of Wagner's handling by the London Press can be read in Ellis, whose praiseworthy industry enabled him to devote nearly the whole of his fifth volume to these four months spent by Wagner in London. Wagner was convinced that most of the critics were in the pay of Meyerbeer. There is no need to assume that: the trouble was simply that they were men of ordinary intelligence brought face to face, for the first time in their professional lives, with a contemporary phenomenon that was extraordinary, and failing to see how much bigger it was than themselves. No suspicion whatever of undue influence can attach to Henry Chorley, the critic of the *Athenaeum*. His musical culture and musical sympathies were alike limited; he wrote penetratingly about the things he really understood — such as singing and interpretation in Italian and French opera — while for the rest, however narrow his range of apprehension may have been he was undeniably honest, though sometimes the spleen of ill-health is evident in his work. When Sydney Smith, not long before his death, was destroying his letters so that no biographer could make indiscreet use of them, a friend asked him if he would mind Chorley reading them first. " No ", said Smith: " Chorley is a gentleman." Whatever we may think of his judgment of what was then the new music, there can be no doubt that Chorley was sincere in his beliefs and honest in his expression of them.

George Hogarth — Dickens's father-in-law, by the way — managed, not unsuccessfully, to square his functions as secretary of the Philharmonic Society with his duties as musical critic of the *Illustrated London News* and the *Daily News*. Here again there can be no question of corrupt influence from any quarter: Hogarth, indeed, was anything but unappreciative of much of Wagner's work. On the *Morning Post* was W. H. Glover; on the *Sunday Times*, Henry Smart. The nominal head of the profession was J. W. Davison, who, besides being the musical critic of *The Times*, was editor of the *Musical World*. The range of his musical or his general intelligence was on the whole no wider than that of Chorley, though he wrote with a blustering cocksure belief in himself and a knockabout comedian's gusto in his journalism that attracted to him a larger public than Chorley's. He was undoubtedly on terms of greater intimacy with a number of composers and performers than it was wise for any critic to be, even in those days, when the standard of propriety in these matters was not so high as it is now: but although malice might make capital out of more than one incident in his career there is no reason to doubt his general honesty. He was of the journalistic type that finds no difficulty in persuading itself that its own rather small intelligence is the measure of all things musical, and therefore regards each of its naïve repulsions as the expression of a taste so pure that God alone can have been the creator of it.

Of Wagner at first hand these gentlemen knew very little: [17] but they were mostly prejudiced against him from the first,[18] partly on the strength of the garbled accounts of his theories that were floating about in the musical world — he was popularly credited, for instance, with not having a good word to say for any music but his own — partly because he was known to have expressed himself contemptuously about Meyerbeer and suspected to have only a tempered admiration for Mendelssohn, and partly because of his association with Liszt. At that time Liszt had produced none of the large-scale orchestral and choral works by which he is now best known, and it is doubtful whether the English critics in general had any close acquaintance with the piano works of his earlier period. There can be no question, then, of a prejudice against him purely on account of his music. The only conclusion we can come to is that there was something in his personality and his career that did not commend itself to many worthy people: we must remember that the maturer Liszt of the modern popular imagination, the Liszt who showed so much nobility interwrought with his failings, the Liszt who commands our sympathy and pity for the endless struggle within him of the noble and the ignoble elements in his nature, the Liszt who faced with such earnestness so many new problems of composition, was at that time quite unknown. That generation knew, for the most part, only the Liszt who had mingled so much that was shoddy with the brilliance of his virtuosity as a pianist, and the Liszt whose name stank in the nostrils of thousands of quiet, sober people because it had so often been associated with

---

[17] Perhaps the best-informed of them was Chorley, who had heard *Lohengrin* at Weimar in 1850 and *Tannhäuser* in Dresden in 1852. But he evidently could not grasp anything whatever of either the new spirit or the new form of these works.

Some months after Wagner had left England, Davison heard *Tannhäuser* in Cologne. He had to admit that "there was a full house, and the opera was much applauded", and that "the success of *Tannhäuser* here, with the public, is considerable." But, he adds, "the musicians will not tolerate it" — the said "musicians", of course, being professional mediocrities of the Hiller type.

[18] Chorley, for instance, broke out ill-temperedly in the *Athenaeum* as soon as the news of Wagner's engagement was made public. "Supposing", he said, "that we were to be spiritedly shown that no competent conductors exist in England, we submit that it was not needful to pick out from among all the continental musicians the man of men whose avowed and published creed is contempt for all such music as the English love. . . . The appointment of Herr Wagner can be regarded as nothing short of a wholesale offence to the native and foreign conductors resident in England. . . ."

the escapades of the boudoir and the bedchamber. No student of the byways of the musical literature of the time can avoid the conclusion that he was an object of suspicion and dislike to many people. Apart from personal considerations of this kind there was a vague sense in the minds of many that music was taking a new direction, that the old values were being questioned, that the new values were as yet dubious, and that the flamboyant Liszt and his hot-headed young Weimar disciples were beginning to be a danger to " classical " art.

Wagner's well-known association with Liszt, then, made him also an object of suspicion with many who as yet knew next to nothing about him at first hand. Praeger, in his new-found zeal for Wagner, did him no service by contributing to an American paper an article, reproduced with malicious glee by Davison in the *Musical World*, in which he hailed Wagner and Berlioz as " the two most ultra-red republicans in music ", and rejoiced at the disturbing effect they were likely to have in " the musical world of this classical, staid, sober, proper, exclusive, conservative London." For Mendelssohnian London in general, and Davison in particular, to whom Praeger had referred disparagingly in his article, looked upon themselves as the heaven-appointed custodians of the ark of the musical covenant. Even before Wagner had come to London, Davison had told his readers that

" it is well known that Richard Wagner has little respect for any music but his own "; that " he is earnestly bent on upsetting all the accepted forms and canons of art . . . in order the more surely to establish his doctrines that rhythm is superfluous, counterpoint a useless bore, and every musician ancient or modern, himself excepted, either an impostor or a blockhead. Now such rhodomontade may pass muster in the dreary streets of Weimar, where Franz Liszt reigns, like a musical King Death, and quaffs destruction to harmony and melody . . . but in England, where Liszt was never much thought of . . . it can hardly be. If the brilliant meteor, Berlioz, failed to entice the musical mind of this country from its devotion to the bright and pure spheres of art into his own erratic and uncertain course, what chance can there be for the duller Richard, with his interminable pamphlets? " [19]

---

[19] Verdi, who by that time had got no further than *Il Trovatore* and *La Traviata*, was also regarded by this precious denizen of the "bright and pure spheres of art" as "a red republican of music".

Wagner had from the first refused to follow the practice of the day and pay duty calls on the critics; and these gentlemen would perhaps have been less than human, in the then state of musical criticism, had they not been offended with him for this: it could only look to them like a combination of stiff-necked arrogance and pre-resolved enmity. Davison in particular was accustomed to being courted and flattered by composers and performers.[20] Further, Ellis has given good grounds for believing that Praeger's foolish American articles, in which he fell foul of Davison in particular, were answerable for the gradual increase of malice towards Wagner in the London Press as the concerts proceeded. Praeger's colleagues had never taken the simpleton very seriously — Davison especially losing no opportunity of making a butt of him: and now that Praeger had taken Wagner under his protection, and was using him as a stick with which to castigate Davison and his like, the

---

[20] Jullien once protested to him that "if *The Times* is against anything whatever, that thing cannot hold out long. Do you want to ruin me? . . . Speak . . . but I beseech you, do not assassinate me." Berlioz often flattered Davison for diplomatic reasons, even going so far as to dedicate the *Corsaire* overture to him. Such trifling tokens of disinterested regard as snuff-boxes, diamond pins, shirt-studs, and so on frequently came his way. Meyerbeer in particular had an exquisitely sensitive perception of Davison's unique abilities as a critic — at any rate as a critic of Meyerbeer's operas. He could not leave London, he wrote to him in 1859, after the production of *Dinorah*, without expressing his "deep gratitude" for Davison's "admirable article": "such criticism constitutes a *second creation*, and I am proud and happy to have obtained the approbation of a man so eminent as yourself." If Wagner could only have paid a few humble tributes of this kind to the commanding genius of Davison the historian of musical criticism in England might have a different tale to tell to-day. But Wagner could not: nor had he either the inclination or the depth of purse to testify his appreciation of a critic in Meyerbeer's well-known way. "You would double my obligation to you", Meyerbeer's letter continues, "if you would kindly accept the accompanying little souvenir, continue your valued friendship for me, and remember me to the charming Madame Goddard-Davison [the critic's wife, Arabella Goddard]." See DMW, pp. 73, 101, 149, 150, 226, etc.

Perhaps, after all, Davison had not been entirely uninfluenced, in his public utterances about Meyerbeer, by the latter's dinners, flatteries, and "little souvenirs". The tenor Gustave Roger, who was in England in the summer of 1848, records in his diary on the 27th July that "that crazy fellow Davison, who is not unversed in music, has just been maintaining that Meyerbeer and Halévy are not musicians, that they cannot write correctly!" In September, after hobnobbing with Davison in Scotland, Roger says again that the journalist's gods are Bach, Handel, Gluck, and — greatest of all — Mendelssohn. "I find it vain to talk to him about our French school — Herold, Auber, Meyerbeer, Halévy: the last two simply exasperate him; he rejects them, finds them beneath criticism. I have done all I can to inoculate him with my admirations." (RCT, pp. 82–3, 146–7).

temptation at once to make a laughing-stock of him and to harass Wagner was irresistible. (The feeling at the back of their minds, no doubt, was that Praeger's articles had been inspired by Wagner).

A good deal of the criticism of the concerts, however wrong-headed it may appear now, had at first been quite legitimate — honest attempts on the part of the writers to assess musical values according to the current standards. They naturally felt that wherever Wagner departed from the readings of Mendelssohn or Costa, but especially of Mendelssohn, he must be wrong. The delicate nuancing which he tried to get from the orchestra seemed to the critics merely affectation. Used as they were to the grotesque tempi that Mendelssohn had made the tradition in the Beethoven symphonies, and the headlong pace of Costa,[21] they could not reconcile themselves to Wagner's tempi. His flexibility of rhythm, that subtle ebb-and-flow combined with the preservation of the firm line of the phrase that is the ideal of the modern conductor, seemed to them improper. They thought his beat " uncertain " — great importance was attached to the " beat " in those days. His way of stressing the more poetic second subjects, in contrast to the sometimes more dramatic first subjects, either made him take them more slowly or gave his listeners the impression that he was so doing. His bringing-out of the contrasting dramatic elements in Weber's overtures seemed to them " forced ". Anything in his readings that departed, in tempo or in shading, from what they had grown accustomed to was " taking unwarrantable liberties with the music ". In taking these views the critics were perfectly within their rights: all that we have against them to-day is the crudity and the vulgarity with which some of them, particularly the buffoon of *The Times*, expressed their opinions, and their uniform and lamentable failure — which marks them out for the commonplace intelligences they mostly were — to recognise that they were being faced with something vitally new in music, and to sit down and do some hard thinking and self-questioning about it.

---

[21] What Costa's tempi were like we may surmise from a letter of Sterndale Bennett's to Davison in 1836: "Do not take my new overture too fast. . . . Is it true that Costa will conduct the Philharmonic concerts next year? I hope not: the only advantage would be that we might have the whole of Beethoven's symphonies in one night and still have time for supper." DMW, p. 30.

We of to-day can perhaps visualise the situation as it appeared to the more thoughtful of them. Henry Smart had four main faults to find with Wagner: " Firstly, he takes all quick movements faster than anyone else; secondly, he takes all slow movements slower than anyone else; thirdly, he prefaces the entry of an important point, or the return of a theme — especially in a slow movement — by an exaggerated *ritardando;* and fourthly, he reduces the speed of an allegro — say in an overture or the first movement of a symphony — fully one-third, immediately on the entrance of its cantabile phrases." This seems, on the face of it, a reasoned statement of facts observed. But the question arises, from what point of view were they observed? We need have little hesitation in taking it for granted that Wagner's tempi sometimes differed markedly from those in current use. From his brochure of 1869 *On Conducting* we learn that he had been dissatisfied from the beginning of his career with the tempi of the ordinary conductor, especially in Beethoven: Mendelssohn in particular had started a bad tradition of taking whole works at a uniformly brisk pace in order, as he himself confessed, to cover up defects in the playing. Wagner's main contentions, as regards tempi, were that most conductors in the first place did not make sufficient distinction between a fast movement and a slow one, and in the second place that they did not see the difference in spirit between, say, a Mozart and a Beethoven adagio. And as he had an unusually acute sense of the *drama* implicit in many orchestral works we can readily believe that his tempi seemed to the London critics too fast at one point, too slow at another: they could not place themselves at his inner point of view. Apart from that, he held that " tempo " in itself is not much more than an abstraction — a matter on which many modern conductors will agree with him. A performance can be perfectly correct according to the metronome marks and yet be altogether bad: he was always amused, indeed, when after a poor performance of one of his own operas he was solemnly assured by the Kapellmeister that the tempi had been precisely as indicated in the score. Tempo is a matter, as he says, not merely of time but of *melos* — the singing soul of the melody: " the right conception of the melos alone ", he says, " can give the right tempo; the two are one and indivisible; the one conditions the other." [22] The *life* of a musical phrase is something subtly compounded of tempo, of dynamics, and of all that we mean by *song* — the suffusion of the melodic line with accents and nuances that make it *live*, in correspondence with the life it had within the brain of the composer who poured out his heart in it.

It was from Schröder-Devrient's instinctive artistry in this respect in the phrasing of the melodies she sang, he says, that he divined the true rendering, for example, of the moving oboe cadenza in Beethoven's C minor symphony; and as he matured, both in his understanding of music and in his knowledge of conducting, he came to see ever more and more clearly that the quintessence of interpretation resided in this giving at once plastic form and changeful play of feeling to the melos of the music. But this was a matter not simply of tempo but of the careful modelling of each phrase to the desired end; and we can easily understand that neither had he the time for all this at a single rehearsal nor could the London players rid themselves in a moment of their old habits and acquire new ones. It is quite conceivable, then, that many of his performances really did miss fire because they were neither one thing nor the other, had the virtues neither of the old straightforward kind, such as they were, nor of the new Wagnerian kind; for the one thing that could have made the novel points of his tempi clear — the securing of organic inter-relations between the tempo and the nuancing — were impossible under London Philharmonic conditions. The critics, therefore, were presumably often right as regards externals: what they failed to realise — and indeed, under the circumstances could hardly be expected to realise — was that the performances were falling between two stools, and that the fault was not Wagner's.

8

He had not been able to enforce his demand for what he regarded as adequate rehearsals; and he was often in despair over the impossibility of doing justice to any of the works in a long programme in the limited time allotted to him. A good deal of time must have been lost at rehearsals by his inability to speak English: he mastered,

---

[22] *On Conducting*, in RWGS, VIII, 274.

indeed, one allocution — " Once more, please! " — but that of it-self would not carry him far. Sainton, of course, had to do the inter-preting in general. On the whole Wagner seems to have got on well with the orchestra and to have earned its respect, though they were chary of showing it in public for fear of offending Costa, on whom they depended for their engagements at the Opera. Probably what distressed Wagner even more than the length of the programmes and the insufficient time allotted him for the rehearsals was the miscellaneous character of them. He especially objected to the sometimes paltry vocal solos. His ill-humour over these and other matters came to a head at the fourth concert, at which a Herr Reichardt, having made a false entry in an aria from the *Hugue-nots,* made gestures to the audience suggesting that the fault was the conductor's. This was the last bitter drop in a cup already full: at the end of the first part of the concert he told everyone who was within hearing that he was sick to death of " these endless pro-grammes, with their mass of vocal and instrumental pieces ", which " tired me out and tortured my aesthetic feelings." [23] His friends succeeded in talking him over; but the bitterness remained, and the conviction deepened within him that his acceptance of the London offer had been one of the most grievous mistakes of his life.

He was not cut out, indeed, for any post as a concert conductor. It was characteristic of his uncompromising nature that he had no interest whatever in the small change of life, literature or art: he lived only for the great things of other men and for his own great goal. He had from the first, by instinct, the wisdom that comes to most of us only late in life through experience and reflection, the wisdom that urges a man to deal with his soul as with his body, giving it to eat only what will nourish it, not perpetually forcing it to eat for mere eating's sake, or because other people, of grosser appetite but less refined palate, are not happy unless they are eat-

---

[23] To Fischer on the 15th June: RWUF, p. 329. As Lucas had conducted his own symphony, and, one gathers, Spohr's Nonet was given without a conductor, Wagner had nothing to do during the long first half of this concert but to conduct a Beethoven aria, the Meyerbeer aria, and, as final piece, Weber's overture *The Ruler of the Spirits.* He may well have asked himself whether it had been worth his while to come from Switzerland just for this. But an encore of the overture had been demanded: and *this,* I conjecture, was the main cause of his anger. To have to stand up like a per-forming dog and do his tricks for an audience that could demand a repetition of a second-rate work of this kind must have been gall and wormwood to him.

ing, no matter what. The minor things in music never interested him very much, even as matters of historical study. " I am not a learned musician ", he said in one of his talks with friends in his old age.

> " I never had occasion to pursue antiquarian researches; and periods of transition did not interest me much. I went straight from Palestrina to Bach, from Bach to Gluck and Mozart — or if you choose, along the same path backwards. It suited me to rest content with the acquaintance of the principal men, the heroes and their main works. For aught I know this may have had its drawbacks; any way, my mind has never been stuffed with ' music in general ' ".

The professional conductor, however, *has* to have his mind stuffed with " music in general ": he has to eke out his programmes with a number of works of the second or third order. If he is a genuine artist, he cannot possibly feel a consuming interest in such works: he can only pump up a momentary show of interest in them, applying to them certain recipes for " expression " that have become second nature to him. To Wagner this kind of thing was impossible. He simply could not conduct *Fidelio* or *Don Giovanni* one night and *Martha* the next: he could throw himself only into music that came from a profound experience in the composer and therefore made him also live through an experience as profound when he was conducting it.

Being interested, then, only in " the heroes and their main works ", it must have been torture to him to have to occupy himself not only with the usual small vocal and instrumental trimmings of a concert but with large-scale works by composers who could by no stretching of the meaning of the word be regarded as giants. Praeger seems to be telling the truth when he says that he and Wagner, a day or two after the latter's arrival in London, called on Anderson to discuss the programmes, and Anderson told him of the Committee's intention of including a recent " prize symphony " by Lachner. Wagner flew into a rage: " Have I therefore left my quiet seclusion in Switzerland to cross the sea to conduct a prize symphony by Lachner? No; never! If that be a condition of the bargain I at once reject it, and will return." But certain other works, he found, he could not refuse to conduct, the usual kind of British work, given for the usual kind of British reason — that the composer is a professor at this academy of music or the other, or that recognition has to be given to native talent, or simply that the composer is a decent fellow who has done so much for others that they feel themselves under an obligation to do something in return for him. Charles Lucas, about whom, by the way, Wagner says nothing in *Mein Leben*, conducted his own symphony; [24] but Wagner was in charge of Cipriani Potter's symphony, Macfarren's *Chevy Chase*, and Onslow's *L'Alcalde de la Vega*. It is evident that, although these works could have meant next to nothing to him, he did his conscientious best for them. He tells us in *Mein Leben* [25] of the care he took over Potter's symphony, which was simple and modest enough not to provoke any unpleasant reactions in him, while he seems to have felt a certain sympathy and pity for the gentle old recluse. Hogarth, in his notice of the Macfarren overture, admitted that the work " received the greatest justice from the conductor and was warmly applauded "; Davison said that " although the time was a little too quick, the performance generally was strikingly good: Herr Wagner — to his credit be it said — took as much pains with it as he did with Mr. Potter's symphony at the sixth concert." As we have seen, there was a touch of the elemental in Macfarren's overture that appealed to Wagner; but in the case of none of these works, we may be sure, could he feel that it had been worth his while to come from Zürich to conduct music of that order. It is greatly to his credit, then, that he should have taken the trouble over them which he manifestly did.

9

As a composer he was at this time virtually unknown to the English public. He had hoped, when he went to London, to do something for his *Lohengrin:* but he found to his astonishment, when he arrived there, that he had no English publishing rights in his own

---

[24] Even Davison saw no reason for inflicting this work on the audience, a work already some twenty-five years old. "Mr. Lucas", he said in his notice of the concert, "was then a young man, and great hopes were entertained of his career — hopes, it is scarcely necessary to add, which, as in so many other instances, have been disappointed."

[25] See also his remarks on the subject in *On Conducting*, RWGS, VIII, 278.

works. A recent decision of the House of Lords had deprived foreign composers of copyright in any of their works that had not been written for or in this country, and had been first published here. Blithely accepting this parliamentary invitation to publishers to take part in the ancient and merry game of legalised robbery of composers, the firm of Ewer had brought out the " Abendstern " song from *Tannhäuser* and Lohengrin's " Reproof to Elsa " (as Wagner calls it in a letter to Wesendonk). " I am assured ", he says, " that a further selection of my vocal pieces will appear shortly. Anyone has the right to reprint them if he wishes to do so." Once more one is moved to comment that there must have been something fundamentally wrong with the ethics of a world that could permit publishers and others to rob a man in this rascally fashion of the fruits of his labour, and then hold up its hands in pious horror at his borrowing in order to live. In the preceding year the same publishers had issued a pirated piano arrangement of the *Tannhäuser* March; and it was by means of this March, *orchestrated for the occasion by some unknown local hack*, that Wagner was introduced to the London public at a concert of the Amateur Musical Society on the 10th April of that year! There had followed, on May 1st, a performance of the *Tannhäuser* overture, under Lindpaintner, at a concert of the New Philharmonic Society; while this work was included two or three times in the programmes of Jullien's concerts of the following winter. It seems to have been quite incomprehensible to many worthy people and to have aroused furious hatred in others, especially in Davison and his colleagues of the Press.

It was at the request of the Philharmonic Committee that Wagner included in the programme of his second concert the *Lohengrin* Prelude and two other pieces from the opera. Public opinion was divided as to the value of these: to no one, of course, could the situation have presented the comic aspect it does to us to-day — the Wagner who had already written the *Rhinegold* and the *Valkyrie* being solemnly discussed as if he himself were putting forward the *Bridal Chorus* as a typical specimen of " the music of the future ". One's final impression, after reading the contemporary criticisms of the concert that Ellis has reprinted for us, is that not merely were the critics mostly ignorant of Wagner's earliest operas but that they would have been incapable of understanding them if they had known them. Yet in spite of the general hostility of the Press towards both his music and his conducting, the audiences in general had been favourably impressed by him. The attendance, however, seems occasionally to have been small. This may have been due, in part, to the facts that the Philharmonic was already looked upon, before the season began, as moribund, that the Crimean War, rather than music, occupied the minds of many people just then, and that the " Old " Philharmonic concerts were expensive in comparison with those of the " New "; but it is evident also that the critics had succeeded only too well in prejudicing large numbers of people against Wagner. Glover, summing the season up in the *Morning Post,* asked the directors what else but public disapproval they could expect after they had deliberately turned their backs on their previous noble conservatism

> " to place the guardianship of Art's sacred temple in the hands of an unbeliever in its divinities . . . could the directors see nothing between blind reverence for the used-up ideas of a bygone period and the wildest innovation and licentiousness of the degenerate present? . . . It is truly ludicrous to observe how a professedly conservative society can throw itself into the arms of a desperate musical democrat like Herr Wagner. . . ."

Early Victorian England, with its moral prejudices and its general remoteness from the main stream of European culture, was ill-prepared to withstand pious rant of this kind.

It was a sure sign, however, of the commotion he had created in the musical life of London that the Queen and Prince Albert, accompanied by various royalties and ladies of the Court, should have attended his seventh concert, at which the *Tannhäuser* overture was repeated " by command ". During the interval the Queen sent for Wagner, and she and the Prince Consort talked with him for some time. Writing to Minna the next day, Wagner described the Queen as not so stout as rumour alleged: he had not been too overcome to notice that she was " short and not very pretty ", and that her nose was regrettably inclined to be red. She and Albert seem to have indulged in the amiable, condescending generalities customary with royal personages on these occasions; and Wagner was not greatly impressed by the Queen's suggestion that his operas might perhaps be given in London in Italian. But the royal couple un-doubtedly meant well; and Wagner found some satisfaction in the fact that he, a proscribed revolutionary in his own country, had been thus publicly recognised by the rulers of England; he hoped the lesson would not be lost on his enemies in high places in Ger-many. " I should think ", he writes ironically to Minna, " the Ger-man police might let me pass in peace now! " But for all his irony he was genuinely appreciative of the good-heartedness of the Queen, and the courage that had prompted her to show him public favour in spite of his political record and the enmity of the Press.

<h2 style="text-align:center">10</h2>

But nothing could alleviate his misery in this London hell. He was pining to see Mathilde Wesendonk again. Partly from physical and mental exhaustion, partly because of his profound spiritual wretchedness, he could make little progress with the scoring of the *Valkyrie:* the inner connection of the threads of the work was momentarily lost to him, and he would sometimes stare in blank hopelessness at the notes as at so many hieroglyphics to which he could not find the key. All joy in creative work being lost, his thoughts became more and more sombre. He wrote to Röckel at great length about Schopenhauer's philosophy and the doctrine of Buddha: he read Dante, concerning whose *Inferno* and *Purgatorio* he wrote to Liszt in a way that foreshadows the innermost moods of *Tristan:* he had already come to regard the world as " a sin of Brahma's ", a sin which Brahma, " having transferred himself into this world, has to expiate in the monstrous sufferings of the world, redeeming himself in those saints who, through complete denial of the Will to Live, and possessed through and through by sympathy for all suffering things, pass over into Nirvana, the land of Being-no-more." [26] London materialism had brought to full flower the mystic in him.

Towards the end of his stay he once more came into contact with Berlioz, who had arrived in London on the 9th June. (On the 2nd June, a week before setting out from Paris, he had written to his

---

[26] See his long and profoundly interesting letter of the 7th June to Liszt.

friend Auguste Morel, " Wagner, who is in London conducting the ' Old ' Philharmonic Society . . . , is succumbing to the attacks of the entire English Press; but he remains calm, they say, assured as he is that *in fifty years* he will be the master of the musical world "). Wagner attended a New Philharmonic concert at which Berlioz conducted the G minor symphony of Mozart and a portion of his own *Romeo and Juliet.* He was not impressed by the reading of the Mozart,[27] and he sympathised with Berlioz in having to be satisfied with so poor a performance of his own work. Berlioz, in turn, heard Wagner's last concert: his comment was that Wagner " conducts in free style, as Klindworth plays the piano." The two men, it thus appears, were the antithesis of each other not only in their root-conception of the nature and the end of music but in their methods of conducting. Wagner, like Liszt, favoured a flexible handling of the melodic line. To Berlioz, any departure from strict time was abhorrent: he could not even endure Chopin's rubato when playing his own music.

Notwithstanding these and other points of difference between them, the two men were undoubtedly attracted to each other during these last few days of Wagner's stay in London. " One really good thing I bring with me out of England ", Wagner wrote to Liszt from Zürich on the 5th July — " a cordial, heartfelt friendship for Berlioz." The Frenchman, for his part, had assured Liszt, on the 25th June, that " Wagner is superb in his ardour, his warmth of heart; and I confess that even his violences carry me away. . . . We dined together before the [last] concert. There is something singularly attractive about him; and if we both of us have our asperities, at any rate they fit into each other —

"

---

[27] "I was astonished", he said later in *Mein Leben,* "to find the man who conducted his own works with such energy sinking [in the Mozart symphony] into the commonest rut of the ordinary time-beater."

[477]

They dined together two or three times at Sainton's, Wagner's improved French now enabling him to converse with Berlioz with comparative ease. They found a subject congenial to both of them in Meyerbeer, especially the charlatan's regular campaign of oily flatteries and charming briberies before each new production; Meyerbeer's *dîner de la veille* was by now one of the standard jokes in musical circles from Paris to Vienna. But Berlioz's non-speculative Latin mind could not follow the Teutonic Wagner in his more metaphysical flights; and it must have been an awkward moment for the company when, after an exposition by Wagner of the theory that " life's impressions hold us captive, as it were, until we rid ourselves of them by the formation of inner soul-forms, which are by no means called forth by those impressions but are only roused by them from their deep slumber, so that the artistic image is not the result of the impressions but, on the contrary, a liberation from them ", Berlioz " smiled in a condescending, sagacious way ", and said, " Nous appelons cela: digérer."

What really drew the two men together at this time was the sense of their common misery in a world that seemed to them to be bent on misunderstanding and frustrating them. Berlioz was generous enough to resent the persecution that the other had undergone at the hands of the London Press; while Wagner, with still greater generosity, pitied Berlioz as being, as he wrote to Liszt, even more unhappy than himself. " He gave me the impression ", he says in *Mein Leben,* " of utter weariness and hopelessness; and I was suddenly seized with a profound sympathy for this man whose vast superiority to all his rivals was so manifest." The *rapprochement* between them would have gone even further than it did but for the unfortunate fact that Madame Berlioz — the former Marie Recio — was present at their meetings. Disappointment at her failure as a singer had brought out all that was worst in a nature that was vinegarish to the core.[28] She was jealous of Wagner, in whom she sensed a " rival " to Berlioz; and although the worst results of her evil influence upon her unfortunate husband were not to become manifest for some time yet, it is clear that she was already bent on

---

[28] See, for one manifestation of it, the appalling story told by Ernest Legouvé (who had it from Berlioz himself) of her treatment of Berlioz's discarded wife, Harriet Smithson. BMEN, p. 509.

not allowing the friendship of the two men to develop any further than she could help.

It is unfortunate that immediately after Wagner had left London the translation of *Opera and Drama* which Davison was running in the *Musical World* should have reached the point at which Wagner had dealt with the tendencies represented by Berlioz as a composer. One gathers that Berlioz had long ago acquired a roundabout knowledge of these passages and had not been particularly put out by them. But the partisans whose interest it was to disturb the pleasant relations between him and Wagner no doubt made the most of this unexpected windfall; and so we find Berlioz writing to his friend Théodore Ritter, with evident annoyance, " Wagner embraces me fervently, weeps, stamps his feet. Scarcely has he left when the *Musical World* publishes the passages in his book in which he knocks me about in the most comical and witty fashion. . . . Delirious joy of Davison in translating this for me." The hand behind the letter is undoubtedly that of Madame Berlioz: Adolphe Boschot cites an unpublished letter of the lady in which she avers that poor Hector has been " the dupe of the effusions of the traitorous Wagner." [29] For a while, after each of them had returned home, it looked as though a closer communion between them as composers might be brought about. In September, Wagner asked Berlioz to send him some of his full scores. Berlioz replied that his publishers were not generous with free copies of those already published: but he promised Wagner the scores of the *Te Deum*, *L'Enfance du Christ*, and *Lélio*, which were then in the press. " I have your *Lohengrin*", he added: " if you could send me *Tannhäuser* you would give me great pleasure." He admits, though, the justice of Wagner's contention that his complete ignorance of German would be an obstacle to his full understanding of the works. The tone of the letter is admirably courteous; but it is certainly not markedly cordial. One suspects that Berlioz was already hardening against Wagner, though the open breach between them was not to come until much later.

Meanwhile Wagner, having left London on the 26th June, was back again in Zürich on the 30th. His all-but-four months in Lon-

[29] See BHB, III, 408.

don, and all they had cost him in work and misery, had left him with a net saving of only 1,000 francs out of his £200 — a matter of some £2 10s. per week! " This is the hardest money I have ever earned ", he wrote to Sulzer; " in comparison, my drudgery in days gone by for the Paris music-dealers, humiliating as it was, seems mere child's-play. I assure you that I have had to pay for every one of these 1,000 francs with a feeling of bitterness which I hope it will never be my lot to experience again." [30] The ovation given him by audience and orchestra at the conclusion of his final concert — an ovation which would have sent any other man away in the seventh heaven of happiness, and which, at the time, had moved even him — seemed to him now only dust and ashes in the mouth.

[30] SRWZ, III, 9.

CHAPTER XXIII

NEARING THE END IN ZÜRICH

1

ON THE 10th July poor Peps died, to the great grief of Wagner, whose faithful and, it almost seemed, understanding little friend he had been for thirteen years. The next day Wagner and Minna set off for Seelisberg, where Minna was to take a whey-cure: there went with them the new parrot, Jacquot — the successor to old Papo, who had died in 1851. (Jacquot, however, was always Minna's friend rather than Richard's). Wagner's physical vitality was low, as the result of his labours and annoyances in London; and though Seelisberg itself once more struck him as the nearest thing to Paradise he had met with on earth, the weather turned out to be not quite what he would have desired. He consequently made relatively slow progress with the fair copying of so much of the *Valkyrie* score as was by now completed. Hornstein came to spend a few weeks with him, and the pair talked much of Schopenhauer: Hornstein noted that Wagner had nothing but disparagement now for Feuerbach.[1] By the middle of August, Wagner and Minna were back in Zürich again, poor Minna not much better for her " cure ": and Wagner plunged once more into the scoring of the *Valkyrie*.

He was heartened a little by the news of the steady conquest of the German theatres by *Tannhäuser* and *Lohengrin,* though he could rarely persuade himself that their " success " was due to much more than the high notes of this or that tenor. So agonising, indeed, had the thought of the imperfections of the ordinary German performance of his operas now become to him that he actually shrank from the idea of being amnestied, for a return to Germany would mean that he would be compelled to see and hear in person the horrors committed, in all good faith, in his name.[2] It is rather odd, at

---

[1] See Hornstein's account of these days in HM.
[2] See his letter of the 30th July, 1855, to Schindelmeisser, in RWFZ, p. 170.

first sight, that in *Mein Leben* he should pass over almost in silence the production of *Tannhäuser* in Munich; the explanation seems to be that by the time he came to write his autobiography he had no feeling towards Franz Lachner but one of sullen anger. All he says about the matter in *Mein Leben* is that

> " Dingelstedt, who was the Intendant of the Munich Court Theatre, undertook to introduce my *Tannhäuser* there, though, thanks to Lachner's influence, that *terrain* was not particularly well disposed towards me. Dingelstedt, however, seemed to have brought it off pretty well, although, according to him, not so well as to permit of his fulfilling promptly his promises to me with regard to the honorarium."

But this is only one of many instances of the bitterness and injustice engendered in Wagner by his Munich experiences of some ten years later. The fact is that Lachner, though not cut out by nature to be an ardent Wagnerian, had carried out his duties in connection with *Tannhäuser* with the most commendable conscientiousness.

For the fact that the work had not been given in Munich in 1854 " not Lachner was guilty but the cholera ", says Sebastian Röckl.[3] When the proposition was taken up again in the following year, Lachner, knowing that Wagner and Dingelstedt could not agree about the fee, and being afraid that the consequent delay might be put down to *his* account, took the trouble to write to the Frankfort Kapellmeister, Schmidt, asking him to use his good offices with the composer to smooth matters over. Schmidt's letter was rather long in reaching Wagner, as the latter was in London at the time; so that Wagner's reply to Lachner of the 3rd July, 1855 (after his return to Zürich), did not reach Munich until after the rehearsals had begun. In this letter he made impossible conditions — that he should receive a fee of 100 Louisdor and that he should be summoned to Munich to superintend the production. Finally he agreed to accept 50 Louisdor: and Lachner at once threw himself into the work of rehearsal with such zeal that the orchestra grumbled at the strain put upon it.[4] After the first performance, in reply to Lach-

---

[3] RLW, I, 5.

[4] Rehearsals began on the 10th July, and continued on the 12th, 13th, 16th, 20th, 26th, 27th, August 3rd, 6th, 7th, 8th, 9th, 10th, and 11th. For a conductor

ner's letter of felicitation on the success of the work, Wagner wrote him a letter of warm thanks for his unsparing exertions, " which had made the success possible ", and hoping that the result of it all would be " an extension of the *rapprochement* " between them.

Interest in Wagner had for some time been steadily increasing in Munich; [5] and whatever Dingelstedt's personal feelings about *Tannhäuser* may have been it was clear enough to him, as to everyone else, that it would mean good " business " for the theatre, and that the Bavarian Court Opera could not face much longer the obloquy of shutting its doors to a highly popular work that had by now been given even in the smallest German theatres. He himself says in his memoirs that it " kept its promise " to be a " box-office attraction of the first order ", for it was repeated nine times between the 12th August and the end of the year,[6] eight times at raised prices, — and this in spite of the agitation begun long before in some journalistic quarters against the " red-republican " composer who had behaved so badly, in the days of the Dresden rising, to the " King of Bavaria's close relation, the King of Saxony." [7] The work was so continuously successful that when Liszt was in Munich in December, 1856, he found a charity performance of it being given for the poor — a sure indication of its box-office value. Liszt could not feel that the performance was in all respects ideal; but he paid a tribute to the zeal of Lachner, who, he assured Wagner,

---

whom Wagner imagined to be antagonistic to him this seems fairly zealous! The Munich *Punsch*, indeed, came out with two humorous drawings of a player before the rehearsals and after — in the one case erect and plump, in the other much shrunken in body, leaning exhaustedly on a crutch, and wearing an eye-shade. See the reproduction in RLW, I, 8, 9.

[5] The Bavarian Duke Max had long been very keen to have *Tannhäuser* given there. He had seen it in Frankfort and in Würzburg, and had been entranced by it. "This is magnificent, sublime music", he wrote to a friend. "One hears tones and harmonies that never existed before. His *Lohengrin* is even more individual." (RLW, I, 5).

[6] What these figures really mean the reader can better estimate when he learns that at that time there were only two opera performances each week in Munich.

[7] See *supra*, p. 305. There seem to have been some disturbances in the house at the first performance; but the evening ended in a triumph for Wagner — and for Lachner, who thanked the audience in the composer's name. (See ZGMO, pp. 394 ff.). Zenger himself, then a young man of eighteen, was present at this performance, which seems to have been, on the whole, not much more than passable, except in the orchestral part; Zenger testifies, as others had done, to the great pains Lachner had taken over the work. Glasenapp's remark that *Tannhäuser* was at last given in Munich "in spite of Lachner's bitter antagonism" is pure calumny.

" had rehearsed the score with the utmost pains and accuracy, for which we owe him all thanks and praise." Whatever reason Wagner may have had later for doubting Lachner's goodwill towards him, there was certainly none at this time.

Nor does there appear to be any justification for Wagner's spleen against Dingelstedt in the matter of the fee. He found himself financially embarrassed again during the latter half of 1855, and in the following January had to make a desperate appeal to Liszt for a loan of 1,000 francs.[8] It becomes evident, in the course of the correspondence, that one of the expenses Wagner found it difficult to meet was that of a copyist for the stupendous *Ring* score: a man who could not balance his ordinary domestic budget could hardly afford to pay a copyist 800 francs a year for three years — which was the sum Wagner calculated would be necessary. Fretted as he was by all this, it was natural that he should think Dingelstedt a little unkind to him. But a letter of Dingelstedt to Liszt of the 1st February, 1856, shows that the Intendant could not do more than he had already done. Wagner, he says, had received a fee of 50 Louisdor in the preceding August, after the first performance of *Tannhäuser*. This was a large fee for Munich, though apparently unsatisfactory to Wagner. Dingelstedt accordingly agreed to pay him in addition a percentage on the *profits* of the later performances; but as the expenses of the production were abnormally high there had as yet been no profits. In these days we should regard Wagner as entitled to a royalty on the gross receipts; but since he had consented to the other arrangement he necessarily had to stand or fall by it, and so he agreed to let the question of supplementary fees lie over until June or December, 1856. Dingelstedt, however, was willing, if Wagner's need at the moment was great, to pay him 50 Louisdor at once for *Lohengrin,* though there was no likelihood of Munich being able to produce that work at present.[9] " I dislike

---

[8] The letter, dated 15th January, 1856, in which this request was made is not included in the Wagner-Liszt correspondence. It was published recently, for the first time, in RLL, p. 175. Wagner thought he would soon be able to repay the loan out of his Munich receipts. Later he asked Liszt to rescue him from ruin by making the 1,000 francs a *gift*, and guaranteeing him a similar sum for two years.

[9] Röckl says that *Lohengrin* was not immediately taken in hand because of (1) King Maximilian's languid interest in opera, (2) the difficulty of finding an adequate Ortrud, (3) the cabals against Dingelstedt that resulted in his having to

and am ashamed ", Dingelstedt wrote to Liszt, " to play the haggler, especially with men of talent. But I am bound to definite Civil Lists and norms of payment, subjected to a rigorous audit by the Royal Exchequer, and consequently not a free agent in such details, either as regards the total or the reckoning." [10]

To Dingelstedt's offer regarding *Lohengrin* Wagner made no reply, having, perhaps, other ideas with regard to that work in the more distant if not in the immediate future. But in the light of all the facts as we know them it is impossible to accept Wagner's disparagement of Dingelstedt's conduct in the matter. The recently published letter of the 15th January, 1856, to Liszt makes it probable that Wagner had misunderstood Dingelstedt's original terms. " Dingelstedt asked me, last July, with regard to my request for a fee of 100 Louisdor for *Tannhäuser,* to be satisfied with the following arrangement — (1) 50 Louisdor the day after the first performance, (2) at the new year [1856] a further payment, in case of a real success, of the same amount." [11] Evidently Wagner had not realised at the time that the further payment was contingent not upon " success " in the ordinary sense of the term but upon the actual profits of the performances. The truth is that we are approaching that period in the *Mein Leben* story when every statement in it that concerns other people has to be tested by collateral evidence, so much deliberate concealment of the truth, or at all events the full truth, is there, and so grievously is Wagner's judgment coloured by resentment against people who had either opposed him or failed, in his opinion, to do all for him that they might have done.

2

With Zürich music he had now totally finished. A fresh attempt on the part of the Music Society to get him to co-operate in their concerts of the season 1855–6 met with an emphatic refusal, though he publicly declared himself, in February, 1856, willing to conduct

---

resign his post in February, 1857. It was at last produced on the 28th February, 1858, after nine *full* rehearsals under Lachner. The work so pleased the King that he attended four of the six performances of that year. RLW, I, 15.

[10] LZBHZ, II, 64.
[11] RLL, p. 175.

Mozart's *Requiem* [12] if the town would guarantee him an adequate orchestra, chorus and concert hall. As this last stipulation meant the erection of a new building, we need hardly be surprised that nothing came of his offer. London had no doubt sickened him for the time being of public music-making, [13] his whole mental bent was now towards a complete withdrawal inwards upon himself, and he was no longer in the mood to try to induce the rich people of the town to be more generous with their money for a local cause that concerned them far more than him. But his final alienation from Zürich society in general and Zürich's public life was undoubtedly due, in part, to the recognition, at last, that the town would never provide him with the temporary theatre he had planned for the *Ring*. Henceforth Zürich, as Zürich, meant nothing to him: and in one of those bitter retrospects in which the later pages of *Mein Leben* are so rich he endorses Goethe's estimate of the Swiss — " smug bourgeois ", " suburban Philistines ", imprisoned equally by their mountains and their customs. He spent the remainder of the year 1855 working, when he could, at the orchestration of the *Valkyrie*, studying Buddhism, talking to Herwegh and Semper (the latter was now installed at the Zürich Polytechnic), [14] and brooding more and more intensely over the Tristan subject. This last was linked in his mind with another — *Die Sieger* (*The Victors*) — which he was tempted to cast into dramatic form; the hope of still doing so had not left him some twelve years later, when he was engaged upon his autobiography. His sketch for the drama has survived: it is dated " Zürich, 16th May, 1856 ", and runs thus:

" The Buddha on his last journey. — Ananda given water from the well by the Tchandala maiden Prakriti. Her passionate love for Ananda; he is deeply moved. —

" Prakriti racked by the agony of love: her mother brings Ananda to her: love's desperate battle: Ananda, distressed and moved to tears, released by Chakya [the Buddha].

" Prakriti goes to Buddha, under the tree at the city gate, to plead for union with Ananda. He asks if she is willing to fulfil the con-

---

[12] In 1856 the centenary of Mozart's birth was being celebrated everywhere in the usual way.

[13] In the summer of 1855 he had refused an invitation to conduct in America.

[14] Keller joined the circle later, after his return to Zürich about Christmas, 1855. Karl Ritter settled in the town once more in October of that year.

ditions of such a union. Dialogue with two-fold meaning, interpreted by Prakriti in the sense of her passion: she sinks horrified and sobbing to the ground when at length she hears that she must share Ananda's vow of chastity. Ananda persecuted by the Brahmins. Reproofs of Buddha for his commerce with a Tchandala maiden. Buddha's attack on the spirit of caste. He tells of Prakriti's previous incarnation: she was the daughter of a haughty Brahmin; the Tchandala King, remembering a former existence as Brahmin, desires the Brahmin's daughter for his son, who had conceived a violent passion for her; in pride and arrogance the daughter had refused to return his love and mocked at the unfortunate one. This she had now to expiate, — reborn as Tchandala to feel the torments of hopeless love; withal to renounce, and be led to full redemption by reception into Buddha's flock. — Prakriti answers Buddha's final question with a joyful Yea. Ananda welcomes her as a sister. Buddha's last teachings. All are converted by him. He departs to the place of his redemption." [15]

Further light on the subject is thrown by a passage in the diary Wagner kept, in Venice, for the future perusal of Frau Wesendonk: the entry is of the 5th October, 1858. He there explains that the Buddha was at first against the admittance of women into the community of the saints, for women, by reason of their too great subjection by Nature to the functions of sex, are " too prone to caprice and attachment to personal existence ever to attain that concentration and breadth of contemplation whereby the individual being cuts itself loose from the nature-drift to arrive at redemption." It was Ananda who finally induced the Master to relax his severity in this regard and admit women into the flock; and it is this " motive ", Wagner explains, that solves his problem for him — the problem of how to adapt the Buddha, himself uplifted above all passion, for not only dramatic but musical treatment; out of compassion for Ananda's despair something stirs within the Buddha that leads him also one step further towards perfection: stung by the reproaches of the Brahmins for his intercourse with such a maiden as Savitri, he " recognises in her sufferings the whole vast concatenation of the sufferings of the world ", and, on her declaring herself willing to take any vow, " admits her among the saints, as if for his own final apotheosis, thus regarding his world-course for the redeeming of

---

[15] RWGS, XI, 325.

all things as completed, since he has been able — directly — to accord redemption to Woman also. Happy Savitri! now canst thou follow the beloved everywhere, be ever near him, ever with him. Happy Ananda! she is nigh thee now, won never to be lost." [16]

All this was no doubt clearer to Wagner than it is to us. But we may surmise that the basic reason why he never went any further with the scheme was that he did not quite see how to realise it in terms of drama. Some features of it were undoubtedly carried over later into the conception of Kundry; and it is possible that here and there in *Parsifal* there are musical motives that had their first vague origin in Wagner's broodings over the *Sieger* subject. Glasenapp tells us, moreover, that Wagner himself informed him that the so-called motive of " World-Inheritance " in the third act of *Siegfried* (given out by the orchestra during the scene between Wotan and Erda, after the God's words,

> What, when my mind was torn with anguish,
> despairing once I resolved,
> gay and gladsome
> freely I will to befall),

was originally intended for *Die Sieger*.[17]

3

The Munich fortress having at last capitulated, there remained only the entry into Vienna and Berlin to make Wagner's triumph complete. The Vienna fortress was not to fall for some time yet; but Berlin opened its gates not long after Munich. Liszt having re-established friendly relations with Hülsen, *Tannhäuser* was produced in Berlin, under Dorn, on the 7th January, 1856: [18] Liszt seems to have been present unofficially at a couple of the piano rehearsals. The extent of public interest in Wagner at this time may be gauged from the fact that no fewer than 10,172 applications were received for seats for the first performance. Johanna Wagner,

---

[16] RWMW, pp. 57 ff.
[17] GRW, III, 119.
[18] It is curious, by the way, that Wagner should make no mention whatever in *Mein Leben* of this production.

HOW "TANNHÄUSER" COMES TO THE CONTEST OF SONG ON THE BERLIN WARTBURG

THE TOURNAMENT MASTER (*to Wagner, who is riding on Liszt's back*): All right, Honoured Herr Minstrel!
On foot, with pleasure! But the steed must be left outside!

*The figures on the right are Meyerbeer, Dorn and Taubert; the Tournament Master is Hülsen. The reference is to Wagner's wish
that Liszt should control the Berlin production of the opera. (From Erich W. Engel's "Richard Wagners Leben und Werke
im Bilde", by courtesy of Fr. Kistner and C. F. W. Siegel, Leipzig)*

according to Liszt, who was present at the first performance, was " superb " as Elisabeth: Theodor Formes [19] seems to have been reasonably good as Tannhäuser, Radwaner as Wolfram, and Leopoldine Tuczek as Venus.[20] All accounts agree as to the magnificence of the scenery and costumes, on which no expense had been spared: Gropius, the designer, had made, says Liszt, " veritable works of art of Venus's grotto, the Wartburg landscape, and the Hall of Song in the Wartburg. . . . The seats alone in the Hall of Song scene cost 800 écus. I have never seen such noble splendour."

But seemingly the musical part of the performance had left a good deal to be desired in the eyes of those who, like Liszt and Bülow, knew not only the notes of the score but Wagner's intentions in the work. The chorus was too weak for the large house and for the orchestra, while in the latter the strings were relatively undermanned. Dorn had seen fit to double the trombones in the overture and to increase the wind unnecessarily in other places. There had been two serious errors in the tempo, one in the G major section before the entry of the B major ensemble in Act II, the other in the song of the sirens in the first scene of Act I. Both these passages were taken much too fast; but the fault in the second case was Wagner's own, not Dorn's — though there was no excuse for the latter obstinately continuing to indulge in the wrong tempo after the error had been pointed out to him by Bülow. In the original score of the opera Wagner had forgotten to indicate that the sirens' chorus is to be taken only half as fast as the hectic music that precedes it.

To outward appearance the opera had been a popular success, in spite of the raising of a dissentient voice here and there. But Bülow, in an article in the Berlin *Feuerspritze* of the 14th January, fell foul of the audiences, in his usual vigorous way, for having been, as he thought, more impressed by the splendours of the stage production than by the music and the drama. On this occasion, as on many another, he no doubt overshot the mark, and did Wagner more harm than good: but we can have nothing but admiration for

---

[19] Not to be confused with his brother, the celebrated bass, Karl Formes.
[20] See Liszt's contemporary accounts of the performance in his letters to Wagner (RWLZ, II, 104 ff.), the Princess (LZB, IV, 295), and Agnes Street (LZB, III, 56).

the spirit that urged him on, as it did so often in his later life, to disregard every consideration of personal prudence in order to serve Wagner. His enthusiasm for the cause of Wagner and Liszt in Berlin involved him in incessant warfare with the more conservative musical elements in the town, and nearly ruined his career at the commencement of it. Wagner, who was almost as indifferent to polemic on his own behalf as to polemic against him, had already warned his young disciple of the folly and the uselessness of journalistic controversy:

" If it gives you a lot of pleasure to write in journals ", he said, " do so; but on the whole by doing this kind of thing one derogates too much from one's dignity, for it means associating with the most deplorable ruffians that our civilisation has produced — the littérateurs and journalists. I find it no longer possible to do anything at all that might create the impression that I paid any attention to this absurd and nauseous crew. Believe me, even the apparent victories we win on this field are no more than the most lamentable self-delusion. Among this rabble, only he will pretend to understand us who finds it to his personal advantage to do so: but in reality no one will understand us — that, at any rate, is my experience. So accustom yourself, when you rush into print, to look upon it only as a piece of thoughtlessness which you will regret later." [21]

At no time of his stormy life was Bülow able to take this philosophical view of the inutility of polemic about art, and least of all now, at the age of twenty-five. To him the triumph of the Wagner cause was a matter of life and death: he actually went so far as to pay a little claque to applaud at the *Tannhäuser* performances, even though this meant his running into debt. On the whole, Wagner and his friends had little cause to be dissatisfied with the results of Berlin having at last taken up the opera: twenty performances of it were given in the first twelve months or so, and another twenty by April, 1858. Wagner himself wrote a letter of warm thanks to Hülsen for his zeal for the work, and assured him that his [Wagner's] previous withholding of it had been entirely due to certain difficulties inherent in the Berlin operatic situation, not to any distrust of the Intendant. He concluded by saying that he hoped some

[21] RWHB, 70. Liszt, on the other hand, encouraged Bülow to keep up his attacks on the Philistines.

day to be able to thank Hülsen in person for a kindness for which he would ever be profoundly in his debt. Of all this, not a word of mention in *Mein Leben!* By the time the autobiography was written he had become once more mistrustful of Hülsen and all that he and the other German Intendants stood for.

4

At the beginning of October, 1855, Wagner had been able to send the fair copy of the full score of Acts I and II of the *Valkyrie* to Liszt, who, after reading the first few pages, declared the music " a miracle ". The third act was not completed until the 23rd March, 1856. Ever since his return from London he had found work difficult. A malady which he had felt coming on in London declared itself in Zürich as erysipelas.[22] Against these attacks, of which he had no fewer than thirteen between the summer of 1855 and the summer of 1856, he could do nothing: they reduced him to complete exhaustion, besides causing him a good deal of pain, and while they lasted they made work virtually impossible. The twelfth or thirteenth attack came on at the end of May, 1856, during an excursion to Brunnen, on Lake Lucerne, with Tichatschek, whom he now saw for the first time since 1849. Once more Wagner was delighted by the childlike temperament of his old Dresden friend, and astonished to find, when the tenor sang him some pieces from *Lohengrin,* how much of its brilliance his voice had retained. From Tichatschek he learned of a young tenor, Ludwig Schnorr von Carolsfeld (son of the celebrated painter, Julius Schnorr von Carolsfeld), who, at the age of twenty, had just made a promising début at the Carlsruhe Court theatre. Nine years later he was the Tristan in the first production of the opera, in Munich.

Liszt had been unable to respond to Wagner's piteous appeal for financial help in the preceding January. In May, however, he sent him 1,000 francs (possibly the gift of the Princess, for Liszt himself had no superfluous funds at this time), though he could hold out no hopes of any yearly sustentation. Wagner's broken health

---

[22] This is the customary English translation of the German "Gesichtsrose". Ellis, however, preferred to regard Wagner's trouble as "eczema" or "herpes", "as nowadays the word erysipelas conveys a much graver meaning."

necessitated using part of this sum for a cure at Mornex, on Mont Salève, whither he went immediately after Tichatschek's departure — in the early days of June. At Mornex he had the good fortune to come under the care of a Dr. Vaillant, who, calming him with the assurance that there was little wrong with him but overwrought nerves, put him upon a moderate water-regimen that restored him to something like health; with erysipelas, at any rate, he was not troubled again for some twenty-three years. Creative work being out of the question at Mornex, Wagner amused himself with reading a little of Byron and a good deal of Walter Scott, removing uninvited insects from Fips's coat, studying the scores of the six symphonic poems of Liszt that had lately been published (*Mazeppa, Orpheus, Les Préludes, Festklänge, Prometheus* and *Tasso*), and designing, as well as he could, a house which he hoped might some day be his own. For at the hint of a willingness on Breitkopf & Härtel's part to consider the publication of the score of the *Ring* his inveterate optimism with regard to the future had surged up in him again.

On the 15th August, his cure being finished, he went for a few days to Lausanne, where Karl Ritter and his wife were staying for the summer. On his return to Zürich he found not only Minna, who had already returned from the Seelisberg, but his sister Klara. Her two months' visit was welcome not only in and for itself but because while she was with them there was a diminuendo in the " scenes " that were by now unfortunately frequent in his household, Minna's diseased heart making her, as he says, " more and more suspicious, hot-tempered, and capricious ", while Natalie's incurable commonness, in combination with Minna's perpetual nagging of the wretched young woman, seems to have been making life so unbearable for them all at this time that Wagner thought of shipping Natalie off permanently to Minna's relations in Zwickau. From his letters of this period to Liszt we realise how sick of soul he was: reading between the lines, we suspect that to anxiety about his health and his finances, and the strain of his work — for *Tristan* and *Die Sieger* were jostling the *Ring* in his too active brain — was added now a torturing passion for Mathilde Wesendonk. On no other hypothesis can we explain the depth of his longing to see Liszt again and to pour out his heart to him.

" Try, best and dearest friend," he had cried in the letter of the 15th January that has only recently seen the light, " to arrange another meeting of us two: my whole life depends upon this. I cannot go on living under such conditions as the present. We must find, by word of mouth, a solution of the dominant problem: either things must change for me this year or I must wholly, fundamentally change in myself. I cannot keep my head up in my present situation; it will mean the end of my art. The only change I get from the agonising ill-health that hampers me in everything I have to do is a transition to gloomy vacuity and dull discomfort. Never anything to comfort or refresh me." [23]

In the light of all we know now of Wagner's life during this period, this seems to point to a desire on his part to pour out his soul to Liszt on another matter besides that of his finances.

On the 22nd September, 1856, he began work upon *Siegfried*, with the first scene of which he had made good progress by the time of Liszt's arrival in Zürich — the 13th October — in spite of the incessant hammering of a tinsmith who had established himself in the opposite house. It is to the exasperation engendered by the hammer of this tinsmith that we owe, indirectly, the melody to which Siegfried rails petulantly at the incompetent smithying of Mime: [24]

Liszt, who was joined in a day or two by Princess Carolyne and her daughter (now nineteen years old), stayed six weeks in Zürich. In spite of the ceaseless racket which Carolyne, as usual, imposed upon everyone, Liszt and Wagner found opportunities now and then to talk quietly about the things that lay closest to their hearts. From a letter of Wagner's of about a year later it appears that one evening, full of pity for himself, he told Liszt and the Princess what he calls his " mournful Bordeaux story ", and that Liszt had been even more than usually sympathetic and comforting on the walk back with Wagner from the Hôtel Baur to the Zeltweg. The

---

[23] RLL, p. 175.

[24] He finally came to an agreement with the tinsmith, under which the latter was not to hammer on the mornings when Wagner was composing. It goes without saying that Wagner kept *his* part of the compact — not to compose while the rival rhythmist was hammering.

subject seems to have been brought up in the first place by a letter received by Liszt from Madame Laussot, in which she told him of her plan for founding an educational institution of some kind, by way of giving her troubled life a solid basis and centre.[25] That Wagner should still be so moved by news of Jessie is an indication of how much she had meant to him six years before, and how tragic had been the disillusionment her apostasy then had brought him. But we may surmise that on that walk back to his house he opened out his heart to Liszt on the subject of Mathilde Wesendonk also; for she was by now the only thing that reconciled him to the hard world of actuality.

Carolyne turned Zürich upside down. She indulged to the full her passion for what Wagner called " this appalling professor-hunting ", and many others of the provincial notabilities besides the professors were not only delighted but flattered to be argued with by one who was not only the most voluble of blue-stockings but a Princess — if only a Russian " Princess ". Wagner, who would have preferred to be alone with Liszt, found " this devil's brood of professors " a sore trial to his peace of mind: a temperament like his, he wrote to Bülow when it was all over, could not stand " this eternal racket ". But the racket was very much to the liking not only of the Princess but of Liszt: it no doubt gave him as much pleasure as it did her to see plaster medallions of himself being distributed among the admiring throng. But there were occasional compensations for it all. At a large party at the hotel on Liszt's birthday (the 22nd October) the first act of the *Valkyrie* was run through, with Liszt at the piano, Emilie Heim taking the part of Sieglinde, and Wagner those of Siegmund and Hunding.[26] On the 1st November the same three performed the scene in the second act in which Brynhilde brings the death-message to Siegmund; while shortly before Liszt left Zürich the second half of the third act was given, the versatile Wagner this time transforming himself into Wotan. Wagner's hunger to hear something of Liszt's music

[25] See Wagner's letter of the 30th November, 1856, to Julie Ritter, in RWJR, p. 104. " It would be a real consolation for me ", he says, " to be able to extend my hand to Jessie in friendship now that passion can no longer trouble our relations."

[26] Frau Heim and Wagner had already sung the first act at Wagner's house in the preceding April. On that occasion Baumgartner probably played the piano part.

was satisfied by a piano performance — perhaps more than one, indeed — of the *Dante Symphony*, which was still in manuscript. It was on one of these occasions that Wagner protested against the marring of the finale — in which Paradise, as he says, had originally been " just hinted at in the Magnificat, with its delicate shimmer " — by the addition of a noisy coda with a kind of Hallelujah chorus. Liszt agreed with him, but, as usual, weakly allowed his own judgment to be overruled by that of the Princess, to whose crude taste the more pompous ending made more appeal.[27]

On the 23rd November the two friends took part in a concert at St. Gallen, partly out of complaisance towards the deserving local music director, Sczadrowsky, but still more in order that Wagner, for the first time, might hear one of Liszt's works on the orchestra. Liszt conducted the *Orpheus* and *Les Préludes:* apparently these were the only works of his of which Wagner ever heard orchestral performances. He himself conducted the Eroica, thereby giving great offence in Zürich circles, which took it ill of him that he should bestow his favours on a rival town after having refused so positively to have anything more to do with Zürich music.

5

Liszt's visit to Zürich had brought much consolation to Wagner. But it also brought in its train, indirectly, a serious misfortune for him — the cessation of the pension he had enjoyed for five years from Frau Ritter.

The saintly character of Liszt is a myth that owes its creation to

---

[27] In the published score as we now have it, the coda is marked *ad libitum* — a singular confession, on Liszt's part, of dubiety with regard to his own work.

In a letter of the 7th June, 1855, just after he heard that Liszt was engaged on a setting of Dante, Wagner had set out in full his reasons for holding that the Paradise section, which is the weakest in the *Divina Commedia*, would not lend itself to musical treatment. Recognising the soundness of Wagner's argument, Liszt had decided on ending his work with the Magnificat. He may have felt later that this was not altogether satisfactory from the point of view of "musical form"; but the determining factor was undoubtedly supplied by the pious Princess, who wanted the ending of the symphony to conform to her religious prepossessions. In this connection the preface to the score (the signature is Richard Pohl's, but the voice is Carolyne's) is interesting and instructive.

It is to the Princess's rather flamboyant taste in matters of this kind that we owe also the more "effective" choral ending of the *Faust Symphony*.

the biographers and to his own correspondence, in which he almost invariably wears a mask. It was only occasionally, in moments of unusual strain, that the mask fell, revealing under it a face with quite the normal marks of human frailty. Already in Weimar, in 1849, Wagner had been astounded and distressed by a volcanic outburst of temper on the part of this man whom he had regarded as a model of gentleness and sweetness.[28] On more than one occasion during this visit of his to Zürich, says Wagner in *Mein Leben*, Liszt showed a " thoroughly ill-humoured and even quarrelsome excitability." A quarrel with Wagner over Goethe — of whom neither Liszt nor the Princess ever had much appreciation — was only averted by the tight hold Wagner was able to keep over his own sharp temper through his personal knowledge of his friend's little failings and the warnings he had had with regard to them from others. " We never came to blows ", he records; " but from that time forward there remained with me, for the rest of my life, a vague feeling that this might some day happen, and that the combat would be terrific."

Liszt was in bad physical health during his stay, and indeed for some time later: and his mind was even more ill at ease than his body. For a long time he had been fretted by the problem of his children Blandine and Cosima, who had been taken out of the charge of his mother in 1850 and placed under the care, in Paris, of the Princess's former Russian governess, the aged and austere Madame Patersi, who naturally enough shared all the prejudices of the Princess against the children's mother, the Countess d'Agoult. As the girls grew to womanhood [29] they had been attracted more and more to their mother, with whom they were forbidden by Liszt to associate, although she, too, lived in Paris. We have long known, on the sober testimony of Cosima herself in her old age, that Liszt's severity towards his children during their early years was the result of pressure put upon him by the implacable Princess, who was incapable of any feeling towards her predecessor in Liszt's affec-

---

[28] See RWML, I, 563. For other testimony to Liszt's "mask" and as to his fury when crossed, or more especially when his vanity was hurt, see NML, *passim*.

[29] Blandine had been born on the 18th December, 1835, Cosima on the 25th December, 1837. A son, Daniel, who died on 13th December, 1859, was born on the 9th May, 1839.

tions but one of normal feminine malice reinforced by abnormal pious self-esteem: Cosima has pointed out the difference in tone between the stern letters written to the children by Liszt with the Princess, as it were, standing over him, and the more genial letters written when he was away from her. It is only lately, however, that we have been able to realise the full extent of Carolyne's malevolence where Madame d'Agoult was concerned, and of Liszt's feeble subservience to her will. The letters from Liszt to the two girls that have recently been published by M. Daniel Ollivier [30] breathe a harshness — at times, indeed, a brutality — that will surprise those whose notions of Liszt have been derived from the legend regarding him that was for so long imposed upon the world by the Princess and her chosen Liszt-biographer Lina Ramann.[31] No one who has

[30] Blandine's son, born in July, 1862. Blandine died on the 11th September following.

[31] In the late summer and autumn of 1855 the three children had stayed for some time with Liszt in Weimar. Their mother naturally protested against the "indelicacy" of Liszt's conduct in compelling them to live in the same house with his present mistress. This charge of indelicacy was of itself sufficient to irritate Liszt. But something still worse happened. After the girls had left Weimar, Liszt received from Madame Patersi copies of three letters from their mother which she had come across in the process of rummaging amongst their papers while they were away. Daniel was still in Weimar. Liszt showed the copies to his son, and the boy, to his father's astonishment and anger, broke out into indignant remonstrances against what he called Madame Patersi's "espionage", "police procedure", and so on: his view of the lady's conduct was that it was "disgusting". As Blandine and Cosima took the same view of it, Liszt emptied out on them the vials of his rancour against their mother.

What made matters supremely difficult for the two girls, who were made of exceptionally fine substance, was their unshakeable love for both their mother and their father. Young as they were, they were already wiser in this matter than he: they saw his tragedy for what it was, and mourned over it. When Blandine, in September, 1859, told her father of her engagement to the young French lawyer-politician, Emile Ollivier, and asked him for his blessing, she must have touched his heart to the quick with one sentence in her letter that must have reminded him, as it reminds us, of Brynhilde's cry to Wotan:

When Fricka had made thee
false to thy purpose,
when to her own will she bent thee,
foe wert thou to thyself......

. . . .
'Twas because so clearly
mine eyes could discern
what thou wouldst in thy sorrow
hide from thyself,
torn by thy own will's dissension!

"I can only ask you", Blandine wrote him, "to bless our union, and in particular to bless me, your child, your eldest born, who has given you all that was purest

studied the problem of Liszt's psychology as a whole, or who has any knowledge of the respective styles of Liszt and the Princess, can have the slightest doubt that not only the spirit but the substance of these unpleasant letters is hers. Bitter as he was towards Madame d'Agoult, one finds it difficult to believe that Liszt of his own free will would have treated his daughters with such unrelenting harshness for no offence on their part but the love they could not help feeling for the beautiful and attractive woman who was their mother. The sense of his subservience to the Princess in this matter must have been, in secret, a constant exasperation to him: and it so happened that it was at the period of his visit to Zürich that the correspondence between him and his daughters had reached its maximum of acerbity.

But there was perhaps yet another reason for the fretted state of his nerves at this time. Liszt's orchestral works were now beginning to venture outside their Weimar shelter, and already there were hints, in the Press and in circles that had formerly been friendly with him, of that storm of dislike and mistrust of his music and of himself that was soon to break over his head and to last to the end of his days. It was a sick and fretted man that Wagner had to humour in Zürich.

6

It was apparently on the first evening of his visit, before, as yet, the Princess and her daughter had arrived in Zürich, that there occurred an unfortunate scene in Wagner's house between Liszt and Karl Ritter. Karl, whose complex nature, one gathers, sometimes made him rather trying, managed, says Wagner, to bring Liszt into one of those moods in which it needed little to irritate him. Piecing together the complementary accounts of the episode given by Wagner in *Mein Leben* and in his contemporary letters to Frau Ritter, we gather that Liszt had been holding forth on the subject of the Jesuits, and had been annoyed by the constant smile on Karl's face and by his attitude of implied opposition. (Liszt was

---

and warmest in her heart, and who, even when she seemed to be opposing you, has done so only the better to fulfil your secret intentions, which she thought she had divined. . . ."

The illuminative correspondence between Liszt and his daughters was published in the *Revue des Deux Mondes* of the 15th December, 1935, and the 1st January, 1936.

always inclined to resent what he took to be disrespectful behaviour towards him on the part of young men, for the attitude towards him of the majority of the young people who gathered round him at all periods of his life was one of ecstatic adoration). Later in the evening the conversation turned on the French Emperor, for whom Liszt had an admiration which few of his friends were able to share with him. Liszt lost his temper over the ironic smile with which Karl again greeted his pontifyings. Wagner told Frau Ritter that " Liszt became so violent that he concluded with a remark that would have been personally insulting had it not been just a generality." What that remark was we learn from *Mein Leben*. Liszt had burst out with " If we are not prepared to admit this, what do we prove ourselves to be? Baboons! " Karl smiled again, but this time " with deadly embarrassment ": Wagner afterwards learned from Bülow that once before, in some dispute or other of his youth, Karl's adversary had hurled " Baboon-face " at him. The young man appears, however, to have passed Liszt's remark by for the moment as not having a personal application.

Still later in the evening Liszt maintained, as against Wagner and Herwegh, that Bakunin was a Russian spy. His prejudice against Russia — the result, perhaps, of the Tsar's sequestration of Princess Wittgenstein's Russian estates — no doubt inflamed his temper once more, and he addressed Karl in a way which the latter did not like. " Herr Doktor," interrupted Karl, " I will not discuss with you in this tone "; and he left the company in a rage. Liszt maintained that he had been justified in speaking as he had done; but on Wagner's reminding him that his manner of speech had contained real cause for offence he at once calmed down, his natural amiability and generosity asserted itself, and he promised to call on Karl the next day but one. He did so, and came away with the impression that peace had been concluded; as a matter of fact, Karl accepted an invitation to a gathering at Liszt's hotel for the following evening. At this, to Wagner's surprise, the young man suddenly reverted, for no apparent reason, to his former attitude of hostility towards Liszt. A few days afterwards, when Wagner called on him to try once more to smooth matters over by explaining and apologising for Liszt's well-known weaknesses, Karl was so bitter against Wagner himself that the latter left the house in tears. It was the last time the pair were to see each other for nearly two years.[32]

Karl had of course given his mother his own version of the affair, and naturally enough she felt that the right was on his side. Apparently she reproached Wagner for not having protected her son: it was the first time in their lives that the smallest shadow had crept over their friendship, and Wagner was deeply hurt. Frau Ritter opined that the bitterness towards Wagner shown in her son's letters must have been only the final bursting into flame of a long-smouldering resentment. Wagner, in self-defence, pointed out that for some time past he had been particularly watchful of himself, in view of Karl's " capricious humours, singularities and really offensive rudenesses ". In Dresden recently, he had been informed, Karl had spoken unkindly of him, mocking at his own former devotion to Wagner; and Karl's behaviour at Sitten had been quite in keeping with all this. Since then the young man had been alternately conciliatory and unfriendly, but Wagner had not only been patient with him but had defended him on several occasions recently in Zürich when his manner had given offence to others. The upshot of it all was that Wagner felt he could no longer accept monetary help from Frau Ritter: what had been given him in love and faith would have a different taste in his mouth if it were now merely cold and, as it were, obligatory charity. With great dignity, therefore, and without a word of reproach or resentment, he voluntarily renounced the pension he had enjoyed since 1851. For a man circumstanced as he was then, the sacrifice was no small one: the pension had been his sheet anchor.

---

[32] The editor of Wagner's letters to Frau Ritter surmises that it was on the second evening at Wagner's house that Liszt made his unfortunate remark about baboons. On the whole, however, the evidence seems to me to justify the account given above of the sequence of events. Wagner naturally refrains from repeating the reflection on Karl's looks to Karl's mother. It is natural, again, that to her he should lay stress on Liszt's temper, at the same time that he makes excuses for it. There were certain subjects, he tells her, so notoriously certain to make Liszt quarrelsome — Louis Napoleon, for instance, or Goethe, or the Russian character — that he [Wagner] always kept careful guard over his tongue when the conversation happened to turn on them. The day after the final breach with Karl, he says, the young Princess Marie "called on me to tell me that for some time past the tendency had been markedly growing upon Liszt to be violent and combative in argument, especially on certain subjects, and — though this was hardly necessary — to make excuses for it."

Wagner's letters concerning the affair will be found in RWJR, pp. 105 ff.

It was fortunate for him that Berlin had taken up *Tannhäuser*, and that the Berlin Opera paid royalties. In 1856 the work had had twenty-two performances there, for each of which he had received, on the average, 300 francs (against which, however, there had to be set off the advance payment of about 2,000 francs made in May, 1855). This means that one of his operas in Berlin alone had brought him more than £260 in English money in the course of a single year — a sum that represented a fair income in those days. It is evident, then, that if he had received even small royalties from the forty German theatres that had already given either *Rienzi*, the *Flying Dutchman*, *Tannhäuser* or *Lohengrin*, or in some cases more than one of these, he would have been positively rich.[33]

On the 27th November Wagner accompanied Liszt and the Princess to Rorschach, whence they made their way to Munich. From the depression that seized upon him after his friend's departure he found a partial escape in a long " Letter " to the young Princess Marie, dealing with Liszt's works, which he sent to Weimar on the 15th February, 1857. This was published in the *Neue Zeitschrift für Musik* of the 10th April, under the title, *On Franz Liszt's Symphonic Poems: A Letter to M. W.* It deals, in the main, with general questions of aesthetics and the new musico-poetic forms rather than specifically with Liszt's musical achievement; but there is evidence enough, both in the *Letter* and in Wagner's private correspondence, that he by no means underrated his friend's talent as a composer. He was no doubt repelled by the theatrical gestures that mar some of the works, but *Orpheus*, at any rate, he thought a " quite unique masterpiece of the highest perfection." [34] His sincere affection for Liszt, and his gratitude to him, which made him tolerant of many things that would have aroused his anger had they emanated from anywhere else but the Altenburg, are shown by the easy way he

---

[33] A single example will suffice to give some idea of what Wagner would have earned had all the German theatres paid royalties in that epoch. For reasons with which the reader is by now acquainted, his operas were not taken up in earnest by the Dresden theatre until 1858. In that year *Rienzi* and *Tannhäuser* had between them 18 performances. In 1859 there were in all 22 performances of *Rienzi*, *Tannhäuser* and *Lohengrin*. The figures for the next few years, either for these three works or for these plus the *Flying Dutchman*, are as follows: 15 performances in 1860, 19 in 1861, 14 in 1862, 12 in 1863, 12 in 1864, 13 in 1865, 9 in 1866, 23 in 1867. (KDW, p. 45).

[34] See his letter of the 29th November, 1856, to Bülow, in RWHB, p. 75.

took the Princess's cavalier handling of his manuscript for publication purposes. Apparently Carolyne, instead of sending the document as it stood to Brendel, had handed it to Richard Pohl and a certain Fräulein Riese (a former pupil of Liszt) to be copied; and during the process of that copying, one gathers, Carolyne made several alterations in the original. Wagner, when the *Neue Zeitschrift* reached him, protested vigorously to Brendel against the many departures from his own text in the printed version. He was polite enough to profess to believe that most of these were only printers' errors; but the fact that he straightway sent a corrected copy to Zellner, in Vienna, for publication in his *Blätter für Musik*, hints at a suspicion on his part that the Princess had been at work, and that he resented her manipulation of the *Letter*. He refrained, however, from sending Brendel a list of corrigenda to be printed in the *Neue Zeitschrift*, giving as his reasons the fact that " such corrections are never read along with the text "; while if it were Brendel, he says, who had deliberately altered such expressions as " *purer* art-form " into " newer ", the misunderstanding had been so gross that correction on the author's part would look like public censure of Brendel himself. Reading between the lines, we can have little doubt that the reprimand was intended not for the editor of the *Neue Zeitschrift* but for Liszt, to whom Wagner sent the letter of protest with a request that he would forward it to Brendel. Liszt, who, for all his pose of dignified resignation and of philosophical superiority to public opinion, was always avid of praise, and who in days gone by had " fed " the Press with matter complimentary to himself with a zeal and a thoroughness which no modern press agent could surpass, was so delighted with Wagner's *Letter* that he had fifty or sixty copies of it struck off on superior paper for private distribution in quarters that would be likely to be impressed by it.

7

In December, 1856, and January, 1857, it looked as if war might break out between Switzerland and Prussia over the latter's claims in respect of the canton of Neuchâtel. Wagner became a little concerned for his personal safety in the event of a Prussian invasion; but the storm soon blew over, and he was able to address himself to a problem that had now become a vital problem for him — that of his maintenance until the *Ring* should be completed. For a time he cherished hopes of a permanent pension from the Grand Duke of Weimar, or a grant for at least three years. But the Grand Duke, as usual, was more willing to angle for the reputation of a Maecenas than to incur the expenditure necessarily involved in being a royal patron of the arts: and so Wagner had to make another attempt at a business deal with a publisher.

Six months or so previously — during his stay in Mornex in June, 1856 — he had broached with Breitkopf & Härtel the subject of the publication of the four scores of the *Ring*, which at that time he was confident of completing by the summer of 1858. No less confident was he, he assured the Leipzig firm, of being able to realise his plan for a " festival " production of the great work in some suitable spot. The German theatres everywhere would be sure to take it up, no doubt in the first place in the form of repetitions of the original production by the company trained by him for the " festival ", though some of the better equipped theatres, such as that of Berlin, might prefer a production on their own account. Once the tetralogy had been given in its entirety the theatres could perform this or that section of it as they chose; so that what he is offering to Breitkopf & Härtel, he says, is really four new operas. Had he any heirs, he would propose merely a royalty arrangement with them; but as his pressing need is for money to keep him alive while he is finishing the work, and above all to enable him to buy a small property in which he can hope for the necessary quiet for composition, he suggests to them a sale outright on his part for the sum of 10,000 thalers: half of this is to be paid to him now, against the already completed scores of the *Rhinegold* and the *Valkyrie*, and 2,500 against each of the remaining two as they are delivered, with a terminal date for the final one of December, 1858. In case of the non-delivery of the whole by the appointed time, by reason of his death or from any other cause, the firm is to be at liberty to issue as many sections of the whole as are in their hands by then, for each part is a self-contained opera. He wishes not only the piano arrangements but the full scores to be engraved, the expenses of the latter to be met if necessary, in whole or in part, by a public subscription.

That Breitkopf & Härtel should be willing to entertain at all the idea of publishing a four-barrelled work that might never be finished, and the production of which would present unheard-of difficulties to the theatres, is a proof of the hold that Wagner had by now obtained over the German public. The firm, of course, threw a certain amount of cold water on his enthusiasm. The success of *Tannhäuser* could not be denied; but that of *Lohengrin*, they hinted, was still in the future. The music trade was not what it had been: the public was not buying vocal scores as it used to do; and that of the *Ring* would be a hard nut for it to crack. What the dilettante public liked was arrangements for the piano alone, for two or four hands; and the firm already knew his objections to these. The future both of his works and of the German operatic stage was uncertain: and so on at considerable length, in the best publishers' style when discussing business with an author or a composer. It went without saying, they assured him, that the ardent wish of their hearts was to close with him on his own terms; but things being as they were, would he consider the postponement of part of the payment to that future in which he had such confidence? In other words, would he reduce his terms for immediate cash by one half, the remainder to be paid out of actual sales? On these lines they would be delighted to send him a contract. They stipulated, however, reasonably enough, that the publication of the separate parts should not be held over until the whole work was complete: the public, they said, was used to paying 8, 10, or 12 thalers for an opera, but it would jib at being asked to pay 32, 40, or 48 thalers in a lump for four operas. He might try also to overcome his objection to arrangements for piano alone. The firm was evidently quite willing to take, on what it conceived to be reasonable terms, this work which they knew in advance would create extraordinary difficulties for the theatres, the work of a composer who, according to the nonsensical modern legend, had no success until after his death.

Wagner, in his reply, thanked them for their readiness to meet him, and suggested a slight modification of the alternative terms they had put forward: they were to pay him 5,000 thalers down, while the remaining 5,000 thalers were to be regarded as capital of his lying in their hands, on which they were to pay him five per cent. per annum during his or Minna's lifetime, the capital sum reverting to the firm on the death of the survivor. This, in its turn, was a reasonable proposition. As he pointed out, he needed money while he was alive, not after he was dead; *their* business, on the other hand, would continue after the demise of any or all of the partners. His health and that of his wife being what it was, it was improbable that the interest payments would continue very long; but if the firm thought otherwise, he would suggest their placing a limit of twenty years on them — that is to say, the second 5,000 thalers were to be liquidated in twenty yearly payments of 250 thalers each, this arrangement also being subject to the proviso that if both he and Minna died at any time before the twenty years were out the firm's liability would forthwith be at an end. He had no objection to the issue of each score as it was ready, though he would desire no single part to be published until the whole had been written and production was in sight: and on the subject of piano arrangements he made what to us to-day is a very interesting pronouncement. His objection to those they had issued of selections from *Lohengrin* (in 1854) had been that they had been made irrationally: there was no sense in including, in an arrangement for piano solo, passages of a so-called " recitative " character that could have little meaning or interest for the player without the words that elucidate them.

> " But I have an idea for a kind of arrangement that shall dexterously set forth in its entirety the true melodic complex of the various scenes, all rhetorical phrases being passed over, so that each scene becomes a flowing musical piece, very much as I myself would have shaped the melodic content had I been working it out not in connection with a dramatic action but for itself alone, symphonically as it were."

He ended by saying that he hoped some member of the firm would come to Zürich in the autumn, when Liszt would be there, so that with the latter at the piano, and he himself taking the voice parts, he would be able to give them a better idea of the *Rhinegold* and the *Valkyrie* than some pianist or other in Leipzig was likely to do.

8

But now the firm drew timorously back. Their next letter raises the suspicion that they had already repented of their first offer, and were glad of the technical pretext to withdraw it afforded them by Wagner's suggested modification of their terms. He had to ask them for a definite explanation of their somewhat evasive letter: were they merely trying to bring him to their way of thinking with regard to the second 5,000 thalers, or were they closing the negotiations down for good? If only the former, he could set their minds at rest: a friend [Otto Wesendonk] had made him an offer that would enable him to meet them on this point. Their reply of the 30th August was conclusive: they were as anxious as ever to publish a work of his, they assured him, but their first offer had been made without due consideration of all the circumstances of the music publishing world as it was just then. They managed to state quite a plausible case for themselves, and the upshot of it all was decisive: the *Ring* proposition was one that bristled with difficulties for everyone, especially for the theatres, and so — they jumped at the excuse offered them by his non-acceptance of their terms to withdraw their original offer. Once again a fortune was to be lost to people whose business instincts were a guide to nothing but the immediate future. The *Ring* scores were ultimately published not by Breitkopf & Härtel but by Schotts.

It has been conjectured that the firm allowed themselves to be prejudiced against the prospects of the Wagnerian cause by Otto Jahn, or some other Leipzig Philistine of the same type. But apart from that there must have been a general belief at that time that the *Ring* was merely a fantastic dream of Wagner's. The poem seemed to almost everyone unrealisable in music, while Wagner himself had never made any secret of his conviction that the German theatres would have to be reformed from root to branch before they could cope with the work. His idea of a specially constructed theatre to which an elect few were to be " invited " for a festival production must have seemed to most people the delusion of a megalomaniac. The word was now going round that his long seclusion in Zürich from the larger world of music had meant the impairment of his sense of the realities and practicabilities both of opera composition and of opera production.[35]

Whether Wagner met the firm's refusal with dignified silence, or whether the temperature of his answer was too high to permit of its publication, even after the lapse of sixty-five years, we cannot say. Their decision had been communicated to him on the 30th August, 1856; his next letter to them is dated the 22nd September, and the tone of it leaves no doubt as to what he thought of them. In June he had sent them a copy of the poem to assist them in coming to a decision. He now asks for the return of this:

> " With the exception of my personal copy ", he says, " it is the last of those I had destined to be communicated to people in whom I might have presupposed it would awaken understanding and sympathy. But I cannot be indifferent to the reflection that it is precisely this copy that is in the hands of people who now, before my work can be submitted to public judgment, find it to their interest to justify the fact that this understanding, this sympathy have not been stirred in them, or have been destroyed by the opinion of third persons." [36]

There, then, the matter rested for the present. Princes and publishers alike had failed him in his need. In any rational slave state, the masters, in their own interest, see to it that the slaves' bodies are at least nourished sufficiently to permit of their doing their work: but to neither princes nor publishers, nor indeed to the world of comfortable citizens at large, did it seem to be a vital concern that the creator of the *Ring* should have at any rate food to eat and a roof over his head so that he might complete his work. To Wag-

---

[35] "This fear", he wrote fifteen years later, "became at last a definite opinion, nay, with all who thought they had grounds for giving up any further connection with me, a hopeful consolation. They needed to follow me no further; and that had its agreeable side for those who felt themselves called to fulfil on their own account the expectations aroused by my earlier works. Our most renowned reviewers of theatre music regarded me as no longer in the land of the living." See the *Epilogue dealing with the Circumstances and Fates that accompanied the Production of the Ring* . . . in RWGS, VI, 266.

[36] The whole of the correspondence will be found in RWBV, I, 85–103. Writing on the 7th May, after negotiations with Breitkopf & Härtel had been re-opened through Liszt, he again refers to this "third person": it had wounded him, he says, that instead of accepting his invitation to come to Zürich to hear the work the firm preferred to "rely on the judgment and the counsel of a third person who knows nothing of the music, nor of the poem anything more than what seems to him its impossibility."

ner, with his unshakeable — and, as we now see, thoroughly justified — faith that the success of his works was certain if only he
could bring them before the public, the situation must have seemed
fantastically incredible: like Henry Murger he might have cried
out to the world, " Give me what my monument will cost you! " He
would have fallen into the depths of despair had not Otto Wesendonk, on his own initiative, offered him help. At home Wagner had
to bear as best he could the often uncongenial company of Minna:
work was made difficult for him by the absence of quiet in the
Zeltweg: Zürich, which had responded so ill to his efforts to expand
its musical life, had become hateful to him; the one thing that still
bound him to the town was the friendship of Otto and his wife.
For some time past Otto had been building himself a magnificent
house on a hill in the Enge suburb, and he seems to have offered
Wagner shelter there when it should be ready, or alternatively to
help him to acquire a little plot of land on which he could build a
house of his own. In February, 1857, however, circumstances suddenly arose that led to a solution of their common problem that
seemed to both of them, at the time, ideal. Adjoining Otto's new
estate was a small piece of land with a cottage on it. He had already thought of buying this for Wagner's use; but he had been
too slow to move in the matter, with the result that one day he
learned that the ground had passed into other hands, and that the
new proprietor, a mental specialist, intended to erect on it an
asylum for his afflicted patients. Appalled at this prospect, Otto
gave orders for the land to be bought for him at any price. The
little house, which was situated only a few yards from his new
mansion, he placed at Wagner's disposal for life at a nominal rent.

The financial relations between Wagner and Otto are set forth
in a letter of the former to Liszt in February. Against his advances
to Wagner of three years ago [37] Otto had been given a lien on
Wagner's household goods: these, along with the house and the
land, were now re-assigned to Wagner for his and Minna's lifetime
for a yearly rent of 1,000 francs. A sum of 2,000 francs having
recently come into Otto's possession as administrator of Wagner's
affairs, this, instead of being retained by him, was to be regarded
as two years' rent paid in advance. This friendly arrangement per-

[37] See *supra*, p. 415.

THE WESENDONK HOUSE ON THE GREEN HILL

mitted Wagner to feel that he was now independent of Wesendonk's guardianship, and that their neighbourly relations need not be clouded by questions of money.

Wagner was in the seventh heaven of happiness: he would have complete quiet for his work, magnificent views over the Lake, a little garden in which he could take his ease and in which Minna could raise vegetables for domestic use, and the proximity of the human being most dear to him in all the world.[38] There can be no question that at this time he was greatly attached not only to Mathilde Wesendonk but to Otto, whom he saw for what he undoubtedly was — a man of fine feeling and generous instincts; and one of the saddest blots on *Mein Leben* is the unpleasant tone of his references to Otto there. The explanation of that tone is no doubt a double one. In the bitter Munich and Triebschen years it was Cosima's conviction, and perhaps his own, that Mathilde, by influencing her husband, could have " saved " him.[39] In addition there was the curious strain in him that always made him comparatively inappreciative of financial help that was given not to the deserving artist in him but merely to the impecunious man. In no matter is his complex and unusual character so difficult to understand as in this; the current standards of the world offer us no guide here. From many a passage in his letters, however, it is clear that he made a subtle distinction between money that was offered him out of a burning faith in his work and his mission on the part of the donor, and money which, welcome as it was, amounted to no more than the ordinary willingness of a rich man to open his purse, on request, to a poor one. The cynical epigrammatists have assured us that charity leaves a secret resentment in the breast of the recipient of it. Charity of the common kind certainly left Wagner, in general, comparatively unresponsive: a genuine sacrifice for his art alone, however, like that of Frau Ritter, he valued highly and

---

[38] It is greatly to be regretted that the little house — the Asyl, as Wagner called it — no longer exists. A later owner of the Wesendonk mansion on the Green Hill pulled down the Asyl and erected the present larger house on the site.

[39] After taking down from his dictation the story of those years, Cosima wrote in her diary: "It seems to me that the year 1858 was the real turning-point in Richard's destiny, and that if Frau Wesendonk had acquitted herself well then, he would have been spared all the perplexities of his life until the appearance of the King [Ludwig]." See MECW, I, 432.

never forgot. " The world ", he wrote in a fragment found among his papers after his death, " is taught how to behave itself properly towards all others: but how to behave towards a man of my sort it can never be taught, because such a case occurs too rarely." There were certainly ways in which he was unique.

9

The future Asyl having been originally not much more than a summer house, much internal work had to be done at it in order to adapt it to occupation all the year round. Part at least of the expense of all this fell on Wagner — to say nothing of that fresh expenditure on furnishing that is inseparable from removals; and presumably he had to incur in consequence further debts to tradesmen in Zürich. As he had given up his apartments in the Zeltweg too soon, he and Minna had to live for ten days in the Hôtel Baur, where they had for company the Wesendonks, who had recently returned to Zürich after something like a year in Paris, and were waiting, as he was, for their new home to be made ready; during these ten days Frau Wesendonk gave birth (on the 18th April) to a son, Karl. Wagner and Minna took possession of the Asyl at the end of April: the weather was cold and damp, the newly installed heating apparatus did not function, and until warmer weather set · in they were ill and uncomfortable. Wagner tells us in *Mein Leben* that he awoke on Good Friday to find the sun at last streaming into the house, and the garden green and gay with the song of birds: he suddenly remembered that the day was Good Friday, his memories of the Parsifal subject revived in him, and he rapidly made a sketch for a three-act drama on the theme. As Good Friday fell, in 1857, on the 10th April, however, on which date he had not yet taken up his residence in the Asyl, it has been assumed that his memory was at fault, and that the Parsifal sketch must belong to the following year.

The first letter he wrote from the Asyl was in reply to one from Frau Ritter, who had at last broken a silence that had endured for nearly six months. Apparently she had voluntarily offered to resume the pension he had renounced in the preceding December: he gratefully accepts it as being the only sustentation he can reckon on as certain at present, for a sense of delicacy withholds him from making himself chargeable to his friend and neighbour Wesendonk.[40] But Karl's loan of 400 thalers for the purpose of paying off Hiebendahl [41] being still unliquidated by the people in Dresden who had charge of the Meser business, he asks Frau Ritter to earmark the first 400 thalers of the revived pension for Karl's benefit. In July, however, the debt was discharged out of the receipts from the publishing business, Pusinelli and Kriete assenting to this course.

His financial position, always desperate, had certainly not been improved by the expense in which the Asyl had involved him. In January, as we have seen, he had had to beg Liszt to sound the Grand Duke of Weimar once more on the question of a pension, or at least of a grant for three years to enable him to finish the *Ring*. Failing that, Liszt was begged to do what he could to induce Breitkopfs to resume negotiations for the scores. Wagner was confident just then that he would be amnestied in 1858, and that, once more free to enter Germany, and with the *Ring* ready for the theatres, his financial troubles would soon be at an end; it was therefore, he held, merely a question of maintaining himself until then without incurring any further debts. If Breitkopfs, he writes to Liszt, will give him 1,000 thalers now for the *Rhinegold* score and 1,000 for that of the *Valkyrie,* and a third 1,000 for *Siegfried,* which should be in their hands by the end of the present year (1857), he will be free from anxiety for some years to come, since in future he will place his expenditure under the control of Minna. Liszt accordingly talked the *Ring* matter over with Breitkopf & Härtel during his visit to Leipzig in February. He assured them of his own belief that the work would prove a popular success; and Wagner again voiced his faith in *Siegfried* in particular when, in May, he broached the matter once more with the firm, this time expressing his willingness

---

[40] To Liszt he had written, on the 8th February, immediately after Otto's offer of the Asyl for life: "He has had to pay a high price for it, and he would like now to feel sure that no assaults against me — and consequently upon him — are to be apprehended from my Dresden creditors. . . . Other considerations, having their ground partly in my friend's character, partly in other, very tender, relations [Mathilde], have made me resolve firmly not to take his property unless I can feel pecuniarily quite independent of Wesendonk, and can give him the most convincing assurance as to this."

[41] See *supra,* p. 420.

to agree to the lower terms they had orginally put forward. But it soon became evident that Breitkopfs had no intention of retracting their emphatic refusal of the preceding August. Wagner made a last desperate attempt to remove the prejudice they had plainly conceived against the work. He urged them to send someone to him in the Asyl to hear it: he was expecting visits, he said, from Tichatschek, Niemann (from Hanover) and Luise Meyer (from Vienna); with these assistants, and Klindworth or Kirchner at the piano, he could promise them a performance that would be representative. The firm drily replied, on the 3rd June, that none of the partners would be free to make the journey before the middle of August at the earliest, and they would let him know when a visit would be possible. This was the last straw: on the 29th Wagner told Liszt that he would trouble no more about Breitkopfs: he had decided, he said, " to give up the obstinate undertaking to complete my *Nibelungen.*" Virtually only Liszt, he continued, believed in it, perhaps because Liszt too had not sufficiently weighed the difficulties of it: Breitkopfs he excused with the bitter reflection that now their disbelief in the possibility of it will be justified, seeing that " the composer cannot even complete it without their help."

" I have led my young Siegfried into the beautiful forest solitude ", he had written to Liszt: " there I have left him under a linden tree, and, with tears from the depths of my heart, said farewell to him: he is better there than anywhere else." As Siegfried seats himself under the linden tree *twice* — immediately after his entry in the second scene of the second act, and again later, near the end of the second act, just after he has slain Mime — there was at one time much speculation as to the precise point at which Wagner laid down his pen. We know definitely now that he broke off in the *first* of these two situations: after the setting of Siegfried's words " Dass der mein Vater nicht ist " he continued, in the Composition Sketch, with a half-bar of the orchestral figure that runs through this scene, and added " etc."; underneath the bar he has written " 27th June 57. R. W. (Wann sehn wir uns wieder??) " ("When shall we see each other again?? ").[42] But this is not the whole story. His letter to Liszt is dated the 28th — the day after

---

[42] A facsimile of the page is given in DM, Vol. 25, No. 5 (February, 1933).

he had made his melancholy decision to go no further with his " obstinate undertaking ". He evidently soon repented of his decision, however, for a fortnight later he took up his work again, completing the Composition Sketch *down to the end of the second act* by the 30th July. (He finished the orchestral sketch on the 9th August). No doubt he had felt an irresistible impulse to complete at any rate this act before he began serious work upon the poem of *Tristan,* which he did on the 30th August: he may have feared that after the long separation from his score which the carrying out to the end of this new operatic scheme of his would involve he would have lost his hold upon the threads of the *Siegfried* music, as had happened to him in London in the case of the *Valkyrie.*[43]

10

Of some slight consolation but considerable financial help to him during the spring of this year (1857) had been the success of *Tannhäuser* in Vienna. The Austrian capital had not hitherto been regarded by him or by his followers as a propitious *terrain* for his art: Vienna loved to bask complacently in the glory shed on it in former days by Gluck, Mozart, Schubert and Beethoven, but since the death of the last two of these it had become, as far as opera was concerned, more and more an Italian preserve; many Germans, indeed, looked upon the town as almost a foreign enclave. After 1848 the general musical taste of Vienna had improved considerably, partly as an indirect result of the political reaction, which, by suppressing all political activity, left the public with little but the arts to expend its mental energies upon. The Court Opera, however, remained very conservative; and even had it been inclined to open its doors to Wagner the musical innovator, they would have re-

---

[43] He puts it in *Mein Leben* that "in order to prove to myself that I was not to be scared away from the older work by any feeling of disgust with it, I determined at all events to finish the lately-begun composition of the second act." It is rather odd that he should not have mentioned his completion of the act in any of his later letters to Liszt. The result was that until *Mein Leben* was published the whole musical world believed that the remainder of the second act was not written until he took up *Siegfried* again in 1869. The authentic dates of composition of the final portion of the act are given by Otto Strobel in an article on *Die Kompositionsskizzen zum Ring des Nibelungen,* in BFF, 1930, p. 120.

mained closed to Wagner the notorious political revolutionary of 1849. He was the subject of close observation in Zürich by the Austrian police department: even Liszt sometimes became on object of suspicion by reason of his association with the Saxon fugitive. There appears, however, to have been a growing interest in Wagner in Vienna during the early 1850's: the more progressive Austrian music-lovers could not be deaf to the commotion he was making in Germany, while his reputation as a revolutionary of itself commended him to certain circles that were perhaps more interested in politics than in art.

He seems to have owed the first introduction of his music in Vienna to the composer of the *Blue Danube* Waltz. Johann Strauss and his brother Eduard were among the earliest Austrian Wagnerians, and to the end they remained among the most faithful: in 1863 Eduard generously cancelled one of his own popular concerts so as not to draw any part of the audience from a concert of his own which Wagner had put down for the same evening. In March, 1853, Johann had given selections from *Tannhäuser* and *Lohengrin*, following these up with the *Tannhäuser* and *Rienzi* overtures in 1854, and by other Wagner pieces in the later years of that decade.[44] In July, 1854, the Gesellschaft der Musikfreunde performed the *Rienzi* overture, and in November, 1856, the *Faust Overture* was given at a concert of the Vienna Akademie: it called forth a characteristically stupid " criticism " from Hanslick, who had already begun to make himself a power in the Vienna Press by his fluent, superficial journalism, the secret of whose vogue lay in its presenting the reader with bright reading matter that had the minimum of connection with the work of art under discussion.

The first performance of a Wagner opera in Austria took place in a small provincial theatre — that of Graz, where *Tannhäuser* was produced on the 20th January, 1854: eight performances were given in two months in spite of an unfriendly Press. Prague followed Graz's example in the late autumn of that year. It was not until 1857 that *Tannhäuser* was given in Vienna, and then not at

---

[44] He broke more than one lance for Liszt also. "It is an interesting fact, and characteristic of our [Viennese] musical conditions", said a local journal in 1856, "that the music lover who wants to become acquainted with Wagner or Liszt has to go to a dance orchestra's concert." See MWK, I, 107.

THE THALIA THEATRE, VIENNA

(From Erich W. Engel's "Richard Wagners Leben und Werke im Bilde", by
courtesy of Fr. Kiftner and C. F. W. Siegel, Leipzig)

the Court Opera (the Kärntnertor Theatre) but on a suburban stage.

Students of Beethoven will remember that in October, 1882, he wrote an overture, *Zur Weihe des Hauses*, for the opening of a theatre in the Josefstadt suburb of Vienna. Allied with this institution, in 1856, was the newly constructed Thalia Theatre in the Lerchenfeld quarter, a large wooden structure, used only in the summer months, in which the spectators — sitting in their shirtsleeves — could alternately enjoy the light Viennese musical and dramatic fare that was put before them and muse upon the prospect of being roasted alive in case of fire. Both theatres were in 1856 under the control of Johann Hoffmann, a one-time tenor who had been alternately director of the opera in Riga,[45] Prague and Frankfort-on-the-Main before returning to his native Vienna.

In February, 1857, Hoffmann conceived the bold idea of giving the universally popular *Tannhäuser* in the Thalia Theatre. Wagner could have no illusions as to the quality of the performances likely to be given on so ill-equipped a stage, by a company that could boast of no singers of distinction. He made no secret of the fact that he consented to the carrying out of the plan only because the realisation of it would be a smack in the face for the Court Opera,[46] and because of his dire need of money at the time: it was " a somewhat frivolous piece of behaviour " on his part, he confessed, which he humorously justified, in a letter to Liszt which appears to be lost, by a comparison of himself with Mirabeau, who, not having been elected by his peers to the Assembly of Nobles, sought the suffrages of the electors of Marseilles as a linendraper. His normal attitude now towards these early works of his is set forth in a letter to Kapellmeister Stolz. He knows, he says, that the operas are nowhere given in a way which he can regard as corresponding to his intentions; still, they go on from " success " to " success ", and at least he can turn, with an indulgent, ironic smile, his " popularity " into cash, and so manage to keep himself alive while he writes new and better works. These, however, will be produced under his

<hr />

[45] On his connection there with Wagner in 1839 see Vol. I, p. 236.

[46] "I detest the Kärntnertor Theatre so much", he wrote to the Thalia Kapellmeister, Stolz, "that I would love to feel it had had a fine one in the face (*eine noble Schlappe*) through this success."

own direction or not at all: and as he sees no immediate likelihood of an amnesty he looks upon both himself and these new works of his as having no real connection with the world.

11

He treated Hoffmann *de haut en bas* so far as business was concerned: he could afford to wait tranquilly, he told him, till the Court Opera should choose to take up his works,[47] but meanwhile, if Hoffmann was really keen to give *Tannhäuser* he could have it for a fee of 100 francs for each performance, on the understanding that 2,000 francs on account were to be paid to the composer in advance on receipt of the score; for the next thirty his royalties were to be remitted quarterly; while he would expect no payment for any performances after the fiftieth. These fees, he said, were justified by his experiences with Berlin: from the Kärntnertor he would demand at least twice what he was asking from Hoffmann: even Kroll, when he planned to give the work in a minor theatre in Berlin, had guaranteed him thirty performances at six Louisdor each. If Hoffmann jibbed at his terms, he would take it that the impresario's heart was not really in the matter: and the result would be a poor production and general denigration of the work in the Vienna Press. He further stipulated that Niemann (of Hanover) should be engaged as Tannhäuser. Hoffmann's capital was too modest for him to rejoice at the prospect of having to pay his old friend 2,000 francs in advance, nor did he think the formality of a written contract was necessary. Wagner replied that he needed the 2,000 francs for his expenses in connection with the Asyl, gaily urged Hoffmann to put up with a little inconvenience to spare *him* a much greater one, and insisted on a written contract as a safeguard for him in case Hoffmann turned the theatre over to someone else: he further recommended the Zürich singer Philippi for the part of Wolfram. Hoffmann's reluctance to sign a legally binding contract was no doubt due in part to his inability to go through with the matter at all if his daring gamble did not succeed from the first, in part also to that reluctance to disgorge that is characteristic

---

[47] It appears that the Vienna soprano Luise Meyer was making active propaganda on his behalf at the Opera.

of the tribe of impresarios. Wagner, for his part, played quite straight with him. Director Ernst, of Mainz, had just then conceived a plan for taking a specially formed company of his own to Vienna in the summer of 1858 and giving performances of the *Flying Dutchman, Tannhäuser* and *Lohengrin:* but although this would have meant handsome fees for Wagner he refused to countenance it, in order not to subject Hoffmann to dangerous competition.

The upshot of it all was that *Tannhäuser* was at last given in the Thalia Theatre on the 28th August, 1857. Stolz seems to have done relative wonders with the orchestra, but the singers were a poor lot, both vocally and intellectually; as Wagner had feared, the slipshod Viennese operatic methods of the day, combined with the mental effects of a repertory that was largely made up of Verdi, Donizetti and Auber, had not been calculated to give the singers much insight into the new style. (Nothing had come, of course, of Wagner's recommendations of Niemann and Philippi). At the very last minute the Landgrave (Reichmann) was not merely hoarse — that appears to have been his normal condition — but too hoarse to think of going on the stage; the situation was only saved by Hoffmann catching sight, in the foyer, of the Hanover bass, Schott, in the act of asking for a free ticket for the performance, and persuading him to play the Landgrave at literally a moment's notice.[48] Everyone in Hoffmann's troupe seems to have been more or less hoarse, no doubt as the result of attempting Wagner parts with an inadequate vocal technique: and the local wits did not fail to repeat to each other what had by now become a punning catchword in Germany — " *Tannhäuser,* dann heiser " (" *Tannhäuser,* then hoarse "). The critics were very frank in their summing-up of the singers and of the production in general. The Elisabeth (Fräulein Friedlowsky) looked as if she had come out of a marionette theatre; in the Hall of Song scene she and the Landgrave " received the Thuringian nobility in the way a Philistine and his daughter receive the guests at their tea-party." The aforesaid nobility, as well as the Minstrels, looked as if they had been recruited from among the cobblers, tailors and carpenters of the local public-houses: " if these are the nobles ", said one critic, " I should like

[48] Reichmann's name, of course, appears in the playbill for that evening.

to see the plebs! " The Wolfram (Eghart) " grunted like a wounded boar." The Venus (Fräulein Lieven), whose habit of singing out of tune had already moved some Viennese wit to say that the Government ought to prosecute her for issuing so many false notes, appears to have beaten even her own record on this occasion.

All in all, the performance must have been deplorable; even Hanslick, who had seen the opera under Wagner in Dresden in 1846,[49] felt constrained, ill-disposed as he now was towards the composer, to warn the public that this was not *Tannhäuser* as Wagner intended it to be. Yet even in a gross travesty of this kind the work made its usual mark and achieved its usual " success ". Ten performances were called for in the Thalia by the end of September, after which date the company moved to the Josefstadt Theatre for the winter season. Another fourteen performances followed in October, and another thirteen, making thirty-seven in all, by the beginning of April, 1858, after which the theatre reverted to its normal circus and small comedy fare. The Venus in the Josefstadt performances was Josefa Richter (née Czarczinski), the mother of a fourteen-years-old boy, Hans by name, who was destined to be closely associated with Wagner in later years. The success of the opera naturally filled Hoffmann with the desire to give *Lohengrin* also; but this plan came to nothing, Wagner having found it difficult to extract any money for *Tannhäuser* from him, even after putting legal pressure on him in Vienna.[50]

---

[49] See Vol. I, p. 451.
[50] Wagner's letters to Hoffmann are given in full in W. Nicolai's article *Die erste Tannhäuser-Aufführung in Wien*, in RWJF, 1906, pp. 3–37.

CHAPTER XXIV

BETWEEN ZÜRICH AND PARIS

1

BY THIS time Wagner had virtually given up all hope of assistance from the Grand Duke of Weimar, who professed himself
to be willing enough to produce the *Ring* in Weimar when it should
be ready, but would not dip into his purse to provide the harried
creator of the work with the means to endure to the end: as Wagner
put it in one of his bitter outcries to Liszt, the Grand Duke was de-
luding himself if he thought he was going to be allowed to adorn
himself with the feathers after doing nothing to support the bird
that grew them. Wagner detected more signs of practical sympathy
in the young Grand Duke of Baden, whose passion for music in general, and for Wagner's in particular, had lately been increased by
his marriage with the daughter of the Crown Princess of Prussia,
who brought with her to her new home in Carlsruhe the enthusiasm
for Wagner's works which she had imbibed from Alwine Frommann in Berlin. And as his old Dresden friend Eduard Devrient
was now regisseur in Carlsruhe, the omens for a closer association
with the Baden Court seemed for a time unusually favourable.

To this period belongs the curious episode in which Dom Pedro II, Emperor of Brazil, played a fugitive part. A certain Ferrero, announcing himself as the Brazilian consul in Leipzig, called
on Wagner with an invitation from his master, who, he said, was a
great admirer of his genius, to go to Rio de Janeiro and conduct his
operas there. For a while Wagner seriously thought of producing
Tristan in Rio de Janeiro, naturally in an Italian translation. Even
Semper was somehow or other worked upon by this Ferrero to
the extent of drawing up the plans for a grand new opera house in
the Brazilian capital; while Wagner sent the Emperor expensively
bound copies of the piano scores of the *Flying Dutchman, Tannhäuser* and *Lohengrin,* hoping, as he says, for some tangible ex-

pression of the imperial esteem in return.[1] But this hope proved as illusive as so many others had done; the bright prospect faded as suddenly as it had opened. He heard nothing more, he says, of either the Emperor or his Leipzig consul. *Mein Leben* was written too early, however, for Wagner to be able to add that Dom Pedro, still a Wagner enthusiast, was present at the first *Rhinegold* performance in Bayreuth in 1876, afterwards making the composer's personal acquaintance. He came to the little town quite unheralded, his identity only being revealed when he was signing the hotel book: in the column reserved for visitors' " occupations " he gravely wrote " Emperor ".

On the 28th June, 1857, Wagner had told Liszt that he had

> " torn Siegfried out of his heart, and placed him under lock and key like one buried alive ". . . . " There will I keep him, and no one else shall see anything of him, for I must keep him locked up even from myself. Well, perhaps the sleep will do him good! I have no plans for his awakening, and neither Härtels nor your Grand Duke — not even Councillor Müller! — shall awaken him again without my *bon plaisir*. This decision has meant a cruelly hard fight for me. Let us put ' Paid ' to it all! "

At the same time he informs Liszt that he will embark at once upon *Tristan*, casting the work into a form that will place it within the scope of the ordinary theatre; he has in view a production in Strassburg in the summer of 1858. He fixes upon Strassburg because in this French town he will be able to superintend the production himself: but for the leading parts he will have Niemann and Luise Meyer, while the neighbouring Carlsruhe will lend him, he hopes, its orchestra and the singers for the smaller parts: " and so I hope, by the grace of God, once more to produce something in my own style and on my own account without the Grand Duke of Weimar, thus winning refreshment and consciousness of myself." In the early days of July, however, Devrient came to see him, and brought such encouraging accounts of the goodwill of the Grand Duke of Baden towards him that henceforth he looked forward almost

---

[1] See, in addition to RWML, II, 747, Wagner's contemporary account of the affair in his letter to Liszt of the 8th May, 1857, and his later account in the *Epilogue concerning the Circumstances and Fate . . . of the Ring* (written in 1871), in RWGS, VI, 268.

definitely to Carlsruhe as the birthplace of *Tristan*. Devrient was glad to learn that at last Wagner was bent on doing something "practical". Little idea had he or Wagner himself, at that time, of the musical dimensions this more "practical" opera was to assume!

2

One would have thought that from Liszt, at any rate, the news of the abandonment of the *Ring* would have wrung a cry of the deepest concern and the profoundest sympathy. But all he does is to tell Wagner that he " has to weep " when he thinks of " the interruption of your *Nibelungen* ", assure him once more that he cannot induce the Grand Duke to do anything to help him, express the pious hope that " a more favourable hour will come ", congratulate him on the *Tristan* plan, and promise that " we will all of us come to Strassburg and form a guard of honour for you. No doubt I shall see you again in the early autumn, though I am not in a position to make any definite plans at present. The Princess is still confined to her bed. . . ." In spite of Liszt's protestations, in his later letters of this period, of enduring friendship for Wagner, in spite of Wagner's outpouring of the love of his heart for Liszt, it is difficult to overcome the suspicion that Liszt was cooling somewhat towards his old friend just then. Excuses can easily be found for him. His own poor health, the Princess's illness, the increasing hostility of the Press towards his music, the steady worsening of his position in Weimar, and perhaps the conviction already growing upon him that the alliance with Carolyne had been another of the fatal mistakes of his life where women were concerned, would be reasons enough for his deciding that he had troubles enough of his own, and that Wagner must be left to deal with his as best he could. That the great friendship between them had reached and passed its climax is evident enough to us to-day. Each of them seems to have sensed the change of temperature, and Wagner was more conscious of it, and more concerned by it, than Liszt. Their lives were already drifting apart, their common spiritual centre weakening: the days were not far distant when each of them was to be the object of cooler criticism by the other than had ever been the case as yet.

To no one, perhaps, with the exception of Wagner himself, did the abandonment of the *Ring* project cause a profounder grief than to Frau Ritter. It was to help him to bring this great scheme of his to completion that she had willingly made such sacrifices, and it gave him a pang at heart to have to break the tragic news to her; he remembered that once she had said to him, with a sigh, that she feared she would not live to see the production of the work. He tried now to comfort her with the expression of his hope that the entombment of *Siegfried* would last only a year — till *Tristan* was off his hands: but neither he nor she, in their heart of hearts, could really believe that. She had to resign herself to the gradual fading of all the hopes that had sustained her during those years of hard trial for them both: the noble creature died in 1869, at the age of seventy-five, after having, indeed, seen the man for whom she had done so much rise to a position of extraordinary power under the protection of King Ludwig, but without even a premonition of the crowning triumph of his life of incessant conflict — the creation of Bayreuth.

3

Why did Wagner abandon the *Ring* plan in 1857? To that question no one sufficient answer can be given. There was certainly operative in his mind the idea that a more " practical " work would both lighten his financial hardships and acquaint the world with something at least of the greater Wagner that had been silently maturing since the *Lohengrin* of 1846–8. But he himself never regarded that explanation as covering the whole ground. There may have been, in addition, a little of that weariness and self-doubt that every big artistic or literary scheme brings in its train at a certain point in the protracted execution of it: the *Ring* must have occupied the major part of his thinking for the last nine years, and he probably began to feel the need of a mental change from it. He may have felt also that the imaginative and technical problems ahead of him in the *Götterdämmerung* were so vast that even yet he was not ripe for them: while of course a production of the great work was not within the bounds of possibility until a considerable time after the political ban upon him should have been raised.

But perhaps the profoundest reason of all for his abandoning the *Ring* lay in his subconsciousness. For a long time before the summer of 1857 a deep-seated instinct had been driving him more and more inwards upon himself. The outer world was becoming daily less real to him: the mystic within him was taking more and more complete possession of him. This growing mysticism was not the result of his meeting with the Tristan subject: rather it was the secret cause of his reaching out ever more and more eagerly to that subject: it was upon this theme that his longing for escape from the world of crude daylight illusion into the reality of the night of non-being slowly and silently concentrated. It was not his reading in the literature of Buddhism that gave, for the time being, a Buddhistic tinge to his conception of life and the world: it was his new mystical world-view that led him to the Buddha. His life was always rich in paradoxes: and the greatest paradox of all those it presents to us to-day is his frantic struggle for a foothold in the real world during these years when the profoundest instincts and impulses of his being were urging him towards a mystical withdrawal from the world, a convulsive effort to redeem himself from the curse of existence by that regimen of " silence and purification " that has been the prescription of the wise Pythagoreans in all ages. His letters from about 1853 onwards had been full of complaints of his " loneliness " in Zürich, complaints which his associates there, could they have heard them, would have found it difficult to understand. At the period when he abandoned the *Ring* to sink himself in *Tristan* even they had become dimly conscious that only his body moved about among them, his soul being elsewhere. " I do not often see Wagner ", Frau Wille had written to the Princess Wittgenstein in January, 1857: ". . . I fancy he feels very lonely and sad since he lost Liszt and you all." But the sense of solitude that was rapidly growing upon him had its roots in something deeper than deprivation of the company of Liszt. " Wagner is indescribably lonely here ", Frau Wille continues: " but would he not be lonely almost anywhere? For any man whose mind and whose nature raise him above his fellows must stand *alone,* though in exchange he has the company of higher spirits." [2] The change in him about this time must have been very marked

---

[2] LMG, p. 191.

for even the Zürich " Philistines ", as he not altogether justly called them, to be conscious of it.

Nor, contrary to the popular belief, and even to the belief of the young lady herself, was Mathilde Wesendonk the " onlie begetter " of *Tristan and Isolde*. If ever the Life of Richard Wagner engages the attention of Hollywood, we may be sure that Mathilde will play a leading part in the romantic super-film. But one requires to have an imagination of the film-magnate type to be able to persuade oneself that she was ever one of the really seminal forces of his life, and that, in particular, she " inspired " him with *Tristan*. This is not to imply that she did not mean a very great deal to him at that time: one merely finds no reason to believe that she was anything more than a medium through which the artist and thinker in him could pour out the fullness of his soul — not the generator of the lightning but merely the conductor of it.

4

Mathilde Luckemeyer was born at Elberfeld on the 23rd December, 1828: she was consequently about fifteen and a half years younger than Wagner. Her parents settled in Düsseldorf while she was a girl, and it was there that she married, on the 19th May, 1848, the Rhinelander Otto Wesendonk (born on the 16th March, 1815).[3] He was a partner in a New York house of silk-importers, and appears to have amassed a considerable fortune before he was forty. The year 1850 seems to have been spent by the pair in America. In 1851 they were in Zürich, living at the Hôtel Baur au Lac, where their daughter Myrrha was born on the 7th August of that year.[4] The hotel remained their general headquarters until the summer of 1857, though they spent a considerable portion of each year abroad. They appear to have made Wagner's acquaintance soon after their first arrival in Zürich, and sympathy

---

[3] Mathilde died on the 31st August, 1902, Otto in November, 1896.
The family used to spell its name indifferently "Wesendonk" or "Wesendonck", but ultimately settled on the former.

[4] A first child, a son born in November, 1849, had died four months after birth. Their other children were Guido (born on the 13th September, 1855, died on the 13th October, 1858); Karl (born on the 18th April, 1857); and Hans (born on the 16th June, 1862, died in 1882).

Verlag F. Bruckmann, Munich

MATHILDE WESENDONK

with the struggling artist and idealist developed in Mathilde very quickly. We have seen that Otto's purse was always open to him, both for the furtherance of his musical plans in Zürich and for his personal necessities.

Let it be said at once that the whole matter of the relations of Wagner and Mathilde is wrapped in an obscurity that is at present utterly impenetrable. Those of his letters to her that have already been published are only a selection made by the lady herself in her old age, with a natural insistence on the most ideal aspects of their relationship.[5] But even when the letters are published in full, as they no doubt will be one day, it is improbable that they will tell us all we need to know in order to see the matter as it really was. All we can be sure of is that at an early stage of their acquaintance Wagner was greatly attracted by Mathilde, in whom he found a ready listener to his tales of woe. It is not even certain to what extent she was really able to traverse with him the spiritual lands through which he believed he was leading her. Between 1868 and 1898 she published a number of prose and poetic works of her own, which commanded the admiration of at any rate her family and some of her friends, though they do not seem to have attracted the attention of historians of German literature. In 1871 she wrote, under the emotional influence of the Franco-German war, a drama on the subject of Frederick the Great, and sent a copy of it to Wagner. He refused to read it, leaving to Cosima the task of sending a courtesy letter of acknowledgment; but when he read the letter, in which Cosima had tactfully talked about Frederick and avoided critical discussion of the drama itself, he became rather angry, agreeing in principle with the critic who wondered, if we are to call Mr F.'s aunt a woman of genius, what words of praise we are to find for the talented author of *Hamlet:* " What language is left us for the highest things ", he asked, " if we treat absurdity in this way? " [6] It is fairly evident, then, that in later years, when the mists of illusion had rolled away from his eyes, he had no very high opinion of Mathilde's abilities as an author.

All we can be sure of is that in the 1850's she drank eagerly at his

---

[5] Wagner's letters to Otto were published in 1905. Here again it is unlikely that we are in full possession of all the documents.

[6] MECW, I, 548.

fountain, seeming to be infinitely receptive of his ideas: as she herself expressed it in after years, she was a blank page for him to write on. What her real feelings for him were we have practically no means of knowing at present. It is true that in the letters he addressed to her from Venice, after the flight from Asyl, he more than once speaks of her having expressed her " love " for him: but precisely what that means we do not know. What is quite certain is that he loved her deeply for some years — even more deeply than was at one time suspected. If we are to credit her with the music of *Tristan* we must equally credit her with much of that of the *Valkyrie*, for it is evident now that during the composition of the first act of that work he constantly saw himself and her in his Siegmund and Sieglinde. It has long been known that the manuscript of the prelude to the *Valkyrie* bore the letters " G.s.M." (" Gesegnet sei Mathilde ": " Blessed be Mathilde "); but it is only recently that we have learned that there are no less than sixteen similar references to her in the manuscript of the first act of the opera. At the point, for instance, where the stage directions run " He [Siegmund] looks up, gazes into her eyes, and begins earnestly " (i.e. at the words " Friedmund darf ich nicht heissen "), he has written " W.d.n.w.G!!! " which is taken to signify " Wenn du nicht wärst, Geliebte!!! " (" Were it not for thee, beloved! "). The annotations were always made in a more than Pepysian shorthand, perhaps as a guard against Minna: but there is no reason to question the accuracy of Strobel's interpretation of the letters. After Siegmund's cry to Sieglinde, " Die Sonne lacht mir nun neu " (" But sunlight laughs on me now "), Wagner has written " I.l.d.gr." (" Ich liebe dich grenzenlos ": " I love you infinitely "). At the point where Siegmund and Sieglinde " look into each other's eyes with the utmost emotion " we find " L.d.m.M?? " (" Liebst du mich, Mathilde? "). When Sieglinde, after a yearning glance at Siegmund, goes at Hunding's bidding into the inner room, and Siegmund, left alone, " sinks on to the couch by the fire, and broods silently for a while, in great inward agitation ", Wagner writes " G.w.h.d.m. verl?? " (" Geliebte, warum hast du mich verlassen?? ": " Why hast thou left me, beloved? "). And so on.[7] That Mathilde was

---

[7] See SGW, p. 36, and SWLL, p. 152.

well aware of this association of her (as Sieglinde) in Wagner's mind with himself as Siegmund seems to be indicated by his quotation, in a letter of invitation of his to Otto and herself,[8] of the motive, in intertwining thirds, of " Sieglinde's Compassion " from the opening scene of the *Valkyrie*.

5

There had already been a good deal of gossip in Zürich about his manifest passion for Otto Wesendonk's beautiful young wife: and more than one objective observer must have sensed the danger of the two families now being separated from each other only by a few yards of garden.

> Pyramus et Thisbe ....
> contiguas habuere domos ....
> ....
> notitiam primosque gradus vicinia fecit:
> tempore crevit amor ....
> ....
> conscius omnis abest: nutu signisque locuntur,
> quoque magis tegitur, tectus magis aestuat ignis.

Between this Pyramus and this Thisbe, however, there was not even the trifling difficulty of a wall.

For the moment, however, everything, to the people most immediately concerned, seemed for the best in the best of all possible worlds. The Wesendonks took up their residence in the Green Hill on the 22nd August, 1857. Happy in Mathilde's proximity, and with *Tristan* rapidly taking shape within him, Wagner felt for a while a new interest in life and a new courage for the future. He had several visitors during that summer and early autumn, including the simple-minded Praeger, Eduard Röckel, Richard Pohl, the song-writer Robert Franz, and Bülow and Cosima, who had been married in Berlin on the 18th August. Bülow's notorious lack of qualifications for the rôle of husband, by the way, was perhaps already shown in his desire for company even during the very first days of his honeymoon; after saddling himself and his bride with

---

[8] The missive is undated: it must belong to the middle 1850's.

Pohl a day or two after the marriage, and then touring the Lake of Geneva with Karl Ritter and the latter's wife, Hans arrived at the Asyl with Cosima about the 29th, and remained there some three weeks.

The man whom Wagner was really longing to see — Liszt — did *not* come. It may be, as Ellis suggests, that he was not pleased with Wagner for looking not to Weimar but to Carlsruhe for the first performance of *Tristan;* but he could hardly fail to see that Wagner was justified in refusing to lean any longer on so sagging a lath as the Weimar Grand Duke. The real root of the slowly developing coolness between the two old friends was undoubtedly the Princess's growing animosity towards Wagner. As he did to his children, so to Wagner also Liszt wrote much more cordial and human letters when away from Carolyne: it was when he was alone in Dresden, for instance, in November, 1857, that he wrote Wagner that letter of sincere affection in which he spoke of his emotions in once more being in the same room in the Hôtel de Saxe " where we first drew nearer to each other as your genius flashed upon me." In September, 1860, he made his will, in which he wrote, " In contemporary art there is a name already glorious and destined to become more so — that of Richard Wagner. His genius has been a torch to me: I have followed it, and my friendship for Wagner has preserved the character of a noble passion." There spoke the real Liszt; and it is perhaps not without significance that this document was drawn up when he was alone in Weimar, Carolyne having left the town for ever in the preceding May. The continuation of the passage seems also to have an inner significance. Liszt speaks of the frustration of his hopes to make Weimar, through Wagner and himself, what the old Weimar of Karl August had been under Goethe and Schiller. Then he adds, " but my feelings remain unchanged, as well as my conviction . . . and I beg Carolyne to fall in with it by continuing, after my death, our affectionate relations with Wagner." This rather broad hint would hardly have been given, one conjectures, had there not been signs already that the Princess was no longer as friendly towards Wagner as she had been.[9]

---

9 LZB, V, 56. Carolyne did not see the document until nine months later.
"I have now only one feeling where Liszt is concerned", Wagner had written to Bülow in 1857, "distress over the decline of his health, and wrath, fury and hatred of

All Wagner's visitors found him in high spirits. The most sympathetic and discerning of them all, Bülow, saw a kind of *Verklärung* in him that brought out all that was warmest and loftiest in his nature. It is about Wagner, not about his own felicity as a newly-married man, that Bülow grows lyrical in a letter of the 19th September to his Berlin friend Julius Stern:

> "For the last fortnight my wife and I have been staying with Wagner, and I can think of nothing more calculated to bring me a sense of blessing and refreshment than to be with this glorious, unique man, whom one must venerate like a god. In the presence of this Great and Good all the *misère* of life melts away, I rise above it. I cannot talk to you about the *Nibelungen:* in face of that, all the resources of expression of admiration fail one. I will just say this — that even the 'specific' musicians, if they have a particle of honesty in them, if they have not turned into petrefacts of stupidity and baseness, must be *amazed* by it. Nothing like it, nothing approaching it, has ever been produced in any art, in any tongue, anywhere, at any time. From it one looks right down, right *over*, everything else. It is a veritable deliverance from the mire of the world. . . ." [10]

Pohl, however, observed that all was not well between Richard and Minna. Quiet enough in general company, when she was alone with Pohl she opened out her heart to him: she could see no sense in her husband's devoting himself, year in, year out, to projects that stood not the least chance of being realised on the stage, still less, perhaps, of bringing in any money. With Minna in this unsympathetic mood, the many dangers inherent in the Asyl situation could hardly be warded off for long: the obvious connection in Richard's mind between his newest work and Mathilde Wesendonk was bound to bring to a head, sooner or later, the jealousy that had been smouldering in Minna for years.

---

everything that drags him deeper down to ruin. Or ought I to remain indifferent when it is clear to anyone with eyes in his head that Liszt is due before very long for a breakdown unless he withdraws himself radically from *every* excitement and undertakes the most drastic and enduring cure? I communicated to the unhappy Princess, and finally to Liszt himself, my painful anxiety and my urgent warning: and since then, — only silence from Weimar!" (RWHB, p. 81). But Liszt's condition was the result not only of his troubles in connection with the Weimar theatre and his tendency to fly for comfort to alcohol and tobacco, but to his secret consciousness that the Princess's stronger will was shaping his life in a way he did not like.

[10] BB, III, 114 ff.

6

We have seen that the idea of an opera on the subject of Tristan and Isolde had occurred to Wagner at least as early as December, 1854. The detailed Prose Sketch [11] (now available in RWGS, XI, 326–43), was begun on the 20th August, 1857. The poem itself must have been embarked upon a few days later: he was working at it each morning during the visit of Bülow and Cosima, and at the end of each week he read an act to them as it was completed. (The actual date of completion was probably the 18th September). A little later he read the poem to an audience consisting of the Wesendonks, Herwegh, Semper, Keller and Ettmüller and his wife; all of them, with the exception of Mathilde, seem to have been puzzled and rather wearied by it: once more Wagner, in his burning enthusiasm for a work that meant so much to him, had made the mistake of communicating to others a completely new dramatic conception without the music that was to elucidate and vivify it.

The prelude was written, apparently, on the 1st October, and the music to the first act finished on the last day of the year 1857: the whole of this Composition Sketch was at once taken over to the Green Hill with the following verses addressed to Mathilde:

> Hochbeglückt,
> Schmerzentrückt,
> frei und rein
> ewig Dein —
> was sie sich klagten
> und versagten,
> Tristan und Isolde,
> in keuscher Töne Golde,
> ihr Weinen und ihr Küssen
> leg' ich zu Deinen Füssen,
> dass sie den Engel loben,
> der mich so hoch erhoben!

---

[11] Ellis (ELW, VI, 309) thought that a scenario must have been drafted about July, 1856, as Wagner, in a letter to Liszt, speaks of "its third act, with the black flag and the white." But as the opera could only have been planned for three acts, and as "the black flag and the white" came, at that time, into the closing scene, he could surely speak already of "its third act" without his having written an actual scenario of the work.

("Thrice happy, beyond the reach of pain, free and purely ever thine — Tristan and Isolde, what they bewailed and renounced, their tears and their kisses, in music's chaste gold I lay at thy feet, that they may praise the angel who has lifted me so high.")

During this winter of 1857–8 he set to music five poems by Mathilde — *Der Engel* on the 30th November, *Träume* on the 4th December (sixteen introductory bars being added on the 5th), *Schmerzen* on the 17th (this also was remodelled slightly a few days later), *Stehe still* on the 2nd February, 1858, and *Im Treibhaus* on the 1st May. *Träume* is based in part on the thematic material of the duet " O sink' hernieder, Nacht der Liebe " in the second act of the opera, and *Im Treibhaus* on the orchestral prelude to the third act: when the five songs were published (in 1862) Wagner described these two as " Studies for *Tristan and Isolde* ". Wolfgang Golther thought he had detected some " significant " references, in *Der Engel*, to the melody of Loge's song in praise of woman's charm in the *Rhinegold*, and to Wolfram's " Abendstern " song in *Tannhäuser*; but it is extremely doubtful whether these slight resemblances were intentional on Wagner's part, or whether they merely came from the tendency of all composers to revert to essentially the same musical formula whenever they are confronted with essentially the same poetic idea.

It is clear enough that there are several veiled references in these poems to the secret sympathy between Mathilde and Wagner. In *Der Engel* she speaks of hearts that languish in care, hiding themselves from the world, praying with tears for salvation, to whom there descends an angel that bears them on its shining wings to heaven. (Wagner frequently addresses her in his letters as the " Angel "). In *Stehe still* we read —

> Let me swoon in tranquil rapture,
> And sweet oblivion recapture!
> With eye from eye enchantment drinking,
> Soul in soul in transport sinking;
> Spirit with spirit again be blended,
> And Hope's long weary waiting be ended;
> Our lips are mute, vain speech doth perish,
> Not a wish now can our bosoms cherish. . . .

The melody to which Wagner has set the first two of these lines is obviously taken from *Tristan*.

Wagner having scored *Träume* for a small orchestra, eighteen players from Zürich performed it under Mathilde's window as a birthday greeting to her on the 23rd December, 1857; Minna no doubt watching it all as suspiciously as Melot watched the lovers in the opera. The Orchestral Sketch of the first act of the opera was begun on the 5th November, 1857, and completed on the 13th January, 1858. The full score of this act was finished in April of that year.

7

Agreeing with Wagner that the public was eagerly expecting a new work from him, and that *Tristan* would be a much easier proposition for the theatres than the *Ring*, Breitkopf & Härtel consented after very little discussion to publish the full score, the poem, and Bülow's piano arrangement. They beat him down, it is true, from 600 Louisdor to 200 (with a further 100 in case of " an extraordinary success "), but paid him half of this amount in advance (in March), as he was in urgent need of money. (He was certain, at that time, that the second act would be in their hands by the end of June and the third by the end of September, while the stage production would take place in November, or in December at the latest). That they should have undertaken the publication at all of a work most of which was still unwritten is still further evidence of the commanding position Wagner had by now obtained in the musical world.[12] Breitkopfs not only sent him a further 50 Louisdor later but even coquetted again, for a while, with the idea of bringing out the *Ring*. It was not until August, 1859, that the whole of the *Tristan* manuscript was in their possession. The score and the poem were thus published some years before the work was performed (in June, 1865).

Meanwhile, in January, 1858, Wagner had paid a flying visit to Paris. The ostensible reason was to look into the matter of his copyrights there; but his letters make it clear that this was not the real reason. On the 11th of the month he wrote agitatedly to Liszt

---

[12] See the correspondence in RWBV, I, 109 ff.

asking him to meet him in Paris, or, if that should be impossible, in Strassburg. He needs, he says, to pour out his soul to his friend.

> " I am at the end of a conflict in which everything that can be holy to a man is involved. I must come to a decision, and every choice that lies open to me is so cruel that when I do decide I must have by my side the one friend that heaven has given me."

He cannot, he says, go into details in his letter; but Liszt will understand the matter without explanation. Two days later he writes that it is unnecessary for Liszt now to put himself out to meet him: for himself, however, a temporary absence from Zürich is imperative. He can assure Liszt, with a good conscience, that he has not lost his head, and that he is still stout of heart: all he needs is patience and endurance. But, he repeats, he *must* get away, if only for a time, from where he now is: it had been a cause of great distress to him that he could not leave on the day he had first written to Liszt. The latter, who was well acquainted already with the lie of the land, guessed at once that some crisis in connection with Frau Wesendonk had suddenly developed. " Is your wife remaining in Zürich? " he wrote back. " Are you thinking of returning later? Where is Mme W—? "

The exact nature of this crisis has always been a mystery. Ellis pointed out that " an outward ' storm ' of any sort is disproved by the mere fact of his being able to make his opera affairs ' a pretext at home ' for his journey to Paris ", that on the 27th December " we find Minna uniting with her husband in a homely message " [to the Wesendonks], and that " we also find her forwarding his correspondence when he has started." To this it may be added that Wagner's letters from Paris to Minna, which were published after the sixth volume of Ellis's work, are couched in his usual tone of domestic good-fellowship, though there is a passage at the end of the letter of the 17th January that seems to hint obscurely at her jealousy of Mathilde. An open " scene " of any kind seems to be ruled out by these and other considerations. The crisis was apparently an inner one on the part of Wagner, and perhaps, to a lesser degree, of Mathilde and Otto: Minna evidently knew little or nothing of it. The explanation of it all is perhaps to be found in a passage in *Mein Leben*. After saying that at the beginning of the new year (1858) he felt it an imperative necessity to make a break in his work, he continues thus:

" Even the immediate and apparently so agreeable proximity of the Wesendonk family only increased my discomfort, for it became really intolerable to me to give up whole evenings to conversations and entertainments in which my good friend Otto Wesendonk thought himself bound to take part at least as much as myself and the others. His anxiety lest, as he imagined, everything in his house would soon go my way rather than his gave him, moreover, that peculiar burden-someness [*Wucht*] with which a man who thinks himself slighted throws himself into every conversation in his presence, something like an extinguisher on a candle. All this soon became oppressive to me; only someone who could perceive this, and show some signs of understanding it, could awake in me an interest which in the cir-cumstances still could not be exhilarating. So I made up my mind in the middle of the severe winter, notwithstanding that at the moment I was totally unprovided with the means for it . . . to carry out my plan for an excursion to Paris. The dim thought, always within me, of a departure from which there would be no return took clearer shape within me."

This unpleasant passage — one of several that reveal how little gratitude he felt in later years towards the kindly man who had done so much for him — seems to make the matter clear. It is sig-nificant that it should occur in *Mein Leben* just where it does — at the very point in the story where he begins to tell us of his need to escape for a while to Paris: the passage may be based on some phrases actually jotted down in his diary at the time, in the full flood of his irritation with Otto.[13] Absorbed in *Tristan* and in Mathilde, and identifying the one with the other, he resented more and more the intrusion of the husband into the ideal world he had built about himself and her: and presumably on some evening about the end of the year there had been an explosion of temper on his part, with considerable embarrassment for the other two. He seems, when he had calmed down in Paris, to have realised that Otto had good reason for feeling aggrieved; for in his letter of the 18th (or 20th?) January to Liszt he says he now sees how right he

---

[13] These pages of *Mein Leben* were dictated in 1868 or 1869, only ten or eleven years after the event. That Wagner's memory not only of episodes but of the actual wording of conversations and letters was very accurate is shown by the close cor-respondence between his account of it all in *Mein Leben* and his letters of 1858.

was in going away, so that time might do its healing work. A final, or even a long, removal from the Zürich scene was out of the question; but it was necessary for him to " do something to help to alleviate the sufferings of the good-natured man: this will come about, and I hope to return in a few weeks."

8

As usual, he had no money, either to maintain himself for several weeks in Paris or to provide for Minna while he was away. He still could not extract anything of his Vienna dues from the reluctant Hoffmann, nor could he ask Breitkopfs for an advance until at least a section of the *Tristan* score was in their hands. For his travelling expenses he had to borrow, he told Liszt, from Semper; while in a letter to Praeger, appealing for a loan, he speaks of Müller as the good Samaritan. Perhaps he laid them both under contribution. From Liszt, after he had arrived in Paris, he received 1,000 francs, nominally by way of an advance fee for the intended production of *Rienzi* in Weimar. He had first written to Liszt about his new crisis on the 11th January. He evidently made haste, during the next few days, to complete the orchestral sketch of the first act of *Tristan;* and he left for Paris on the 14th, travelling through Basel, Strassburg, and Epernay — where he saw Kietz. In Strassburg he was astonished to see a theatre poster announcing a performance of the *Tannhäuser* overture as a preface to a French play. He took a ticket, and found himself in a stall near the front. There he was recognised by the kettledrummer, who had taken part in the Zürich festival of 1853: the news spread that the composer was in the house, and at the end of the performance, which seems to have been a good one,[14] he received an ovation from orchestra and audience. He left the house, he says, in tears.

On the 16th he arrived in Paris, and after a night in a little hotel in the Rue des Filles St.-Thomas, off the Rue de Richelieu, where he was unable to sleep for the noise of the traffic, he settled down in a quiet room, overlooking the courtyard, on the third floor of the newly opened Grand Hôtel du Louvre, where, by the way, about

---

[14] The conductor was Joseph Hasselmans.

the end of the month, a waiter stole his hard-borrowed money. He had at first thought of going to a small hotel in the Rue Le Pelletier. It was well for him that he had changed his mind: for it was just here that Orsini had made his attempt on the Emperor's life on the 14th, and it was in this very hotel that the principal conspirators had been arrested. It might have gone hard with Wagner had he, a notorious political refugee, been found in such a place at such a time. He sought out Emile Ollivier, who was already a parliamentary deputy and a lawyer of distinction, and gave him a power of attorney to act for him in the matter of his French copyrights: the fear had sprung up in him that now his fame was extending to Paris some crafty French publisher would rob him of the French rights in his property by the simple process of printing pirated editions of his scores before he could give a performance of any of them on his own account.

He stayed in Paris nearly a month, reading Calderon, enjoying the company of Ollivier and Blandine, and discussing politics with the former, who was one of the most confirmed of Napoleon's enemies, though he refused to take an active part in revolutionary propaganda, holding that in time the Empire would collapse of its own inner rottenness and make way for a republic. One day, strolling with Ollivier in the Salle des Pas-Perdus, Wagner was introduced to a number of the leading Parisian lawyers, to whom he was delighted to hold forth on his purposes in *Tannhäuser*. He was warmly befriended by Mme Herold, the widow of the composer, whose daughter and son-in-law had become ardent Wagnerians after hearing *Tannhäuser* in Vienna: at her house he met the influential critic of the *Revue des Deux Mondes*, Scudo, for whom he at once felt the comprehensive contempt he had for most critics. Through the Olliviers he met also Mme Erard, with whom was her sister-in-law, Spontini's widow: Mme Erard delighted him with the present of a fine Erard grand piano, worth 5,000 francs. He called on Berlioz, who read to him the libretto — his own work — of *Les Troyens*, upon the music of which he was then engaged. The characteristically French poem made, as might have been expected, no appeal to Wagner, and matters were made worse for him, he says, by Berlioz's " singularly dry and theatrically affected delivery." He jumped to the hasty conclusion that the music, of which, of course, he knew nothing, would be bound to have all the faults he saw in the text, which reminded him of Dorn's *Nibelungen*. He seems to have realised at last that Berlioz and he were unfitted by nature to understand each other, and that the less they saw of each other in future the better for both of them.

" As he read it to me ", he wrote to Bülow, " I was filled with a dismay that made me wish that we might never meet again, for I could not delude myself and the world so artfully as would be necessary to keep Berlioz deceived as to myself and him. To see him sitting there like that, brooding over the fate of this unspeakable absurdity, as though the salvation of the world and of his own soul hung upon it, was too much for me." [15]

It was probably not unknown to Wagner that the driving force in the inception and execution of *Les Troyens* had been the Princess Wittgenstein, who, it is generally agreed now, hoped to use Berlioz as a counterpoise to the rapidly growing vogue of Wagner. But personal considerations had very little to do with his contempt, which Berlioz must have sensed, for the text of the new work: the real root of it all was the perception on the part of both men, as they grew older and more fixed in their mental habit, that neither of them could exist in the mental world of the other. It was perhaps because Berlioz had been conscious of Wagner's discomfort that he made no reference to the reading in a letter to the Princess in which he told her of Wagner's call on him — unless, of course, the dots in his letter at one point indicate a discreet omission on the part of the editor of the correspondence. All that Berlioz appears to say is that " nevertheless we passed several hours together ": the unrelated " nevertheless " after the dots certainly raises the suspicion that something has been omitted. Boschot is probably right in holding that Berlioz would not be pleased to learn that one of Wagner's ultimate objects in coming to Paris was to float his works at either the Opéra or the Théâtre-Lyrique, which happened to be the only two theatres in which there was any hope of *Les Troyens* being given, and that his jealous wife had warned him once more against cultivating the " false friendship " of the man who had criticised him in *Opera and Drama*.[16]

---

[15] RWHB, p. 92.
[16] BHB, III, 453–4.

In the preceding September, Leopold Amat, the director of music at the Wiesbaden, Homburg, Ems and other festivals, had given a successful performance of *Tannhäuser* in Wiesbaden, with Tichatschek as tenor, and the event had received a good deal of attention in the French Press: the notice for the *Courrier de Paris* had been written by Ernest Reyer, and that for the *Moniteur* by no less a person than Théophile Gautier. In December, Amat sounded Wagner on the question of bringing about a performance of the work at the Paris Opéra: this was the matter which had made it imperative for Wagner to see without delay to the protection of his copyright in France. He soon found, however, that Amat was not likely to make much impression on the Opéra just then; whereas Carvalho, the director of the Lyrique, who was a personal friend of Ollivier, professed to be keen to bring out something of Wagner's at his own theatre. Wagner would have been willing to let him have *Rienzi* for this purpose, on the quaint grounds, as he told Liszt, that as he no longer felt much interest in this work of his youth he did not greatly care whether it was " bungled a bit " or not, so long as it brought him in some money; and that in any case *Rienzi* seemed to him the opera of his most suited, both in its plot and its music, to French taste, of which he had no very high opinion. A young littérateur, de Charnal, was authorised to make a translation of *Rienzi;* but Carvalho seems to have felt no particular enthusiasm for this opera. He believed sincerely enough in *Tannhäuser*, at any rate as a box-office draw; and if he were to produce anything of Wagner's it would be this. Wagner, as usual, indulged himself in the most optimistic dreams for the future — there was a fair prospect next winter, he told Minna, of *Rienzi* at the Lyrique and *Tannhäuser* at the Opéra, with fabulous royalties. But all that happened, for the time being, was that the *Tannhäuser* overture was given (on the 29th January) at one of the Concerts de Paris: he attended the rehearsal, and finding that the conductor — Arban, the cornet professor at the Conservatoire — had no full score and not much idea of the meaning of the work, he drilled the orchestra himself for a couple of hours.

He left Paris on the 2nd February, travelling back by way of Epernay in order to see Kietz once more. The artist was staying with M. Paul Chandon, and painting a portrait in oils: " the opinion entertained by everyone ", says Wagner, who knew the ways of his old friend, " that it would soon be finished interested me very much."

CHAPTER XXV

THE ASYL CATASTROPHE

1

HE REACHED Zürich on the 5th, and at once plunged into the full score of the first act of *Tristan*. On the 28th February *Lohengrin* was given in Munich, under Lachner, with the usual success so far as the public was concerned and the usual display of stupidity and malevolence on the part of some sections of the Bavarian Press. " The barbarians ", the critic of the Augsburg *Allgemeine Zeitung* had written some time before, " are at the gates — have even penetrated into our towns. All the more is it the duty of all good people to keep the temple clean as against insolent intruders who, with their dull, vain rigmarole and barricade-humour, their libidinous bacchanalian frenzy, would fain sweep the ancient, pious, noble spirit out of the stupefied world." [1] The production was destined to have an unlooked-for influence on Wagner's fortunes eight years later. It was attended by the Baroness Meilhaus, the governess of the thirteen-years-old Crown Prince Ludwig: her enthusiasm over it infected the impressionable boy, who had already succumbed to the charm of the Lohengrin saga, with a passion for Wagner's opera and an interest in the composer of it.

On the 31st March Frau Wesendonk gave a serenade to her husband — nominally for his birthday, but actually not till some little time afterwards — at which Wagner took an orchestra of thirty [2] musicians from Zürich through a programme of selections from the third, fourth, fifth, seventh, eighth, and ninth symphonies of Beethoven in the spacious vestibule of the Wesendonk villa; a hundred guests were accommodated in the surrounding rooms. As the concert died away with the strains of the adagio of the Ninth Symphony, Wagner had a melancholy intuition that he had come to the end of a chapter:

---

[1] RLW, I, 16.   [2] Not eighteen, as in *Mein Leben*.

"I had a feeling", he says in *Mein Leben*, "that the highest possible point of my life had been reached, and, indeed, passed, that the string of the bow was stretched to breaking-point."

Frau Wille, who was present, told him later that she too had had a premonition of this: perhaps the evidence of a conflict of emotions within him had been too plain. The storm-clouds were obviously gathering; and soon the lightning struck.

On the 7th April, after having despatched to Breitkopf four days before, for engraving, the full score of the first act of *Tristan*, he sent over to Mathilde the original pencil sketch he had long ago promised her of the prelude, accompanied, he tells us, by "a little note in which I communicated to her, seriously and calmly, the mood that filled me at the time." Minna, whose jealousy had been increasing for a long while, intercepted the servant, took the package from him, and read the letter. Its contents, Wagner told his sister Klara a fortnight later, were of a nature which, if Minna had had any real understanding of himself and Frau Wesendonk, ought to have reassured rather than alarmed her, for its theme was resignation. To Minna it seemed something very different. The account she gave of the letter to one of her lady friends runs thus:

> "After a wild night of love that he had had,[3] he writes to her — 'Thus it went on the whole night through. In the morning I was rational again, and from the depth of my heart could pray to my angel, and this prayer is Love! Love! Deepest soul's joy on this love, the source of my redemption! Then came the day with its evil weather, the joy of seeing you was denied me, my work would not go at all. Thus my whole day was a struggle between melancholy and longing for you', etc. The letter ended in this way: 'Be good to me: the weather seems mild: to-day I will come again to your garden as soon as I see you. I hope to find you undisturbed for a moment'."[4]

2

Minna never parted with the fatal eight-page letter, which went at her death to Natalie, and is now in the Burrell Collection. A

---

[3] This merely means that on the preceding evening but one he had been annoyed at finding the Italian scholar De Sanctis occupying Mathilde's time and attention with his talk, and his annoyance had caused him a sleepless night.

[4] JKWF, p. 148.

translation of a portion of it has been given by Messrs. Hurn and Root in *The Truth about Wagner;* and from this one is at last able to see the oft- and long-debated matter as it really was. Wagner was justified in describing the theme of the letter as " resignation " even though that word itself does not seem to occur in it. He calls himself a fool for having sought " to win peace and the world from without. . . . Only inside, within, only in depths does salvation dwell! Even to you I can only speak and explain myself when I don't see you — or may not see you." Half the letter was devoted to a discussion of a conversation they had had on the subject of Goethe's *Faust*.[5] Anything less like a " love-letter " in the common acceptance of the term could hardly be imagined: Wagner is mysticising, Tristanising, as he had done for a year past and was to do for another year to come. The Wesendonk-*Tristan* affair is a cardinal example of his ability to exist mentally in two dimensions at once: he saw nothing incongruous in being completely absorbed in Mathilde as his " Muse " and at the same time living affectionately on the ordinary domestic plane with Minna. The spheres of the ideal and the real were almost completely distinct for him. But Minna, in whose nature there was not a trace of mysticism, while she had scant understanding of the psychology of an artist, lived only in one dimension. " Love " as a poetic, mystical conception, " lovers " who found their consolation in " resignation " and understood each other best in absence or in silence — these things were beyond her comprehension. She was an illiterate, unimaginative woman, whose mind, such as it was, was all foreground without perspective. She was now nearing fifty, incurably sick, unable to reconcile herself to the loss of the physical charm that had brought men fluttering round her in her youth. She was tied to a man who, in spite of the strain that life had always been on him, was younger than she not merely in years but in spirit and in body. She knew that women were a necessity to his nature, but did not see that what he sought in women was, for the most part, sympathy with him as an artist rather than the ordinary satisfactions of sex. She was already becoming mentally a little abnormal, owing to the drugs that had been unwisely prescribed for her heart disease and insomnia.

---

[5] This section is not translated in Messrs. Hurn and Root's book. It is a pity we cannot be given the whole letter in its German form.

Verlag F. Bruckmann, Munich

MINNA WAGNER IN MIDDLE LIFE

The situation, as she saw it, was simply the common one of a volatile husband passing over an ageing wife for a younger and prettier woman; while his habit of closing up his mind towards her where his art was concerned, yet opening it in full to Mathilde, must have given her a galling sense of her own intellectual inferiority.

She told him at once that she had opened and read the letter, and then played her cards according to the established rules of bourgeois morality, as she had no doubt learned them from the dramas in which she had acted as a girl. She would not tolerate, she said, this " deception " of the good Otto: she herself would go away, but Richard must make an honest woman of Mathilde by " calling her his own for ever ". Wagner tried in vain to explain the true nature of his relations with Mathilde. Fine-spun distinctions in the concept of " love " were beyond her comprehension; the more subtly analytical he became the more convinced she was that she had to deal with an inveterate casuist, and so the more furiously she raged against what she called his " marvellous gift of the gab ".[6] The next day, full of pity for her no less than for himself, he made the sensible suggestion that as she was visibly very ill she should go away for a cure; on her return they would be able to talk it all over more quietly. She confessed afterwards that nothing had angered her so much as the calmness of his manner and his speech during the crisis. Had he flown into one of the passions with which she was familiar in their domestic " scenes ", and indulged in the violent language usual with him on those occasions, she would have been better able to hold her own. But for Wagner the thing was too serious for temper: the sense that the bottom had suddenly dropped out of the ideal world he had built around himself and his *Tristan* made the ordinary reactions to the abuse of the furious woman impossible for him.

3

It was arranged that she should go for her cure to Brestenberg, on the Hallwyler Lake, which had a reputation for success in the treatment of cases of heart trouble. But before she left she could

---

[6] "Seine vortreffliche Suade." Perhaps "his wonderful blarney" would convey Minna's meaning better.

not refrain from calling on Mathilde and " warning " her, as she put it, " against the consequences of any imprudent intimacy " with Richard. She showed the fatal letter to Mathilde and said, " If I were an ordinary woman I would take this to your husband." She returned to the Asyl exceedingly pleased with herself at not only having done what she took to be the correct thing, but having played the leading lady well. But irreparable mischief had now been done. Mathilde, who had never had any secrets from Otto, at once told him what had happened; and later she reproached Wagner for not having assured Minna from the first of the innocence and lofti-ness of their relations.[7] He had difficulty in making her realise that to a mentality like Minna's no amount of assurance on his or any one else's part would have carried conviction on a matter at which she looked from a completely different angle from his.

None of them, as yet, realised that the situation was fundamen-tally hopeless: Wagner in particular felt that with the restoration of Minna's mental health she would see how mistakenly she had judged and acted, and he would be able once more to settle down to happy work at *Tristan*. His letters to her during April and the following months are affectionate and wise: his only unwisdom consisted in believing that forces irreconcilable by nature, once unleashed and coming to a clash, could result in anything but catastrophe. He im-plored her to think of nothing but the recovery of her health: " Without that there is no hope for any of us. . . . Only patience and courage! Everything will come right, for sure, and after all storms and cares there will be, in the end, a peaceful, contented old age! " But the more he tried to soothe her, the more he sought to make clear to her the true nature of his relations with the Wesen-donks, the more angrily suspicious she became: the poor creature's mind was not merely penned within its natural limitations but poisoned by disease and drugs.

On the 27th April the cry is wrung from him, evidently in an-swer to something she had written him, that he is ready not for a hydropathic institution but for a mad-house:

" Whatever I say or write, even with the best intentions, I stir up nothing but misfortune and misunderstanding. If I keep silence about

---

[7] Thus in *Mein Leben*. According to one of his letters to Minna while she was away it was Otto who made these reproaches to him.

certain things, you become distrustful and suspicious — you imagine I am trying to dupe you: if I write seriously and frankly, and at the same time — as I, poor ass, believed — thoroughly reassuringly, I learn that I have been hatching a crafty plot to hurry you to your grave! . . . I am so in doubt concerning everything I say or do that very soon I shall be carried about like a child. No matter, though, if only you will rid yourself once for all of these terrible fancies, and recognise that at least I have the best, most honest will to show myself good and grateful to you, faithful and attached, affectionate and thoughtful. . . . God only grant that I am not exciting you again with this letter: I literally know no longer what I am doing! You worry a black meaning out of everything."

He exhorts her not to " fall back always into black self-torturing fancies ", not to fasten misconceivingly on single words and expressions of his, to take him as a whole and see him as a whole, to recognise that he is not dissimulating with her, to join with him in being " lenient towards each other's weaknesses ", and " honestly to help each other to fulfil life's heavy task in cheerful, untroubled fashion."

Gradually, with Minna not there to fret him, able, as always when she was at a distance from him, to think of her with genuine sympathy and affection, he manages to take up his inner life again, and, in spite of his bad health, to find delight once more in the easy way that the music of *Tristan* is spinning itself out from his pen,[8] and in the growing beauty of his garden. " When I cast my eye around ", he tells her on the 28th May, " I really must rejoice in the lovely Asyl that has been prepared for us. It is and will be saved for us: [9] we have to do with pure and noble people." He assures her again and again of his sincere affection, exhorts her to give up her brooding, and looks forward to a happy old age with her. The *Tristan* mood, in fact, the mood of mystic, entranced absorption in the ideal world of his own inner creating, has taken possession of him again in these weeks of freedom — though he visited Minna occasionally in Brestenberg — from the fret and nag of daily inter-

---

[8] The composition of the second act was begun on the 4th May, and finished on the 1st July.

[9] Under the first shock of the "scene" with Minna, Mathilde had declared it to be impossible for her ever to enter the Asyl again, but neither she nor Otto was willing to admit that this would mean that Wagner could no longer make his home there. See RWML, II, 768.

course with this woman to whom he was in all sincerity attached and grateful, whose misfortune was that she was not his intellectual equal, and whose chief fault was her constitutional inability to see that there was not one man but two in him. He is resuming his normal outer life, he tells her. The sixteen-years-old Tausig is staying in the neighbourhood, and he is growing fond of the wayward young imp of genius, with his amusing mixture of the child and the man of the world, his marvellous piano-playing, his swaggering Lisztian airs, his strong cigars. The Bülows are to visit him again soon. The Wesendonks would not hear of his leaving the Asyl, even if it means that communications between the two households shall be broken off. The great thing is for Minna to get well, to give up her opium, be sensible, and in future handle the difficult problem of his life and hers with calm and dignity. His material affairs, he assures her, are shaping promisingly. He indulges himself in rosy hopes of being amnestied before long. The Vienna Court Opera intends to give *Lohengrin*, and has offered him 1,000 gulden for the first 20 performances, another 500 gulden after the 20th, and a further 500 after the 30th. Kapellmeister Esser has been to see him, and they have run through the opera together; the contract has been signed, and he has already received the first 1,000 gulden. *Tannhäuser* has at last been revived in Dresden with immense success. A rich enthusiast who has taken over the Basel theatre intends to produce *Lohengrin* there. Berlin is waking up again: he has received a first royalty of 255 thalers for *Lohengrin* from Hülsen.[10] He will soon be able to pay off all his debts, and a new life will begin for them both if only she can restore her body's health, and with it her mind's. She was undeniably improving; but it suffices, in July, for him to defer writing to her for two days for the old crazy suspicions and reproaches to break out once more.

---

[10] On the 23rd June he was given an audience in Lucerne by the Grand Duke of Weimar, who was apparently perturbed at the news that *Tristan* would be produced in Carlsruhe, and wanted an assurance that Weimar should have the first performance of the *Ring*. Nothing came, of course, of all this. Wagner found Carl Alexander a pleasant-mannered and cultivated young man, but saw no reason to change the opinion he had already formed as to his talent being for talking about great deeds rather than performing them.

4

He brought Minna back from Brestenberg on the 15th July. She found Tichatschek installed in the only spare room of the Asyl,[11] and the Bülow couple waiting in a Zürich hotel until he should leave. On the 17th the young Wendelin Weissheimer called with a letter of introduction from Schindelmeisser: apparently he observed no signs of strain in the Asyl atmosphere. A closer observer might have seen that clouds were still hanging over the Green Hill; but these would probably have rolled away in time had Minna been more normal. It had been Wagner's original plan that after her cure in Brestenberg she should go for a while to her friends in Saxony: manifestly the longer she was away from Zürich the more chance there would be of her irritation with Frau Wesendonk working itself out. Wagner had some justification for hoping that the worst was already over. At the end of May she had returned to the Asyl for a day or two to attend to some household affairs; and she then gave him the impression that she regarded the incident of the 7th April as at an end. The view she took of it was that there had been just a little " love affair " which she, as an experienced woman of the world, had known how to put straight. Richard talked to her earnestly, begging her to reflect seriously upon what she had already done and to be careful what she did in the future, for the situation was delicate; any further imprudence on her part would mean their having to leave the Asyl, in which case, he told her frankly, a separation between them was inevitable. For the moment she seems to have realised that she was her own worst enemy as well as Richard's: for the first time in their lives, he says, she broke into a low wail; and when they were parting for the night she humbly kissed his hand. He was deeply touched, and encouraged to believe that with restored health her mental outlook would change. As on the Laussot occasion, the thought of a final separation from him was more than she could bear.

---

[11] He had been there for some time. During his visit Wagner received a call from the Hanover tenor, Niemann, who was accompanied by his bride, the actress Marie Seebach. From what he had heard of Niemann from others, Wagner thought him the only likely tenor for his Siegfried and Tristan. But as neither of the two star tenors in the Asyl would sing in the presence of the other, he was still unable to get any idea of Niemann's voice.'

The Wesendonks, deeply pained at being dragged into an atmosphere of bourgeois vulgarity that was hateful to them, had been spending some weeks in Italy, but had returned before Wagner brought Minna back from Brestenberg. Everything now depended on her: all would have been well had she been able to see the difficult situation as everyone else saw it, to make in future no demands on her husband outside the narrow circle of their domestic life but leave him free to find elsewhere the intellectual communion that was essential to him as an artist. But this, it soon became manifest, she could not resign herself to doing. She lacked at once the diplomatic tact of Cosima and the latter's unselfish recognition that in the long run nothing mattered where Wagner was concerned but his art: Cosima, in the later Bayreuth days, looked with a benevolent, philosophic eye on the old man's romantic infatuation with Judith Gautier. Minna's one-track mind took no account of the psychological complexities of more highly-organised beings than herself: the situation, as she saw it, was simply the old one of one woman against another, and of an honest woman, with all the legalities and moralities on her side, against a designing siren. Perhaps Mathilde, during all these years, had been lacking in tact in her general dealings with her — had hurt her by tacitly ruling her out of the intellectual world in which Wagner and his " Muse " met on apparently equal terms. Minna certainly hated Mathilde, " that cold woman, spoiled by happiness " as she described her to one of her own friends; and the hatred was shared by Natalie, to whom, to her dying day, Mathilde was " the super-devilish Helen Mathilde Wesendonk." [12]

5

The demons of ill-will were soon at their fell work again. A foolish and perhaps malicious servant had rigged up a floral arch to celebrate the return of the mistress of the house. Minna insisted on its remaining up for several days, as visible evidence to the enemy that she had returned not in humiliation but in triumph. Mathilde, angry at the crudity of it all, expressed her feelings in

---

[12] She so describes her in a letter of 1891 to Mrs Burrell. See CBC, No. 299.

passionate terms to the Bülows, who repeated her words to Wagner. A premonition of the coming doom now came over him: peace would be for ever impossible with only a few yards separating Mathilde from Minna. Bülow and Cosima had come to stay with him after Tichatschek's departure, and on the very day of their entry into the Asyl they were the sadly perturbed witnesses of a scene of horrible recrimination between Minna and Richard: he had told her, we learn from *Mein Leben,* that it was no longer possible for them to remain in the Asyl, and that he was only deferring his departure till his young friends had left. " This time ", he says, " I had to admit to her that the reasons for my departure were not entirely contained in her behaviour." What lies behind that remark it is difficult to decide now.

The same events, looked at through eyes that are the windows of very different minds, can bear a very different aspect to each beholder of them. What Minna had seen during the first weeks after their removal to the Asyl had been a constant interchange of letters and packets and visits between her husband and Mathilde. To the latter and Richard, all this was justified by the ideal nature of these communications — poems on both sides, music on his, reports of his progress in his work and his delight in it. To Minna it all looked like an intrigue of the commonest kind. She occupied the ground floor of the house, Wagner the upper floor.

" Mme Wesendonk ", she wrote to a friend, " used to visit my husband secretly, as he did her, and forbade my servant, when he opened the door for her, to tell me that she was above. I calmly let it all go on. Men so often have an affair; why should I not tolerate it in the case of my husband? I did not know jealousy. Only the commonnesses, the mortifications, might have been spared me, and my ludicrously vain husband should have concealed it from me." [13]

But precisely because Minna could have been trusted, by any one who knew her, to see all this intercourse in the commonest light, Frau Wesendonk must have been either somewhat thick-skinned by nature or utterly blinded by her infatuation for Wagner to have persisted in it under the circumstances. A woman of any natural delicacy would surely have refrained from wounding, as

---

[13] JKWF, p. 147.

she constantly did, the susceptibilities of another woman over whom she had all the tactical advantages of age, looks, social position and culture, a woman, moreover, whom she must have known to be smarting under the sense of pecuniary obligation to the rich couple on whose property she was living. It is difficult for the impartial observer to believe that Mathilde Wesendonk was made of such particularly fine stuff as Wagner at that time thought and would have us think. A rather false idea of the situation as it must have been on the material side during these years has been given us by the letters of a later date in which Wagner idealises her. It is evident that in the matter of coarse feminine recrimination Mathilde sometimes gave as good as she took: in the Bayreuth days Wagner amused Cosima with an account of how the two women used to do their best to annoy and anger each other, " while I — I was thinking of neither of them." [14]

Minna, for her part, could see it all from no angle but her own bourgeois one. The final impression we get from a study of all the documents open to us is that both she and Wagner are, from first to last, telling the simple truth as they saw it: the tragedy came from the fact that not a single incident, a single motive, a single conversation, bore the same appearance for both of them. There is not the slightest reason to doubt Wagner's story of the moving scene between them on her temporary return from Brestenberg, when she had a momentary glimpse of the pain there was in the depths of him, and she broke into lamentation and kissed his hand. But she had only to be a few days away from him again, a few days in which she suffered tortures from the incessant thumping of her heart, for the inveterate, monomaniac sense of grievance to rise uppermost in her once more, and for her to be convinced that he had behaved brutally to her on that very occasion.

" It is really horrible ", she wrote to Emma Herwegh on the 14th June, " how shabbily Richard behaves towards his wife, whom he has made so ill. May God help me! A week last Sunday I was at home, but only for twenty-three hours, so that I had no time to call on you. I wish I had not gone there: dear Richard vented his spleen on me until two in the morning." [15]

---

[14] MECW, I, 860.
[15] JKWF, p. 153.

The dates show that it is the same occasion that is being referred to by each of them. Could any two descriptions of the same conversation by two people differ more absolutely? And would any judge, hearing either side alone, hesitate to give his verdict to the appellant? It is evidently the same occasion to which Wagner refers again in a letter [16] to Alwine Frommann, in which he goes on to say how, after that sign of tenderness and understanding in her, he had again tried to get her to see that the case which she " so odiously misrepresented " was in reality " one of *suffering*, noble and tender suffering, without anything in it to cause solicitude." This is what Minna represents as his venting his spleen on her until two in the morning!

6

Even at the time he seems to have recognised despairingly that he was making no real impression on her, so few and fixed were her ideas about the matter, so restricted and unimaginative her outlook upon it. " Yet how was *I* to make this clear to her? " he asks Alwine. " Any attempt to do so from *my* mouth was sure to be regarded as a new injury to her, a new complaint against her. For on this point her whole feeling was simply one of excitement: reason and insight could make no headway towards an understanding against the fact that it was *my* voice that was urging her to be just." In this the gravest crisis of his whole domestic life he found himself confronted by a woman who had never had more than the minimum of understanding of him as an artist, and was now all the less able to be tolerant of his peculiarities because her mind was by this time far from normal. During her stay in Brestenberg his letters had been studiously patient, conciliatory, and kindly; he knew he had to deal not only with a woman who was suffering grievously but with one who, as the Brestenberg doctor had privately warned him, might die suddenly at any time. Any woman in a normal condition

---

[16] Even the same expressions occur in this letter as in the *Mein Leben* story of so many years later — in the one case, "Sie war . . . zum erstenmal ganz weich, und nur noch klagend, was mir das Herz zerriss"; in the other, "So dass ich sie hier, zum ersten Male in unsrem Leben, in eine weiche und würdige Klage ausbrechen hörte. Zum ersten und einzigen Male gab sie mir das Zeichen einer liebevollen Demut, indem sie mir, als ich in tiefer Nacht von ihr mich zurückzog, die Hand küsste. Dieses rührte mich ausserordentlich. . . ."

of mental health would have recognised that whatever grievance she might feel she had against him on the ground that he would not recast his views of the Wesendonk affair to agree with hers, at any rate he had shown himself full of solicitude for her in her sufferings. But in this letter of hers of the 14th June to Frau Herwegh we find her saying,

> " My dear husband might be really kind and ease my pain if he did not allow himself to be got round by certain people: his heart is good, but very weak! That is why he sometimes writes me really nice comforting letters, but more often hurls the basest and commonest things at me in them, exalts other people to heaven and treads me underfoot. That, my dearest Emma, is what is still eating my heart away! It is only rarely that I can weep over these grossnesses, and that is very bad for me: my heart chokes as if it were being twisted round. . . . It is really horrible how Richard behaves to his wife, when it is he who has made her so ill."

If now we turn to Wagner's letter to her of the 11th, which she must have had plenty of time to think over when she was writing in this strain on the 14th to Frau Herwegh, we find him exhorting her to be patient and sensible, as there was really no reason, in spite of what had happened, why their whole lives should be ruined by their having to leave the Asyl. " She whom you hate so much wishes nothing more than that I should retain this pretty Asyl, even if she never sees me or has any intercourse with me. . . . Just comprehend, then, with *whom* you have to do "; and he exhorts her again to concentrate on the first thing needful — to restore her health, and above all renew her body, " which has been quite undermined by the frightful mass of opium and physic." This is what Minna regards as hurling the basest and commonest things at her, exalting other people to heaven and treading her underfoot!

Even apart from her hatred of Mathilde, she was not psychologist enough to realize that she invariably saw the workings of her husband's mind the wrong way round. It was not that he let women influence his art, but that the urge of his art constantly made him idealise the woman who, at the moment, seemed to harmonise most perfectly with his inner world. And not only women, indeed, but men, as is shown by his remark in later years that " Bismarck is certainly a great politician but not a great man, for he has no comprehension of Bayreuth." [17] It is necessary to insist once more on the cardinal fact in his psychology that it was not his life that determined his art so much as his art that coloured his life. Liszt's pupil Kellermann, who saw a good deal of him in the Bayreuth period, noted that

> "Richard Wagner was a man who was absolutely dependent on his moods: what he was turning into poetry or music reflected itself instantly in his daily life. If he was dealing with some great conflict, he came into conflict and quarrel with the people round him. If he was working at something beautiful and winning, he was exceptionally friendly and enchantingly sweet. . . . His art was to him the highest and weightiest thing on earth: everything had to be subordinated to it."

Hence his resentment against those who did not further his financial plans as ardently as he could have wished: " he was convinced that it was all a mere matter of bad will." [18] When he was writing *Parsifal* he felt the need of surrounding himself with subtle odours and fine fabrics if there was to be no rude shattering of the world of soft outlines and shifting colours in which his characters lived and moved and had their being. Hence what seems to us the strange episode in which Judith Gautier figured. Cosima, like the wise woman she was, sank her personal feelings and humoured him in this as in everything else: the child of genius could have any toy or sweetmeat it liked that would keep it happy: the end was so great that the means did not matter. But Minna was incapable not only of this magnanimous behaviour towards him but even of grasping the fundamental law of his nature as an artist.

7

In the *Tristan* period the material world in which he stumbled about so blindly was only an outward projection of the Buddhistic mood within him. He talked incessantly at that time of resignation and renunciation as the law of life: it was one of the emotional formulae, the verbal counters, that for the time being had become

---

[17] This was after Bismarck had opposed a State contribution to the Bayreuth fund. See KEK, p. 77.
[18] KEK, pp. 76, 77.

second nature to him: and it was with blank amazement that he discovered now and then that to other people, and to Minna in particular, his conduct seemed pure selfishness, his " renunciation " just an egoistic grasping at what he most wanted and would on no account deny himself. Minna could not follow the intricate workings of his mind and what appeared to her to be the sophistical subtleties of his speech: she no doubt read the fatal letter of the 7th April again and again in the vain effort to find in it the " resignation " which he assured her was the ground-motive of it. Yet to him the resignation and renunciation were there — as poetic concepts if not as materialities — and they were the secret source of his consolation in the lofty beauty of it all: thus it was, he felt, that his Tristan conceived *his* relations with Isolde. While Minna was in Brestenberg he wrote Mathilde a letter in which he enlarged upon this very theme. He had already told Otto that he had resolved to break off personal communion with both of them.[19] " Hereby the necessity of our renunciation took on of itself another character: the conclusion resolved itself into a gentle reconcilement"; and again, " The stupendous conflicts we have passed through, how could they end but with the victory over every wish and craving? In the most ardent moments of approach, did not we know that this was our goal? " He had realised that

" there is only one salvation for me that I can think of; and this can come only from the innermost depth of the heart, not from any outer contrivance whatever. Its name is Rest! An end to longing! Stilling of every desire! Worthy, noble overcoming! Life for others, for others — thus solace for ourselves! "

Highly imaginative artists can make almost any situation tolerable for themselves, and not merely tolerable but subtly desirable, by thus poetising themselves and their experiences: great is the power of words over those who plume themselves on being the mas-

---

[19] See also his letter to Minna of the 3rd June: " The Wesendonks returned the evening before last. He called on me yesterday and invited me to tea; whereupon I very delicately explained to him in writing that for the future we would remain on friendly terms, but without personal intercourse. Let it stop at that! I most earnestly beg you to abstain from *any* kind of interference, which would only have results I should be obliged to regard positively as a fresh breach of your trust."

OTTO WESENDONK, 1865

FROM A RELIEF BY JOSEPH KOPF

(From Erich W. Engel's " Richard Wagners Leben und Werke im Bilde ", by courtesy of Fr. Kijtner and C. F. W. Siegel, Leipzig)

ters of words! They weave and weave fine words till the poetic concepts at the back of them come to seem to them the only realities. Wagner was soon roughly reminded that for poets, no less than for other men, there are hard realities in life. In Minna there was none of this casuistry of the emotions, this virtuoso delight in dialectic for its own sake: to her it was a matter purely and simply of beating a woman she hated or being beaten by her; a situation that might have righted itself in time had she gone at once from Brestenberg to Germany, leaving Wagner to purge his soul of the *Tristan* music and by that very process discover that Mathilde was no longer necessary to him, became impossible as soon as the two women, each nursing a sense of grievance against the other, were once more separated only by a few yards of garden. A wretched month dragged on, the evil hour being postponed only because the Asyl was full of visitors — the Bülows, the Countess d'Agoult, Tausig, Klindworth, Lachner, Karl Ritter and others. But there must have been many " scenes ", in private and in public, between Richard and Minna;[20] and he had already decided that an end would have to be made of a situation that had grown utterly impossible. As he told Frau Ritter later, his life ever since he had gone to the Asyl had been " a veritable hell ", owing to the increasing irritability of Minna as the result of her insomnia and drug-taking. To a winter with her in the Asyl he could look forward only with apprehension: having no intellectual resources, she could not exist without company and entertainments of her own type, and on the Green Hill in Enge she was rather cut off from these. She would be better, they agreed, with her kin in Saxony. As for him, any further progress with *Tristan* would be impossible with this pathetic fury always tearing at his patience and his temper. Had not something drastic been done, he wrote to Frau Ritter more than a year later, all of them on the Green Hill would have gone mad.

---

[20] " Perpetual *Gewitterschwüle* " (the sultriness that precedes a storm) was Bülow's description of the Asyl atmosphere in a letter of the 9th August to Pohl. He stayed on only because he felt that Wagner needed him: Bülow found his nature as "fundamentally noble " as ever, in spite of his trials. The friends had found some relief from their cares in running through the *Rhinegold* and *Valkyrie* scores, Klindworth playing the piano magnificently and Wagner singing all the vocal parts "with colossal self-forgetfulness, expending all his forces."

He had hoped that Liszt would come to him and help him with the advice of a man of the world; but Liszt, who had apparently no desire to be mixed up with so delicate and complicated an affair, put him off with a vague promise to be in Zürich — to meet the Princess on her return from Munich — at the beginning of September. But by the 4th August Wagner's resolution was taken: " I leave Zürich on the 15th ", he wrote to Liszt, " never to return there. My wife will go a little later to Germany." Manifestly alarmed, Liszt now offered to come earlier than he had intended, and asked Wagner to postpone his departure for a fortnight. But it was too late.

> " For weeks ", he wrote back briefly on the 11th, " I have been longing for the day when I could leave here. I *can* leave on the 15th — which is the same thing as I *must*. I will let you know later where I settle down. It was very painful to me that I could not have you with me in this momentous catastrophe of my life."

We can see now that, in the deepest sense, it was *Tristan*, rather than Minna and Mathilde, that drove him from the Asyl. It was one of the strangest features of his strange nature that his creative imagination did not suffer by material annoyances but positively throve on them: the explanation probably is that the shock raised the temperature of his mind, and, at the raised temperature, it functioned more swiftly, though not within the sphere of the crude annoyance itself but within the sphere of his art. He told Cosima, in later years, of an episode that had occurred on one of his rambles with Wille and Herwegh. Feeling too tired to go any further, he had asked the others to go on without him. Wille, surmising that he was merely lazy, slapped him roughly on the back and urged him on. Wagner cursed him soundly — and at once there came to his mind both the words and the music for Loge's apostrophe to the Rhine Maidens! He said also that Minna was always infuriated by his inexplicable calm when she was making the most fearful " scenes ": he was calm because the raising of the temperature sent ideas for *Tristan* or the *Valkyrie* flashing across his brain. His own explanation of it all was that anger increases the vital powers for the moment, and that then the " most essential nature " of a man gets to work in its own way, regardless of the immediate surroundings. For the working-out of the ideas thus generated, however, the slow shaping of them into an organic tissue, the profoundest quiet is necessary.[21] It was largely because his whole being called out for this quiet in order to complete his *Tristan* that further life at the Asyl had now become impossible for him.

---

[21] MECW, I, 705.

CHAPTER XXVI

CALM IN VENICE

1

THE BÜLOWS, however, did not leave until the 16th, Bülow bathed in tears, Cosima sombre, silent, thoughtful. What she had seen and heard in the Asyl was her first initiation into the sheer ugliness of life, and perhaps we may date from that visit the dawning of her immeasurable sympathy for Wagner; something must have torn at her heart as Amfortas's cry of pain tore at the heart of Parsifal, bringing with it a blinding spiritual illumination. Wagner, who had bidden a final farewell to Mathilde in Bülow's presence, left Zürich by the five o'clock train on the morning of the 17th. Minna had made him some tea: after that, in a dawn of wonderful beauty, husband and wife paced sadly up and down the garden they were never to look upon together again. On both of them there had descended an unearthly calm. She accompanied him to the station, and there she broke down: he remained dry-eyed.

> " Once more ", he wrote to Frau Wesendonk later, " I exhorted her to be gentle and noble and win Christian comfort for herself; and once more the old revengeful vehemence flamed up in her. She is past all helping, I could not help saying to myself; yet I cannot revenge myself on the unhappy woman: she must work out her own sentence."

In the train a merciful serenity of spirit took possession of him: the very violence of the storm that had lasted so many months had brought in its wake a feeling of relief that the end had really come — that now at last he could devote himself, unfretted, to his art. He had had enough of the world of ugly reality: now he would have the solitude he longed for, an outer solitude if possible, but at any rate an inner one.

Italy had been his ultimate objective from the first, though he had intended to remain for a month or so in Geneva until cooler weather set in. From Geneva he wrote to Minna on the 19th and the 25th, quietly, sensibly and kindly. Evidently he still did not mean the separation to be permanent: he told her of his hope of winning peace of soul in the only way possible for him, and exhorted her to make a fresh effort to rebuild her own world about her, and, as a prerequisite to happiness, to strive for the re-establishment of her health. Her reply, judging from his next letter to her, was not very encouraging.

> " I have been feeling particularly wretched for some days past ", he says, " especially after receiving your letter, from which I realised that it will probably be always impossible for you to see clearly and correctly. For you, a definite blame always should and must be borne by a definite person: you do not understand the nature of things and Fate, but simply think that if this person or thing had never been, everything would have happened otherwise."

Once more he tried to make her see that further life on the Green Hill would have been possible for all concerned only if there had been a complete severance of communications between the two households, which in the nature of the case was impracticable. But he has no hope of enlightening her as to the deeper significance, for him, of all that has happened, and can only suggest finally that each of them shall try to conquer the past and remake the future in his own way. She was clearly unteachable. He had hoped that their departure from Zürich would be accomplished quietly, so that evil tongues would not be set wagging any more than was inevitable. But she went clumsily about the business of selling their superfluous belongings, with the result that the air became thick with gossip and scandal, and the aggrieved Wesendonks soon had new wounds to lick.

His stay at Geneva [1] lasted no longer than a week, Karl Ritter, whom he had come across in Lausanne, persuading him to go with him at once to Venice. After a night there in a second-rate hotel, Wagner found ideally quiet and secluded quarters in one of the dilapidated Giustiniani palaces on the Grand Canal, near the Palazzo Foscari (Campiello Squillini, No. 3228). The building was rather out of favour with visitors, its aspect making it very cold

---

[1] He stayed at the Maison James Fazy (later the Hôtel de Russie), at the corner of the Quai du Leman and the Rue du Montblanc.

in the winter. He obtained a very large salon and an only slightly smaller bedroom: he at once had the grey walls of the former covered with inexpensive dark red hangings, and portières of the same colour placed over the doors. The reason he gave for doing this was that the original handsome doors of the apartment had been taken away and replaced by others of common wood, which offended his eye; but the real explanation no doubt was that, as usual when he had a composition in hand, he wished to give himself the illusion of being insulated from the outer world. His Erard arrived in October, and the second act of *Tristan* was soon well under way again. To support himself and Minna during the seven months he spent in Venice was no easy matter: there were occasional royalties from the theatres — generally spent in advance, of course — and Breitkopf & Härtel paid him 25 Louisdor for the publishing rights in his version of *Iphigenia in Aulis*; but his letters show him to have been in grievous difficulties at times. There are hints that his Zürich creditors had swooped on his furniture at the Asyl, and that the prompt intervention of his friends had been necessary to redeem the Erard, which was indispensable to him in his work. But as some at least of the furniture followed Minna to Germany, and turned up again later in Paris, it seems likely that Otto Wesendonk or some other Zürich friend saved the essential things for him.

2

Although he had one or two bad illnesses during these seven months, they were probably, on the whole, the serenest of his life until then. The world, when it succeeded in piercing the armour of his spirit, indeed wounded him sorely; but the very intensity of his sufferings for so many years had developed in him a stoical indifference to many things. Thus he could assure Bülow that Liszt, who was wincing under the attacks of the Press enemies of his music, seemed to him enviably fortunate in that he could still feel pain over such matters. For his own part, he said, the moral crisis he had been through had brought him so much torture that he had become completely indifferent to attacks on him as an artist. When, in the early weeks of 1859, attempts were made by the Saxon authorities to have him driven out of Venice, what pained him most was not the possible consequences to himself but the sense of the incredible heartlessness of men towards men.[2] But from his material cares during this Venice period he found a blissful escape in work at his *Tristan* and in philosophical brooding upon the constitution of the universe.

" My late heart-rending experiences of life ", he wrote to Bülow in September, " have made my attitude towards the world more and more a negative one. I feel myself set almost entirely free from wish and longing. I want only to cause as little suffering as possible to others: my own sufferings pass from me when I know that theirs are being mitigated. . . . If I were not an artist I could become a saint: this redemption, however, is not assigned to me." [3]

He found, as Goethe had done seventy years before, that in Venice one could enjoy the spectacle of crowds and incessant movement and yet feel deliciously alone. Karl Ritter, who was reconciled to him by now, and showing once more the best side of his complex nature, was an intelligent companion always at hand when wanted, and with plenty of occupations of his own, among the pictures and the churches, when he was not. No one else was allowed to encroach seriously on Wagner's solitude. Liszt's pupil Winterberger happened to be there for some time, but Wagner saw as little of him as possible. He was more attracted by a new acquaintance, a handsome Venetian piano teacher named Tessarin who described himself as a " white raven " in Italy, for his passion was German music, especially that of Wagner and Liszt. One day, on the Riva, Wagner was accosted by two strangers who waxed very enthusiastic over *Lohengrin,* which they had just heard in Vienna: they were Count Edmund Zichy and Prince Dolgoruki. The former left Venice soon afterwards, but Dolgoruki remained for the winter: he was a man of fine culture, to whom Wagner became quite attached.

As usual with him, he organised his time on routine lines — till two in the afternoon, work; then down the Grand Canal in a gondola to the Piazzetta, for a meal in the Piazza San Marco; then a walk, either alone or with Karl, along the Riva to the Giardino Pubblico; at nightfall back to the Palazzo Giustiniani by gondola; then a little more work and a chat over tea with Karl. Occasionally

---

[2] RWHB, p. 115.   [3] Ibid., p. 106.

he would go to a theatre, taking especial pleasure in the Goldoni performances at the Camploi: he saw also Ristori as Medea and as Marie Stuart, and was impressed by her virtuosity, though finding her lacking, according to German notions, in imagination and ideality. The opera did not attract him often. If he wanted music, there were excellent Austrian military bands playing in the evenings on the Piazza San Marco: he made the acquaintance of some of the bandsmen and officers, who treated him with great respect; and the overtures to *Rienzi* and *Tannhäuser* frequently figured in the programmes.

He does not mention by name, in *Mein Leben*, a man to whom, had he only known it, he was in reality indebted for being allowed to remain in Venice and so make the progress he did with the scoring of the second act of *Tristan*. Venice at that time was under the dominion of Austria, and Austria was a member of the German Confederation; and though Venice was not part of that Confederation, it was in the power of his enemies in Germany to make his residence there unpleasant, if not impossible. No sooner did Baron von Kempen, the Vienna Chief of Police, discover that Wagner was in Venice than he consulted the Austrian Minister of Foreign Affairs, Count von Buol-Schauenstein, as to what ought to be done in the matter, having regard to " the consideration due to the Saxon Government ". The Minister was not disposed to take any steps beyond informing the Saxon Government, as a matter of courtesy, that the notorious Richard Wagner had arrived in Venice with a Swiss passport, having ostensibly gone there for reasons of health, and that he contemplated staying for six months. As Dresden in turn did not at the moment seem to think that the German Confederation was in any grave danger from this new turn of affairs, there the matter would have rested but for the direct pressure now put on the Venice police by von Kempen: this " political refugee ", who had " markedly compromised himself during the revolutionary period " and associated with " the coryphées of revolutionary propaganda in Zürich ", was to be " kept under the closest surveillance during his residence in Venice "; moreover a watchful eye was to be kept on his health, and as soon as this showed signs of improvement the proper steps were to be taken to hasten his removal not only from Venice but from Austrian territory in general.

Obviously it would have gone hard with Wagner had the local police knuckled under to von Kempen. But the Venice Councillor of Police, Angelo Crespi, seems to have been not only an unusually sensible and human official but a man interested in music and in Wagner. After an interview with the latter he placidly reported to von Kempen that the supposed revolutionary had abstained from all political activities in Zürich, devoting himself exclusively to his profession, " in which his genius as composer, musical essayist and critic has enabled him to open out a new path: as the creator of the so-called music of the future he stands at the head of the musical and aesthetic movement of to-day." He had come to Venice, said Crespi, solely in quest of health and quiet; he received few letters and kept very much to himself. Fume and fret as he might, von Kempen could make no impression on the doughty Crespi, thanks to whom Wagner, though his movements were evidently watched, was allowed to remain in peace.[4] The musical world owes a great deal to Angelo Crespi: good Wagnerians ought to drink his health after each performance of the second act of *Tristan*.

3

Separation from Mathilde made the flame of Wagner's love for her burn, at first, the more fiercely. Had there ever been any signs of an equal ardour on her part, indeed, a drastic breach with convention might have occurred long before this; and even during the first portion of his stay in Venice he seems to have thought he might still make her entirely his own. But Mathilde was not built of the heroic stuff that would have been necessary for a bold stroke of that kind:[5] away from the physical presence of the magician she was much less susceptible to his spell. The pull of husband and children and home and comfort upon her was too strong to be resisted. It was the perception of this that made Wagner so bitter

---

[4] See the official correspondence in LWV, Chapter V.

[5] In 1873 he told Cosima that "during that dreadful time when Mathilde Wesendonk was jealous of my wife" he had suggested to the former a double divorce and a marriage between himself and her. Her reply was that this would be "a sacrilege". The epithet had struck him at the time as "stupidly inappropriate". But, he added with a smile, "the incomprehensible word suited the proposal very nicely, for unconsciously, in the depths of me, I was not serious." MECW, I, 654.

towards Otto; and though he was deeply moved by the death of little Guido on the 13th October, he even resented the strength of Mathilde's affection for her children, so convinced was he that she ought to have given up everything to fly to him.

> " Duties of parents to children — how remote all this sounded to me in my hallowed mood of solemn serenity! Whenever I thought of you, parents, children and duties never entered my mind: I only knew that you loved me and that everything noble in the world must be unhappy."

It did not occur to him that his own unhappiness, profound and genuine as it was, was really overridden by the luxury of the fine thoughts in which his artistic ideals and his self-pity enabled him to find refuge, and the fine words and still finer music in which he knew how to clothe these thoughts. It must have gradually dawned upon him that Mathilde, like Jessie Laussot, had failed him because, when the acid test came, what he called the Philistine world had won a victory in her over the ideal; and it needed only the ebbing of the *Tristan* lava-tide in him — which was bound to come in due course — for him to see her no longer as a haloed vision in an artist's dream of paradise but as she really was.

At the Green Hill it had been decided, for prudence' sake, that communication with him must cease, at any rate for the time being. His letters were returned to him unopened: but he and Mathilde each kept a diary which was read by the other at a later date. Wagner's diary, kept in the form of letters to Mathilde, gives us an incomparable picture of his inner life during his Venice sojourn.[6]

---

[6] These are the finest of all his letters. It is a thousand pities that to the English reader who does not know German they are accessible only in the often grotesque translation of Ashton Ellis. No one who has had occasion to work in detail at Wagner's life and letters can have anything but respect for Ellis's untiring industry and his patience in disentangling complicated threads. But unfortunately the peculiar kind of English he employs in his versions of the prose works and some of the letters gives a touch of the ridiculous to them that is not in the original. As long ago as 1893 Houston Stewart Chamberlain had to express to Cosima his regret that the task of Englishing Wagner had fallen into the hands of Ellis, for whom, as a man, he had considerable respect — "the good Ellis", as he calls him in a letter of the 4th October of that year. "But ah!" he continues, "that is a sad business! Only now have I been able to examine his work as translator [of the prose works], and I look upon it as a pure calamity." Later he wrote to Cosima, "I must talk to you some other time about Ellis's translations. I did not mean, as you appear to think, that they are not faithful; but they are *not English*. No Englishman who does not understand German

For a long time before his flight his absorption in the inner world of his dreams had made the outer world seem unreal to him. He himself had been acutely conscious of this during his interview with the Grand Duke of Weimar in June, 1858: the bare possibility of entering into any binding material obligation with him or any other German prince had appalled him.

> " Having fled from the world once before ", he had written to Mathilde on the 6th July, " can you delude yourself that I could now return to it? Now, when everything within me has grown so excessively tender and sensitive through the ever-lengthening of my period of weaning from it? . . . I cannot — cannot — go into it again: to settle down permanently in a large town is inconceivable to me. Could I think again of founding a new refuge [*Asyl*], a new hearth, after having had to break up this scarcely acquired one, founded for me in this bewitching paradise by friendship and noblest love? No, no! To go forth from here is, for me, tantamount to — going under."
> " I had been painfully but more and more definitely disentangling myself from the world ", he wrote in retrospect on the 18th September. " All had turned to negation, to warding-off, within me. Even my artistic creation was painful to me; for it was longing, an unstilled longing, to find for that negation, that warding-off, the affirmative, the positive, the wedding of me to my own self [*Sich-mir-vermählende*]."

4

In his Venice solitude of soul he could indulge himself to the full in this mystical self-absorption. Commerce with the world, even to the extent of writing the most necessary letters, revolted him:

> " this constant, ignoble care for life ", he wrote, " — and at bottom so deep a disgust for life; a life I always have to arrange artificially so as not to see it constantly before me in all its repulsiveness! If people only knew what lies between me and the possibility of a final rest for work! "

Now and then there dawns upon him a faint perception that for those who cross his orbit he is fated to be a force of disturbance

---

can understand this Ellis-style. Ellis is faithful enough to the word — too faithful; but not to the sense." (WHSC, pp. 354, 363). A new translation of Wagner's more vital prose works and letters, and especially of his letters to Frau Wesendonk, is urgently called for.

and destruction. He smiles at the simple creatures around him who were terrified by the great comet of September. " I chose it with a certain haughty defiance for my star. I could see in it nothing but the unaccustomed, the dazzling, the marvellous. Am I such a comet myself? Have I brought misfortune? Was that *my* fault? " But in the main he manages, in his mystical moods, to persuade himself that he has no concern with others, except as fellow-sufferers with him under the primal curse of existence. He sinks a deeper shaft than ever into Schopenhauer, Calderon, the Buddha. The ill-treatment of helpless animals no longer stirs him, as it had done in London, to passionate physical intervention, but fills him with a mournful, resigned sense of the suffering that is inextricably inwrought with the very structure of the world. A magical Good-Friday-peace takes possession of his soul: what place can there be for bitterness in the heart of one who has realised that the world of seeming reality is but Maya, illusion?

> " Silent and tranquil ", he writes on the 29th September, " I reached the gaily-lighted, ever-lively Piazzetta. I am taken down the grave, melancholy Canal: to right and left are splendid palaces. Not a sound anywhere but the gentle gliding of the gondola and the plashing of the oar. The moon casts broad shadows. I disembark at the steps of my dumb palace. Wide halls and spaces, inhabited by me alone. My lamp is burning: I take up my book, read a little, muse a good deal. All is still."

He is full of pity and sympathy, less for individuals than for humanity itself, doomed to suffering by the very law of its being: this feeling, he says, " I recognise as the strongest feature in my moral being: presumably it is also the well-spring of my art." His sympathy, he says, is more profound for lower natures than for higher, because the higher has more capacity for raising itself, by the philosophic perception of the cosmic meaning of its suffering, to serene heights of resignation: more profound, again, for beasts than for men, for the beast's suffering is just dull, hopeless pain, without possibility of redemption from it by the philosophic imagination. All this, he tells Mathilde, will be made clearer to her some day in the Good Friday scene in his *Parsifal*. For lower natures he can feel sympathy [*Mitleid*], but not community of joy [*Mitfreude*]: this, he says, was the real cause of his final trouble with his wife. Inwardly detached from the world, he sees it now only objectively, like a spectator at a play: he feels neither hope nor despair — only a profound peace.

Henceforth he will be able to tolerate the world, therefore, only in the mass, forming no ties of mind or heart in it. When *Tristan* is finished he will settle in some large town — the larger the better, for there he need form no ties, but only make superficial contacts. Never again a Weimar or a Zürich! All he desires is to hear tolerably good performances of his works now and then. The two dearest things in the world to him are silence and sleep: *Tristan* is " the profound art of silence in sound." Karl Ritter had left Venice at the end of August, and did not return till near the end of November. For three weeks Wagner was blissfully alone, hearing no voices but those of his servants and his doctor. All was peace, within him and without.

5

" Richard ", Minna had written to Frau Herwegh on the 2nd August, after it had been decided to break up the Asyl home, " has two hearts; he is ensnared on the other side, and clings to me from habit, that is all." His possession not only of two hearts but of two minds becomes almost bewilderingly evident when we compare his letters of this period to Mathilde with those to Minna. In the case of anyone else it would be difficult to believe that they all come from the same man; but the dualism causes no surprise where he is concerned. Of no one is it so true as it is with Richard Wagner that we tend to cast our letters in the mould of the mind of our correspondent of the moment. As soon as he turns from the thought of Mathilde and *Tristan* and takes up his pen to write to Minna, he is in another world, one constructed on a different principle and calling for a different regulation of one's life. Sometimes the starkest contradiction seems to reign between the letters to the one woman and those to the other. Thus to Mathilde he sings the praises of " community of joy, reverence, worship "; this is his consolation when he thinks of her.

> " So do not contemn my pity where you see me exercise it, for to yourself I can now pour out nothing but community of joy. . . .

From the commoner nature to which I gave pity [Minna] I must
quickly turn away as soon as it demands community of joy of me."

This was on the 1st October. But three days before that he had
written to Minna,

" The essence of love consists in community of grief and of joy: but
community of joy is most illusory, for in this world there is little
ground for joy, and our sympathy only has real durability when it is
directed to another's grief."

He was equally sincere in both moods: the apparent contradiction
comes from his unconsciously defining " joy " in different ways
on the two occasions. Any community of joy with Minna was impossible for him, because that would have meant living on the same
mental plane as she; they were linked together only by their common suffering: a community of joy was possible in the other case
because he felt that he and Mathilde inhabited the same world of
the spirit.

The dualism of his nature makes it perfectly easy for him to urge
Minna to make in time a new home for them both, a " peaceful
retreat " to which " I also could withdraw when all the storms of
life were weathered, there at last to find enduring repose beneath
your care ", and at the same time to assure Mathilde that he knows
" that it is still granted to me to die in your arms." How this double
performance was to be accomplished he does not pause to consider;
he saw nothing incongruous in the Flying Dutchman having not
one Senta but two. He tells Mathilde that physical remoteness from
Minna is a necessity if he is to be just and sympathetic towards her:
" When I am near her I become incapable of it; only from a distance can I tranquillise her, as then I can choose the time and the
mood for my communications, so as to be always mindful of my
task towards her." Yet to Minna he writes, at nearly the same time,
" Think of nothing but our reunion; and to make that thoroughly
good and enduring and beneficial for both of us, simply attend to
nothing now but your health." At Zürich

" we were far too buried and thrown too much on our own resources;
that was bound in time to be injurious and to set us bickering. When
once we are in a large town again, where I can have performances
to look after, and you can tend me when I am exhausted, and rejoice

with me over their success, it will be to you a dream that we were ever packed into a little den like that [the Asyl]. . . . Well, well! All that will be altered, and a quite new life will begin, full of fame, honours and recognition, as much as I shall desire; so get in good trim to enjoy that harvest with me after a long and painful seedtime."

He was manifestly doing all he could to soothe the poor creature and bring her back to health; but it would be an error to suppose that everything he said to her was not said in all sincerity. He meant to link his life again with hers at the first appropriate moment: that, however, could not come until *Tristan* was off his hands, for he needed, for the completion of that, a spiritual solitude which he knew he could never obtain in Minna's company. But when *Tristan* was finished there would have to come a period of residence in some large town in which he could produce his new works; and for that, Minna and domesticity were virtually a necessity to him. He no doubt hoped that by that time the memory of her grievance over Mathilde would have faded from her mind, while there was little probability at the moment of a similar complication ever occurring again. Had he also, one wonders, already an intuition that when he had purged his artist's soul of *Tristan*, Mathilde herself would come to mean much less to him than she had done, that after all she was not the inspirer of his poetry and his music but only the temporary outlet for the overwhelming flood of the moment?

After the completion of *Tristan* his correspondence with Mathilde reveals a steady decline of temperature. As for the lady herself, when it became unmistakeably clear to her that she was no longer the lodestar of his life and that she would " inspire " no more *Tristans*, she turned her attentions to — Brahms, whose acquaintance she had made at a concert of his works in Zürich in 1865. Nine years later she offered him, as poetic material for his Muse, the text of a cantata she had written on the subject of cremation, which she now held to be the most vital question of European culture — so vital, indeed, that, it appeared, the arts must be called in to its assistance. Brahms must have shaken his mighty midriff with laughter. " Dear friend ", he writes to the surgeon Billroth, enclosing Mathilde's masterpiece, " isn't this uncommonly interesting? Don't you feel an urge to send an expression of thanks to the lady genius? I should be so delighted to append a greeting to my letter! Or, on the other hand, my famous surgeon, can you tell me of a method of death for an author's good opinion of himself? Anyhow, the enclosure will give you and your wife a quarter-of-an-hour's delicious amusement." To which Billroth replied, " Ja! Ja! When one wants to discover the right thing, one has only to apply to noble women. Oh! Mathilde! Where have you landed yourself? She seems to have no one to save her from the consequences of such bad taste. My wife and I have had a hearty laugh over it. Many thanks for sending it to me! The flames blaze through the smoke! [7] Away! Away! One suffocates in smoke of this sort! " [8]

It must always be remembered to Mathilde's credit that at any rate she did not offer to write the text of *Tristan* for Wagner.

---

[7] This would appear to be a quotation from the cantata.
[8] See the letters, recently published, in BBBW, pp. 214–5.

CHAPTER XXVII

FROM VENICE TO LUCERNE

1

D URING THE autumn of 1858 Breitkopfs were proceeding with the engraving of the full score of the first act of *Tristan*, as well as of Bülow's arrangement of it for the piano. The poem was issued in an edition of 2,000 copies, about Christmas, though the title-page bears the date 1859. A copy was sent to Schopenhauer, but the reactions of the nearly seventy-years-old philosopher to it are not known. No one else's approval of the work would have meant so much to Wagner as his, for there is much in the second act of it that gives poetic form to the Schopenhauerian doctrine. The Frankfort sage had been a good deal in Wagner's thoughts in Venice. Among his papers there was found, after his death, the never-completed draft of a letter to Schopenhauer in which he propounds a solution of a metaphysical problem — that of the joint suicide of lovers — by which the philosopher had confessed himself baffled.[1] Wagner's solution of it would obviously have run on the lines of the colloquy of his Tristan and Isolde in the second act; and we can have little difficulty in deciding that the draft dates not from 1857, as Hans von Wolzogen thought, but from the Venice period, when, as always happened with Wagner, the profounder implications of his poem were being made manifest to him by his music.

Bülow was lost in admiration of the musical marvels of the *Tristan* score; but he sweated blood over his task of reducing it to the capacity of the piano. He seems also to have been puzzled by some of Wagner's harmonies and counterpoints; the correspondence of the two men shows us Bülow surmising " errors " in the engraving of the full score, and Wagner gently assuring him that he really meant what he had said in the passage in question. Bülow queries,[2]

---

[1] The fragment will be found in BBW, 1866, IV, 101.   [2] BNB, p. 419.

for instance, the bars in the orchestra that conclude Tristan's words (in the second act) —

> Wie könnte die Liebe mit mir sterben,
> die ewig lebende mit mir enden?

He condenses the orchestral score thus —

and says, " The passage has cost me many a headache: as many things that sound good and smooth in the orchestra become harsh and unpleasant on the piano, I have permitted myself to trivialise this in the following way " —

Bülow was evidently alienated by such things as the clash of the F sharp in the oboe melody with the F naturals in the strings.[3] " Ask yourself ", says Wagner in reply, " whether the upper G in

---

[3] Matters are further complicated harmonically by the ascending "Isolde's magic" motive — F, G, G sharp — in the cor anglais and bassoon (shown in the lower part of Bülow's topmost stave). These two bars may be taken as typical of the impossibility of making a piano score of *Tristan* that shall be quite representative of the orchestral score.

the oboes does not carry, in your conception of the string passages, a mild and comfortable sound, whereas to my thinking it acquires a quite other, urgent character by reason of the fact that it is dissonant, not consonant, with the rest. Must I say this to *you* — the composer of the Suicide Fantasia? [4] I beg, at least,"

instead of the amiable " — [5]

And he gently twits Bülow with desiring, perhaps, to accompany the shepherd's cor anglais melody (at the beginning of the third act) with harmonies in the *Oberon* style —

" You will have your work cut out! " he adds grimly.[6]

---

[4] In 1854 Bülow had asked for Wagner's criticism of an orchestral fantasia of his own, dealing with the subject of suicidal mania. Finding much to praise in the work, Wagner gave the younger man a warning against harmonic complexities that look impressive enough on paper but really mean nothing, merely giving the hearer the impression that an ordinary piece of harmony is being played on instruments that are out of tune. He recognises that there may be points in a musical conception that can be expressed only in dissonances that offend the ear of the musical Philistine; but it is a youthful weakness to pile up dissonances for the mere purpose of avoiding what seems to be the obvious. His own theory is that the hearer must not be asked to listen to dissonance for mere dissonance' sake, but led insensibly to a perception and acceptance of the *idea* that justifies the dissonance. See RWHB, pp. 61 ff.

[5] Wagner confuses the matter still further — or the printer of the letters has done so for him — by reversing the proper order of these two quotations!

In the Bülow score of *Tristan* the first part of the 'cello arpeggio in the first bar of the passage quoted above is after all correctly given as B, D, G sharp, A, but the second part, which should be B, D, F natural, G, is watered down to B, D, G natural, D. Evidently Bülow was still unable to reconcile himself to an F natural in the alto against an F sharp in the treble! The whole arpeggio is given correctly in the Klindworth arrangement, except that one note is dotted.

One or two discrepancies between the manuscript (a facsimile of which was published a few years ago) and the piano arrangement may be due either to errors on Bülow's part or to "correction" by him (or by Wagner). See my article in the *Sunday Times* of the 12th April, 1936.   [6] RWHB, pp. 122, 123.

Bülow had indeed his work cut out with this complex score, the like of which had never been seen until then. He certainly did some strange things with it here and there; in bars 28 and 29 of the prelude, for example, he has the following —

It will be seen that he ties the C in the bass at the end of bar 28 to the D sharp in bar 29. He was evidently unaware that the B, C and D sharp are a single entity, not merely a bass but a motive — none other than the " Death " motive that plays so large a part in the work. He has even gone to the length of disregarding Wagner's own tie, which embraces all three notes! [7] But his piano version was in the main a miracle of condensation: he got so much of the original upon the piano, indeed, that his version was afterwards regarded as unplayable, and a more " simplified " one had to be made by Klindworth.[8] For his colossal labours upon the work Bülow received from Breitkopfs the magnificent fee of about £20 in English money.

---

[7] In a letter of the 24th August, 1859, to Hans von Bronsart he refers to this phrase as "a very characteristic bass", without, apparently, even yet recognising it as an important motive. See BB, III, 257.

[8] Bülow's problem, indeed, was an insoluble one, in view of the fact that man has only five fingers on each hand. Wagner criticised the frequently scanty tone in the bass of the piano arrangement: he urged the octave doubling of the bass in many places where Bülow had used a single line, and a comparison of their correspondence with the published score shows that Bülow adopted the suggestion wherever possible. Bülow, however, had deliberately thinned out the top and bottom parts in order to include more of the inner harmonic reinforcements or counterpoints. Clearly it had to be, for the piano, either one thing or the other; and Wagner confessed that it was easier for him to talk about what should be done than to do it. See, in particular, his letter of the 21st October and 1st November, 1859, in RWHB, pp. 132–4. There are evidently great gaps in the published edition of Bülow's letters in BNB; there is no letter from Bülow to Wagner, for instance, between that of the 24th August, 1859, and the 20th September, 1860.

2

In the winter of 1858–9 Wagner made yet another attempt to induce Breitkopfs to publish the *Ring* scores, but the firm would do so only on conditions that were unacceptable to him: on receiving an assurance as to the date of the stage production they would engrave the scores, paying him nothing in advance, however, but sharing future profits with him. Once more it all seemed incomprehensible to him. The profits, he foresaw, would ultimately be considerable: but as he had no heirs, and did not reckon on many more years of life, of what use to him was a slow annual trickle of profits at some distant date? It was *now* that the distracted artist needed money — money to keep him alive while he completed the works he had in hand. In his despair he begged Liszt to try to persuade the Grand Duke of Weimar to buy the publishing rights in the scores from him for 300 Louisdor each, he retaining only the right to performing fees from the theatres. But once more a German royal house failed him in his need.

Meanwhile his financial affairs had come to a desperate pass, and at the turn of the new year an outburst of bitter humour over the matter had led to the first open estrangement between himself and Liszt. The latter's affairs in Weimar had recently come to a crisis. In the autumn of 1857 Dingelstedt had been brought from Munich to be the new Intendant of the theatre. The personal relations of Liszt and Dingelstedt had hitherto been good, but it soon became evident that there was no room in Weimar for more than one of them. The amiable Grand Duke wanted both a first-rate theatre and a first-rate opera, but, as usual, was unwilling to dip deeply enough into his pocket to pay for both. Dingelstedt, a man of considerable ability and full of enthusiasm for his work, quickly realised that if the drama, which was his main interest, was to become what he wanted it to be in Weimar, more money would have to be spent on it, which of necessity meant less being spent on the musical side. It was inevitable, then, that two parties should form in the town, and that many people's dislike of Liszt as a man should now be reinforced by a desire to relegate him to a second place in the theatre. The storm came to a head on the 15th December, 1858, when Cornelius's *Barber of Bagdad* was produced under

Liszt: even the presence of the Grand Duke could not procure a decent hearing for the work. There seems no reason to believe that Dingelstedt himself had any part in organising the opposition to it; and it is fairly evident that the demonstration throughout was directed not so much against Cornelius as against Liszt. For the latter it was the last straw. He never conducted another opera in Weimar; and though he remained some time longer in the town his official connection with music there was now at an end. Personal as well as artistic considerations played their part in his withdrawal; as he told the Grand Duke, the *Barber* incident was only the drop that made a cup already full at last overflow. In after years Cornelius held that there was no real need for Liszt to have turned his back on Weimar, and that he had been wrong in doing so; and it is clear enough to us to-day that Liszt had seized upon the affair as the best of pretexts for doing what it was already in his mind to do. He was an unhappy man, and his spirit had long been wilting under the combined strain of his public and his private griefs.

It was at this very time that Wagner's financial troubles were coming to a head. Until *Tristan* could be ready, it was mostly only to *Rienzi* that he could look now for fees from the theatres; and difficulties of one kind and another were springing up in connection with that work. Dresden had indeed given it on the 25th August; but Hanover, Prague and Darmstadt were slow to move; Munich [9] had turned it down " for religious reasons ", whereby Wagner lost 50 Louisdor on which he had reckoned; at Weimar, Dingelstedt was haggling about the fee. On the 5th December Wagner wrote to Liszt to the effect that since, as he learned, the work was not likely to be given in Weimar for some time he had no further interest in it: the only thing that had mattered to him was the fee, and desperate as his condition was he would somehow or

---

[9] In the light of the unfriendly feeling shown by Wagner towards Lachner in *Mein Leben*, it is interesting to note that after the performance of *Lohengrin* Lachner expressed the hope that Munich might be the first to produce *Tristan*. In a letter of the 26th September, 1858, from Venice, Wagner told him that the work was not yet far enough advanced for any definite plan to be formed for its production, and suggested that he should give *Rienzi* instead. Lachner took up the idea with alacrity. It was decidedly not his fault that the work was not given in Munich. See RLW, I, 17–21.

other manage to last out until Easter. At Christmas Liszt received from Breitkopfs a set of proofs of the first act of *Tristan*, his delight in which he expressed to Wagner. Unfortunately in the same letter he advised Wagner to accept the proposed dedication to him of an opera, *Diana de Solange*, by Duke Ernst II of Sachsen-Coburg-Gotha: " accept it in a friendly spirit ", he urged, " even though you will find yourself in the somewhat strange company of Meyerbeer. The composer — the brother-in-law of the Grand Duchess of Baden — is well disposed towards you. . . ." This roused Wagner's fury.

> " In the name of God ", he wrote to Liszt on the 31st December, " what can I do with *Diana de Solange?* " " You answer me too pathetically. Let me comment my last letter to you humorously-realistically. Dingelstedt! Grand Duke! *Rienzi!* All stuff and nonsense! What I want is money. . . . Tell them that Wagner does not care a curse for you all, your theatres, even his own operas; he needs money; that is all! "

He had been reduced to pawning his watch, a bonbonnière given him by the Princess Wittgenstein, and a snuff-box that had been a present from the Grand Duke of Weimar; these, however, he managed to redeem later. Between him and his rent and starvation he had at the moment less than 10 gulden, and there was Minna to be provided for; and at a time like this the best that a German art-loving prince could do for him was to offer him the dedication of one of his own miserable operas! " Send me your *Dante* and your Mass ", Wagner cries to Liszt. . . . " But don't write to me again earnestly and pathetically! My God! I have told you all lately that you are tiresome. Hasn't that been any use? "

3

The bitter, grimacing humour was of the type that can be carried off in conversation between friends, but is apt to be misunderstood in a letter, especially if your correspondent happens at the moment to be himself fretted beyond endurance by troubles of his own. On the 2nd January Wagner wrote again, explaining " the storm I let loose on you, no doubt to your sorrow ", in his previous letter.

" Such storms must not occur again . . . even this last sudden attack was possible to me only in a moment of the utmost excitement." He proceeds to state calmly what had been in his mind in the earlier letter. He turns once more to Liszt as his best and most understanding friend. He has reached a major crisis in his life. An amnesty would mean little to him now apart from the fact that if he were free to enter Germany again he could see Liszt oftener. Nothing binds him to so miserable an existence as his but the urge to complete the art-works he has begun; even the performance of them is a matter of indifference to him. The haphazard nature of such income as he has hitherto enjoyed has been a dire evil. For a time receipts come in abundantly; they give him a false sense of security; they suddenly fall off, plunging him into poverty and care; then they burst upon him again, and the fatal cycle begins anew. He must be placed in a position in which his livelihood is secured in another way, the chance receipts from the theatres being treated as windfalls; only if this is done can he be free at once to create and to deny his works to theatres that cannot or will not give them in accordance with his intentions. He can live comfortably on 2,000 or 3,000 thalers a year. Certain German princes in combination could easily provide him with this; he has in mind the Grand Dukes of Weimar and Baden, the Grand Duke of Coburg, the Prince of Prussia, and possibly the King of Hanover and the Grand Duke of Hesse-Darmstadt. In return for such a pension the Court theatres of these princes will have the right to perform gratis all his present and future works; he will also, if amnestied, superintend at any time in person the study and production of his operas at any of their theatres, and even take charge of other works the performance of which would be for the benefit and honour of art.

The request would have been modest enough had it been purely and simply a matter of charity: as a business proposition it would have turned out very much to the advantage of these notables had they accepted it. Nothing came of it, however, in spite of Liszt's diplomatic offices: more than five years were still to elapse before a German prince could be found who thought it one of the duties attendant on his high office to save from want the greatest German genius of his epoch.

By a sad mischance, Liszt had replied (on the 4th January) to

Wagner's passionate letter of New Year's Eve before that of the 2nd reached him. He had inexplicably misread the earlier one, taking the words " You answer me in much too pathetic a tone " and " Never write me again earnestly and pathetically " as a rough rejection of the glowing congratulations he had sent Wagner after the receipt of the *Tristan* music. In one of those sudden accesses of temper that were not infrequent with him, he sent Wagner a curt missive of studied insult:

> " In order not to expose myself again to the danger of boring you with a pathetic, serious way of speaking, I am sending back to Härtel the first act of *Tristan,* and soliciting the favour of not making the acquaintance of the remainder until it is published. Since the *Dante Symphony* and the Mass are not valid as bank stock, it would be superfluous to send them to Venice. Not less superfluous is it, in my opinion, to receive in future any telegrams [10] of distress or wounding letters from there."

The misunderstanding was soon cleared up. Wagner explained, on the 7th January, that in the letter he had received from Liszt on the 31st December he had expected to find at least the promise of 25 Louisdor in connection with the projected performance of *Rienzi* in Weimar. Instead of that, he found only a serious exposition of Liszt's difficulties with Dingelstedt, and he had been enraged that Liszt also should be dragged, on his account, into the mire of theatre chicanery; his angry protest had been against Liszt thinking it necessary to write him so " earnestly and pathetically " about the wretched business of *Rienzi*. Liszt's congratulations on the first act of *Tristan* had thrown him into " a paroxysm of joyous excitement "; and it had been in a mood of reckless and bitter irony not towards Liszt but towards the world that he had written the explosive letter that had caused all the mischief.

> " It is you, my friend," he concludes, " whom I see to be suffering and needing comfort, for the extraordinary letter which you found it possible to send me must have sprung from a terrible inward irritation. . . . Let me assure you that you have in no way hurt me, for

---

[10] A telegram, which has not survived, had been sent by Wagner to Liszt, apparently on the 1st January. In this, Wagner had used the expression "wunderbar miserabel."

Neither Wagner's letter of the 31st December nor Liszt's of the 4th January was included in the first edition of their correspondence.

your arrows did not hit me; their barbs stuck in your own heart. May this letter of mine free you of them! "

But the mischief had been done. Though the old friendly tone was soon resumed in their correspondence, Wagner had had a startling revelation of the poisons working in Liszt's soul, poisons generated not only by his unhappy experiences in Weimar but by the machinations of the Princess, as to whose enmity Wagner was by this time no longer in any doubt. A shadow had suddenly fallen between him and Liszt, a shadow that was to go on lengthening and darkening in the succeeding years. Liszt had shown too plainly his irritation — and that of the Princess — at being expected to take a passionate interest in the affairs of a " rival " whose star had by now eclipsed his own. Wagner, for his part, felt that he could never again be quite frank with Liszt. " I see more clearly than ever ", he wrote to Bülow, " that I cannot let myself go where he is concerned, that I must employ a certain circumspection in my dealings with him. My humour is utterly alien to him." Once more he had occasion to regret that they met in the flesh so seldom, while the Princess was with Liszt always.[11]

4

Breitkopfs must often have been worried by the slow progress Wagner was making with *Tristan;* as usual, all kinds of hindrances were cropping up, and the prospective day of stage production was receding further and further into the distance. They could not have been more anxious than he was to finish the work, for he was looking to the performing fees for it to bring some sort of order into his finances. Frau Ritter had generously offered help, and Wagner had gratefully agreed to accept the stipend again, though only for a year. Berlin gave *Lohengrin* for the first time, under Taubert, on the 23rd January, 1859; this meant a mild tonic for the Wagner

---

[11] "We [i.e. Cosima and himself] have only just learned something about your unpleasant interim with Liszt", Bülow wrote to Wagner on the 5th February. "Thank God that all is now in order again! You are right to diplomatise a little with him here and there. He has become in the highest degree mistrustful. He is betrayed and disowned day after day: and now this hail of stones on him in all the papers! It is a pity and a shame." BNB, p. 425.

budget. Bülow, who had given the prelude at his Berlin concert nine days earlier, thought the opera performance very bad, apart from one or two bright spots such as Johanna Wagner's acting as Ortrud. For the rest, it was the now familiar story of enthusiasm on the part of the public and obscurantism on the part of most of the Press: " criticism so pitiable ", Bülow reported to Alexander Ritter, " that it has dealt itself a terrible blow in the eyes of the majority of the public." The Dresden management, finding that it had been possible to bring *Rienzi* into the repertory again without the earth opening and swallowing the Saxon kingdom, now thought of giving *Lohengrin;* but this proved impossible until the 6th August, 1859, when the valiant Tichatschek, who was now fifty-two, sang the title-rôle. In the following November, the magnificent sum of 283 thalers was paid to Minna, who was then living in the town, in full discharge of the theatre's indebtedness to the composer of the work.

During the winter of 1858–9 the question of an amnesty became a more pressing one than ever for Wagner, for he could not reconcile himself to the idea of *Tristan* being produced under any direction but his own. The Saxon authorities, one gathers, would not have been unwilling to put an end to the long tragi-comedy, but they stubbornly insisted that the formal procedure should run along what they regarded as the proper lines. Private hints were given Wagner in January, 1859, that if he would surrender in Dresden and let formal action be taken against him the King would pardon him.[12] This suggestion he rightly turned down in a long letter of the 9th February to Lüttichau. It would mean, he foresaw, months of legal examination and legal hair-splitting on points that were now merely shadows in his memory, a strain that his health would not be able to bear, and the complete interruption of his work on *Tristan.* It is interesting in the first place to note that he more than once addresses Lüttichau as his " benefactor ", and in the second place that he makes no attempt whatever to deny that his activities in May, 1849, warranted his being placed on trial. He does not protest his perfect innocence: he only pleads that now, after ten years, he is " no longer, politically speaking, the same

---

[12] Minna, who, after a brief stay with her relations in Zwickau, had settled in Dresden in September, 1858, had called, on her own initiative, on Lüttichau, and had been kindly received.

man ", that he can " only shake his head and wonder " as he thinks of " those wretched, exciting days ", and that he cannot take any steps now that might possibly lead to his imprisonment for " an act of folly long ago repented." This is not the language of a man whose interest in the revolt of 1849 had been merely that of spectator and poetic dreamer.

He recalls the loan of 5,000 thalers granted him more than ten years before from the Theatre Pension Fund, which he proposes to liquidate by giving the Dresden theatre the right to perform any of his future works, and further, if invited to do so, by rehearsing and conducting any of these works without payment. To all this Lüttichau replied in half-a-dozen official lines on the 16th: in view of the rule that an applicant for pardon must first submit himself for examination and judgment, which Wagner refused to do, he himself could not intervene: it was still open to Wagner, however, to apply directly to the King for clemency. Lippert surmises, perhaps rightly, that Wagner's well-meant offer in connection with his old debt may actually have prejudiced the King against him: to the high-principled if rather rigid-minded Johann there would probably be something offensive in the suggestion that a question of justice should be mixed up with a business deal.

On the 22nd, Wagner addressed a letter to the new Minister of Justice, von Behr, in which he appealed for clemency on the ground mainly of his health. Once more, be it observed, he does not take up the attitude of an innocent person protesting against being wrongly suspected, but as good as admits that the authorities are legally right in taking the view of the case they had always done.

> " I may take it for granted ", he says, " that you know of my impru
> dent conduct during the disturbances of 1849, and the charges made
> against me owing to my conspicuous [13] behaviour during the lamen
> table catastrophe in Dresden in May of that year, from which I be
> lieved I ought to escape by flight."

But the flight had not been *from the charges*, for none had been made against him either at the actual time of his flight or in the days

---

[13] The German word is " auffällig ", which means conspicuous, striking, remarkable, strange, unusual, and sundry other things. In view of all the circumstances of the case, "conspicuous" seems to me to express Wagner's meaning best.

preceding it; the plain inference is that he had fled the country in such haste because he knew his conduct had made the charges inevitable if he were captured.

" I unreservedly admit the justice of the conditions which his Majesty has laid down for granting me a pardon ", he continues; " I confess, with sincere repentance, as I did years ago, that my behaviour laid me open to punishment [*mein sträfliches Verhalten*]; I acknowledge now the justice of the attitude maintained towards me, and, in view of this perception, regard any attempt to modify this attitude as inadmissible."

He accordingly begs the King to exercise his pure clemency on his behalf. Behr's reply of the 10th March, which was sent to Minna, was clearly made by command of the King. It ran thus:

" The principle that Saxon political fugitives shall be granted permission to return only on the condition that they submit to the trial which they evaded by flight has repeatedly been maintained and applied. I am therefore not in a position to give your husband any hope of an exception being made in his favour. In accordance with your offer, I beg you will communicate the above to your husband, and so spare me the necessity of a further reply to his letter." [14]

The door at which Wagner had been knocking so long seemed closed on him for good.

5

The already homeless wanderer was by this time faced with the necessity of uprooting himself once more, for other than political reasons, however. Renewed attempts on the part of the Saxon police, towards the end of 1858, to have him expelled from Venice had culminated, on the 3rd February, 1859, in a courteous intimation from the Venice authorities that he must leave the town: at the same time they advised him to apply direct to the Governor-General (the

---

[14] The official documents relating to this period are given in full in LWV.

One gathers from some of them that all his letters from Venice were opened by the police. "His correspondence", says a report of the Venice Chief of Police to the Governor of the town on the 20th December, 1858, "is fairly extensive, but confined to the directors of the principal theatres — Weimar, Berlin, Zürich, Dresden, Darmstadt, Leipzig — and the well-known composer Liszt." Two days later Crespi reported that Wagner had sent his new opera, *Tristan* [i.e. the poem] "with a dedication to the Grand Duchess of Baden, who not only deigned to accept the dedication but was further pleased to express her gratification".

Archduke Maximilian, brother of the Austrian Emperor), for permission to remain in consideration of his delicate health. He easily obtained the necessary permission, but it was by now becoming evident to him that, for other reasons, he would soon have to leave Venice. The drinking water did not agree with him: he missed the tramps over hill and dale that he had been accustomed to in Switzerland: he dreaded the heat of Venice in the coming summer. The second act of *Tristan* had been completed in the full score on the 9th March, and he was reluctant to begin work on the third act until he could be sure of freedom from interruption until it was finished. This freedom was threatened by the imminence of war between Austria on the one side and Sardinia, backed by France, on the other.

He decided to settle in Lucerne. Having said farewell on the 23rd March to Karl Ritter,[15] who had returned to Venice in January, Winterberger, Dolgoruki and his other friends, and arranged for his Erard to be sent over the Gotthard, he was in Milan on the 24th. After three days' sight-seeing and the enjoyment of some Goldoni comedies in the Teatro Re, and being disillusioned as regards Italian music by a performance at the Scala of an opera so worthless, in his eyes, that in later years he could not even remember the name of it, he went by way of Como and Lugano and the Gotthard to Lucerne. The season there not yet having begun, he was fortunate enough to obtain a whole floor to himself at the Hotel Schweizerhof. Service he had to provide for himself: he found a woman whose services and whose character he appreciated so highly that some years later he engaged her as his housekeeper.[16] At the moment he had funds, or prospective funds, sufficient to

---

[15] He and Karl never met again.

[16] She was Vreneli Weitmann, afterwards Frau Stocker. She re-entered his service in the first Munich days, and remained with him throughout the Triebschen period: she had consented to marry Stocker only on condition that he also would enter Wagner's service. She survived Wagner twenty-three years, dying in 1906. She left behind her a manuscript of reminiscences of which Glasenapp was able to avail himself; and he notes that while practically everyone else who gave the world his reminiscences of Wagner laid stress on what *he* had been to the great man, Vreneli talked not of herself but only of the master whom she adored. She was a woman of education, and occasionally answered letters for him, signing them "*pro* R. Wagner." Her summing-up of him was that " in the whole of my life I have never met a man who was so full of gratitude for anything that was done for him." See GRW, IV, 28, 440–1, and Hans von Wolzogen's article on her in BBW, 1906, pp. 199–200.

relieve him from anxiety for a little while, what with the Ritter pension, the payment from Breitkopfs for the second and third acts of *Tristan*, and royalties from Berlin and elsewhere. At this period he could easily have made money by accepting invitations to conduct in America; but apart from his general objection to work of that kind he needed all his time and strength for the completion of *Tristan*.

Lucerne remained his headquarters for nearly six months. Soon after his arrival he went, at Otto Wesendonk's invitation, to the Green Hill, staying there for a few days: the visit was repeated more than once later, while Otto and Mathilde called on him twice in Lucerne. The object of these meetings was to give a more or less public *démenti* to the malicious gossip that had been current in Zürich after Wagner's departure from the Asyl. The reunion, of course, called forth some comments from Minna that reveal the incurable monomaniac she had become by this time. Blind to the spiritual agonies through which Richard had passed during the last twelve months, she saw in the diplomatic visits merely a further duping of the weak and innocent Otto, the prospect of another " scandal ", and, if not an actual desire on Richard's part to " insult " her, at any rate a regrettable refusal on his part to protect her from such " insults ".

Wagner had few other visitors while he was in Lucerne. In July, the twenty-four-years-old Felix Draeseke called on him with a letter of introduction from Liszt: Wagner was at first a little bored by his facetious anecdotes about the smaller musical world, but afterwards, when the conversations had begun to take a more serious turn, took a liking to him and spent part of each day with him. Baumgartner came over from Zürich for a few weeks simply to be with his old friend; while from St. Petersburg came the composer Alexander Serov, who had conceived a passion for Liszt's music and Wagner's in Russia, and had lately heard *Lohengrin* twice in Dresden. Wagner found him intelligent and likeable.

Over Weimar, evidently, a cloud still hung. Though Liszt's *Dante* and *Die Ideale* had been published in February or March, no copy of either of them reached Wagner, in spite of his urgent appeals for them. The *Dante* was sent him towards the end of April: the printed score bore only the dedication " To Richard Wagner ", but in a renewed glow of the old emotion Liszt added to this, in his own hand: " As Virgil guided Dante, so have you guided me through the mysterious regions of the life-imbued worlds of tone. From the depths of his heart calls to you —

' Tu se lo mio maestro, e il mio autore! '

and dedicates this work to you in unchangeably faithful love,

Your

F. LISZT."

Wagner, in his letter of acknowledgment, duly praises the " peculiar grandeur " of the work, and — perhaps having found, that morning, that the *Tristan* music was not flowing easily from his pen — flatteringly contrasts Liszt's facility with his own slowness. " Believe me ", he adds humorously, " I am not up to much. I really believe now that Reissiger must have helped me with *Tannhaüser* and *Lohengrin!* " With a side-glance at the Princess, he tells his friend how Karl Ritter had heard — evidently from Weimar — that in the published *Letter concerning Franz Liszt's Symphonic Poems* he had expressed himself " evasively ", and how astonished Karl had been, when he came to read the Letter for himself, at the " *enormous* significance " there attributed to Liszt.[17] Having himself read the Letter again, Wagner says, he was " compelled to chime in with K.R.'s animated outburst over the incredible obtuseness, superficiality and triviality of the people who could possibly misunderstand the meaning of that Letter." This was hardly distinguishable from a declaration of war against the Princess, who by this time — and Liszt must have been well aware of it — was regarded by most of Liszt's friends as his evil genius. A new tone has obviously crept into the correspondence of the two men. Wagner could still hope that if they could meet and talk together they would re-establish something of the old spiritual communion: but the Princess took good care that they should not meet if she could help it.

---

[17] The final truth of it all seems to be that while Wagner could not honestly profess to like certain elements in Liszt's music — especially the theatricality of much of it — he was sincerely appreciative of Liszt's significance as an innovator in the matter of form and an explorer of new territories of musical expression. In a conversation with Cosima in 1872, apropos of the *Lorelei*, he praised the "drastic" quality of Liszt's themes, and said of his work as a whole, "It is always interesting, even when it does not amount to much." (MECW, I, 639). That is a fair summing-up of the whole matter.

CHAPTER XXVIII

PREPARING FOR THE SIEGE
OF PARIS

1

THE FULL score of *Tristan* was completed early in August; and now Wagner had to face the awkward questions, what and whither next? He had humorously compared himself, during the difficult days since his departure from the Asyl, to Leto, who had been hunted about the earth, unable to find a place in which to give birth to Apollo and Artemis, until Poseidon in compassion caused the island of Delos to rise from the sea. Wagner's painful delivery of what he had always called his " child of sorrow " having at last been accomplished, his Delos had no further attraction for him. He was still not without hope that he might be pardoned in time to permit of his producing *Tristan* in person under the protection of the Grand Duke of Baden, in Carlsruhe in December. But where was he to live in the meantime? Mystics rarely have a very good time of it in a world so actual as ours; and Wagner succeeded no better than the average of them in balancing the rival demands of mysticism and actuality. As an artist he longed for nothing but seclusion in which to create. But the Fates had been unkind enough to make him a musician and a dramatist, which meant that before his creations could reach the public they had to pass through the complicated apparatus of the theatre. With the theatre, then, and all that it meant in the way of correspondence and personal contacts, he had to concern himself willy-nilly. Moreover, once this stage in connection with a work had been reached, he was torn in opposite directions by the joy of external self-realisation and disgust at the chicanery of the theatre and the incompetence of most of those with whom it brought him in contact.

Now, in the summer of 1859, solitude no longer being the prime necessity it had been to him when writing *Tristan*, he was attracted to the idea of living in some large town where he could both produce a work of his own again and satisfy his longing to hear some good performances of other men's music. Liszt had once more suggested Paris, though only a year before he had assured Wagner that not Paris but Germany was the proper field for him. Wagner had never any great love for France or the French, but at the moment Paris seemed to have certain advantages over the few other places open to him, including that of the chance of seeing Liszt there occasionally; while there was always the possibility of Carvalho producing *Tannhäuser* there. For Paris, accordingly, he decided. He was now, in the late summer of this year, well provided with funds. Otto Wesendonk had generously offered him another loan, but this he had refused. He suggested, instead, a business deal — Otto to buy the publishing rights in the *Ring* on the same terms as those agreed upon with Breitkopfs for *Tristan*, i.e. 6,000 francs for each score. Otto having agreed, Wagner found himself in immediate possession of 12,000 francs for the *Rhinegold* and the *Valkyrie*, with the prospect of a further 6,000 in the not very distant future, for he hoped to complete *Siegfried* before long. Otto was perhaps not greatly impressed by Wagner's confidence that time would prove him to have acquired a gold mine very cheaply: his delicate motive was probably to relieve the harassed artist of his material cares for the future without submitting him to the ignominy of charity.

2

On the eve of his departure from Lucerne Wagner spent three days at the Green Hill, where a dispute with Herwegh, Semper and Keller on the subject of the war between France and Austria led to a quarrel with Semper, which, however, was soon made up. He left Switzerland in the second week of September. In Paris he took lodgings at No. 4 in the Avenue de Matignon, Champs-Elysées, until he could find a permanent home for himself and Minna, who, it had been arranged, was to rejoin him as soon as possible. A month later he took a three-years' tenancy, at 4,000 francs a year, of a house in the Rue Newton (No. 16) that had formerly been occupied by the novelist Octave Feuillet: standing in its own garden in a cross street between two of the larger avenues branching out from the Etoile, it was sufficiently secluded to promise him immunity from the plague of piano-strumming.[1] The proprietor, though he would not spend a sou in putting the somewhat dilapidated place in order, insisted on the rent for the two final terms being paid in advance. The reason became apparent later; the street had already been marked out for reconstruction in accordance with Baron Haussmann's plans for rebuilding this part of Paris. In a few months, after Wagner had put himself to considerable expense in restoring and decorating the house, he had to leave it: he received no compensation, and thought himself lucky in being released from the remainder of the agreement. The omens for his financial future were already bad.

It was in October of the following year (1860) that he and Minna left the house in the Rue Newton — which their visitors had found charming in itself and very tastefully furnished — and took an apartment on the second floor of the Rue d'Aumale, No. 3. "Judging by the salon", Madame Eugénie Fétis wrote to her friend Emma Herwegh, "they are magnificently lodged: and there are five fine rooms on the second floor. However, Madame [Minna] does not think much of it: has she caught a little of her husband's malady of vanity?"[2] In the Rue Newton, Minna, who had always been used to doing much of her own house-work, had had a man-servant and a maid: in the Rue d'Aumale she was reduced to a *bonne à tout faire*.[3] The change of residence had a significance beyond that of Baron Haussmann's reconstruction of Paris. At first Wagner had meant to devote himself, while in Paris, to the completion of the composition of *Siegfried*; and for this he needed a quiet retreat. By the autumn of 1860 he had been caught once more in the coils of the actual theatre: the imperial ukase had gone forth that *Tannhäuser* was to be given at the Opéra, and residence

---

[1] According to Challemel-Lacour, who attended some of Wagner's "evenings" in the Rue Newton, the house was in "lost country, at the foot of the muddy steppes that lie between the Etoile barrier and Passy."

[2] HBD, pp. 72–3. Marcel Herwegh's book contains a number of hitherto unknown letters from his father's and mother's friends.

[3] There may have been a touch of feminine malice in Mme Fétis's account. Both Malwida von Meysenbug and the tenor Niemann thought the Rue d'Aumale quarters rather shabby. Wagner himself describes them as "not very spacious, but comfortably fitted up."

within convenient distance of the theatre was now a necessity for him.

Disappointments, disillusionments and anxieties of all kinds had begun to crowd upon him soon after his arrival in Paris. The management, the singers and the orchestra at Carlsruhe took fright at the unprecedented difficulties of *Tristan*. His enemies rejoiced.

> " The chief event in our musical life ", said a Berlin paper, " is the laying-aside of Richard Wagner's *Tristan and Isolde* as *unproduceable*. It had to come to this: now at last the title of ' music of the future ', about which there has been so much fighting, is justified: the present cannot even perform this music! Ostensibly the shelving of the work was on the singers' account; but according to trustworthy reports the demands made on the orchestra are equally exorbitant and impossible to be met."

The difficulties could no doubt have been overcome had Wagner been able to take control in person; as a matter of fact, the Tristan (Schnorr von Carolsfeld) and the Isolde (Malwina Garrigues, later Frau Schnorr) of the first Munich production of the opera some six years later were already members of the Carlsruhe personnel. But Devrient was by now anything but well disposed towards Wagner, perhaps dreading not only the excessive work that would be thrown on his forces by this " impracticable " work but the virtual passing of the control of the theatre, for a time, out of his own hands into those of Wagner: and though the Grand Duke of Baden was still, in theory, anxious to do anything within his powers for Wagner, he had neither the desire nor the will to take a bold line with his own theatre. These German princelings, indeed, cut a sorry figure in the long Wagner story. In later years, when he was nearly beaten to the ground by the difficulties attendant on the establishment of Bayreuth, and the princes were refusing to help him, Wagner remarked to Cosima, " The reason why the princes are so hostile to me is that they behaved so badly to me in the past, and they hate me because I have not succumbed. As the old proverb has it, it is curious how we hate those whom we have injured." [4] " I will not give a sou to Bayreuth ", said the Duke of Weimar to Liszt in 1872.[5] A little while before that, Wagner, meeting the

---

[4] MECW, I, 634.   [5] Ibid., I, 628.

Grand Duke of Baden in Mannheim, had told him bluntly that if the *Ring* was at last finished the King of Bavaria was to be thanked for it, whereupon the Duke, we are told, " turned red in the face." [6]

In 1859, however, the time had not yet come when Wagner could tell the German princes what he thought of them. For the moment the rejection of *Tristan* by Carlsruhe looked like a deadly blow to all his hopes for not only *Tristan* but the *Ring*. It is true that in October he received a hint from Dresden that the King might order the production of *Tristan* there and grant him permission to return for it; in no case, however, could this happen before the summer of 1860. The plan, of course, like so many others, came to nothing in the end. Sorrowfully he had to admit, in a letter of the 27th October to Otto Wesendonk, that in all that he was and all that he was doing he was " too far outside the possibilities of the present." He could only call up the reserves of his indomitable spirit for a frontal attack on Paris.

3

Carvalho was still enamoured of the idea of producing *Tannhäuser;* but his theatre, the Lyrique, was soon to be pulled down — another victim to Haussmann's passion for town-planning — and its successor in the Place du Châtelet was not likely to be ready for some time. Meanwhile there was the question of the translation to be settled.

When Wagner had attended at the douane to obtain some furniture that had been sent on from Zürich he had been touched by the courtesy and helpfulness of a young customs official, Edmond Roche, who, it seems, had long been an ardent student of Wagner's scores, and had pricked up his ears at the mention of the name " Richard Wagner ". To this Roche, in the end, the translation of *Tannhäuser* was entrusted; but the goal was reached only after many détours.

Bülow had advised Wagner to make the acquaintance of a young friend of his, Agénor de Gasperini, a young physician, no longer in practice, who cultivated literature and the arts. Gasperini, being

---

[6] Ibid., I, 593.

in Marseilles when Wagner arrived, asked his friend Léon Leroy to call on the composer: and in the course of a two hours' conversation the question of a *Tannhäuser* translation cropped up. Thinking it over later, it occurred to Leroy to suggest Gustave Roger for the task. Roger, the leading French tenor of his day, had recently, at the age of forty-four, had his stage career suddenly terminated by a shooting accident that had necessitated the amputation of an arm. He had frequently sung in Germany, and had a good working knowledge of the German language.[7] Roger took with alacrity to the idea of making a translation. Wagner called on him two or three times at his sumptuous estate in Villiers, found much to commend in so much of the work as Roger had completed in the first flush of his enthusiasm, and liked his singing of some of the music. But his keen judgment of men made him doubt whether Roger would endure to the end, or at all events complete his work within a reasonable time; the tenor's proneness to rush away from the piano to the domino table impressed him unfavourably. It was not long before he had to rule Roger out as a translator. A certain M. de Charnal, to whom the translation of *Rienzi* had been entrusted some time before, also soon proved a broken reed. Later still, a native of Magdeburg, one Lindau, undertook the work in collaboration with Roche, who possessed a certain poetic talent but unfortunately knew little or no German: Wagner himself, whose French by this time was fairly good, lent a hand when the other two were gravelled. When, in 1860, a production of the opera at last seemed likely, the translation was finally revised by a friend of Emile Ollivier's, a young lawyer, Charles Truinet, who dabbled in literature under the pseudonym of Nuitter. Truinet himself knew no German, but his father, he assured Wagner, had travelled in Germany often enough to pick up the essentials of the language! With the version finally obtained as the result of all this dubious collaboration Wagner had to be content.

Meanwhile the acquaintance with Gasperini had been ripening. In 1866 Gasperini published a volume on Wagner that was in part biographical, in part expository. It is clear from this that Wagner

---

[7] His diary, *Le Carnet d'un Ténor*, shows him to have been gifted with an amount of intelligence not usually credited by an unkind world to tenors.

had told him plainly that, Germany being closed to him, he had come to Paris determined to introduce himself to the French public as composer. At their first meeting Gasperini was astonished to find that, in spite of the incessant *Sturm und Drang* of his life, Wagner looked ten years younger than his actual age. At first his manner was reserved, his features impassible; but as he warmed to his new friend he became more like the volcano that Gasperini had conceived him to be from his music. The Frenchman was struck by the size of his forehead, the strength of his chin, the " indomitable will " that revealed itself as " the very basis of his nature ". He was conscious also of the strain of asceticism and mysticism that ran through the granite tissue of the man: as soon, however, as Wagner began to talk about his bold plans not only for the morrow but for the distant future, Gasperini saw before him " a man still young, enthusiastic, full of vitality and faith, and, for all his theories, far removed from the Buddha and his sterile contemplations." [8]

Gasperini soon had reason to fear that Wagner's course would be anything but easy, for the Paris theatres and theatre directors were no different from what they had been when he had tried to work upon them twenty years before. Wagner almost succeeded in prejudicing Carvalho against *Tannhäuser* by the Dionysiac frenzy he put into a single-handed performance of the finale of the second act: " he sang ", says Gasperini, " he shouted, he threw himself about, he played the piano with his hands, his wrists, his elbows, he smashed the pedals, he ground the keys. M. Carvalho remained throughout the chaos as impassible as Horace's man, waiting with a patience worthy of the antique for the witches' sabbath to come to an end. When the last page was reached, M. Carvalho stammered out a few polite words, turned on his heels, and disappeared. Assuredly it is permissible to a composer to play the piano badly, even not to play it at all; he can with impunity sing out of tune or not sing at all — but only among intimate friends. In front of a director who does not know a note of the work he is listening to he should be rather particular." [9] Carvalho did not come to a second audition of the kind. We are fortunate enough

---

[8] GW, pp. 52, 53.   [9] Ibid., p. 53.

to possess his own account of the affair. " I can still see Wagner, wearing a blue jacket with red braid, and a yellow Greek cap adorned with a green fringe. He was waiting for me in a drawing-room in which were two grand pianos set out for the performance of his work. With a fire, an *entrain* that I shall never forget, he began by giving me the first part of *Tannhäuser:* then, dripping with perspiration, he disappeared, to return this time in a red cap decorated with yellow braid; his blue coat had been replaced by a yellow one embellished with blue braid. In this new costume he sang for me the second part of his opera. He howled, he threw himself about, he hit all kinds of wrong notes, and to crown it all he sang in German! And his eyes! The eyes of a madman! I did not dare to cross him; he frightened me." [10]

4

Nor was Wagner any greater success in French society. He and Minna " received " on Wednesdays, his most frequent visitors being Roche, Ollivier and the charming Blandine, Frédéric Villot, the conservator of the imperial museums (who was fortunate enough later to receive the dedication of the French translations of the Wagner operas), Jules Ferry, Leroy, and writers such as Champfleury, Lorbac and Baudelaire; Berlioz dropped in occasionally. Company of this kind Wagner found tolerable, for there he could talk seriously. But in more general society, and especially that of the fashionable women on whom he had sometimes to call, he was bored to the point of exasperation, and sometimes showed it only too openly; he never had much taste, and less than ever just now, for the tittle-tattle and fiddle-faddle that constitute the substance of the conversation when people who are " fond of music " get together. He found a congenial spirit in Malwida von Meysenbug, who, finding herself in front of him at a concert, had ventured timidly to remind him of their meeting in London: he apologised for his cold behaviour on that occasion, which he put down to " the London fogs ", and the two discovered for the first time how much they had in common. Malwida, in spite of her genuine liking for

---

[10] TLFW, p. 179.

Minna, saw with regret how utterly unsuited the pair were to each other, and how the differences between them were increasing daily. In the eyes of her bourgeois acquaintances it was Minna who deserved most sympathy; but Malwida was under no illusions with regard to her. Minna had no idea whatever of the sorrow and the pain in her husband's soul, or of her duty towards him as an artist: even now, after his terrible experiences of trial by fire in the Dresden and Zürich days, she could still urge him to " make concessions " to the public. Malwida often tried to enlighten her as to the real nature and necessities of the man to whom she was tied, but in vain.

Minna, it should be said, had rejoined him, with the parrot and the dog, in mid-November, 1859. In *Mein Leben* he says that he " could only regard it as a freak of fate " that Minna had announced her readiness to rejoin him in Paris and that he was to expect her shortly. Precisely what lies behind that remark we do not know; what we do know, from his letters, is that for a long time past he had been urging her to return. His motive in doing so was not simply that she could look after him. He was sincerely concerned about her health, and still more so about the bad influence of her Dresden female associates upon her: apparently they not only kept her jealousy always on the boil but led her into a way of living that was bad for her. He had urged Pusinelli, who acted as her doctor in Dresden, to persuade her to join him in Paris, where, he said, he would do all he could to soothe her excitable nerves and make existence pleasant for her. She brought with her a letter from the good Pusinelli in which, as physician and friend in one, he gave Wagner a grave warning that Minna's very life lay in his hands. He exhorted him not to let himself be dragged into the " little squabbles " that " wear us out and in the end break down our resistance." " Therefore let your daily prayer be: Lord, give me meekness, steadfastness, benevolence and indulgence! " Minna was to be kept from excitement and not burdened with too many household cares.[11]

She was tactless enough to open this confidential letter and read it in the train. Wagner was so annoyed with her in consequence

---

[11] The letter is in the Burrell Collection. It has lately been published for the first time in RWAP, pp. 110 ff.

that he refused to take it from her and read it: he wrote to Pusinelli a month or so later (the 12th December), asking him to repeat the contents of it to him direct. It was a bad beginning to their reunion.

It is probably a safe conjecture that Minna made full use, in the differences that in time arose between them once more, of the strategic advantages her knowledge of the letter conferred on her: now more than ever she might be trusted to play her trump card of the sick good wife whose sufferings were all her selfish husband's work. That card had always won the game for her with friends and acquaintances of her own mental type: it had, however, considerably less effect on women like Malwida and Blandine Ollivier, who, while full of human sympathy for Minna, realised that Wagner also had a case. There is no reason to doubt his account of their meeting at the station, when " she at once gave me to understand that she did not come to me out of need, and that if I treated her badly she knew quite well where to go back to." It was not long before he could once more sigh, with his own Wotan as Fricka approaches him,

> Der alte Sturm,
> die alte Müh!
> Doch Stand muss ich hier halten.

The servants he had engaged to ensure her comfort left him, finding it impossible to live with her: for himself, he realised that the gulf between Minna and him had widened and deepened during their separation — that she was becoming, as he puts it, " more and more a stranger to him."

5

As was always the way with him, Wagner tried to induce some of his friends to settle near him to console him with their company: Bülow, he thought, might be willing to uproot himself in Berlin and find a new sphere of activity in Paris. What pained Wagner most was the manifest indifference of Liszt towards him in his new need. Liszt had turned aside a suggestion that they should meet for a couple of days in Strassburg: the Princess had actually been in Paris without making any effort to see Wagner. Liszt, about this time, was suffering keenly under the blows of fate. His son Daniel had died on the 13th December, 1859: a few weeks later, his work and his activities were publicly denounced as a menace to German art in the famous manifesto issued by Brahms, Joachim and others; in May, 1860, the Princess left for Rome to make a desperate attempt to influence the Pope to sanction her marriage with Liszt. The pair did not meet again for some seventeen months; in the interval, the strong hand of the Princess being lifted from him, he reverted to type, seeking in the usual narcotics and stimulants a refuge from his troubles, and in tuft-hunting and the flattery of sycophants an anodyne for his wounded amour-propre as an artist, and, through it all, despising himself for his incurable weaknesses. The months between December, 1858, when he crashed with Cornelius in Weimar, and May, 1860, when Carolyne went to Rome, were undoubtedly the most crucial of his whole life. His friends saw clearly that only a miracle could save him from going under.

" I hope to hear from you ", Wagner wrote to Bülow on the 22nd December, 1859, after the news of Daniel's death, " that Liszt has not suffered too greatly in his sorrow. I fear terribly for him, for it was clear from his last passionate disturbance that now, more than ever, he is in need of the peace that unfortunately has always so harshly been denied him. I fear that he is irresponsibly allowing his life to be interfered with: he will lose in the end the strength to withstand the *unavoidable* encroachments upon his nature. I am very concerned about him."

Each of the two old friends saw the other now as a fine instrument badly out of tune. The latest documents bearing on the subject show Liszt to have been slowly losing sympathy with Wagner: that, at any rate, would have been Wagner's view of the matter. It was natural, indeed, that Liszt, like so many others of his contemporaries, should take a purely contemporary view of certain aspects of Wagner's life. To us, looking back at it all from the vantage point of posterity, the clearness of Wagner's long-distance vision and the singleness of his purpose are the things that stand out most clearly from the frequent murk of his daily life: he stands illumined for us by the bright light of his ultimate triumph. To his contemporaries it must often have seemed that he was his own enemy, multiplying difficulties and annoyances for himself as an artist by his imprudent management of some of the most ordinary affairs of life. Liszt's ill-temper towards him in January, 1859, is now more easily understood when we read a letter of Liszt's to Blandine — recently published for the first time — of the 1st May, 1858:

> " A certain one (who is indeed someone) of our friends sometimes embarrasses me as to what I can do for him, seeing that he has a peculiar talent for managing his affairs badly. You will not guess whom I mean; do not be surprised when I say it is Wagner. With his immense genius, which becomes more incontestable through all the silly combats he has to sustain, he unfortunately does not succeed in freeing himself from the most grievous domestic worries,[12] to say nothing of all the evil consequences of his fantastic calculations. He resembles those high mountains that are radiant at the summit, but wrapped in mists up to the shoulder — with this difference, that imaginary mists are much more truly inconvenient than real ones." [13]

Manifestly Liszt's feelings towards him were already changing, though Wagner was as yet unaware of it.

On the 29th December, 1859, Blandine gave her father some particulars of Wagner's struggle to establish himself in Paris musical life.

> "He is in great torment", she writes. "He has got it into his head that the year 1859 must not end without something definite being done for him, so that St. Sylvester means for him a mass of drudgeries, journeys, visits, letters, and so on. There is nothing more frightful than to see genius locked in combat with the common obstacles of life. It is the eternal and pathetic story of Gulliver enmeshed in the thousand-and-one little threads of the Lilliputians." [14]

Liszt's reply to this shows that little now remained of whatever real understanding he had ever had of the total Wagner. He had little confidence, he told Blandine, in the way Wagner was going about his business. His advice to him would be to " hasten slowly ", and not plunge into negotiations for which his character and habits of mind unfitted him. It was no doubt deplorable to see a great genius in combat with common obstacles; but then why cannot a great genius bring a little of the procedure of good sense into the practi-

---

[12] This, it will be noted, was written at the time when matters were coming to a crisis at the Asyl.

[13] OLPF, 1st January, 1936, p. 124.

[14] Ibid., p. 128.

cal matters of life? " This would greatly simplify things for Wagner, whom it pains me to see embroiling himself more and more in fantastic combinations that will bring him only bitter deceptions." He admits that he had more than once advised Wagner to establish himself in Paris, but he had also tried to make it clear to him that there was no *immediate* likelihood of the production of his operas there, and that,

> " to my thinking, the best thing he could do would be to preserve a calm, dignified, and rather proud reserve. . . . I sincerely wish him all imaginable success; at the same time, as I have the conviction that the rôle he is playing at the moment is not the one he ought to be playing, I will abstain completely from mixing myself up at all in his procedure and his pursuits, confining myself to enduring in silence his bad humour towards me for as long as he likes to continue it." [15]

There can be no doubt that Liszt failed Wagner in sympathy in his hour of trial. He, if anyone, ought to have realised what it meant to an exquisitely sensitive man of genius, anxious only to communicate to the world the treasures of his spirit, to have three masterpieces and part of a fourth lying in a drawer without any hope of production, to have virtually the whole of the Press against him, to be banished from his native land without apparent hope of return. To counsel a man fighting, as Wagner was just then, not only for his existence as an artist but for his very subsistence as a man to " preserve a calm, dignified, and rather proud reserve " was to talk mere pious platitude. Wagner had not Liszt's capacity for striking noble theatrical attitudes and, where hard realities were concerned, duping himself and others with fine phrases — nor, as he bitterly commented to Bülow, had *he* a rich Princess at the back of him. He knew well that he would obtain nothing from the world except by fighting for it; and though the combat sickened him he had no choice but to launch an attack against the forces entrenched against him. Did Liszt, one feels bound to ask in all sobriety, urge Wagner into the Paris venture because he saw in it a means of shifting from his own shoulders a burden of which, thanks largely to the Princess, he had become weary? What is certain is that Wagner, tired, ill, once more heading for financial dis-

[15] Ibid., pp. 128–9.

aster, and engaged in a life-or-death struggle with alien musical conditions, felt acutely the cooling of his old friend's feelings towards him. Liszt had definitely promised that he would visit him frequently in Paris; [16] as it was, he never even wrote to him any oftener than he could help.

Wagner, for his part, fell below his best self when, in a moment of irritation, he protested to Bülow against a passage in an article on the *Tristan* prelude by Pohl, in which the latter had referred to Liszt's influence on Wagner as a harmonist. There were things, Wagner wrote angrily to Bülow, that could be agreed upon among themselves, but which there was no call to talk about in public.

> " For instance, that since my acquaintance with Liszt's compositions I have become quite another being harmonically from what I was before. But when friend Pohl blurts out this secret before the whole world right at the head of a short notice of the *Tristan* prelude, this is, to say the least, indiscreet; and I am not to assume that he was authorised to commit such an indiscretion? "

This passage has often been gleefully quoted against Wagner, but without a perception of its true significance. This resides in the note of interrogation after the sentence just quoted. Wagner goes on to say that, regarding as " an excess of friendship " Liszt's eulogy of him as his " guide and master " in the dedication to him of the *Dante*, he could accept such praise in private, but it would be foolish of him to try to insist on it appearing in the printed copies; had that been done, indeed, he would have protested publicly.[17] What he is driving at is that Pohl's remark betrayed the Princess's hand at the back of it; [18] hence the interrogation mark. He took the passage as an attempt on the part of the Princess to belittle him publicly and exalt Liszt — which no doubt it was. A sense of his own immense achievements as a harmonic innovator ought to have saved him from his peevish outburst to Bülow; but at any rate it is desirable that we should understand what motived the peevishness.

---

[16] See Wagner's letter of the 17th December, 1859, to Bülow.

[17] RWHB, pp. 125–6.

[18] " Herr Pohl ", he concludes, " might be recommended by both of us [i.e. himself and Liszt] to exercise more discretion, since I believe he is compromising Liszt, even though he gratifies the Princess."

6

Paris was still Meyerbeer's stronghold, and the assault on it was a hazardous one, for the rich Jew had not only the theatres but the bulk of the Press in his pocket. The Press campaign against Wagner began as soon as it became manifest that he had come to Paris in order to produce his own works: Wagner found himself described as the Marat of music, with the consolatory addition that Berlioz was the Robespierre. Wagner's ultimate aim, seeing that there was now no likelihood of *Tristan* being produced in Germany, had been to float it in Paris. Before this could be possible, however, the Parisians would have to be made acquainted with his earlier music. At first he had had in his mind a bold scheme for starting a German theatre in Paris, giving in turn *Tannhäuser*, *Lohengrin*, and *Tristan*. The Théâtre Italien (the Salle Ventadour) would have been available in the May of 1860, after the close of the Italian season; and he could confidently count on the co-operation of such singers as Tichatschek, Niemann, Mitterwurzer, and Luise Meyer; the nucleus of the chorus would of course have to be German.

The primary consideration, however, was finance. Gasperini introduced him to a rich man named Lucy, at that time Receiver-General in Marseilles, who took to the idea with enthusiasm. It was settled that first of all Wagner should give three concerts of his music, in order to pave the way for the larger scheme. From that time onwards he was plunged up to the neck in the troubled sea of business; his days and nights were spent in writing letters, interviewing people likely to be friendly to his plan, and the wire-pulling of every description that is necessary before anything can be done in connection with music. Belloni, who knew every inch of the Parisian ground, was called in to help: the editor of a theatrical journal, one Giacomelli, proved very friendly, and at his office Wagner met, he says, " all the strange beings with whom, for the purpose of theatrical and similar matters, one has to mix in Paris." The concerts would of course receive the greatest *éclat* by being given with the orchestra and chorus of the Opéra, but the necessary permission for this would have to be obtained direct from the Emperor. Lucy, fearing the opposition of Fould, the Minister of the Household, who was a friend of Meyerbeer, appealed for help to a former friend of his youth, the Emperor's secretary, Moquard. But as neither Lucy's letter to Moquard nor Wagner's to Napoleon himself received any answer, Wagner had in the end to be content with the Salle Ventadour. The director of the Italian Opera, Calzado, was at first coy; but by holding out to him glowing hopes of the success some day of *Tristan*, Wagner at last managed to obtain the theatre, at the high rent of 4,000 francs a night, for three concerts to be given in January, 1860. Dissolved into thin air were all his hopes of tranquil days devoted to the completion of the *Ring*. He was committed now to many months of frenzied struggle with the musical, theatrical and journalistic world of Paris. " You know me well enough ", he wrote to Otto Wesendonk on the 12th February, 1860, " to realise that along this path there lies no joy for me. I do not seek applause and triumphs, but only the possibility of putting my new works clearly before the public, so that I can die in peace."

WAGNER AND MEYERBEER

IN KBWM of the 15th November, 1934 (see the list of Sources and References at the commencement of the present volume) — too late, therefore, to be available for my first volume — Georg Kinsky published in full five letters from Wagner to Meyerbeer that were previously known only by extracts from them in an autograph dealer's catalogue. They are dated Paris, 18th January and 15th February, 1840, Dresden, 26th December, 1844, 27th December, 1845, and 4th January, 1846. The first two are concerned with Wagner's attempts to get a footing in the Paris theatres. (See Vol. I, pp. 278–85). They show him expressing a lively sense of all that had been done for him by Meyerbeer. He is Meyerbeer's " protégé ": he looks forward to " salvation from all evil through God and you; if you remain well disposed towards me, then God too is near me ": he feels he can count on Meyerbeer's grace and favour, " for your kindness has already been too deeply engaged on behalf of one so necessitous as myself." He has no hope on earth except from Meyerbeer, whom he urges to keep putting pressure on Joly (the director of the Renaissance Theatre) to produce *Das Liebesverbot,* for Wagner " cannot pick up even a pin " in Paris without Meyerbeer's help and protection. Joly's excuses, it seems, for not doing anything for Wagner in spite of Meyerbeer's recommendation of him, were that (1) Wagner was a German, and the young French composers would be very indignant were the Renaissance to be opened again to a German, (2) he could not give works that had not been written expressly for his theatre and his singers, (3) he could not give translated operas, (4) in general, German music was too difficult and too learned for his theatre.

Wagner sees the force of these excuses, but for all that is not inclined to give up the struggle. But a special effort will be required, and Meyerbeer alone has the artillery to back up that. " Anténor [Joly] thinks, ' God is good, the Tsar is a long way off, and Monpou also isn't bad '. What is to be done in these circumstances? Terrorism is the only means, and you, my honoured sovereign of all tones, alone can apply it. . . . Well then, if you still remember me, take pity on me and write the bad Anténor a letter, a sort of ukase or bull. . . . Tell him that I am indeed a German, but a Leipziger, not a Mainzer. . . ." A good deal of the earlier letters is in this humorous tone.

Later we find that it was at Meyerbeer's request that Habeneck had rehearsed the Columbus Overture at the Conservatoire. (See Vol. I, p. 283). The whole orchestra, says Wagner, had applauded it warmly, and Habeneck had promised him a second rehearsal, so that there was a likelihood of the work being accepted for performance at a concert. " This would be the first and a really weighty success, for which I should have no one to thank but you. But why *thank* you for it? May heaven only grant that some opportunity may arise for me to render you even a thousandth part of what thanks I owe you. I can hardly hope, however, that Heaven will be so generous to me: on the contrary, I see that I shall follow you from aeon to aeon stammering my thanks, until in the end, exasperated at not being able to get any peace from me even in heaven, you will consign me to hell. Then, indeed, you will hear nothing of me; but I can assure you that I will still be stammering thanks there."

Nearly five years later, on the 26th December, 1844, we find Wagner congratulating Meyerbeer on the success of his latest opera, *Ein Feldlager in Schlesien,* and praising his " mastery ": he would have gone to Berlin for the first performance had not Meyerbeer told him it was doubtful whether he would be able to find a seat. Then he proceeds to the real business of the letter. Is there any hope of a speedy production of *Rienzi* in Berlin? Cannot a heroic tenor be found? On Berlin now rest all his hopes for the spread of *Rienzi* beyond Dresden; but if it should be impracticable there at the moment, cannot Meyerbeer persuade Küstner to keep his promise to repeat the *Flying Dutchman* in the new opera house? (It had been given in unsatisfactory style in the preceding January in the Playhouse, the Court Opera House having been burnt down in August, 1843. It was the new house that had opened on the 7th

December, 1844, with *Ein Feldlager in Schlesien*). Meyerbeer had evidently offered Wagner his good offices in the Küstner matter, and Wagner now asks him to do what he can for him. At their next meeting he promises to make his benefactor split his midriff with the humorous things he will have to tell him about Spontini, who had been producing *La Vestale* in Dresden that winter. (See Vol. I, pp. 390–3). The reader will recall that Meyerbeer had gone to Dresden in September, 1844, to hear *Tannhäuser*, had apparently been impressed by it, and had promised to do all he could to bring about a performance of it in Berlin. It had certainly been owing to his recommendation that the *Flying Dutchman* had been given there.

In the fourth letter Wagner is still seen trying his utmost to get a footing in Berlin: his success in Dresden has been flattering, but Dresden in comparison with Berlin is only a provincial town, whose verdict does not count much with Germany as a whole. He had evidently hoped to produce in Berlin, with Meyerbeer's assistance, the new work (*Lohengrin*) on which he was then engaged; but it had turned out that Lüttichau particularly wanted this for Dresden; besides, it would call for a better tenor and two better women singers than Berlin possessed at present. But as it is a matter of the greatest importance to him to establish himself in Berlin, so as to impress the rest of Germany, he asks for Meyerbeer's assistance in bringing about a production of *Rienzi*.

In the last letter of the series he urges Meyerbeer to arrange for the production of (the still unfinished) *Lohengrin* in Berlin. He sends him a copy of the poem, on the strength of which he asks Meyerbeer to petition the King of Prussia to commission the opera for his Court Theatre. If there is any hope of his being allowed to read the poem to the King he will come to Berlin at once. He ends by trusting that Meyerbeer will continue to show his sympathy with him, and remains his " for ever greatly beholden Richard Wagner."

There is no reason to suppose that Wagner was not sincere in his many expressions of gratitude to Meyerbeer; it is clear that he believed, between 1839 and 1847,[1] that he was under real obliga-

---

[1] We have seen him telling Hanslick, on the 1st January, 1847, that while he no

tions to him. Nor, in view of all the evidence, is there any reason to doubt that Meyerbeer had shown him considerable kindness and done him several services not only in Paris but in Berlin. It remains a mystery why, within the next two or three years, Wagner should have conceived so intense a dislike for him, and in later life have been so unwilling to acknowledge any indebtedness to him. His Paris letter of the 5th June, 1849, to Liszt shows that, like many other people, he had come to the conclusion that he had been mistaken about Meyerbeer. Perhaps, by about 1848, what had once been only private talk about the element of calculation in Meyerbeer's beneficences had swelled to something like a public scandal, and Wagner, disappointed in his hopes for Berlin, and feeling, in his customary way, that whatever Meyerbeer had done for him he might and ought to have done more, lent too ready an ear to his friends' suggestions that Meyerbeer had all along been a jealous enemy concealing his machinations under a mask of friendship. Certainly Meyerbeer, apart from the ill odour into which his notorious bribery of the Press had brought him, inspired distrust and repugnance in many detached observers, who felt him to be fundamentally insincere. The French tenor Roger hit him off in a penetrating sentence or two in his diary for 1848: " I have passed the evening with Meyerbeer, who received me with open arms. His conversation is charming; he has a way that is all his own of saying the most biting things in the sweetest style, his eyes full of tenderness, his lips pursed as if for a kiss."

Still, insincere and calculating as he may have been, base as the methods were by which he consolidated, if he did not gain, his European power, there can be no doubt that he exerted himself for Wagner both in Paris and in Berlin. Meyerbeer's friendliness to him in Paris can hardly have been the result of calculation, for at that time he could not have foreseen a future rival in this quite unknown young man of twenty-seven or so. In the Meyerbeer case it becomes more and more difficult to put up any defence against the oft-repeated charge against Wagner of ingratitude to his benefactors. If, as seems probable, Meyerbeer had really done him sev-

longer has a "high estimate" of Meyerbeer as a composer, he is "personally friendly" with him, and has "every reason to prize him as a sympathetic, amiable man." See Vol. I, p. 436.

eral services out of pure kindness of heart, we can readily understand how impossible it was for Meyerbeer, in later life, to hear Wagner's name mentioned without a grimace passing over his face, " as if he had been jarred by a dissonance ". If ever Meyerbeer's diary is published in full, it ought to make interesting reading.

WAGNER'S ORIGINS

I · THE GEYER QUESTION

1

IN VOL. I there was quoted a statement by Glasenapp to the effect that " Wagner repeatedly expressed as a possibility in conversation with intimate friends, of whom we could name several ", that Geyer " might even have been his real father." Knowing as we do the conditions under which Glasenapp's biography was constructed, in the closest association with Cosima, and with access to many documents only available at Wahnfried, it is tolerably certain that this sentence could have been inserted only with Cosima's sanction; the inference is that Wahnfried itself, about 1905, had no objection to the world knowing that Wagner himself regarded it as a " possibility " that Geyer was his father.

In the *Bayreuther Festspielführer* for 1933, however, Dr. Otto Strobel, the keeper of the Wahnfried archives, to whose researches we are indebted for a vast amount of new information about Wagner, disclosed a hitherto unknown passage in Cosima's diary for the 26th December, 1878: " I ask R[ichard]: Vater Geyer was probably your father? Richard replied: ' That I don't believe — my mother loved him — elective affinities '." [1] Dr. Strobel regards this as " authentic testimony that Richard Wagner absolutely did *not* regard himself as Ludwig Geyer's son ". [2]

I cannot agree, however, that this citation disposes of the matter. It may well be that on this subject, as on so many others, Wagner's opinion remained anything but steadfast during his later years. The citation does not dispose of Glasenapp's plain testimony as to what *he* had heard from " several intimate friends " of the com-

---

[1] "Wahlverwandtschaften" had become a common term in German literature after Goethe's book bearing that title.

[2] BFF, 1933, p. 32.

poser. It was in the summer of 1878 that Glasenapp went to Bayreuth in order to collect, with Cosima's assistance, the material for his biography; the inference, then, is that it was *after* the date of the entry in Cosima's diary — any time between 1878 and 1905 — that he collected the information upon which he based his statement. Moreover, we are told by Cosima's biographer, Du Moulin Eckart, that Glasenapp had had access to her diaries for his own work.[3] It is true that the wording of Du Moulin's sentence might be taken to imply that it was for the *final months of Wagner's life* that Glasenapp had had access to the diaries; but there are features of the biography that make that limited application of the words difficult to justify. There is reason to believe that he was familiar with more of the contents of the diaries than that: and if that were so, the chances are that he knew of the entry of the 26th December, 1878. It is surely not without significance, on this view, that he should not regard that passage as at any rate qualifying the statement in his volume of 1905. But even putting all this aside as a matter for conjecture rather than one of irrefragable evidence, the fact remains that whereas, as I have already pointed out (Vol. I, pp. 7 ff.), as late as the third edition of his book (1894) Glasenapp was concerned to conceal or confuse certain aspects of the story, in the fourth edition (1905) he at last came out boldly with the statement that Wagner himself had " expressed the possibility " of Geyer having been his father. That statement, as I said, would hardly have been made without Cosima's approval: we are driven, therefore, to the conclusion that about that time Cosima herself did not attach a vast amount of importance to the conversation of December, 1878.

2

The true facts of Wagner's paternity, of course, will never be known: we can do no more than marshal the available evidence and use our reason upon it. We may note, however, that all the trails lead back ultimately to Nietzsche. In *Der Fall Wagner* (1888) he had written the following, every word of which calls for careful

---

[3] MECW, I, 986.

examination: " Was Wagner a German at all? We have some reasons for asking this. It is difficult to discover in him any German
trait whatever. Being the great learner he was, he has learned to
imitate much that is German — that is all. His nature [*Wesen*]
itself is contradictory of what has hitherto been regarded as German — not to speak of the German musician! His father was an
actor named Geyer. A Geyer is almost an Adler.[4] What has hitherto been put into circulation as the ' Life of Wagner ' is *fable
convenue,* if not something worse. I confess my mistrust of every
point which rests solely on the testimony of Wagner himself. He
had not pride enough for any truth whatever about himself. Nobody was less proud: he remained just like Victor Hugo, true to
himself even in matters biographical — he remained an actor."

To this one paragraph can be traced back all the errors and
rumours that have gathered about the Wagner-Geyer subject during the last fifty years. Because Nietzsche was known to have seen
the opening chapters of Wagner's privately printed autobiography
through the press, it was everywhere assumed that that work began with the words " I am the son of Ludwig Geyer ". When *Mein
Leben* was published (in 1911), and it was seen that it began by
a reference to " my father, Friedrich Wagner ", the story went
round that Cosima had garbled the opening words of Wagner's
manuscript for her own purposes. We now know that there was no
garbling at all — that in both the privately printed edition and the
public issue the opening sentences are precisely as they are in the
manuscript. Yet Nietzsche undoubtedly knew *something* on which
he based his famous passage in *Der Fall Wagner*. What was that
something? In my *Fact and Fiction about Wagner* I have adduced
a variety of evidence all pointing to the fact that about Christmas,
1869, he had been the recipient of an *oral confidence* on the subject on Wagner's part.[5]

Having learned that Wagner believed, or half-believed, himself
to be the son of Geyer, Nietzsche was astonished to find, when the
manuscript of *Mein Leben* came into his hands in 1870, to be
passed on to the Basel printer, that the opening page (written, by
the way, in 1865, when perhaps Wagner's ideas on the subject were

---

[4] Geyer (vulture) and Adler (eagle) are both German-Jewish names.
[5] I must refer the reader to the book itself for details.

not so definite as they had become by Christmas, 1869) spoke of "my father, Friedrich Wagner", and that this was obviously the story it was deemed advisable that posterity should officially be told. In the light of what Nietzsche now knew privately — let us not lose sight, by the way, of the express testimony of Frau Förster-Nietzsche that "my brother told me that *Wagner had indicated* [italics mine] his stepfather Geyer as his real father" — he could only regard the opening page of *Mein Leben* as a deliberate concealment of truth on Wagner's part, due to a lack of the "pride" that would have boldly faced any truth about himself. Almost every sentence in the passage quoted above from *Der Fall Wagner* obviously shoots straight at the mark from very close quarters. When Nietzsche asks whether Wagner was a German at all, he says boldly that "there are reasons for this question". And one of those "reasons" was not simply that his character, in Nietzsche's opinion, was not really German, but the statement, put forward as a fact, that "his father was a stage-player named Geyer." Nietzsche goes on to say that he distrusts every point that rests solely on Wagner's own testimony; that Wagner remained an actor even in *the matter of biography;* and that what has hitherto been in circulation as the "Life of Wagner" is "*fable convenue,* if not something worse" — the "something worse" obviously meaning calculated deception. Now Nietzsche was not in a position to sift out fact from fiction in Wagner biography *as a whole;* that has proved anything but an easy matter for present-day biographers, with a thousand documents before them of the very existence of which Nietzsche was wholly ignorant. Nietzsche was not generalising: he had his mind fixed on a definite point, and was speaking of something he *knew.* He had been told, we are practically driven to assume, by Wagner himself that Geyer was in all probability his real father, and when he saw that, by means of *Mein Leben,* a legend of another kind was to be imposed upon the world, he was angry at what he took to be a fraud, and at the lack of "pride" in Wagner that made him shrink from the truth about his origin being known; and so he declares his distrust of every biographical detail that rests on Wagner's authority alone.

It seems to me highly probable that, as he gradually drifted apart from his former idol during the late 1870's, Nietzsche blabbed to other people about the confidence with which Wagner had favoured him, and so a belief in Wagner's Semitic origin began to spread through European musical circles. For it is surely significant that it is in the late 1870's, for the first time so far as I have been able to discover, that Wagner's enemies began to make public play with this supposedly damaging fact. It is about this time that the German caricaturists begin to give a Jewish turn to his features. A cartoon in the Vienna *Floh* of 1879 shows him surrounded by children of a markedly Jewish cast of feature: on the piano is a bust of the Jewish Offenbach, while Wagner's own nose is made exaggeratedly Jewish.[6] A drawing in the Vienna *Kikeriki* of 1882 shows an audience of Jews applauding *Parsifal*.[7]

About 1880 the Viennese journalist Daniel Spitzer published a malicious but amusing novel, *Verliebte Wagnerianer*, in which Wagner unmistakably figures as the composer Goldschein. There is no mistaking at whom the ironic passage is directed in which a " Germanist " scholar, a great admirer of Wagner, appears as the author of a work " in which he had contradicted the statement that Wagner was born in the house in the Brühl at Leipzig which bears a tablet recording his birth there. For the Brühl has always been Leipzig's Jewish quarter, and it is impossible to place *there* the birthplace of the most glorious fighter against the Jews since the Emperor Titus — unless one wants to agree with certain adversaries of the Master who assert that he is himself of Jewish origin." [8] Manifestly the story that Wagner was really the son of Geyer was by this time in general circulation among his enemies.

In 1876 another Viennese journalist, Ludwig Speidel, had said bluntly in an article in the *Fremdenblatt* that " Wagner, who was born in the Jewish quarter of Leipzig, is of Semitic origin: a Saxon scholar is seriously occupied with the task of establishing his Jewish

---

[6] See KFW, p. 95, where the cartoon is reproduced.
[7] Reproduced in KFW, p. 111. Wagner, say the authors apropos of the cartoon, "has become the God of the Jews, to whom they pour out their adoration."
[8] SVW, pp. 51-2.

pedigree." [9] In 1879 Spitzer had contended that the "continual putting of questions and answering them with another question [in the *Ring*] is another of the little Jewish traits of the Rabbi von Bayreuth,[10] or, as the German translation has it, the Master." [11] It is true that before that, in the late 1860's, there had been mutterings here and there that the author of *Judaism in Music* was himself a Jew: Albert Hahn, for instance, in 1869, had asserted that Wagner's nose was "not German".[12] But it is towards 1880 that the journalists and novelists and caricaturists begin to play exultantly with the thesis that Wagner was of Jewish origin. That thesis was evidently widely current by then; and it is not improbable that it owed its diffusion to talk by Nietzsche, who by that time had drifted far apart from his former idol. Once more be it said that nothing of all this is clearly demonstrable: all one can do is to assemble the facts and the dates and suggest the further facts to which they seem to point. It was in 1878, be it recalled, that Cosima asked Wagner point-blank whether he now thought that Geyer was his father. Does not this of itself suggest that somehow or other the question had "come into the air" about that time? And in view of the fact that Wagner's enemies were now using his supposed Semitic origin to denigrate his national German art-work, is it not conceivable that he himself should be less inclined to countenance the Geyer theory in 1878 than he had been at Christmas, 1869?

II · THE PRINCE CONSTANTIN QUESTION

1

In an article entitled *Briefe einer Mutter, Johanna Geyer an ihren Sohn Richard Wagner*, in BFF, 1933, Dr. Otto Strobel quotes the

---

[9] TWSK, p. 38.

[10] This expression is met with elsewhere in the journalism of the period. Kreowski and Fuchs cite one wit as saying that "Richard Wagner is arranging for an extra performance of *The Nibelung's Ring* for the benefit of the Jews expelled from Russia, in which only Kosher Valkyries will appear, and the fire flickers under the supervision of the Bayreuth Higher-Rabbinate." (KFW, p. 138). "Whereas formerly", say Kreowski and Fuchs, "they could not say enough by way of reflection on Wagner's anti-semitic leanings, he was now reviled as a bondsman of the Jews."

[11] Ibid., p. 69.

[12] TWSK, p. 38.

passage from *Mein Leben* a translation of which has been given by me in Vol. I, p. 23, and comments on it thus: " Here Wagner clearly points to a problem the solution of which, strange to say, has till now been overlooked by researchers: for it can no longer be doubted, in the light of what Wagner says, that Johanna Rosine Paetz was *not* the daughter of the Weissenfels baker, however diffi-cult it may be to establish her real origin." Dr. Strobel had evi-dently not seen the first volume of the present Life when he wrote this, for I had already suggested there that Wagner's words are in-tended to convey that Johanna was actually the daughter not of the Weissenfels baker but of this " exalted fatherly friend ".

It now appears that in the inner Wagnerian circles the suggested aristocratic paternity of Johanna has never been questioned, for Dr. Strobel quotes a letter from Houston Stewart Chamberlain to one Hellmundt, of the 12th December, 1913, in which occurs the following passage: " The ancestral line of Wagner's mother is de-monstrable without a break, and the little secret that is embedded here is no secret for the initiated; it enables us to trace her pedigree back to the twelfth century." The " little secret " is that Johanna was the natural daughter of Prince Friedrich Ferdinand Constantin of Weimar, the only brother of the then reigning Grand Duke Karl August (the patron of Goethe). This young man was born on the 8th September, 1758, and died on the 6th September, 1793. As Dr. Strobel says, " like his brother Karl August he matured early "; so that there is *a priori* nothing incredible in his having become Johanna's father at the age of about fifteen and a quarter. Wagner, it will be remembered, refers to Johanna's education at the " select educational institution in Leipzig " (not the kind of school to which a small-town baker's child would normally be sent) as having been terminated by " the sudden death of the ' fatherly friend ' ". Here again the dates seem to fit in: Johanna would be just nineteen at the death of Prince Constantin in 1793. When we further learn that Prince Constantin was notable both for his exceptional musical gifts and for the wildness of his life, we find it still less difficult to believe that he may have been the grandfather of Wagner. If this were the case, and if, in addition, there was the blood of the gifted Geyer in Wagner's veins, it is little wonder that the composer was the many-sided, dynamic creature his life and work show him to

PRINCE CONSTANTIN OF WEIMAR

FROM A PASTEL PAINTING BY GEORG OSWALD
MAY, IN THE GOETHE NATIONAL MUSEUM,
WEIMAR

FROM A BUST BY AN UNKNOWN SCULPTOR,
IN THE GOETHE NATIONAL MUSEUM,
WEIMAR

(By courtesy of the Goethe National Museum, Weimar)

have been. It is decidedly a piquant reflection that Wagner and the Grand Duke Carl Alexander of Weimar who played so considerable a part in his life may have been cousins.

2

For the information of the reader of the present volume the following details of the Weimar house of that and a later period may be given here:

1. Grand Duke Ernst August (died January, 1748) was succeeded by his young son Ernst August Constantin, who formally ascended the throne in December, 1755.

2. Ernst August Constantin married, in March, 1756, the sixteen-years-old Princess Anna Amalie of Brunswick. Their son Karl August was born in September, 1757. In the following May the Grand Duke Ernst died, before he had completed his twenty-first year. Karl August, who succeeded him (attaining his majority in 1775), was later to become famous as Goethe's Grand Duke.

3. A few months after Ernst August's death, his widow gave birth to a second son, Friedrich Ferdinand Constantin. It is he who, according to Chamberlain, was Wagner's grandfather.

4. Karl August died in June, 1828, and was succeeded by his son Karl Friedrich, who married Maria Pavlovna, sister of the Tsar of Russia, Nicholas I.

5. Karl Friedrich died in July, 1853. His son Carl Alexander (born June, 1818), figures in the Wagner story of the present volume first of all as Hereditary Grand Duke, then, from 1853 onwards, as Grand Duke. He died in January, 1901.

Little is known about Prince Constantin, owing to his early death and the fact that he never ascended the throne. He appears to have spent most of his youthful years in Schloss Belvedere, the famous country retreat of the Grand Ducal family.[13] It lies a few miles south of Weimar. Weissenfels is a small town on the route from

---

[13] Such information as is to be had about Prince Constantin, together with a mass of interesting details of the Weimar royal family and Belvedere, will be found in Hans Wahl's *Tiefurt* (Leipzig, 1929) and Werner Deetjen's *Schloss Belvedere* (Leipzig, 1926).

Weimar to Leipzig, about 50 miles from the former and 20 from the latter.

The tanner's daughter Dorothea Erdmuthe Iglisch (mother of Wagner's mother, Johanna) married on the 11th January, 1763, the Weissenfels baker J. G. Paetz. Johanna, born on the 19th September, 1774, was her fourth child. Frau Paetz died on the 5th January, 1789, when Johanna was fourteen-years-and-a-quarter old. Prince Constantin at that time would be thirty-one. Let us now look again at Wagner's account of his mother. " She never ", he says, " gave any of her children any definite information about her extraction. She came from Weissenfels, where, she admitted, her parents had been bakers. . . . The curious thing was that she had been placed in a select educational institution in Leipzig, where she enjoyed the advantage of the care of one whom she called an ' exalted fatherly friend ',[14] to whom she afterwards referred as being a Weimar prince who had been of service to her family in Weissenfels. Her education in this establishment seems to have been interrupted by the sudden death of this fatherly friend."

3

It will be seen that Wagner twice uses the expression " fatherly friend ", and once puts it in inverted commas. Can we detect a touch of irony in this — a sly smile at the " fatherly "? We have to note further that (1) the story came from Johanna herself; (2) she could not give her children " any definite information about her extraction ", although one cannot see what difficulty there could be about the matter if she were the plain and simple daughter of the baker whose name she bore; (3) that it was a " curious thing " that a girl of that ostensible origin should have been placed in a select school for young ladies in Leipzig; (4) that Johanna herself referred to the " exalted fatherly friend " who had provided for her education as " a Weimar prince ". Weissenfels was not in the Weimar territory, but in Saxony. Why should a Weimar prince, unless for very good reasons of his own, take up the daughter of a Weissenfels baker and send her to Leipzig to receive an education above the

---

[14] *Eines von ihr sogenannten "hohen väterlichen Freundes". Hohe* means "high up in the world": a Royal Highness is a *Königliche Hoheit.*

average of that of her class? And this education was " interrupted
by the sudden death of the fatherly friend ". The only " Weimar
prince " the date of whose death fits in with this was Constantin.

That Johanna's name was associated in some way or other with
the Weimar Court we gather from other sources. Mrs Burrell, in
the 1890's, " heard from more than one source ", " with variations ", that Johanna Rosine had been chosen by Karl August and
Goethe for the Weimar stage, and that it was through Goethe that
Friedrich Wagner made her acquaintance and married her." [15] The
object of sending the child to the Leipzig school (perhaps after the
death of her mother in January, 1789, and the second marriage of
the baker in the following October) may indeed have been to fit her
for a stage career; but if so, that design must surely have been
abandoned when it became clear that Johanna would always be of
exceedingly small stature.[16] If she left the school when Constantin
died (the autumn of 1793) we perhaps have an explanation of that
" very faulty " education of which Wagner speaks. Karl Friedrich
Wagner married her in June, 1798. In 1803, when they were at
Lauchstadt (for the first performance of Schiller's *Die Braut von
Messina*), he "rebuked her warmly ", Wagner tells us, for her ignorance of Goethe and Schiller, whom he " pointed out to her on the
promenade ". As no one could possibly have lived in Weimar without knowing Goethe by sight — still less have had anything to do
with the Weimar theatre, with which Goethe was so closely associated, — this seems to dispose of Mrs Burrell's theory that Johanna
" was chosen by Karl August and Goethe for the Weimar stage, and
that it was through Goethe that Friedrich Wagner made her acquaintance." What is pertinent to our subject in the story as told to
Mrs Burrell is the association, by later tradition, of Johanna with

[15] BRW, p. 19. It is rather extraordinary that Mrs Burrell, who had obtained
possession of the privately-printed edition of *Mein Leben*, never sensed the significance of Wagner's account of his mother's origin; for once Mrs Burrell fell below her
high level of acuity. She owed the many extraordinary "finds" of her Collection to
the fact that, having a copy of *Mein Leben* in her hands as early as 1892 (less than
ten years after Wagner's death), she was able to interview a large number of still
living people who are mentioned there, and so acquire a host of first-hand documents
before they could come into the market. With her gift for research, and her large income to back it up, she might have ferreted out, before it was too late, a good deal
of information concerning the Constantin mystery had she perceived what lay behind Wagner's words. The irony of the "exalted fatherly friend" never seems to have
dawned on her.   [16] See Vol. I, p. 24.

the Weimar royal family. After all, it is not surprising that a legend of that association should have persisted down to Mrs Burrell's time. It would have been surprising, under the circumstances, if it had not; for in so tiny a place as Weissenfels was in the 18th century the whole population could hardly fail to know that a Weimar prince took so keen an interest in one of the local baker's children as to send her to an expensive school in Leipzig. Many people in Weissenfels in later years must have heard from their parents that the Richard Wagner who had sprung into fame about 1842 was the son of Johanna Paetz of that hamlet; and the story of Karl August's interest in Johanna, as Mrs Burrell heard it, was perhaps the final vague form into which the local legend of the " Weimar prince " had crystallised.

4

There is nothing inherently improbable, it may be added, in the notion of a youth of royal blood conferring motherhood on a female of the lower classes, either in his own territory or in that of some other German ruler. It was the commonest phenomenon imaginable in those days. Many of the women regarded it as an honour done them: some looked upon it as a source of easy and not unpleasurable profit: others, and their fathers, brothers, lovers and husbands along with them, accepted it philosophically as the will of Providence, which in its infinite wisdom had created certain people to rule in Germany and others to serve. One surmises from the contemporary records that most of the maidens and matrons concerned put into practice, without ever having heard of it, the sage precept of Chinese philosophy that declares that " When raping is inevitable, it is best to submit and enjoy it." It was not every German prince the arithmetic of whose achievements so nearly approached the astronomic as did that of August the Strong, of Saxony, who endowed his kingdom with no less than 354 illegitimate children; but the others also did their modest best.[17] Some districts of modern Germany can perhaps boast of a more aristo-

---

[17] On this subject of the view of the German princes that their female subjects were material for their harems see Leo Balet, *Die Verbürgerlichung der deutschen Kunst und Musik im 18. Jahrhundert* (1936). "Karl Eugen of Württemberg", says Balet (p. 53), "kept a whole harem of Italian and French girls, to whose numbers

cratic population than any other European state: quite a large proportion of the inhabitants must have at least a drop or two of royal blood in their veins. And if Prince Constantin really conferred his royal favour on the baker's wife of Weissenfels, and, in God's good time, Richard Wagner was the ultimate result, then he builded, so to speak, wiser than he knew.

5

Portraits of Prince Constantin are not plentiful; but by the courtesy of Dr. Hans Wahl, the curator of the Goethe National Museum in Weimar, I am able to reproduce a portrait bust and a pastel that are in the possession of that institution. But for one rather awkward fact, we might be disposed to fancy we see in the ample nose and pronounced chin of the young man the origin of those notable organs in Wagner. Could we accept the theory of the Constantin heredity, indeed, one of our difficulties in connection with the Geyer problem would disappear. It has often been pointed out that Richard Wagner's features strongly resemble those of his fourteen-years-older brother Albert, who was born long before the family had made Geyer's acquaintance. It is not very clear, of course, why resemblances between brothers should be attributed only to their father; still, the argument, such as it was, against the Geyer paternity in Richard's case could not be brushed aside. What, however, if both Albert and Richard inherited their features, through their mother, from Constantin? That deduction may appear not improbable to those who see, not a striking total resemblance between Constantin and Richard, but a certain similar emphasis on the part of nature on the chin and nose of each of them. Against this, however, has to be set the awkward fact that there is a very strong resemblance between the features of Richard and his Uncle Adolf — brother of Karl Friedrich Wagner. The physiognomical evidence thus fails us.

Hunters for suggestions of the Constantin nose and chin in Wagner may perhaps find what they want in the portraits of the latter given on pp. 183, 237, 472, 482, 597, and 629 of EWLW.

---

were added many of the seduced daughters of his vassals. When one of his female subjects became pregnant the Duke sent her back to her home with the 'princely' compensation of 50 gulden in full discharge."

INDEX

Liszt, Franz (*continued*)
4; Wagner's "ingratitude" to, 248, 440, 463; suggests commissioning of *Siegfrieds Tod*, 252–4, 258–61; *Lohengrin* article of, 257, 259–60; and expansion of Siegfried plan, 262, 264–5, 267–70; revives *Benvenuto Cellini*, 294–300; "diplomacy" of, 295–6, 401, 424; "Wagner evenings" of, 301; and negotiations for Wagner productions in Berlin, 309–10, 373, 424–7, 440–2, 488–9; out of sympathy with opera form, 314; advises Wagner against Paris production, 321; and *Ring* poem, 364–7, 370; recommends consolations of religion, 366; seeks amnesty for Wagner, 378, 379; visits Wagner in Zürich, 384–7, 407, 493–6, 498–9; and "festival" scheme, 385; conducts at Carlsruhe, 391; young bodyguard of, 392; and Joachim, 392, 597; in Paris, 393; children of, 394, 496–7; and sale of rights in *Lohengrin*, 399, 410–11; and Leipzig *Lohengrin*, 400–3; mishandles Wagner's affairs, 402, 424, 426–7, 440–2; Princess's influence over, 440–2, 495–8, 528, 586; article of, on *Rhinegold*, 443–4; prejudice against, in London, 466; on Munich *Tannhäuser*, 483; Dingelstedt's letters to, 484–5; on Berlin *Tannhäuser*, 488; on *Valkyrie*, 491; Wagner hears works of, 494–5; mask of, 496; quarrelsome temper of, 496, 498–9; Press attacks on, 498, 560, 580 (note); his avidity for praise, 502; negotiates for sale of *Ring* score, 511; police suspicion of, 514; and abandonment of *Ring*, 521–2; drifts away

Liszt, Franz (*continued*)
from Wagner, 521, 528, 586; will of, 528; Wagner's anxiety over, 528–9 (note), 597; puts off going to Zürich, 556; estrangement between Wagner and, 575, 577–80, 596–600; turns his back on Weimar, 576; Wagner and *Dante* of, 585–6, 600; manifesto against, 597; Princess leaves, 597; on Wagner's mismanagement of affairs, 596–7; influence of, on Wagner as harmonist, 600

Lobe, J. C., 258 (note)

Lohengrin, 21, 33, 46; scoring of, 3; performance of fragment of, 41; rejected by Dresden theatre, 44–6, 48, 101, 127; staging of, 78 (note); Dresden performances of, 102, 581; attempts to sell score of, 122–3, 197; passages from, played in Zürich, 180–1, 188; Liszt and, 196–7, 200–3; score of, sent to Liszt, 201; Weimar performance of, 201–3, 204, 213–17, 225, 231–3, 249–50, 264, 297, 303, 308 (note); Raff on, 226–7; singers slow down the time of, 231–2; publication of score of, 243, 301; Wagner anxious to hear, 251–2, 283, 321, 323, 379; cutting of, 252, 401; increasing popularity of, 257, 481; Liszt's article on, 257, 259–60; Leipzig negotiates for, 306; Berlin performances of, 308 (note), 414, 546, 580; withheld from the theatres, 316; and Johanna, 320; attempt to sell performing rights of, 399, 411–13; Leipzig performance of, 400–2, 413; "lyrical pieces for solo voices" from, 412; prelude of, in London, 474; and Munich, 484–5, 540; piano selections from, 505; selections

A NOTE ON THE TYPE IN WHICH
THIS BOOK IS SET

This book is composed on the linotype in Bodoni, so called after Giambattista Bodoni (1740–1813), son of a printer of Piedmont. After gaining experience and fame as superintendent of the Press of the Propaganda in Rome, Bodoni became in 1766 the head of the ducal printing house at Parma, which he soon made the foremost of its kind in Europe. His Manuale Tipografico, *completed by his widow in 1818, contains 279 pages of specimens of types, including alphabets of about thirty foreign languages. His editions of Greek, Latin, Italian, and French classics, especially his Homer, are celebrated for their typography. In type-designing he was an innovator, making his new faces rounder, wider, and lighter, with greater openness and delicacy. His types were rather too rigidly perfect in detail, the thick lines contrasting sharply with the thin wiry lines. It was this feature, doubtless, that caused William Morris's condemnation of the Bodoni types as "swelteringly hideous." Bodoni Book, as reproduced by the Linotype Company, is a modern version based, not upon any one of Bodoni's fonts, but upon a composite conception of the Bodoni manner, designed to avoid the details stigmatized as bad by typographical experts and to secure the pleasing and effective results of which the Bodoni types are capable.*

THE BOOK WAS COMPOSED, PRINTED, AND BOUND BY THE PLIMPTON PRESS, NORWOOD, MASS. THE PAPER WAS MADE BY S. D. WARREN CO., BOSTON. THE BINDING WAS ADAPTED FROM DESIGNS BY W. A. DWIGGINS.

DATE DUE			